# *Solaris 8 Advanced System Administrator's Guide, Third Edition*

Janice Winsor

*Sun Microsystems Press*
*A Prentice Hall Title*

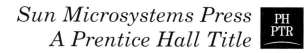

**Sun Microsystems Press**
**A Prentice Hall Title**

# PREFACE

This book is for system administrators who are familiar with basic system administration and with the tasks described in the *Solaris System Administrator's Guide*, Third Edition, cited in the bibliography at the end of this book.

## A Quick Tour of the Contents

This book is divided into seven parts, two appendixes, a glossary, and a bibliography.

Part 1, "Mail Services," describes the Solaris mail services in four chapters. Refer to the chapters in this part if you need to set up a new mail service or expand an existing one.

Chapter 1, "Understanding Mail Services," describes the components of the mail service, defines mail service terminology, and explains how the programs in the mail service interact.

Chapter 2, "Customizing sendmail Configuration Files," describes how `sendmail` works, introduces the m4 macro processor, and describes how to write a custom macro configuration file and generate the `sendmail` configuration file.

Chapter 3, "Planning Mail Services," describes how to create `sendmail` configuration files for a number of different mail services configurations.

Chapter 4, "Setting Up and Administering Mail Services," describes how to set up, test, administer, and troubleshoot mail services.

Part 2, "NIS+," introduces the NIS+ nameservice environment. Refer to the chapters in this part if you want to familiarize yourself with the basics of the NIS+ nameservice and its administrative commands. Also refer to these chapters for instructions for setting up an NIS+ client. This part provides only the basic information for a system administrator who must set up and support an NIS+ environment.

Chapter 5, "Introducing the NIS+ Environment," provides an overview of NIS+, explains how NIS+ differs from the NIS nameservice, and introduces the NIS+ commands.

Chapter 6, "Setting up NIS+ Servers and Clients," describes how to use the `nisserver`, `nispopulate`, and `nisclient` scripts to set up one Solaris system as a root master server and others as NIS+ clients.

Part 3, "Automounter and WebNFS Services," describes the Solaris automount services and introduces WebNFS. Refer to the chapters in this part if you need to set up a new automount service or modify an existing one.

Chapter 7, "Understanding the Automounter," describes automount terminology and the components of automounting, explains how the automounter works, recommends automounting policies, and tells you how to plan your automount services.

Chapter 8, "Setting Up the Automounter," describes how to set up and administer automount maps.

*New!*  Chapter 9, "Introducing WebNFS," contains a description of how WebNFS works and describes how to set up WebNFS files.

Part 4, "Service Access Facility," describes the Solaris Service Access Facility (SAF). Refer to the chapters in this part if you need to set up a new SAF service for terminals, modems, or printers or if you need to modify an existing one.

Chapter 10, "Understanding the Service Access Facility," provides an overview of SAF and describes the port monitors and services used by the SAF.

Chapter 11, "Setting Up Modems and Character Terminals," describes how to set up and administer SAF for modems and terminals.

Chapter 12, "Setting Up Printing Services," describes how to set up and administer SAF for printers and how to troubleshoot printing problems.

Part 5, "Application Software," describes how to install and delete application software. Refer to this part for guidelines on setting up an application server and for information on installing and removing application software and patches.

Chapter 13, "Installing and Managing Application Software," provides an overview of the installation, introduces the package commands and the Software Manager for installation, recommends a policy for installing software on an application server, and describes how to access files from a CD-ROM drive.

Chapter 14, "Package Commands," describes how to use the package commands to administer application software and how to set up the users' environment.

Chapter 15, "Admintool: Software Manager," describes how to use Admintool to administer application software.

Chapter 16, "Solaris Product Registry," describes how to use Solaris Product Registry to install and uninstall software.

Chapter 17, "Installing and Managing Software Patches," describes how to use the `patchadd` and `patchrm` commands.

Part 6, "Introduction to Shell Programming," familiarizes you with the basics of shell programming. Use the information in this part to decide which shell language you want to use to perform a specific task. This part does not provide in-depth instructions for writing scripts in the three basic shells.

Chapter 18, "Writing Shell Scripts," introduces the basic concepts of shell programming and the three basic shells available with the Solaris Operating Environment. It describes how shells work and describes the programming elements.

Chapter 19, "Reference Tables and Example Scripts," provides reference tables comparing shell syntax. It also contains examples of shell scripts.

Part 7, "System Security," provides information about creating and administering secure systems. Refer to these three chapters if you want to familiarize yourself with the basics of system security and if you want to use authentication services and ASET security.

Chapter 20, "Understanding System Security," introduces the basic concepts of system security, including file, system, and network security.

Chapter 21, "Using the Automated Security Enhancement Tool (ASET)," describes how to set up and use automated security enhancement tool (ASET).

Chapter 22, "Using Authentication Services," describes how to use authentication services. It provides an overview of secure RPC and explains how to use pluggable authentication modules (PAM).

*New!*    Chapter 23, "Role-Based Access Control," introduces the Role-Based Access Control (RBAC) security feature, new in the Solaris 8 Operating Environment, that enables you to assign a subset of superuser privileges to one or more users. It also describes new RBAC functionality added with the Solaris 8 Update 3 (01/01) release.

Appendix A, "Volume Management," describes the volume management feature introduced in the Solaris 2.2 system software. Volume management automates the mounting of CD-ROMs, diskettes, and DVD-ROM drives. You no longer need to have superuser permission to mount a CD-ROM, a diskette, or a DVD-ROM drive.

*New!*    Appendix B, "Celeste's Tutorial on Solaris 2.x Modems and Terminals," describes how to set up modems and character terminals if the basic configuration instructions provided in Chapter 11, "Setting Up Modems and Character Terminals," are not sufficient.

This book also provides a glossary of common system administration terms and a bibliography of useful reference books and URLs.

## Important: Read This Before You Begin

Because we assume that the root path includes the /sbin, /usr/sbin, /usr/bin, and /etc directories, the steps show the commands in these directories without absolute path names. Steps that use commands in other, less common directories show the absolute path in the example.

The examples in this book are for a basic Solaris software installation without the Binary Compatibility Package installed and without /usr/ucb in the path.

*CAUTION. If /usr/ucb is included in a search path, it should always be at the end. Commands like ps or df are duplicated in /usr/ucb with formats and options different from those of Solaris commands.*

This book does not contain all the information you need to administer systems. Refer to the complete system administration documentation for comprehensive information.

Because the Solaris Operating Environment provides the Bourne (default), Korn, and C shells, examples in this book show prompts for each of the shells. The default C shell prompt is *system-name%*. The default Bourne and Korn shell prompt is $. The default root prompt for all shells is a pound sign (#). In examples that affect more than one system, the C shell prompt (which shows the system name) is used to make it clear when you change from one system to another.

# Conventions Used in This Book

## Commands

In the steps and the examples, the commands to be entered are in bold type. For example: "Type **su** and press Return." When following steps, press Return only when instructed to do so, even if the text in the step breaks at the end of a line.

## Variables

Variables are in an italic typeface. When following steps, replace the variable with the appropriate information. For example, to print a file, the step instructs you to "type **lp** *filename* and press Return." To substitute the file named quest for the *filename* variable, type **lp quest** and press Return.

## Mouse-Button Terminology

This book describes mouse buttons by function. The default mouse button mapping is shown below.

- SELECT is Left.
- ADJUST is Middle.
- MENU is Right.

Use the SELECT mouse button to select unselected objects and activate controls. Use the ADJUST mouse button to adjust a selected group of objects, either adding to the group or deselecting part of the group. Use the MENU mouse button to display and choose from menus.

## Platform Terminology

*New!*

In this document, the term IA (Intel Architecture) is used instead of x86 to refer to the Intel 32-bit processor architecture, which includes the Pentium, Pentium Pro, Pentium II, Pentium II Xeon, Celeron, Pentium III Xeon processors, and comparable microprocessor chips made by AMD and Cyrix.

## Storage-Medium Terminology

In this book, we distinguish between three different types of media storage terminology in the following way.

- *Disc* is used for an optical disc, CD-ROM, or DVD disc.
- *Disk* is used for a hard-disk storage device.
- *Diskette* is used for a floppy diskette storage device. (Note: Sometimes, screen messages and mount points use the term *floppy*.)

## Icons

*New!*

Marginal icons mark information that is new in this edition. The new information may be new with the Solaris 7 Operating Environment, the Solaris 8 Operating Environment, or simply new in this edition.

Other new information may have been available in previous releases but was not included in the second edition. Where possible, the text indicates the release number where the command or functionality was added.

# SPARC and IA Information

This book provides system administration information for both SPARC and IA systems. Unless otherwise noted, information throughout this book applies to both types of systems. Table 1 summarizes the differences between the SPARC and IA system administration tasks.

**Table 1**     *SPARC and IA System Administration Differences*

| Category | SPARC Platform | IA Platform |
|---|---|---|
| System operation before kernel is loaded | A programmable read-only memory (PROM) chip with a monitor program runs diagnostics and displays device information. The PROM is also used to program default boot parameters and to test the devices connected to the system. | The basic input/output system (BIOS) runs diagnostics and displays device information. A Solaris Device Configuration Assistant boot diskette with the Multiple Device Boot (MDB) program is used to boot from nondefault boot partitions, the network, or the CD-ROM. |

**Table 1**    *SPARC and IA System Administration Differences (Continued)*

| Category | SPARC Platform | IA Platform |
|---|---|---|
| System booting | Commands and options at the PROM level are used to boot the system. | Commands and options at the MBD, primary, and secondary boot subsystems level are used to boot the system. |
| Boot programs | `bootblk`, the primary boot program, loads `ufsboot`. `ufsboot`, the secondary boot program, loads the kernel. | `mboot`, the master boot record, loads `pboot`. `pboot`, the Solaris partition boot program, loads `bootblk`. `bootblk`, the primary boot program, loads `ufsboot`. `ufsboot`, the secondary boot program, loads the kernel. |
| System shutdown | The `shutdown` and `init` commands can be used without additional operator intervention. | The `shutdown` and `init` commands are used but require operator intervention to type any key to continue the prompt. |
| Disk controllers | SCSI and IDE. | SCSI and IDE. |
| Disk slices and partitions | A disk may have a maximum of eight slices, numbered 0–7. | A disk may have a maximum of four `fdisk` partitions. The Solaris `fdisk` partition may contain up to 10 slices, numbered 0–9, but only 0–7 can store user data. |
| Diskette drives | Desktop systems usually contain one 3.5-inch diskette drive. | Systems may contain two diskette drives: a 3.5-inch and a 5.25-inch drive. |

# Solaris Operating Environment Evolution

To help you understand how Solaris is evolving, Table 2 provides a list of the major system administration feature differences for each release.

**Table 2**      *Solaris Operating Environment Evolution*

| Release | New Features |
| --- | --- |
| Solaris 1.0 (SunOS 4.x) | Berkeley (BSD) UNIX contains SunOS 4.x functionality. |
| Solaris 2.0 (SunOS 5.0) | A merger of AT&T System V Release 4 (SVR4) and BSD UNIX. To facilitate customer transition, Solaris uses SVR4 as the default environment, with BSD commands and modes as an option. Administration Tool provides a graphical user interface Database Manager and Host Manager. |
| Solaris 2.1 (SunOS 5.1) | Administration Tool adds a graphical user interface Printer Manager and User Account Manager. |
| Solaris 2.2 (SunOS 5.2) | Volume management integrates access to CD-ROM and diskette files with the File Manager and provides a command-line interface. Users no longer need superuser privileges to mount CD-ROMs and diskettes. Solaris 2.0 and 2.1 procedures do not work with volume management because volume management controls and owns the devices. |
| Solaris 2.3 (SunOS 5.3) | Volume management changes Solaris 2.2 mount point naming conventions. |
|  | Administration Tool adds a graphical user interface Serial Port Manager with templates that provide default settings, which makes adding character terminals and modems much easier. |
|  | The automounter is split into two programs: an `automountd` daemon and a separate `automount` program. Both are run when the system is booted. The `/tmp_mnt` mount point is not displayed as part of the path name, and the local path is displayed as `/home/`*`username`*. Additional predefined automount map variables are provided. (Refer to the *Solaris Advanced System Administrator's Guide.*) |
|  | Online: Backup 2.1 is included with the release. (Not documented in this book.) |

**Table 2**    *Solaris Operating Environment Evolution (Continued)*

| Release | New Features |
|---|---|
| | Pluggable Authentication Model (PAM) is included with the release. PAM provides a consistent framework to enable access control applications, such as `login`, to be able to choose any authentication scheme available on a system, without concern for implementation details. (Not documented in this book.) |
| | C2 Security is included in this release. (Not documented in this book.) |
| | The `format`(1) command changes for SCSI disks. (Not documented in this book.) |
| | PPP network protocol product that provides IP network connectivity over a variety of point-to-point connections is included in this release. (Not documented in this book.) |
| | Cache File System (CacheFS) for NFS is included in this release. CacheFS is a generic, nonvolatile caching mechanism to improve performance of certain file systems by using a small, fast, local disk. |
| | New NIS+ setup scripts are included in this release. The `nisserver`(1M), `nispopulate`(1M), and `nisclient`(1M) scripts enable you to set up an NIS+ domain much more quickly and easily than if you used the individual NIS+ commands to do so. With these scripts, you can avoid a lengthy manual setup process. |
| Solaris 2.4 (SunOS 5.4) | New Motif GUI for Solaris software installation is added. (Not documented in this book.) |
| Solaris 2.5 (SunOS 5.5) | New `pax`(1M) portable archive interchange command for copying files and file systems to portable media is added. |
| | Admintool is used to administer only local systems. Solstice AdminSuite product is available for managing systems in a network for SPARC and IA systems. |
| | New process tools are available in `/usr/proc/bin` that display highly detailed information about the active processes stored in the process file system in the `/proc` directory. |

**Table 2**    *Solaris Operating Environment Evolution (Continued)*

| Release | New Features |
|---------|--------------|
| | Telnet client is upgraded to the 4.4 BSD version. `rlogin` and `telnetd` remote login capacity are improved. (Not documented in this book.) |
| Solaris 2.5.1 (SunOS 5.5.1) | The limit on user ID and group ID values is raised to 2147483647, or the maximum value of a signed integer. The `nobody` user and group (60001) and the no access user and group (60002) retain the same UID and GID as in previous Solaris releases. |
| Solaris 2.6 (SunOS 5.6) | Changes to the Solaris 2.6 printing software provide a better solution than the LP print software in previous Solaris releases. You can easily set up and manage print clients by using the NIS or NIS+ nameservices to enable centralization of print administration for a network of systems and printers. New features include redesign of print packages, print protocol adapter, bundled SunPrint™ client software, and network printer support. |
| | New `nisbackup` and `nisrestore` commands provide a quick and efficient method of backing up and restoring NIS+ namespaces. |
| | New patch tools, including `patchadd` and `patchrm` commands, add and remove patches. These commands replace the `installpatch` and `backoutpatch` commands that were previously shipped with each individual patch. (Refer to the *Solaris Advanced System Administrator's Guide*.) |
| | New `filesync` command ensures that data is moved automatically between a portable computer and a server. (Not documented in this book.) |
| | The previous flat `/proc` file system is restructured into a directory hierarchy that contains additional subdirectories for state information and control functions. This release also provides a watchpoint facility to monitor access to and modifications of data in the process address space. The `adb`(1) command uses this facility to provide watchpoints. |

**Table 2**  *Solaris Operating Environment Evolution (Continued)*

| Release | New Features |
|---------|-------------|
| | Large files are supported on UFS, NFS, and CacheFS file systems. Applications can create and access files up to one Tbyte on UFS-mounted file systems and up to the limit of the NFS server for NFS- and CacheFS-mounted file systems. A new -mount option disables the large-file support on UFS file systems. Using the -mount option enables system administrators to ensure that older applications that are not able to safely handle large files do not accidentally operate on large files. |
| | NFS Kerberos authentication now uses DES encryption to improve security over the network. The kernel implementations of NFS and RPC network services support a new RPC authentication flavor that is based on the Generalized Security Services API (GSS-API). This support contains the hooks for future stronger security of the NFS environment. (Refer to the *Solaris Advanced System Administrator's Guide.*) |
| | The PAM authentication modules framework enables you to "plug in" new authentication technologies. (Refer to the *Solaris Advanced System Administrator's Guide.*) |
| | Font Admin enables easy installation and use of fonts for the X Window System. It supports TrueType, Type0, Type1, and CID fonts for multibyte languages and provides comparative font preview capability. It is fully integrated into the CDE desktop. (Not documented in this book.) |
| | TrueType fonts are supported through X and Display PostScript. Font Admin enables easy installation and integration of third-party fonts into the Solaris environment. (Not documented in this book.) |
| | The Solaris 2.6 Operating Environment is year 2000 ready. It uses unambiguous dates and follows the X/Open guidelines where appropriate. (Not documented in this book.) |
| | WebNFS software enables file systems to be accessed through the Web with the NFS protocol. This protocol is very reliable and provides greater throughput under a heavy load. (Not documented in this book.) |

**Table 2**    *Solaris Operating Environment Evolution (Continued)*

| Release | New Features |
|---|---|
| | The Java Virtual Machine 1.1 integrates the Java platform for the Solaris Operating Environment. It includes the Java runtime environment and the basic tools needed to develop Java applets and applications. (Not documented in this book.) |
| | For IA systems, the Configuration Assistant interface is part of the new booting system for the Solaris (Intel Platform Edition) software. It determines which hardware devices are in the system, accounts for the resources each device uses, and enables users to choose which device to boot from. |
| | For IA systems, the kdmconfig program configures the mouse, graphics adapter, and monitor. If an owconfig file already exists, kdmconfig extracts any usable information from it. In addition, kdmconfig retrieves information left in the devinfo tree by the defconf program and uses that information to automatically identify devices. (Not documented in this book.) |
| | Release is fully compliant with X/Open UNIX 95, POSIX standards. (Not documented in this book.) |
| Solaris 7 (SunOS 5.7) | Solaris 64-bit operating environment is added (SPARC Platform Edition only). (Not documented in this book.) |
| | UFS logging improves file system support. |
| | Lightweight Directory Access Protocol (LDAP) protocol improves managing name databases. (Not documented in this book.) |
| | Java Development Kit for Solaris significantly improves scalability and performance for Java applications. (Not documented in this book.) |
| | Dynamic reconfiguration significantly decreases system downtime. |
| | AnswerBook2 server runs on a Web server. (Not documented in this book.) |
| | Unicode locales enhanced with multiscript capabilities and six new Unicode locales are added. |

*New!* (margin note beside Solaris 7 row)

**Table 2**    *Solaris Operating Environment Evolution (Continued)*

| Release | New Features |
|---------|--------------|
| | RPC security is enhanced with integrity and confidentiality. (Not documented in this book.) |
| | The Solaris Common Desktop Environment (CDE) contains new tools to make it easy to find, manipulate, and manage address cards, applications, e-mail addresses, files, folders, hosts, processes, and Web addresses. (Not documented in this book.) |
| Solaris 8 (SunOS 5.8) | IPv6 adds increased address space and improves Internet functionality by using a simplified header format, support for authentication and privacy, autoconfiguration of address assignments, and new quality-of-service capabilities. |
| | The Solaris Operating Environment provides the Naming Service switch back-end support directory service based on Lightweight Directory Access Protocol (LDAP). (Not documented in this book.) |
| | The Java2 Software Development Kit for Solaris significantly improves scalability and performance of Java applications. (Not documented in this book.) |
| | The Solaris 8 Installation CD provides a graphical, wizard-based, Java-powered application to install the Solaris Operating Environment and other software. (Not documented in this book.) |
| | The Solaris 8 Operating Environment supports the Universal Disk Format (UDF) file system, enabling users to exchange data stored on CD-ROMs, disks, diskettes, DVDs, and other optical media. |
| | The Solaris Smart Card feature enables security administrators to protect a computer desktop or individual application by requiring users to authenticate themselves by means of a smart card. (Not documented in this book.) |
| | The PDA Synchronization (PDA Sync) application synchronizes the data from applications such as Desktop Calendar, Desktop Mail, Memo, and Address, with data in similar applications on a user's Personal Digital Assistant (PDA). (Not documented in this book.) |

New!

**Table 2**    *Solaris Operating Environment Evolution (Continued)*

| Release | New Features |
| --- | --- |
| | The Solaris 8 Software CDs and Languages CD include support for more than 90 locales, covering 37 languages. (Not documented in this book.) |
| | The Solaris Common Desktop Environment (CDE) contains new and enhanced features that incorporate easy-to-use desktop productivity tools, PC interoperability, and desktop management tools. (Not documented in this book.) |
| | The X Server is upgraded to the X11R6.4 industry standard that includes features to increase user productivity and mobility, including remote execution of X applications through a Web browser on any Web-based desktop, Xinerama, Color Utilization Policy, EnergyStar support, and new APIs and documentation for the developer tool kits. (Not documented in this book.) |
| | Role-Based Access Control (RBAC) enables system administrators to create specific roles by which they can assign superuser privileges for specific tasks to one or more individual users. |
| Solaris 8 Update 3 | Role-Based Access Control (RBAC) functionality is enhanced with the addition of a complete set of Solaris Management Console tools used to manage RBAC. |
| | Solaris AdminSuite 3.0 functionality, previously available as a separate free download, has been integrated with the Solaris 8 Update 3 release. This functionality is now provided with the Solaris Management Console set of tools. |
| | Internet Protocol version 6 (IPv6) adds increased address space and improved Internet functionality with support for authentication and privacy and autoconfiguration of address assignments. IPv6 uses a simplified header format and enables new quality-of-service capabilities. |
| | The CDE mailer provides the capability to add attachments to mail messages in the Compose window. |
| | The UFS file system has been enhanced to improve the performance of direct I/O to enable concurrent read and write access to regular UFS files. |

*New!*

**Table 2**   *Solaris Operating Environment Evolution (Continued)*

| Release | New Features |
| --- | --- |
| | During installation, systems can be configured by the system identification commands to be LDAP clients. Previous releases enabled only the configuration of a system as an NIS, NIS+, or DNS client. |
| | The Solaris WebStart 3.0 installation has been updated to enable you to modify selected Solaris Software Group by adding or removing packages. |
| | A new version of the Solaris Product Registry enables you to uninstall individual system packages, display all installed localized Solaris system products in the System Software Localizations folder, and make registry compatible with more installation wizards. |
| | Diskless Client management provides the new smosservice(1M) and smdiskless(1M) commands to manage diskless clients. |

# Freeware

*New!*

The following freeware tools and libraries are included in the Solaris 8 release.

- bash—sh-compatible command language interpreter.
- bzip2—Block-sorting file compressor.
- gpatch—Applies patch files to originals.
- gzip—GNU zip compression command.
- less—A pager similar to more.
- libz—Also known as zlib. A library that performs compression, specifically, RFCs 1950-1952.
- mkisofs—Builds a CD image, using an iso9660 file system.
- rpm2cpio—Transforms a package in RPM format (Red Hat Package Manager) to a cpio archive.
- tcsh—C shell with file-name completion and command-line editing.
- zip—Compression and file packaging command.
- zsh—Command interpreter (shell) usable as an interactive login shell and as a shell script command processor.

# ACKNOWLEDGMENTS

## Third Edition

Sun Microsystems Press would like to acknowledge the following people for their contributions to the third edition of this book.

Gordon Mahler for his excellent technical input and especially for providing substantial revisions and examples for the Mail Services part of this book. Gordon unpacked his first Sun workstation in 1987, and has been fascinated by UNIX ever since. He has worked as a UNIX System Administrator and Architect in Texas, Washington state and New York City for various firms in the pharmaceutical, telecommunications, and financial fields, as well as a government contract here and there. He is currently a UNIX consultant in the New Jersey/New York area.

Sally Beach, Larissa Brown, Maria Santiago, and Beauty Shields of Sun Microsystems, Inc., for enabling me to participate in the Solaris 8 beta programs and for answering numerous questions.

John Beck, Member of Technical Staff, Sun Microsystems, Inc., for providing information about new `sendmail` features, mail use statistics, and for technical review.

Sandy Carrigan, Sun Microsystems, Inc., for reviewing the RBAC chapter.

Khary Funchess, UNIX/WINDOWS Customer Service, Sun Microsystems, Inc, for answering questions about bugs in the `rmformat` command.

Linda Gallops, Sun Microsystems, Inc., for help identifying technical resources at Sun.

Peter H. Gregory, author of *Solaris System Security* and *Sun Certified System Administrator for Solaris 8 Study Guide,* for permission to include and modify an illustration from his security book and for recommending Gordon Mahler as a technical reviewer.

Mary Lautman, Sun Microsystems, Inc., for providing answers to questions about the new Role-Based Access Control (RBAC) features.

Wil Mara, at Prentice Hall PTR, for his production support.

Eric Nielsen, Manager, Solaris OS, Sun Microsystems, Inc., for reviewing the Volume Management appendix.

Jim Paugh, Sun Microsystems, Inc., for answering questions about NIS+ and for technical review.

William Reeder, Sun Microsystems, Inc., for suggesting John Beck as a technical resource.

Celeste Stokely, Stokely Consulting, for permission to include her *Modems and Terminals Tutorial* as an appendix to this book.

Rama Yalamanchili, Sun Microsystems, Inc., for answering questions about Solaris 8 Beta installation problems.

Those writers from Sun Technical Publications who contributed to the *Solaris System Administration Guide Volumes I, II, and III*, which were used as a technical reference resource.

The author would especially like to thank Rachel Borden, Publisher, Sun Microsystems Press; Michael Alread, Marketing Manager of Sun Microsystems Press; and Greg Doench, Senior Editor, Prentice Hall, for their unfailing enthusiasm, support, and friendship. She would also like to thank Mary Lou Nohr for editing this manuscript with her usual skill and tact and Lisa Iarkowski of Prentice Hall for production support.

The author would also like to thank her husband, Maris, for his continued love and support.

## Second Edition

Sun Microsystems Press would like to acknowledge the following people for their contributions to the second edition of this book.

Bret Bartow, Acquisitions Editor, Macmillan Computer Publishing, for his enthusiasm and support on this project.

Mary Lautner, Program Manager, Sun Microsystems, Inc., for her invaluable help and assistance in providing the author with documentation and answers to numerous questions. Without Mary's help and the information she provided, the author would have been unable to complete this project.

Those writers from Sun Technical Publications who contributed to the *Solaris System Administration Guide* and the documentation on the Solaris Server Intranet Extension CD-ROM, which were used as technical reference resources.

Lisa Gebken of Macmillan Computer Publishing for editing this manuscript.

Peter Gregory for technical review comments.

Tobin Crockett for networking the author's SPARCstatio™ 10 and Macintosh Power PC and for setting up a network printer.

Rob Johnston, System Support Specialist, Sun Microsystems, Inc., for installing Solaris 2.6 and for troubleshooting hardware and software problems.

Tien Nguyen, System Support Specialist, Sun, Inc., for help in troubleshooting hardware and software problems.

Linda Gallops, Sun SQA, for help in tracking down information about modems.

Ken Erickson of Sun Microsystems, Inc., for allowing the author to pester him with occasional technical questions.

The author would especially like to thank Rachel Borden and John Bortner of Sun Microsystems Press for their unfailing enthusiasm and friendship.

## First Edition

Many people contributed to the design, writing, and production of the first edition of this book. Sun Microsystems Press would particularly like to acknowledge the following people for their contributions.

Connie Howard and Mike Rogers, Sun Information Technology and Products managers, and Bridget Burke for their support and encouragement.

Karin Ellison, Sun Press, deserves special thanks for her can-do attitude and her willingness to help out with all kinds of issues related to this book.

Don Charles, Sun Engineering Services Organization, for help in setting up a two-SPARCstation network for this project, and for general system administration support.

Lori Reid, Sun Engineering Services Organization, for providing a Solaris® 2.1 CD-ROM.

Because this book contains different subject areas, specific acknowledgments are listed by part.

# Part 1: Mail Services

Tom Kessler, Sun Engineering, for technical review and helpful discussions about different mail services configuration.

Dave Miner, Sun Engineering, for help with information about the `Aliases` database in Admintool.

Mike Gionfriddo, Sun Engineering, for answering questions about Admintool.

Don Brazell for technical review.

# Part 2: NIS+

Rick Ramsey, Sun Information Technology and Products, for writing a great book about NIS+, providing me with background information, and answering many questions about NIS+.

Vipin Samar, SunSoft Engineering, for providing the engineering perspective for NIS+ and for technical review.

Saquib Jang, Sun Marketing, for providing the marketing perspective and information about the benefits of NIS+.

Bob LeFave, Sun Engineering Services Organization, for last-minute technical input and technical review.

John Auer, SMCC Enterprise Information Services, for additional technical review.

Don Brazell for technical review.

Scott Mann and SunU for permission to sit in on lab classes about NIS+.

## Part 3: Automounter Services

Brent Callaghan, Sun Engineering, for background information and technical review.

Don Brazell for technical review.

## Part 4: Service Access Facility

Patrick Moffitt, Sun Training, for technical review.

Scott Mann and SunU for permission to sit in on lab classes about SAF.

Neil Groundwater, Sun Engineering, for answering questions about modem connections and for technical review.

Tom Fowler, Sun Technical Marketing, for spending lots of time and effort figuring out how printing works in the Solaris 2.x releases and for providing most of the printing troubleshooting examples.

Mary Morris, Sun Engineering, for technical review.

Bruce Sesnovich, Sun Information Technology and Products, for providing background information about SAF and modem procedures.

Tom Amiro, Sun Information Technology and Products, for providing background information about administering user accounts and printers.

## Part 5: Application Software

Steve Shumway, Sun Marketing, for technical review.

Davis Weatherby, Sun Information Resources system engineer, for taking time off from his vacation to provide excellent background information on implementing wrapper-based application servers.

Wayne Thompson, Sun Information Resources systems engineer, for technical review and for facilitating the quality technical input on Sun's implementation of application servers.

Scott Mann and SunU for permission to sit in on lab classes about pkgadd and Software Manager.

Charla Mustard-Foote, Sun Information Technology and Products, for providing me with a CD-ROM of SearchIt™ sofware to use in the examples and for answering questions about Software Manager.

MacDonald King Aston and Julie Bettis, Sun Information Technology and Products, for patiently answering questions about Software Manager.

Keith Palmby, Sun Information Technology and Products, for providing background information about the Online: DiskSuite™ product.

Terry Gibson, SunTech Technical Publications, for providing background information about software licensing.

Dan Larson, SunTech Engineering Support Organization, for discussions about the engineering implementation of application servers.

Bill Petro, Sun Marketing, for background information about installing application software.

Linda Ries, Sun Engineering, for answering questions about the package commands and Software Manager.

# Part 6: Introduction to Shell Programming

Sam Cramer, Sun Engineering, for doing two technical reviews of this part, even though his newest family member arrived right in the middle of the review cycle.

Ellie Quigley, Learning Enterprises: Chico, California; for providing me with her class notes for the Bourne, Korn, and C shells, and for permission to use examples from her course notes.

Wayne Thompson, SMCC Sun Information Resources, for technical review and for providing sample scripts for Chapter 16.

# Appendix A: Volume Management

Howard Alt, Sun Engineering, for background information and for technical review.

Lynn Rohrer, Sun Information Technology and Products, for background information and for technical review.

Robert Novak, Sun Marketing, for technical review.

Mary Lautner, Sun Information Technology and Products, for letting me use her system to test the remote CD-ROM procedures.

## Appendix B; Solaris Server Intranet Extension Products

Neil Groundwater, Sun Engineering, for background information and for technical review.

Lynn Rohrer, Sun Technical Information Technology and Products, for background information and for technical review.

Robert Novak, Sun Marketing, for technical review.

## Glossary

Craig Mohrman, Sun Engineering, for technical review.

Thanks are also due to the following people at Ziff-Davis Press for being so easy to work with: senior development editor Melinda Levine, copy editor Ellen Falk, managing editor Cheryl Holzapfel, and project coordinator, Ami Knox.

The author would like to thank her three cats for lap sitting, keyboard walking, and general company keeping while this book was in progress.

# CONTENTS

# 3 Planning Mail Services  77

## 21 Using the Automated Security Enhancement Tool (ASET)   559

# *Part One*

# Mail Services

Refer to the chapters in this part if you need to set up a new mail service or expand an existing one.

This part describes the Solaris mail services in four chapters. Chapter 1 describes the components of the mail service, defines mail service terminology, and explains how the programs in the mail service interact. Chapter 2 describes several common mail configurations and provides guidelines for setting up each configuration. Chapter 3 describes how to set up and administer mail services. Chapter 4 describes the sendmail configuration file and explains how to customize it if you need a more complex configuration file for your mail system.

# 1

# UNDERSTANDING MAIL SERVICES

As system administrator, you may need to expand an existing mail service or set up a new one. To help you with these tasks, this chapter introduces what's new with Solaris 8 mail services, defines mail services terminology, and describes the components of the mail service.

*NOTE. The information in this chapter has been extensively revised and updated.*

New!

This chapter defines the following terms and describes how they are used in the mail services.

- Systems in a mail configuration.
  - Gateway.
  - Mail hub.
  - Mail client.
- Mail user agent (MUA).
- Mail transport agent (MTA)
- Mail delivery agents (sometimes called mailers).
- Domains.
- Mail addressing.
- Mailbox.
- Aliases.

## New! New Mail Service Features

The Solaris™ 8 mail services use the Version 8.9.3 `sendmail` mail-transport agent. The following list describes some of the important changes that are included in this new version.

- You no longer edit the `sendmail.cf` file directly. You should treat it as a binary that is not editable. Instead, you start with a file with an `.mc` (mail configuration) suffix and use the m4 macro processor together with the m4 macro files included with `sendmail` to "compile" the file with a `.cf` suffix. See "Generating the sendmail Configuration File" on page 53 for more information.

- The new `MaxHeadersLength` configuration file option limits the length of the sum of all header lines in a message. The default value is 32786 bytes. Incoming messages with headers that exceed the `MaxHeadersLength` value are rejected. See "Processing Options" on page 61 for more information. Note that even processing options such as these are controlled from the `.mc` file. *Never* change any of these options in the `.cf` file as long as the m4 macro files enable you to set them in the `.mc` file. See Chapter 2, "Customizing sendmail Configuration Files" for more information.

- You can use the new `/etc/default/sendmail` file to store options used to start `sendmail`. In previous releases, the options were stored in an init script. When you use the `/etc/default/sendmail` file, upgrading systems is easier because you do not need to change the init scripts.

  The new `/etc/default/sendmail` file is handy for client `sendmail` systems. For example, you use this file to leave out the `-bd` option when running `sendmail` on a client system. Without the `-bd` option, `sendmail` delivers e-mail sent only from inside the system—sent by users currently logged in locally. `sendmail` does *not* listen to TCP port 25 in this case, so this system cannot have e-mail transported *through or into it*, only *from inside* it. This feature improves security because only a very few `sendmail` servers have the `-bd` option turned on in this file and only those hosts have `sendmail` listening on TCP port 25 for incoming e-mail transmissions.

- The `mail.local` program is extended to use the Local Mail Transfer Protocol (LMTP). This protocol returns error codes for each recipient so that the message is re-sent only to the recipients that did not receive the message. In previous releases, the message was requeued to all of the recipients so that everyone who had previously received the message would receive duplicates. This protocol was added to `sendmail` in the Solaris 7 release.

- You can use the new `/usr/bin/praliases` command to turn the data in the alias database into plain text. If you specify an argument on the command line, the command displays any matching key:value pair.

- You can use the new `smrsh` shell to limit the number of commands that can be run with the `"|program"` syntax of `sendmail`. When this feature is enabled—by adding `FEATURE(`smrsh')` in the `*.mc` file—only programs included in `/var/adm/sm.bin` can be run. See "Using the sendmail Restricted Shell" on page 55 and the `smrsh(1M)` manual page for more information.

- The `vacation` program has new options. You can use the `-f` option to select an alternate database instead of `~/.vacation.ext`. You can use the `-m` option to specify an alternate message file instead of `~/.vacation.msg`. You can use the `-s` option to specify the reply address instead of the UNIX `From` line in the incoming message.

- With the `mailx` program you can use the `From:` header as the basis of the sender instead of the envelope sender. This change to `mailx` makes it consistent with `mailtool` and `dtmail`.

- The `/usr/lib/sendmail.mx` program—previously used to access DNS mail exchange records—has been removed. This functionality is now included in `sendmail` by default. `/etc/nsswitch.conf` file simply turns on the system's ability to use DNS. It does not affect `sendmail` directly. If DNS is available, `sendmail` uses it. Make sure DNS is available on all systems that run `sendmail` by modifying the `hosts:` entry in the `/etc/nsswitch.conf` file. See "Configuring Hosts to Use DNS Mail Exchange Records" on page 112 for more information.

You can find additional information on the Solaris version of `sendmail` at `http://www.sendmail.org/sun-specific/migration+sun.html`.

# Systems in a Mail Configuration

A mail configuration requires a minimum of two elements, which can be combined on the same system or can be provided by separate systems: a mail hub and mail clients. When you want users to be able to communicate with networks outside of your domain, you must also have a gateway. `mailhost` is a common DNS host alias assigned to the mail hub in any domain.

Figure 1 shows a typical electronic mail configuration that uses all elements. Each of these elements is identified and described in the following sections.

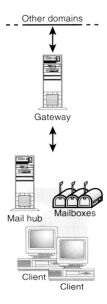

*Figure 1*     *A Typical Electronic Mail Configuration*

## Gateway

A *gateway* is a system that handles connections between your network(s) and networks external to your site(s) such as the Internet, as shown in Figure 2. Note that both domains have a `sendmail` gateway host that is the only path out of their networks onto the Internet and, from there, to any other domain. You must customize the `*mc` file used to create the `sendmail.cf` file on the gateway system.

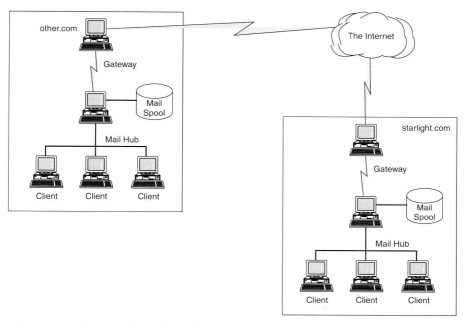

*Figure 2    A Gateway Can Handle Connections Between Different Communications Protocols*

If you have to set up a gateway, find a gateway configuration file that is close to what you need and modify it to fit your situation. Refer to the default `/usr/lib/mail/cf/main-v7sun.mc` file as an example if you want to write your own `.mc` file to use on a gateway system.

> *NOTE. The process you use to create* `sendmail` *configuration files has been changed. You must create a file with a* `.mc` *suffix and use the m4 macro processor and provided* `sendmail` *m4 macro files to build the* `sendmail.cf` *file. See "Testing the Rewriting Rules—the -bt Flag" on page 54 for more information.*

## Mail Hub

A *mail hub* is a system that you designate as the main mail system on your network. The mail hub is the system to which other systems at the site forward mail that they cannot deliver. You designate a system as a mail hub by adding the word `mailhost` to the Internet Protocol (IP) address line in the system's `/etc/hosts` file or by adding a `mailhost A` (address) record to DNS for the mail hub in question. You should also write a `*.mc` file specific to your domain for your mail hub.

A mail hub is any system that stores mailboxes in the `/var/mail` directory. The mail hub is responsible for routing all of the mail from a client. When a client sends mail, the mail hub puts it in a queue for delivery. Once the mail is in the queue, the client can reboot or turn off the system without losing the mail messages. When the recipient gets mail from a client, the path in the `From:` line of the message contains the name of the mail hub. If the recipient chooses to respond, the response goes to the user's mailbox on the server.

When the mailbox is on a mail hub, messages are delivered to the server, not directly to the client's system. When the mailbox is on the user's local system, the local system acts as its own mail hub if it does not mount `/var/mail` from another system.

If the mail hub is not the user's local system, users with NFS can mount the `/var/mail` directory in the `/etc/vfstab` file, use the automounter, or log in to the mail hub to read their mail.

A good candidate for a mail hub is a system with good network connectivity with a large amount of disk space for spooling incoming e-mail. The system should be backed up regularly. If your mail hub also doubles as your gateway, it should have connectivity to the Internet. If you have a stand-alone system that is not networked but is in a time-sharing configuration, you can treat the stand-alone as the mail hub of a one-system network. Similarly, if you have several systems on an Ethernet and none have phone lines, you can designate one as the mail hub. The mail hub can also provide home directories for users.

If the mail hub for a domain does not also store user home directories, it should at least be able to automount the home directories for all users. The mail hub needs to examine the `.forward` file in a user's home directory when trying to deliver messages to that user in case the user's e-mail is being forwarded to another location. If each user's home directory is not available to the mail hub, such forwarding does not work properly.

Table 1 shows some sample statistics about the size of mail messages and mail traffic at a computer company with about 200 employees who transmit large numbers of binaries (PDF files, executables, Excel spreadsheets, PowerPoint presentations) as attachments.

*Table 1     Sample Statistics for Mail Messages and Traffic*

| Statistic | Description |
| --- | --- |
| 10 Kbytes | Average size of an e-mail message. |
| 1 Mbyte | Amount of mail received by an average user in one day. |
| 1 Mbyte | Small mailbox size (user reads mail regularly and stores messages elsewhere). |

*Table 1     Sample Statistics for Mail Messages and Traffic (Continued)*

| Statistic | Description |
|-----------|-------------|
| 200 Mbytes | Large mailbox size (user stores long-term mail in /var/mail mailbox). |
| 50-75 Mbyte | Recommended spooling space to allocate for each user's mailbox, based on the figures in this table. |

## Mail Client

A *mail client* is any system that enables a user's mail spool file to be read through an NFS mount of /var/mail from a mail hub and, therefore, does not have a local /var/mail directory. You must make sure the mail client has the appropriate entry in the /etc/vfstab file and a mount point to mount the mailbox from the mail server or that it automounts the /var/mail directory.

> *NOTE. Mail clients often run* sendmail, *but they do not (or should not) listen for incoming* sendmail *connections from the network. Mail clients simply run* sendmail *so that* sendmail *can transmit e-mail sent from within the mail client to the nearest mail hub for processing.*

# Mail Service Programs

Mail services are provided by a combination of programs that interact, as shown by the simplified diagram in Figure 3.

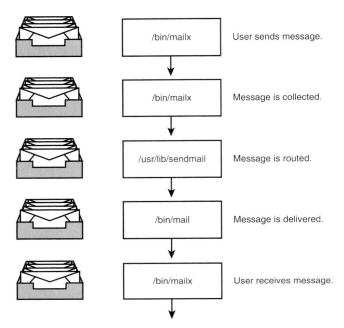

*Figure 3     How Mail Programs Interact*

Users send messages with programs—known as mail user agents (MUAs)—such as `mailx`, `mailtool`, or `dtmail`. See the manual pages for information about these programs.

The message is collected by the program that was used to generate it and is passed to the `sendmail` daemon or mail transport agent (MTA). The `sendmail` daemon *parses* (divides into identifiable segments) the addresses in the message, using information from the configuration file `/etc/mail/sendmail.cf` to determine network name syntax, aliasing, forwarding information, and network topology. Using this information, `sendmail` determines the route a message must take to get to a recipient.

The `sendmail` daemon passes the message to the appropriate mail hub, where it is handed off to a mail delivery agent. The `/usr/lib/mail.local` program—an example of a mail delivery agent—on the mail hub delivers the mail to the mailbox in the `/var/mail/username` file of the recipient of the message.

The user is notified that mail has arrived and retrieves it using an MUA such as `/bin/mail`, `/bin/mailx`, `mailtool`, `dtmail`, or a similar program.

## Mail User Agents (MUAs)

The *mail user agent* is the program that acts as the interface between the user and the `sendmail` program. The MUAs for the Solaris Operating Environment are `/usr/bin/mail`, `/usr/bin/mailx`, `$OPENWINHOME/bin/mailtool`, and `/usr/dt/bin/dtmail`.

## Mail Transport Agent (MTA)

The *transport agent* actually receives and deliveres messages. The transport agent for the Solaris Operating Environment is `sendmail`.

Open source `sendmail` is available at the `www.sendmail.org` Web site, which is maintained by the Sendmail Consortium. At the time of writing, the current version of `sendmail` is 8.11.3. Sun compiles `sendmail` version 8.9.3 and provides it as part of Solaris.

The transport agent performs the following functions.

- Accepts messages from the mail user agent.
- Understands destination addresses.
- Hands off mail originating on the local system to the proper delivery agent.
- Receives incoming mail from other MTAs and hands it off to delivery agents for delivery to local users.

If you want to use a more current version of `sendmail` than Sun provides, you can download it from `www.sendmail.org`. Two additional Web sites provide additional information about `sendmail`. A forum at `www.sendmail.net` disseminates information about and discuss `sendmail`. It has many useful articles and publishes news related to `sendmail`. `www.sendmail.com` sells a commercial version of `sendmail`. This version has nice graphical tools to help you customize `sendmail`.

### The sendmail Configuration File (sendmail.cf)

A *configuration file* controls the way that `sendmail` performs its functions. The configuration file determines the choice of delivery agents, address-rewriting rules, and the format of the mail header. It also enables you to specify options that modify the functionality of different features or to turn the features on or off.

The sendmail program uses the information from the `/etc/mail/sendmail.cf` file to perform its functions. Each system has a default `sendmail.cf` file installed in the `/etc/mail` directory. You *may* not need to build a customized configuration file for your mail clients, but you do need to build them for your gateways and mail hubs.

The Solaris Operating Environment provides two default configuration files, which are also in the /etc/mail directory.

- A configuration file named main.cf for the system (or systems) you designate as the mail hub or a gateway.
- A configuration file named subsidiary.cf (a duplicate copy of the default sendmail.cf file).

Which configuration file you use on any individual system depends on the role the system plays in your mail service.

- For mail clients, you do not need to do anything to set up or edit the default configuration file.
- To set up a mailhost, a relay host, or a gateway, copy the /usr/lib/mail/cf/main-v7sun.mc file and rename it with a .mc (mail configuration) suffix. Next, edit the .mc file to set parameters needed for your mail configuration: gateway and mail hub. You must then "compile" the file, using the m4 macro processor. See "Generating the sendmail Configuration File" on page 53 for more information. Refer to Chapter 2, "Customizing sendmail Configuration Files" for information on editing configuration files.

The following list describes some configuration parameters you may want to change, depending on the requirements of your site.

*NOTE. You change these parameters in the .mc file that is used to generate the sendmail.cf file, not in the sendmail.cf file itself. The parameters are mentioned here so that you know what they look like in the resulting configuration file.*

- Time values.
  - Specify how often sendmail runs the queue. The interval is typically set to between 15 minutes and 1 hour.
  - Specify read timeouts.
  - Specify how long a message remains in the queue before it is returned to the sender.
- Delivery modes specify how quickly mail is to be delivered.
- Load limiting prevents wasted time during loaded periods because it does not attempt to deliver large messages, messages to many recipients, or messages to sites that have been down for a long time.
- Log level specifies what kinds of problems are logged.

*New!*

- File modes.
  - `setuid` for `sendmail`.
  - Temporary file modes.
  - `/etc/mail/aliases` permissions.

The `sendmail` program receives a message from a program such as `mailx`, `mailtool`, or `dtmail`, edits the message header as required by the destination mailer, and calls appropriate delivery agents to make the delivery. If delivery cannot be made immediately, `sendmail` requeues the request and tries to hand off delivery to the proper delivery agent at regular intervals until delivery is successful or until a timeout value is reached.

*NOTE. The* `sendmail` *program never edits or changes the body of a message. Any changes that it makes to interpret e-mail addresses are made only in the header of the message.*

**Argument Processing and Address Parsing**    When `sendmail` processes a message, it collects recipient names (either from the command line or from the SMTP protocol) and generates two files. One is an envelope that contains a list of recipients and information about delivery. The other file contains the header and the body of the message. The `sendmail` program expands aliases, including mailing lists, and validates as much as possible the remote recipient; `sendmail` checks syntax and verifies local recipients. Detailed checking of host names is deferred until delivery. As local recipients are verified, messages are forwarded to them.

After parsing the recipient lists, `sendmail` appends each name to both the envelope and the header of the message. When a name is aliased or forwarded, it retains the old name in the list and sets a flag to tell the delivery phase to ignore this recipient. The lists are kept free from duplicates, preventing "alias loops" and duplicate messages delivered to the same recipient, which can occur if a recipient is in two different alias groups.

*NOTE. Users may receive duplicate copies of the same message when alias lists contain e-mail addresses for the same person (who is using different syntax). The* `sendmail` *program cannot always match the duplicate e-mail addresses.*

**Message Collection**    The `sendmail` program then collects the message. The message has a header at the beginning. The header and the body of the message must be separated by a blank line. The only formatting requirement imposed on the message body is that its lines of text must be no greater than 1,024 bytes. The `sendmail` program stores the header in memory and stores the body of the message in a temporary file. To simplify the program interface, the message is collected even if no names are valid—in which case the message is returned with an error.

*NOTE. Until now,* `sendmail` *could not transmit binary data as part of mail messages. With the advent of the multimedia mailtool, users can now transmit binary data. It must, however, be encoded by a mail user agent.* `sendmail` *does not do any automatic encoding of binary data. Refer to the documentation for Mail Tool or* `dtmail` *for information on how to encode and decode electronic mail messages.*

**Message Delivery**    For each unique mailer and host in the recipient list, `sendmail` calls the appropriate delivery agent. Each invocation of a delivery agent sends a message to all of the users on one host. Delivery agents that accept only one recipient at a time are handled properly.

The `sendmail` program sends the message to the delivery agent with one of the same interfaces used to submit a message to `sendmail` (using the conventional UNIX argument vector/return status, speaking over a pair of UNIX pipes and speaking SMTP over a TCP connection). Each copy of the message has a customized header attached to the beginning of it. The delivery agent catches and checks the status code, and a suitable error message is given as appropriate. The exit code must conform to a system standard. If a nonstandard exit code is used, the message `Services unavailable` is used.

**Queuing for Retransmission**    When the delivery agent returns a status that shows it might be able to handle the mail later (for example, the next host is down or the phone is busy for UUCP), `sendmail` stores it in a queue and tries again later.

**Return to Sender**    If errors occur during processing, `sendmail` returns the message to the sender for retransmission. The letter may be mailed back or written to the `dead.letter` file in the sender's home directory.

## .forward Files

Users can create a `.forward` file in their home directory that `sendmail` uses to temporarily redirect mail or send mail to a custom set of programs. With a `.forward` file, users can redirect their mail without needing to bother a system administrator with frequent alias change requests. When troubleshooting mail problems, particularly problems of mail not being delivered to the expected address, always check the user's home directory for a `.forward` file.

## Mail Delivery Agents

A mail delivery agent (or delivery agent) specifies a program external to `sendmail` that `sendmail` uses to deliver messages to various locations and for various purposes. The following list provides examples of delivery agents.

- `local`—This delivery agent actually delivers an e-mail message into a user's mailbox, usually on a central mail hub system.

- `prog`—This delivery agent enables an e-mail message to be passed into a program instead of into a mailbox.

- `smtp`—This delivery agent does not actually call a program. Instead, it instructs `sendmail` to open a TCP network connection with another `sendmail` program running on another host. `smtp` enables `sendmail` to transmit messages to users that don't have a mailbox on the local system.

Delivery agents return the status of their deliveries to `sendmail`. If the delivery is successful, `sendmail` does no further work. If the delivery fails, then `sendmail` determines whether to requeue the message for another delivery attempt later or to bounce the message back to the original sender. `sendmail` makes this decision based on the status returned by the delivery agent.

Delivery agents are sometimes called *mailers*. This terminology is confusing because the m4 macros used to specify delivery agents in `.mc` files are called `MAILER`s. Therefore, we use the term delivery agent here. For more information, see "Mailers" on page 51.

# Mailbox

A *mailbox* is a file on a mail server that is the final destination for e-mail messages. The name of the mailbox can be the user name or a place to put mail for someone with a specific function, such as the postmaster. Mailboxes can be in the `/var/mail` directory on the user's local system or on a mail server. The `/var/mail` directory is often called the *mail spool*. The files contained within that directory are called *mailboxes*.

Mail should always be stored in `/var/mail`. If `/var/mail` is NFS-mounted, it must be mounted with the `actimeo=0` option.

The `Aliases` database, the `/etc/mail/aliases` file, and nameservices such as NIS and NIS+ provide mechanisms for creating aliases for electronic mail addresses so that users do not need to know the precise local name of a user's mailbox. Mail aliases provide aliases for names to the left of the @ sign.

Some common naming conventions for special-purpose mailboxes are shown in Table 2.

*Table 2      Conventions for the Format of Mailbox Names*

| Format | Description |
|---|---|
| *username* | User names are frequently the same as mailbox names. |
| *Firstname.Lastname,* *Firstname_Lastname,* *Firstinitial.Lastname* *Firstinitial_Lastname* | User names can be identified as full names with a dot (or an underscore) separating the first and last names or by a first initial with a dot (or an underscore) separating the initial and the last name. |

# DNS and sendmail

Domain Name Service (DNS) is a required part of the mail services infrastructure. sendmail depends on DNS to transmit e-mail outside of internal networks. sendmail looks for DNS MX records to determine which system is used to transmit e-mail to each destination domain. DNS provides host names to the IP address service and serves as a database for mail administration. Networks generally organize their hosts into a hierarchy of administrative domains.

A *domain* is a directory structure for electronic mail addressing and network address naming. The domain address has the following format.

```
mailbox@subdomain. . . . . subdomain2.subdomain1.top-level-domain
```

The part of the address to the left of the @ sign is the *local address*. The local address may contain information about routing using another mail transport. For example, if you are on the Internet and you want to send e-mail to a person (jim) who lives in a UUCP domain (joebob.uucp) that is hiding behind a domain that has direct Internet connectivity and DNS (starlight.com), you would use the address jim%joebob.uucp.@starlight.com.

Generally, this kind of addressing is no longer needed and is strictly prohibited by sendmail by default because it is used by spammers to send e-mail through other sites (called *spam relaying*). For example, suppose you want to send e-mail to ralph at idiot.com but you want to go through starlight.com to get there. Both domains are on the Internet and both run DNS, but you can still address the e-mail to `ralph%idiot.com@starlight.com`. This syntax sends the message(s) to `starlight.com`, whose `sendmail` converts the address to `ralph@idiot.com`. This conversion eats up time on the `starlight.com` gateway or mail hub.

The part of the address to the right of the @ sign shows the *domain address* for the local address. A dot (.) separates each part of the domain address. The domain can be an organization, a physical area, or a geographic region. Domain addresses are case-insensitive. It makes no difference whether you use upper, lower, or mixed case in the domain part of an address.

The order of domain information is hierarchical, with the locations more specific and local the closer they are to the @ sign (although certain British and New Zealand networks reverse the order).

*NOTE. Most gateways automatically translate the reverse order of British and New Zealand domain names into the commonly used order. The larger the number of subdomains, the more detailed the information that is provided about the destination. Just as a subdirectory or a file in a file system hierarchy is inside the directory above, each subdomain is considered to be inside the one located to its right.*

Table 3 shows the top-level domains in the United States.

*Table 3      Top-Level Domains in the United States*

| Domain | Description |
|--------|-------------|
| `.com` | Commercial sites. |
| `.edu` | Educational sites. |
| `.gov` | Government installations. |
| `.mil` | Military installations. |
| `.net` | Networking organizations. |
| `.org` | Nonprofit organizations. |

Because of the increasing popularity of the World Wide Web, the International Ad Hoc Committee (IAHC), a coalition of participants from the broad Internet community, has implemented a proposal to add seven new generic top-level domains (gTLDs) to the existing set. The new gTLDs are listed in Table 4.

*Table 4*      *New Generic Top-Level Domains*

| Domain | Description |
|--------|-------------|
| .arts | Entities emphasizing cultural and entertainment activities. |
| .firm | Businesses or firms. |
| .info | Entities providing information services. |
| .nom | Entities that want individual or personal nomenclature. |
| .rec | Entities emphasizing recreation and entertainment activities. |
| .store | Businesses offering goods to purchase. |
| .web | Entities emphasizing activities related to the World Wide Web. |

In addition to the new gTLDs, up to 28 new registrars will be established to grant registrations for second-level domain names. To guide future registrar developments, under Swiss law a Council of Registrars (CORE) association will be established to create and enforce requirements for registrar operations. The full text of the IAHC report is available at `http://www.iahc.org`.

> *NOTE. The IAHC was dissolved in 1997. Its successor, linked from the IAHC site, deals exclusively with DNS.*

Table 5 shows the top-level domains for the United States and European countries.

*Table 5*      *Top-Level Country Domains*

| Domain | Description |
|--------|-------------|
| .au | Australia. |
| .at | Austria. |
| .be | Belgium. |
| .ch | Switzerland. |
| .de | West Germany. |
| .dk | Denmark. |
| .es | Spain. |

*Table 5 Top-Level Country Domains (Continued)*

| Domain | Description |
|--------|-------------|
| .fi | Finland. |
| .fr | France. |
| .gr | Greece. |
| .ie | Ireland. |
| .is | Iceland. |
| .it | Italy. |
| .lu | Luxembourg. |
| .nl | The Netherlands. |
| .no | Norway. |
| .pt | Portugal. |
| .se | Sweden. |
| .tr | Turkey. |
| .uk | United Kingdom. |
| .us | United States. |

The following examples show education, commercial, and government domain addresses.

```
roy@shibumi.cc.columbia.edu
rose@haggis.ssctr.bcm.tmc.edu
smallberries%mill.uucp@physics.uchicago.edu
day@concave.convex.com
paul@basic.ppg.com
angel@enterprise.arc.nasa.gov
```

The following address is for a French domain.

```
hobbit@ilog.ilog.fr
```

The following address is for a British domain.

```
fred@uk.ac.aberdeen.kc
```

Note that some British and New Zealand networks write their mail addresses from top level to lower level, but most gateways automatically translate the address into the commonly used order (that is, lower level to higher).

# Aliases

An *alias* is an alternative name. For electronic mail, you can use aliases to assign additional names to a user, to route mail to a particular system, to define mailing lists, to send e-mail through programs for processing, and to append e-mail messages to a file for later use.

You can create a mail alias for each user at your site to specify where the mail is stored. Providing a mail alias is like providing a mail stop as part of the address for an individual at a large corporation. If you do not provide the mail stop, the mail is delivered to a central address. Extra effort is required to determine where the mail is to be delivered within the building, and the possibility of error increases. For example, if two people named Kevin Smith work in the same building, the probability is high that each Kevin will receive mail intended for the other.

Use domains and location-independent addresses as much as possible when you create alias files. To enhance the portability and flexibility of alias files, make your alias entries as generic and system independent as possible. For example, if you have a user named `ignatz` on system `oak` in domain `Eng.sun.com`, create the alias as `ignatz` instead of `ignatz@Eng` or `ignatz@oak`. If the user `ignatz` changes the name of the system but remains within the engineering domain, you do not need to update any alias files to reflect the change in the system name.

When creating aliases that include users outside your domain, create the alias with the user name and the domain name. For example, if you have a user named `smallberries` on system `privet` in domain `Corp.sun.com`, create the alias as `smallberries@Corp`.

> *NOTE. You can set an option in the* `*.mc` *file that generates the* `sendmail.cf` *file to translate the e-mail address to a fully qualified domain name—a domain name that contains all of the elements needed to specify where an electronic mail message should be delivered or where an NIS+ table is located—when mail goes outside the user's domain. See Chapter 2, "Customizing sendmail Configuration Files" for more information.*

Figure 4 shows how `sendmail` uses aliases. Programs that read mail, such as `/usr/bin/mailx`, can have aliases of their own, which are expanded before the message reaches `sendmail`.

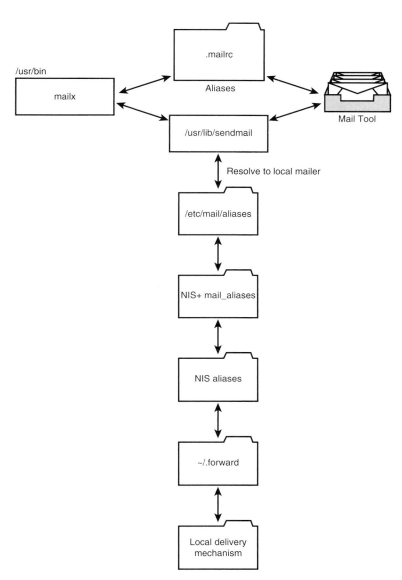

*Figure 4     How sendmail Uses Aliases*

As system administrator, you should choose a policy for updating aliases
and forwarding mail messages. You might set up an aliases mailbox as a
place for users to send requests for mail forwarding and changes to their
default mail alias. If your system uses NIS or NIS+, you can administer
forwarding instead of forcing users to manage it themselves. A common
mistake users make is to put a .forward file in the home directory of Host A
that forwards mail to user@host-b. When the mail gets to Host B,

`sendmail` looks up the user in the NIS or NIS+ aliases and sends the message back to `user@host-a`, resulting in a loop and more bounced mail.

## Uses for Alias Files

You create mail aliases for global use in the NIS+ `aliases` table, in the NIS `aliases` map, or, if your site does not use a nameservice, in local `/etc/mail/aliases` files. You can also create and administer mailing lists with the same alias files.

Depending on the configuration of your mail services, you can administer aliases with the NIS or NIS+ nameservice to maintain a global aliases database or by updating all of the local `/etc/mail/aliases` files to keep them in sync. See Chapter 4, "Setting Up and Administering Mail Services" for information on how to create aliases.

In general, only the mail hub for an e-mail domain contains the full list of aliases. The client systems and gateways have no idea how to deliver e-mail to individuals. They forward or relay e-mail to the mail hub for handling. Unless you have multiple mail hubs, you don't need to put aliases into NIS or NIS+.

### Creating User Aliases

Users can also create and use aliases. They can create aliases either in their local `.mailrc` file, which only they can use, or in their system's local `/etc/mail/aliases` file, which anyone can use. Users cannot create or administer NIS or NIS+ alias files. Users cannot administer the local `/etc/mail/aliases` file unless they have access to the root password on their system.

### Including Files in Aliases

You can keep an alias list in a separate file and include a reference to it in the aliases file with the following syntax.

```
mailinglistname: :include:pathname
```

The following example includes an alias named `engineers` that is located in the `/etc/mail/includes/engineers` file.

```
engineers:  :include:/etc/mail/includes/engineers
```

If you want to delegate the administration of aliases to others, use the `chown` command to change the ownership of the included file to the name of the user.

Then, with the following syntax, create an alias that designates the owner of the alias.

```
owner-mailinglistname: username
```

*mailinglistname* is the name of the mailing list and *username* is the login name of the person responsible for administering the alias. The following example assigns ownership of the alias named `engineers` to user `winsor`.

```
owner-engineers: winsor
```

Individuals can then use the `owner-engineers` alias to send e-mail to the person responsible for administering the alias.

### Sending Mail to Files and Programs

You also can have aliases send e-mail to files and programs.

The following example appends all e-mail sent to `listings-log` to `/proj/dev/logs/listings-log`.

```
listings-log:   /proj/dev/logs/listings-log
```

The following example sends all e-mail sent to `weblogs` as standard input to the program `/usr/local/bin/analyze-web-logs`.

```
weblogs:   "/usr/local/bin/analyze-web-logs"
```

For program aliases, the program must provide an appropriate exit status that is returned to `sendmail`; otherwise `sendmail` bouces all e-mails sent to this kind of aliases. `sendmail` is very picky about these return values. The appropriate values are listed in `/usr/include/sysexits.h`.

## Syntax of Aliases

The following sections describe the syntax of NIS+, NIS, and `.mailrc` aliases.

### NIS+ Aliases

The NIS+ aliases table contains all of the names by which a system or person is known, except for private aliases listed in users' local `.mailrc` files. The `sendmail` program can use the NIS+ `Aliases` database instead of the local

/etc/mail/aliases files to determine mailing addresses. See the aliasadm(8) and nsswitch.conf(4) manual pages for more information.

The NIS+ aliases table has the following format.

```
alias: expansion [options#   "comments"]
```

The NIS+ aliases table columns, are described in Table 6.

*Table 6      Columns in the NIS+ Aliases Database*

| Column | Description |
|--------|-------------|
| alias | The name of the alias. |
| expansion | The value of the alias as it would appear in a sendmail /etc/aliases file. |
| options | Reserved for future use. |
| comments | Use to add specific comments about an individual alias. |

The NIS+ Aliases database should contain entries for all mail clients. You list, create, modify, and delete entries in the NIS+ Aliases database with the aliasadm command. If you are creating a new NIS+ aliases table, you must initialize the table before you create the entries. If the table already exists, no initialization is needed.

When creating alias entries, enter one alias per line. You should have only one entry that contains the user's system name. For example, you could create the following entries for a user named winsor on system castle.

```
winsor: janice.winsor
jwinsor: janice.winsor
janicew: janice.winsor
janice.winsor: winsor@castle
```

You can create an alias for local names or domains. For example, an alias entry for the user fred, who has a mailbox on the system oak and is in the domain Trees, could have the following entry in the NIS+ aliases table.

```
fred: fred@Trees
```

To use the aliasadm command, you must be root, a member of the NIS+ group that owns the Aliases database, or the person who created the database.

See Chapter 4, "Setting Up and Administering Mail Services" for information on how to create NIS+ alias tables.

## NIS Aliases

Aliases in the NIS aliases map have the following format.

```
name: name1, name2, . . .
```

## .mailrc Aliases

Aliases in a .mailrc file have the following format.

```
alias aliasname name1 name2 name3 . . .
```

## /etc/mail/aliases Aliases

Distribution list formats in a local /etc/mail/aliases file have the following format.

```
aliasname: name1,name2,name3 . . .
```

The aliases in the /etc/mail/aliases file are stored in text form. When you edit the /etc/mail/aliases file, run the newaliases program to create a DBM database to make the aliases available to the sendmail program in binary form.

The Solaris 8 release provides the new /usr/bin/praliases command that you can use to display the contents of the /etc/mail/aliases file as key:value pairs. If you specify an argument on the command line, the command displays any matching key:value pair.

The following example uses the praliases command to display all of the aliases on the system paperbark.

```
paperbark% praliases
mailer-daemon:postmaster
postmaster:root
winsor:winsor@paperbark
nobody:/dev/null
ignatz:ignatz@paperbark
@:@
paperbark%
```

The following example uses the praliases command with a username argument to display the alias for user ignatz.

```
paperbark% praliases ignatz
ignatz:ignatz@paperbark
paperbark%
```

# Mail Addressing

The *mail address* contains the name of the recipient and the system where the mail message is delivered. When you are administering a small mail system that does not use a nameservice, addressing mail is easy: Login names uniquely identify users.

Mail addressing for more complex sites is also easy when you use DNS Mail Exchange (MX) records.

## UUCP Route-Based Addressing

*UUCP route-based addressing* requires the sender of an e-mail message to specify not only the local address (typically a user name) and its final destination but also the route that the message must take to reach its final destination.

> *NOTE. UUCP route-based addressing is shown here for historical reasons. These days, almost no one uses this form of addressing.*

Route-based addresses, which are fairly common on UUCP networks, use the following format.

```
host!path!user
```

Whenever you see an exclamation point (bang) as part of an e-mail address, all (or some) of the route was specified by the sender. Route-based addresses are always read from left to right. For example, the following e-mail address is sent to user `winsor` on the system named `ucbvax` by going first from `castle` to the address `sun`, then to `sierra`, then to `hplabs`, and finally to `ucbvax`. (Note that this is an example and not an actual route.) If any of the four mail handlers is out of commission, the message is delayed or returned as undeliverable.

```
castle!sun!sierra!hplabs!ucbvax!winsor
```

## Route-Independent Addressing

*Route-independent addressing* requires the sender of an e-mail message to specify the name of the recipient and the final destination address. Route-independent addresses usually indicate the use of a high-speed network, such as the Internet. In addition, newer UUCP connections frequently use domain-style names. Route-independent addresses use the following format.

```
user@host.domain
```

The increased popularity of the domain hierarchical naming scheme for computers across the country is making route-independent addresses more common. In fact, the most common route-independent address omits the host name from the address and relies on DNS MX records in the destination domain to properly identify the final destination of the e-mail message.

```
user@domain
```

Route-independent addresses are read by searching for the @ sign and then reading the domain hierarchy from the right (the highest level) to the left (the most specific address to the right of the @ sign). For example, an e-mail address such as winsor@Eng.sun.com is resolved starting with the .com commercial domain, then the sun company name domain, and finally the Eng department domain.

## How Mail Addressing Works

Assuming that you use the default rule set in the sendmail.cf file, the following examples show the routes an e-mail message can take. The route is determined by how the e-mail is addressed.

- Mail within a domain addressed with only the user's login name goes to the aliases file on the mail hub (or to the Aliases database) and is sent to the address found in the database. In the example shown in Figure 5, mail addressed to the user winsor goes to the mail hub and is forwarded to the host named castle.

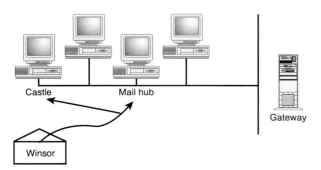

*Figure 5    Delivery Path for Mail Addressed with a User Name Only*

- Mail within a domain addressed with the user's login name and host name goes directly to the host system without any additional processing. In the example shown in Figure 6, mail addressed to the user `winsor` at the host named `castle` goes directly to the host named `castle`.

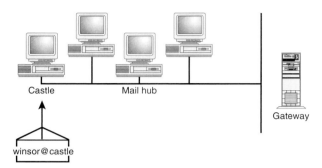

*Figure 6     Delivery Path for Mail Addressed with the User Name and the Host Name*

- Mail within a domain addressed with the user's login name and domain name goes to the `aliases` file on the mail hub (or to the `Aliases` database). If the mail hub has an alias, it redirects the message to the host system. In the example shown in Figure 7, mail addressed to the user `winsor@Eng` goes to the mail hub and is then forwarded to the host named `castle`.

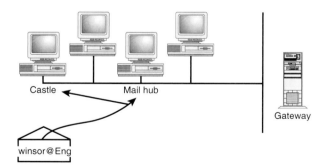

*Figure 7     Delivery Path for Mail Addressed with the User Name and the Domain Name*

Mail addressed with the user's name and a fully qualified domain name goes to the mail hub, which sends it to the gateway. The gateway sends the message to the host system. When the mail comes from the recipient's domain, however, the mail hub recognizes the domain name and does not send the message to the gateway host. In the example shown in Figure 8, mail addressed to the user `ignatz@Eng.sun.com` from outside the engineering domain goes to the sender's mail hub and then to the sender's gateway host. It is then forwarded to the recipient's gateway host, the recipient's mail hub, and finally to the host named `oak`.

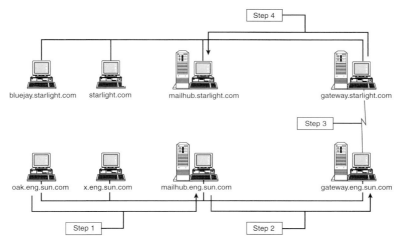

*Figure 8     Delivery Path for Mail Addressed with a User Name and a Fully
                Qualified Domain Name*

In Step 1, the e-mail is sent by a user on `oak.eng.sun.com` to `jim@starlight.com`. Note that the recipient's personal system is `bluejay.starlight.com` but the mail spool for `jim` is NFS mounted from `mailhub.starlight.com`. The e-mail is picked up by `sendmail` on `oak.eng.sun.com` and transmitted to `mailhub.eng.sun.com`.

In Step 2, local `sendmail` determines that the e-mail is to someone outside the `eng.sun.com` DNS domain, so the e-mail is sent to `sendmail` on `gateway.eng.sun.com` for delivery over the Internet.

In Step 3, `sendmail` on `gateway.eng.sun.com` looks up the DNS MX record for `starlight.com`. In this case, it points to `gateway.starlight.com`, so `sendmail` transmits the message to the `sendmail` program on `gateway.starlight.com`.

The `sendmail` program on `gateway.starlight.com` is programmed to forward all e-mail to *user*`@starlight.com` to `mailhub.starlight.com`, which is done in Step 4. On `mailhub.starlight.com`, the message is handed off to the local delivery agent and the message is appended to Jim's mailbox.

# Mail Services Files and Programs

Files for the mail service are located in three directories: `/bin`, `/etc/mail`, and `/usr/lib`. Users' mailboxes are located in the `/var/mail` directory. Table 7 lists the mail services programs.

*Table 7     The Components of Mail Services*

| Command or File | Description |
|---|---|
| `$OPENWINHOME/bin/mailtool` | MUA. |
| `.sendmailvars.org_dir` | NIS+ version of `sendmailvars` table. |
| `/etc/default/sendmail` | Store options used to start `sendmail`. This command is new in the Solaris 8 release. In previous releases, `sendmail` options were added to the init script. Because you no longer need to edit init scripts to add `sendmail` options, upgrading systems is easier. See Chapter 2, "Customizing sendmail Configuration Files" for more information. |
| `/etc/mail/aliases` | Mail-forwarding information. |
| `/etc/mail/main.cf` | Sample configuration file for main systems. |
| `/etc/mail/sendmail.cf` | Configuration file for mail routing. |
| `/etc/mail/sendmail.subsidiary.cf` | Sample configuration file for subsidiary systems. |
| `/etc/mail/sendmailvars` | Table that stores macro and class definitions for lookup from `sendmail.cf` file. |
| `/usr/bin/mail` | MUA. |
| `/usr/bin/mailq` | Symbolic link to `/usr/lib/sendmail` that is used to print the headers of messages in the mail queue. |

*Table 7* *The Components of Mail Services (Continued)*

| Command or File | Description |
|---|---|
| `/usr/bin/mailstats` | File that stores mail statistics generated by `sendmail` into `/etc/mail/sendmail.st` (if present). |
| `/usr/bin/mailx` | MUA. |
| `/usr/bin/mconnect` | Connect to the mailer for address verification and debugging. |
| `/usr/bin/newaliases` | Symbolic link to `/usr/lib/sendmail` that is used to rebuild the database for the mail aliases file. |
| `/usr/bin/praliases` | Display aliases in the `/etc/mail/aliases` file as key:value pairs. You can also specify an argument on the command line to display a matching key:value pair. |
| `/usr/dt/bin/dtmail` | CDE window-based MUA. |
| `/usr/dt/bin/dtmaillpr` | CDE electronic mail messaged print filter. |
| `/usr/lib/mail.local` | Delivery agent that delivers mail to mailboxes. |
| `/usr/lib/sendmail` | MTA. |
| `/usr/lib/smrsh` | Limit the number of commands that can be used to run the `"|program"` syntax of `sendmail`. This freeware `sendmail` restricted shell is new in the Solaris 8 release. |
| `/usr/sbin/in.comsat` | Mail notification daemon. |
| `/usr/sbin/syslogd` | Daemon that implements the UNIX logging subsystem. `sendmail` sends logging information to this subsystem. |

*NOTE. Sites that used DNS with older releases of Solaris used the* `/usr/lib/sendmail.mx` *file to access mail exchange records. In the Solaris 8 release, this functionality is included in* `sendmail`, *and the* `/usr/lib/sendmail.mx` *file has been removed. You can configure the DNS nameservice with the* `/etc/nsswitch.conf` *file.*

With `sendmail` version 8.9.3, you can use the `/etc/mail` directory to store tables that you activate with various m4 `FEATURE` macros.

You can create tables such as the following.

- `/etc/mail/genericstable`
- `/etc/mail/mailertable`
- `/etc/mail/virtusertable`
- `/etc/mail/userdb`

For example, to reference the `/etc/mail/mailertable` map, you include the following line in your `.mc` file.

```
FEATURE(`mailertable', `hash -o /etc/mail/mailertable')dnl
```

See `http://www.sendmail.org/m4/cf-readme.txt` and Chapter 2, "Customizing sendmail Configuration Files" for more information on the purpose of each of these files.

Table 8 shows the contents of the `/usr/lib/mail` directory. These subdirectories are used with `sendmail` version 8.9.3 to customize and "compile" the `sendmail` configuration file. Refer to Chapter 2, "Customizing sendmail Configuration Files" for more information.

*Table 8      Contents of the /usr/lib/mail Directory*

| Directory | Description |
|-----------|-------------|
| m4 | General support routines. These very important routines process `.mc` files so that they can be used as configuration files. Do not change these routines without very careful consideration. |
| cf | Configuration files. The files have `.mc` suffixes, and must be processed with the m4 macro processor to be complete. The resulting output has a `.cf` suffix. |
| ostype | Definitions describing a particular operating system type. Use the `OSTYPE` macro in the `.mc` file to reference operating system types. Examples include `"bsd4.3"`, `"bsd4.4"`, `"sunos3.5"`, and `"sunos4.1"`. |

*Table 8     Contents of the /usr/lib/mail Directory (Continued)*

| Directory | Description |
|---|---|
| domain | Definitions describing a particular domain. Use the DOMAIN macro in the .mc file to reference domains. Domain definitions are site dependent; for example, "CS.Berkeley.EDU.m4" describes hosts in the CS.Berkeley.EDU subdomain. |
| mailer | Descriptions of mailers. Use the MAILER macro in the .mc file to reference mailer descriptions. |
| sh | Shell scripts used when building the .cf file from the .mc file in the cf subdirectory. |
| feature | Special features that you might want to include. Use the FEATURE macro to reference special features. |

Table 9 shows the contents of the /bin directory that are used for mail services.

*Table 9     Contents of the /bin Directory That Are Used for Mail*

| Name | Type | Description |
|---|---|---|
| mail | File | A mail user agent. |
| mailcompat | File | A filter to store mail in SunOS 4.x mailbox format. |
| mailq | Link | Link to /usr/lib/sendmail. |
| mailstats | File | Mail statistics generated by the /etc/mail/sendmail.st file (if present). |
| mailx | File | A mail user agent. |
| newaliases | Link | Link to /usr/lib/sendmail that is used to rebuild the database for the mail aliases file. |

Table 10 shows the contents of the /etc/mail directory.

*Table 10     Contents of the /etc/mail Directory*

| Name | Type | Description |
|---|---|---|
| Mail.rc | File | Default settings for the mailtool user agent. |
| aliases | File | Mail-forwarding information. |
| aliases.dir | File | Binary form of mail-forwarding information (created by running newaliases). |

*Table 10     Contents of the /etc/mail Directory (Continued)*

| Name | Type | Description |
|------|------|-------------|
| aliases.pag | File | Binary form of mail-forwarding information (created by running newaliases). |
| mailx.rc | File | Default settings for the mailx user agent. |
| main.cf | File | Sample configuration file for main systems. |
| sendmail.cf | File | Configuration file for mail routing. |
| sendmail.hf | File | Help file used by the SMTP HELP command. |
| sendmail.pid | File | File containing the /usr/lib/sendmail -b -q1h command. |
| sendmail.st | File | The sendmail statistics file. (If this file is present, sendmail logs the amount of traffic through each mailer.) |
| sendmailvars | File | Table that stores macro and class definitions for lookup from sendmail.cf. |
| sendmailvars. org_dir | Table | NIS+ version of sendmailvars table. |
| subsidiary.cf | File | Sample configuration file for subsidiary systems. |

Table 11 shows the mail files in the /usr/lib directory.

*Table 11     Mail Files in the /usr/lib Directory*

| Name | Description |
|------|-------------|
| mail.local | Mailer that delivers mail to mailboxes. |
| sendmail | The routing program, also known as the mail transport agent. |

Spooling directories for delivered mail are located in the /var/mail directory, as shown in Table 12. Mail that has not been delivered is stored in the /var/spool/mqueue directory.

*Table 12     Contents of the /var/mail Directory*

| Name | Type | Description |
|------|------|-------------|
| mailbox1 | File | Mailboxes for delivered mail. |
| mailbox2 | File | Mailboxes for delivered mail. |
| mailbox3 | File | Mailboxes for delivered mail. |

# 2

# CUSTOMIZING SENDMAIL CONFIGURATION FILES

The `sendmail` program is a mail-transport agent and message router that uses a configuration file to provide aliasing and forwarding, automatic routing to network gateways, and flexible configuration. The Solaris environment supplies the standard configuration files that most sites can use.

With sendmail version 8.9.3, you no longer edit the `sendmail.cf` file *New!* directly. You should treat it as a binary that is not editable. Instead, you start with a file with a `.mc` (macro configuration) suffix and use the m4 macro processor to "compile" the `.mc` file into the final `sendmail` configuration file, which has a `.cf` suffix. See "Generating the sendmail Configuration File" on page 53 for more information.

Because the m4 macro processor automatically generates the rules and *New!* rulesets in the `sendmail.cf` file from the macros you specify in the `.mc` file, you no longer need to write your own rules or rulesets.

## How the sendmail Program Works

The following sections describe how the `sendmail` program works.

When a sender wants to send a message, the program issues a request to `sendmail`. The `sendmail` program then goes through the steps listed below, which are described in detail in the following sections.

1.  Arguments are processed and the address is then parsed.
2.  The message is collected.
3.  The message is delivered.
4.  If instructions are received from the mailer, the message is queued for retransmission.
5.  If errors occur during processing, the message is returned to the sender.

## Argument Processing and Address Parsing

If `sendmail` is called by means of the argument vector or is connected to through a pipe, the arguments are first scanned and option specifications are processed. Recipient names are then collected, either from the command line or from the SMTP command, and a list of recipients is created. Aliases, including mailing lists, are expanded at this step. As much validation as possible of the remote recipient is done at this step: Syntax is checked and local recipients are verified, but detailed checking of host names is deferred until delivery. Forwarding is also performed as the local recipients are verified.

The `sendmail` program appends each name to the recipient list after parsing. When a name is aliased or forwarded, the old name is retained in the list and a flag is then set to tell the delivery phase to ignore this recipient. This list is kept free from duplicates, thus preventing alias loops and duplicate messages from being delivered to the same recipient, as might occur when a person is in two alias lists.

*NOTE. Users may receive duplicate copies of the same message when alias lists contain e-mail addresses for the same person but with different syntaxes. The* `sendmail` *program cannot always identify the e-mail addresses as duplicates of one another.*

## Message Collection

The `sendmail` program then collects the message, which has a header at the beginning. The message body does not need to be formatted in any special way except that it must be composed of lines of text. (In other words, binary data is not allowed.) The header is stored in memory, and then the body of the message is saved in a temporary file.

To simplify the program interface, the message is collected even if no names were valid. The message subsequently is returned with an error.

## Message Delivery

For each unique mailer and host in the recipient list, `sendmail` calls the appropriate mailer. Each mailer invocation sends the message to all users receiving it on one host. Mailers that accept only one recipient at a time are handled properly.

The message is sent to the mailer through one of the same three interfaces used to submit a message to `sendmail`. Each copy of the message has a customized header added to the beginning of the message. The mailer status code is caught and checked, and a suitable error message is given if appropriate. The exit code must conform to a system standard or the generic message `Service unavailable` is displayed.

### Retransmission Queuing

When the mailer returns a status indicating that it might be able to handle the mail later, `sendmail` queues the mail and tries again later.

### Return to Sender

When errors occur during processing, `sendmail` returns the message to the sender for retransmission. The letter can be mailed back (when the mail comes from a different site) or written to the `dead.letter` file in the sender's home directory.

## Message-Header Editing

The `sendmail` program does some automatic editing of the message header. Header lines can be inserted under control of the configuration file. Some lines may be merged; for example, a `From:` and a `Full-name:` line may be merged under certain circumstances. A `Received` header is added to the header lines.

## Configuration File

Almost all configuration information is read at runtime from a text configuration file.

- Macro definitions (defining the value of macros used internally) are encoded.
- Header declarations (the format of header lines that are specially processed and lines that are added or reformatted) are embedded.
- Mailer definitions (with information such as the location and characteristics of each mailer) are included.
- Name-rewriting rules (a limited pattern-matching system used to rewrite names) are defined.

# How sendmail Is Implemented

The following sections provide an overview of the syntax used in `sendmail` and describe some implementation details.

You can follow flag arguments with recipient name arguments unless you run in SMTP mode. In brief, the following format is used for recipient names.

- Anything in parentheses is thrown away (as a comment).
- Anything in angle brackets (< >) is preferred over anything else. This rule implements the Internet standard that writes names in the form of *username <system-name>* and sends to the electronic *system-name* instead of to the human *username*.
- Double quotes (`"`) denote phrases; backslashes (`\`) denote characters. Backslashes compare otherwise equivalent phrases differently—for example, *user* and *"user"* are equivalent, but *\user* is different from either of them.

Parentheses, angle brackets, and double quotes must be properly balanced (that is, used in pairs) and nested. The rewriting rules control the rest of the needed processing.

## Mail to Files and Programs

Files and programs are legitimate message recipients. Files provide archival message storage, which is useful for project administration and history. Programs are useful as recipients in a variety of situations—for example, to use `mailsort` to sort mail or to have the `vacation` program respond with an informational message when users are away.

Any name passing through the initial parsing algorithm as a local name is scanned for two special cases.

- If the prefix is a vertical bar (`|`), the rest of the name is processed as a shell command.
- If the user name begins with a slash (`/`), the name is used as a file name instead of a login name.

## Message Collection

After all of the recipient names are parsed and verified, the message is collected. The message comes in two parts: a message header and a message body. The header and the body are separated by a blank line. The header is formatted as a series of lines of the following form.

```
field-name: field-value
```

The following example shows a header for John Smith at `Podunk.edu`.

```
From: John Smith <Smith@Podunk.edu>
```

You can split `field-value` across lines by starting the subsequent lines with a space or a Tab. Some header fields have special internal meaning and have appropriate special processing. Other headers are simply passed through. Some header fields, such as timestamps, can be added automatically.

The body is a series of text lines. It is completely uninterpreted and untouched, except that lines beginning with a dot have the dot doubled when transmitted over an SMTP channel. This extra dot is then stripped by the receiver.

## Message Delivery

The send queue is grouped by the receiving host before transmission to implement message batching. An argument list is built as the scan proceeds. Mail to files is detected during the scan of the send list. The interface to the mailer is performed with one of the techniques described in "Introducing the m4 Macro Processor" on page 40.

After a connection is established, `sendmail` makes the per-mailer changes to the header and sends the result to the mailer. If any mail is rejected by the mailer, a flag is set to invoke the return-to-sender function after all delivery is complete.

## Queued Messages

If the mailer returns a `Temporary failure` exit status, the message is queued. A control file describes the recipients and various other parameters. This control file is formatted as a series of lines, each describing a sender, a recipient, the time of submission, or some other parameter of the message. The header of the message is stored in the control file so that the associated data file that is in the queue is simply the original temporary file.

# New! Introducing the m4 Macro Processor

Although Solaris provides prebuilt default configuration files for `sendmail`, these configuration files make certain assumptions about the e-mail architecture of a site that may not be true for your site. Because these assumptions are not documented and often have subtle side effects, it is best to build your own `sendmail` configuration file(s) with the prepackaged m4 macros provided with the `sendmail` distribution. When you do so, you can design the e-mail architecture for your entire site and implement it the way you want.

> *NOTE. This section is a basic introduction to the m4 macro processor, and not a comprehensive reference. We describe the constructs that lend themselves directly to creating* `sendmail` *configuration files.*

The m4 macro processor is a standard UNIX tool, unrelated to `sendmail`. Historically, the m4 macro processor was used as a front end to different compilers, to expand easy-to-remember macro expressions into "canned" complex constructs.

m4 expects two things as input.

- A file that specifies macros, much like function calls.
- A file that defines what the macros translate into, which is generally something *very* complex.

Usually these input files are not fed into m4 separately; instead, the first file uses m4's ability to include another file within itself. The included file can then include any number of other files that define the macros specified in the original file. This construct enables you to create arbitrarily complex macro definitions.

m4 then creates an output file that is the result of translating the macros that were sent to it according to the macro definitions that were also sent to it.

> *NOTE. In addition to the macro definitions that you supply, m4 has a group of built-in macros. See the* m4*(1) manual page for more information.*

## Comments

Comments in an m4 macro file can begin either with a hash mark (#) or with the word `dnl`, which is a built-in macro that means "delete to newline." The `dnl` construct deletes all subsequent characters up to the next newline. You will notice that many lines in an m4 macro line end with the dnl construct; this practice keeps the resulting output of m4 as clean as possible.

The following example shows a regular comment with the # mark.

```
# This line is a comment.
```

The following example shows the same comment with the dnl construct.

```
dnl This line is a comment.
```

The following example of an m4 macro uses the dnl construct to keep the m4 output clean.

```
OSTYPE(`solaris2')dnl
```

## Quoting

The use of quotes in an m4 macro file differs from their use in many other languages, mostly because any quoted phrase begins with one type of quotation mark and ends with another. A quoted phrase always begins with a backquote ( ` ) and ends with a regular quote ( ' ). Many people make the mistake of trying to use two matching backquotes or regular quotes.

The following example shows a quoted phrase in a sendmail m4 macro file.

```
OSTYPE(`solaris2')
```

## Including Macro Files

An m4 macro file can ask the m4 macro processor to include the contents of other m4 macro files with the built-in include macro, as shown in the following example.

```
include(`../cf/m4/cf.m4')dnl
```

## Diversions

The m4 macro processor can have 10 buffers (numbered 0–9) open simultaneously, but the macro file can specify only one at a time to send output to. The macro file uses the built-in `divert` macro to specify which buffer to direct the current output to. Normally, stream 0 is specified as the default buffer. If a stream other than 0 through 9 is specified by `divert`, then all output until the next valid `divert` is discarded. Thus, you often see the following construct in a `sendmail` macro file.

```
divert(-1)
# Some comments here that are not intended for the final output file
# but are useful only to someone editing this original macro file
divert(0)
...valid macros from here on in the file...
```

This use of `divert` keeps comments you enter in the macro file from ending up in the final file generated by the m4 macro processor.

## New! Writing a Custom Macro Configuration File

Why go to the trouble to generate a `sendmail` configuration file? Because writing or even modifying an existing `sendmail` configuration file can waste many hours of your time, and you're still likely to make subtle mistakes. The developers of `sendmail` have, over time and through much trial and error, collected all of the necessary rulesets to implement virtually any `sendmail` behavior and "canned" them for use in the `sendmail` m4 macro definition files. These macro definitions also include methods for modifying all `sendmail` configuration options. This arrangement is desirable for the following reasons.

- It enables administrators to write a short macro configuration file that generates a large and complex `sendmail` configuration file whose components have been tested over many years.
- The macro configuration file can be easily managed under source code control.
- As `sendmail` is gradually improved, changes are made to the macro definition files, `sendmail` option names change, and so on. These changes could make maintaining a `sendmail` configuration file a nightmare. In actuality, these changes affect your macro configuration file very little, if at all, after a `sendmail` upgrade. The only thing that usually changes is the final `sendmail` configuration file generated from your original macro configuration file.

Now, on to creating the actual macro configuration file.

*NOTE. The information contained in the rest of this section is not exhaustive. The goal is to walk you through the creation of your own* `sendmail` *macro configuration file for common* `sendmail` *configurations. For unusual configurations, you'll need a deeper grasp of* sendmail's *inner workings than can be provided here. See* /usr/lib/mail/README *for the complete current list of all of* sendmail *m4 macro configuration directives. Use the O'Reilly Sendmail book as a complete reference. Although that book covers only* sendmail *v8.8 and earlier, it is valuable for its insight into the* sendmail *m4 macro directives and their interactions.*

## Including the Sendmail m4 Macro Definitions

*NOTE. This directive or the method specified in "Generating the sendmail Configuration File" on page 53 is mandatory.*

First, you need to include the sendmail m4 macro definition files so that m4 knows how to expand the rest of the macros in your macro configuration file. You include a single m4 macro definition file—/usr/lib/mail/m4/cf.m4—that then includes all of the other macro definition files. The following example shows the directive you use to include the /usr/lib/mail/m4/cf.m4 file.

```
include(`/usr/lib/mail/m4/cf.m4')dnl
```

## Defining Your OS Type

*NOTE. This directive is mandatory.*

sendmail needs to know what operating system you are running because each UNIX OS vendor puts the various files used to configure and control sendmail in slightly different locations that must to be reflected in the final sendmail configuration file. The following example shows the directive for Solaris 2.x.

```
OSTYPE(`solaris2')dnl
```

## Masquerading

Under normal circumstances, the sender's address in an e-mail message from a host in a domain like starlight.com contains the fully qualified return address (for example, *user@host*.starlight.com). This address sends any replies to this e-mail message to the system where it originated instead of to your mail hub. To make managing an e-mail infrastructure simpler, you may want to configure sendmail to rewrite all outgoing messages from a domain as coming from the domain itself instead of from any specific host within that domain. `sendmail` can rewrite the sender's e-mail addresses in outgoing e-mail messages as *user@*`starlight.com`. This behavior is known as *masquerading*.

The `sendmail` m4 macro directives that affect masquerading are listed in Table 13.

*Table 13*    *Masquerade Directives*

| Directive | Description |
|---|---|
| MASQUERADE_AS | |
| | This directive defines the host or domain that all sender's addresses appear to be coming from. The following example defines the directive for the `starlight.com` domain.<br><br>`MASQUERADE_AS(`starlight.com')dnl` |
| MASQUERADE_DOMAIN | |
| | If you have control over other domains and want them to masquerade under the same host/domain specified in the MASQUERADE_AS directive, you can mention them each separately with this directive, as shown in the following example.<br><br>`MASQUERADE_DOMAIN(`old-starlight.com eng.starlight.com prod.starlight.com')dnl`<br><br>Any e-mail sent from hosts in the `old-starlight.com`, `eng.starlight.com,` or `prod.starlight.com` domains have return addresses that look like *user@*`starlight.com`. |
| MASQUERADE_DOMAIN_FILE | |
| | Instead of using a long MASQUERADE_DOMAIN directive, you can use a MASQUERADE_DOMAIN_FILE directive that references a file. The file contains a list of all the domains you want to masquerade as the domain mentioned in MASQUERADE_AS. For example, you could specify the following directive.<br><br>`MASQUERADE_DOMAIN_FILE(`/etc/mail/masq-domains')dnl`<br><br>The file `/etc/mail/masq-domains` would contain the following entries. |

*Table 13    Masquerade Directives (Continued)*

| Directive | Description |
|---|---|
| | `old-starlight.com`<br>`eng.starlight.com`<br>`prod.starlight.com` |
| EXPOSED_USER | |
| | Certain users should always be "exposed." That is, their internal host name should always be revealed so that tracing the ultimate origin of the e-mail for administrative purposes is easy. By default, the root, daemon, and mail user names are always exposed. You can use the `EXPOSED_USER` directive to change this default or to add other users to this list, as shown in the following example.<br><br>`EXPOSED_USER(`root daemon mail news')dnl` |

## Features

The `FEATURE` macros each activate some capability or feature of `sendmail` by inserting the "canned" rulesets and options associated with these `FEATURE`s into the final configuration file. As new `FEATURE`s are added, their corresponding macros are added to the `sendmail` m4 macro definition files.

> *NOTE. Not all of the available* `FEATURE`s *are listed below, just the most commonly used ones. Refer to* `/usr/lib/mail/README` *for the list of* `FEATURE` *macro directives currently supported on your version of Solaris.*

Some `FEATURE`s take an argument. This argument falls into one of two categories.

- A constant string—Usually used to describe a host or file name. For example, the `nullclient` feature takes as an argument the name of the host that receives all e-mail messages, as shown in the following example.

```
FEATURE(nullclient,`mailhost.starlight.com')dnl
```

In this case, the quoted string `mailhost.starlight.com` is the argument.

- A database map type—Many features activate the use of an external database map file related to the feature. These external files contain information that changes `sendmail` behavior related to the specified

feature. These files are usually DBM database maps generated by the
makemap(1) command. Because makemap(1) can generate database map
files in several different formats, you must specify the format for each of
these files so that sendmail knows how to read them. See "External
Configuration Files" on page 52 for more information on using
makemap(1) to generate these database map files. Note that these
database map type arguments also specify whether these external files
are mandatory or optional for the sendmail configuration. If the
argument uses the -o option, the map (and thus the feature) is optional,
as shown in the following example.

```
FEATURE(mailertable,`hash -o /etc/mail/mailertable')dnl
```

However, if you omit the -o option, the database map created by
makemap(1) *must* exist for sendmail to run at all, as shown in the
following example.

```
FEATURE(mailertable,`hash /etc/mail/mailertable')dnl
```

Table 14 lists commonly used FEATURE directives and describes any
required arguments and the formats of any required external files.

*Table 14     FEATURE Directives*

| Directive | Description |
| --- | --- |
| FEATURE(allmasquerade) | |
| | Normally the MASQUERADE_AS masquerading option rewrites only *sender* addresses in an outgoing e-mail. This feature turns that functionality on for *recipient* addresses too. |
| FEATURE(always_add_domain) | |
| | If e-mail is sent between users in the same domain, the e-mail tends to be addressed to *username* instead of *username@domain*. This feature makes sure that all e-mail headers for *recipients* are rewritten to be fully qualified. The *domain* is the domain specified in the MASQUERADE_AS option. |
| FEATURE(domaintable) | |
| | When a site needs to transition from an old domain name to a new one (such as after a company name change or merger), this feature enables an external database map to map e-mail |

*Table 14* *FEATURE Directives (Continued)*

| Directive | Description |
|---|---|
| | sent to the old domain to the new domain(s). The format of the file is shown below.<br><br>```\noldname1.com      newname.com\noldname2.com      newname.com\n```<br><br>The feature takes a database map as an argument, as shown in the following example.<br><br>```\nFEATURE(domaintable,`hash -o /etc/mail/domaintable')dnl\n``` |
| FEATURE(genericstable) | |
| | This feature enables an external database map to specify translations of *sender* addresses. This feature might be useful when you want to make a sender's e-mail address seem to originate from another domain under your control. The following example shows the format of the file.<br><br>```\n# We are in starlight.com domain but we want\n# all e-mail sent from news@starlight.com to\n# seem to come from\n# news-admin@eng.starlight.com, so that replies\n# go to the proper administrator.\n\nnews    news-admin@eng.starlight.com\n```<br><br>The feature takes a database map as an argument, as shown in the following example.<br><br>```\nFEATURE(genericstable,`dbm -o /etc/mail/genericstable')dnl\n``` |
| FEATURE(mailertable) | |
| | This feature uses an external file to map e-mail sent to *host.domain* or just *domain* to a particular delivery agent on another host. This feature is useful if you have multiple domains under your control but want e-mail coming from the Internet for all of them to be funneled through a single gateway host. This central host would use this feature to direct e-mail to the proper mail hub or gateway for each domain under your control. The format of the file is shown below. |

*Table 14     FEATURE Directives (Continued)*

| Directive | Description |
|---|---|
|  | ```# All e-mail received on this gateway host bound```<br>```# for starlight.com or *.starlight.com will be```<br>```# relayed to mailhost.starlight.com```<br><br>```starlight.com          relay:mailhost.starlight.com```<br>```.starlight.com         relay:mailhost.starlight.com```<br><br>```# All e-mail received on this gateway host bound```<br>```# for eng.starlight.com or *.eng.starlight.com```<br>```# will be relayed to mailhost.eng.starlight.com```<br><br>```.eng.starlight.com relay:mailhost.eng.starlight.com```<br><br>The feature takes a database map as an argument, as shown in the following example.<br><br>```FEATURE(mailertable,`hash -o /etc/mail/mailertable')dnl``` |
| FEATURE(masquerade_entire_domain) | |
|  | Normally, if you used macro directives in your macro configuration file like those shown below, all outgoing mail from hosts in the ```starlight.com``` and ```eng.starlight.com``` domains are rewritten as coming from *user*@starlight.com.<br><br>```MASQUERADE_AS(`starlight.com')dnl```<br>```MASQUERADE_DOMAIN(`eng.starlight.com')dnl```<br><br>However, e-mail coming from hosts *under* these domains, such as ```mech.starlight.com``` or ```nw.eng.starlight.com```, would *not* masquerade. You can turn on the ```masquerade_entire_domain``` FEATURE to masquerade all of the domains your specify in MASQUERADE_AS and MASQUERADE_DOMAIN directives, as well as any of their subdomains. |
| FEATURE(masquerade_envelope) | |
|  | Normally, ```sendmail``` masquerade only e-mail headers. You can use this feature to treat envelopes in the same way as e-mail headers. |
| FEATURE(nullclient) | |
|  | Usually ```nullclient``` is the only FEATURE listed in an e-mail client's macro configuration file. It sends all e-mail to a |

*Table 14    FEATURE Directives (Continued)*

| Directive | Description |
|---|---|
| | central mail hub for processing. No processing of any kind takes place on the system running the configuration file generated with this feature, so you should never use this feature on a mail hub or gateway. |
| | This feature takes the name of the central mail hub as an argument, as shown in the following example. |
| | `FEATURE(nullclient,'mailhost.starlight.com')dnl` |
| `FEATURE(rbl)` | |
| | Reject all e-mail from any host listed in the `Realtime Blackhole List` database maintained by the Mail Abuse Prevention System (`MAPS-http://maps.vix.com`). This DNS-based database lists all of the world's known spamming organizations. |
| `FEATURE(relay_entire_domain)` | |
| | Accept e-mail relayed from any host within your domain, instead of just the hosts and domains listed in `/etc/mail/relay-domains`. |
| `FEATURE(use_cw_file)` | |
| | To prevent e-mail loops, `sendmail` needs to know all names that a particular host is known by. Use this feature to list all of the names for a host in `/etc/sendmail.cw`. For example, if a mail hub has all of the following names |
| | `mailhub.starlight.com`<br>`mailhost.starlight.com`<br>`rosebud.starlight.com` |
| | and it receives all e-mail for the `starlight.com domain`, then `/etc/sendmail.cw` should contain the following entries. |
| | `mailhub.starlight.com`<br>`mailhost.starlight.com`<br>`rosebud.starlight.com`<br>`starlight.com` |

*Table 14    FEATURE Directives (Continued)*

| Directive | Description |
|---|---|
| | If e-mail addressed to users at any of these hosts or domains is received by this host, then `sendmail` recognizes that the e-mail has reached its final destination.<br><br>Note that `/etc/sendmail.cw` is one of the few `sendmail` configuration files that is not a database map; it is a plain text file. |
| `FEATURE(virtusertable)` | |
| | Enable a domain-specific form of aliasing, allowing multiple virtual domains to be hosted on one machine. For example, if the `virtuser` table contained the entries<br><br>`info@foo.com      foo-info`<br>`info@bar.com      bar-info`<br>`@baz.org          jane@elsewhere.net`<br><br>then mail addressed to `info@foo.com` is sent to the address `foo-info`, mail addressed to `info@bar.com` is delivered to `bar-info`, and mail addressed to anyone at `baz.org` is sent to `jane@elsewhere.net`. The user name from the original address is passed as `%1` allowing the syntax<br><br>`@foo.org          %1@elsewhere.com`<br><br>meaning `someone@foo.org` is sent to `someone@elsewhere.com`.<br><br>All the host names on the left side (`foo.com`, `bar.com`, and `baz.org`) must be contained in `/etc/sendmail.cw`.<br><br>This feature takes a database map as an argument, as shown in the following example.<br><br>`FEATURE(`virtusertable', `dbm -o /etc/mail/virtusers')` |

## Configuration Options

The final `sendmail` configuration file contains options that control many aspects of `sendmail` behavior, such as path names to critical files, network timeout counters, and `FEATURE` capabilities. Instead of editing the `sendmail` configuration file directly, you can set the values of certain m4 variables in your `sendmail` m4 macro configuration file. That way the options are already set to the values you want when you generate your final `sendmail` configuration file.

The m4 variables that you can change, the `sendmail` configuration options they affect, and their default values are listed in `/usr/lib/mail/README` in the section titled "TWEAKING CONFIGURATION OPTIONS." The file also describes quoting rules for these variables. All of the variables start with `conf`, for example, `confLOG_LEVEL`.

To change one of the `conf` variables in your macro configuration file, you use the built-in m4 macro `define`, as shown in the following example.

```
# Change the default location of sendmail.cw to be located in
# /etc/mail/sendmail.cw, and make the existence of the file optional
# by using the -o option.
define(`confCW_FILE',`-o /etc/mail/sendmail.cw')dnl
# Change the default SMTP login message to reflect the starlight.com
# domain name
define(`confSMTP_LOGIN_MSG',`[$j Sendmail $v/$Z; $b, starlight.com]')dnl
# Change initial connection timeout from default of 5 minutes to 2 minutes
define(`confTO_INITIAL',`2m')dnl
```

# Mailers

`MAILER` macros generate the delivery agent sections in the final `sendmail` configuration file. These sections configure `sendmail` to know how to hand off messages for delivery. Always list `MAILER` macros last in the macro configuration file. The `/usr/lib/mail/README` file describes quite a few mailers under the section "MAILERS." Some of the most commonly used mailers are listed below.

## MAILER(local)

Defines the following delivery agents.

- `local`—Delivers into local mail folders.
- `prog`—Handles delivery of e-mail messages into programs for processing.

## MAILER(smtp)

Defines the following delivery agents.

- `smtp`—The basic SMTP delivery agent.
- `esmtp`—The enhanced SMTP delivery agent.
- `smtp8`—An SMTP delivery agent that assumes an 8-bit clean path.

- `relay`—An SMTP delivery agent that does minimal header manipulation.

### MAILER(uucp)

Defines the following delivery agents.

- `uucp-old`—Traditional (Version 7) UUCP interface.
- `uucp-new`—Same as `uucp-old` with the added benefit of handling multiple recipients per message transaction.
- `uucp-uudom`—Envelopes use UUCP syntax, but headers use domain-based syntax.
- `uucp-dom`—Envelopes and headers use domain-based syntax.

## External Configuration Files

`sendmail` uses several external configuration files with different FEATUREs that have already been discussed. Most of these external configuration files are, by default, some type of NDBM database map; you can change the type. The use of the NDBM database maps improves performance, especially if these files are large. But how do you create these database maps?

First, you must activate the FEATUREs that use these files and the FEATURE directives must specify the type and the final location of these database map files. For example, use the following directive to activate the `mailertable` FEATURE and to specify that the database map file is present at `/etc/mail/mailertable` and that it is a *hash* map.

```
FEATURE(mailertable,`hash -o /etc/mail/mailertable')dnl
```

But this directive allows `sendmail` to use this map only if it exists (note the `-o` option makes this map optional). Next, we need to actually create the database map.

At this point, you can create the plain text version of the map—which you will edit from time to time—in `/etc/mail/mailertable`. `sendmail` never sees this file; it's for administrative use only. You can now add the properly formatted lines for this particular FEATURE to this file.

Finally, use the `makemap(1)` command to convert the plain text file to a hash database map file:

```
makemap hash /etc/mail/mailertable < /etc/mail/mailertable
```

makemap(1) reads in the contents of /etc/mail/mailertable, creates an NDBM hash database from it, then writes the results to /etc/mail/mailertable.db.

*NOTE. The* FEATURE *directive specified the location of the map as* hash -o /etc/mail/mailertable. *This directive implies to* sendmail *that the database map it actually opens is located at* /etc/mail/mailertable.db, *because all hash database maps end with a* .db *suffix.*

# Generating the sendmail Configuration File

Once you have completed your m4 macro configuration file editing, you use the m4 macro processor to create the final sendmail configuration file. For the following examples, we assume that your macro configuration file is located at /usr/lib/mail/myconfig.mc.

If you used the built-in include directive mentioned in "Including the Sendmail m4 Macro Definitions" on page 43, run the following command.

```
# m4 /usr/lib/mail/myconfig.mc > /tmp/sendmail.cf
```

If you *did not* use the built-in include directive, you can still run m4, using the following arguments.

```
# m4 /usr/lib/mail/m4/cf.m4 /usr/lib/mail/myconfig.mc > /tmp/sendmail.cf
```

Now that you have a sendmail configuration file located at /tmp/sendmail.cf, you need to relocate it to /etc/mail/sendmail.cf so that sendmail can see it. To do so, as root, run the following command.

```
# cp /tmp/sendmail.cf /etc/mail/sendmail.cf
```

You can now stop and restart the sendmail daemon to make your changes take effect. Make sure that you have already created any necessary external database map files with makemap(1) (described in "External Configuration Files" on page 52) before you carry out the next step.

```
# /etc/init.d/sendmail stop
# /etc/init.d/sendmail start
```

## Testing the Rewriting Rules—the -bt Flag

When you build a configuration file, you can perform a certain amount of testing by using the test mode of sendmail. For example, you can invoke sendmail as

```
% sendmail -bt -Ctest.cf
```

which then reads the configuration file test.cf and enters test mode. For example,

```
ADDRESS TEST MODE
Enter <ruleset> <name>
>
```

In this mode, you enter lines of the following form, where *rwset* is the rewriting set you want to use and *name* is a name to which the set is applied.

```
ADDRESS TEST MODE
Enter <ruleset> <name>
> rwset name
```

Test mode shows you the steps it takes as it proceeds, finally showing you the name it ends up with. You can use a comma-separated list of *rwsets* for sequential application of rules to an input; ruleset 3 is always applied first. The following example first applies ruleset 3 to the input monet:bollard. Ruleset 1 is then applied to the output of ruleset 3, followed similarly by rulesets 21 and 4.

```
ADDRESS TEST MODE
Enter <ruleset> <name>
> 1,21,4 monet:bollard
```

If you need more detail, you can also use the -d21.99 flag to turn on more debugging. The following example turns on an incredible amount of information; a single word name can result in several pages of information.

```
% sendmail -bt -d21.99
```

# Using the sendmail Restricted Shell

*New!*

The Solaris 8 release provides the `sendmail` restricted shell, `smrsh`. Using `smrsh` instead of `/bin/sh` for mailing to programs improves control of what gets run with e-mail.

`smrsh` runs only the programs in the `/var/admin/sm.bin` directory, enabling you to choose the set of acceptable commands. Reasonable additions to the `sm.bin` directory are commands such as `vacation(1)` and `procmail`. Never include any shell or shell-like program (for example, Perl) in the `sm.bin` directory. The absence of `perl` in the `sm.bin` directory does not restrict the use of shell or Perl scripts in the `sm.bin` directory. It simply disallows the execution of arbitrary programs.

You activate `smrsh` in the `sendmail` configuration file with a `FEATURE` macro in your macro configuration file. The following line specifies the `smrsh` shell.

```
FEATURE(`smrsh')
```

*NOTE. The first character following the opening parenthesis must be a backquote ( ` ).*

Specify `FEATURE` definitions in the configuration file after the `DOMAIN` definition and before local macro definitions.

If you provide an argument, it is used as the path name to `smrsh`; otherwise, the path defined by `confEBINDIR` is used. The default path is `/usr/libexec/smrsh`.

# Reference Tables

This section includes reference tables for `sendmail` command-line arguments, configuration options, mailer flags, and processing options.

## Command-Line Arguments

The following sections describe the arguments for sendmail that you can use on the command line. The arguments are briefly described in Table 15.

*Table 15     Command-Line Arguments for sendmail*

| Argument | Description | |
|---|---|---|
| -bx | Set operation mode to x. Operation modes are listed below. | |
| | m | Deliver mail (default). |
| | a | Run in Arpanet mode. |
| | s | Speak SMTP on input side. |
| | d | Run as a daemon. |
| | t | Run in test mode. |
| | v | Just verify recipients. |
| | i | Initialize the Aliases database. |
| | p | Print the mail queue. |
| | z | Freeze the configuration file. |
| -C*file* | Use a different configuration file. | |
| -d*level* | Set debugging level. | |
| -f *name* | An obsolete form of -r. | |
| -F*name* | Set the full name of this user to *name*. | |
| -h *cnt* | Set the hop count to *cnt*. Show the number of times this message has been processed by sendmail (to the extent that it is supported by the underlying networks). During processing, *cnt* is incremented; if it reaches the value of configuration option h, sendmail returns the message with an error. | |
| -M *msgid* | Run given message ID from the queue. | |
| -n | Do not do aliasing or forwarding. | |
| -ox*value* | Set configuration option x to the specified *value*. | |
| -q*time* | Try to process the queued-up mail. If you specify *time*, sendmail repeatedly runs through the queue at the specified interval to deliver queued mail; otherwise, it runs only once. | |

*Table 15    Command-Line Arguments for sendmail (Continued)*

| Argument | Description |
|---|---|
| `-r name` | The sender's name is *name*. This option is ignored unless the real user is listed as a "trusted user" or if *name* contains an exclamation point (because of certain restrictions in UUCP). |
| `-R recipient` | Run messages for given recipient only from the queue. |
| `-t` | Read the header for `To:`, `CC:`, and `BCC:` lines, and send to everyone listed in those lists. Delete the BCC: line before sending. Delete any names in the argument vector from the send list. |

These arguments are described in the next section.

You can specify several configuration options as primitive flags. These flags are the `c`, `e`, `i`, `m`, `T`, and `v` arguments. Also, you can specify the `f` configuration option as the `-s` argument.

## Configuration Options

You can set the options shown in Table 16 by using either the `-o` flag on the command line or the `O` line in the configuration file.

*Table 16    Configuration Options for sendmail*

| Option | Description |
|---|---|
| `Afile` | Use the named *file* as the alias file instead of `/etc/mail/aliases`. If you specify no file, use `aliases` in the current directory. |
| `Atime` | Specify the time to wait for an `@:@` entry to exist in the `Aliases` database before starting up. If the entry does not appear after that time, rebuild the database. |
| `Bvalue` | Substitute blanks. Default is the dot (`.`) character. |
| `bn` | Disallow empty messages to more than *n* recipients. |
| `c` | If an outgoing mailer is marked as being expensive, do not connect immediately. A queue process must be run to actually send the mail. |
| `cn` | Checkpoint after *n* recipients. |

*Table 16     Configuration Options for sendmail (Continued)*

| Option | Description | | |
|---|---|---|---|
| D | Rebuild the `Aliases` database if necessary and possible. If this option is not set, `sendmail` never rebuilds the `Aliases` database unless explicitly requested with `-bi`. | | |
| d*x* | Deliver in mode *x*. Legal modes are shown below. | | |
| | `i` | Deliver interactively (synchronously). | |
| | `b` | Deliver in background (asynchronously). | |
| | `q` | Just queue the message (deliver during queue run). | |
| e | Mail back errors and give zero exit status always. | | |
| e*x* | Dispose of errors using mode *x*. The values for *x* are shown below. | | |
| | `p` | Print error messages (default). | |
| | `q` | No messages, just give exit status. | |
| | `m` | Mail back errors to sender. | |
| | `w` | Write back errors (mail if user is not logged in). | |
| f | Save UNIX-style `From:` lines at the front of headers. Normally, they are assumed redundant and are discarded. | | |
| F*n* | Set the temporary queue file mode in octal. Good choices are `644` (rw-r--r--) and `600` (rw-------). | | |
| g*n* | Set to *n* the default group ID in which mailers are run. | | |
| H*file* | Specify the help file for SMTP [Postel82]. | | |
| h *n* | Set maximum hop count to *n*. | | |
| i | Ignore dots in incoming messages. | | |
| L*n* | Set the default log level to *n*. | | |
| m | Send to me too, even if I am in an alias expansion. | | |
| M*xvalue* | Set the macro *x* to *value*. Use this option only from the command line. | | |
| o | Assume that the headers may be in old format; that is, spaces delimit names. This flag actually turns on an adaptive algorithm. If any recipient name contains a comma, parentheses, or angle brackets, it is assumed that commas already exist. If this flag is not on, only commas delimit names. Headers are always output with commas between the names. | | |

*Table 16*     *Configuration Options for sendmail (Continued)*

| Option | Description |
|---|---|
| P*name* | Set the name of the local postmaster. If defined, error messages from the MAILER-DAEMON send the header to this name. |
| Q*dir* | Use the directory named in the *dir* variable as the queue directory. |
| q*limit* | Set size limit of messages to be queued under heavy load. Default is 10,000 bytes. |
| R*server* | Remote mode. Deliver through remote SMTP server. Default is location of /var/mail. |
| r*time* | Time out reads after *time* interval. |
| s | Be supersafe when running things; that is, always create the queue file, even if you are going to try immediate delivery. The sendmail program always creates the queue file before returning control to the client under any circumstances. |
| S*file* | Save statistics in the named file. |
| T*time* | Set the queue timeout to *time*. After this interval, messages that have not been sent successfully are returned to the sender. |
| u*n* | Set the default user ID for mailers to *n*. Mailers without the S flag in the mailer definition run as this user. |
| v | Run in verbose mode. |
| X*n* | Set the load average value so that the sendmail daemon refuses incoming SMTP connections to reduce system load. Default is 0, which disables this feature. |
| x*n* | Set the load average value so that sendmail simply queues mail (regardless of the d*x* option) to reduce system load. Default is 0, which disables this feature. |
| y*n* | Recipient factor. Lower the delivery priority of messages with the specified number of bytes per recipient. |
| Y*name* | Set NIS map name to be used for aliases. Default is mail.aliases. |
| Z*n* | Lower the delivery priority of messages with the specified number of bytes per delivery attempts. |

*Table 16     Configuration Options for sendmail (Continued)*

| Option | Description |
|--------|-------------|
| z*n* | Lower the delivery priority of messages with the specified number of bytes per class. |

## Mailer Flags

The flags you can set in the mailer description are described in Table 17.

*Table 17     Flags You Can Set in the Mailer Description for sendmail*

| Flag | Description |
|------|-------------|
| C | If mail is received from a mailer with this flag set, any names in the header that do not have an at sign (@) after being rewritten by ruleset 3 have the @*domain* clause from the sender tacked on. This flag allows mail with headers of the following form.<br><br>`From: usera@local`<br>`To: userb, userc@remote`<br><br>to be automatically rewritten as<br><br>`From: usera@local`<br>`To: userb@local, userc@remote` |
| D | Set a `Date:` header line for this mailer. |
| E | Escape `From:` lines to be `>From` (usually specified with `U`). |
| e | Try to avoid connecting normally because this mailer is expensive to connect to; perform any necessary connection during a queue run. |
| F | Set a `From:` header line for this mailer. |
| f | Set the `-f` from flag for this mailer, but only if this is a network forward operation. (That is, the mailer gives an error if the executing user does not have special permissions.) |
| h | Preserve upper case in host names for this mailer. |
| L | Limit the line lengths as specified in RFC 821. |
| l | Set this mailer as local (that is, final delivery is performed). |

*Table 17    Flags You Can Set in the Mailer Description for
          sendmail (Continued)*

| Flag | Description |
|---|---|
| M | Set a `Message-Id:` header line for this mailer. |
| m | Send to multiple users on the same host in one transaction for this mailer. When a `$u` macro occurs in the `argv` part of the mailer definition, that field is repeated as necessary for all qualifying users. The `L=` field of the mailer description can be used to limit the total length of the `$u` expansion. |
| n | Do not insert a UNIX-style `From:` line on the front of the message. |
| P | Set a `Return-Path:` line for this mailer. |
| p | Always add local host name to the `MAIL From:` line of SMTP, even if there already is one. |
| r | Same as `f`, but send the `-r` flag. |
| S | Do not reset the user ID before calling the mailer. Use this flag in a secure environment in which `sendmail` runs as root. This flag can be used to avoid forged names. |
| s | Strip quote characters from the name before calling the mailer. |
| U | Set UNIX-style `From:` lines with the UUCP-style remote from `<host>` on the end for this mailer. |
| u | Preserve upper case in user names for this mailer. |
| X | Use the *hidden dot* algorithm as specified in RFC 821 for this mailer; basically, insert an extra dot at the front of any line beginning with a dot (to be stripped at the other end). This flag ensures that lines in the message containing a dot do not terminate the message prematurely. |
| x | Set a `Full-Name:  header` line for this mailer. |

## Processing Options

*New!*

You can set a number of configuration file options from the command line with the `-o` option. If you want to set these options permanently, include them in your macro configuration file. Options are represented by a single character or by multiple-character names. The syntax for the single-character names sets option $x$ to `value`.

```
Oxvalue
```

Depending on the option, `value` can be a string, an integer, a boolean (with legal values t, T, f, or F; the default is `true`), or a time interval.

The multiple-character or long names use the following syntax, which sets the option `Longname` to `argument`.

```
O Longname=argument
```

Long names are beneficial because they are easier to interpret than the single character names.

Not all processing options (see Table 18) have single-character names. In Table 18, the multiple-character name is presented first, followed by the single-character syntax enclosed in parentheses.

*Table 18*     *Processing Options for sendmail*

| AliasFile (A`file`) | |
|---|---|
| | Specify possible alias file(s). |
| AliasWait (a *N*) | |
| | Wait up to *N* minutes for an `@:@` entry to exist in the `Aliases` database before starting up. If it does not appear in *N* minutes, rebuild the database (if the `AutoRebuildAliases` option is also set) or issue a warning. Default is 10 minutes. |
| AllowBogusHELO | |
| | Allow a HELO SMTP command that does not include a host name. By default this option is disabled. |
| AutoRebuildAliases (D) | |
| | Rebuild the `/etc/mail/aliases` database if necessary and possible. If this option is not set, `sendmail` never rebuilds the `aliases` database unless explicitly requested with –bi or newaliases(1). |
| | Note that for the database to be rebuilt, root must own and have exclusive write permission to the `/etc/mail/aliases*` files. |

*Table 18    Processing Options for sendmail (Continued)*

| BlankSub (B*c*) | |
|---|---|
| | Set the blank substitution character to *c*. Replace unquoted spaces in addresses with this character. Default is space (that is, no change is made). |
| CheckAliases (n) | |
| | Validate the RHS of aliases when rebuilding the `aliases`(4) database. |
| CheckpointInterval (C*N*) | |
| | Checkpoint the queue every *N* addresses sent. If your system crashes during delivery to a large list, this option prevents retransmission to any but the last *N* recipients. Default is 10. |
| ClassFactor (z*fact*) | |
| | Multiply the indicated factor *fact* by the message class (determined by the `Precedence:` field in the user header and the `P` lines in the configuration file) and subtract from the priority. Thus, favor messages with a higher `Priority:`. Default is 1800. |
| ColonOkInAddr | |
| | Treat colons as a regular character in addresses. If not set, they are treated as the introducer to the RFC 822 group syntax. This option is `on` for version 5 and lower configuration files. |
| ConnectionCacheSize (k*N*) | |
| | Cache the maximum number of open connections at a time. The default is 1. Delay closing the current connection until either this invocation of `sendmail` needs to connect to another host or it terminates. Setting this option to 0 default is the old behavior, that is, connections are closed immediately. |
| ConnectionCacheTimeout (K*timeout*) | |
| | Set the maximum amount of time a cached connection is permitted to idle without activity. If this time is exceeded, immediately close the connection. This value should be small (on the order of 10 minutes). Before `sendmail` uses a cached connection, it always sends a `NOOP` (no operation) command to check the connection; if this command fails, `sendmail` reopens the connection. This behavior keeps your end from |

*Table 18     Processing Options for sendmail (Continued)*

| | | |
|---|---|---|
| | failing if the other end times out. This option enables you to be a good network neighbor and avoid using up excessive resources on the other end. The default is 5 minutes. | |
| ConnectionRateThrottle | | |
| | Set the maximum number of connections permitted per second. After this time, many connections are accepted, further connections are delayed. If not set or ≤ 0, there is no limit. | |
| DaemonPortOptions (O*options*) | | |
| | Set server SMTP options. The options are *key=value* pairs. The following keys are known. | |
| | Addr | Address mask. Default is INADDR_ANY. The address mask can be a numeric address in dot notation or a network name. |
| | Family | Address family. Default is INET. |
| | Listen | Size of listen queue. Default is 10. |
| | Port | Name/number of listening port. Default is smtp. |
| | ReceiveSize | The size of the TCP/IP receive buffer. |
| | SendSize | The size of the TCP/IP send buffer. |
| DefaultCharSet | | |
| | Set the default character to use when converting unlabeled 8-bit input to MIME. | |
| DefaultUser (g*gid*) or (u*uid*) | | |
| | Set the default group ID for mailers to run in to *gid*, or set the default user ID for mailers to *uid*. Default is 1. The value can also be given as a symbolic group or user name. | |
| DeliveryMode (d*x*) | | |
| | Deliver in mode *x*. The following modes are legal. | |
| | i | Deliver interactively (synchronously). |
| | b | Deliver in background (asynchronously). |
| | d | Deferred mode. Defer database lookups until the actual queue run. |

*Table 18    Processing Options for sendmail (Continued)*

| | | |
|---|---|---|
| | q | Just queue the message (deliver during queue run). |
| | Default is b if you specify no option, i if you specify it with no argument, that is, Od is equivalent to Odi. | |
| DialDelay | If a connection fails, wait the specified number of seconds and try again. 0 means do not retry. | |
| DontBlameSendmail | | |
| | Override the file safety checks. This option compromises system security and should not be used. See http://www.sendmail.org/tips/DontBlameSendmail.html for more information. | |
| DontExpandCnames | | |
| | Do not expand CNAME records $[... $] in DNS-based lookups. | |
| DontInitGroups | | |
| | Never invoke the initgroups(3C) routine. If you set this option, agents that are run on behalf of users have only their primary (/etc/passwd) group permissions. | |
| DontProbeInterfaces | | |
| | Do not insert the names and addresses of any local interfaces into the $=w class. If set, you must also include support for these addresses; otherwise, mail to addresses in this list bounces with a configuration error. | |
| DontPruneRoutes (R) | | |
| | Do not prune route-addr syntax addresses to the minimum possible. | |
| DoubleBounceAddress | | |
| | If an error occurs when an error message is being sent, send that "double bounce" error message to this address. | |
| EightBitMode (8) | | |
| | Use 8-bit data handling. This option requires one of the following keys. You can specify the key by using just the first character, but using the full word is better for clarity. | |
| | mimify | Do any necessary conversion of 8BITMIME to 7-bit. |

*Table 18*     *Processing Options for sendmail (Continued)*

| | | |
|---|---|---|
| | `pass` | Pass unlabeled 8-bit input through as is. |
| | `strict` | Reject unlabeled 8-bit input. |
| `ErrorHeader` (`E`*file*/*message*) | | |
| | Append error messages with the indicated message. If the message begins with a slash, assume it to be the path name of a file containing a message (this is the recommended setting). Otherwise, it is a literal message. The error file might contain the name, e-mail address, or phone number of a local postmaster who could provide assistance to end users. If the option is missing or null or if it names a file that does not exist or is not readable, then print no message. | |
| `ErrorMode` (`e`*x*) | | |
| | Dispose of errors by using mode $x$. You can specify the following values for $x$. | |
| | `e` | Mail back errors and always return `0` exit status. |
| | `m` | Mail back errors. |
| | `p` | Print error messages (default). |
| | `q` | No messages, just give exit status. |
| | `w` | Write back errors (mail if user not logged in). |
| `FallbackMXhost` (`V`*fallbackhost*) | | |
| | Act like a very low priority `MX` on every host. This option is intended for sites with poor network connectivity. | |
| `ForkEachJob` (`Y`) | | |
| | Deliver each job that is run from the queue in a separate process. Use this option if you are short of memory because the default tends to consume considerable amounts of memory while the queue is being processed. | |
| `ForwardPath` (`J`*path*) | | |
| | Set the path for searching for `.forward` files. The default is `$z/.forward`. Some sites that use the automounter may prefer to change this path to `/var/forward/$u` to search a file with the same name as the user in a system directory. | |

*Table 18    Processing Options for sendmail (Continued)*

| | |
|---|---|
| | You can also set it to a sequence of paths separated by colons; `sendmail` stops at the first file it can successfully and safely open. For example, `/var/forward/$u:$z/.forward` searches first in `/var/forward/username` and then in `~username/.forward` (but only if the first file does not exist). |
| `HelpFile (Hfile)` | |
| | Specify the help file for SMTP. |
| `HoldExpensive (c)` | |
| | If an outgoing mailer is marked as being expensive, don't connect immediately. |
| `HostsFile` | Set the file to use when doing "file" type access of host names. |
| `HostStatusDirectory` | |
| | Keep host status on disk between `sendmail` runs in the named directory tree. If you do not use a full path, then interpret the path relative to the queue directory. |
| `IgnoreDots (i)` | |
| | Ignore dots in incoming messages. This option is always disabled (that is, dots are always accepted) when SMTP mail is read. |
| `LogLevel (L`*n*`)` | |
| | Set the default log level to *n*. Default is 9. |
| `MatchGECOS (G)` | |
| | Try to match recipient names by using the `GECOS` field. This option allows mail to be delivered with names defined in the `GECOS` field in `/etc/passwd` as well as the login name. |
| `MaxDaemonChildren` | |
| | Set the maximum number of children the daemon permits. After this number, reject connections. If not set or ≤0, there is no limit. |
| `MaxHeadersLength` | |
| | Limit the length of the sum of all header lines in a message. Default is 32768. Reject incoming messages with headers that exceed this value. |

*New!*

*Table 18      Processing Options for sendmail (Continued)*

| | |
|---|---|
| `MaxHopCount` (h*N*) | |
| | Set the maximum hop count. Assume that messages have been processed. Default is `25`. |
| `MaxMessageSize` | |
| | Set the maximum size of messages that are accepted (in bytes). |
| `MaxMimeHeaderLength=`*M*[`/`*N*] | |
| | Set the maximum length of certain `MIME` header field values to *M* characters. For some of these headers that take parameters, the maximum length of each parameter is set to *N* if specified. If you do not specify `/`*N*, use one half of *M*. By default, these values are `0`, meaning no checks are done. |
| `MaxQueueRunSize` | |
| | Limit the maximum size of any given queue run to this number of entries. Stop reading the queue directory after this number of entries is reached; do not use job priority. If not set, there is no limit. |
| `MeToo` (M) | Send to me too, even if I am in an alias expansion. |
| `MaxRecipientsPerMessage` | |
| | Permit no more than the specified number of recipients in an SMTP envelope. Further recipients receive a 452 error code and are deferred until the next delivery attempt. |
| `MinFreeBlocks` (b*N*/*M*) | |
| | Insist on at least *N* blocks free on the file system that holds the queue files before accepting e-mail sent through SMTP. If there is insufficient space, `sendmail` gives a 452 response to the `MAIL` command. This response invites the sender to try again later. The optional *M* is a maximum message size advertised in the `ESMTP` `EHLO` response. It is currently otherwise unused. |
| `MinQueueAge` | |
| | Specify the amount of time a job must sit in the queue between queue runs. This option enables you to set the queue run interval low for better responsiveness without trying all jobs in each run. The default is `0`. |

*Table 18      Processing Options for sendmail (Continued)*

| MustQuoteChars | | |
|---|---|---|
| | Automatically quote characters in a full name phrase: `&,;:\()[]`. | |
| `Mxvalue` | Set the macro `x` to `value`. This option is intended for use only from the command line. | |
| NoRecipientAction | | |
| | Set action if there are no legal recipient files in the message. The following values are legal. | |
| | `add-apparently-to` | |
| | | Add an `Apparently to:` header with all the known recipients may expose blind recipients. |
| | `add-bcc` | Add an empty `Bcc:` header. |
| | `add-to` | Add a `To:` header with all the known recipients may expose blind recipients. |
| | `add-to-undisclosed` | |
| | | Add a `To: undisclosed-recipients:` header. |
| | `none` | Do nothing, leave the message as it is. |
| OldStyleHeaders (o) | | |
| | Assume that the headers may be in old format, that is, spaces delimit names. This option actually turns on an adaptive algorithm: if any recipient address contains a comma, parenthesis, or angle bracket, assume that commas already exist. If this option is not on, only commas delimit names. Headers are always output with commas between the names. | |
| OperatorChars ($o) | | |
| | Define the list of characters that can be used to separate the components of an address into tokens. | |
| PostmasterCopy (Ppostmaster) | | |
| | Send copies of error messages to the named postmaster. Send only the header of the failed message. Because most errors are user problems, it is probably not a good idea to use this option on large sites. It arguably contains all sorts of | |

*Table 18    Processing Options for sendmail (Continued)*

| | | |
|---|---|---|
| | privacy violations, but it seems to be popular with certain operating systems vendors. | |
| `PrivacyOptions (popt,opt,...)` | | |
| | Set privacy options. Privacy is really a misnomer; many of these options are simply a way of insisting on stricter adherence to the SMTP protocol. | |
| | The `goaway` pseudoflag sets all flags except `restrictmailq` and `restrictqrun`. If `mailq` is restricted, only people in the same group as the queue directory can print the queue. If queue runs are restricted, only root and the owner of the queue directory can run the queue. `authwarnings` adds warnings about various conditions that can indicate attempts to spoof the mail system, such as using a nonstandard queue directory. | |
| | You can specify the following options. | |
| | `authwarnings` | Put `X-Authentication-Warning:` headers in messages. |
| | `goaway` | Disallow essentially all SMTP status queries. |
| | `needexpnhelo` | Insist on `HELO` or `EHLO` command before `EXPN`. |
| | `needmailhelo` | Insist on `HELO` or `EHLO` command before `MAIL`. |
| | `needvrfyhelo` | Insist on `HELO` or `EHLO` command before `VRFY`. |
| | `noetrn` | Disallow `ETRN` entirely. |
| | `noexpn` | Disallow `EXPN` entirely. |
| | `noreceipts` | Prevent return receipts. |
| | `novrfy` | Disallow `VRFY` entirely. |
| | `public` | Allow open access. |
| | `restrictmailq` | Restrict `mailq` command. |
| | `restrictqrun` | Restrict `-q` command-line flag. |
| `QueueDirectory (Qdir)` | | |
| | Use the named *dir* as the queue directory. | |

*Table 18    Processing Options for sendmail (Continued)*

| QueueFactor (q*factor*) | |
|---|---|
| | Use *factor* as the multiplier in the map function to decide when to just queue up jobs instead of run them. This value is divided by the difference between the current load average and the load average limit (xflag) to determine the maximum message priority that is sent. Default is 600000. |
| QueueLA (x*LA*) | |
| | When the system load average exceeds *LA*, just queue messages (that is, do not try to send them). Default is 8. |
| QueueSortOrder | |
| | Select the queue sort algorithm. The default value is Priority. Other values are Host or Time. |
| QueueTimeout (T*rtime*/*wtime*) | |
| | Set the queue timeout to *rtime*. After this interval, return to sender all messages that have not been successfully delivered. Default is five days (5d). The optional *wtime* is the time after which a warning message is sent. If it is missing or 0, then send no warning messages. |
| RecipientFactor (y*fact*) | |
| | Add the indicated factor *fact* to the priority (thus lowering the priority of the job) for each recipient; that is, this value penalizes jobs with large numbers of recipients. Default is 30000. |
| RefuseLA (X*LA*) | |
| | When the system load average exceeds *LA*, refuse incoming SMTP connections. Default is 12. |
| RemoteMode (>[RemoteMboxHost]) | |
| | Enable remote mode by using this host. If you do not specify RemoteMboxHost and if /var/mail is remotely mounted, then enable remote mode by using the remote mount host. If you do not specify RemoteMboxHost and /var/mail is locally mounted, then disable remote mode. |
| | When remote mode is enabled, all outgoing messages are sent through that server. |
| ResolverOptions (I) | |
| | Tune DNS lookups. |

*Table 18      Processing Options for sendmail (Continued)*

| RetryFactor (Z*fact*) | |
|---|---|
| | Add the indicated factor *fact* to the priority every time a job is processed. Thus, each time a job is processed, decrease its priority by the indicated value. In most environments, this value should be positive because hosts that are down are all too often down for a long time. Default is `90000`. |
| RunAsUser | Become this user when reading and delivering mail. Intended for use on firewalls where users do not have accounts. |
| SafeFileEnvironment | |
| | Do a `chroot` into this directory before writing files. |
| SaveFromLine (f) | |
| | Save UNIX-style `From:` lines at the front of headers. Normally, they are assumed redundant and are discarded. |
| SendMimeErrors (j) | |
| | Send error messages in `MIME` format (see RFC 1341 and RFC 1344 for details). |
| ServiceSwitchFile | |
| | Define the path to the service-switch file. Because the service-switch file is defined in the Solaris operating environment, this option is ignored. |
| SevenBitInput (7) | |
| | Strip input to seven bits for compatibility with old systems. This option should not be needed. |
| SingleLineFromHeader | |
| | Unwrap `From:` lines that have embedded newlines onto one line. |
| SingleThreadDelivery | |
| | If this option and the `HostStatusDirectory` option are both set, use single-thread deliveries to other hosts. |
| SmtpGreetingMessage or $e | |
| | Set the initial SMTP greeting message. |
| StatusFile (S*file*) | |
| | Log statistics in the named file. |

*Table 18     Processing Options for sendmail (Continued)*

| SuperSafe (s) | | |
|---|---|---|
| | Be supersafe when running things; that is, always instantiate the queue file, even if you are going to try immediate delivery. sendmail always instantiates the queue file before returning control to the client under any circumstances. | |
| TempFileMode (Fmode) | | |
| | Set the file mode for queue files. | |
| Timeout (rtimeouts) | | |
| | Time out reads after time interval. The *timeouts* argument is a list of *keyword=value* pairs. All but command apply to client SMTP. For backward compatibility, a timeout with no *keyword=* part sets all of the longer values. The following list contains recognized timeouts, their default values, and their minimum values specified in RFC 1123 section 5.3.2. | |
| | command | Command read [1h, 5m]. |
| | connect | Initial connect [0, unspecified]. |
| | datablock | Data block read [1h, 3m]. |
| | datafinal | Reply to final . in data [1h, 10m]. |
| | datainit | Reply to DATA command [5m, 2m]. |
| | fileopen | File open [60sec, none]. |
| | helo | Reply to HELO or EHLO command [5m, none]. |
| | hoststatus | Host retry [30m, unspecified]. |
| | iconnect | First attempt to connect to a host [0, unspecified]. |
| | ident | IDENT protocol timeout [30s, none]. |
| | initial | Wait for initial greeting message [5m, 5m]. |
| | mail | Reply to MAIL command [10m, 5m]. |
| | misc | Reply to NOOP and VERB commands [2m, none]. |
| | queuereturn | Undeliverable message returned [5d]. |
| | queuewarn | Deferred warning [4h]. |

*Table 18     Processing Options for sendmail (Continued)*

| | | |
|---|---|---|
| | `quit` | Reply to `QUIT` command [2m, none]. |
| | `rcpt` | Reply to `RCPT` command [1h, 5m]. |
| | `rset` | Reply to `RSET` command [5m, none]. |
| `TimeZoneSpec (ttzinfo)` | | |
| | Set the local time zone to `tzinfo`, for example, `PST8PDT`. Actually, if this option is not set, the `TZ` environment variable is cleared (so the system default is used); if set but null, use the user's `TZ` variable, and if set and non-null, set the `TZ` variable to this value. | |
| `TryNullMXList (w)` | | |
| | If you are the "best" (that is, lowest preference) `MX` for a given host, you should normally detect this situation and treat that condition specially by forwarding the mail to a UUCP feed, treating it as local or whatever is appropriate. However, in some cases (such as Internet firewalls) you may want to try to connect directly to that host as though it had no `MX` records at all. Setting this option tries a direct connection. The downside is that errors in your configuration are likely to be diagnosed as "host unknown" or "message timed out" instead of something more meaningful. This option is deprecated. | |
| `UnixFromLine or $l` | | |
| | Use the `From:` line when sending to files or programs. | |
| `UnsafeGroupWrites` | | |
| | Consider group-writable `:include:` and `.forward` files unsafe; that is, programs and files cannot be directly referenced from such files. | |
| `UseErrorsTo (l)` | | |
| | If there is an `Errors-To:` header, send error messages to the addresses listed there. They normally go to the envelope sender. Use of this option violates RFC 1123. | |
| `UserDatabaseSpec (U)` | | |
| | Define the name and location of the file containing User Database information. | |

*Table 18    Processing Options for sendmail (Continued)*

| Verbose (v) | Run in verbose mode. Adjust the `HoldExpensive` and `DeliveryMode` options so that all mail is delivered completely in a single job so that you can see the entire delivery process. You should never set the `verbose` option in the configuration file; it is intended for command-line use only. |
| --- | --- |

You can specify all options on the command line with the `-o` option, but most relinquish `sendmail` setuid permissions. The options that do not do this are b, d, e, E, i, L, m, o, p, r, s, v, C, and 7. Also considered "safe" is M (define macro) when you are defining the r or s macros.

If the first character of the user name is a vertical bar, use the rest of the user name as the name of a program to pipe the mail to. You may need to quote the name of the user to keep `sendmail` from suppressing the blanks between arguments.

If invoked as `newaliases`, `sendmail` rebuilds the alias database as long as the `/etc/mail/aliases*` files are owned by root and root has exclusive write permission. If invoked as `mailq`, `sendmail` prints the contents of the mail queue.

# 3

# PLANNING MAIL SERVICES

This chapter describes the following four basic mail configurations and outlines the tasks required to set up each configuration. All of the information in this chapter is new in this edition.

- Single DNS domain with an Internet connection and a combined mail hub and gateway.
- Single DNS domain with Internet connection and separate gateway.
- DNS domain and a subdomain with one Internet connection.
- DNS domain with a UUCP gateway.

You may find the following sections useful if you need to set up a new mail system or are expanding an existing one. The configurations start with a basic case (a single DNS domain connected to the Internet) and increase in complexity to a two-domain configuration with Internet and UUCP gateways. More complex systems are beyond the scope of this book.

To set up a mail system, regardless of its configuration, you need the following elements.

- A `sendmail.cf` configuration file on each system.
- Alias files with an alias for each user to point to the place where mail is to be delivered.
- A mailbox to store (or spool) mail files for each user.
- A `postmaster` alias for the person who administers mail services.

See Chapter 4, "Setting Up and Administering Mail Services," for detailed information on how to set up these elements.

How you set up the configuration file and the alias file and where you put the mailboxes depend on the configuration you choose.

# Single DNS Domain with an Internet Connection

The simplest and most common type of e-mail configuration you can build is a single DNS domain with an Internet connection and a system that acts as a combined mail hub and a gateway. To support this simple configuration, you need only two different `sendmail` configuration files.

1. One configuration file is used on a single server that acts as both a mail hub and a gateway to the Internet.
2. The second configuration file is used on all other hosts. These hosts are dumb clients that defer all decisions to the domain's mail hub and gateway.

For this example, the domain name is `starlight.com`, and the system that acts as the mail hub and gateway is named `mailhost.starlight.com`. All outgoing e-mail is rewritten to appear as though it comes from *username*@`starlight.com`, even if it is going from one local user to another, and all e-mail from the Internet will be addressed to *username*@`starlight.com`.

## The Client Configuration

Begin by first creating a `/usr/lib/mail/client.mc` client macro configuration file with the following contents.

```
dnl
dnl client.mc:
dnl Client macro configuration file for starlight.com
dnl
include(`/usr/lib/mail/m4/cf.m4')
OSTYPE(`solaris2')
FEATURE(`nullclient',`mailhost.starlight.com')
```

Notice that only one feature, `nullclient`, is activated. This feature tells all clients to send all e-mail generated locally to `mailhost.starlight.com` without doing any header rewriting.

Next, create the client `sendmail` configuration file from the
`/usr/lib/mail/client.mc` file with the following command.

```
# m4 /usr/lib/mail/client.mc > /usr/lib/mail/client.cf
#
```

Finally, copy the resulting `client.cf` configuration file to
`/etc/mail/sendmail.cf` on all of the client workstations.

## The Mail Hub/Gateway Configuration

The following example shows the `/usr/lib/mail/hub-gateway.mc` macro
configuration file for the system that acts as the mail hub and gateway.

```
dnl
dnl hub-gateway.mc
dnl Mail Hub/Gateway macro configuration file for starlight.com
dnl
include(`/usr/lib/mail/m4/cf.m4')dnl
OSTYPE(`solaris2')dnl
dnl
dnl Now make everything look like it comes from username@starlight.com
dnl
MASQUERADE_AS(`starlight.com')dnl
dnl
dnl Masquerade header recipients too
dnl
FEATURE(allmasquerade)dnl
dnl
dnl And the envelope as well
dnl
FEATURE(masquerade_envelope)dnl
dnl
dnl Activate DNS-based black hole, to drop mail from known spammer sites
dnl Activate Realtime black hole, to drop mail from known spammer sites
dnl When upgrading to sendmail 8.10, change this to the `dnsbl' feature
dnl
FEATURE(rbl)dnl
dnl
dnl Turn on mailertable feature so that we can relay to certain domains
dnl by using gateways WE define in the /etc/mailertable file. (in 8.10, this
dnl file will move to /etc/mail/mailertable, so we're putting it there
dnl manually for now)
dnl
FEATURE(use_cw_file)dnl
FEATURE(`mailertable',`hash -o /etc/mail/mailertable')dnl
FEATURE(`domaintable',`hash -o /etc/mail/domaintable')dnl
FEATURE(`virtusertable',`hash -o /etc/mail/virtusertable')dnl
FEATURE(`access_db',`hash -o /etc/mail/access')dnl
dnl
dnl Allow relaying of hosts in the starlight.com domain, but also
dnl allow us to specify more domains that we will relay in
dnl /etc/mail/relay-domains
dnl
FEATURE(relay_entire_domain)dnl
RELAY_DOMAIN_FILE(`-o /etc/mail/relay-domains')dnl
dnl
dnl Configurable options are modified here
dnl
define(`confSMTP_LOGIN_MSG',`[$j Sendmail $v/$Z; $b, starlight.com]')dnl
define(`confCW_FILE',`-o /etc/mail/sendmail.cw')dnl
dnl
dnl define MAILERs here
dnl
MAILER(`local')
```

```
MAILER(`smtp')
```

Let's break down the components of this file.

The first section contains comments and the regular heading for macro configuration files.

```
dnl
dnl hub-relay.mc
dnl Mail Hub/Gateway macro configuration file for starlight.com
dnl
include(`/usr/lib/mail/m4/cf.m4')dnl
OSTYPE(`solaris2')dnl
```

The masquerading section comes next. The first MASQUERADE_AS directive makes all e-mail look as though it comes from *username*@starlight.com instead of from *username* or *username*@*hostname*.starlight.com. Without this directive, the DNS MX records (discussed later) won't work properly. The allmasquerade feature also rewrites recipients that are in the starlight.com domain, converting them from *username* to *username*@starlight.com. The masquerade_envelope feature rewrites the enclosing envelope of all messages.

```
dnl
dnl Now make everything look like it comes from username@starlight.com
dnl
MASQUERADE_AS(`starlight.com')dnl
dnl
dnl Masquerade header recipients too
dnl
FEATURE(allmasquerade)dnl
dnl
dnl And the envelope as well
dnl
FEATURE(masquerade_envelope)dnl

Next we activate a SPAM reduction feature:
dnl
dnl Activate DNS-based black hole, to drop mail from known spammer sites
dnl Activate Realtime black hole, to drop mail from known spammer sites
dnl When upgrading to sendmail 8.10, change this to the `dnsbl' feature
dnl
FEATURE(rbl)dnl
```

The next section activates several external configuration files that change *how* sendmail carries out certain activities and decisions. The first line activates the use of the /etc/sendmail.cw file (but, later in this file we change the location to /etc/mail/sendmail.cw). Then, we activate the mailertable, domaintable, virtusertable, and access_db features.

*NOTE. These features are all hash maps that you create with the* makemap *command. However, you make all these maps optional with the* -o *option.* sendmail *now recognizes the maps if they exist and ignores them if they do not exist.*

```
dnl
dnl Turn on mailertable feature so that we can relay to certain domains
dnl by using gateways WE define in the /etc/mailertable file. (in 8.10, this
dnl file will move to /etc/mail/mailertable, so we're putting it there
dnl manually for now)
dnl
FEATURE(use_cw_file)dnl
FEATURE(`mailertable', `hash -o /etc/mail/mailertable')dnl
FEATURE(`domaintable', `hash -o /etc/mail/domaintable')dnl
FEATURE(`virtusertable', `hash -o /etc/mail/virtusertable')dnl
FEATURE(`access_db', `hash -o /etc/mail/access')dnl
```

The next section defines the relaying policy. For this domain, we relay e-mail sent from any system in the starlight.com domain. For the future, we also allow the file /etc/mail/relay-domains to list any other domains for which we will relay.

*NOTE. The* /etc/mail/relay-domains *file is a text file and you do not need to process it with the* makemap *command. The* -o *option specifies that the file is optional.*

```
dnl
dnl Allow relaying of hosts in the starlight.com domain, but also
dnl allow us to specify more domains that we will relay in
dnl /etc/mail/relay-domains
dnl
FEATURE(relay_entire_domain)dnl
RELAY_DOMAIN_FILE('-o /etc/mail/relay-domains')dnl
```

You make any changes to the sendmail default options in the next section. Here, we simply customize the SMTP login message to include the starlight.com domain name and change the default location of the sendmail.cw file from /etc/sendmail.cw to /etc/mail/sendmail.cw.

```
dnl
dnl Configurable options are modified here
dnl
define(`confSMTP_LOGIN_MSG', `[$j Sendmail $v/$Z; $b, starlight.com]')dnl
define(`confCW_FILE', `-o /etc/mail/sendmail.cw')dnl
```

The final section includes the mailers we want to activate. In this case, the mail hub needs to be able to deliver mail locally to the mail spool and to transfer e-mail via the SMTP mailer.

```
dnl
dnl define MAILERs here
dnl
MAILER(`local')
MAILER(`smtp')
```

When you have finished creating the hub-gateway.mc file, you use it to generate the sendmail configuration file with the following command.

```
# m4 /usr/lib/mail/hub-gateway.mc > /usr/lib/mail/hub-gateway.cf
#
```

Then, copy the resulting hub-gateway.cf file to /etc/mail/sendmail.cf on mailhost.starlight.com.

## Customizing the External Databases

Before you can start sendmail on mailhost.starlight.com, you must minimally configure some of the external databases. These databases and their contents are listed below.

- /etc/mail/mailertable

  Because this system is the mail hub, use this file to ensure that all incoming e-mail for username@starlight.com is ultimately delivered on this system. This file also deals with the unlikely event that e-mail may arrive addressed to username@hostname.starlight.com.

```
#
# Locally handle anything ending with starlight.com on this system.
# Also, locally handle any e-mail addressed to
# username@hostname.starlight.com in case such a format is used.
starlight.com      local:
.starlight.com     local:
```

  Use the makemap command to process this file into a hash map, as shown below.

```
# makemap hash /etc/mail/mailertable > /etc/mail/mailertable
#
```

- /etc/mail/relay-domains

  Use this file to ensure that e-mail originating from within your domain is accepted for delivery by this gateway to any location anywhere. The relay-domains file must contain your domain name.

```
# List domains for which we actually relay mail.
# If a domain is not listed here, relaying of mail from that domain is denied.
starlight.com
```

  Because sendmail treats relay-domains as a plain text file, you need take no other action to process it.

- `/etc/mail/sendmail.cw`

  Use this file to list all of the names by which this host is known so that `sendmail` recognizes that e-mail sent to any of those host names is truly intended for this system. Also, list the domain name here because most e-mail is sent to *username*@`starlight.com`, and you want `sendmail` to recognize that `starlight.com` is another way of referring to this host.

```
# List all the names by which the mail hub is known so
# that sendmail doesn't get confused into thinking that it shouldn't
# deliver mail into the proper spool on this system. Note
# that you list the DNS domain itself at the end of the list because
# most e-mail will be addressed to username@starlight.com
mailhost.starlight.com
starlight.com
```

  Because `sendmail` treats `sendmail.cw` as a plain text file, you need take no other action to process it.

Now that you have customized all of these files, restart `sendmail` so that it reads the files and uses their settings to make decisions for incoming and outgoing e-mail.

## The DNS Configuration

To ensure that all e-mail sent from any Internet site directly reaches the system acting as the `starlight.com` e-mail gateway and hub, put entries like those shown in the following example in the `starlight.com` DNS server tables.

```
starlight.com    IN  MX  10  mailhost
mailhost         IN  A       205.172.3.45
```

This example assumes that the IP address of the system that acts as the mail hub and gateway is `205.172.3.45`. Any Internet site trying to send e-mail to *username*@`starlight.com` performs a DNS lookup and discovers that the mail exchanger (MX) record for all e-mail destined for `starlight.com` should be sent directly to `mailhost.starlight.com`, with a preference of `10`.

# Single DNS Domain with Internet Connection and Separate Gateway

Although the previous section describes a completely valid `sendmail` configuration, it is often desirable to separate the function of the mail hub from the mail gateway. This separation enables you to put the mail hub inside a protective firewall, shielding it from direct attacks on sendmail. You would put the gateway on the firewall's DMZ network (preferred) or outside the firewall. In this way, you can monitor any attacks on the gateway. If compromised, the gateway has only its sendmail configuration file stored on it.

The following example still uses the starlight.com domain with three sendmail configuration files to implement this change.

1. One for the gateway named gw.starlight.com.
2. One for the mail hub named mailhost.starlight.com.
3. One for all clients of the starlight.com domain. This file has exactly the same macro configuration file as shown in "The Client Configuration" on page 78, because mailhost.starlight.com is still the mail hub for the site.

## The Gateway Configuration

The macro configuration file for the gateway contains the same directives as shown in "The Mail Hub/Gateway Configuration" on page 79; it simply has a different name, /usr/lib/mail/gateway.mc. For your convenience, the contents of the file are repeated below.

```
dnl
dnl gateway.mc
dnl The Gateway macro configuration file for starlight.com
dnl
include(`/usr/lib/mail/m4/cf.m4')dnl
OSTYPE(`solaris2')dnl
dnl
dnl Now make everything look like it comes from username@starlight.com
dnl
MASQUERADE_AS(`starlight.com')dnl
dnl
dnl Masquerade header recipients too
dnl
FEATURE(allmasquerade)dnl
dnl
dnl And the envelope as well
dnl
FEATURE(masquerade_envelope)dnl
dnl
dnl Activate DNS-based black hole, to drop mail from known spammer sites
dnl Activate Realtime BLack hole, to drop mail from known spammer sites
dnl When upgrading to sendmail 8.10, change this to the `dnsbl' feature
dnl
FEATURE(rbl)dnl
dnl
dnl Turn on mailertable feature so that we can relay to certain domains
dnl by using gateways WE define in the /etc/mailertable file. (in 8.10, this
dnl file will move to /etc/mail/mailertable, so we're putting it there
dnl manually for now)
dnl
FEATURE(use_cw_file)dnl
FEATURE(`mailertable',`hash -o /etc/mail/mailertable')dnl
FEATURE(`domaintable',`hash -o /etc/mail/domaintable')dnl
FEATURE(`virtusertable',`hash -o /etc/mail/virtusertable')dnl
FEATURE(`access_db',`hash -o /etc/mail/access')dnl
```

```
dnl
dnl Allow relaying of hosts in the starlight.com domain, but also
dnl allow us to specify more domains that we will relay in
dnl /etc/mail/relay-domains
dnl
FEATURE(relay_entire_domain)dnl
RELAY_DOMAIN_FILE('-o /etc/mail/relay-domains')dnl
dnl
dnl Configurable options are modified here
dnl
define(`confSMTP_LOGIN_MSG',`[$j Sendmail $v/$Z; $b, starlight.com]')dnl
define(`confCW_FILE',`-o /etc/mail/sendmail.cw')dnl
dnl
dnl define MAILERs here
dnl
MAILER(`local')
MAILER(`smtp')
```

You use the entries in the external databases to explicitly instruct sendmail that the gateway is a separate system, not a system that acts as a combined gateway and mail hub.

## The Gateway's External Databases

Make the following changes, at a minimum, to the gateway's external databases.

- /etc/mail/mailertable

  Use this file to enable the gateway to deal properly with all *incoming* e-mail from the Internet bound for the common addresses of the form *username*@starlight.com or the much rarer case of *username*@*hostname*.starlight.com. In either case, the e-mail is transmitted through SMTP to mailhost.starlight.com for final handling. The [ ] characters surrounding mailhost.starlight.com tell sendmail *not* to consult DNS for MX records to determine where to send e-mail bound for mailhost.starlight.com. Instead, sendmail should simply send the e-mail directly to that host. If you don't use this construct, the e-mail loops back to the gateway again and again, forming an e-mail loop. Also, note that, because no e-mail is ever delivered into a mail spool on this machine, you don't have the local: entries. You include the local: entries only on the final mail hub.

```
# This system acts as a sendmail gateway for all the DNS domains
# listed below.
# Note the []'s that surround the mail hub names. They ensure that
# MX records are not looked up again by this gateway, thereby preventing
# a nasty MX record loop!
#
starlight.com    smtp:[mailhost.starlight.com]
.starlight.com   smtp:[mailhost.starlight.com]
```

Remember to use the makemap command on this file so that sendmail can use it.

- `/etc/mail/relay-domains`

  Use this file to relay all e-mail with a source or destination address in the `starlight.com` domain by this gateway.

```
# Domains listed in this file are those for which we
# actually relay mail. If a domain is not listed
# here, relaying of mail from that domain is denied.
starlight.com
```

- `/etc/mail/sendmail.cw`

  List only the names this host is known by. Don't list the `starlight.com` domain because only the host where the mail ultimately is delivered to the mail spool needs to do this.

```
# List all the names by which the mail gateway is known so
# that sendmail doesn't get confused into thinking that it shouldn't
# deliver mail to this system.
gw.starlight.com
```

## The Mail Hub Configuration

The macro configuration file for the mail hub is identical to that for the gateway. Thus, the final `sendmail` configuration file is also identical. The behavior of this mail hub is governed by the `sendmail` external databases listed below.

### The Mail Hub's External Databases

- `/etc/mail/mailertable`

  Because this system is the mail hub, use the `mailertable` file to ensure that all incoming e-mail for *username*@`starlight.com` ultimately is delivered on this system. This file also deals with the unlikely event of e-mail that is addressed to *username*@*hostname*`.starlight.com`. Finally, because this system is not the e-mail gateway for this domain, ensure that all e-mail sent from inside this domain to the Internet is forwarded to the gateway machine (`gw.starlight.com`) for handling.

```
#
# Locally handle anything ending with starlight.com.
# Also, locally handle any e-mail addressed to
# username@hostname.starlight.com, in case such a format ever appears.
starlight.com      local:
.starlight.com     local:
# Relay EVERYTHING else to gw.starlight.com for handling
.                  relay:gw.starlight.com.
```

The `.` at the beginning of the last line acts as the final dot in a fully qualified DNS name, such as `sun.com`. With nothing before it, this dot (`.`) is interpreted as *anything*.`{com,gov,net,org,etc.}`. Because any previous, more specific rules in the configuration file override this file, we can put in rules that prevent mail that originates inside `starlight.com` bound for someone else inside `starlight.com` from going to the gateway and thus onto the Internet, where it might be intercepted by unscrupulous persons.

Note also that the host name has a dot (`.`) at the end of it to ensure that it is a fully qualified host name.

Use the `makemap` command to process this file into a hash map, as shown in the following example.

```
# makemap hash /etc/mail/mailertable > /etc/mail/mailertable
#
```

- `/etc/mail/relay-domains`

  Put your domain name in this file to ensure that e-mail originating from within your domain is accepted for delivery to any location anywhere by this gateway.

```
# List domains in this file for which we actually will relay mail.
# If a domain is not listed here, relaying of mail from that domain is denied.
starlight.com
```

  Because `sendmail` treats `relay-domains` as a plain text file, you need take no other action to process it.

- `/etc/mail/sendmail.cw`

  Use this file to list all of the names by which this host is known so that `sendmail` recognizes that e-mail sent to any of those host names is truly intended for this system. Because this system is the mail hub for that domain, also list the domain name here; most e-mail is sent to *username*`@starlight.com`, and you want `sendmail` to recognize that `starlight.com` is another way of referring to this host.

```
# List all the names by which the mail hub is known so that sendmail
# doesn't get confused into thinking that it shouldn't
# deliver mail into the proper spool on this system. Note
# that the DNS domain itself is at the end of the list because
# most e-mail will be addressed to username@starlight.com
mailhost.starlight.com
starlight.com
```

  Because `sendmail` treats `sendmail.cw` as a plain text file, you need take no other action to process it.

As always, after you make these changes you need to restart `sendmail`.

## The DNS Configuration

To ensure that all e-mail sent from any Internet site reaches the `starlight.com` domain correctly, put entries that look like the following example in the `starlight.com` DNS server tables.

```
starlight.com    IN  MX  10  gw
gw               IN  A       205.172.3.46
```

This example assumes that the IP address of the gateway is `205.172.3.46`. Any Internet site trying to send e-mail to *username*`@starlight.com` performs a DNS lookup and discovers that the mail exchanger (MX) record for all e-mail destined for `starlight.com` should be sent directly to `gw.starlight.com` with a preference of `10`.

As you can see, all incoming e-mail goes through the gateway to get to the mail hub. This action does not affect outgoing e-mail because it is handled directly by `sendmail` on the mail hub and gateway without involving DNS. Remember that the e-mail clients in this domain just send everything to the mail hub for processing, so they don't look at DNS either.

# DNS Domain and a Subdomain with One Internet Connection

This section describes a more complex example with a parent DNS domain—`starlight.com`—for the corporate headquarters of the Starlight company, and a child DNS domain—`eng.starlight.com`—for the engineering division of the company. Consider the following issues for this configuration.

- Each domain needs to send internal and external e-mail independently of the other.
- The two domains must be able to send e-mail to each other.
- Only one of the domains (`starlight.com`) has a connection to the Internet but both need to send and receive e-mail with Internet sites. The networks of both domains are interconnected.

At first, this example looks quite complex but you can handle it with five configuration files.

1.  One for the gateway named `gw.starlight.com`.
2.  One for the corporate mail hub named `mailhost.starlight.com`.
3.  One for the engineering mail hub named `mailhost.eng.starlight.com`.
4.  One for each client of the `starlight.com` domain.
5.  One for each client of the `eng.starlight.com` domain.

## The Gateway Configuration

This gateway uses the same macro configuration file as "The Gateway Configuration" on page 84. Again, you specify the differences with the external database files.

### The Gateway's External Databases

-   `/etc/mail/mailertable`

    Use this file to enable the gateway to deal properly with all *incoming* e-mail from the Internet bound for the common addresses of the following forms: *username*@`starlight.com`, *username*@`eng.starlight.com`, or the much rarer cases of *username*@*hostname*.`starlight.com` and *username*@*hostname*.`eng.starlight.com`. When bound for the corporate domain, the e-mail is transmitted through SMTP to `mailhost.starlight.com` for final handling. When bound for the engineering domain, the e-mail is transmitted through SMTP to `mailhost.eng.starlight.com` for final handling.

```
# This systems acts as a sendmail gateway for all the DNS domains
# listed below.
# Note the []'s that surround the mail hub names ensure that
# MX records are not looked up again by this gateway, thereby preventing
# a nasty MX record loop!
#
starlight.com       smtp:[mailhost.starlight.com]
.starlight.com      smtp:[mailhost.starlight.com]
eng.starlight.com   smtp:[mailhost.eng.starlight.com]
.eng.starlight.com  smtp:[mailhost.eng.starlight.com]
```

    Remember to run the `makemap` command on this file so that `sendmail` can use it.

-   `/etc/mail/relay-domains`

    Use this file to ensure that `sendmail` relays all e-mail to this gateway with a source or destination address in the `starlight.com` or `eng.starlight.com` domains.

```
# List domains in this file for which we actually relay mail.
# If a domain is not listed here, relaying of mail from that domain is denied.
starlight.com
eng.starlight.com
```

- /etc/mail/sendmail.cw

  List the names by which this host is known. Don't list the
  starlight.com or eng.starlight.com domains because only the
  host(s) where the mail ultimately is delivered to the mail spool needs to
  do this.

```
# List all the names by which the mail gateway is known so
# that sendmail doesn't get confused into thinking that it shouldn't
# deliver mail to this system.
gw.starlight.com
```

## The Corporate Mail Hub Configuration

The macro configuration file for the mail hub is identical to that for the
gateway. Thus, the final sendmail configuration file is also identical. The
behavior of this mail hub is governed by the sendmail external databases
listed below.

### The Corporate Mail Hub's External Databases

- /etc/mail/mailertable

  Because this system is the mail hub, use this file to ensure that all
  incoming e-mail for *username*@starlight.com is ultimately delivered
  on this system. This file also deals with the unlikely event that e-mail
  arrives addressed to *username*@*hostname*.starlight.com. Because
  this system is not the e-mail gateway for this domain, make sure that
  all e-mail sent from inside this domain to the Internet is forwarded to
  the gateway machine (gw.starlight.com) for handling.

  Finally, if e-mail originates within this domain bound for the
  engineering domain, don't send it through the gateway, Instead, send it
  directly to the engineering mail hub.

```
#
# Locally handle anything ending with starlight.com
# Also, locally handle any e-mail addressed to
# username@hostname.starlight.com,
starlight.com      local:
.starlight.com     local:
# Send all e-mail bound for the Engineering domain to the engineering mail
# hub
eng.starlight.com  relay:mailhost.eng.starlight.com
.eng.starlight.com relay:mailhost.eng.starlight.com
# Relay EVERYTHING else to gw.starlight.com for handling
.                  relay:gw.starlight.com.
```

The . at the beginning of the last line acts as the final dot in a fully qualified DNS name, such as sun.com. With nothing before it, this dot (.) is interpreted as *anything*.{com,gov,net,org,etc.}. Because any previous, more specific rules in the configuration file override this file, we can put in rules that prevent mail that originates inside starlight.com bound for someone else inside starlight.com from going to the gateway and thus onto the Internet, where it might be intercepted by unscrupulous persons.

Note also that the host name has a dot (.) at the end of it to ensure that it is a fully qualified host name.

Process this file into a hash map with the makemap command, as shown in the following example.

```
# makemap hash /etc/mail/mailertable > /etc/mail/mailertable
#
```

- /etc/mail/relay-domains

  Include your domain name in this file to ensure that e-mail originating from within your domain is accepted by this gateway for delivery to any location anywhere. Also, relay anything to or from the eng.starlight.com domain.

```
# List domains in this file for which we actually relay mail.
# If a domain is not listed here, relaying of mail from that domain is denied.
starlight.com
eng.starlight.com
```

Because sendmail treats relay-domains as a plain text file, you need take no other action to process it.

- /etc/mail/sendmail.cw

  List all of the names by which this host is known so that sendmail recognizes that e-mail sent to any of those host names is truly intended for this system. Also, because this system is the mail hub for the domain, list the `starlight.com` domain name here. Most e-mail is sent to *username*`@starlight.com`, and you want `sendmail` to recognize that `starlight.com` is another way of referring to this host.

```
# List all the names by which the mail hub is known so that sendmail
# doesn't get confused into thinking that it shouldn't
# deliver mail into the proper spool on this system. Note
# that the DNS domain itself is at the end of the list because
# most e-mail is addressed to username@starlight.com
mailhost.starlight.com
starlight.com
```

Because `sendmail` treats `sendmail.cw` as a plain text file, you need take no other action to process it.

As always, once you make these changes, restart `sendmail`.

## The Corporate Client Configuration

Use the following macro configuration file to generate `sendmail.cf` files for each of the clients in the `starlight.com` corporate domain.

```
dnl
dnl corp-client.mc:
dnl Client macro configuration file for starlight.com
dnl
include(`/usr/lib/mail/m4/cf.m4')
OSTYPE(`solaris2')
FEATURE(`nullclient',`mailhost.starlight.com')
```

Notice that only the `nullclient` feature is activated. This feature tells all clients to send all e-mail generated locally to `mailhost.starlight.com` without doing any header rewriting.

Use the following command to create the client `sendmail` configuration file.

```
# m4 /usr/lib/mail/corp-client.mc > /usr/lib/mail/corp-client.cf
#
```

Copy the `corp-client.cf` configuration file to `/etc/mail/sendmail.cf` on each of the corporate client workstations.

## The Engineering Mail Hub Configuration

The macro configuration file for the corporate mail hub is identical to that for the gateway. Thus, the final `sendmail` configuration file is also identical. The behavior of this mail hub is governed by the `sendmail` external databases listed below.

## The Engineering Mail Hub's External Databases

- `/etc/mail/mailertable`

  Because this system is the mail hub for the domain, use the `mailertable` file to ensure that all incoming e-mail for *username*@eng.starlight.com is ultimately delivered on this system. This file also deals with the unlikely event that e-mail arrives that is addressed to *username*@*hostname*.eng.starlight.com. Because this system is not the e-mail gateway for this domain, ensure that all e-mail sent from inside this domain to the Internet is forwarded to the gateway machine (gw.starlight.com) for handling.

  Finally, if e-mail originates within this domain bound for the corporate domain, don't send it through the gateway. Instead, send it directly to the corporate mail hub.

```
#
# Locally handle anything ending with eng.starlight.com
# Also, locally handle any e-mail addressed to
# username@hostname.eng.starlight.com,
eng.starlight.com        local:
.eng.starlight.com       local:
# Send all e-mail bound for the Corporate domain to the corporate mail
# hub
starlight.com            relay:mailhost.starlight.com
.starlight.com           relay:mailhost.starlight.com
# Relay EVERYTHING else to gw.starlight.com for handling
.                        relay:gw.starlight.com.
```

  The . at the beginning of the last line acts as the final dot in a fully qualified DNS name, such as sun.com. With nothing before it, this dot (.) is interpreted as *anything*.{com,gov,net,org,etc.}. Because any previous, more specific rules in the configuration file override this file, we can put in rules that prevent mail that originates inside eng.starlight.com bound for someone else inside eng.starlight.com from going to the gateway and thus onto the Internet, where it might be intercepted by unscrupulous persons.

  Note also that the host name has a dot (.) at the end of it to ensure that it is a fully qualified host name.

  Use the makemap command to process this file, as shown in the following example.

```
# makemap hash /etc/mail/mailertable > /etc/mail/mailertable
#
```

- `/etc/mail/relay-domains`

  Include your domain name in this file to ensure that e-mail originating from within your domain is accepted for delivery to any location anywhere by this gateway. Also, relay anything to or from the `starlight.com` domain.

```
# List domains in this file for which we actually relay mail.
# If a domain is not listed here, relaying of mail from that domain is denied.
starlight.com
eng.starlight.com
```

  Because `sendmail` treats `relay-domains` as a plain text file, you need take no other action to process it.

- `/etc/mail/sendmail.cw`

  Use this file to list all of the names by which this host is known so that `sendmail` recognizes that e-mail sent to any of those host names is truly intended for this system. Also, because this system is the mail hub for the domain, list the domain name here because most e-mail is sent to *username*@`starlight.com` and you want `sendmail` to recognize that `starlight.com` is another way of referring to this host.

```
# List all the names by which the mail hub is known so
# that sendmail doesn't get confused into thinking that it shouldn't
# deliver mail into the proper spool on this system. Note
# that the DNS domain itself is at the end of the list because
# most e-mail is addressed to username@eng.starlight.com
mailhost.eng.starlight.com
eng.starlight.com
```

  Because `sendmail` treats `sendmail.cw` as a plain text file, you need take no other action to process it.

As always, once you make these changes, restart `sendmail`.

## The Engineering Client Configuration

Use the following macro configuration file to generate `sendmail.cf` files for each of the clients in the `eng.starlight.com` corporate domain.

```
dnl
dnl eng-client.mc:
dnl Client macro configuration file for eng.starlight.com
dnl
include(`/usr/lib/mail/m4/cf.m4')
OSTYPE(`solaris2')
FEATURE(`nullclient', `mailhost.eng.starlight.com')
```

Notice that only the `nullclient` feature is activated. This feature tells all clients to send all e-mail generated locally to `mailhost.eng.starlight.com` without doing any header rewriting.

Use the following command to create the client `sendmail` configuration file.

```
# m4 /usr/lib/mail/eng-client.mc > /usr/lib/mail/eng-client.cf
#
```

Copy the `eng-client.cf` configuration file to `/etc/mail/sendmail.cf` on each of the engineering client workstations.

## The DNS Configuration

Put entries like those in the following example in the `starlight.com` DNS server tables to ensure that all e-mail sent from any Internet site reaches the `starlight.com` or `eng.starlight.com` domains correctly.

```
starlight.com        IN MX  10   gw
eng.starlight.com    IN MX  10   gw
gw                   IN  A       205.172.3.46
```

This example assumes that the IP address of the gateway is `205.172.3.46`. Any Internet site trying to send e-mail to *username*`@starlight.com` or *username*`@eng.starlight.com` performs a DNS lookup and discovers that the mail exchanger (MX) record for all e-mail destined for these domains is sent directly to `gw.starlight.com` with a preference of `10`.

As you can see, all incoming e-mail goes through the gateway to get to the mail hubs. This behavior does not affect outgoing e-mail because it is handled directly by `sendmail` on the mail hubs and gateway without involving DNS. Remember that the e-mail clients in both domains just send everything to their respective mail hubs for processing, so they don't look at DNS either.

# DNS Domain with a UUCP Gateway

Adding the capability of dealing with UUCP addresses to a gateway is easily done. Just add the following line to the end of the macro configuration file for the gateway in question.

```
MAILER(uucp)dnl
```

Run the macro configuration file through the m4 macro processor and copy the generated `sendmail` configuration file to `/etc/mail/sendmail.cf` on your gateway. Restart `sendmail`; your gateway can now deal with UUCP addresses.

# 4

# SETTING UP AND ADMINISTERING MAIL SERVICES

This chapter describes how to set up, test, administer, and troubleshoot mail services. If you are not familiar with administering mail services, read Chapter 1, "Understanding Mail Services," for an introduction to the terminology and structure of the mail services. Read Chapter 3, "Planning Mail Services," for descriptions of several mail services configurations.

## Preparing to Set Up Mail Services

You can set up a mail service relatively easily if your site does not provide connections to electronic mail services outside of your company or if your company is in a single domain. Setting up complicated sites with multiple domains is beyond the scope of this book. Chapter 2, "Customizing sendmail Configuration Files," contains information about how to create the more complicated configuration files required for sites with multiple domains.

Mail requires two types of configurations for local mail and a third for communication with networks outside of your domain. These configurations

*New!*

can be combined on the same system or provided by separate systems. Table 19 describes each of these configurations.

*Table 19    Mail Configurations*

| Configuration | Description |
| --- | --- |
| Mail hub | You need at least one mail hub. The mail hub stores mailboxes in the `/var/mail` directory. |
| Mail client | Mail clients are users who have mailboxes either locally or on a mail server. |
| Gateway | A gateway is a connection between different communications networks. A relay host manages communication with networks outside of your domain. A relay host can also act as a gateway. You must add rules to the `*.mc` file used to generate the `sendmail.cf` file to set up a gateway. See Chapter 2, "Customizing sendmail Configuration Files," for information about creating a `*.mc` file. |

Before you begin to set up your mail service, choose the systems that will act as mail hubs and gateways. You should also make a list of all of the mail clients you will be providing service for and indicate the location of their mailboxes. This list will help you when you are ready to create mail aliases for your users. See Chapter 1, "Understanding Mail Services," for more information about the function each of these systems provides. For your convenience, guidelines about which systems are good candidates for mail hubs and gateways are described in the following sections.

# Setting Up Mail Services

To simplify the setup instructions, the following sections tell you how to set up individual mail hubs, mail clients, and gateway hosts. If a system in your mail services configuration is acting in more than one capacity, simply follow the appropriate instructions for each type of system. For example, if your mail hub and gateway are the same system, follow the directions for setting up that system as a mail hub and then follow the directions for setting up the same system as a mail gateway.

*NOTE. The following procedures for setting up a mail server and a mail client apply when mailboxes are NFS-mounted. You do not need to follow these procedures when mailboxes are maintained in locally mounted /var/mail directories.*

## Setting Up a Mail Hub

**New!**

The *mail hub* is responsible for routing all of the mail from a client. The only resource requirement for a mail hub is that it have adequate spooling space for client mailboxes. See Chapter 1, "Understanding Mail Services," for recommendations about spooling space.

To set up a mail hub, you must export the `/var` directory. On Solaris systems, type **share** and press Return to check whether the `/var` directory is exported. In the following example, the `/var/mail` directory is not exported.

```
cinderella% share
cinderella%
```

If the `/var` directory is not exported, become superuser and then type **share -F nfs -o rw /var/mail** and press Return. You can type **share** with no arguments to verify that the directory is exported. You can also add the line to the `/etc/dfs/dfstab` file so that the file system is shared when the system is rebooted.

```
cinderella% share
cinderella% su
Password:
# share -F nfs -o rw /var/mail
# share

-               /var/mail    rw    ""
# vi /etc/dfs/dfstab
Add the line:
share -F nfs -o rw /var/mail
```

> *NOTE. The* `mail.local` *program automatically creates mailboxes in the* `/var/mail` *directory the first time a message is delivered. You do not need to create individual mailboxes for your mail clients.*

A mail hub resolves difficult e-mail addresses and reroutes mail within your domain. A good candidate for a mail hub is a system that connects you to the outside world or to a parent domain.

Use the following steps to set up a mail hub.

1.  Become superuser on the mail hub system.
2.  Type **/usr/lib/mail/sh/check-hostname** and press Return.

    The `check-hostname` script verifies whether `sendmail` can identify the fully qualified host name for this server. If the script is not successful in identifying the fully qualified host name, you must add the fully qualified host name as the first alias for the host in the

/etc/hosts file. The following example shows a host name that is not fully qualified.

```
paperbark% su
Password:
# /usr/lib/mail/sh/check-hostname
Hostname paperbark could not be fully qualified.
We recommend changing the /etc/hosts entry:

172.16.8.22 paperbark loghost

to:

172.16.8.22 paperbark paperbark.pick.some.domain loghost
#
```

3.  Use admintool to edit the /etc/hosts file and add the words **mailhost** and **mailhost.domainname** after the IP address and system name of the mail hub system.

    The domain name must be identical to the subdomain string in the output of the **/usr/lib/sendmail -bt -d0 </dev/null** command.

    The following example shows the output of the command for the system paperbark which is part of the eng.wellard.com subdomain.

```
paperbark% /usr/lib/sendmail -bt -d0 < /dev/null
Version 8.9.3+Sun
 Compiled with: LDAPMAP MAP_REGEX LOG MATCHGECOS MIME7TO8 MIME8TO7
                NAMED_BIND NDBM NETINET NETINET6 NETUNIX NEWDB \NIS NISPLUS
                QUEUE SCANF SMTP USERDB XDEBUG

============ SYSTEM IDENTITY (after readcf) ============
      (short domain name) $w = paperbark
  (canonical domain name) $j = paperbark.eng.wellard.com
         (subdomain name) $m = eng.wellard.com
              (node name) $k = paperbark
=======================================================
paperbark%
```

    The following example shows the entry in the /etc/hosts file that designates paperbark as the mail hub for domain eng.wellard.com.

```
# cat /etc/hosts
#
# Internet host table
#
127.0.0.1       localhost
172.16.8.22     paperbark mailhost mailhost.eng.wellard.com       loghost
```

4.  Create an entry for the new mail hub in the appropriate hosts file.

If you are using NIS or NIS+, add an entry including a host alias called `mailhost` and `mailhost.`*`domainname`* to the host entry for the new mail host.

If you are not using NIS or NIS+, create an entry in `/etc/hosts` for each system on the network, using the format `IP:`*`address`* *`mailhost_name`* `mailhost mailhost.`*`domainname`*.

5. Type **cp /etc/mail/main.cf /etc/mail/sendmail.cf** and press Return.

   The `main.cf` file is copied to the file `sendmail.cf`.

```
# cp /etc/mail/main.cf /etc/mail/sendmail.cf
#
```

6. Type **pkill -HUP /usr/lib/sendmail** and press Return.

   `sendmail` is restarted.

7. Test your mail configuration.

   See "Testing Your Mail Configuration" on page 114 for instructions on how to test your mail configuration.

## Setting Up a Mail Client from a Command Line

A *mail client* is a mail services user that has a mailbox on a mail hub and a mail alias in the `Aliases` database or local `/etc/mail/aliases` file. This alias indicates the location of the mailbox.

Use the following steps to set up a Solaris mail client with a mailbox on a mail server.

1. Become superuser on the mail client's system.

2. Create a `/var/mail` mount point on the mail client's system.

3. Edit the `/etc/vfstab` file and add an entry to mount the `/var/mail` directory from the mail hub on the local `/var/mail` directory—type ***servername*:/var/mail - /var/mail nfs - yes rw,hard,actimeo=0** and press Return.

   You must use the `actimeo=0` option or locking of the mailbox files fails.

```
server:/var/mail - /var/mail nfs - yes rw,hard,actimeo=0
```

With an entry in the client system's `/etc/vfstab` file, the client's mailbox is automatically mounted any time that system is rebooted.

*New!*

Alternatively, you can edit the `/etc/auto_direct` file and add an entry like the following one to mount `/var/mail` automatically.

```
/var/mail -rw,hard,actimeo=0 server:/var/mail
```

4.  Type **mountall** to mount the mailbox.

    The client's mailbox is mounted.

5.  Use `admintool` to edit the `/etc/hosts` file and add an entry for the mail hub.

    This step is not required if you are using a nameservice.

6.  Add the user accounts for the client system to the `Aliases` database.

    See "Creating Mail Aliases" on page 103 for information on how to create mail aliases for different types of mail configurations.

*New!*

*NOTE. The* `mail.local` *program automatically creates mailboxes in the* `/var/mail` *directory the first time a message is delivered. You do not need to create individual mailboxes for your mail clients.*

*New!*

7.  Type **pkill -HUP /usr/lib/sendmail** and press Return.

    `sendmail` is restarted.

The following example sets up the Solaris system `newton` as a mail client of the system `cinderella`.

```
newton% su
Password:
# mkdir /var/mail
# vi /etc/vfstab
Add the line:
cinderella:/var/mail  -  /var/mail  nfs  -  yes  rw
# mountall
# pkill -HUP /usr/lib/sendmail
#
```

## Setting Up a Gateway Host

A *gateway host* manages communications with networks outside of your domain that use the same relay mailer. The mailer on the sending gateway host must match the mailer on the receiving system.

For example, a good candidate for a gateway host is a system attached to an Ethernet and to phone lines. Another good candidate is a system configured as a router to the Internet. You may want to configure the mail hub as the gateway host or to configure another system as the gateway host. You may choose to configure more than one gateway host for your domain. Each gateway host you configure must use a mailer that matches the mailer on the connecting system. If you have UUCP connections, you should configure the system (or systems) that have the UUCP connections as the gateway host.

> *NOTE. The procedure for creating a* `sendmail` *configuration file is changed in the Solaris 8 Operating Environment. Refer to Chapter 3, "Planning Mail Services," for instructions.*

*New!*

# Creating Mail Aliases

The mail hub for each DNS domain or subdomain must have a complete list of aliases for all users in that DNS domain. The mail hub for the domain uses these aliases to properly deliver e-mail for users in that domain. Mail aliases must be unique within a domain.

This section describes how to create mail aliases for NIS+, for NIS, or on the local system. Use the `aliasadm` command to create, modify, and delete aliases from a command line. See the `aliasadm`(1M) manual page for more information.

## Listing the Contents of an NIS+ mail_aliases Table

*New!*

Use the `aliasadm` command to list the contents of an NIS+ aliases table. To use the `aliasadm` command, you must be root, a member of the NIS+ group that owns the `mail_aliases` table, or the person who created the table.

To list all of the NIS+ `mail_aliases` entries, type **aliasadm -l** and press Return.

> *NOTE. If you have a large aliases table, listing the contents can take some time. To search for a specific entry, pipe the output through the* `grep` *command (*`aliasadm -l | grep` *entry).*

You can use the `aliasadm -m` *alias* option to list individual entries in the NIS+ `mail_aliases` table. The `-m` option matches only the complete alias name. It does not match partial strings.

The following example lists the alias entry for user `ignatz`.

```
# aliasadm -m ignatz
ignatz: ignatz@paperbark  # Alias for Iggy Ignatz
#
```

*New!*      ## Creating a New NIS+ mail_aliases Table

If the mail_aliases table does not exist, you must first initiate it. To initiate a new mail_aliases table, type **aliasadm -I** and press Return.

*New!*      ## Adding Aliases to an NIS+ mail_aliases Table

Use the aliasadm command to add aliases to an existing NIS+ mail_aliases table.

Use the following steps to add aliases to an NIS+ mail_aliases table.

1. Compile a list of each of your mail clients, the location of their mailboxes, and the name of the mail server systems.
2. Become superuser on any system.
3. For each alias, type **aliasadm -a *alias expanded-alias [options "comments"]*** and press Return.

   Each alias is added to the NIS+ aliases table. The following example adds an alias for user iggy.

```
# aliasadm -a iggy iggy.ignatz@paperbark "Iggy Ignatz"
```

4. Type **aliasadm -m *alias*** and press Return.

   The entry you created is displayed.
5. Check to make sure the entry is correct.

If you are adding many aliases, you can edit the NIS+ table directly with the aliasadm -e command.

Use the following steps to edit the NIS+ mail_aliases table directly.

1. Compile a list of each of your mail clients, the location of their mailboxes, and the name of the mail server systems.
2. Become superuser on any system.
3. Type **aliasadm -e** and press Return.

   The aliases table is displayed in the editor program specified with the $EDITOR environment variable. If this variable is not set, vi is the default editor.
4. Type each alias on a separate line, using the format ***alias expanded-alias # ["options" # "comments"]***. If you leave the options column blank, type an empty pair of quotation marks ( " " ) and then add the comments. Press Return at the end of each line.

You can enter the aliases in any order. The order of the aliases is not important to the NIS+ `mail_aliases` table. The `aliasadm -1` command sorts the list and displays it in alphabetical order.

5. Check to make sure the entry is correct.

6. Save the changes.

## Changing Aliases in an NIS+ mail_aliases Table

Use the `aliasadm` command to modify aliases in an existing NIS+ `mail_aliases` table.

Use the following steps to modify aliases to an NIS+ `mail_aliases` table.

1. Become superuser on any system.

2. Type **aliasadm -m** *alias* and press Return.

The information for the alias is displayed.

3. Type **aliasadm -c** *alias expanded-alias* **[***options* **"***comments***"]** and press Return.

The alias is changed using the new information you provide.

4. Type **aliasadm -m** *alias* and press Return.

The information for the alias is displayed.

5. Check to make sure the entry is correct.

## Deleting Entries from an NIS+ mail_aliases Table

Use the `aliasadm -d` command to delete aliases in an existing NIS+ `mail_aliases` table.

Use the following steps to delete aliases from an NIS+ `mail_aliases` table.

1. Become superuser on any system.

2. Type **aliasadm -d** *alias* and press Return.

The alias is deleted from the NIS+ `mail_aliases` table.

## Setting Up the NIS mail.aliases Map

This section describes how to set up mail aliases on an NIS master server.

The `/etc/mail/aliases` file on a Solaris NIS master contains all of the names by which a system or person is known. The NIS master is searched if there is no match in the local `/etc/aliases` or `/etc/mail/aliases` file.

The `sendmail` program uses the NIS master file to determine mailing addresses. See the `aliases(5)` manual page for more information.

*New!*

The `/etc/mail/aliases` file on the NIS master should contain entries for all of the mail clients. You edit the file on the NIS master server and propagate the changes to NIS slave systems.

Aliases have the following form.

```
name: name1, name2,...
```

You can alias local names or domains. For example, an alias entry for the user `fred`, who has a mailbox on the system `oak` and is in the domain `Trees`, would have the following entry in the `/etc/aliases` file.

```
fred: fred@Trees
```

Use the following steps to set up the NIS `mail.aliases` map.

1. Compile a list of each of your mail clients, the locations of their mailboxes, and the names of the mail server systems.
2. Become superuser on the NIS master server.
3. Edit the `/etc/aliases` file and make the following entries.
   - Add an entry for each mail client.
   - Change the entry `Postmaster: root` to the mail address of the person who is designated as postmaster. See "Setting Up the Postmaster Alias" on page 113 for more information.
   - If you have created a mailbox for the administration of a mail server, create an entry for `root: ` *mailbox@mailserver*.
   - Save the changes.
4. Edit the `/etc/hosts` file on the NIS master server and create an entry for each mail server.
5. Type **cd /var/yp** and press Return.
6. Type **make** and press Return.

   The changes in the `/etc/hosts` and `/etc/aliases` files are propagated to NIS slave systems. It takes a few minutes, at most, for the aliases to take effect.

## Setting Up Local Mail Alias Files

The `/etc/mail` aliases file on a local Solaris system contains all of the names by which a system or person is known. The `sendmail` program uses this file to look up mailing addresses. See the aliases(5) manual page for more information.

The /etc/mail/aliases file of each system should contain entries for all mail user accounts. You can either edit the file on each system or edit the file on one system and copy it to each of the other systems.

You can use the SMC Users: Mailing Lists tool—available in the Solaris 8 Update 3 release—to edit local /etc/mail/aliases files. *New!*

Use the following steps to set up local mail aliases files with the SMC Users, Mailing Lists tool.

1. Compile a list of each of your mail clients and the locations of their mailboxes.
2. From the CDE Applications menu, open the Application Manager.

   The Application Manager window is opened, as shown in Figure 9.

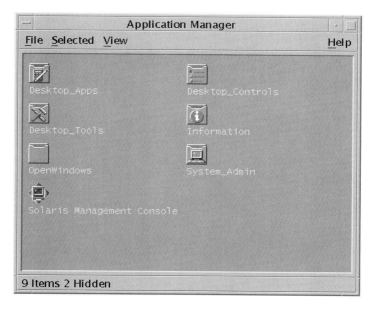

*Figure 9    Application Manager Window*

You can also access SMC from the Tools menu on the CDE Front Panel.

3. Double-click on the Solaris Management Console icon.

   The Solaris Management Console window is displayed, as shown in Figure 10.

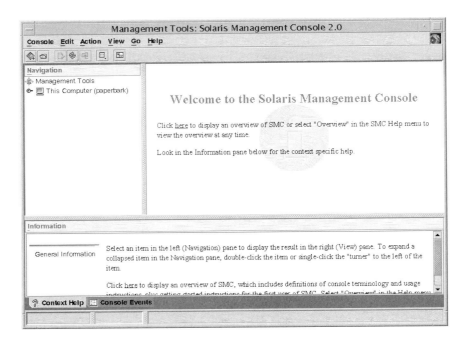

*Figure 10    Solaris Management Console Window*

4. From the Console menu, choose Open Toolbox.

The Open Toolbox window is displayed, as shown in Figure 11.

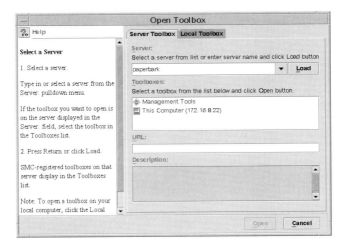

*Figure 11    Open Toolbox Window*

5. Type the name of the mail server or click on the name of the mail server in the list and then click on the Load button.

The toolbox for the system you chose is displayed.

6. Click on the control to the left of the This Computer icon, then click on the control next to the System Configuration item in the navigation pane.

The Users tool is displayed. Figure 12 shows all of the SMC tools in the navigation pane.

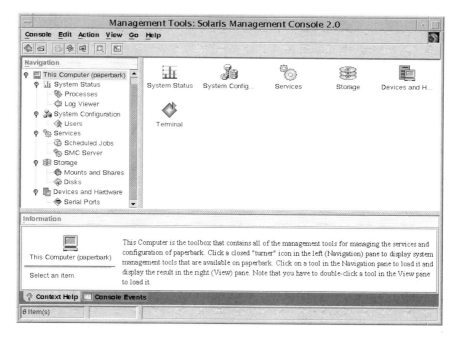

*Figure 12   SMC Tools*

7. Double-click on the Users icon.

The Users Login window is displayed, as shown in Figure 13.

*Figure 13    Users Login Window*

8.  Log in with your user name if you have rights to edit mail aliases, as a role name that has rights to edit mail aliases, or as root, and type the appropriate password.

    See Chapter 23, "Role-Based Access Control," if you need more information about rights.

    After a few moments, the Users tools are displayed in the right pane, as shown in Figure 14.

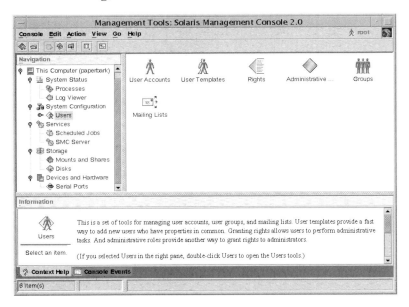

*Figure 14    Users Tools*

9.  Double-click on the Mailing Lists icon.

The mailing lists for this computer are displayed, as shown in Figure 15.

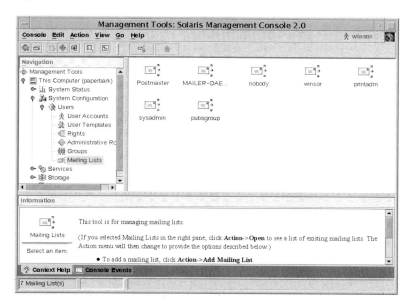

*Figure 15    Mailing Lists*

10. From the Action menu, choose Add Mailing List.

The Add Mailing List window is displayed, as shown in Figure 16.

*Figure 16    Users Tools*

11. Add an entry for each mail user account and click on the OK button.

12. In the Mailing Lists window, double-click on the Postmaster mailing list.

    The properties for the Postmaster alias are displayed.

13. Change the entry for Postmaster from root to the mail address of the person who is designated as postmaster and click on the OK button.

    See "Setting Up the Postmaster Alias" on page 113 for more information.

14. If you have created a mailbox for the administration of a mail server, create a new mailbox entry for root with the address `mailbox@mailserver`.

    It is a good idea to create an administrative account for each mail server. You do this by assigning root a mailbox on the mail server and adding an entry to the `/etc/mail/aliases` file for root. For example, if the system `paperbark` is a mailbox server, add a root mailbox with the address `sysadmin@paperbark`.

    An alias file is created in binary form that `sendmail` can use. The file is stored in the `/etc/mail/aliases.dir` and `/etc/mail/aliases.pag` files.

15. Use the `rpc` or `rdist` commands, a script that you create for this purpose to copy the `/etc/mail/aliases`, `/etc/mail/aliases.dir`, and `/etc/mail/aliases.pag` files to each of the other systems. Alternatively, use the SMC Mailing Lists tool to create the `/etc/mail/aliases` files on each of the other systems.

    Remember that you must update all of the `/etc/mail/aliases` files each time you add or remove a mail client.

## Configuring Hosts to Use DNS Mail Exchange Records

The DNS nameservice does not use aliases for individuals. It does use aliases for hosts or domains, which are called *Mail Exchange (MX) records*. The `/etc/named.boot` file on the DNS server(s) for the domain or subdomain contains a list of other configuration files in DNS, one of which contains MX host information. You can specify host names or domain names in this file. Domain names can contain wildcards; for example, `*.sun.com` is an acceptable domain name.

New!

*NOTE. Releases before Solaris 2.4 included a binary called* `sendmail.mx` *that was used with the DNS nameservice.* `sendmail.mx` *is now included in the* `sendmail` *program; you turn the functionality on by adding the* `dns` *flag to the* `hosts` *entry in the* `/etc/nsswitch.conf` *file.*

Use the following steps to enable DNS host and MX record lookups for a host that already uses the NIS+ nameservice.

1. Become superuser.
2. Edit the /etc/nsswitch.conf file and remove the comment (#) from the hosts definition.
3. Add the dns flag after nisplus in the hosts entry, as shown below.

```
hosts:    nisplus dns []NOTFOUND=return] files
```

## Setting Up the Postmaster Alias

Every system should be able to send mail to a postmaster mailbox. You can create an NIS or NIS+ alias for postmaster or create one in each local /etc/mail/aliases file. The following example shows the default /etc/mail/aliases entry.

```
# Following alias is required by the mail protocol, RFC 822
# Set it to the address of a HUMAN who deals with this system's mail problems.
Postmaster: root
```

To create the postmaster alias, edit each system's /etc/mail/aliases file and change root to the mail address of the person who will act as the postmaster.

You may want to create a separate mailbox for the postmaster to keep postmaster mail separate from personal mail. If you create a separate mailbox, use the mailbox address instead of the postmaster's mail address when you edit the /etc/mail/aliases files.

Follow these steps to create a separate mailbox for the postmaster.

1. Create a user account named postmaster and put an asterisk (*) in the password field.
2. Type **mail -f postmaster** and press Return.

   Mail can be read and written to the mailbox name.

Follow these steps to add the postmaster mailbox to the alias.

1. Become superuser and edit the /etc/mail/aliases file on each system.

   You can use the SMC Users: Mailing Lists tool to edit the /etc/mail/aliases file. See "Setting Up Local Mail Alias Files" on page 106 for more information.

2. Change the `postmaster` alias from root to **Postmaster:** **postmastermailbox@postmasterhost** and save the changes.

3. On the postmaster's local system, create an entry in the `/etc/mail/aliases` file that defines the name of the alias (`postmaster`, for example) and includes the path to the local mailbox.

4. Type **newaliases** and press Return.

Alternatively, you could change the `Postmaster:` entry in the aliases file to `Postmaster:` `/usr/somewhere/somefile`.

# Testing Your Mail Configuration

When you have all of the systems in your mail configuration set up, use the suggestions in this section to test the setup to make sure mail messages can be sent and received.

1. Become superuser on the system for which you have changed a configuration file.

2. Type **pkill -HUP /usr/lib/sendmail** and press Return.
   `sendmail` is restarted.

3. Send test messages from each system by typing **/usr/lib/sendmail -v *names* </dev/null** and press Return.
   Specify a recipient's e-mail address in place of the *names* variable. This command sends a null message to the specified recipient and displays messages while it runs.

4. Run the following tests.
   - Send mail to yourself or to other people on the local system by addressing the message to a regular user name.
   - If your system is on an Ethernet, send mail to someone on another system. Do this in three directions: from the main system to a subsidiary system, from a subsidiary system to the main system, and from a subsidiary system to another subsidiary system.
   - If you have a mail gateway, send mail to another domain from the mail host to ensure that the gateway is configured properly.
   - If you have set up a UUCP connection on your phone line to another host, send mail to someone at that host and have that individual send mail back or call you when the message is received.

- Ask someone to send you mail over the UUCP connection. The `sendmail` program cannot tell whether the message gets through because it hands the message to UUCP for delivery.
- Send a message to the postmaster on different systems and make sure that it comes to your postmaster's mailbox.

# Administering Your Mail Configuration

The following sections describe how to keep mail services running smoothly.

## Duties of Postmaster

As postmaster, your responsibilities for administering mail include the following tasks.

- Check the mail queues to make sure that mail is flowing in and out.
- Check any down systems where mail is backing up. If the system is not needed, delete it from the mail system or bring it up to keep mail moving.
- Fix personal aliases, as requested.
- Administer the `Aliases` databases as people move in and out of the domain.
- Set up temporary forwarding files.
- Contact owners of mailing lists and help them fix mailing list problems.
- Go through postmaster mail daily and look for problems, broken `.forward` files, and mail alias loops. Fix the problem or tell people how to fix it.
- Answer questions about mail delivery problems from outside of the company.
- Truncate log files periodically.

## The Mail Queue

Under high load or temporary failure conditions, `sendmail` puts a message into a job queue in the `/var/spool/mqueue` directory instead of delivering it immediately. Ordinarily, the mail queue is processed automatically. Sometimes, however, you may have to intervene manually. For example, if a major host is down for a period of time, the queue may become clogged. Although `sendmail` ought to recover gracefully when the host comes up, you may find performance unacceptable in the meantime.

## Printing the Mail Queue

You can print the contents of the queue by specifying the `-bp` flag to
`sendmail`. Type **/usr/lib/sendmail -bp | more** and press Return.
Alternatively, you can print the contents of the queue with the `mailq`
command. **/usr/bin/mailq | more** is equivalent to the `sendmail -bp`
command. A list of the queue IDs, the size of the message, the date the
message entered the queue, the message status, and the sender and
recipients are displayed.

## Format of Queue Files

The `sendmail` program stores temporary queue files in
`/var/spool/mqueue`. All such queue files have the form `xAA99999`, where
`AA99999` is the ID for the file and `x` is the type. Table 20 shows the types of
queue files.

*Table 20     Types of Queue Files*

| Type | Description |
|------|-------------|
| d | A data file. The message body (excluding the header) is kept in this file. |
| l | A lock file. If this file is present, the job is currently being processed, and running the queue will not process it. For this reason, an extraneous lock file can make a job seem to disappear. |
| n | This separate file is created whenever an ID is created. It ensures that no mail can ever be destroyed because of a race condition. This file should not exist for more than a few milliseconds at any given time. |
| q | The queue control file. This file contains the information needed to process the job. |
| t | A temporary file. This file is an image of the `qf` file when it is being rebuilt. When the rebuild is complete, the file is renamed `qf`. |
| x | A transcript file that exists during the life of a session and shows everything that happens during that session. |

The qf file contains a series of lines, each beginning with a code letter, as shown in Table 21. See Chapter 2, "Customizing sendmail Configuration Files," for more information about qf file codes.

*Table 21     Codes for the qf File*

| Code | Description |
|------|-------------|
| P | The current message priority, which is used to order the queue. The higher the number, the lower the priority. The priority increases as the message sits in the queue. The initial priority depends on the message class and the size of the message. |
| T | The job creation/submission time in seconds, which is used to compute the time when the job times out. |
| D | The name of the data file. |
| M | A message. This line, which is printed by sendmail with the -bp flag, is generally used to store status information. It can contain any text. |
| S | The sender name. |
| E | Error recipient name. Error messages are sent to this user instead of to the sender. This line is optional. |
| H | A header definition. Any number of these lines can be present. The order is important: It represents the order in the final message. The syntax is the same as in the header definitions in the configuration file. |
| R | A recipient name. Each recipient has one line. The recipient name normally is completely aliased, but it is actually re-aliased when the job is processed. The recipient name must be at the end of the qf file. |

The queue is automatically run at the interval specified in the sendmail.cf file. (The default is every hour.) The queue is read and sorted by message priority, and then sendmail tries to process all jobs in order. The sendmail program first checks to see if a job is locked. If locked, it skips the job; if not locked, sendmail processes it.

If a major host goes down for several days, the queue may become prohibitively large, and sendmail spends lots of time sorting the queue. You can fix this problem by moving the queue to a temporary place and creating a new queue. You can run the old queue later, when the host is returned to service.

*New!*

## Forcing the Queue

To process the mail in the queue now, type **/usr/lib/sendmail -q -v** and press Return. The queue is forced and the progress of the jobs in the queue is displayed as the queue is cleared.

## Moving the Mail Queue

Use the following steps to move the mail queue.

*New!*

1.  Become superuser on the mail hub.
2.  Type **/etc/init.d/sendmail stop** and press Return.

    The `sendmail` daemon is stopped to keep it from trying to process the old queue directory.
3.  Type **cd /var/spool** and press Return.
4.  Type **mv mqueue omqueue; mkdir mqueue** and press Return.

    The `mqueue` directory and all of its contents are moved to the directory `omqueue`, and a new empty `mqueue` directory is created.
5.  Type **chmod 755 mqueue; chown daemon.daemon mqueue** and press Return.

    Permissions of the directory are set to read/write/execute by others and read/execute by group and by others. Owner and group are set to daemon.
6.  Type **/etc/init.d/sendmail start** and press Return.

    A new `sendmail` daemon is started, with a queue runtime of one hour.

## Running the Old Mail Queue

Use the following steps to run the old mail queue.

1.  Type **/usr/lib/sendmail -oQ/var/spool/omqueue -q** and press Return.

    The `-oQ` flag specifies an alternate queue directory, and the `-q` flag says to run every job in the queue. Use the `-v` flag if you want to see the verbose output displayed on the screen.
2.  When the queue is finally emptied, type **rmdir /var/spool/omqueue** and press Return.

    The empty directory is removed.

You can run a subset of the queue at any time with the `-R`*string* option (run queue where any recipient name matches *string*) or with the `-M`*nnnnn* option to `sendmail`. (Run just one message with queue ID *nnnnn*.)

To run a subset of the mail queue, type **/usr/lib/sendmail -R*string***
and press Return. In the following example, everything in the queue for
recipient wnj is processed.

```
oak% /usr/lib/sendmail -Rwnj
```

## The System Log

The mail service uses the syslogd program to log most errors. The default is
for syslogd to send messages to a system identified as the log host.

Just as you define a system called mailhost as a mail hub to handle mail
relaying, you can define a system called loghost in the /etc/hosts file to
hold all logs for an entire NIS domain. The system log is supported by the
syslogd program. You can specify a loghost in the Hosts database. If you
specify no loghost, then error messages from syslogd are not reported.

The following example shows the default /etc/syslog.conf file.

```
#ident   "@(#)syslog.conf      1.5     98/12/14 SMI"    /* SunOS 5.0 */
#
# Copyright (c) 1991-1998 by Sun Microsystems, Inc.
# All rights reserved.
#
# syslog configuration file.
#
# This file is processed by m4 so be careful to quote (`') names
# that match m4 reserved words.  Also, within ifdef's, arguments
# containing commas must be quoted.
#
*.err;kern.notice;auth.notice                  /dev/sysmsg
*.err;kern.debug;daemon.notice;mail.crit       /var/adm/messages

*.alert;kern.err;daemon.err                     operator
*.alert                                         root

*.emerg                                         *

# if a non-loghost machine chooses to have authentication messages
# sent to the loghost machine, un-comment out the following line:
#auth.notice                    ifdef(`LOGHOST', /var/log/authlog, @loghost)

mail.debug                      ifdef(`LOGHOST', /var/log/syslog, @loghost)

#
# non-loghost machines will use the following lines to cause "user"
# log messages to be logged locally.
#
ifdef(`LOGHOST', ,
user.err                                        /dev/sysmsg
user.err                                        /var/adm/messages
user.alert                                      `root, operator'
user.emerg                                      *
)
```

You can change the default configuration by editing the
/etc/syslog.conf file. You must restart the syslog daemon for the

*New!*

*New!*

changes to take effect. You can define the following entries in the
`/etc/syslog.conf` file to gather information about mail.

- `mail.alert`—Messages about conditions that should be fixed now.
- `mail.crit`—Critical messages.
- `mail.warning`—Warning messages.
- `mail.notice`—Messages that are not errors but might need attention.
- `mail.info`—Informational messages.
- `mail.debug`—Debugging messages.

The following entry sends a copy of all critical, informational, and debug
messages to `/var/log/syslog`.

```
mail.crit;mail.info;mail.debug     /var/log/syslog
```

When the `syslogd` daemon starts up, it creates the file
`/etc/syslog.pid`, which contains its process ID number. The following
example shows a `syslog.pid` file.

```
oak% more /etc/syslog.pid
179
oak%
```

The following example shows the end of a system log file.

```
oak% tail /var/log/syslog
Apr  4 09:47:41 oak sendmail[14192]: AA14190: to=<uucp>, delay=00:00:01,
 stat=Sent

Apr  4 09:47:50 oak sendmail[14195]: AA14195: message-id=<9304041647
 .AA195@oak.Eng.Sun.COM>

Apr  4 09:47:50 oak sendmail[14195]: AA14195: from=<uucp>, size=378, class=0,
 received from ignatz (129.144.52.69)

Apr  4 09:47:51 oak sendmail[14197]: AA14195: to=<uucp>, delay=00:00:01,
 stat=Sent

Apr  4 10:44:27 oak sendmail[14280]: AA14280: message-
 id=<93040401748.AA06975@castle.Eng.Sun.COM>

Apr  4 10:44:27 oak sendmail[14280]: AA14280: from=<winsor@castle>, size=892,
 class=0, received from zigzag (129.144.1.38)

Apr  4 10:44:27 oak sendmail[14282]:AA14280: to=lautner@oak, delay=00:00:01,
 stat=Sent

Apr  4 10:52:43 oak sendmail[14307]: AA14307: message-
 id=<9304041753.AA05638@pigglet.Eng.Sun.COM>

Apr  4 10:52:43 oak sendmail[14307]: AA14307: from=<nixed@pigglet>,
 size=918,class=0, received from piglet (129.144.154.7)
```

```
Apr  4 10:52:44 oak sendmail[14309]: AA14307: to=lautner@ oak, delay=00:00:01,
  stat=Sent
oak%
```

*NOTE. Because of the length of each entry, space has been added between entries in this example to improve readability.*

Each line in the system log contains a timestamp, the name of the system that generated it, and a message. `syslog` can log a large amount of information. The log is arranged as a succession of levels. At the lowest level, only unusual occurrences are logged. At the highest level, even the most mundane and uninteresting events are recorded. As a convention, log levels under 10 are considered useful. Log levels higher than 10 are usually used for debugging.

# Troubleshooting Your Mail Configuration

The following sections provide some tips and tools that you can use for troubleshooting mail.

## Checking Aliases

To verify aliases and determine whether mail can be delivered to a given recipient, type **/usr/lib/sendmail -v -bv *recipient*** and press Return. The command displays the aliases and identifies the final address as deliverable or not. The following example shows the output from this command.

```
% /usr/lib/sendmail -v -bv shamira@raks
shamira... aliased to   mwong
mwong... aliased to              shamira@raks
shamira@raks... deliverable
%
```

*CAUTION. Take extra care to avoid loops and inconsistent databases when both local and domain-wide aliases are used. Be especially careful when you move a user from one system to another to avoid creating alias loops.*

## Testing sendmail

Use the following steps to run `sendmail` in test mode.

1. Type **/usr/lib/sendmail -bt** and press Return.
   Information is displayed.

2. At the last prompt (>), type **3,0** *e-mail-address* and press Return.
   See Chapter 2, "Customizing sendmail Configuration Files," for a complete description of the diagnostic information.

## Verifying Connections to Other Systems

To verify connections to other systems, you can use the `mconnect` program to open connections to other `sendmail` systems over the network. The `mconnect` program runs interactively. You can issue various diagnostic commands. See the `mconnect`(1) manual page for a complete description.

The following example verifies that mail to user `winsor` is deliverable.

```
$ mconnect castle
connecting to host castle (172.16.8.19), port 25
connection open
220 castle.Eng.Wellard.COM Sendmail 8.98.0+Sun/8.9.0; Tue, 19 Sep 2000
  12:45:35 -0700
vrfy winsor
250 Janice Winsor <winsor@castle.Eng.Wellard.COM>
>
```

If you cannot use `mconnect` to connect to an SMTP port, check the following conditions.

- Is the system load too high?
- Is the `sendmail` daemon running?
- Does the system have the appropriate `/etc/mail/sendmail.cf` file?
- Is TCP port 25 (the port that `sendmail` uses) active?
- Is the network connection down?
- Is a firewall blocking the connection?

## Obtaining Other Diagnostic Information

For other diagnostic information, check the following sources.

- Look at the `Received` lines in the header of the message. These lines trace the route the message took as it was relayed, reading from the bottom up. Note that in the UUCP network many sites do not update these lines, and in the Internet the lines often get rearranged. To straighten them out, look at the date and time in each line. Remember to account for time zone differences, and beware of clocks that have been set incorrectly.

- Look at messages from MAILER-DAEMON. These messages typically report delivery problems.

- Check the system log that records delivery problems for your group of workstations. The sendmail program always records what it is doing in the system log. You may want to modify the crontab file to run nightly a shell script that searches the log for SYSERR messages and mails any that it finds to the postmaster.

- Use the mailstats program to test mail types and determine the number of messages coming in and going out.

# *Part Two*

# NIS+

This part introduces the NIS+ (Network Information Service Plus) nameservice environment. Chapter 5 provides an overview of NIS+, explains how NIS+ differs from the NIS nameservice, and introduces the NIS+ commands. Chapter 6 describes how to use the NIS+ commands to set up an **New!** NIS+ root master server and to add a system as an NIS+ client.

Refer to the chapters in this part if you want to familiarize yourself with the basics of the NIS+ nameservice and its administrative commands and for instructions on how to set up an NIS+ root master server and an NIS+ client.

# 5

# *INTRODUCING THE*
# *NIS+*
# *ENVIRONMENT*

NIS+ is a network information service that was introduced with the first
Solaris release. NIS+ is a repository of administrative information, the
foundation for the Solaris Management Console applications, and a storage
place for network resource information that users can access without
knowing the specific location of the resource. NIS+ is a component of ONC+™
(Open Network Computing Plus). ONC+ consists of a set of new and
enhanced core services for enterprise-wide distributed computing. ONC+
services—including NIS+, TI-RPC (transport-independent RPC), and
enhanced NFS—are completely compatible and will interoperate with the
installed base of ONC services, including NFS, NIS, and RPC services. NIS+,
which replaces NIS, is compatible with it. When run in compatibility mode,
NIS+ serves NIS requests as well as NIS+ requests. NIS+ is designed to
manage resources for distributed systems, make it easier to administer in
complex organizations, and provide more security than was possible with
NIS.

   The main function of NIS+ is to simplify system and network
administration, including tasks such as adding and relocating systems and
users. A second function is to act as directory assistance for the network by
enabling users and applications to easily find other network entities. For
example, when using NIS+, you can easily locate other users and resources in
the corporate network, regardless of the actual physical location of the entity.

   One important benefit of NIS+ is scalability: NIS+ simplifies the
administration of both small and large networks. As organizations grow and
decentralize, NIS+ continues to provide administrative efficiency. Another

key enhancement in NIS+ is update performance. Changes made to the NIS+ information base are automatically and instantaneously propagated to replica servers across the network. You can perform tasks such as adding new systems and users much more rapidly than with NIS. NIS+ provides improved security over NIS. NIS+ enables you to flexibly control access to network resources by preventing unauthorized sources from reading, changing, or destroying nameservice information.

This chapter describes the differences between NIS and NIS+; how NIS+ information is organized, stored, and distributed; how NIS+ security mechanisms work; and how NIS+ information is updated. It also describes the nameservice switch file and introduces the NIS+ commands. Chapter 6, "Setting Up NIS+ Servers and Clients," describes how to use the nisserver(1M), nispopulate(1M), and nisclient(1M) NIS+ scripts to set up basic NIS+ root master server and NIS+ client system. Describing NIS+ completely and providing installation and setup instructions for master and replica servers are beyond the scope of this book.

## Comparison of NIS and NIS+

To help you understand the differences between NIS and NIS+, Table 22 compares the features of the two programs.

*Table 22     Comparison of NIS and NIS+ Features*

| Capability | NIS Features | NIS+ Features |
| --- | --- | --- |
| Namespace | Flat. | Hierarchical. |
| Database | Centralized for each independent network domain. | Partitioned into directories to support each network subset or autonomous domain. |
| Data storage | Multiple bicolumn maps with key-value pairs. | Multicolumn tables with multiple searchable columns. |
| Replication | Minimum of one replica server per IP subnetwork. | Each replica server can serve clients on multiple IP subnets. |
| Update privileges | Requires superuser privileges on the master server. | Performed remotely by authorized administrators; no superuser privileges required. |

*Table 22    Comparison of NIS and NIS+ Features (Continued)*

| Capability | NIS Features | NIS+ Features |
|---|---|---|
| Update propagation | Initiated by administrator; whole maps transferred. | Automatic and high-performance updating, using only updated information. |
| Authorization | Anyone can read all of the information stored in the NIS database. | Access control to individual elements within the NIS+ directories, tables, columns, and entries. |
| Resource access across domains | Not supported. | Permitted for authorized users. |

# The NIS+ Namespace

The *NIS+ namespace* is the arrangement of information stored by NIS+. You can arrange the information in the namespace in a variety of ways to suit the needs of your organization. The hierarchical namespace of NIS+ is similar to that used by DNS and by the UNIX file system. With a hierarchical namespace, you can decentralize administration and improve security. When NIS was developed, the basic assumption was that the network and organization-wide namespace would be small enough for one person to administer. The growth of networked computing has resulted in a need to change this assumption.

NIS+ works best when the information in the NIS+ namespace is arranged into configurations called *domains*. An NIS+ domain is a collection of information about the systems, users, and network services in a portion of an organization. In the sample network shown in Figure 17, the domains for a fictitious company, Starlight Corporation, are organized by division.

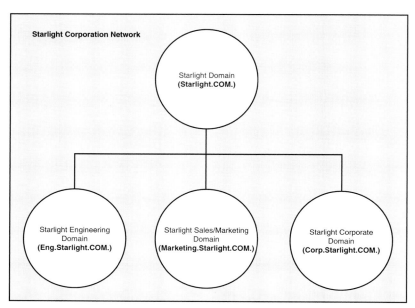

*Figure 17    Creation of Administrative Domains*

As Starlight Corporation grows beyond a few hundred systems, the corresponding growth of its NIS+ directory begins to affect manageability and performance. Functional groups, such as Engineering and Sales/Marketing, may choose to create local subdomains and appoint (or hire) autonomous system administrators for these subdomains. These local administrators take responsibility for administering their own subdomains, thus relieving the central administration group of some of its workload.

As Starlight Corporation continues to grow, further decentralized administrative requirements may emerge. Administrators will be able to continue to subdivide the domains along functional groups or other natural administrative lines, such as by location or by building. Figure 18 shows how the Starlight network has decentralized the Sales domain.

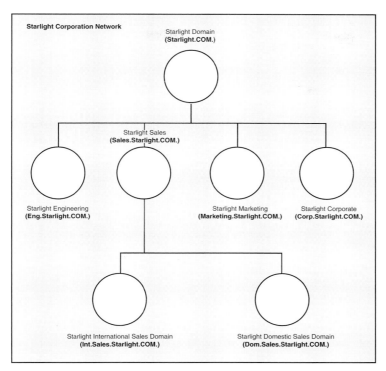

*Figure 18    Hierarchical Domains*

Each domain can be administered either locally or centrally. Alternatively, some portions of domain administration can be performed locally while others remain under the control of a central administrator. A domain can even be administered from within another domain. As more domains are created, NIS+ clients continue to have the same access to the information in other NIS+ domains of the company.

The NIS+ commands enable authorized administrators to interactively administer and add, delete, or change information in NIS+ servers from systems across the domain or enterprise network. Administrators do not need to remotely log in to or have superuser privileges on these servers to be able to perform administrative functions. The following sections describe the components of the NIS+ namespace. NIS+ security is discussed in "NIS+ Security" on page 137.

## Components of the NIS+ Namespace

The NIS+ namespace contains the following components.

- Directory objects.
- Table objects.
- Group objects.
- Entry objects.
- Link objects.

Directory, table, and group objects are organized into NIS+ domains. Entry objects are contained in tables. Link objects provide connections between different objects. Directory and table objects are described in detail in the following sections.

### Directory Objects

*Directory objects,* which are the framework of the namespace, divide the namespace up into separate parts. Each domain consists of a directory object; its two administrative directories, `org_dir` and `groups_dir`; and a set of NIS+ tables, as shown in Figure 19.

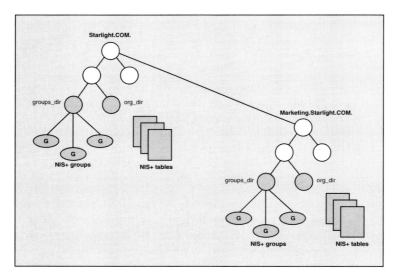

*Figure 19    The org_dir and groups_dir Directories for Two Domains*

The `org_dir` directory contains NIS+ tables that store information about users and systems on your network. The tables are described in "Table Objects" on page 135. The `groups_dir` directory stores information about the NIS+ groups for the domain. A directory object is considered a domain only if it contains its own administrative tables in the `org_dir` and `groups_dir` subdirectories. The NIS+ scripts that are run when NIS+ is set up create these two default directories. Figure 20 shows the contents of the `org_dir` directory for the Starlight Corporation top-level domain and two subdomains.

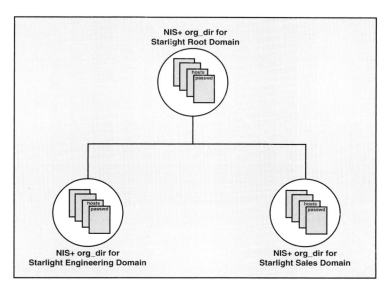

*Figure 20*    *An Example of the Domains, Directories, and Tables in an NIS+*
    *Namespace*

The top-level domain in an NIS+ hierarchy is called the *root domain*. The root domain is the first NIS+ domain installed. Each directory contains administrative information on resources local to that domain.

## Domain Name Syntax

NIS+ domain names consist of a string of ASCII characters separated by a dot ( . ). These character sequences, which identify the directories in an NIS+ domain, are called *labels*. The order of labels is hierarchical. The directory at the left of the sequence is the most local, and the directories identifying the parts of the domain become more global the closer they are to the right, as is the convention for most e-mail domain addresses. You must use a dot at the end of a fully qualified NIS+ domain name. The dot identifies the global root of the namespace. NIS+ names are fully qualified when the name includes all of the labels that identify all of the directories. Figure 21 shows examples of some fully qualified names in an NIS+ namespace. Note that an *NIS+ principal* is a user or system whose credentials have been stored in the NIS+ namespace. See "NIS+ Security" on page 137 for more information.

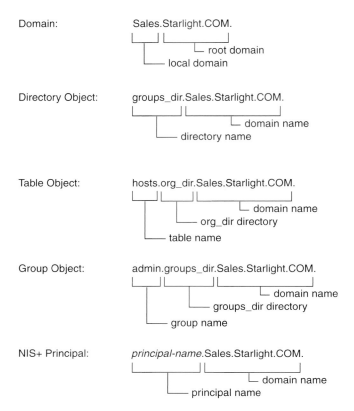

*Figure 21    Fully Qualified Names of NIS+ Namespace Components*

> *NOTE. If an NIS+ command requires a fully qualified domain name and you omit the global root dot from the end of the name, a syntax error message is displayed.*

Names without a trailing dot are called *partially qualified*. For example, hosts.org_dir is a partially qualified domain name that specifies the hosts table in the org_dir directory of the default domain.

Figure 22 shows a more detailed example of a hierarchical namespace. In Figure 22, Starlight.Com. is the root domain, Sales and Corp are subdomains of the root domain, Int is a subdomain of Sales, and hostname.int.sales.starlight.com. is a client system in the int.sales.starlight.com. domain. The system hostname.corp.starlight.com. is a client of the Corp domain.

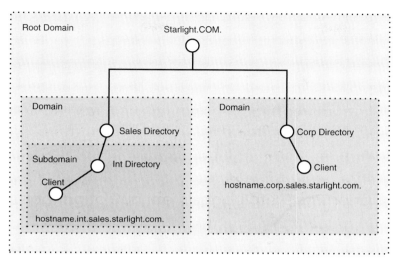

*Figure 22    An Example of the Directories and Domains in an NIS+ Namespace*

> *NOTE. Domain names for NIS+ are not case sensitive. You do not need to type the names with exact capitalization. The names* `esg.eng.starlight.com.` *and* `ESG.Eng.Starlight.COM.` *are identical in NIS+.*

## Table Objects

NIS+ table objects use columns and entries (rows) to store information for NIS+ domains. NIS+ tables provide two major improvements over the maps used by NIS.

- You can access any searchable column in an NIS+ table; with NIS maps you could search only in the first column. Duplicate maps (which were used by NIS) are unnecessary. Instead of providing NIS `hosts.byname` and `hosts.byaddr` as separate maps, NIS+ commands can search any column (name or address) marked searchable in the `hosts.org_dir` table.

- An NIS+ principal's access to NIS+ tables can be controlled at three levels: at the object level of the table itself, at the column level, and at the row or entry level. If access is given at the table level, it cannot be restricted at the column or entry level. Any access granted at the column level cannot be taken away at the entry level.

In addition, you can specify a search path for each table, and you can create symbolic links between table objects and entries with the `nisln` command. See the `nisln`(1) manual page for more information about creating links.

Each table object has its own access security information that controls whether a principal has access to the table object itself. Table security is similar to UNIX file security. See "NIS+ Security" on page 137 for more information.

## NIS+ org_dir Tables

The tables in `org_dir` provide much of the functionality that you need to administer your network. Although you can create your own tables, you do most of the standard NIS+ table administration with the tables in the `org_dir`.

Table 23 lists the tables in the `org_dir` directory in alphabetical order and briefly describes the contents of each table.

*Table 23    NIS+ org_dir Tables*

| Table | Description |
|---|---|
| aliases | Information about the e-mail aliases in the domain. |
| auto_home | The location of automounted home directories in the domain. |
| auto_master | The `master` automount map. |
| bootparams | Location of the root, swap, and dump partitions of every diskless client in the domain. |
| cred | NIS+ credentials for principals who have permission to access the information or objects in the domain. |
| ethers | The Ethernet address for systems in the domain. |
| group | Group password, group ID, and the list of members for every UNIX group in the domain. Note that the `group` table is for UNIX groups and should not be confused with the NIS+ groups in the `groups_dir` directory. |
| hosts | IPv4 network address and host name of every system in the domain. If you use DNS, leave the `hosts` table empty. |
| ipnodes | IPv4 and IPv6 addresses for the host. You must manually keep the `ipnodes` table consistent with the `hosts` table. If you use DNS, leave the `ipnodes` table empty. |
| netgroup | The netgroups to which systems and users in the domain may belong. |
| netmasks | The networks in the domain and their associated netmasks. |
| networks | The networks in the domain and their canonical names. |

*New!* (beside hosts row)

*New!* (beside ipnodes row)

*Table 23    NIS+ org_dir Tables (Continued)*

| Table | Description |
|---|---|
| `passwd` | Password information about every user in the domain. |
| `protocols` | The list of IP protocols used in the domain. |
| `RPC` | The RPC program numbers for RPC services available in the domain. |
| `services` | The names of IP services used in the domain and their port numbers. |
| `timezone` | The time zone of the domain. |

See "Table Information Display" on page 153 for a brief explanation of how to display information about these tables.

The following sections briefly describe how the `org_dir` tables are created and populated. Creating and populating these tables is part of the procedure for setting up NIS+.

As part of setting up NIS+, a set of empty tables is created in the `org_dir` directory. Once the tables are created, authorized principals can add information from existing NIS maps or text files with the `nispopulate(1M)` NIS+ script, or with the `nisaddent` or the `nistbladm` command. If NIS+ entries already exist in the table, authorized principals can use the `nisaddent` command to merge NIS map information with existing NIS+ information. See the `nispopulate(1M)`, `nisaddent(1)`, and `nistbladm(1)` manual pages for more information.

# NIS+ Security

NIS+ is designed to protect the information in its directories and tables from unauthorized access. For example, an authorized user can create a table listing the home telephone number and address of members of the Starlight Engineering domain as part of the domain's NIS+ directory. Access to this table can be limited to all or part of the Engineering organization. In another example, a desktop application can create NIS+ tables of application-specific information that must be available to the entire network. In a third example, confidential personnel information, such as the company identification number and job category for employees, can be stored in an NIS+ table with access authorized only on a very selective basis.

NIS+ controls access to servers, directories, and tables in two ways.

- Authentication verifies the identity of a system or a user of NIS+.
- Authorization controls access to information stored in NIS+.

In addition to authentication and authorization of access rights, you can run the NIS+ daemon, `rpc.nisd`, at three different levels of security, as described in Table 24.

*Table 24     Levels of NIS+ Security*

| Security Level | Description |
| --- | --- |
| 0 | Do not check the principal's credentials at all. Any client can perform any operation. Level 0 is designed for testing and setting up the initial NIS+ root domain. |
| 1 | Check the principal's credentials and accept any authentication. Because some credentials are easily forged, do not use this level on networks to which untrusted servers may have access. Level 1 is recommended only for testing. |
| 2 | Check the principal's credentials and accept only DES authentication (described in the next section). Level 2 is the highest level of security currently provided and is the default level assigned to an NIS+ server. |

You control the level of security with the `-S` option when you start the `rpc.nisd` daemon. If a system is configured as an NIS+ server, the `rpc.nisd` daemon is automatically started when a system boots. When `rpc.nisd` is started with no arguments, the default security level is 2. To start the daemon with security level 0, use `rpc.nisd -S 0`. To start the daemon with security level 1, use `rpc.nisd -S 1`.

## NIS+ Authentication

Every request to an NIS+ server is made by an *NIS+ principal*. An NIS+ principal can be a user or a workstation. *Authentication* is the process of identifying the principal who made a request to the NIS+ server by checking the principal's credentials. These credentials are based on encrypted verification information stored in the NIS+ `cred` table.

The purpose of authentication is to obtain the principal's name so that access rights to information in the nameserver can be looked up and verified. All interactions that an NIS+ principal has with an NIS+ server are authenticated.

The benefit of authentication is the protection of NIS+ information from access by untrusted principals, thereby providing more flexible and secure administration of NIS+ servers.

*NOTE. Protection of resource information in NIS+ does not imply protection of the resource itself. For example, protecting information about a server does not protect the server itself.*

Principals can have two types of credentials: LOCAL and DES. A LOCAL credential consists of the UID of an NIS+ principal. An NIS+ server uses the LOCAL UID credential to look up the identity of the principal who sent the request so that the NIS+ server can determine the principal's rights to access the requested object.

A DES credential is more complicated, and both users and systems can have such credentials. The DES credential consists of the principal's secure RPC netname and a verification field.

Table 25 shows the columns in the `cred` table and describes the type of information stored for LOCAL and DES authentication.

The first column, `cname`, contains the fully qualified credential name of an NIS+ principal. When the authentication type is LOCAL, the first column can only contain user names because client systems cannot have LOCAL credentials. When the authentication type is DES, the principal name can be either a user name or a system name.

*Table 25     Columns in the cred Table*

| cname | auth_type | auth_name | public_data | private_data |
|---|---|---|---|---|
| NIS+ principal name of a client user. | LOCAL. | UID. | GID list. | None. |
| NIS+ principal name of a client user or client system. | DES. | Secure RPC netname. | Public key. | Encrypted private key. |

The following example shows the contents of the `cred` table on the system named `castle`. The fields are separated by colons.

```
castle% niscat -h cred.org_dir
# cname:auth_type:auth_name:public_data:private_data
castle.starlight.com.:DES:unix.castle@starlight.com:c7f431834d42a23600e72bac676ba12
   a6b9621530e246cab:02528567109f39cd3873dfde50eb441395f6d49ff75f5b9970d2f6bd764cc3cc
```

```
winsor.starlight.com.:LOCAL:1001:10,14:
winsor.starlight.com.:DES:unix.1001@starlight.com:a07ca94a979c9681add77e75d27298417
  014880af4a93347:fbfaace3b1b5d23fb142a69f81d3b5e312811c2d7d65b78a37521288b40d7b48
ignatz.starlight.com.:LOCAL:1005:1:
castle%
```

The first entry shows the names of the columns in the `cred` table. The second entry is the DES authentication for the system `castle`. The third and fourth entries are LOCAL and DES authentication entries for the user `winsor`. The fifth entry is LOCAL authentication for user `ignatz`, who has an account on the system. User `ignatz` does not have DES authentication credentials in the local domain. Only a LOCAL `cred` entry is needed if the user's home domain is not the local one.

NIS+ security privileges are assigned in two stages: The principal is authenticated (identified) as an authorized user, and the access rights are checked.

Figure 23 shows a simplified view of how NIS+ security works.

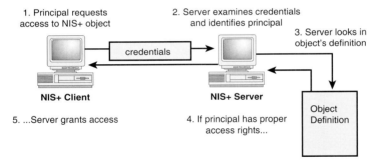

*Figure 23    How NIS+ Security Works*

NIS+ classifies NIS+ principals into four authorization categories, as described in Table 26.

*Table 26    NIS+ Authorization Categories*

| Abbreviation | Authorization | Description |
|---|---|---|
| n | Nobody | A category reserved for unauthenticated requests. |
| o | Owner | A single NIS+ principal, who was the creator of the object. You can change the ownership of existing objects with the `nischown` command. |

*Table 26    NIS+ Authorization Categories (Continued)*

| Abbreviation | Authorization | Description |
|---|---|---|
| g | Group | A collection of NIS+ principals, grouped to provide access to the namespace. When an object is created, it is by default assigned to the NIS+ principal's default group. NIS+ group information is stored in the NIS+ group object in the `groups_dir` subdirectory of every NIS+ domain. |
| w | World | All NIS+ principals who are authenticated by NIS+. |

## Access Rights

Access rights are granted not to specific NIS+ principals, but to four categories of NIS+ principals: Nobody, Owner, Group, and World, as previously described. The four types of NIS+ access rights are Read, Modify, Create, and Destroy, as described in Table 27.

*Table 27    NIS+ Access Rights*

| Abbreviation | Access Right | Description |
|---|---|---|
| r | Read | Principal can read the contents of the object. |
| m | Modify | Principal can modify the contents of the object. |
| c | Create | Principal can create new objects in a table or a directory. |
| d | Destroy | Principal can destroy objects in a table or a directory. |
| – | No access | Principal cannot access the object. |

Each object grants access rights to the four categories of NIS+ principals: Nobody, Owner, Group, and World. Access rights for each object consist of a string of 16 characters, 4 for each principal category. In the example shown in Figure 24, all access rights are permitted for each authentication category.

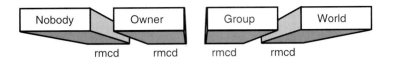

*Figure 24    NIS+ Authentication Categories and Access Rights*

In the following example, Nobody has read permission (`r---`); Owner has read, modify, create, and destroy permissions (`rmcd`); Group has read and modify permissions (`rm--`), and World has read permission (`r---`).

```
r---rmcdrm--r---
```

An NIS+ table or directory can grant one or more access rights to one or more categories of clients. For example, a directory could grant Read access to the World category but only Modify access to the Group and Owner. NIS+ authorization supports flexible and secure administration. For example, the Group access right enables finer control for NIS+ administration. It can be used to maintain security and control as administrative authority becomes more decentralized. When NIS+ domains are first created, a group consisting of central administrative personnel could have only Modify and Create access rights to directories across the network. As the domain evolves and decentralizes, directories could grant these access rights to new groups that contain both local and central administrative personnel. Expanding access rights while maintaining access to existing administrators permits the smooth transition of control.

When you create an object, NIS+ assigns the object a default owner, group, and set of access rights. The default owner is the NIS+ principal who creates the object (in this case, you). The default group is the group named in the `NIS_GROUP` environment variable. The default set of access rights is shown below.

```
----rmcdr---r---
```

You can change these default values in several different ways. One way to change the access rights of an NIS+ object or table entry is to use the `nischmod` command. To use the `nischmod` command, you must already have Modify rights to the object or entry. The `nischmod` command syntax is much like the syntax for the `chmod` command. You add access rights with the + operator and remove access rights with the - operator. For example, you would use the following syntax to add Read and Modify rights to the Group of the `esg.eng.starlight.com.` directory.

```
oak% nischmod g+rm esg.eng.starlight.com.
```

See the manual page for `nischmod(1)` for more information. See "NIS+ Commands" on page 148 for a list of the NIS+ commands.

Once they are set, the access rights for a table object define the level of security for that table object. The only way to make entries or columns in a table more secure is to change the access rights for the table object itself. You can, however, provide additional access to the information stored in a table object by extending the rights to additional principals or by providing additional access rights to existing principals.

For example, your company may have a policy that permits anybody in the company to create, modify, or delete entries for a particular e-mail alias. Access to all other aliases is restricted to the owner of the `aliases` table. To implement this policy, you would create the most restrictive rights for the `aliases` table object itself (`----rmcdr---r---`) and grant free access to the entry that contains the particular alias (`rmcdrmcdrmcdrmcd`).

You can use the `nistbladm` command to set access rights to a table when it is created, to set access rights to an entry and a column when you create the entry, or to modify the access rights of an existing table. See the `nistbladm(1)` manual page for more information.

# The NIS+ Updating Model

The NIS+ updating model is more reliable and efficient than the NIS updating model. NIS+ stores a primary copy of a directory on a master server. Zero or more replica servers store replicas of the primary copy. When you use the NIS+ commands to administer NIS+, changes are made only to the directory on the master server. When a master server receives an update to an object—whether a directory, group, link, or table—the server waits about two minutes for other updates so that it can batch the updates. When the waiting period is complete, the server stores the updates on disk and in a transaction log, along with a timestamp, and propagates the changes to its replica servers. In contrast to NIS updates, which usually take a day or more to propagate in large organizations, NIS+ incremental updates are automatically and quickly propagated to the replicas.

The NIS+ updating model enables more efficient use of network bandwidth because only the changes are transmitted from the master to the replica servers. In addition, replica servers are contacted only once, with an aggregate update to all tables occurring within a short time. If replicas are out-of-date, they ask for updated information.

The NIS+ transaction log model provides rollback recovery and consistency of NIS+ databases, even when a server fails during an update. NIS+ master and replica servers can use the transaction log to automatically repair databases to their state before the failure occurred.

## NIS and NIS+ Compatibility

NIS+ provides an NIS compatibility mode. This mode lets an NIS+ server running the Solaris Operating Environment answer requests from NIS as well as NIS+ clients. After the NIS+ server is set up, you can select NIS compatibility mode. You do not need to do any additional setup or changes for the NIS client. The NIS+ compatibility mode is one way that you can gradually make the transition from NIS to NIS+.

The comparison between master servers and slave servers is as follows. NIS master servers know about NIS slave servers only; NIS does not know about NIS+. NIS+ master servers interact with NIS+ replica servers only. NIS+ does not convert NIS+ tables into maps and push them to NIS slave servers.

## The Nameservice Switch

Solaris provides the `/etc/nsswitch.conf` nameservice switch file that you can use to tailor the nameservice policy of individual systems to use multiple nameservices in the Solaris environment. You can specify the following configurations with the `/etc/nsswitch.conf` file.

- Which nameservices are used for each type of configuration information, such as password or host IP address.
- The order in which the different nameservices are used for each type of information.
- The criteria for search continuation if information is not found or if a nameservice is not available.

You can use the `/etc/nsswitch.conf` file to set flexible policies for nameservice use and to describe and change these policies after site requirements change. For example, a system running the Solaris Operating Environment could obtain its host's information from DNS, its group information from NIS maps, and its password information from the local `/etc/passwd` file.

The `/etc/nsswitch.conf` file also simplifies migration from NIS to NIS+, because both Solaris 1.x and Solaris 2.x systems can be clients of Solaris 1.x NIS servers. In addition, Solaris 2.x systems can be clients of both NIS and NIS+, which enables the two nameservices to coexist during the transition. If you combine NIS and NIS+ domains, make sure that they both use the same domain name. The NIS/NIS+ domain name is usually, but not always, the same as the DNS domain name.

> NOTE. *The Solaris 8 Operating Environment supports the* `printers` *database in the* `/etc/nsswitch.conf` *nameservice switch file. The* `printers` *database provides centralized printer configuration information to print clients on the network. With the* `printers` *database and corresponding sources of information in the nameservice switch file, print clients can automatically access printer configuration information without having it added to their own systems. The* `printers` *database is configured by the Solaris Print Manager when you add a printer to a system.*
>
> *New!*

When you install the Solaris Operating Environment, the `/etc` directory contains a default `nsswitch.conf` file and the files `nsswitch.files`, `nsswitch.nis` and `nsswitch.nisplus`. The Solaris 8 release also provides *New!* `nsswitch.dns` and `nsswitch.ldap`, which provide default settings for each of these possible sources of nameservice information: files, NIS, NIS+, DNS, and LDAP. The default `nsswitch.nisplus` file is shown below.

*New!*

```
#
# /etc/nsswitch.nisplus:
#
# An example file that could be copied over to /etc/nsswitch.conf; it
# uses NIS+ (NIS Version 3) in conjunction with files.
#
# "hosts:" and "services:" in this file are used only if the
# /etc/netconfig file has a "-" for nametoaddr_libs of "inet" transports.

# the following two lines obviate the "+" entry in /etc/passwd and /etc/group.
passwd:     files nisplus
group:      files nisplus

# consult /etc "files" only if nisplus is down.
hosts:      nisplus [NOTFOUND=return] files
ipnodes:    files
# Uncomment the following line and comment out the above to resolve
# both IPv4 and IPv6 addresses from the ipnodes databases. Note that
# IPv4 addresses are searched in all of the ipnodes databases before
# searching the hosts databases. Before turning this option on, consult
# the Network Administration Guide for more details on using IPv6.
#ipnodes:    nisplus [NOTFOUND=return] files

#Uncomment the following line, and comment out the above, to use both DNS
#and NIS+.  You must also set up the /etc/resolv.conf file for DNS name
#server lookup.  See resolv.conf(4).
#hosts:      nisplus dns [NOTFOUND=return] files

services:   nisplus [NOTFOUND=return] files
networks:   nisplus [NOTFOUND=return] files
protocols:  nisplus [NOTFOUND=return] files
```

```
rpc:         nisplus [NOTFOUND=return] files
ethers:      nisplus [NOTFOUND=return] files
netmasks:    nisplus [NOTFOUND=return] files
bootparams:  nisplus [NOTFOUND=return] files

publickey:   nisplus

netgroup:    nisplus

automount:   files nisplus
aliases:     files nisplus
sendmailvars:    files nisplus

printers:        user nisplus files xfn

auth_attr:   files nisplus
prof_attr:   files nisplus
```

When you set up an NIS+ server or client system, you must copy the `/etc/nsswitch.nisplus` file to `/etc/nsswitch.conf`. After you have copied the file, you can either use the default file or customize it to suit the needs of your site. For example, if your site uses DNS, change the `hosts` entry in the `/etc/nsswitch.conf` file to `hosts: files dns`. Sun suggests that you start by using the default file and customize it only if you need to do so.

Table 28 lists the locations that the `/etc/nsswitch.conf` file can search for information.

*Table 28     Location of Name Service Information*

| Location | Description |
|----------|-------------|
| `files` | File on the client's local system. |
| `nisplus` | An NIS+ table. |
| `nis` | An NIS map. |
| `compat` | Supports old-style "+" syntax for `passwd` and `group`. |
| `dns` | Applies only to the `hosts` entry. |
| `ldap` | Lightweight Directory Access Protocol (LDAP) nameservice. |

*New!*

When NIS+ searches one or more of these locations, it returns one of the four status messages listed in Table 29.

*Table 29     Name Service Switch Status Messages*

| Status Message | Description |
|----------------|-------------|
| `SUCCESS` | Found a valid result. |
| `UNAVAIL` | Could not use the source. |

*Table 29    Name Service Switch Status Messages (Continued)*

| Status Message | Description |
|---|---|
| NOTFOUND | Information not in the source. |
| TRYAGAIN | Source returned an "I'm busy, try later" code. |

In the `/etc/nsswitch.conf` file, you can specify what action NIS+ should take when it returns one of these status messages. The actions you can specify are the following.

- `continue`—Try the next source.
- `return`—Stop trying, and return this result.

If no action is specified in the `/etc/nsswitch.conf` file, NIS+ uses the default value [NOTFOUND=continue].

The entries in the `/etc/nsswitch.conf` file have the following syntax.

```
table: location [location...] [status=action] [location]
```

The `table` variable contains the name of the NIS map, the NIS+ table, or the `/etc` file. The `location` variable specifies the first place for the system to search, using any of the locations shown in Table 28. If you want, you can specify additional locations to search. You can also specify an `action` (`continue` or `return`) if one of the status messages shown in Table 29 is encountered.

In the default NIS+ file, local `/etc` files are not consulted for `hosts`, `services`, `networks`, `protocols`, `rpc`, `ethers`, `netmasks`, and `bootparams` unless NIS+ is down. If the entry is not found, the [NOTFOUND=return] entry prevents NIS+ from consulting the `/etc` files. If you want NIS+ to consult the appropriate `/etc` file on the local system when an entry is not found in the NIS+ table, edit the default file and remove the [NOTFOUND=return] entries.

# NIS+ Administration

When NIS+ is configured on the network, you can use the NIS+ commands to administer NIS+. Sun recommends that at least one administrator be familiar with all of the NIS+ commands.

## NIS+ Commands

A major advantage of NIS+ over NIS is that you have direct read-write access to information served by NIS+ through the command-line and programmatic interface. You can further fine-tune control of this access with the NIS+ security authentication and access mechanisms.

The command-line interface lets you change NIS+ tables and directories on servers significantly more easily and quickly without first creating text files and converting them into databases.

Tasks such as adding users and systems to a domain require changing information only in that domain's NIS+ directory. You can also perform these operations remotely—from systems around the domain—without needing superuser privileges or `rlogin` access to the NIS+ master servers.

Because you have read-write programmatic access to NIS+ information, you can develop interactive and innovative system administration applications on top of NIS+. NIS+ is used by all Solaris distributed system management applications as the storage facility for administrative data.

Table 30 alphabetically lists the NIS+ commands, shows the NIS equivalent command (if appropriate) and where the command can be used, and describes how the command is used.

*New!*

*NOTE. Starting with the Solaris 2.6 release, the NIS* `ypmake`, `ypserv`, `ypupdated`, *and* `ypxfrd` *commands are included in the Solaris Operating Environment. In previous releases, you had to install these commands from the NSKit.*

See the appropriate manual pages for more information about these commands.

*Table 30      NIS and NIS+ Commands*

| NIS+ Command | NIS Command | Used For | Description |
|---|---|---|---|
| `nisaddcred*` | N/A | Authentication | Maintain credentials for NIS+ principals and store them in the `cred` table. |
| `nisaddent` | N/A | Tables | Put information from ASCII files or NIS maps into NIS+ tables. |

Table 30    NIS and NIS+ Commands (Continued)

| NIS+ Command | NIS Command | Used For | Description | |
|---|---|---|---|---|
| nisauthconf | N/A | Tables | Control which authentication flavors NIS+ uses when communicating with other NIS+ clients and servers. | New! |
| nisbackup | N/A | Backing up NIS+ master server | Back up NIS+ master server running Solaris 2.5 release or later. | |
| nis_cachemgr | N/A | NIS+ directories | Start the NIS+ cache manager on an NIS+ client. | |
| niscat* | ypcat | Tables | Display the format or the content of NIS+ tables and directory objects. | |
| nischgrp | N/A | Objects | Change the NIS+ group owner of an NIS+ object. | |
| nischmod | N/A | Objects | Change the access rights that an NIS+ object grants. Access can be changed for four categories of NIS+ principal: Nobody, Owner, Group, and World. | |
| nischown | N/A | Objects | Change the owner of an NIS+ object. | |
| nischttl | N/A | Objects | Change the time-to-live value for an NIS+ object. | |
| nisclient | N/A | Tables | Create NIS+ credentials for hosts and users, initialize NIS+ hosts and users, and restore the network service environment. | New! |

*Table 30     NIS and NIS+ Commands (Continued)*

| NIS+ Command | NIS Command | Used For | Description |
|---|---|---|---|
| nisdefaults | N/A | Objects | Show the default values for an NIS+ principal: domain name, group name, system name, NIS+ principal name, access rights, directory search path, and time to live. |
| niserror | N/A | NIS+ error message numbers | Print the NIS+ error message text for the specified NIS+ error number. |
| nisgrep* | ypmatch | Tables | Search for entries in an NIS+ table. |
| nisgrpadm | N/A | Administration | Display information for, create, or destroy an NIS+ group; also, add, remove, or test for members of existing groups. |
| nisinit | ypinit | Administration | Initialize an NIS+ client or server. |
| nisln | N/A | Objects | Create a symbolic link between two NIS+ objects. |
| nislog | N/A | Transaction logs | Display the contents of the NIS+ server transaction log. |
| nisls* | N/A | NIS+ directories | List the contents of an NIS+ directory. |
| nismatch* | ypmatch | Tables | Search for entries in an NIS+ table. |
| nismkdir | N/A | NIS+ directories | Create an NIS+ directory and specify its master and replica servers. |
| nisopaccess | N/A | Access control | Enforce access control for NIS+ operations that, by default, perform no access checking. |

New! (niserror)

New! (nislog)

New! (nisopaccess)

*Table 30    NIS and NIS+ Commands (Continued)*

| NIS+ Command | NIS Command | Used For | Description | |
|---|---|---|---|---|
| nispasswd* | yppasswd | Authentication | Change NIS+ password information. | |
| nisping* | yppush yppoll | NIS+ directories | Update or checkpoint updates to domain replicas. | |
| nispopulate | N/A | Tables | Populate NIS+ tables in a specified domain from corresponding files or NIS maps. | *New!* |
| nisprefadm | N/A | Cache manager | Define which servers are to be preferred by NIS+ clients. | *New!* |
| nisrestore | N/A | Restore NIS+ master server | Restore NIS+ master server running Solaris 2.5 release or later. | |
| nisrm | N/A | Objects | Remove NIS+ objects from the namespace. | |
| nisrmdir | N/A | NIS+ directories | Remove NIS+ directories from the namespace. | |
| nisserver | N/A | Tables | Set up a root master, non-root master, or replica NIS+ server with level 2 security (DES). | *New!* |
| nissetup | N/A | Domains | Create org_dir and groups_dir directories and a complete set of standard, unpopulated NIS+ tables for an NIS+ domain. | |
| nisshowcache | N/A | Administration | List the contents of the NIS+ shared cache that the NIS+ cache manager maintains. | |
| nisstat | N/A | Tables | Query an NIS+ server for various statistics about its operations. | *New!* |

*Table 30     NIS and NIS+ Commands (Continued)*

| NIS+ Command | NIS Command | Used For | Description |
|---|---|---|---|
| nistbladm* | N/A | Tables | Create or delete NIS+ tables and modify or delete entries in an existing NIS+ table. |
| nistest | N/A | Tables | Enable shell scripts and other programs to test for the existence, type, and access rights of objects and entries. |
| nisupdkeys | N/A | Directories | Update the public keys stored in an NIS+ directory object. |

*New!*

* An asterisk indicates an NIS+ command that you are likely to use frequently.

Because NIS+ uses a completely different way to propagate new information, no NIS+ equivalents to the ypbind, ypwhich, ypxfr, and ypset NIS commands exist.

Refer to Chapter 6, "Setting Up NIS+ Servers and Clients," for examples of how to use NIS+ commands to set up NIS+ systems. Refer to Chapter 8, "Setting Up the Automounter," for examples of how to use NIS+ commands to administer automount maps.

For some NIS+ commands, such as nistbladm -m (used to modify a specific entry in an existing entry), you must identify information in the table by using a format called an *indexed name.* An indexed name has the following syntax.

```
'[column=value,column=value]'table-name.directory-name
```

You must include the indexed name in single quotes (') to prevent the shell from interpreting the information between the square brackets as wildcard characters for expansion.

*NOTE. The NIS+ manual pages incorrectly show a comma after the final bracket and before the table name.*

For example, if you want to change only one column for an existing entry, you can use the nistbladm -m command. To change just the IP address for a system in the hosts table, first you specify the new IP address you want, then you provide an indexed name for the current entry. In the following example, the IP address for `cinderella` is changed from `129.144.52.75` to `129.144.52.80`.

```
oak% nistbladm -m addr=129.144.52.80 '[addr=129.144.52.75]'hosts.org_dir
oak%
```

## Table Information Display

This section describes several ways that you can use NIS+ commands to display information about table objects and view the contents of the tables.

The NIS+ commands require either a directory name or a fully qualified name to follow the name of the table in the argument. The fully qualified name is the name of the table, followed by the directory where the NIS+ tables are stored and the domain name, respectively.

*NOTE. With NIS+ commands, a fully qualified name has a dot at the end of the domain name. For example,* `auto_master.org_dir.starlight.com.` *is the fully qualified name for the* `auto_master` *table, which is in the directory* `org_dir` *in the domain* `starlight.com.`.

If you use the name of the table only, the NIS+ commands use the information from the NIS+ `NIS_PATH` environment variable to complete the name. You set the `NIS_PATH` environment variable just as you set any other shell environment variable—from a shell for the current session, or in the user's `.cshrc` file (C shell) or `.profile` file (Bourne or Korn shell). For example, to set the `NIS_PATH` environment variable to `org_dir.starlight.com.` for the C shell, type **setenv NIS_PATH org_dir.starlight.com.**. For the Bourne or Korn shell, type **NIS_PATH=org_dir.starlight.com.;export NIS_PATH**.

The following Bourne shell examples show three possible `NIS_PATH` variable values for an NIS+ client that is in the `starlight.com.` NIS+ domain. The `/etc/defaultdomain` file contains the NIS+ domain name. (Note that the domain name in the `/etc/defaultdomain` file does not have a trailing dot.) If `NIS_PATH` is not set, NIS+ uses the value from the `/etc/defaultdomain` file. In the following examples, the value in the `/etc/defaultdomain` file is `starlight.com` because that is the default NIS+ domain.

You have the option of setting `NIS_PATH` to actually search through a path of NIS+ domains or (shudder!) directories under those domains. The following `NIS_PATH` setting means the same thing as `NIS_PATH=starlight.com.`.

```
$ NIS_PATH=$;export NIS_PATH
$
```

The following example applies all NIS+ commands first to the org_dir.starlight.com. directory. If no matches or appropriate responses are found, the commands apply to starlight.com..

```
$ NIS_PATH=org_dir.$:$;export NIS_PATH
$
```

Setting the NIS_PATH variable to the above value can save lots of typing.

The following example first searches starlight.com., then org_dir.starlight.com., then groups_dir.starlight.com.. Then, if nothing is found in the default NIS+ domain, it searches sales.starlight.com., org_dir.sales.starlight.com., and finally, group_dir.sales.starlight.com..

```
$ NIS_PATH=$:org_dir.$:groups_dir.$:sales.$:org_dir.sales.$:groups_dir.sales.$
$ export NIS_PATH
$
```

Setting this kind of value for the NIS_PATH variable can be very useful for an administrator who maintains multiple NIS+ domains in some distributed environments.

You can display the contents of the org_dir directory with the nisls command. When you type **nisls *directory-name***, the directory and domain name are displayed, followed by a list of the contents of the directory. In the following example, the client is in the domain starlight.com..

*New!*

```
castle% nisls org_dir
org_dir.starlight.com.:
passwd
group
auto_master
auto_home
bootparams
cred
ethers
hosts
ipnodes
mail_aliases
sendmailvars
netmasks
netgroup
networks
protocols
rpc
services
timezone
client_info
```

```
auth_attr
exec_attr
prof_attr
user_attr
audit_user
castle%
```

*NOTE. If you set the* `NIS_PATH` *variable to* `NIS_PATH:org_dir.$,`
*you would simply type* `nisls` *to display the contents of*
`org_dir.starlight.com..` *If you typed* `nisls org_dir,` *the*
*command would still work because NIS+ commands look in* $ *if they*
*fall off the end of the path without finding the requested path.*

The `nisls -1` command displays a long listing of the contents of the
directory. The client is in the domain `starlight.com.`. The `T` in the left
column identifies each entry as a table object. The second column displays the
access rights for the table; the third column displays the owner of the table;
the fourth through eighth columns display the date the tables were created;
and the ninth column displays the name of the table.

```
castle% nisls -1 org_dir
org_dir.starlight.com.:
T ----rmcdrmcdr--- castle.starlight.com. Fri Dec 22 16:04:45 2000 passwd
T ----rmcdrmcdr--- castle.starlight.com. Fri Dec 22 16:04:46 2000 group
T r---rmcdrmcdr--- castle.starlight.com. Fri Dec 22 16:04:46 2000 auto_master
T r---rmcdrmcdr--- castle.starlight.com. Fri Dec 22 16:04:46 2000 auto_home
T r---rmcdrmcdr--- castle.starlight.com. Fri Dec 22 16:04:46 2000 bootparams
T r---rmcdrmcdr--- castle.starlight.com. Fri Dec 22 16:04:46 2000 cred
T r---rmcdrmcdr--- castle.starlight.com. Fri Dec 22 16:04:46 2000 ethers
T r---rmcdrmcdr--- castle.starlight.com. Fri Dec 22 16:04:46 2000 hosts
T r---rmcdrmcdr--- castle.starlight.com. Fri Dec 22 16:04:46 2000 ipnodes
T r---rmcdrmcdr--- castle.starlight.com. Fri Dec 22 16:04:46 2000 mail_aliases
T r---rmcdrmcdr--- castle.starlight.com. Fri Dec 22 16:04:46 2000 sendmailvars
T r---rmcdrmcdr--- castle.starlight.com. Fri Dec 22 16:04:46 2000 netmasks
T r---rmcdrmcdr--- castle.starlight.com. Fri Dec 22 16:04:47 2000 netgroup
T r---rmcdrmcdr--- castle.starlight.com. Fri Dec 22 16:04:47 2000 networks
T r---rmcdrmcdr--- castle.starlight.com. Fri Dec 22 16:04:47 2000 protocols
T r---rmcdrmcdr--- castle.starlight.com. Fri Dec 22 16:04:47 2000 rpc
T r---rmcdrmcdr--- castle.starlight.com. Fri Dec 22 16:04:47 2000 services
T r---rmcdrmcdr--- castle.starlight.com. Fri Dec 22 16:04:47 2000 timezone
T r---rmcdrmcdr--- castle.starlight.com. Fri Dec 22 16:04:47 2000 client_info
T r---rmcdrmcdr--- castle.starlight.com. Fri Dec 22 16:04:47 2000 auth_attr
T r---rmcdrmcdr--- castle.starlight.com. Fri Dec 22 16:04:47 2000 exec_attr
T r---rmcdrmcdr--- castle.starlight.com. Fri Dec 22 16:04:47 2000 prof_attr
T r---rmcdrmcdr--- castle.starlight.com. Fri Dec 22 16:04:47 2000 user_attr
T ----rmcdrmcd---- castle.starlight.com. Fri Dec 22 16:04:48 2000 audit_user
castle%
```

*New!*

You can display information about each table object with the `niscat -o`
*table-name.directory-name* command. Information about the `hosts`
table object is displayed in the following example.

```
castle% niscat -o hosts.org_dir
Object Name   : "hosts"
Directory     : "org_dir.starlight.com."
Owner         : "castle.starlight.com."
Group         : "admin.starlight.com."
Access Rights : r---rmcdrmcdr---
Time to Live  : 12:0:0
Creation Time : Fri Dec 22 16:04:46 2000
```

```
Mod. Time       : Fri Dec 22 16:04:46 2000
Object Type     : TABLE
Table Type      : hosts_tbl
Number of Columns    : 4
Character Separator :
Search Path     :
Columns         :
        [0]     Name        : cname
                Attributes  : (SEARCHABLE, TEXTUAL DATA, CASE INSENSITIVE)
                Access Rights : ----------------
        [1]     Name        : name
                Attributes  : (SEARCHABLE, TEXTUAL DATA, CASE INSENSITIVE)
                Access Rights : ----------------
        [2]     Name        : addr
                Attributes  : (SEARCHABLE, TEXTUAL DATA, CASE INSENSITIVE)
                Access Rights : ----------------
        [3]     Name        : comment
                Attributes  : (TEXTUAL DATA)
                Access Rights : ----------------
castle%
```

The access rights for the table object are displayed on the fifth line. This table has four named columns: cname, name, addr, and comment. Each column has its own access rights, which are displayed after the name and attributes of the column. In this example, no additional access to the columns has been granted, and owner and group have read, modify, create, and delete permissions for the table object.

If you have read permission, you can display the values for a table with the niscat *table-name.directory-name* command. In the next example, the auto_master.org_dir map has four entries.

```
castle% niscat auto_master.org_dir
+auto_master
/net -hosts              -nosuid,nobrowse
/home auto_home -nobrowse
/xfn -xfn
castle%
```

You can display the names of the columns and the contents with the niscat -h *table-name.directory-name* command. In the following example, the auto_master table has two columns, named key and value, and the separator is a space. The auto_master.org_dir map has four entries.

```
castle% niscat -h auto_master.org_dir
# key value
+auto_master
/net -hosts             -nosuid,nobrowse
/home auto_home -nobrowse
/xfn -xfn
castle%
```

*NOTE. When an NIS+ table has many entries, the output of the* niscat *command can be quite long. If you're searching for specific entries, you may want to use* nismatch *or* nisgrep *instead.*

You can create or delete tables with the `nistbladm` command. You can also use the `nistbladm` command to create and modify entries. See the `nistbladm(1)` manual page for more information. You can also look in Chapter 8, "Setting Up the Automounter," for examples of how to use the `nistbladm` command to create and edit automount maps.

## NIS+ Installation Scripts

*New!*

Use the NIS+ installation scripts described in Table 31 as the preferred way to configure NIS+ servers and clients in standard NIS+ domains and NIS-compatible domains.

*Table 31    NIS+ Installation Scripts*

| NIS+ Script | Description |
| --- | --- |
| `nisserver` | Set up root master, non-root master, or replica NIS+ server with level 2 security (DES). Create the NIS+ directories (including `groups_dir` and `org_dir`) and system table objects for the specified domain. |
| `nispopulate` | Populate NIS+ tables in a specified domain from corresponding files or NIS maps. The tables must have already been created with the `nisserver(1M)` or `nissetup(1M)` command. |
| `nisclient` | Create NIS+ credentials for hosts and users, to initialize NIS+ hosts and users, and to restore the network service environment. |

Chapter 6, "Setting Up NIS+ Servers and Clients," describes how to use these NIS+ installation scripts.

# 6

# SETTING UP NIS+ SERVERS AND CLIENTS

This chapter describes how to use the `nisserver`, `nispopulate`, and `nisclient` NIS+ scripts to set up a Solaris system as an NIS+ server and to set up NIS+ client systems. Using these scripts is the recommended way to set up NIS+. For complete information about using the NIS+ commands and administering NIS+, refer to Sun's *Solaris Naming Setup and Configuration Guide*.

*NOTE. All of the information in this chapter is new in this edition.*

## Setting Up an NIS+ Namespace

This section summarizes the steps for setting up an NIS+ namespace.

1. Set up the root master server.
   Use the `nisserver` NIS+ installation script, as described in "Creating a Root Master Server" on page 164.
2. Populate the root domain tables.
   Use the `nispopulate` script, as described in "Populating the NIS+ Tables" on page 166.
3. Set up the clients of the root domain.

Set up a few clients in the root domain to test its operation. Use full DES authentication. Use the `nisclient` script, as described in "Setting Up NIS+ Client Systems" on page 171.

This chapter describes how to perform the first three steps. Describing how to perform the rest of the tasks in this list is beyond the scope of this book. Refer to the *Solaris Naming Administration Guide* for more information.

4. Create or convert site-specific NIS+ tables.

   If your site requires custom, site-specific NIS+ tables, use the `nistbladm` command to create them and use the `nisaddent` command to transfer NIS data into them.

5. Add administrators to root domain groups.

   Use the `nisaddcred` command to create LOCAL and DES credentials for administrators. Administrators' workstations should be clients of the root domain, and their root identities should also be NIS+ clients with DES credentials.

6. Update the `sendmailvars` table if necessary.

   If your e-mail environment changes because of the new domain structure, populate the root domain's `sendmailvars` table with the new entries. If you use DNS, migrating to NIS+ should not affect e-mail.

7. Set up root domain replicas.

   First convert some of the clients into servers. For NIS compatibility, run `rpc.nisd -Y` and edit the `/etc/init.d/rpc` file to remove the comment (#) from the EMULYP line. For DNS forwarding, use `rpc.nisd -B`. Then, run `nisserver -R` on the clients you want to convert to NIS+ replica servers so that they are associated with the root domain.

8. Test the operation of the root domain.

   Develop a set of test routines to verify that the clients are functioning. Operate this domain for about a week before you convert other users to NIS+.

9. Set up the remainder of the namespace.

10. Test the operation of the namespace.

11. Customize the security configuration of the NIS+ domains.

    You may not need to customize the security configuration if everything is working well. However, if you want to protect some information from unauthorized access, you can change the default permissions of NIS+ tables and rearrange the membership of NIS+ groups and the permissions of NIS+ objects to suit your site requirements.

# Introducing the NIS+ Installation Scripts

To set up an NIS+ server and NIS+ clients, use the `nisserver`, `nispopulate`, and `nisclient` scripts. The NIS+ scripts are Bourne shell scripts that execute groups of NIS+ commands so you do not have to type the commands individually. Table 32 describes the tasks each script performs.

*Table 32    NIS+ Scripts*

| NIS+ Script | Description |
|---|---|
| `nisserver` | Set up the root master, non-root master, and replica servers with level 2 security (DES). |
| `nispopulate` | Populate NIS+ tables in a specified domain from their corresponding system files or NIS maps. |
| `nisclient` | Create NIS+ credentials for hosts and users; initialize NIS+ hosts and users. |

In combination with a few NIS+ commands, you can use the NIS+ scripts to perform all the tasks to set up an NIS+ namespace. To see the commands that the scripts call and their approximate output without executing the command, you can run each of the scripts with the -x option. When you first run the scripts with the -x option, you can minimize unexpected surprises.

Although the NIS+ scripts streamline the creation of an NIS+ namespace, the scripts implement only a subset of NIS+ features. The `nisserver` script sets up an NIS+ server only with the standard default tables, permissions, and authorizations. It does *not* do the following tasks.

- Set special permissions for tables and directories.
- Add extra NIS+ principals to the NIS+ `admin` group.
- Create private tables.
- Run an NIS+ server at a security level other than level 2.
- Start the `rpc.nisd` daemon on remote replica servers, which is required to complete server installation.

# Preparing for Setup and Configuration

Before configuring your NIS+ namespace, you must complete the following tasks.

- The `nisserver` and `nisclient` commands automatically copy the `/etc/nsswitch.nisplus` file to `/etc/nsswitch.conf`. If you do not use the `nisserver` or `nisclient` commands, you must install a properly configured `nsswitch.conf` file on each system that uses NIS+
- Plan your namespace, determining the following factors.
    - Decide on your NIS+ domain name. Your NIS+ domain name may be the same as your DNS domain name, although it does not need to be. If you plan to create a hierarchy of NIS+ domains that map to your existing DNS domains, using existing DNS domain names is easier. In this way you can delegate control of NIS+ in the same way you do with DNS.
    - Determine whether you have subdomains and how they will be organized.
    - Decide which systems will be in each NIS+ domain.
    - Determine whether your domain will be connected to a higher domain or to the Internet.
- Plan your server requirements.
    - Determine how many replica servers are needed for each domain.
    - Determine what type of server, processor speed, and memory is required.
    - Determine how much server disk space is required.
- Prepare your existing namespace (if any).
- Choose a root server system.
- Make sure that you have at least one system already running that you can use as your root master server. This system must contain at least the root user in the system information files such as `/etc/passwd`. Systems are usually configured with root in the system files, so this requirement should not be a problem.

## Preparing an Existing Namespace

If your site has an existing NIS domain, you can use the same flat domain structure for your NIS+ namespace. You can later change it to a hierarchical structure. Refer to Sun's *NIS+ Transition Guide* for more planning and preparation information. You can use the NIS+ scripts to start NIS+ with data from NIS maps.

For the NIS+ scripts to run smoothly, you must prepare the existing namespace for conversion. Key preparations are summarized below.

- Domains and hosts must have different names. For example, if you have an `eng` domain, you cannot have a system named `eng`. You also cannot name the domain the same name as any host system in that domain. In addition, subdomain names must be different from system names.

- Because NIS+ uses dots (periods) to delimit between system names and domains and between parent and subdomains, you cannot use a dot in a system name. Before using the scripts to convert an NIS namespace to NIS+, you must eliminate any dots in your host names. Convert any name dots to dashes. For example, you cannot have a machine named `hr.main`. You can convert the name to `hr-main`.

- The system designated as the root server must be up and running and you must have superuser access to it.

- View any existing local `/etc` files or NIS maps that will be used as a source for NIS+ data. Make sure no incorrect entries are present. Make sure that the data is in the correct place and has the right format. Remove any outdated, invalid, corrupt, or partial entries. You can always add individual entries after configuration is complete.

*NOTE. In Solaris 2.4 releases and earlier, the* `/var/nis` *directory contained two files named* `hostname.dict` *and* `hostname.log`. *It also contained a* `/var/nis/hostname` *subdirectory. Starting with the 2.5 release, the* `hostname.dict` *and* `hostname.log` *files are named* `trans.log` *and* `data.dict` *and the subdirectory is named* `/var/nis/data`. *In addition, the content of the files has been changed and the files are not backward compatible. Do not rename either the directories or the files, because they will not work with the Solaris 2.5 and later versions of* `rpc.nisd`.

# Setting Up an NIS+ Root Server

The first step in establishing an NIS+ domain is to set up the root master server. The following section describes how to set up an NIS+ root server by using the `nisserver` script with default settings, which are listed below.

- Security level 2 (DES)—The highest level of NIS+ security.

- NIS compatibility set to OFF (instructions are provided for setting NIS compatibility).

- `/etc` files or NIS maps used as the source of nameservice information.

- `admin.`*domainname* is used as the NIS+ group.

Setting up an NIS+ root master server requires the following tasks.

- Running the `nisserver` script.
- Preparing `/etc` files or NIS maps used to transfer data to NIS+ tables.
- Running the `nispopulate` script to populate the NIS+ tables created by the `nisserver` script.

## Preparing to Run the nisserver Command

Before you run the `nisserver` command, you need the following information.

- The superuser password for the system you are configuring as the root master server.
- The name of the new root domain. The root domain name must have at least two elements and end in a dot (for example, `something.com.`) You can name the trailing element anything you want, but to maintain Internet compatibility, it should be either an Internet organizational name or a two- or three-character geographic identifier such as `.au.` for Australia. See Table 3 on page 17, Table 4 on page 18, and Table 5 on page 18 for examples of organizational and country domain abbreviations.
- Check that the `/etc/passwd` file on the root master server system contains an entry for root.

*NOTE. The* `nisserver` *command has a known bug that prevents a clean shutdown of the root master server. At the time of writing, the bug was not fixed in any of the Solaris 8 Update releases.*

## Creating a Root Master Server

Use the following steps to create a root master server.

1. Add `/usr/lib/nis` to superuser's path.

   The following example adds `/usr/lib/nis` to the superuser path on the command line.

```
paperbark% su
Password:
# PATH=$PATH:/usr/lib/nis;export PATH
# echo $PATH
/usr/sbin:/usr/bin:/usr/lib/nis
#
```

2.  (Optional) If using DES authentication, specify the Diffie-Hellman key length. If you skip this step, the default 192-bit key value is used.

    The following example specifies 640-bit Diffie-Hellman keys as well as the default 192-bit keys.

```
# nisauthconf dh640-0 des
#
```

The following example allows only 640-bit keys and rejects 192-bit keys.

```
# nisauthconf dh640-0
#
```

3.  Type **nisserver -r -d *domainname*** and press Return.

    The -r option configures the root master server and the -d option specifies the domain name. The following example configures the system castle as the root master server with the wellard.com. domain name.

```
# nisserver -r -d wellard.com.
This script sets up this machine "paperbark" as an NIS+
root master server for domain wellard.com..

Domain name              : wellard.com.
NIS+ group               : admin.wellard.com.
NIS (YP) compatibility   : OFF
Security level           : 2=DES

Is this information correct? (type 'y' to accept, 'n' to change) y

This script will set up your machine as a root master server for
domain wellard.com. without NIS compatibility at security level 2.

Use "nisclient -r" to restore your current network service environment.

Do you want to continue? (type 'y' to continue, 'n' to exit this script)
```

The NIS+ group is the group of users who are authorized to modify the information in the wellard.com. domain. The default group is admin.wellard.com. You can change this name after the script is completed.

NIS compatibility determines whether an NIS+ server accepts information requests from NIS clients. The default is OFF.

4.  Type **n** if you want to change the information; the script prompts you for the correct information. Type **y** if the information is correct.

*NOTE. You can change the domain name and the NIS compatibility setting with this script. You cannot, however, change the DES default security level. If you choose to make the server NIS compatible, you*

*must also edit the* /etc/init.d/rpc *file and restart the* rpc.nisd
*daemon before it will work.*

The following example uses the default settings.

```
setting up domain information "wellard.com." ...
mv: cannot access /etc/defaultdomain

setting up switch information ...

running nisinit ...
This machine is in the "wellard.com." NIS+ domain.
Setting up root server ...
All done.

starting root server at security level 0 to create credentials...

running nissetup to create standard directories and tables ...
org_dir.wellard.com. created
groups_dir.wellard.com. created
passwd.org_dir.wellard.com. created
group.org_dir.wellard.com. created
auto_master.org_dir.wellard.com. created
auto_home.org_dir.wellard.com. created
bootparams.org_dir.wellard.com. created
cred.org_dir.wellard.com. created
ethers.org_dir.wellard.com. created
hosts.org_dir.wellard.com. created
ipnodes.org_dir.wellard.com. created
mail_aliases.org_dir.wellard.com. created
sendmailvars.org_dir.wellard.com. created
netmasks.org_dir.wellard.com. created
netgroup.org_dir.wellard.com. created
networks.org_dir.wellard.com. created
protocols.org_dir.wellard.com. created
rpc.org_dir.wellard.com. created
services.org_dir.wellard.com. created
timezone.org_dir.wellard.com. created
client_info.org_dir.wellard.com. created
auth_attr.org_dir.wellard.com. created
exec_attr.org_dir.wellard.com. created
prof_attr.org_dir.wellard.com. created
user_attr.org_dir.wellard.com. created
audit_user.org_dir.wellard.com. created

adding credential for paperbark.wellard.com...
Enter login password:
Type the root login password
creating NIS+ administration group: admin.wellard.com. ...
adding principal paperbark.wellard.com. to admin.wellard.com. ...

restarting NIS+ root master server at security level 2 ...
starting NIS+ password daemon ...
starting NIS+ cache manager ...

This system is now configured as a root server for domain wellard.com.
You can now populate the standard NIS+ tables by using the
nispopulate script or /usr/lib/nis/nisaddent command.
#
```

## Populating the NIS+ Tables

After you run the nisserver script to configure the root master server, you
can use the nispopulate script to populate the standard NIS+ tables. The
following section describes how to populate the NIS+ tables by using the
nisserver script with default settings, which are listed below.

- The domain created by the `nisserver` script.
- `/etc` files or NIS maps as the source of the nameservice information.
- The standard NIS+ tables: `auto_master`, `auto_home`, `ethers`, `group`, `hosts`, `ipnodes`, `networks`, `passwd`, `protocols`, `services`, `rpc`, `netmasks`, `bootparams`, `netgroup`, and `aliases`.

*NOTE. When* `/etc` *files are the source of the nameservice information, the contents of the* `/etc/shadow` *file are merged with the* `/etc/passwd` *file to create the* `passwd` *table. No* `shadow` *table is created.*

## Preparing to Run the nispopulate Command

Before you run the `nispopulate` command, you need to perform the following tasks.

- View each local `/etc` file or NIS map to make sure no incorrect or incomplete entries are present.
- Make sure the domain and host names are different.
- Remove all dots and underscores from host names.
- Make copies of the `/etc` files and—if you are not using DNS—the `/etc/inet/hosts` and `/etc/inet/ipnodes` files, and use the copies to populate the tables. The following example uses files from a directory called `/tmp/nisplusfiles`.

*NOTE. The new* `ipnodes.org_dir` *table has been added to handle IPv6 addresses. It contains both IPv4 and IPv6 addresses for a host. The existing* `hosts.org_dir` *table remains to facilitate existing applications. You must keep both the* `hosts.org_dir` *and* `ipnodes.org_dir` *tables consistent with the IPv4 addresses. These tables are not automatically synchronized. Administering the* `ipnodes.org_dir` *table is similar to administering the* `hosts.org_dir` *table.*

- Edit the `passwd`, `shadow`, `aliases`, `hosts`, and `ipnodes` files. Remove the `root`, `daemon`, `bin`, `sys`, `adm`, `lp`, `smtp`, `uucp`, `nuucp`, `listen`, `nobody`, and `noaccess` entries so that they are not made available across the namespace.
- The domain must be configured and the master server must be running.
- The domain's server must have enough disk space to accommodate the new table information.
- You must be logged in as root because the NIS+ `cred` table has not yet been populated to establish NIS+ principal credentials.

You need the following information if populating from /etc files.

- The NIS+ domain name.
- The path of the edited text files from which data will be transferred.
- The root password.

You need the following information if populating from NIS maps.

- The NIS+ domain name.
- The NIS domain name.
- The name of the NIS server.
- The IP address of the NIS server.
- The root password for the NIS+ root server.

*NOTE. The NIS domain name is case sensitive. The NIS+ domain is not.*

## Populating the Root Master Server Tables from Files

The nispopulate script can fail if the system has insufficient /tmp space. You can set the TMPDIR environment variable to a different directory. If TMPDIR is not set to a valid directory, the script uses the /tmp directory.

*NOTE. Once you type* **y** *to start running the script, do not interrupt it because you can leave the tables only partially populated. The script does not automatically recover or clean up. You can rerun the script safely, but the existing tables will be overwritten with the latest information.*

1. Become superuser on the root master server.
2. Type **mkdir /nisplus-name** and press Return.
3. Copy the /etc files to the NIS+ directory you created in the previous step.

   The following example copies some of the key /etc files to the /nisplusfiles directory. Be sure to copy the /etc/shadow file as well as the /etc/passwd file or the NIS+ passwd table will not populate correctly. Also be sure to copy the /etc/inet/hosts and /etc/inet/ipnodes files.

```
paperbark% su
Password:
# cd /etc
# mkdir /tmp/nisplustables
# cp auto_master /tmp/nisplustables
# cp auto_home /tmp/nisplustables
# cp group /tmp/nisplustables
```

```
# cp inet/hosts /tmp/nisplustables
# cp inet/ipnodes /tmp/nisplustables
# cp networks /tmp/nisplustables
# cp passwd /tmp/nisplustables
# cp shadow /tmp/nisplustables
# cp protocols /tmp/nisplustables
# cp services /tmp/nisplustables
#
```

4. Type **nispopulate -F -p /*tabledirectory* -d *domainname***
and press Return.

The -F option takes the data from files. The -p option specifies the
directory search path for the source files. The -d option specifies the
NIS+ domain name.

The script displays the files directory and domain name and asks you
if you want to proceed. The following example uses a directory named
/tmp/nisplustables for the wellard.com. domain.

```
# nispopulate -F -p /tmp/nisplustables -d wellard.com.

NIS+ domain name            : wellard.com.
Directory Path              : /tmp/nisplustables

Is this information correct? (type 'y' to accept, 'n' to change)
```

5. If you want to change any of this information, type **n**; otherwise,
type **y**.

The following message is displayed.

```
This script will populate the standard NIS+ tables for domain
wellard.com. from the files in /tmp/nisplustables:
auto_master auto_home ethers group hosts ipnodes networks passwd protocols
 services rpc netmasks bootparams netgroup aliases timezone auth_attr
 exec_attr prof_attr user_attr audit_user shadow

**WARNING:  Interrupting this script after choosing to continue
may leave the tables only partially populated.  This script does
not do any automatic recovery or cleanup.

Do you want to continue? (type 'y' to continue, 'n' to exit this script)
```

6. Type **n** to exit or **y** to continue.

Messages such as the following are displayed.

```
populating passwd table from file /tmp/nisplustables/shadow...
passwd table done.



Credentials have been added for the entries in the
hosts and passwd table(s).  Each entry was given a default
network password (also known as a Secure-RPC password).
This password is:

        nisplus
```

```
Use this password when the nisclient script requests the
network password.
```

7. Note and remember the Secure RPC password (`nisplus`, by default). Use this password when prompted for your network or Secure RPC password by the `nisclient` script.

   The script displays a list of tables that the `nispopulate` script failed to populate, as shown in the following example.

```
nispopulate failed to populate the following tables:
 ethers ipnodes bootparams netgroup timezone auth_attr exec_attr prof_attr
 user_attr audit_user
#
```

8. (Optional). Add yourself and other users to `admin` group of the root domain.

   The following example adds user `winsor` to the `admin.wellard.com.` domain.

```
# nisgrpadm -a admin.wellard.com. winsor.wellard.com.
Added "winsor.wellard.com." to group "admin.wellard.com.".
#
```

## Populating the Root Master Server Tables from NIS Maps

The procedure for populating NIS+ tables from NIS maps is similar to that for populating from files.

1. Become superuser on the root master server.
2. Type **nispopulate -Y -d *domainname***

   **-h *nis-server* -a nis-ip -y *nis-domainname*** and press Return.

   The `-Y` option takes the data from NIS maps. The `-d` option specifies the NIS+ domain name. The `-h` option specifies the NIS server name, the `-a` option specifies the IP address for the NIS server. The `-y` option specifies the NIS domain name.
3. Verify the information and type **y** to continue or **n** to correct the information.
4. After the warning message, type **y** to continue or **n** to exit the script.

You can ignore any parse error warnings. Such errors indicate that the script found empty or unexpected values in an NIS map. You may want to verify the data after the script completes.

5. Add yourself and other users to the `admin` group of the root domain.

# Setting Up NIS+ Client Systems

After you have populated the tables for the root master server from files or NIS maps, you can initialize NIS+ client systems. You do not need to do any further steps to initialize the root master server because it is already an NIS+ client of its own domain.

The following section describes how to set up an NIS+ client with the `nisclient` script.

## Preparing to Run the nisclient Command

Before you run the `nisclient` command, the following conditions must be met.

- The domain must already be configured and its master server must be running.
- The master server NIS+ tables must be populated. At a minimum, the `hosts` or `ipnodes` table must have an entry for the client system. If you are using DNS, the NIS+ `hosts` and `ipnodes` tables should be empty and the `hosts` entry in `/etc/nsswitch.conf` should be `hosts: files dns`.
- You must be logged in as superuser on the system that is to become an NIS+ client. In the following example, the new client system is named `paperbark`.

You need the following information before you run the `nisclient` command.

- The domain name.
- The default Secure RPC password (`nisplus`)
- The root password of the client system
- The IP address of the NIS+ server in the client's home domain.
- If you use DES authentication, note the Diffie-Hellman key length used on the master server. Use `nisauthconf` to ascertain the master server Diffie-Hellman key length.

## Security Considerations

Both the administrator and the client must have the proper credentials and access rights. The administrator can have either:

- DES credentials in the client's home domain.
- A combination of DES credentials in the administrator's home domain and LOCAL credentials in the client's domain.

See Chapter 5, "Introducing the NIS+ Environment," for more information about DES and LOCAL credentials.

After you create the client's credentials in the NIS+ domain, you can complete the setup process on the client system. The directory object for its home domain on the NIS+ server must have Read access for the World and Nobody categories. If you are adding a client to an NIS+ domain that has existing clients, the directory object probably has the proper access permissions.

You can check the access rights for the directory object with the niscat -o command. The access rights are displayed on the fifth line of the output. In this example, the World category has Read access, as shown by the r--- at the end of the access rights string:

```
rootmaster# niscat -o ESG.Eng.wellard.COM.
Object Name      : ESG
Owner            : oak.ESG.Eng.sun.COM.
Group            : admin.ESG.Eng.sun.COM.
Domain           : Eng.sun.COM.
Access Rights : r---rmcdrmcdr---
Time to Live  : 12:0:0
Object Type      : DIRECTORY
Name : 'ESG.Eng.sun.COM.'
Type : NIS
Master Server :
        Name         : oak.ESG.Eng.sun.COM.
        Public Key : None.
        Universal addresses (6)
        [1] - udp, inet, 127.0.0.1.0.111
        [2] - tcp, inet, 127.0.0.1.0.111
        [3] - -, inet, 127.0.0.1.0.111
        [4] - -, loopback, oak.rpc
        [5] - -, loopback, oak.rpc
        [6] - -, loopback, oak.rpc
Time to live : 12:0:0
Default Access rights :
```

If you have Modify rights, you can change the access rights for the directory object, with the nischmod command. See the nischmod(1) manual page for more information.

## DES Authentication

The DES authentication must match on the root master server and the client systems. Use the `nisauthconf` command on the root master to determine the DES authentication.

The following example shows that the default DES authentication is configured.

```
# /usr/lib/nis/nisauthconf
des
#
```

The following example shows that 640-bit Diffie-Hellman keys has been configured as well as the default 192-bit keys

```
# /usr/lib/nis/nisauthconf
dh640dh-0 des
#
```

If you need to specify the Diffie-Hellman key length (it is configured to something other than the default), on the client system, use the `nisauthconf` command to configure the client to match the setting on the root master server.

The following example configures the client system, `paperbark`, with `dh640dh-0 des`.

```
paperbark% su
Password:
# /usr/lib/nis/nisauthconf dh640dh-0 des
#
```

## Initializing a New Client System

Use the following steps to initialize a new client NIS+ system.

1. Become superuser on the client system.
2. All on one line, type **/usr/lib/nis/nisclient -i -d**
   **domainname -h NIS+-master** and press Return.

   The -i option initializes a client system. The -d option specifies the NIS+ domain name. If you do not specify the domain name, the default is the current domain name. The -h option specifies the name of the NIS+ server.

The following example initializes the system paperbark in the
wellard.com. domain from the castle NIS master server.

```
# /usr/lib/nis/nisclient -i -d wellard.com. -h castle

Initializing client paperbark for domain "wellard.com.".
Once initialization is done, you will need to reboot your
machine.

Do you want to continue? (type 'y' to continue, 'n' to exit this script) y


setting up domain information "wellard.com."...
Can't open /etc/defaultdomain
cp: cannot access /etc/defaultdomain

setting up the name service switch information...


At the prompt below, type the network password (also known
as the Secure-RPC password) that you obtained either
from your administrator or from running the nispopulate script.
Please enter the Secure-RPC password for root:
Please enter the login password for root:

Your network password has been changed to your login one.
Your network and login passwords are now the same.

Client initialization completed!!
Please reboot your machine for changes to take effect.
#
```

3. Type **init 6** to reboot the system.

# Verification of the Setup

The following sections describe some ways to verify that the system has been
properly configured as an NIS+ client.

## Verifying That the Cache Manager Is Running

Check to see whether nis_cachemgr is running. Type **ps -ef | grep
nis_cachemgr** and press Return. In the following example, the cache
manager is running on the system paperbark.

```
paperbark% ps -ef | grep nis_cachemgr
    root   128     1  0 16:40:01 ?        0:00 /usr/sbin/nis_cachemgr
    winsor 440   414  0 16:41:51 pts/4    0:00 grep nis_cachemgr
```

## Checking the Contents of the /var/nis Directory

When an NIS+ client is set up properly, the `/var/nis` directory has one or more files. Type **ls  /var/nis** and press Return. The contents of `/var/nis` should look like the following example.

```
paperbark% ls /var/nis
NIS_COLD_START        NIS_SHARED_DIRCACHE
paperbark%
```

## Verifying That the NIS+ Commands Succeed

When an NIS+ client is set up properly, you can use the NIS+ commands. For example, type **nisls  org_dir** and press Return. When the command is successful, a list of the tables in the `org_dir` directory is displayed, as shown in the following example.

```
paperbark% nisls org_dir
org_dir.wellard.com.:
passwd
group
auto_master
auto_home
bootparams
cred
ethers
hosts
ipnodes
mail_aliases
sendmailvars
netmasks
netgroup
networks
protocols
rpc
services
timezone
client_info
auth_attr
exec_attr
prof_attr
user_attr
audit_user
paperbark%
```

# Part Three

# Automounter and WebNFS Services

This part describes the Solaris automounter services in two chapters. It also introduces WebNFS™ services in a third chapter.

Chapter 7 describes automount terminology and the components of automounting, explains how the automounter works, recommmends automounting policies, and tells you how to plan your automounter services. Chapter 8 describes how to set up and administer automounter maps. Chapter 9 introduces WebNFS services.

Refer to the chapters in this part if you need to set up a new automount service or modify an existing one or if you need information about the WebNFS service.

# 7

# UNDERSTANDING
# THE AUTOMOUNTER

The automounter works with the NFS (network file system) to automatically mount and unmount directories from other systems on the network as they are needed. The automounter supplements the virtual file system table (/etc/vfstab) and manual mount and unmount activities with an automatic, on-demand facility. When the user types a command that accesses a remote file or directory, the automounter consults a series of *maps*—described in detail later in this chapter—to determine which directories to mount, which system to mount them from, which mount parameters to use, and where to mount them on the user's local system. The directory remains mounted as long as it is in use. When the user exits from the file or the directory, the resource is automatically unmounted if it has not been accessed for 5 minutes.

Although you could administer the automounter by editing local automount maps in the /etc directory, Sun recommends that you use the NIS, NIS+, or LDAP nameservice with the automounter. Using a nameservice *New!* creates a consistent global namespace for your users and a centralized control model for your administrators, and it provides a consistent automounter configuration throughout the domain.

This chapter describes some automount terminology, the automount maps and mount points, and the way in which automounting works. It also provides some example maps and suggests policies you can use to implement automounting in your network environment. (Chapter 8, "Setting Up the Automounter," discusses how to create and edit automount maps.)

# NFS Terminology

NFS, which is the Solaris distributed network file system, is the industry's most widely available file-sharing system and has been adopted and shipped by more than 300 vendors. The terms in this discussion are commonly used to describe how resources are shared with NFS and how these terms relate to the automounter.

## Server and Client Systems

The terms *server* and *client* describe the roles that systems perform when they interact to share resources. These terms are part of general distributed computing terminology and are not specific to either NFS or the automounter.

- A *server* is a system that shares (exports) file systems so that they are accessible to other systems on the network.
- A *client* is a system that accesses some or all of its files from one or more servers.

You do not need to set up server file systems in a special way for access by the automounter. As long as the file systems are shared for NFS access, the automounter software can mount and unmount them.

## Mount Points

*Mount points* are directories on a client system that are used as places to attach (or mount) other file systems. When you mount or automount a file system on a mount point, any files or directories that are stored locally in the mount point directory are hidden and inaccessible as long as the file system is mounted. These files are not permanently affected by the mounting process, and they become available again when the file system is unmounted. However, mount directories are usually empty so that existing files are not obscured.

*New!*

NOTE. *If the top-level automount mount points do not exist, the automounter creates them.*

## The Virtual File System Table

Each system has a virtual file system table (`/etc/vfstab`) that specifies which file systems are mounted by default at system boot. This file specifies local UFS (UNIX file system) and NFS file systems that are mounted automatically when a system boots. The `/etc/vfstab` file has additional entries for file systems, such as `swap` and `proc`, that are used by the system.

In addition, the `/etc/vfstab` file may have entries for `pcfs` (personal computer file system) and `cdrom` file systems.

The automounter is an alternative to the `/etc/vfstab` file for specifying which file systems to mount and unmount. The automounter uses maps because they are more flexible than the `/etc/vfstab` file and they enable a consistent network-wide view of all file names.

You can, without any conflict, mount some file systems with the `/etc/vfstab` file and other files with the automounter.

*CAUTION. Do not create entries in the* `/etc/vfstab` *file for file systems that will be automounted. Conversely, do not put file systems that are included in the* `/etc/vfstab` *file into any of the automount direct maps.*

## Mount and Unmount

Without the automounter, user file systems are mounted when the system boots from entries in the `/etc/vfstab` file. When file systems are not automounted, users employ the `mount` and `umount` commands—which require superuser privileges—if they need to mount any additional file systems or unmount a mounted file system. The `mount` command is used to mount a file system. The `umount` command is used to unmount a file system. When file systems are automounted, users do not need to use the `mount` and `umount` commands. Instead, the automounter mounts the file systems and makes them available when a user changes into an autofs directory.

For a description of the types of file systems and for information on how to share, mount, and unmount files, refer to *Solaris System Administrator's Guide,* Third Edition, by Janice Winsor. (See the bibliography at the end of this book.)

## The Mount Table (/etc/mnttab)

The Solaris Operating Environment uses a mount table, which is maintained in the `/etc/mnttab` file, to keep track of currently mounted file systems. Whenever users mount or unmount a file system with either the `mount` or `umount` commands or the automounter, the system modifies the `/etc/mnttab` file to list the currently mounted file systems.

In previous Solaris releases, the `/etc/mnttab` mount table was a text-based file that stored information about mounted file systems. This file could get out of sync with the state of mounted file systems. Starting with the Solaris 8 release, `/etc/mnttab` is an MNTFS file system that provides

*New!*

read-only information directly from the kernel about mounted file systems for the local system.

Because of this structural difference, the following `mnttab` behavior is changed.

- Programs or scripts cannot write to `/etc/mnttab`.
- The `mount -m` option for faking `mnttab` entries no longer works.

MNTFS requires no administration. See `mnttab`(4) for more information.

You can display the contents of the `/etc/mnttab` file with the `cat` or `more` commands, but you cannot edit it.

# NIS+ Terminology

NIS+ is the Solaris enterprise nameservice. Information used by NIS+ is stored in tables, also called *databases*, which can be administered with the `nistbladm` (NIS+ table administration) command. NIS+ implementations of automount maps also are called databases or *tables*. For example, you use the `nistbladm` command to administer the NIS+ `auto_home` database, the NIS+ `auto_master` table, and any other NIS+ automounting tables you create.

# Automount Terminology

This section describes terms that are specific to the automounter.

## Automounter

New!

The automounter has three components.

- The `automount` program.
- The `automountd` daemon.
- The autofs file system.

The `automountd` daemon and the `automount` program are started at boot time by the `/etc/init.d/autofs` script. The daemon runs in the background and automatically mounts and unmounts NFS file systems as requested by autofs. The autofs file system sends request to the `automount` program, which processes the requests and then terminates, leaving the `automountd` daemon to do the work. Information provided in maps in the

/etc directory with the prefix auto_ is used to mount and unmount directories and subdirectories that are listed in the automount maps. The term *automounter* in this context refers to the automount programs and the functionality that they provide, and the term *automounting* describes the activities of the automount programs and autofs. See "Components of the Automounter" on page 196 for more information about the automounter components.

## Automount Maps

The automounter uses maps to determine which file systems to mount and where to mount them. The automounter uses three kinds maps: master, indirect, and direct. By convention, map names have auto_ as a prefix.

> *NOTE. SunOS 4.x automount maps used the* auto. *prefix naming convention. You do not need to rename your SunOS 4.x automount maps for them to be compatible with the Solaris automounter. The Solaris automounter looks first for files with an* auto_ *prefix. If none are found, it looks for files with an* auto. *prefix.*

### The Master Map

The *master map*, named auto_master, is the master file consulted by the automounter when the system starts up or whenever you run the automount program to register changes you have made to the auto_master map or to any other automount maps. The auto_master map contains the default mount points /net and /home and the names of the direct or indirect maps that the automounter consults.

### Indirect and Direct Maps

The *indirect* and *direct* maps contain detailed information that the automounter uses to mount and unmount the file systems. You specify indirect maps with a simple path name; you specify a direct map with an absolute path name. See "Indirect Maps" on page 184 and "The Direct Map" on page 190 for more information.

The most commonly used indirect maps are the auto_master map and the *home directory map*. The home directory map contains the mount point and the names of the home directories that are to be mounted automatically.

# Automount Maps and Mount Points

The following sections describe the syntax of automount maps, the `auto_master` default mount points, and the mount point required for direct maps.

## Indirect Maps

In an *indirect map*, you can specify a simple name (no slashes) as the mount point for each indirect map—in other words, you specify a relative path name for each indirect map entry in the `auto_master` map. You can create as many other indirect maps as you like so that you can provide users access to files exported from one or more servers.

The syntax for indirect maps is shown below.

```
key      [mount-options]      server:pathname
```

The simple path name is *key*, which is used as the mount point for the resource. An optional, comma-separated list of options, [*mount-options*], controls the mounting of the resource. If no options are specified, the resource is mounted read-write. The name of the server and the path to the resource is *server:pathname*.

Map entries can describe any number of resources—from different locations and with different mount options. For example, you can create an indirect map named `auto_local` to make FrameMaker and OpenWindows available from different servers. You put an entry in the `auto_master` map that references the `auto_local` map. For example, the `auto_master` file can contain the following line.

```
/usr/local     auto_local
```

This `auto_master` entry points to the following `auto_local` indirect map.

```
# Indirect map for executables: auto_local
#
openwin     -ro  oak:/usr/openwin
frame.6.0   ash:/usr/local/frame.6.0
```

You can include an integer in parentheses to specify more than one server location, use shortcuts and wildcard characters to shorten entries with similar characteristics, and set weighting factors for each server named. The most likely to be selected is (0); progressively higher values decrease the chance of being selected. For more information, see "Syntax and Shortcuts for Map Entries" on page 191.

## The Default Automount Maps

The Solaris Operating Environment provides you with two default indirect automounter maps: auto_master and auto_home.

**The Master Map**     The master map is located in the /etc directory. As indicated earlier, this indirect map contains the default mount points /net and /home. Use the default mount points as a convenient way to maintain a consistent namespace.

The auto_master map has the following syntax.

```
mount-point      map-name       [mount-options]
```

The full path name of a directory is *mount-point*. If the directory does not exist, the automounter creates it if possible. The map used by the automounter to find the mount points and locations of the server's file systems is named *map-name*. Finally, *mount-options* is an optional list of comma-separated options that control the mounting of the entries specified by *map-name*. Options specified in the *map-name* map take precedence over options specified in the auto_master map. The *mount-options* used by the automounter are the same mount options used in the /etc/vfstab file. Table 33 shows the most common mount options. See the mount_nfs(1M) manual page for a complete list of NFS mount options.

*Table 33     Mount Options*

| Option | Description |
|--------|-------------|
| rw | Mount resource read-write. If no option is specified, the resource is mounted rw. |
| ro | Mount resource read-only. |
| suid | Allow set user ID execution. If no option is specified, the resource is mounted suid. |
| nosuid | Do not allow set user ID. |
| soft | Return an error if the server does not respond. |
| hard | Continue retrying the mount request until the server responds. |

*Table 33*   *Mount Options (Continued)*

| Option | Description |
|--------|-------------|
| intr | Allow keyboard interrupts to kill a process that is hung while waiting for a response on a hard-mounted file system. The default is intr. |
| nointr | Do not allow keyboard interrupts to kill a process that is hung while waiting for a response on a hard-mounted file system. |

The default auto_master map is shown below.

```
# Master map for automounter
#
+auto_master
/net        -hosts        -nosuid,nobrowse
/home       auto_home     -nobrowse
/xfn        -xfn
```

**New!**

You can also have an /- entry for an auto_direct map, as shown below.

```
# Master map for automounter
#
+auto_master
/net        -hosts        -nosuid,nobrowse
/home       auto_home     -nobrowse
/xfn        -xfn
/-          auto_direct   -ro
```

See "The Direct Map" on page 190 for more information about the direct map.

**New!**

Starting with the Solaris 2.6 release, the automounter supports browsability of indirect maps. The browse feature enables all of the potential mount points to be visible, regardless of whether they are mounted. You can turn off the browse feature with the -nobrowse option. By default, the auto_master map specifies the -nobrowse option to the entries for /home and /net. See "Disabling Automounter Browsability" on page 217 for more information.

Each client system has a copy of the default /etc/auto_master map. The +auto_master entry provides a link to the NIS, NIS+, or LDAP auto_master map. This entry is the first entry in the file, to ensure that the nameservice auto_master map overrides information that is specified locally. The /xfn entry provides a way for the federated nameservice to map composite names to a reference. For more information on xfn, refer to the xfn(3N) manual page.

*NOTE. The automounter provides backward compatibility with SunOS 4.x* auto.master *and other* auto. *files. If the automounter does not find any maps with an* auto_ *prefix, it searches for maps with the* auto. *prefix.*

The automount line of the /etc/nsswitch.conf file specifies the order in which local files and network databases are searched for information. The automounter uses the following entry in the nsswitch.conf file when the system is not using a nameservice.

```
automount: files
```

The automounter uses the following entry in the nsswitch.conf file when the system is using the NIS nameservice.

```
automount: files nis
```

The automounter uses the following entry in the nsswitch.conf file when the system is using the NIS+ nameservice.

```
automount: files nisplus
```

The automounter uses the following entry in the nsswitch.conf file when the system is using the LDAP nameservice.

```
automount: files ldap
```

See "The Nameservice Switch" on page 144 for more information.

The default auto_master map contains a /net mount point as part of an entry that automatically includes all of the systems under the special map -hosts. This built-in map uses the nameservice auto_master map to locate shared file systems on a remote host system when the user specifies a system by name. What this means to users is that they can gain access to any files on systems that are listed in the nameservice Hosts database with the usual Solaris commands. For example, suppose that Fred sends an e-mail telling you that a document is available on his system for review. Fred includes the system name—oak—and the path to the document—/export/home/fred/Newprojects/review.doc—in the e-mail message. He may show the path as /net/oak/export/home/fred/Newprojects/review.doc. To print the file without copying it to your local system, you would type the following command.

```
castle% lp /net/oak/export/home/fred/Newprojects/review.doc
castle%
```

To copy the file to your current working directory on your local system, you would type the following command.

```
castle% cp /net/oak/export/home/fred/Newprojects/review.doc .
castle%
```

If you know that the file is somewhere on the system named oak, but you are not sure of the complete path name, you can work your way down through the file system, as shown in the following example.

```
castle% cd /net/oak
castle% ls
export
castle% cd export;ls
home
castle% cd home;ls
fred ignatz newton magic
castle% cd fred;ls
Newprojects Status Oldprojects
castle% cd Newprojects;ls
review.doc
castle% pwd
/net/oak/export/home/fred/Newprojects
castle%
```

*New!*

*NOTE. This example works only if the home directory is shared.*

*New!*

If the nameservice is not running, the -hosts map consults the /etc/hosts file. For example, if a user types **cd /net/castle** and the system named castle is in the Hosts database, castle is mounted on /net as /net/castle. The -nosuid option prevents users from running setuid programs that are a security threat on the /net mount point. The -nobrowse option prevents users from viewing mount points that are not mounted.

The default auto_master map also contains a /home mount point and the auto_home map name so that you do not need to make a special entry in the auto_master map for auto_home. Sun recommends that you use /home/*username* as your naming convention instead of the /home/*system-name*/*username* convention.

*New!*

The auto_master map is parsed from top to bottom. The top entry takes precedence. Consequently, when you use NIS+ maps to set up a global namespace, the local /etc/auto_master maps should always have the +auto_master entry at the top of the file unless you specifically want to override something in the auto_master NIS or NIS+ map or you want to create a local map for testing.

You can add new entries to the nameservice auto_master map and take them away, although you should be careful when you delete entries from the nameservice auto_master map. For example, if you wanted to change the default mount point of the /net mount point, you could change the

`/net -hosts` entry to `/net -null` and define your new mount point. For example, to change the mount point to `/foo`, you would add the following entry.

```
/net     -null
/foo     -hosts    -setuid
```

*NOTE. Although you can change the default* `/net` *mount point, Sun recommends that you use the* `/net` *mount point to make the automounter easier to administer, to provide a consistent namespace for your users, and to ensure compatibility with future automounter releases.*

When you create new indirect or direct maps, you must add the mount points and map names to the nameservice `auto_master` table so that the automounter knows to look for them. See Chapter 8, "Setting Up the Automounter," for step-by-step instructions for creating indirect and direct maps and updating the `auto_master` map.

**The Home Directory Map**    The home directory indirect map, located in the `/etc` directory, is named `auto_home`. The default map contains a `+auto_home` link to the nameservice `auto_home` database.

The `auto_home` map has the following syntax.

```
username      [mount-options]      server:pathname
```

The user's login name is *username*, which is used as the mount point for the home directory. An optional, comma-separated list of options, [*mount-options*], controls the mounting of the user's home directory. If no options are specified, the home directory is mounted read-write. The *server:pathname* variable specifies the name of the server and the path to the user's home directory.

The default `auto_home` map is shown below.

```
# Home directory map for automounter
#
+auto_home
```

The local path is displayed as `/home/`*username*.

## The Direct Map

In a *direct map*, you can specify an absolute path name as the mount point.

Direct maps have the following syntax.

```
key      [mount-options]     server:pathname
```

The absolute path name, `key`, is used as the mount point. An optional, comma-separated list of options, [`mount-options`], controls the mounting of the resource. If no options are specified, the resource is mounted read-write. The name of the server and the path to the resource are `server:pathname`.

You can have only one direct map—which, by convention, is named `auto_direct`—because you can have only one `/-` entry in the `auto_master` file. Use it for all of the file systems you want to mount with an absolute path name.

Manual pages are a good example of an entry you might want to automount in a direct map. `/var/mail` is another example, especially if you use a central mail hub where you keep all user mailboxes. To show you the difference between indirect and direct maps for manual pages, let's first see how an indirect map would look. If you created an indirect map named `auto_man` to automount manual pages from a server named `oak` on mount point `/usr/man`, you would put the following entry in the `auto_master` file so the automounter knows to look for the `auto_man` indirect map.

```
/usr/man     auto_man     -ro
```

This entry references the following `auto_man` indirect map.

```
# Indirect map for man pages: auto_man
#
man1      oak:/usr/share/man/man1
man1b     oak:/usr/share/man/man1b
man1c     oak:/usr/share/man/man1c
man1f     oak:/usr/share/man/man1f
man1m     oak:/usr/share/man/man1m
man1s     oak:/usr/share/man/man1s
man2      oak:/usr/share/man/man2
man3      oak:/usr/share/man/man3
man3b     oak:/usr/share/man/man3b
man3c     oak:/usr/share/man/man3c
man3e     oak:/usr/share/man/man3e
man3g     oak:/usr/share/man/man3g
man3i     oak:/usr/share/man/man3i
man3k     oak:/usr/share/man/man3k
man3m     oak:/usr/share/man/man3m
man3n     oak:/usr/share/man/man3n
man3r     oak:/usr/share/man/man3r
man3s     oak:/usr/share/man/man3s
man3x     oak:/usr/share/man/man3x
man4      oak:/usr/share/man/man4
man4b     oak:/usr/share/man/man4b
man5      oak:/usr/share/man/man5
```

```
man6       oak:/usr/share/man/man6
man7       oak:/usr/share/man/man7
man9       oak:/usr/share/man/man9
man9e      oak:/usr/share/man/man9e
man9f      oak:/usr/share/man/man9f
man9s      oak:/usr/share/man/man9s
man1       oak:/usr/share/man/man1
mann       oak:/usr/share/man/mann
```

If you do not want to create directories for each manual group, you can instead create a direct map with a single entry to automount manual pages. You would add the following entry in the `auto_master` map.

```
/-            auto_direct  -ro
```

This entry references the following manual page `auto_direct` direct map.

```
# Direct map: auto_direct
#
# Entry for automounting manual pages
#
/usr/man    oak:/usr/share/man
```

This map creates a direct association between the shared directory and the mount point. In this case, you can clearly see the benefits of using a direct map.

> CAUTION. *Be sparing in your use of a direct map. A direct map locks you into a direct path, which is difficult to change on the fly. By contrast, indirect maps are more flexible. You can move the top-level mount points easily by changing the entry in the* `auto_master` *map and running the* `automount` *command on each client to refresh their view of the automounter hierarchy.*

## Syntax and Shortcuts for Map Entries

The following sections describe the syntax and shortcuts you can use for map entries. The examples show indirect maps, but you can also use these same shortcuts for the *mount-options* and *server:pathname* fields of direct maps.

### Specifying Multiple Servers

You can specify more than one server as the resource for one mount point. If you specify more than one server in the *server:pathname* field, the automounter mounts the file system from the first server that replies to the mount request from the local net or subnet. If no server responds, all of the servers on the list are retried.

The following syntax specifies multiple servers that contain identical copies of the same file system. The automounter could mount any of these file systems at the specified mount point on the client.

```
key      [mount-options]      server:pathname \
         [mount-options]      server:pathname \
         [mount-options]      server:pathname
```

The backslash at the end of each line tells the automounter to consider the entire entry as one line, and it makes the entry easier for administrators to read. The last entry line does not have a backslash because it ends the sequence. The following map entry example mounts the OpenWindows executable from one of the three listed servers.

```
openwin    -ro    oak:/usr/openwin \
           -ro    ash:/usr/openwin \
           -ro    elm:/usr/openwin
```

In the following entry, each server would be mounted with the same *mount-options*. You can combine the options after the key with the following syntax.

```
key      [mount-options]\
             server:pathname \
             server:pathname \
             server:pathname
```

The following example mounts any of these servers read-only.

```
openwin      -ro\
             oak:/usr/openwin\
             ash:/usr/openwin\
             elm:/usr/openwin
```

## Specifying Multiple Servers with the Same Path

You can shorten the previous example because each of the locations uses the same path. Use the following syntax to combine the server names on one line and separate them with commas.

```
key    [mount-options] server1,server2,server3:pathname
```

The following example combines *mount-options* for all servers and the names of the servers.

```
openwin      -ro    oak,ash,elm:/usr/openwin
```

## Specifying Weighting Factors for Each Server

You can specify weighting factors for each server in the list by putting a number in parentheses after the name of the server. `Server(0)` is most likely to be selected, with progressively higher values decreasing the chance of being selected. If you do not specify a number, the automounter assumes all servers in the list have a `(0)` weighting, and thus they all have equal priority.

> *NOTE. Versions of the automounter earlier than the Solaris 2.1 release do not recognize the server-weighting values. When the automounter does not recognize the weighting values, servers with such values are ignored. Consequently, if you want to share automount maps among systems of various release levels, do not use the weighting factors.*

The weighting factor syntax is shown below.

```
key        [mount-options]\
           server1(n),server2(n),server3(n):pathname
```

The following example combines `mount-options` for all servers and combines the names of the servers with weighting factors.

```
openwin    -ro\
           oak,ash(1),elm(2):/usr/openwin
```

In the above example, the server `oak` has the highest priority, `(0)`, the server `ash` has the second highest priority, and the server `elm`, the third. The locations of the servers are shown in Figure 25.

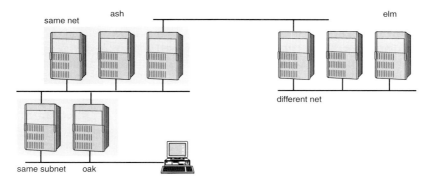

*Figure 25    Specifying Server Weighting Factors*

You can use the weighting factor for any list of servers, whether they are on individual lines or are combined on the same line. Just place the weighting factor number in parentheses after the name of the server.

*NOTE. Server proximity takes precedence over the weighting value. For example, a server on a local subnet is chosen even if it has a higher weighting value than a server on a different subnet. The weighting value is used to choose between servers that have the same network proximity.*

## Using Map Variables

The automounter provides predefined map variables, similar to environment variables, that you can use in defining paths. The Solaris map variables are ARCH and CPU.

When you include $ARCH as part of the path, the map variable returns the name of the system architecture as it would be returned by the uname -m command. In the following example, the uname -m command returns the architecture sun4u.

```
oak% uname -m
sun4u
oak%
```

When you include $CPU as part of the path, the map variable returns the name of the system architecture as it would be returned by the uname -p command. In the following example, the uname -p command returns the architecture sparc.

```
oak% uname -p
sparc
oak%
```

If you have a server exporting binaries for both SPARC and IA architectures from /usr/local/bin/sparc and /usr/local/bin/i486, respectively, you can use the $CPU command to create a map entry that mounts the binaries appropriate for each system's architecture. The entry would look like the following example.

```
bin     -ro     server:/usr/local/bin/$CPU
```

With this entry, the map can be used for clients running all architectures.

Starting with the Solaris 2.3 release, the additional predefined map variables shown in Table 34 are provided.

*Table 34    Predefined Map Variables*

| Variable | Means | Command | Example |
|----------|-------|---------|---------|
| ARCH | Architecture type. | uname -m | sun4, i486pc |
| CPU | Processor type. | uname -p | sparc, i486 |
| HOST | Host name. | uname -n | castle |
| OSNAME | Operating system name. | uname -s | SunOS |
| OSREL | Operating system release. | uname -r | 5.8 |
| OSVERS | Operating system version. | uname -v | Generic |

# Metacharacters

*New!*

The automounter recognizes some special characters to use for substitutions or to protect other characters from the autofs map parser.

## Ampersand (&)

You can use the ampersand (&) as a string substitution character for the key. For example, consider the following example map that specifies many subdirectories.

```
winsor          paperbark:/home/winsor
ray             paperbark:/home/ray
des             castle:/home/des
rob             seachild:/home/rob
```

You can use the ampersand character to substitute the key wherever it appears, as shown in the following example; this action changes the previous map.

```
winsor          paperbark:/home/&
ray             paperbark:/home/&
des             castle:/home/&
rob             seachild:/home/&
```

You can also use key substitutions in a direct map. You can write the following example

```
/usr/man      paperbark,castle,seachild:/usr/man
```

as

```
/usr/man      paperbark,castle,seachild:&
```

The ampersand substitution uses the whole key string, so if the key in a direct map starts with a / (as it should), the slash is carried over.

### Asterisk (*)

You can use the asterisk (*) to match any key. For example, you could use the following map entry to mount the /export file system from all hosts.

```
*      &:/export
```

The value of any given key is substituted for each ampersand. Autofs interprets the asterisk as an end-of-file character.

### Special Characters

The autofs parser is sensitive to names containing colons, commas, spaces, and so on. You should enclose these names in double quotes, as shown in the following example.

```
/vms      -ro    vmserver: -  -  -  "rc0:dk1 - "
/mac      -ro    g3:/ - "Macintosh HD - "
```

# [New!] Components of the Automounter

The automounter uses the following three components.

- The automount command—Installs autofs mount points and associates an automount map with each mount point.
- The autofs file system—Monitors attempts to access directories within the file system and notifies the automountd daemon.
- The automountd daemon—An RPC server that answers file system mount and unmount requests from autofs.

## The automount Command

The `automount` command is called at system startup by the `/etc/init.d/autofs` script. (This script also starts the `automountd` daemon.) The `automount` command reads the `auto_master` map file to create the initial set of autofs mount points, as shown in Figure 26, and then terminates. These mount points are only created at startup time (no file systems are mounted) and are subsequently used to mount file systems as requested by users. These mount points are also known as *trigger nodes*.

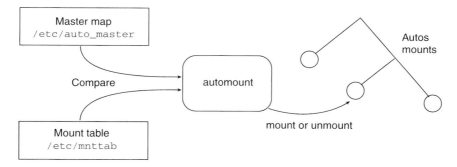

*Figure 26    How Autofs Uses the auto_master Map*

The `automount` command checks the `/etc/nsswitch.conf` file to determine which `auto_master` file to use: `files`, `nis`, `nisplus`, or `ldap`. The automount command does not read the `/etc/vfstab` file.

After system startup, you can run the `automount` command manually, as needed, to re-read the `auto_master` map and update any revised or new indirect maps.

## The Autofs File System

Autofs is a kernel file system that supports automatic mounting and unmounting. When a user makes a request to access a file system at an autofs mount point, autofs performs the following tasks.

1.  Autofs intercepts the request.
2.  Autofs sends a message to `automountd` to mount the requested file system.

    `automountd` locates the file system information in a map, creates the trigger nodes (if necessary), and performs the mount.
3.  Autofs enables the intercepted request to proceed.
4.  After a period of inactivity (the default is five minutes), autofs unmounts the file system.

### The automountd Daemon

Starting with the Solaris 2.5 release, the `automountd` daemon is completely independent of the `automount` command. Because of this separation, you can add, delete, or change map information without needing to stop and start the `automountd` process.

The `automountd` daemon is started at boot time by the `/etc/init.d/autofs` script (which also runs the `automount` command, reads the master map, and installs autofs mount points).

The `automountd` daemon subsequently responds to requests intercepted by autofs, locates the file system information in a map, creates the trigger nodes, and performs the mount.

## How the Automounter Works

*New!*

The descriptions in this section have been revised to reflect the Solaris 8 implementation of the automounter.

Figure 27 illustrates the automounter startup process. In the first step, the `automountd` daemon is started and continues to run as long as the system is up. The `automount` program is started, does the job specified in Figure 27, and then terminates.

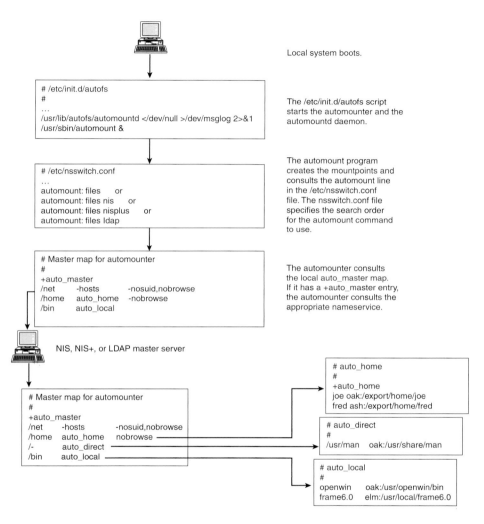

*Figure 27    Starting the Automounter*

## Automounter Behavior

After the startup process, the automounter works in the following way.

- Autofs intercepts any user requests to access file systems on autofs mount points.
- Autofs compares entries in the master map with entries in the mount table.

- If not already mounted, autofs sends a message to the `automountd` daemon to mount the requested file system.
- The `automountd` daemon locates the file system information in a map and mounts it.
- Autofs enables the intercepted request to proceed.
- After a period of inactivity (5 minutes by default), autofs unmounts the file system.

In other words, any time a user changes to a directory that has a mount point controlled by the automounter, autofs intercepts the request and instructs the `automountd` daemon to mount the remote file system if it is not already mounted.

On the other hand, when a user changes out of a directory controlled by the automounter, autofs instructs the `automountd` daemon to wait a predetermined amount of time (the default is 5 minutes) and unmount the file system if it has not been accessed during that time. Figure 28 shows how the automounter uses the automount maps on an NIS+ network to locate the file systems to mount.

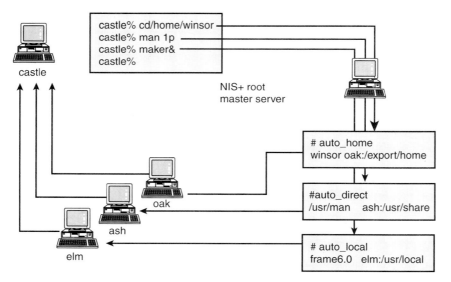

*Figure 28   How the Automounter Works*

- In Figure 28, when the user types **cd**, the automounter looks in the table that was created at boot time—created by the `automount` command from the NIS+ `auto_master` map and NIS+ `auto_home` map—and mounts the user's home directory from the server named `oak`. When the user types **man lp**, the automounter looks in the table that was created at boot time, mounts the manual pages on `/usr/man`, and displays the manual page for the `lp` command. After 5 minutes of inactivity, the manual pages are unmounted. When the user types **maker&**, the automounter looks in the table that was created at boot time and mounts the executable for FrameMaker on `/bin/frame6.0`.

## Hierarchical Mounting and Unmounting

*New!*

When an automounter map defines hierarchical layers, the mount process is essentially the same. When a user changes to the top level of the hierarchy, a trigger node is created. In addition, a trigger node to the next level (or levels) in the hierarchy is created so that the next levels can be mounted if they are accessed.

If hierarchical layers are defined, autofs unmounts the file systems after the specified idle time from the bottom up, that is, in the reverse order of mounting. If a directory at a higher level in the hierarchy is busy, file systems below that directory only are unmounted. During the unmounting process, any trigger nodes are removed and then the file system is unmounted. If the file system is busy, the unmount fails and the trigger nodes are reinstalled.

See "Creating Hierarchical Maps" on page 213 for an example of hierarchical maps.

# How to Plan for Automounting

In these discussions about the automounter, it is assumed that you are administering a network of systems running the Solaris Operating Environment and that you are using the NIS, NIS+, or LDAP nameservice. This configuration provides you with a global namespace so that you can mount file systems that are exported from any server on the network. It also creates host-independent resources so that you can specify a list of servers from which file systems can be mounted, and it enables you to relocate resources from one server to another without disrupting the user environment.

*New!*

*NOTE. Although you can set up the automounter by using local maps (`auto_master` files on a local system instead of with a nameservice), Sun strongly recommends that you do not do so to administer a site. Decentralized and local maps are more complicated and expensive to maintain, and they are difficult to update consistently. Using local automounter maps is, however, encouraged for testing on individual systems.*

## Recommended Automounting Policies

Before you begin planning your automounting, review the list of recommended policies in the following sections. They may affect how you set up your automount maps.

*New!*

- Use the default mount points `/net` and `/home`. If your site uses a different mount point naming scheme, convert your site gradually to use the default mount point names to ensure compatibility with future releases.
- Always use the NIS, NIS+, or LDAP maps. Discourage the use of local maps except for testing and debugging.
- Use indirect maps as much as you can to minimize the excessive network traffic that can be generated by direct maps.
- Use direct maps only when absolutely necessary, such as for `/var/mail` or for `/usr/share/man`.
- Use two-level home directory names (`/home/`*username*) instead of three-level home directory names (`/home/`*server*`/`*username*).
- Because the automounter uses the `/home` directory as a mount point, do not use just `/home` as the top-level directory name on the servers that contain users' home directories. Create a user's home directory as a three-level path (`/export/home/`*username*). Most importantly, make sure that user disk partitions are not mounted on or under `/home`. Multiple partitions may require separate mount points—for example, `/export/home1`, `/export/home2`, and so on.
- Do not automount local file systems or systems that are exported from a server. Mount them from the system's local `/etc/vfstab` file.
- Do not put entries that are already in the `/etc/vfstab` file into automount maps.
- If your site has a mixture of systems running SunOS 4.x and the Solaris Operating Environment, you do not need to change the names of your SunOS 4.x automount maps from `auto.`*variable* to `auto_`*variable*. NIS searches for `auto.master` if it cannot find an `auto_master` map.

*CAUTION. You should never change the SunOS 4.x `auto.master` map name; this name is required by the SunOS 4.x automounter.*

## Prerequisites for Using the Automounter

The following sections describe the prerequisites for using the automounter. Before you create automount maps, the network should be up and running a nameservice.

Each system on the network should have the default `auto_master` and `auto_home` maps in its local `/etc` directory. These maps are automatically installed with the system software.

## Servers and the Automounter

Automounter use is completely transparent to servers. A server has no way of telling whether file systems it shares are accessed by the `mount` command or by the automounter. As long as you set up your server file systems and share (export) them, you do not need to do any additional administration on the NFS server side to plan for or set up the automounter.

When planning for automounter setup on an NFS client, you need a list of servers that have the file systems you want to automount and the path to the resources on each of the servers.

If users can log in to an NFS server, you should set it up as an NFS client as well, and use the automounter to perform the NFS mounts, as needed. The automounter subsystem can deal internally with mounting NFS file systems it exports onto itself at the mount points specified in the automount maps. Do not try to manually mount local file systems at the automount mount points with `/etc/vfstab`; instead, let the automount subsystem handle mounting of local file systems.

*New!*

## Clients and the Automounter

As long as you use a nameservice to store automount maps, you do not need to do anything special to administer client systems of the automounter as long as the `/etc/nsswitch.conf` file is set up properly to access automount nameservice maps. If you use local `/etc/auto_variable` maps, you must manually update them with editors and distribute them with `rcp` or `rdist`.

*New!*

## Nameservice Maps

When you use a nameservice with the automounter, all you need to do to set up and administer the automounter is to create and modify the nameservice automount maps. Chapter 8, "Setting Up the Automounter," describes how to create, modify, and delete entries in nameservice automount maps.

The `auto_master` map must contain a list of mount points, optional mount options, and the names of the maps. The `auto_home` map must contain a list of user names and the server and the path to each user's home directory.

You can create additional indirect maps to provide access to executables, manual pages, source files, project files, or any other set of files that are made available from a server.

For example, you can add entries, such as the following to the
`auto_master` map for indirect maps.

```
/apps        auto_apps     -rw
/project     auto_project   -rw
```

Then, you can create the `auto_apps` and `auto_project` indirect maps to
specify the relevant files to mount. See "Creating Hierarchical Maps" on page
213 for an example of how to create an `auto_project` indirect map.

# 8

# *Setting Up the Automounter*

This chapter describes how to set up the automounter on a network that is running the NIS+ nameservice.

## Setting Up Automount Server Systems

A system that is an NFS server shares one or more of its file systems over the network. A server keeps a list of currently exported file systems and their access restrictions (such as read-write or read-only). You can share a resource by adding an entry to the /etc/dfs/dfstab (distributed file system table) on the server and then typing **shareall**. See the dfstab(4) and the share(1M) manual pages for more information.

You do not need to perform any additional steps on the NFS server to make the shared file systems available to the automounter running on NFS clients.

## Setting Up Automount Client Systems

Client systems that use the automounter need to have the default auto_master and auto_home maps in their local /etc directory. These default files are included in the system software installation. You should not need to edit these default files.

# Displaying Information About NIS+ Automount Maps

The following sections describe how to use the `-o` and the `-v` options to the `niscat` command to display information about the format and the content of NIS+ automount maps. You do not need to be root or a member of the `sysadmin` group (GID 14) to display information with the `niscat` command. You do need to have at least read permission for the NIS+ automount tables. See Chapter 5, "Introducing the NIS+ Environment," for more information about NIS+. For complete information about how to set up and administer NIS+, refer to the *Solaris Naming Setup and Configuration Guide*.

## Displaying the Format of NIS+ Automount Maps

Information used by NIS+ is stored in tables on the NIS+ root master server. Copies of these tables are stored on NIS+ replica servers. The automount maps are instances of NIS+ tables. You can display the format of any existing NIS+ automount map with the `niscat -o` command. The format shows information about the NIS+ table—its ownership and permissions—and the names, attributes, and access rights of each column. Use the `niscat -o` command for information such as the permissions for the map and the names of the columns.

The `niscat -o` command has the following syntax.

```
niscat -o table-name.directory.domain-name
```

The syntax for NIS+ automount tables is shown below.

```
niscat -o auto_name.org_dir.domain-name
```

*NOTE. NIS+ tables require a fully qualified domain name—the name of the map, the directory where the map is stored (`org_dir`), and the domain name, which must be followed by a dot ( . ). If you omit the trailing dot, a syntax error is displayed. If the `NIS_PATH` environment variable is set, then you do not have to specify the complete path to the `org_dir` directory. You can type **table-name.directory** (with no trailing dot) and press Return. The examples in this book use the fully qualified domain name. See Part 2 of this book for more information about NIS+.*

The following example displays format information about the NIS+ auto_home map in the `wellard.COM.` domain.

```
oak% niscat -o auto_home.org_dir.wellard.COM.
Object Name     : auto_home
Owner           : oak.wellard.COM.
Group           : admin.wellard.COM
Domain          : org_dir.wellard.COM.
Access Rights   : ----rmcdrmcdr---
Time to Live    : 12:0:0
Object Type     : TABLE
Table Type          : automount_map
Number of Columns   : 2
Character Separator :
Search Path         :
Columns             :
        [0]     Name        : key
                Attributes  : (SEARCHABLE, TEXTUAL DATA, CASE SENSITIVE)
                Access Rights : ----------------
        [1]     Name        : value
                Attributes  : (TEXTUAL DATA)
                Access Rights : ----------------
oak%
```

See Part 2 for more information on NIS+ security and on how to interpret that information.

## Displaying the Contents of NIS+ Automount Maps

You can display the content (or value) of any existing NIS+ automount map's columns with the `niscat -v` command. Use this command when you want to determine the values set for an automount map or to verify that an entry has been created successfully.

The syntax of the `niscat -v` command is shown below.

```
niscat -v table-name.directory.domain-name
```

The more specific syntax for NIS+ automount tables is shown below.

```
niscat -v auto_name.org_dir.domain-name
```

The `auto_master` file contains the following default entry that references the `auto_home` map.

```
/home     auto_home     -nobrowse
```

The following example uses the `niscat -v` command to show the NIS+ auto_home map for the `wellard.COM.` domain. This auto_home map

contains only one entry; the user `winsor` automounts a home directory from
`castle:/export/home/winsor`.

```
oak% niscat -v auto_home.org_dir.wellard.COM.
winsor   castle:/export/home/winsor
oak%
```

> *NOTE. The* `niscat` *command displays the values for the NIS+ table
> you specify as the argument to the command. The output lists the file
> systems that can be mounted but does not indicate whether the file
> systems are mounted.*

# Setting Up NIS+ Automount Maps

The setup and administration of automounting on a network running NIS+
involves creating and maintaining NIS+ automount maps. The steps in the
following sections describe how to create these maps on the NIS+ root master
server. See "Administering NIS+ Automount Maps" on page 214 for
information on how to modify existing maps.

## Setting Up the auto_home Map

The `auto_home` map is created when you set up the NIS+ root master server
and populated when you run the `nispopulate` command. You do not need to
create it separately. You do not need to make an entry for the `auto_home` map
in the NIS+ `auto_master` map. The entry is already included in the default
`auto_master` map.

## Setting Up Indirect Maps

Use the NIS+ command `nistbladm` to create and edit indirect maps on the
NIS+ root master server.

> *NOTE. The* `nistbladm` *command requires a fully qualified name for
> the table—that is, the name of the table, followed by the directory
> where the NIS+ tables are stored and the domain name. Note that for
> NIS+ commands, the domain name of a fully qualified name ends in
> a period. For example,* `auto_master.org_dir.wellard.COM.` *is
> the fully qualified name for the* `auto_master` *table, which is in the
> directory* `org_dir` *in the* `wellard.COM.` *domain.*

   1.   Decide which indirect maps you want to create. Make a list of the
        mount points, the servers, and the path names for each indirect map.

2. Log in to the NIS+ root master server.

   If you are a member of the group that has permission to edit NIS+ automount tables, you can edit the tables as yourself. Otherwise, you must become superuser on the NIS+ root master.

3. For each indirect map you want to create, all on one line, type **nistbladm -c** *automount_map* **key=S value=S \ auto_***table-name***.org_dir.***domainname* and press Return.

   The -c option creates the automount table, creates two columns named key and value—which are searchable—and assigns the table name auto_*table-name*. Note that any mount options you specify are part of the value.

4. For each entry in the table, all on one line, type **nistbladm -a \ key=***mount-point* **value=***options,pathname* **\ auto_***table-name***.org_dir.***domainname* and press Return.

   The -a option adds the entry to the table you specify, and the values are assigned to the columns.

5. To display the values in the table, all on one line, type **niscat -v \ auto_***table-name***.org_dir.***domainname* and press Return.

6. For each map you create, you must add an entry to the auto_master map.

   a. To display existing entries in the auto_master map, all on one line, type **niscat -o auto_master.org_dir.***domainname* and press Return.

   b. To add a new entry to the auto_master map, all on one line, type **nistbladm -a key=***mount-point* **value=***map-name* **\ auto_master.org_dir.***domainname* and press Return.

7. On each NFS client, type **automount** and press Return.

   Every file system that is currently not mounted by the automounter is updated. Any file system currently mounted is remounted at the new location if it is unmounted and reaccessed after the automount command is run.

*NOTE. The* auto_master *map is read only at boot time or when you manually run the* automount *command. After you have created new indirect maps and have added the mount point and map name to the* auto_master *map, run the* automount *command on any NFS clients to reread the automount maps. If the NFS server is also an NFS client of itself, also run the* automount *command on the NFS server.*

The following example creates an indirect automount map named auto_local in the org_dir domain for wellard.COM.. Two rows are entered in the table and the indirect map is added to the NIS+ auto_master table.

```
oak% su
Password:
oak# nistbladm -c automount_map key=S value=S auto_local.org_dir.wellard.COM.
oak# nistbladm -a key=openwin value=oak:/usr/openwin
  auto_local.org_dir.wellard.COM.
oak# nistbladm -a key=frame6.0 value=ash:/usr/local/frame6.0
  auto_local.org_dir.wellard.COM.
oak# niscat -v auto_local.org_dir.wellard.COM.
openwin  oak:/usr/openwin
frame6.0  ash:/usr/local/frame6.0
oak# niscat -o auto_master.org_dir.wellard.COM.
Object Name    : auto_master
Owner          : oak.wellard.COM.
Group          : admin.wellard.COM
Domain         : org_dir.wellard.COM.
Access Rights  : ----rmcdrmcdr---
Time to Live   : 12:0:0
Object Type    : TABLE
Table Type         : automount_map
Number of Columns  : 2
Character Separator  :
Search Path        :
Columns            :
        [0]     Name       : key
                Attributes   : (SEARCHABLE, TEXTUAL DATA, CASE SENSITIVE)
                Access Rights : ---------------
        [1]     Name       : value
                Attributes   : (TEXTUAL DATA)
                Access Rights : ---------------
oak# nistbladm -a key=/bin value=auto_local auto_master.org_dir.wellard.COM.
oak# niscat -v auto_master.org_dir.wellard.COM.
/bin auto_local
oak#
```

## Setting Up a Direct Map

You can set up a direct map in the same way that you set up indirect maps—with the NIS+ nistbladm command.

*New!*

Use the following steps to set up a direct map.

1. Add the /- entry to the auto_master map if the entry doesn't already exist.

2. Use the nistbladm -c command to add the auto_direct map to NIS+.

3. Use the nistbladm -a command to add entries to the auto_direct map.

4. Reboot each of the NFS clients.

   Regardless of which version of Solaris is running, you need to reboot each NFS client to reset an automount direct map, which is a good reason to use as few direct automount entries as possible. Indirect automount map entries don't have this limitation.

The following example sets up a direct map named `auto_direct`—with one entry for automounting manual pages—and adds it to the `auto_master` map.

```
oak% su
Password:
oak# nistbladm -c automount_map key=S value=S auto_direct.org_dir.wellard.COM.
oak# nistbladm -a key=/usr/man value=-ro,oak:/usr/share/man
  auto_direct.org_dir.wellard.COM.
oak# niscat -v auto_direct.org_dir.wellard.COM.
/usr/man  -ro  oak:/usr/share/man
oak# niscat -o auto_master.org_dir
Object Name    : auto_master
Owner          : oak.wellard.COM.
Group          : admin.wellard.COM
Domain         : org_dir.wellard.COM.
Access Rights  : ----rmcdrmcdr---
Time to Live   : 12:0:0
Object Type    : TABLE
Table Type         : automount_map
Number of Columns  : 2
Character Separator :
Search Path        :
Columns            :
        [0]        Name        : key
                   Attributes  : (SEARCHABLE, TEXTUAL DATA, CASE SENSITIVE)
                   Access Rights : ---------------
        [1]        Name        : value
                   Attributes  : (TEXTUAL DATA)
                   Access Rights : ---------------
oak# nistbladm -a key=/- value=auto_direct auto_master.org_dir.wellard.COM.
oak# niscat -v auto_master.org_dir.wellard.COM.
/- auto_direct
oak#
```

## Setting Up the NIS+ Master Map

When the NIS+ root master server is configured, the NIS+ `auto_master` map is created automatically. You do not need to create it as a separate step.

You do, however, need to provide an entry in the NIS+ `auto_master` map for the single direct map and for any additional indirect maps that you create.

The section "Setting Up Indirect Maps" on page 208 contains information on how to edit the NIS+ `auto_master` map. That information is summarized here for your reference.

Use the following steps to add an entry to the NIS+ `auto_master` map.

1. Display the names of the columns in the `auto_master` map by typing **niscat -o auto_master.org_dir.*domain-name*** and pressing Return.

2. To add each entry, all on one line, type **nistbladm -a \** **key=*mount-point* value=*map-name* \** **auto_master.org_dir.*domain-name*** and press Return.

3. On each NFS client, type **automount** and press Return.

   Every file system that is currently not mounted by the automounter is updated. Any file system currently mounted is remounted at the

new location if it is unmounted and reaccessed after the `automount`
command is run.

## Creating a Project Automount Map

If you are administering a large software development project, you can create
a project automount map to make all project-related files available under a
`/project` directory or a set of directories by project name. The following
example creates a `/project` directory and an `auto_project` map that are
accessible to all workstations on the network.

1. Add an entry for the `/project` directory to the NIS or NIS+
   `auto_master` map.

```
/project      auto_project      -nosuid
```

The `auto_project` map determines the contents of the `/project`
directory. As a security precaution, the `-nosuid` option prevents
users from running any setuid programs.

2. Create the `auto_project` map so that each entry describes a
   subproject, as shown in the following example.

```
compiler\
     /vers1.0      alpha:/export/project/&/vers1.0\
     /vers2.0      gamma:/export/project/&/vers2.0\
     /man          gamma:/export/project/&/man
windows\
     /vers1.0      alpha:/export/project/&/vers1.0\
     /man          gamma:/export/project/&/man
files\
     /vers1.0      alpha:/export/project/&/vers1.0\
     /vers2.0      gamma:/export/project/&/vers2.0\
     /vers3.0      gamma:/export/project/&/vers3.0\
     /man          gamma:/export/project/&/man
drivers\
     /vers1.0      alpha:/export/project/&/vers1.0\
     /man          gamma:/export/project/&/man
tools\
     /             charlie:/export/project/&
```

The ampersand (`&`) at the end of each entry is an abbreviation for the
entry key. See "Metacharacters" on page 195 for more information
about using metacharacters in automount maps.

As the project proceeds, you can relocate and expand various disk
partitions as needed by modifying the `auto_project` map without needing
to notify users. Because the NFS servers view the same autofs map as the
NFS clients, any users who log in to the NFS servers can find the `/project`
namespace. These users are provided with direct access to local files through
loopback mounts instead of NFS mounts.

## Creating Hierarchical Maps

*New!*

Starting with the Solaris 2.4 release, autofs supports hierarchical automount maps.

Do not use the -soft option when specifying hierarchical layers. If you use the -soft option, requests to reinstall the trigger nodes can time out. Failure to reinstall the trigger nodes leaves no access to the next level of mounts. The only way to clear this problem is either to wait for the file systems to be automatically unmounted by the automounter or to reboot the system.

Suppose you have an /etc/auto_master file that contains the following entry.

```
/share    auto_share
```

The auto_share map is shown below.

```
# share directory map for automounter
#
ws     /       castle:/export/share/ws
```

When a user accesses the /share/ws directory, the autofs service creates a trigger node for /share/ws.

The following example expands the auto_share map to contain hierarchical mount points.

```
# share directory map for automounter
#
ws     /       castle:/export/share/ws
       /usr    castle:/export/share/ws/usr
```

When a user accesses the /share/ws mount point, autofs creates the /share/ws trigger node. In addition, it creates a trigger node to the next level (/usr) so that the next level can be mounted if it is accessed.

Hierarchical mounts are unmounted from the bottom up in the reverse order of mounting. If one of the higher-level directories is busy, only file systems below that level are unmounted. Any trigger nodes are removed and then the file system is unmounted. If the file system is busy, the unmount fails and the trigger nodes are reinstalled.

## Administering NIS+ Automount Maps

The following sections describe how to modify entries in existing automount maps and how to delete entries from NIS+ automount maps.

### Modifying NIS+ Automount Maps

You can use the `-A` option for `nistbladm` to force an overwrite of information in an existing NIS+ automount map.

The syntax for the `nistbladm -A` option is shown below. You must specify a value for each of the columns in the table.

```
nistbladm -A column= ... table-name.domainname
```

The more specific syntax for NIS+ automount tables is shown below.

```
nistbladm -A key= value= auto_name.org_dir.domainname
```

In the following example, the administrator typed **key=bin** instead of **key=/bin** for the `auto_local` entry in the `auto_master` table.

```
# nistbladm -A key=bin value=auto_local auto_master.org_dir.wellard.com.
# niscat auto_master.org_dir
+auto_master
/net -hosts              -nosuid,nobrowse
/home auto_home -nobrowse
/xfn -xfn
bin auto_local
#
```

When the system booted, the automounter displayed the following error messages informing the administrator that the name `bin` in the `auto_master` table needed to be changed to `/bin`.

```
automount:  dir bin must start with '/'
automount:  /bin: Not a directory
```

The following entry corrects the problem.

```
# nistbladm -A key=/bin value=auto_local auto_master.org_dir.wellard.com.
# niscat auto_master.org_dir
+auto_master
/net -hosts              -nosuid,nobrowse
/home auto_home -nobrowse
/xfn -xfn
/bin auto_local
#
```

### Deleting Entries from NIS+ Automount Maps

You can delete rows from NIS+ automount maps with the `nistbladm -r` command by specifying one of the columns.

The syntax for the `nistbladm -r` option is shown below.

```
nistbladm -r column= table-name.domainname
```

The more specific syntax for NIS+ automount tables is shown below.

```
nistbladm -r column= auto_name.org_dir.domainname
```

If you create an incorrect entry, you can delete it. The administrator who created the `key=bin value=auto_local` entry in the NIS+ `auto_master` map can delete the entry and then create a new one, as shown in the following example.

```
oak% niscat -v auto_master.org_dir.wellard.COM.
bin   auto_local
/-    auto_direct
oak% nistbladm -r key=bin auto_master.org_dir.wellard.COM.
oak% niscat -v auto_master.org_dir.wellard.COM.
/-    auto_direct
oak% nistbladm -a key=/bin value=auto_local auto_master,org_dir.wellard.COM.
oak% niscat -v auto_master.org_dir.wellard.COM.
/bin   auto_local
/-    auto_direct
oak%
```

# Using a Public File Handle with the Automounter

*New!*

The Solaris 7 release introduced extensions to the `mount` and `automountd` command that enable the mount request to use the public file handle instead of the MOUNT protocol. This access method is the one used by the WebNFS service. By circumventing the MOUNT protocol, you can do the mount through a firewall. In addition, because fewer transactions are needed between the server and the client, the mount is faster. See Chapter 9, "Introducing WebNFS," for more information on the WebNFS protocol.

Follow these steps to use a public file handle with the automounter.

1. Become superuser.
2. In the automounter map, add the entry
   
   **/usr/local     -ro,public     *server:/filesystem***

The following example adds a public file handle for the
`/export/share/local` file system on `castle`.

```
/usr/local     -ro,public     castle:/export/share/local
```

The `public` option forces use of the public handle. If the NFS server does
not support a public file handle, the mount fails.

Mounts can fail with the `-public` option in certain conditions. Adding an
NFS URL can also confuse the situation. The following list describes how a
file system is mounted when the `-public` option is used.

- Using the `public` option with an NFS URL forces the use of the public
  file handle. The mount fails if the public file handle is not supported.
- Using the `public` option with a regular path forces the use of the public
  file handle. The mount fails if the public file handle is not supported.
- With an NFS URL only, use the public file handle if enabled on the NFS
  server. If the mount fails with the public file handle, try the mount with
  the mount protocol.
- Regular path only, do not use the public file handle. Use the MOUNT
  protocol.

The default public file handle (which is `0000`) skips all of the transactions
to get information from the portmap service and to determine the NFS port
number.

## Using NFS URLs with the Automounter

The Solaris 2.6 release introduced an extension to the NFS protocol to make a
file system on the Internet accessible through firewalls. The service is an
extension of the NFS version 3 and version 2 protocol. An NFS server
provides greater throughput under a heavy load than does HyperText
Transfer Protocol (HTTP) access to a Web server. This greater throughput can
decrease the time required to retrieve a file. In addition, the WebNFS protocol
provides the capability of sharing files without the administrative overhead of
an anonymous FTP site.

Use the following steps to use NFS URLs with the automounter.

1. Become superuser.
2. In the automounter map, add the entry
   **/usr/local     -ro     nfs://*server/filesystem*.**

The following example adds an NFS URL for the `/export/share/local` file system on `castle`.

```
/usr/local      -ro       nfs://castle/export/share/local
```

See Chapter 9, "Introducing WebNFS," for more information on the WebNFS protocol.

## Disabling Automounter Browsability

*New!*

Automounter browsability was introduced in the Solaris 2.6 release. The browse feature enables all of the potential mount points to be visible, regardless of whether they are mounted. You can turn off the browse feature with the `-nobrowse` option. Although the default version of the `/etc/auto_master` file specifies the `-nobrowse` option for the `/home` and `/net` entries, you may need to make manual changes or turn off browsability for site-specific autofs mount points after installation.

You can turn off the browsability feature in several ways.

- Disable browsability with the `-n` command-line option to the `automountd` daemon. This command completely disables autofs browsability for the NFS client.
- Disable browsability for each map entry on all clients that use autofs maps in either an NIS or NIS+ namespace.
- Disable browsability for each map entry on each client that uses local autofs maps if no nameservice is used.

### How to Completely Disable Autofs Browsability on a Single NFS Client

Use the following steps to completely disable autofs browsability on a single NFS client.

1. On the NFS client, become superuser.
2. As root, edit the `/etc/init.d/autofs` script and add the `-n` option to the line that starts the `automountd` daemon, as shown below.

```
/usr/lib/autofs/automountd -n < /dev/null > /dev/console 2>&1 # start daemon
```

3. Reboot the NFS client to restart the autofs service.

### How to Disable Autofs Browsability for All NFS Clients

You must use a nameservice such as NIS or NIS+ to disable browsability for all clients.

1. Add the `-nobrowse` option to each indirect map entry in the nameservice `auto_master` file.

2. On each NFS client, run the `automount` command.

   The new behavior takes effect after you run the `automount` command on the client system or after the system is rebooted.

If you are not using a nameservice, for each NFS client, manually edit the automounter maps, add the `-nobrowse` option to the indirect maps that you want to disable, and run the `automount` command.

## New! Troubleshooting Automounter Problems

If the automounter subsystem on an NFS client is not mounting file systems that are listed in your nameservice `auto_*` maps, use the following checklist.

1. Check the settings in the `/etc/nsswitch.conf` file to make sure that the automounter is able to read information from the specified nameservice—`nis`, `nisplus`, or `ldap`.

2. Check to make sure that the NFS client has the default `auto_master` and `auto_home` maps and that they are in the `/etc` directory.

3. If the maps are there, check to make sure that the `auto_master` map contains the `+auto_master` entry and that the `auto_home` map contains the `+auto_home` entry. These entries tell the automounter to use the NIS+ automounter maps. If the entries are not present, the automounter uses only the information from the local `/etc` automount maps.

## New! Automounter Error Messages

This section lists automounter error messages generated by the `automount -v` option and error messages that can appear at any time.

## automount -v Error Messages

When troubleshooting problems with the automounter, use the `automount -v` option. The following list shows the error messages generated by this command.

| |
|---|
| `bad key key in direct map mapname` |
| The automounter has found an entry key without a prefixed / while scanning a direct map. Keys in direct maps must be absolute path names. |
| `bad key key in indirect map mapname` |
| The automounter has found an entry containing a / while scanning an indirect map. Indirect map keys must be relative, not absolute path names. |
| `can't mount server:pathname: reason` |
| The mount daemon on the server refuses to provide a file handle for `server:pathname`. Check the export table on the server. |
| `couldn't create mount point mountpoint: reason` |
| The automounter was unable to create a mount point required for a mount. This condition occurs most frequently when autofs is trying to hierarchically mount all exported file systems of a server. A required mount point can exist only in a file system that cannot be mounted (it cannot be exported) and it cannot be created because the exported parent file system is exported read-only. |
| `leading space in map entry entry text in mapname` |
| The automounter has discovered an entry in an automap that contains leading spaces. This condition usually indicates an improperly continued map entry. Check map entries to make sure continued lines are properly terminated with a backslash (\). |
| `mapname: Not Found` |
| The automounter cannot locate the required map. This message is produced only with the `-v` option. Check the spelling and path name of the map name. |
| `remount server:pathname on mountpoint: server not responding` |
| The automounter has failed to remount a file system it previously mounted. |

| WARNING: *mountpoint* already mounted on |
|---|
| The automounter is trying to mount over an existing mount point. This error message means that an internal automounter error has occurred (an anomaly). |

## Miscellaneous Error Messages

| dir *mountpoint* must start with '/' |
|---|
| The automounter mount point must be an absolute path name. Check the spelling and path name of the mount point. |

| host *server* not responding |
|---|
| The automounter tried to contact *server* but received no response. |

| *hostname*: exports: *rpc_err* |
|---|
| The automounter encountered an error getting export list from *hostname*. This message indicates a problem with a server or network. |

| map *mapname*, key *key*: bad |
|---|
| The map entry is malformed and the automounter cannot interpret it. Recheck the entry; perhaps the entry contains characters that must be escaped. |

| *mapname*: *nis_err* |
|---|
| Error in looking up an entry in an NIS map. This message can indicate problems with NIS. |

| mount of *server*:*pathname* on *mountpoint*: *reason* |
|---|
| The automounter failed to do a mount. This message can indicate problems with a server or network. |

| *mountpoint*: Not a directory |
|---|
| The automounter cannot mount itself on *mountpoint* because it is not a directory. Check the spelling and path name of the mount point. |

| nfscast: cannot send packet: *reason* |
|---|
| The automounter cannot send a query packet to a server in a list of replicated file system locations. |

| nfscast: cannot receive reply: *reason* |
|---|
| The automounter cannot receive replies from any of the servers in a list of replicated file system locations. |

| nfscast: select: *reason* |
|---|
| The automounter encountered problems trying to ping servers for a replicated file system. This message can indicate a problem with the network. |
| pathconf: no info for *server*:*pathname* |
| The automounter failed to get pathconf information for path name. See the pathconf(2) manual page. |
| pathconf: *server*: server not responding |
| The automounter cannot contact the mount daemon on *server* that provides the information to pathconf(). |

## Other Errors with the Automounter

If the execute bit is set on the /etc/auto* files, the automounter tries to execute the maps, thereby creating the following type of error message.

```
/etc/auto_home: +auto_home: not found
```

Each entry in the file generates a similar error message. In this case, you would reset the permissions of the file as superuser by typing **chmod 644 /etc/auto_home** and pressing Return.

# 9

# *INTRODUCING*
# *WEBNFS*

Starting with the Solaris 2.6 release, the WebNFS protocol is added as an extension to the NFS version 3 and version 2 protocol. By default, all file systems that are available for NFS mounting are automatically available for WebNFS access. This chapter introduces WebNFS.

*New!*

## The WebNFS Service

WebNFS provides a standard file system for the Internet, enabling groups of people to collaborate on a document over the Internet or within the corporate intranet. With WebNFS, users can read and write to Web documents instead of simply viewing them.

Without WebNFS, most users access Web data through a browser and switch tasks and cut and paste to incorporate Web data into their local applications. With WebNFS, users can Web-enable any desktop application by providing file access methods that are compatible with the way applications now access local disks.

WebNFS complements HTTP, which is still needed for building Web pages and handles dynamic, multimedia-rich data. Because WebNFS servers can handle huge workloads, WebNFS servers can provide users with more reliable and responsive service than do FTP servers.

The WebNFS service makes files in a directory available to clients by means of a public file handle. A *file handle* is a kernel-generated address that identifies a file for NFS clients. The *public file handle* has a predefined value so the server does not need to generate a file handle for the client. Using the predefined file handle reduces network traffic by eliminating the need for the MOUNT protocol and increases response time for clients.

The default public file handle—established on the root file system of an NFS server—provides WebNFS access to any clients that already have mount privileges on the server. You can change the public file handle to point to any file system with the `share` command.

With the NFS protocol, when the client has the file handle for the file system, the protocol runs a LOOKUP to determine the file handle for the file to be accessed. Only one path name component is evaluated at a time. Each additional level of directory hierarchy requires another LOOKUP. By contrast, a WebNFS server can evaluate an entire path name with a single transaction—called a *multicomponent lookup*—when the LOOKUP is relative to the public file handle. With multicomponent lookup, the WebNFS server can deliver the file handle to the desired file without needing to exchange the file handles for each directory level in the path name.

In addition, an NFS client can initiate concurrent downloads over a single TCP connection, and thereby provide quick access without the additional load required by setting up multiple connections. Although Web browser applications support concurrent downloading of multiple files, each file has its own connection. By using one connection, the WebNFS software reduces the overhead on the server.

Clients can access files that are symbolically linked to another file system if the client already has access through normal NFS activities.

Normally, an NFS URL is evaluated relative to the public file handle. You can change the evaluation to be relative to the root file system of the server by adding an additional slash to the beginning of the path. In the following example, if the public file handle has been established on the `/export/ftp` file system, the following two NFS URLs are equivalent.

```
nfs://server/example
nfs://server//export/ftp/example
```

# WebNFS Security Negotiation

The Solaris 8 release includes a new protocol that enables a WebNFS client to negotiate a selected security mechanism with a WebNFS server. The new protocol uses security negotiation multicomponent lookup, which is an extension to the multicomponent lookup used in earlier versions of the WebNFS protocol.

The WebNFS client has no knowledge of how a path is protected by the server. When a WebNFS client makes a regular multicomponent lookup request with the public file handle, the default security mechanism is used. If the default security mechanism is not sufficient, the server replies with an AUTH_TOOWEAK error stating that the client needs to use a stronger authorization mechanism.

When the client receives the AUTH_TOOWEAK error, it sends a request to the server to determine which security mechanisms are required. If the request succeeds, the server responds with an array of security mechanisms required for the specified path. Depending on the size of the array, the client may have to make more requests to get the complete array. If the server does not support WebNFS security negotiation, the request fails.

After a successful request, the WebNFS client selects the first security mechanism from the array and issues a regular multicomponent lookup request, using the selected security mechanism to acquire the file handle. All subsequent NFS requests are made with the selected security mechanism and the file handle.

# WebNFS Limitations with Web Browsers

The WebNFS service does not support several functions that a Web site using HTTP can provide. The NFS server sends only the file, so any special processing must be done on the client. If you need one Web site configured for both WebNFS and HTTP access, consider the following issues.

- NFS browsing does not run CGI scripts, so a file system with an active Web site that uses many CGI scripts may not be appropriate for NFS browsing.
- The browser might start different viewers to handle files in different file formats. An external viewer is started when these files are accessed through an NFS URL as long as the file type can be determined from the file name. The browser should recognize any file-name extension for a standard MIME type when an NFS URL is used. Because the WebNFS software does not check inside the file to determine the file type, the file-name extension is the only way WebNFS can determine a file type.

- NFS browsing cannot use server-side image maps (clickable images). It can, however, use client-side image maps because the URLs are defined with the location. No additional response is required from the document server.

# Planning for WebNFS Access

To use the WebNFS functionality, you first need an application capable of running and loading an NFS URL (for example, `nfs://server/path`). Then you choose the file system to export for WebNFS access. If the application is a Web browser, often you can use the document root for the Web server. You need to consider several factors when choosing a file system to export for WebNFS access.

- Each server has one public file handle that, by default, is associated with the root file system of the server. The path in an NFS URL is evaluated relative to the directory associated with the public file handle. If the path leads to a file or directory within an exported file system, the server provides access. You can use the `-public` option to the `share` command to associate the public file handle with a specific exported directory. When you use this option, URLs relative to the shared file system are allowed instead of relative to the root file system of the server. By default, the `public` file handle points to the root file system, but this file handle does not enable Web access unless the root file system is shared.

- The WebNFS environment enables users who already have mount privileges to access files through a Web browser regardless of whether the file system is exported with the `-public` option. Because users already can access these files with the NFS setup, no additional security risk should be created. You need to share a file system with the `-public` option only if users who cannot mount the file system with NFS need WebNFS access.

- File systems that are already open to the public are good candidates for the `-public` option. Examples are the top directory in an FTP archive or the main URL directory for a Web site.

- You can use the `-index` option with the `share` command to force the loading of an HTML file instead of listing the directory when an NFS URL is accessed.

After you choose a file system, review the files and set access permissions to restrict viewing of files and directories as needed. Establish the permissions as appropriate for any shared NFS file system. For many sites,

755 permissions for directories and 644 permissions for files provide the correct level of access.

# WebNFS Access

Starting with the Solaris 2.6 release, by default, all file systems available for NFS mounting are automatically available for WebNFS access. The only times you need to explicitly enable WebNFS access is on servers that do not already enable NFS mounting, when you want to reset the -public file handle—which, by default points to the root file system, or when the -index option is required.

Use the following steps to enable WebNFS access.

1. Become superuser.
2. Edit the /etc/dfs/dfstab file and add one entry for each file system by using the -public option.

   The -index option in the following example is optional.

```
share -F nfs -o ro,public,index=index.html /export/ftp
```

   After you edit the /etc/dfs/dfstab file, you can share the file system by stopping and starting the NFS server, by rebooting the system, or by using the shareall command. If you stop and restart the NFS server, you do not need to run the shareall command because the script runs the command.

3. Type **shareall** and press Return.
4. Type **share** and press Return.

   Review the output to check that the correct file systems are shared and the options are correct.

5. (Optionally) Type **/etc/init.d/nfs.server stop** and press Return. Then type **/etc/init.d/nfs.server start** and press Return.

   NFS service is started.

   The following example shows the correct options for /export/ftp.

```
# share
-       /export/ftp      ro,public,index=index.html   ""
#
```

# *Part Four*

# Service Access Facility

This part describes the Solaris Service Access Facility (SAF) in three chapters.

Chapter 10 provides an overview of the SAF and describes the port monitors and services used by the SAF. Chapter 11 describes how to set up and administer the SAF for modems and terminals. Chapter 12 describes how to set up and administer the SAF for printers and how to troubleshoot printing problems.

Refer to the chapters in this part if you need to set up a new SAF service for terminals, modems, or printers, or to modify an existing configuration.

# 10

# *UNDERSTANDING THE SERVICE ACCESS FACILITY*

The service access facility (SAF) is a group of daemons and administrative commands that provide a flexible administrative framework for managing service requests in an open-systems environment. You can use the SAF to set up and administer port monitors so that users can log in from a terminal or a modem and can use network printing resources. The SAF replaces the SunOS 4.x `getty`, `login`, and `stty` commands and the `/etc/gettytab` and `/etc/ttytab` files. SAF controls and configures terminals with the `terminfo` database.

You can use the Admintool: Serial Ports graphical user interface to set up and configure modems and character terminals on a local system. See "Admintool: Serial Ports and SAF" on page 257 for more information. Alternatively, you can use the Solaris Management Console (SMC) Serial Ports graphical user interface—available with the Solaris 8 Update 3 release—to set up and configure modems and character terminals.

> NOTE. *The Solaris Management Console (SMC) tools in the Solaris 8 Update 3 release replace the Solaris AdminSuite 3.0 tools from Solaris Admin Pack.*

## Benefits of the SAF

The SAF is an open-systems solution that controls how users access their UNIX system through TTY devices and local area networks. The SAF offers

231

well-defined interfaces so that customers and value-added resellers can easily add new features and configure existing ones.

Flexibility is an important requirement in an open-systems environment. Service of incoming connection requests must be available regardless of the location or connection path of the requester. As much as possible, both local and remote requests must be handled independently of the available network transports.

Restrictions in previous System V and BSD-based versions of UNIX prevented this type of open-systems computing environment. The following list describes the restrictions.

- Lack of selective access control.
- Inflexible `getty` process. Only the login service was provided because it was hardwired in.
- Difficulty in selectively disabling or enabling login service.
- Impossibility of scaling an increasing number of ports because the model is one `getty` per potential access port.
- Inaccuracy of `/etc/utmpx` in accounting for remote services.
- Mixed or no authentication for non-RPC and TCP/IP requests.

You can use the Solaris SAF framework if you want to create a complex application, such as the banking database service shown in Figure 29.

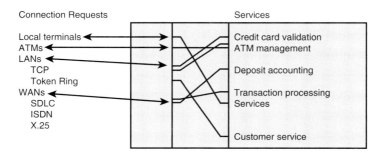

*Figure 29    A Typical Bank Database Server*

The left side of the figure shows incoming connection requests for services—some from local terminals, others from automatic teller machines (ATMs). The right side shows the service that is provided. Many requests come from local area networks that are running a variety of different transport protocols. Bank networks usually have wide-area network connections, such as X.25, SDLC, frame relay, and ISDN, over a variety of datalink layers.

# The SAF Daemons

The SAF uses the Service Access Controller daemon (sac) to oversee all of the SAF port monitors. The sac daemon is started at boot time at run level 2 by init.

The following two port monitors watch for activity on a port.

- The ttymon port monitor handles requests for login services. Solaris provides a default set of ttymon services for use with a stand-alone system. You need to set up a ttymon port monitor to process login requests from modems and additional terminals (such as Wyse or VT terminals) if you configure them for a system.

- The listen port monitor handles requests for network services such as remote printing and remote file access. You need to set up a listen port monitor to provide remote printing services.

After the ports are configured, the port monitors are automatically started any time a system is running in multiuser mode. The ttymon and listen port monitors are described in more detail in "Port Monitors" on page 235.

# The SAF Commands

You can use three SAF commands to administer modems and alphanumeric terminals—sacadm, pmadm, and ttyadm. You can also use three SAF commands to administer printing—sacadm, pmadm, and nlsadmin.

Use the sacadm command to add and remove port monitors. This command is your main link with the Service Access Controller (SAC) and its administrative files /etc/saf/_sactab, /etc/saf/_safconfig, and /etc/saf/pmtag/_config.

*NOTE. Although these configuration files are ASCII text and can be edited, the SAC may not be aware of the changes. Sun recommends that you do not edit these files directly. Instead, use the* sacadm *and* pmadm *commands to make changes to the SAF administrative files.*

Use the pmadm command to add or remove a service and to associate a service with a particular port monitor. Each port monitor has its own administrative file.

You can use two additional commands, ttyadm and nlsadmin, as part of the command-line arguments to pmadm to provide input specific to a port monitor. The `ttyadm` command provides information for the `ttymon` port monitor; the `nlsadmin` command provides information for the `listen` port monitor. SAF commands, which use many options and arguments, can be quite lengthy. See "Reference to SAF Commands, Tasks, and Options" on page 250 for more information.

# SAF Architecture

Figure 30 shows the architecture of SAF. Each of the architectural elements is described in the following paragraphs.

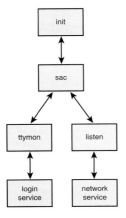

*Figure 30*    *Service Access Facility Architecture*

## The init Process

The init process controls the overall state of the UNIX operating system and creates processes by using the information stored in the `/etc/inittab` file. The init process monitors the `sac`. The `/etc/inittab` file has an entry that restarts the `sac` process if `init` receives a signal indicating that the `sac` process has died.

## Service Access Controller

The `sac` daemon controls the overall state of arbitrary processes that are started in response to connection requests. The `sac` daemon receives all of the requests to enable, disable, start, or stop port monitors and takes the appropriate action. If port monitor processes are terminated, `sac` is responsible for restarting them.

The `sac` is started from the following entry in the `/etc/inittab` file.

```
sc:234:respawn:/usr/lib/saf/sac -t 300
```

*NOTE. The `rc` scripts do not start or control the `sac` process.*

When `sac` is started, it first customizes its own environment by reading the `/etc/saf/_sysconfig` configuration file. Each system has one `/etc/saf/_sysconfig` file. When the `sac` process is started, this file is interpreted and used for all of the port monitors on the system. Modifications to the environment from this file are inherited by all of `sac`'s child processes.

Then, `sac` starts all of the designated port monitors by using information from the `/etc/saf/_sactab` file. For each port monitor to be started, `sac` forks a port monitor child process. The `ttymon` port monitor reads its configuration information from the `/etc/saf/`*pmtag*`/_pmtab` port monitor table. If configured, the `listen` port monitor reads its configuration information from the `/etc/saf/`*pmtag*`/_pmtab` file. You set the value of the *pmtag* variable when you use the `sacadm` command to create the port monitor. The default name for the `ttymon` port monitor for serial ports is `zsmon`; the default name for the `listen` port monitor is `tcp`.

Once the port monitors are running, `sac` polls them periodically for status information. If a port monitor that should be running has stopped, `sac` restarts it if a non-zero restart count was specified with the `-n` *count* option to the `sacadm` command when the port monitor was created.

## Port Monitors

Port monitors monitor a set of homogeneous incoming requests on a system port, detect incoming requests, and connect them to the appropriate service process. As already mentioned, the Solaris Operating Environment provides a TTY port monitor daemon named `ttymon` and a network port monitor daemon named `listen`.

To find out which port monitors are running and to show their status, type **sacadm -l** and press Return.

```
oak% /usr/sbin/sacadm -l
PMTAG          PMTYPE         FLGS RCNT STATUS    COMMAND
zsmon          ttymon         -    0    ENABLED   /usr/lib/saf/ttymon #
oak%
```

In the above example, only the `ttymon` monitor, which is identified by the default port monitor tag of `zsmon`, is started, and the status is ENABLED.

Table 35 describes the fields shown in the output of the `sacadm -l` command.

*Table 35     Fields in the sacadm -l Output*

| Field | Description |
|-------|-------------|
| PMTAG | A unique tag that identifies a particular port monitor. The system administrator assigns the name of the port monitor. `sac` uses the pmtag to identify the port monitor for all ports it administers. Use the default `ttymon` pmtag, `zsmon`, for `ttymon` ports A and B; use the `listen` pmtag, `tcp`, for listen ports in the United States. PMTAG can contain up to 14 alphanumeric characters. |
|  | The default `ttymon` pmtag, `zsmon`, was chosen because SPARCstation serial port chips are made by Zilog. In practice, a server may have hundreds of serial ports. If so, Sun recommends creating one port monitor for each serial port device. For example, consider a server that has two built-in serial ports and two add-in serial port boards, known as *asynchronous line multiplexers*, or *ALMs*. You could set up three port monitors and name them `zsmon`, `alm1`, and `alm2`. The service tag svctag—which specifies the name of the port in the `/dev/term` directory—could be named a and b for `zsmon`, and `0-7` for `alm1` and `alm2`. (An `alm` usually has eight ports, numbered 0 through 7.) |
|  | The default `listen` pmtag, `tcp`, was chosen because the device associated with it is the network. In the United States, the network is usually `tcp`. In Europe, the network is usually `X.25`. Always create the pmtag `listen` variable in such a way that it describes the network. |
| PMTYPE | The type of the port monitor: `ttymon` or `listen`. |
| FLGS | If no flag is specified, the port monitor is started and enabled. The d flag specifies that when the port monitor is started, it is not enabled. The x flag specifies that the port monitor is not to be started. |
| RCNT | Retry count specifies the number of times a port monitor can fail before its state is changed to FAILED. If no count is specified, the field is set to 0 and the port monitor is not restarted if it fails. |

*Table 35* *Fields in the sacadm -l Output (Continued)*

| Field | Description |
|---|---|
| STATUS | The status of activity for the port monitor. Possible states are STARTING, ENABLED, DISABLED, STOPPING, NOTRUNNING, and FAILED. The FAILED message is displayed if SAC cannot start the port monitor after the number of tries specified by RCNT. |
| COMMAND | The complete path name of the command that starts the port monitor, which is followed by a # and any comment that was entered when the port monitor was configured. |

Refer to Chapter 11, "Setting Up Modems and Character Terminals," for information about how to configure, start, and enable the ttymon port monitor. Refer to Chapter 12, "Setting Up Printing Services," for information about how to configure, start, and enable the listen port monitor.

To view the contents of the port monitor administrative file, type **pmadm -l** and press Return.

```
oak% /usr/sbin/pmadm -l
PMTAG           PMTYPE          SVCTAG          FLGS ID        <PMSPECIFIC>
zsmon           ttymon          ttya            u    root      /dev/term/a I -
 /usr/bin/login - 9600 ldterm,ttcompat ttya login:  - tvi925 y  #
zsmon           ttymon          ttyb            u    root      /dev/term/b I -
 /usr/bin/login - 9600 ldterm,ttcompat ttyb login:  - tvi925 y  #
oak%
```

In the above example, the ttymon ports /dev/term/a and /dev/term/b show the default Solaris configuration. Table 36 describes the fields shown in the output of the pmadm -l command.

*Table 36* *Fields in the pmadm -l Output*

| Field | Description |
|---|---|
| PMTAG | A unique tag that identifies a particular port monitor. The system administrator assigns the name of the port monitor. The pmtag is used by sac to identify the port monitor for all of the administration. Use the default pmtag zsmon for ttymon ports; use the pmtag tcp for listen ports. PMTAG can contain up to 14 alphanumeric characters. |
| PMTYPE | The type of the port monitor: ttymon or listen. |
| SVCTAG | A tag unique to the port monitor that identifies a service. The service tags for the serial ports are ttya and ttyb. A service requires both a service tag and a port monitor tag to uniquely identify it. |

*Table 36     Fields in the pmadm -l Output (Continued)*

**New!**

| Field | Description |
|-------|-------------|
| FLGS | If no flag is specified, the port is enabled and no utmpx entry is created for the service. (utmpx replaces the obsolete utmp database file.) The x flag specifies that the port should not be enabled; the u flag specifies that a utmpx entry should be created for this service. Some services, such as login, will not start unless a utmpx entry has been created. |
| ID | The login name of the person who starts the service, typically root. |
| PMSPECIFIC | The address, name of a process, name of a STREAMS pipe, or baud rate and configuration for a login port. |

## The ttymon Port Monitor

The ttymon STREAMS-based port monitor performs the functions provided by the getty process in SunOS 4.x system software. In addition, ttymon initializes and monitors tty ports, sets terminal modes and line speeds, invokes service on serial ports when it receives a connection request, and idles while a service is connected.

> *NOTE. In Solaris 2.x, the serial ports* /dev/term/a *and* /dev/term/b *are provided with a default configuration for the* ttymon *port monitor with a pmtag of* zsmon.

Each instance of ttymon can monitor multiple ports, as specified in the port monitor's administrative file. You configure the administrative file with the pmadm and ttyadm commands.

When an instance of ttymon is started by the sac daemon, ttymon starts to monitor the ports that are under SAF control. For each port, it first initializes the line disciplines, if specified, and the speed and terminal settings. The values it uses for terminal initialization are taken from the appropriate entry in the /etc/ttydefs file, which is maintained by the sttydefs command. Default line disciplines on ports are set up by the autopush(1M) command. You do not need to do anything to configure autopush.

## The listen Port Monitor

The listen process "listens" for network service requests, accepts requests when they arrive, and starts services in response to the requests.

> *NOTE. No* listen *processes are started by default in the Solaris Operating Environment.*

The listen process provides services similar to those provided by the traditional Internet Services daemon, inetd. In Solaris 2.x system software, the inetd daemon is started with the -s option to run stand-alone outside of the SAF.

*CAUTION. The Solaris Operating Environment does not support running* inetd *under SAF. Be sure that the* -s *option is always present.*

## Service Invocations

A *service invocation* is a process that provides the requested service to the incoming connection request. A service invocation can be a process such as login or lp. The ttymon port monitor works with the login process, and the listen port monitor works with the LP print service. The SAF architecture is structured so that programmers can write new port monitors to support other processes specified by the port monitor.

## Port Monitor States

Once added, port monitors can be operational, transitional, or inactive in one of the six states shown in Figure 31.

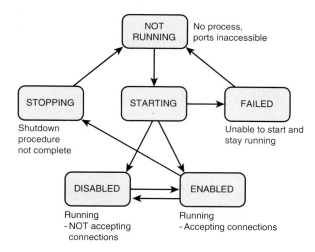

*Figure 31    Port Monitor State Model*

## Operational States

Port monitor operational states are ENABLED and DISABLED. Port monitors are started and enabled by default when you add them. Port monitors are stopped and disabled by default when you remove them. When a port monitor is enabled, it accepts requests for service. When a port monitor is disabled, existing services continue, but new service requests are refused. When a port monitor service is killed, all of its services are terminated.

## Transitional States

A port monitor can be STARTING or STOPPING. When a port monitor is in the process of starting, it is in an indeterminate state in the process of becoming either ENABLED or DISABLED. When a port monitor is stopping, it has been terminated manually but has not yet completed its shutdown procedure. Consequently, it is in an indeterminate state in the process of becoming NOTRUNNING.

## Inactive States

An inactive port monitor is either NOTRUNNING or FAILED. A failed port monitor is unable to start and remain running. When a port monitor is not running, it has been killed. All ports it was monitoring are inaccessible. Unlike the disabled state, when a port monitor is not running, the system cannot write a message on the inaccessible port telling the user that it is disabled.

# The Line Control Model

The line control model for the Solaris Operating Environment is different from that of Solaris 1.x releases. The files /etc/gettytab and /etc/ttytab have been removed. Line settings are stored in the /etc/ttydefs file and in the ttymon configuration files. Table 37 compares the Solaris 1.x and Solaris 2.x line control models.

*Table 37*     *Comparison of Solaris 1.x and Solaris 2.x Line Control Models*

| Feature | Solaris 1.x File | Solaris 2.x File |
|---|---|---|
| Database descriptor. | /etc/termcap /etc/terminfo | /etc/terminfo |
| Set terminal I/O operation. | stty (BSD) | stty (SVR4) |
| Line settings and sequences. | /etc/gettytab /etc/ttytab | /etc/ttydefs |

*Table 37* *Comparison of Solaris 1.x and Solaris 2.x Line Control*
*Models (Continued)*

| Feature | Solaris 1.x File | Solaris 2.x File |
|---|---|---|
| Administer-TTY definitions. | | `ttydef(1M)` |

Figure 32 shows the interaction of the terminal control and the SAF. The
`init` program starts `sac`, which controls the `ttymon` port monitor. In turn,
`ttymon` monitors serial port devices. It connects incoming requests to
services, which are usually login processes. Port monitors keep a close watch
over the device or network transport, add and delete services, and start and
stop services at the appropriate time. You can use the `stty` and `tput`
commands to configure the terminal I/O settings to match the characteristics
of the terminal. When `ttymon` gets a character from the terminal, it starts a
login to the terminal. When the user logs out, `ttymon` hangs up to recycle the
serial port and waits for another service request.

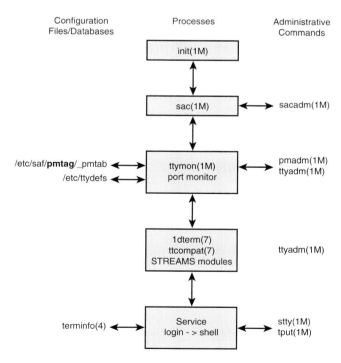

*Figure 32* *Terminal Control Architecture*

## The /etc/ttydefs File

The `/etc/ttydefs` file defines baud rates and terminal settings for TTY ports. When you set up modems, you use the `ttyadm -l` *ttylabel* argument as part of the `pmadm` command-line argument to specify information about the baud rate and the modem settings. The *ttylabel* variable specifies the first field for an entry in the `/etc/ttydefs` file. When `ttymon` initializes a port, it uses the information from the `/etc/saf/`*pmtag*`/_pmtab` file to search the `/etc/ttydefs` file for an entry that contains the *ttylabel* that matches the *ttylabel* for the port. The `ttydefs` file is similar to the old `gettydefs` file. Each entry in the `/etc/ttydefs` file has five fields, which are separated by colons.

```
ttylabel:initial-flags:final-flags:autobaud:nextlabel
```

- The *ttylabel* field contains the TTY label that matches the port.
- The *initial-flags* field contains the initial terminal input and output settings.
- The *final-flags* field contains the terminal input and output values set by `ttymon` after a connections request is made but before the port service is started.
- The *autobaud* field enables `ttymon` to determine the line speed of the TTY port by analyzing the first Return received and setting the speed accordingly. To enable autobaud, the field must contain the character `A`. If the field is empty, autobaud is disabled.
- The *nextlabel* field specifies a hunt sequence that links speeds together in a closed set. For example, 4800 may be linked to 1200, which is linked to 2400, which is linked to 4800. If the current `ttydefs` entry does not provide a compatible line speed, the next speed in the sequence is tried. The default `/etc/ttydefs` file is shown below.

```
# VERSION=1
460800:460800 hupcl:460800 hupcl::307200
307200:307200 hupcl:307200 hupcl::230400
230400:230400 hupcl:230400 hupcl::153600
153600:153600 hupcl:153600 hupcl::115200
115200:115200 hupcl:115200 hupcl::76800
76800:76800 hupcl:76800 hupcl::57600
57600:57600 hupcl:57600 hupcl::38400
38400:38400 hupcl:38400 hupcl::19200
19200:19200 hupcl:19200 hupcl::9600
9600:9600 hupcl:9600 hupcl::4800
4800:4800 hupcl:4800 hupcl::2400
2400:2400 hupcl:2400 hupcl::1200
1200:1200 hupcl:1200 hupcl::300
300:300 hupcl:300 hupcl::460800

460800E:460800 hupcl evenp:460800 evenp::307200
307200E:307200 hupcl evenp:307200 evenp::230400
230400E:230400 hupcl evenp:230400 evenp::153600
153600E:153600 hupcl evenp:153600 evenp::115200
115200E:115200 hupcl evenp:115200 evenp::76800
```

```
76800E:76800 hupcl evenp:76800 evenp::57600
57600E:57600 hupcl evenp:57600 evenp::38400
38400E:38400 hupcl evenp:38400 evenp::19200
19200E:19200 hupcl evenp:19200 evenp::9600
9600E:9600 hupcl evenp:9600 evenp::4800
4800E:4800 hupcl evenp:4800 evenp::2400
2400E:2400 hupcl evenp:2400 evenp::1200
1200E:1200 hupcl evenp:1200 evenp::300
300E:300 hupcl evenp:300 evenp::19200

auto:hupcl:sane hupcl:A:9600

console:9600 hupcl opost onlcr:9600::console
console1:1200 hupcl opost onlcr:1200::console2
console2:300 hupcl opost onlcr:300::console3
console3:2400 hupcl opost onlcr:2400::console4
console4:4800 hupcl opost onlcr:4800::console5
console5:19200 hupcl opost onlcr:19200::console

contty:9600 hupcl opost onlcr:9600 sane::contty1
contty1:1200 hupcl opost onlcr:1200 sane::contty2
contty2:300 hupcl opost onlcr:300 sane::contty3
contty3:2400 hupcl opost onlcr:2400 sane::contty4
contty4:4800 hupcl opost onlcr:4800 sane::contty5
contty5:19200 hupcl opost onlcr:19200 sane::contty

4800H:4800:4800 sane hupcl::9600H
9600H:9600:9600 sane hupcl::19200H
19200H:19200:19200 sane hupcl::38400H
38400H:38400:38400 sane hupcl::2400H
2400H:2400:2400 sane hupcl::1200H
1200H:1200:1200 sane hupcl::300H
300H:300:300 sane hupcl::4800H

conttyH:9600 opost onlcr:9600 hupcl sane::contty1H
contty1H:1200 opost onlcr:1200 hupcl sane::contty2H
contty2H:300 opost onlcr:300 hupcl sane::contty3H
contty3H:2400 opost onlcr:2400 hupcl sane::contty4H
contty4H:4800 opost onlcr:4800 hupcl sane::contty5H
contty5H:19200 opost onlcr:19200 hupcl sane::conttyH

ppp115200:115200 cs8 -parenb hupcl:115200 cs8 -parenb hupcl::uu115200
ppp57600:57600 cs8 -parenb hupcl:57600 cs8 -parenb hupcl::uu57600
ppp38400:38400 cs8 -parenb hupcl:38400 cs8 -parenb hupcl::uu38400
ppp19200:19200 cs8 -parenb hupcl:19200 cs8 -parenb hupcl::uu19200
ppp9600:9600 cs8 -parenb hupcl:9600 cs8 -parenb hupcl::uu9600
ppp4800:4800 cs8 -parenb hupcl:4800 cs8 -parenb hupcl::uu4800
uu115200:115200 cs7 parenb parodd hupcl:115200 cs7 parenb parodd
  hupcl::ppp57600
uu57600:57600 cs7 parenb parodd hupcl:57600 cs7 parenb parodd hupcl::ppp38400
uu38400:38400 cs7 parenb parodd hupcl:38400 cs7 parenb parodd hupcl::ppp19200
uu19200:19200 cs7 parenb parodd hupcl:19200 cs7 parenb parodd hupcl::ppp9600
uu9600:9600 cs7 parenb parodd hupcl:9600 cs7 parenb parodd hupcl::ppp4800
uu4800:4800 cs7 parenb parodd hupcl:4800 cs7 parenb parodd hupcl::ppp2400
```

New!

New!

Figure 33 shows how the ttylabel entry in the
/etc/saf/zsmon/_pmtab file matches an entry in the /etc/ttydefs file.
In this example, the ttylabel is part of the default entry provided by the
Solaris Operating Environment for serial port B.

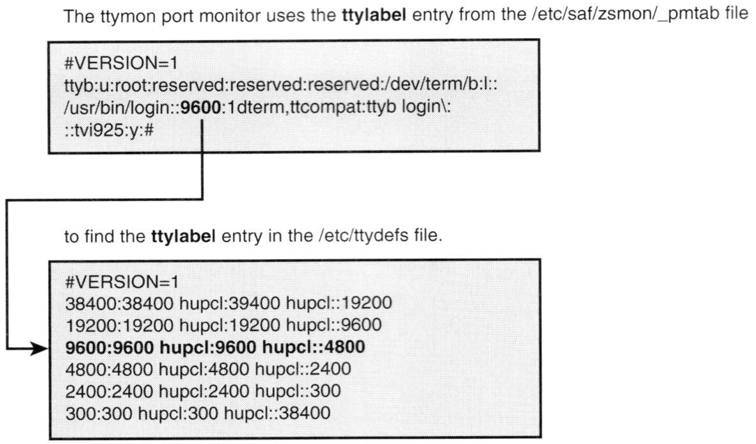

The ttymon port monitor uses the **ttylabel** entry from the /etc/saf/zsmon/_pmtab file

```
#VERSION=1
ttyb:u:root:reserved:reserved:reserved:/dev/term/b:l::
/usr/bin/login::9600:1dterm,ttcompat:ttyb login\:
::tvi925:y:#
```

to find the **ttylabel** entry in the /etc/ttydefs file.

```
#VERSION=1
38400:38400 hupcl:39400 hupcl::19200
19200:19200 hupcl:19200 hupcl::9600
9600:9600 hupcl:9600 hupcl::4800
4800:4800 hupcl:4800 hupcl::2400
2400:2400 hupcl:2400 hupcl::300
300:300 hupcl:300 hupcl::38400
```

*Figure 33    How ttymon Identifies the ttylabel in the /etc/ttydefs File*

The `/etc/ttydefs` file also contains information about speed and terminal settings for the TTY ports on a system. You can use the `sttydefs`(1M) administrative command to create new entries in the `/etc/ttydefs` file. See the `sttydefs`(1M) manual page for information on how to configure the `/etc/ttydefs` file.

## The terminfo Database

The `terminfo` database describes the characteristics of TTY devices. The source files in `terminfo` specify a set of capabilities for a device by quantifying certain aspects of the device and by specifying character sequences that control particular results. This database is often used by applications such as `vi` and `curses`, as well as by the `ls` and `more` commands. Information in the `terminfo` database is stored in a compiled binary format. The `terminfo` compiler, `tic`(1M), translates a `terminfo` file from source format to the required compiled binary format that applications use.

If you have site-specific `termcap` entries for devices, you can use the `captoinfo` command to convert those entries into `terminfo` source format. Then, use the `tic` compiler to translate the data into compiled format. See the `captoinfo`(1M) and `tic`(1M) manual pages for more information.

## The tput Command

Use the `tput`(1M) command to initialize or reset the terminal or to make terminal-dependent capabilities and information available to the shell. The `tput` command sets terminal characteristics, using data in the `terminfo` database. The `tput` command is similar to the SunOS 4.x `tset`(1B) command, which is provided in the SunOS/BSD Compatibility Package. The `tput` command has the following syntax.

```
tput [-Ttype] init
tput[-Ttype] reset
```

## The stty Command

The `/usr/bin/stty` command is the Solaris version of the SunOS 4.x `stty` command. The old `/usr/ucb/stty` command is available in the SunOS/BSD Compatibility Package. Use of the options varies, depending on which version of `stty` you are using. The `stty` command has the following syntax.

```
stty [-a] [-g] [options]
```

The `-a` option lists current options by their `termio` names. The `-g` option lists the same information in a format that can be used as an argument to another `stty` command.

The following examples show the default line settings using first the `/usr/bin/stty` command and then the `/usr/ucb/stty` command.

```
paperbark% /usr/bin/stty
speed 9600 baud; -parity cstopb hupcl loblk
rows = 46; columns = 79; ypixels = 700; xpixels = 721;
erase = ^h; swtch = <undef>;
-inpck -istrip icrnl -ixany ixoff onlcr
echo echoe echok echoctl echoke iexten
paperbark% /usr/ucb/stty
speed 9600 baud; -parity cstopb hupcl loblk
rows = 46; columns = 79; ypixels = 700; xpixels = 721;
erase = ^h; swtch = <undef>;
-brkint -inpck -istrip ixoff
crt iexten
paperbark%
```

Table 38 compares the default global line settings for SunOS 4.x and the Solaris Operating Environment. Note that the dash means not to set the value.

*Table 38     Default Global Line Settings*

| SunOS 4.x | Solaris Operating Environment | Description |
|-----------|-------------------------------|-------------|
| `9600 baud` | `9600 baud` | Set baud rate. |
| `-parity` | `-parity` | Disable parity. |
| `cstopb` | `cstopb` | Use two stop bits per character. |

**New!**

*Table 38    Default Global Line Settings (Continued)*

| SunOS 4.x | Solaris Operating Environment | Description |
|---|---|---|
| `hupcl` | `hupcl` | Hang up connection on close. |
| `rows=46;`<br>`columns=70;`<br>`ypixels=700;`<br>`xpixels=721` | `rows=46;`<br>`columns=70;`<br>`ypixels=700;`<br>`xpixels=721` | Set number of rows, columns, xpixels, and ypixels. |
| `erase=^h` | `erase=^h` | Set erase character. |
| `swtch=<undef>` | `swtch=<undef>` | Set control character assignments. |
| `-brkint` | | Do not signal INTR on break. |
| `crt` | | Enable hardware flow control. |

Table 39 compares the default input/output settings for SunOS 4.x and the Solaris Operating Environment. The i settings are for input, the o settings are for output.

*Table 39    Default Input/output Settings*

| SunOS 4.x | Solaris Operating Environment | Description |
|---|---|---|
| `-inpck` | `-inpck` | Disable input parity checking. |
| `-istrip` | `-istrip` | Do not strip input characters to seven bits. |
| | `icrnl` | Map CR to NL on input. |
| | `-ixany` | Allow only DC1 to restart output. |
| `ixoff` | `ixoff` | Send START/STOP characters when the input queue is nearly empty/full. |
| | `onlcr` | Map NL to CR-NL on output. |

Table 40 compares the default local settings for SunOS 4.x and the Solaris Operating Environment.

*Table 40    Default Local Settings*

| SunOS 4.x | Solaris Operating Environment | Description |
|---|---|---|
| | echo | Echo every character typed. |
| | echoe | Echo ERASE character as a backspace-space-backspace string (BS-SP-BS). |
| | echok | Echo NL after KILL character. |
| | echoctl | Echo control characters as ^char, delete as ^?. |
| | echoke | BS-SP-BS erase entire line. |
| iexten | iexten | Enable extended functions for input data. |

## UUCP Files

To use uucp, tip, or cu with modems and terminals, you must use information from or add information to the /etc/uucp/Dialers and /etc/uucp/Devices files. Each of these files is described in the following sections.

### The /etc/uucp/Dialers File

The /etc/uucp/Dialers file contains information that specifies the initial conversation that takes place on a line before it can be made available for transferring data. This conversation is usually a sequence of character strings that is transmitted and expected. The string often contains a telephone number that is dialed by an *automatic call unit (ACU)*. Each entry in /etc/uucp/Dialers begins with a label identifying the type of the modem. The Solaris /etc/uucp/Dialers file contains support for many different modem types. Each type of caller, except built-in callers, included in the /etc/uucp/Devices file should be contained in the /etc/uucp/Dialers file. You probably do not need to create an entry in this file. You do need to look in this file to verify that it contains an entry appropriate for your modem and to determine the type to use when you edit the /etc/uucp/Devices file.

Each line consists of three parts: the name of the caller, the table that translates the phone number into the code for the particular device, and a chat script to establish the connection. Comments at the beginning of the

/etc/uucp/Dialers file explain the codes shown in the following brief excerpt.

```
penril  =W-P    "" \d > Q\c : \d- > s\p9\c )-W\p\r\ds\p9\c-) y\c : \E\TP > 9\c OK
ventel--=&-%    "" \r\p\r\c $ <K\T%%\r>\c ONLINE!
vadic   =K-K    "" \005\p *-\005\p-*\005\p-* D\p BER? \E\T\e \r\c LINE
develcon ""     "" \pr\ps\c est:\007 \E\D\e \n\007
micom    ""     "" \s\c NAME? \D\r\c GO
direct
##########
#       The following entry is for use with direct connections
#       using ttymon with the -b and -r options on both ends,
#       or the old uugetty with the -r option.
##########
uudirect ""     "" \r\d in:--in:

#  Rixon Intelligent Modem -- modem should be set up in the Rixon
#  mode and not the Hayes mode.
#
rixon   =&-%    "" \r\r\d $ s9\c )-W\r\ds9\c-) s\c : \T\r\c $ 9\c LINE

#    Hayes Smartmodem -- modem should be set with the configuration
#    switches as follows:
#
#       S1 - UP         S2 - UP         S3 - DOWN       S4 - UP
#       S5 - UP         S6 - DOWN       S7 - ?          S8 - DOWN
#
hayes   =,-,    "" \dA\pTE1V1X1Q0S2=255S12=255\r\c OK\r \EATDT\T\r\c CONNECT
```

## The /etc/uucp/Devices File

The /etc/uucp/Devices file contains information for all of the devices that can be used to establish a link to remote systems. Provisions are made for several types of devices, such as ACUs, direct links, and network connections. You need to add an entry to the /etc/uucp/Devices file if you want to set up support for a bidirectional modem. Each entry in the Devices file has the following format.

```
type line line2 class dialer-token-pairs
```

The following excerpt from the /etc/uucp/Devices file shows the default entries.

```
TCP,et - - Any TCP -

ACU cua/b - Any hayes
Direct cua/b - Any direct
```

The *type* argument you supply when editing the /etc/uucp/Devices file is the name of the modem as displayed at the end of the entry from the /etc/uucp/Devices file. It points to an entry in /etc/uucp/Dialers.

## SAF Log Files

The SAF records port monitor behavior in the /var/saf/_log file. In addition, each ttymon port monitor has its own log file, /var/saf/*pmtag*/log, in which it records information, such as messages that it receives from sac and the services that it starts.

An example of the end of the /var/saf/_log file follows. This information shows that the system was rebooted three times and that the ttymon port monitor zsmon was started and enabled successfully each time.

```
paperbark% tail /var/saf/_log
Wed Oct 18 11:33:13 2000; 382; port monitor <zsmon> changed state from
  STARTING to ENABLED
Wed Oct 18 17:11:59 2000; 383; *** SAC starting ***
Wed Oct 18 17:11:59 2000; 393; starting port monitor <zsmon>
Wed Oct 18 17:11:59 2000; 383; port monitor <zsmon> changed state from
  STARTING to ENABLED
Thu Oct 19 08:24:15 2000; 383; *** SAC starting ***
Thu Oct 19 08:24:17 2000; 393; starting port monitor <zsmon>
Thu Oct 19 08:24:17 2000; 383; port monitor <zsmon> changed state from
  STARTING to ENABLED
Fri Oct 20 10:02:47 2000; 381; *** SAC starting ***
Fri Oct 20 10:02:49 2000; 393; starting port monitor <zsmon>
Fri Oct 20 10:02:49 2000; 381; port monitor <zsmon> changed state from
  STARTING to ENABLED
paperbark%
```

Following is an example of the /var/saf/_log file from another system that has a listen tcp port monitor configured.

```
seachild% tail /var/saf/_log
Fri Mar 24 12:06:19 2000; 176; *** SAC starting ***
Fri Mar 24 12:06:20 2000; 181; starting port monitor <tcp>
Fri Mar 24 12:06:20 2000; 182; starting port monitor <zsmon>
Fri Mar 24 12:06:21 2000; 176; port monitor <zsmon> changed state from
  STARTING to ENABLED
Fri Mar 24 12:06:22 2000; 176; port monitor <tcp> changed state from STARTING
  to ENABLED
Sat Mar 25 20:47:44 2000; 177; *** SAC starting ***
Sat Mar 25 20:47:44 2000; 183; starting port monitor <tcp>
Sat Mar 25 20:47:45 2000; 184; starting port monitor <zsmon>
Sat Mar 25 20:47:45 2000; 177; port monitor <zsmon> changed state from
  STARTING to ENABLED
Sat Mar 25 20:47:46 2000; 177; port monitor <tcp> changed state from STARTING
  to ENABLED
seachild%
```

The following example shows the end of the /var/saf/zsmon/log file. The pmtag zsmon is used for ttymon ports. This information shows more detailed information about how the ttymon port monitor zsmon was initialized successfully.

```
paperbark% tail /var/saf/zsmon/log
Fri Oct 20 10:02:49 2000; 393; PMTAG:             zsmon
Fri Oct 20 10:02:49 2000; 393; Starting state: enabled
Fri Oct 20 10:02:49 2000; 393; Got SC_ENABLE message
Fri Oct 20 10:02:49 2000; 393; max open files    = 1024
```

```
Fri Oct 20 10:02:49 2000; 393; max ports ttymon can monitor = 1017
Fri Oct 20 10:02:49 2000; 393; *ptr == 0
Fri Oct 20 10:02:49 2000; 393; SUCCESS
Fri Oct 20 10:02:49 2000; 393; *ptr == 0
Fri Oct 20 10:02:49 2000; 393; SUCCESS
Fri Oct 20 10:02:49 2000; 393; Initialization Completed
paperbark%
```

The following example shows the end of the `/var/saf/tcp/log` file. The pmtag `tcp` is the default name for the `listen` port monitor.

```
seachild% tail /var/saf/tcp/log
04/06/2000 15:11:10; 183; Connect: fd 7, svctag lpd, seq 117, type passfd
04/06/2000 15:11:12; 183; Connect: fd 7, svctag lpd, seq 118, type passfd
04/06/2000 15:26:12; 183; Connect: fd 7, svctag lpd, seq 119, type passfd
04/06/2000 15:26:13; 183; Connect: fd 7, svctag lpd, seq 120, type passfd
04/06/2000 15:34:02; 183; Connect: fd 6, svctag 0, seq 41, type exec
04/06/2000 15:34:03; 3391; NLPS (lp) passfd: /var/spool/lp/fifos/listenS5
04/06/2000 15:50:10; 183; Connect: fd 7, svctag lpd, seq 121, type passfd
04/06/2000 15:50:11; 183; Connect: fd 7, svctag lpd, seq 122, type passfd
04/06/2000 16:05:12; 183; Connect: fd 7, svctag lpd, seq 123, type passfd
04/06/2000 16:05:12; 183; Connect: fd 7, svctag lpd, seq 124, type passfd
seachild%
```

*NOTE. You should periodically clear out or truncate these log files. If you want* cron *to do the cleanup for you, create cron jobs with the* crontab(1) *command. Refer to the* crontab(1) *manual page for more information.*

# Reference to SAF Commands, Tasks, and Options

The following sections provide a quick reference to the variables used in SAF commands; tasks performed with the `sacadm` and `pmadm` commands; and options for the `sacadm`, `pmadm`, `ttyadm`, and `nlsadmin` commands. Refer to Chapter 11, "Setting Up Modems and Character Terminals," for step-by-step instructions on how to use the SAF commands to set up modems and terminals. Refer to Chapter 12, "Setting Up Printing Services," for step-by-step instructions on how to use the SAF commands to set up printers.

## Quick Reference to SAF Variables

Table 41 describes the variables used with the SAF commands.

*Table 41     Variables Used with the SAF Commands*

| Variable | Example | Description |
|----------|---------|-------------|
| *dev-path* | `/dev/term/b` | The full name of the TTY port device file. |
| *pmtag* | `zsmon` | The name of a specific instance of a port monitor. |
| *svctag* | `b` | The name of the port in the `/dev/term` directory. |
| *ttylabel* | `2400H` | The baud rate and line discipline from the `/etc/ttydefs` file. |
| *type* | `ventel` | The type of the modem, as specified in the `/etc/uucp/Devices` file. |

## Quick Reference to Service Access Control (sacadm)

Table 42 provides a task-oriented quick reference to the tasks you perform with the `sacadm` command.

*Table 42     Quick Reference to the Service Access Controller*

| Task | Command Syntax |
|------|----------------|
| Add a port monitor. | `sacadm -a -p` *pmtag* `-t ttymon -c /usr/lib/saf/ttymon -v `ttyadm -V` -y "comment"` |
| Disable a port monitor. | `sacadm -d -p` *pmtag* |
| Enable a port monitor. | `sacadm -e -p` *pmtag* |
| Kill a port monitor. | `sacadm -k -p` *pmtag* |
| List status information for a port monitor. | `sacadm -l -p` *pmtag* |
| Remove a port monitor. | `sacadm -r -p` *pmtag* |
| Start a port monitor. | `sacadm -s -p` *pmtag* |

*Table 42 Quick Reference to the Service Access Controller (Continued)*

| Task | Command Syntax |
|---|---|
| Add a listen port monitor. | `sacadm -a -p` *pmtag* `-t listen -c /usr/lib/saf/listen -v `ttyadm -V` -y "comment"` |

Table 43 describes the options to the `sacadm` command.

*Table 43 Options to sacadm Command*

| | Option | Description |
|---|---|---|
| | `-a` | Add a port monitor. The `-a` option requires the `-c` option. |
| | `-c` *cmd* | Execute the *cmd* command string to start a port monitor. Use only with `-a`. |
| New! | `-d` | Disable the *pmtag* port monitor. |
| New! | `-e` | Enable the *pmtag* port monitor. |
| | `-f dx` | Specify one or both flags. The `x` flag does not enable the specified service. The `u` flag creates a `utmpx` entry for the service. |
| New! | `-k` | Stop the *pmtag* port monitor. |
| New! | `-l` | List service information. |
| New! | `-L` | Same as `-l`, but list output in a condensed format. |
| New! | `-n` *count* | Set the restart count to *count*. If you do not specify a restart *count*, set *count* to `0`. A *count* of `0` indicates that the port monitor is not to be restarted if it fails. |
| | `-p` *pmtag* | Specify an identifying port monitor tag (*pmtag*) for the port monitor. |
| New! | `-r` *pmtag* | Remove the *pmtag* port monitor. |
| New! | `-s` *pmtag* | Start the *pmtag* port monitor. |
| | `-t` *type* | Specify the type of the port monitor—either `ttymon` or `listen`. |
| | `-v` *ver* | Specify the version number of the port monitor. Use `ttyadm -V` to find out the version number to use, or use `` `ttyadm -V` `` as an argument to the `-v` option. |
| New! | `-x` | With no options, read the `_sactab` database file. The `-x` option with the `-p` option reads the *pmtag* administrative file. |

*Table 43    Options to sacadm Command (Continued)*

| Option | Description |
|---|---|
| `-y comment` | Include *comment* in the `_sactab` entry for the *pmtag* port monitor. |

*New!*

## Quick Reference to Port Monitor Administration (pmadm)

Table 44 provides a quick reference to the tasks you perform using the `pmadm` command.

*Table 44    Quick Reference to Port Monitor Administration (pmadm)*

| Task | Command Syntax |
|---|---|
| Add a standard terminal service. | `pmadm -a -p` *pmtag* `-s svctag -i root -v` `` `ttyadm -V` `` `-m "` `` `ttyadm -i 'terminal` `disabled.' -l contty -m ldterm,ttcompat` `-d` *dev-path* `-s /usr/bin/login` `` ` `"` |
| Disable a `ttymon` port monitor. | `pmadm -d -p` *pmtag* `-s svctag` |
| Enable a `ttymon` port monitor. | `pmadm -e -p` *pmtag* `-s svctag` |
| List all services. | `pmadm -l` |
| List status information for one `ttymon` port monitor. | `pmadm -l -p` *pmtag* |
| List status information for a particular service running on one `ttymon` port monitor. | `pmadm -l -p` *pmtag* `-s svctag` |
| Add a `listen` service. | `pmadm -a -p` *pmtag* `-s lp -i root -v` `` `nlsadmin -V` `` `-m "` `` `nlsadmin -o` `/var/spool/lp/fifos/listenS5` `` ` `"` |
| Disable a `listen` port monitor. | `pmadm -d -p` *pmtag* `-s lp` |
| Enable a `listen` port monitor. | `pmadm -e -p` *pmtag* `-s lp` |

Table 45 describes the options to the pmadm command.

*Table 45    Options to the pmadm Command*

| Option | Description |
|--------|-------------|
| -a | Add a service. |
| -d | Add x to the flag field in the entry for the *svctag* service in the port monitor's administrative file to disable the service. This entry is used by the *pmtag* port monitor. |
| -e | Remove x from the flag field in the entry for the *svctag* service in the port monitor's administrative file to enable the service. This entry is used by the *pmtag* port monitor. |
| -f xu | Specify one or both flags. The x flag does not enable the specified service. The u flag creates a utmpx entry for the service. |
| -i *id* | Specify the identity assigned to the service when it is started. |
| -l | List service information. |
| -L | Same as -l, but list output in a condensed format. |
| -m | Identify port monitor-specific options to be included on the -a command line. |
| -p *pmtag* | Specify the port monitor tag (*pmtag*)—for example, zsmon. |
| -r | Remove the entry for the service from the administrative file of the port monitor. |
| -s *svcstag* | Specify the service tag associated with a given service (*svctag*)—for example, ttya for serial port A. |
| -t *type* | Specify the port monitor type. |
| -v *ver* | Specify the port monitor version number. Use ttyadm -V to find the version number, or use `ttyadm -V` as an argument to the -v option. |
| -y *comment* | Associate *comment* with the service entry in the port monitor administrative file. |

*New!* (−d)
*New!* (−e)
*New!* (−l)
*New!* (−L)
*New!* (−r)
*New!* (−t)

Table 46 shows the options to the `ttyadm` command. You usually include the `ttyadm` command and its options in backquotes ( ` ` ) as part of the `pmadm` command.

*Table 46     Options to the ttyadm Command*

| Option | Description | |
|--------|-------------|---|
| `-b` | Set the bidirectional port option so the line can be used in both directions. Users can connect to the service associated with the port, but if the port is free, `uucico(1M)`, `cu(1C)`, or `ct(1C)` can use it for dialing out. | *New!* |
| `-c` | Set the connect-on-carrier option for the port. Invoke the port's associated service immediately when a connect indication is received (that is, print no prompt and search no baud rate). | *New!* |
| `-d` *device* | Specify the full path name of the device file for the TTY port. | |
| `-h` | Set the hangup option for the port. If you do not specify the `-h` option, force a hangup on the line by setting the speed to `0` before setting the speed to the default or specified value. | *New!* |
| `-i` *message* | Specify the inactive (disabled) response message. This message is sent to the TTY port if the port is disabled or the `ttymon` monitoring the port is disabled. | *New!* |
| `-I` | Initialize the service only once. You can use this option to configure a particular device without actually monitoring it, as with software carrier. | *New!* |
| `-l` *ttylabel* | Specify which *ttylabel* in the `/etc/ttydefs` file to use as the starting point when searching for the proper baud rate. | |
| `-m` *modules* | Specify a list of pushable STREAMS modules. The modules are pushed in the order in which they are specified before the service is invoked. *modules* is a comma-separated list of modules with no white space included. Any modules currently on the stream are popped before these modules are pushed. | *New!* |
| `-p` *prompt* | Specify the prompt message, for example, `login:`. | *New!* |
| `-r` *count* | Wait to receive data from the port before displaying a prompt. If *count* is `0`, wait until it receives any character. If *count* is greater than `0`, wait until *count* newlines have been received. | *New!* |

*Table 46* *Options to the ttyadm Command (Continued)*

| Option | Description |
|---|---|
| -s *service* | Specify the full path name of the service to be invoked when a connection request is received. If arguments are required, enclose the command and its arguments in double quotes (" "). |
| -S y\|n | Set the software carrier value. y turns on the software carrier. n turns off the software carrier. |
| -t *timeout* | Close a port if the open on the port succeeds and no input data is received in *timeout* seconds. |
| -T *termtype* | Set the terminal type. The TERM environment variable is set to *termtype*. |
| -V | Display the version number of the current /usr/lib/saf/ttymon command. |

*New!*

*New!*

*New!*

Table 47 shows only the options to the nlsadmin command that can be included as part of the command-line argument for the sacadm and pmadm commands. See the nlsadmin(1M) manual page for further information.

*Table 47* *Options to the nlsadmin Command*

| Option | Description |
|---|---|
| -A | Interpret the address as private for the server. The listener monitors this address and dispatches all calls arriving on this address directly to the designated service. This option may not be used with the -D option. |
| c "*cmd*" | Specify the full path name of the server and its arguments. Use double quotes around the path name to ensure that it is interpreted as a single word by the shell. |
| -D | Dynamically assign a private address that is selected by the transport provider. This option is frequently used with the -R option for RPC services. This option may not be used with the -A option. |
| -o *streamname* | Specify the full path name of a FIFO or named STREAM through which a server is receiving the connection. |

*Table 47    Options to the nlsadmin Command (Continued)*

| Option | Description |
|---|---|
| `-p modules` | If this option is specified, the modules are interpreted as a list of STREAMS modules for the listener to push before starting the service. Modules are pushed in the order they are specified. Specify the modules as a comma-separated list with no spaces. |
| `-R` | Register an RPC service whose address, program number, and version number are registered with the rpcbinder for this transport provider. |
| `-V` | Display the version number of the SAF. |

# Admintool: Serial Ports and SAF

You can configure a serial port for use with a modem or terminal on a local system by using either the Admintool: Serial Ports graphical user interface or the SAF commands described in Part 4 of this book. Sun recommends that you use the Admintool: Serial Ports graphical user interface for these tasks. Alternatively, you can use the SMC Serial Ports tool—available in the Solaris *New!* 8 Update 3 release—to configure serial ports.

Both Admintool: Serial Ports and the SMC Serial Ports tool use the `pmadm` command to configure the serial port software to work with terminals and modems. They provide templates for common terminal and modem configurations and provide a quick visual status of each port. You can also set up multiple ports, modify them, or delete port services.

Once a serial port is configured, use the SAF commands to administer the port.

# Templates

The Serial Port tools provide five templates for the most common terminal and modem configurations; you can then modify the template for a particular device.

- Terminal—hardwired.
- Modem—dial-in only.
- Modem—dial-out only.

- Modem—bidirectional.
- Initialize Only—no connection.

When you choose one of these templates, a set of default values is displayed. These values are optimized for the service that you selected.

# Starting Admintool: Serial Ports

You can use the Admintool: Serial Ports graphical user interface for the following tasks on a local system.

- Initialize a port without configuring the service.
- Add a service.
- Modify a service.
- Disable a service.
- Delete a service.

You perform each task by clicking the SELECT mouse button on the name of each port you want to configure and then choosing an item from the Edit menu. You choose Modify Service for the first four tasks and Delete Service if you want to delete the service for the selected port(s).

*New!*

> *NOTE. Ordinarily, you can run Admintool without requiring root access if you are a member of GID 14. However, if you access Admintool through the Solaris Management Console, you must log in either as root or as a member of a role that grants you superuser permissions to run Admintool. Only then can you use Admintool to edit local password databases. The Solaris Management Console does not recognize membership in GID 14.*

Use the following steps to access the Admintool: Serial Ports graphical user interface.

1. Type **/usr/bin/admintool&** and press Return. The Admintool: Users window is displayed, as shown in Figure 34.

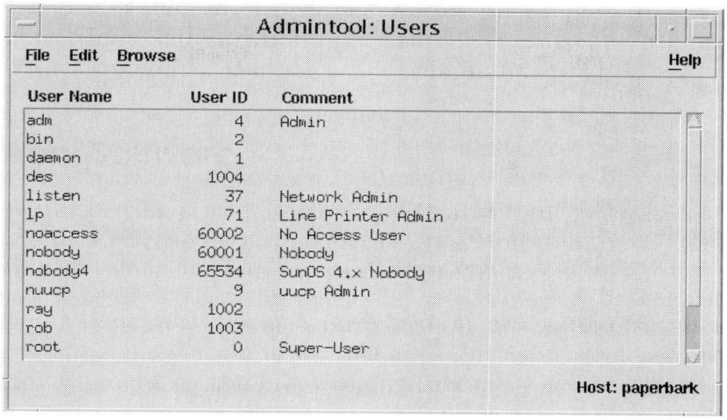

*Figure 34    Admintool: Users Base Window*

    2.   From the Browse menu, choose Serial Ports. The Admintool: Serial Port window is displayed, as shown in Figure 35.

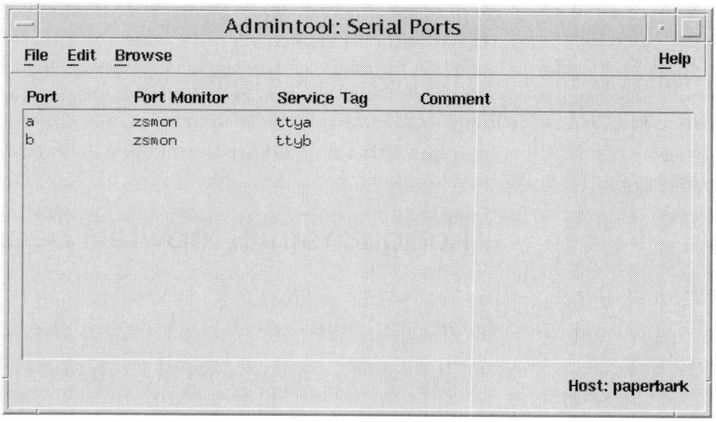

*Figure 35    Admintool: Serial Ports Window*

    3.   Click on the port you want to modify and choose Modify from the Edit menu.

        The Modify Serial Port window displays three levels of information about the port. When the window is first displayed, only Basic information is displayed, as shown in Figure 36. You can click the More radio button to display more information. Clicking the Expert radio button shows all of the possible settings.

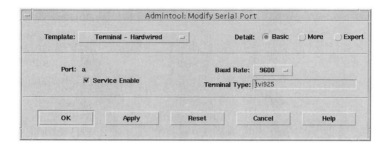

*Figure 36    Admintool: Modify Serial Port window*

See Chapter 11, "Setting Up Modems and Character Terminals," for information on how to set up modems and character terminals.

## Starting the SMC Serial Ports Tool

Use the following steps to start the SMC Serial Ports tool.

See "Setting Up Local Mail Alias Files" on page 106 for complete instructions on how to start SMC and for complete screen illustrations.

1.   From the Tools menu in the CDE Front Panel, choose Solaris Management Console.

     The Solaris Management Console window is displayed.

2.   Click on the control to the left of the This Computer icon, then click on the Devices and Hardware icon in the navigation pane.

     If you have not already logged in to SMC, the login window is displayed.

3.   If necessary, in the login window, log in as a user who has rights to administer serial ports, as a role that has rights to administer serial ports, or with your user name if you are a Primary Administrator. Type the appropriate password, and click on the OK button.

     See Chapter 23, "Role-Based Access Control," for information about rights.

4.   Double-click on the Devices and Hardware icon in the navigation pane or on the Serial Ports icon.

     The Serial Ports icon is displayed in the right pane, as shown in Figure 37.

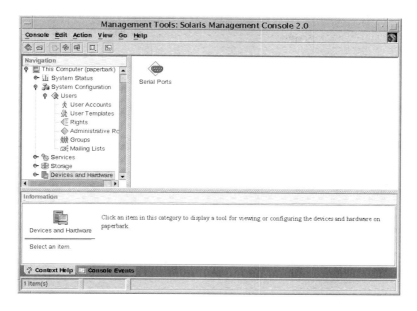

*Figure 37    Serial Ports Icon*

5.  Double-click on the Serial Ports icon.

    The Serial Ports window is displayed, as shown in Figure 38.

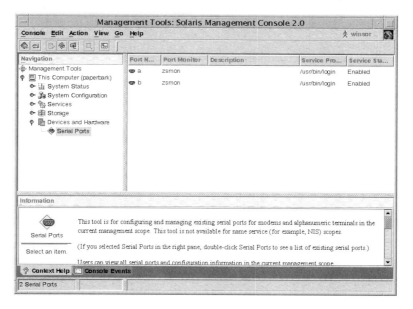

*Figure 38    Serial Ports Window*

Refer to Chapter 11, "Setting Up Modems and Character Terminals," for instructions on how to use the Serial Ports tool to set up modems and character terminals.

# 11

# SETTING UP MODEMS AND CHARACTER TERMINALS

This chapter describes how to use Admintool: Serial Ports, the SMC Serial Ports tool, and the `ttymon` port monitor command to set up the Service Access Facility (SAF) for modems and character terminals.

*New!*

> *NOTE. This chapter contains basic information for configuring modems and character terminals. If you have problems configuring modems and character terminals, refer to Appendix B, "Celeste's Tutorial on Solaris 2.x Modems and Terminals," for more complete and complex instructions.*

*New!*

See Chapter 12, "Setting Up Printing Services," for information on how to use the SAF to set up printers.

## Tools for Setting Up Modems and Character Terminals

You perform three basic tasks to set up a serial port device, such as a modem or a character terminal.

1. Use the `sacadm` command to add a port monitor (if one is not already configured).
2. Use the `pmadm` command to designate a service to be associated with the new port monitor.
3. Edit one or more communications-related files as needed.

The Solaris environment now provides you with two additional tools that provide a graphical user interface to the SAF to manage terminals and modems.

- Admintool graphical user interface. Use this bundled tool to manage terminal and modem setup for local systems only.

New!

- The Solaris Management Console Serial Ports tool provides a graphical user interface that you can use to manage terminals and modems in the current management scope.

Table 48 describes three tasks that are not supported in the Admintool or SMC Serial Port tools. You must use SAF commands to perform these tasks.

*Table 48     Tasks Not Supported by the Serial Port Tools*

| Task | SAF Command | Description |
|---|---|---|
| Inform users that a port is disabled. | `ttyadm -i` | This command specifies the inactive (disabled) response message. The message is sent to a terminal or modem when a user logs in when the port is disabled. This functionality is not provided when you disable a port with the Serial Port tools. |
| Keep the modem connected when a user logs out of a host. | `ttyadm -h` | This command specifies that the system does not hang up on a modem before setting or resetting to the default or specified value. If `ttyadm -h` is not used, the host hangs up the modem when the user logs out of that host. |

*Table 48     Tasks Not Supported by the Serial Port Tools (Continued)*

| Task | SAF Command | Description |
|------|-------------|-------------|
| Require the user to type a character before the system displays a prompt. | `ttyadm -r` | This command specifies that `ttymon` requires the user to type a character or press Return a specified number of times before the login prompt is displayed. When `-r` is not specified, pressing Return one or more times prints the prompt anyway. This option prevents a terminal server from issuing a welcome message that the Solaris host might misinterpret to be a user trying to log in. Without the `-r` option, the host and terminal server might begin looping and printing prompts to each other. |

# Using Variables in SAF Commands

The following sections describe the variables used in the SAF commands in this chapter. When using SAF commands, you supply arguments to specify one (or more) of the variables described in Table 49. These variable names were chosen to match the names of the fields used to display the output of SAF commands. These variables and the files they use are described in the following sections.

*Table 49     Variables Used with the SAF Commands*

| Variable | Example | Description |
|----------|---------|-------------|
| *pmtag* | `zsmon` | The name of a specific instance of a port monitor. |
| *svctag* | `ttyb` | The name of the port. |
| *dev-path* | `/dev/term/b` | The full name of the TTY port device file. |
| *ttylabel* | `2400H` | The baud rate and line discipline from the `/etc/ttydefs` file. |

*Table 49     Variables Used with the SAF Commands (Continued)*

| Variable | Example | Description |
|---|---|---|
| *type* | hayes | The type of the modem, as specified in the /etc/uucp/Devices file. |

## The Port Monitor Tag (pmtag)

You can use the *pmtag* variable to specify the name you assign to a specific instance of a port monitor. You can give port monitors any name you like, provided the name is unique and contains no more than 14 alphanumeric characters. The default *pmtag* variable for the Solaris Operating Environment is zsmon for serial ports A and B. If you install a multiplexer, serial ports are automatically configured as part of the installation process and are given the *pmtag* variable ttymon0. Sun suggests that you use the system-defined *pmtag* variables.

## The Service Tag (svctag)

Each port assigned to a port monitor has its own service tag. By convention, *svctag* is tty followed by the name of the port in the /dev/term directory. For example, for device /dev/term/b, the corresponding svctag is ttyb. For /dev/term/7, the svctag is tty7.

> *NOTE. You can assign any svctag name you like, as long as you use it consistently.*

To display a list of currently active services, type **pmadm -l** and press Return. You do not need to be superuser to display a list of currently active services. In the following example, the first three entries are defined for printing services. The last two entries define the default zsmon services for serial ports A and B.

```
castle% /usr/sbin/pmadm -l
PMTAG           PMTYPE          SVCTAG          FLGS ID       <PMSPECIFIC>
zsmon           ttymon          ttya            u    root     /dev/term/a I -
  /usr/bin/login - 9600 ldterm,ttcompat ttya login:  - tvi925 y  #
zsmon           ttymon          ttyb            u    root     /dev/term/b I -
  /usr/bin/login - 9600 ldterm,ttcompat ttyb login:  - tvi925 y  #
castle%
```

**New!**

In the preceding example, the *pmtag* is zsmon; the *pmtype* is ttymon; the *svctag* is ttya and ttyb; the *flag* is u (which creates a utmpx directory—changed from utmp in the Solaris 8 release—for the service); and the ID, root, is the user identity that is assigned to the service tag when it is started. The port-monitor-specific information includes the device path, I (initialize only), the /usr/bin/login program to run once a connection has been made to this port, the speed entry from `/etc/ttytab`, terminal configuration information, the `login:` prompt, and the terminal type. The `y` at the end of the line indicates that software carrier is on. If the character at the end of the line is an n, software carrier is off.

> *NOTE. A single port monitor can handle multiple requests for the same service concurrently, so it is possible for the number of active login services to exceed the number of* `ttymon` *port monitors.*

## The Device Path (dev-path)

You use the *dev-path* variable to specify the full name of the TTY port device file to which the modem or character terminal is connected. For example, the path name for a character terminal or modem connected to serial port A is `/dev/term/a`. A terminal attached to the first port of a serial port adapter board or multiplexer would be `/dev/term/00`.

## The Baud Rate and Line Discipline (ttylabel)

You can use the *ttylabel* variable to specify which entry in the `/etc/ttydefs` file is used when the SAF searches for the proper baud rate and line discipline. The following example shows the first group of settings from the `/etc/ttydefs` file.

```
460800:460800 hupcl:460800 hupcl::307200
307200:307200 hupcl:307200 hupcl::230400
230400:230400 hupcl:230400 hupcl::153600
153600:153600 hupcl:153600 hupcl::115200
115200:115200 hupcl:115200 hupcl::76800
76800:76800 hupcl:76800 hupcl::57600
57600:57600 hupcl:57600 hupcl::38400
38400:38400 hupcl:38400 hupcl::19200
19200:19200 hupcl:19200 hupcl::9600
9600:9600 hupcl:9600 hupcl::4800
4800:4800 hupcl:4800 hupcl::2400
2400:2400 hupcl:2400 hupcl::1200
1200:1200 hupcl:1200 hupcl::300
300:300 hupcl:300 hupcl::460800
```

## Type of Modem

The type of modem you use is discussed in "Modem Connection and Switch Settings" on page 268.

## Comments

You can add comments (in double quotes) to both the `pmadm` and `sacadm` comments after the `-y` option when you add a port monitor or service. Any comments you add are displayed when you use the `-1` option to the `sacadm` or `pmadm` command to display port monitors or services.

Use comments to specify the ports with which the various port monitors are associated.

# Setting Up Modems

You can set up a modem in three ways.

- Dial-out service—You can access other systems, but nobody outside can gain access to this system.
- Dial-in service—People can access this system from remote sites, but this system does not permit calls to the outside world.
- Bidirectional service—This service provides both dial-in and dial-out capabilities.

## Modem Connection and Switch Settings

Connect the modem to a serial port with an RS-232-C cable that has pins 2 through 8 and pin 20 wired straight through. You can also use a full 25-pin cable to connect the modem to the system. Ensure that all of the connections are secure.

The Solaris Operating Environment supports many popular modems. The following modems have been tested and qualified for use with Solstice PPP.

- AT&T DataPort Express.
- BocaModem V.34 DataFax.
- Cardinal V.34/V.FC 28.8 data/fax.
- Cardinal MVP288I 28.8 Kbps V.34 Fax Modem.
- Hayes Accura 144B and 288V.FC.
- Megahertz XJ2288 PCMCIA.
- Motorola Codex 326X V.34.
- MultiModem MT2834BLF.
- MultiModem MT1432BF.
- Olitec 288.

- Practical 14400 V32bis.
- SupraFaxModem 288.
- USRobotics Sporter 14400.
- USRobotics Sporter 288.
- USRobotics Courier V.34.
- Zoom V34.

*NOTE. This information does not imply a support contract or warranty from Sun Microsystems, Inc., for any of the listed devices.*

## Hayes-Compatible Modem Settings

Hayes-compatible modems that use the Hayes AT command set may work with cu and UUCP software. Use the following configurations.

- Use hardware data terminal ready (DTR). When the system drops DTR (for example, when someone logs out), the modem should hang up.
- Use hardware carrier detect (CD). The modem raises the CD line only when there is an active carrier signal on the phone connection. When the carrier drops, either because the other end of the connection is terminated or the phone connection is broken, the system is notified and acts appropriately. The CD signal is also used for coordinating dial-in *and* dial-out use on a single serial port and modem.
- Respond with numeric result codes.
- Send result codes.
- Do not echo commands.

# Using Admintool: Serial Ports to Configure Modems

You can use the Admintool: Serial Ports graphical user interface to configure SAF for modems on a local system. Sun recommends that you use either Admintool or the SMC Serial Ports tool to configure SAF for modems. These tools issue the appropriate SAF commands to complete the configuration. See "Using the SMC Serial Ports Tool to Configure Modems" on page 273 for instructions on how to use the SMC Serial Ports tool.

*New!*

Table 50 shows the Admintool default values for a dial-in modem.

*Table 50     Modem—Dial-In Only Default Values*

| Item | Default Value |
|------|---------------|
| Port | a \| b \| other port identifier |
| Service | enabled |
| Baud rate | 9600 |
| Terminal type | tvi925 |
| Option: Initialize only | no |
| Option: Bidirectional | no |
| Option: Software carrier | no |
| Login prompt | ttyn login: |
| Comment | Modem—Dial-In Only |
| Service tag | ttyn |
| Port monitor tag | zsmon |
| Create utmpx entry | yes |
| Connect on carrier | no |
| Service | /usr/bin/login |
| Streams modules | ldterm,ttcompat |
| Timeout (secs) | never |

Table 51 shows the Admintool default values for a dial-out modem.

*Table 51     Modem—Dial-Out Only Default Values*

| Item | Default Value |
|------|---------------|
| Port | a \| b \| other port identifier |
| Service | enabled |
| Baud rate | 9600 |
| Terminal type | tvi925 |
| Option: Initialize only | yes |
| Option: Bidirectional | no |
| Option: Software carrier | no |
| Login prompt | ttyn login: |

*Table 51    Modem—Dial-Out Only Default Values (Continued)*

| Item | Default Value |
|---|---|
| Comment | `Modem—Dial-Out Only` |
| Service tag | `ttyn` |
| Port monitor tag | `zsmon` |
| Create `utmpx` entry | `yes` |
| Connect on carrier | `no` |
| Service | `/usr/bin/login` |
| Streams modules | `ldterm,ttcompat` |
| Timeout (secs) | `never` |

Table 52 shows the Admintool default settings for bidirectional modem service.

*Table 52    Modem—Bidirectional Default Values*

| Item | Default Value |
|---|---|
| Port | `a` \| `b` \| other port identifier |
| Service | `enabled` |
| Baud rate | `9600` |
| Terminal type | `tvi925` |
| Option: Initialize only | `no` |
| Option: Bidirectional | `yes` |
| Option: Software carrier | `no` |
| Login prompt | `ttyn login:` |
| Comment | `Modem—Bidirectional` |
| Service tag | `ttyn` |
| Port monitor tag | `zsmon` |
| Create `utmpx` entry | `yes` |
| Connect on carrier | `no` |
| Service | `/usr/bin/login` |
| Streams modules | `ldterm,ttcompat` |
| Timeout (secs) | `never` |

Use the following steps to configure SAF for a modem from the Admintool Serial Ports window.

1.  Start Admintool.

    Refer to "Starting Admintool: Serial Ports" on page 258 if you need instructions on how to start Admintool.

2.  In the Admintool: Serial Ports window, click on the port that will be used with the modem.

3.  From the Edit menu, choose Modify.

    The Admintool: Modify Serial Port window is displayed, as shown in Figure 39.

*Figure 39    Admintool: Modify Serial Port window*

4.  Click the Expert radio button to display all of the settings, as shown in Figure 40.

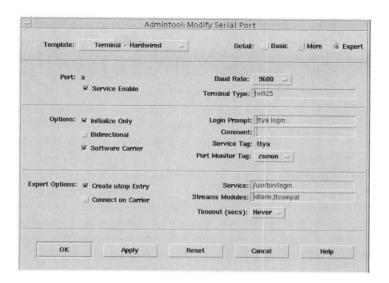

*Figure 40   Admintool: Modify Serial Port Window with Expert Options*

5. From the Template menu, choose the modem configuration that meets or most closely matches your modem service.

6. Change the values of template entries if desired. If you change the values, make sure that you change the comment field so that other users know that you have changed the default values.

7. Click OK to configure the port.

## Using the SMC Serial Ports Tool to Configure Modems

*New!*

You can use the SMC Serial Ports tool—available starting with the Solaris 8 Update 3 release—to configure SAF for modems within the current SMC management scope. The SMC tools replace Solaris AdminSuite 3.0 tools.

The default settings for the SMC Serial Ports tool are the same as for Admintool. See "Using Admintool: Serial Ports to Configure Modems" on page 269 for more information.

Use the following steps to configure SAF for modems with the SMC Serial Ports tool.

1. Start SMC.

   See "Starting the SMC Serial Ports Tool" on page 260 if you need instructions on how to start SMC.

2. Double-click on the Serial Ports icon.

The Serial Ports window is displayed, as shown in Figure 41.

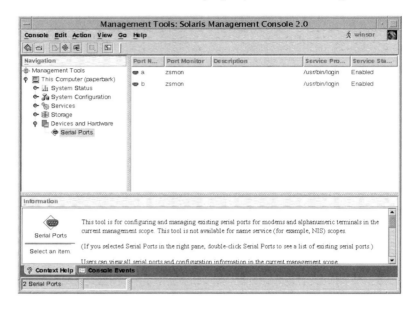

*Figure 41    SMC Serial Ports Window*

3. Click on the port to which the modem is connected and, from the Action menu, choose the configuration you want for your modem.

You can choose Modem (Dial In), Modem (Dial Out), or Modem (Dial In/Out).

The Serial Port Basic properties are displayed, as shown in Figure 42.

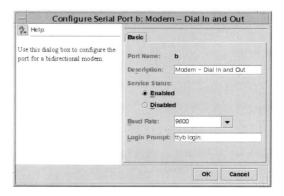

*Figure 42    SMC Serial Port Properties*

*NOTE. If you click on a port and choose a configuration option from the Action menu, only the Basic options tab is displayed. You can display the Advanced options only by double-clicking on a port, by highlighting a port, or by highlighting a port and clicking on the properties icon to the right of the View menu. First configure the modem with the default settings. If they don't work, display the properties for the serial port and modify the Advanced settings.*

4. Change the values of template entries if desired. If you change the values, make sure that you change the comment field so that other users know that you have changed the default values.

5. Click OK to configure the port.

   The port is configured and the configuration information is displayed in the Serial Ports window, as shown in Figure 43.

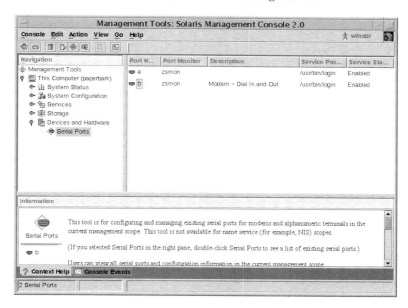

*Figure 43    SMC Serial Ports Window*

## Using SAF Commands to Set Up Modems

The following sections describe how to use the SAF commands to set up modems.

*NOTE. Sun recommends that you use either Admintool or the SMC Serial Ports tool to set up modems.*

You can find an excellent resource for information about using SAF to set up modems and terminals at the following URL.
`http://www.stokely.com/unix.serial.port.resources/modem.html`

For your convenience—with permission—this document is included completely in this book as Appendix B, "Celeste's Tutorial on Solaris 2.x Modems and Terminals."

## Variables Used to Set Up Modems

To set up a modem, you need information for the variables listed in Table 53.

*Table 53     Modem Variables*

| Variable | Description |
|----------|-------------|
| `svctag` | The name of the port the modem is connected to (typically `ttya` or `ttyb`). |
| `pmtag` | The name of the port monitor service (for Sun Microsystems, `zsmon`). |
| `dev-path` | The name of the device for the port (typically `/dev/term/a` or `/dev/term/b`). |
| `ttylabel` | The entry in the `/etc/ttydefs` file that is used to set the proper baud rate and line discipline. |
| `type` | The type of the modem from the `/etc/uucp/Dialers` file (for example, the type for a Hayes modem is `hayes`). |

## SAF Configuration for Modems

To configure the SAF for modems, you use the `pmadm` and `ttyadm` commands. You can use the Admintool: Serial Ports graphical user interface to configure SAF for modems on a local system. See "Using Admintool: Serial Ports to Configure Modems" on page 269 for more information. You can use the SMC Serial Ports tool to configure SAF for modems on a local or remote system. See "Using the SMC Serial Ports Tool to Configure Modems" on page 273 for more information.

Follow the steps in this section to set up the SAF to use a modem for dial-in or bidirectional service.

1. Become superuser.
2. Type **pmadm -l** and press Return.

   A list of all of the available port monitors is displayed. Note the PMTAG, PMTYPE, and SVCTAG values for the modem port. Substitute these values for the appropriate variables in the next steps.
3. Type **pmadm -r -p *pmtag* -s *svctag*** and press Return.

You must remove the existing configuration for the service tag before you can create a new one. If the message Invalid request, pmtag: not found comes up, then the port monitor is not configured. Continue to the next step.

4. To set up the port monitor for use with the modem, type **pmadm -a -p** *pmtag* **-s** *svctag* **-i root -fu -v `ttymon -V` -m "`ttyadm -t** *terminfo-type* **-b -d** *dev-name* **-l** *ttylabel* **-m ldterm,ttcompat -s /usr/bin/login -S n`"** and press Return.

The -a option adds the service, the -p option specifies the port monitor tag, the -s option specifies the service tag, and the -i option sets root as the ID of the owner. The -fu option creates a utmpx directory for the service (changed from utmp in the Solaris 8 release), the -v option specifies the version number, and the -m option specifies the information specific to the port monitor, using input from the ttyadm command. The ttyadm -t option specifies the type of the terminal, as specified by the terminfo database; the -b option specifies that the service is bidirectional; and the -d option specifies the device name. The -l option specifies the TTY label; the -m ldterm,ttcompat command specifies the STREAMS modules to be pushed; the -s option specifies a login service; and the -S n option sets the hardware carrier on.

5. Type **pmadm -l** and press Return. Check the output to ensure that you configured the port monitor service properly.

6. Type **grep cua***n* **/etc/remote** and press Return, where *n* represents the port letter.

   This entry in the /etc/remote file sets the correct baud rate for the port. In the following example, the information for cuab is correct.

```
# grep cuab /etc/remote
cuab:dv=/dev/cua/b:br#2400
#
```

If the entry is not in the /etc/remote file, edit the file to include the entry.

7. If using the port for UUCP, edit the /etc/uucp/Devices file and add the following entry, where *n* is the name of the device in the /dev/term directory (for example, b for /dev/term/b).

```
ACU term/n,M - ttylabel type
```

*NOTE. If you are setting up service on a bidirectional port, you must enable login individually for each port. To enable logins, type* **pmadm -e -p** *pmtag* **-s** *svctag and press Return.*

In the following example, a Hayes-compatible 2400 baud modem is configured for bidirectional service on serial port B. Note that the `contty3H` entry is an entry for a 2400 baud modem.

```
oak# pmadm -l
PMTAG          PMTYPE        SVCTAG        FLGS ID       <PMSPECIFIC>
zsmon          ttymon        ttya          u    root     /dev/term/a I -
  /usr/bin/login - 9600 ldterm,ttcompat ttya login:  - tvi925
y  #
zsmon          ttymon        ttyb          u    root     /dev/term/a I -
  /usr/bin/login - 9600 ldterm,ttcompat ttyb login:  - tvi925
y  #
oak# pmadm -r -p zsmon -s ttyb
oak# pmadm -a -p zsmon -s ttyb -i root -fu -v `ttyadm -V` -m "`ttyadm -t
  tvi925 -b -d /dev/term/b -l contty3H -m ldterm,ttcompat -s /usr/bin/login -S
  n`"
oak# pmadm -l
PMTAG          PMTYPE        SVCTAG        FLGS ID       <PMSPECIFIC>
zsmon          ttymon        ttya          u    root     /dev/term/a I -
  /usr/bin/login - 9600 ldterm,ttcompat ttya login:  - tvi925
y  #
zsmon          ttymon        ttyb          u    root     /dev/term/b b -
  /usr/bin/login - contty3H ldterm,ttcompat login:  - - n  #
oak# sacadm -l
PMTAG          PMTYPE        FLGS RCNT STATUS       COMMAND
zsmon          ttymon        -    0    ENABLED      /usr/lib/saf/ttymon #
oak# grep cuab /etc/remote
cuab:dv=/dev/cua/b:br#2400
oak# vi /etc/uucp/Devices
```

If using the port for UUCP, add the following line to the end of the file.

```
ACU cua/b,M - contty3H hayes
```

## Dial-Out Modem Service Configuration

If you want to dial out on the modem, you do not need to configure SAF files. Once the modem is connected to the system and its switches are properly set, follow these steps to configure dial-out service.

1.  Edit the `/etc/uucp/Devices` file and add the following line, where `n` is the name of the device in the `/dev/cua` directory.

    Use the type `hayes` for Hayes-compatible modems.

```
ACU cua/n,M - ttylabel type
```

2.  Type **pmadm -d -p** *pmtag* **-s** *svctag* and press Return.

    Login service is disabled. (Permitting logins for a modem that is set up to provide dial-out service only is a security hole.)

## Troubleshooting Modem Connections

When troubleshooting problems with modem connections, first check the following list with the user.

- Was the correct login ID or password used?
- Is the serial cable loose or unplugged?
- Is the serial cable verified to work properly?

Sometimes the SAF settings don't work. In that case, you have to remove the port monitor completely and reinstall it. Even then, the hardware can get into a state that requires you to reboot the system for the port monitor to start properly. See Appendix B, "Celeste's Tutorial on Solaris 2.x Modems and Terminals," for a set of commands to work around these problems.

Continue troubleshooting by checking the configuration of the modem.

- Was the proper `ttylabel` used?
- Does the `ttylabel` setting of the modem match the `ttylabel` of the SAF?
- If you have changed any modem switches, turn off the power to the modem, wait a few seconds, and turn it on again.

If the problem persists, check the system software.

- Was the port monitor configured to service the modem?
- Does it have the correct `ttylabel` associated with it?
- Does the `type` definition match a setting in the `/etc/ttydefs` file?
- Is the port monitor enabled? (Use the `sacadm -l -p` *pmtag* command.)
- Is the service enabled? (Use the `pmadm -l -p` *pmtag* command.)

If the Service Access Controller is starting the `ttymon` port monitor, the service is enabled, and the configuration matches the port monitor configuration, continue to search for the problem by checking the serial connection. A serial connection consists of serial ports, cables, modems, and terminals. Test each of these parts by using it with two other parts that are known to be reliable.

To check for cable problems, a breakout box is helpful. It plugs into the RS-232-C cable. A patch panel lets you connect any pin to any other pins. A breakout box often contains light-emitting diodes that show whether a signal is present on each pin.

Continue troubleshooting by checking each of the following:

- If you cannot access a port and the `ps` command shows that a process is running on it, make sure that pin 8 in the cable is connected. If the pin is connected, check that the device driver is configured properly to set the correct flag for the line to Off.

- If the error message `can't synchronize with hayes` is displayed when a Hayes-compatible modem is used, check the `/etc/remote` file and make sure that you have changed `at=ventel` to `at=hayes`.

- If the message `all ports busy` is displayed, the port may actually be busy running a dial-in user. Use the `ps` command to see what is running. You should also check to ensure that the carrier detect is set up properly. Type **pmadm -l** and press Return. If the last flag in the `PMSPECIFIC` field is `y`, delete the entry and reconfigure it, making sure that you use `-S n` (not `-S y`) as the last argument for *ttymon*.

- If the message `all ports busy` still displays after you have followed the above steps, the message may be bogus. Check the `/var/spool` and `/var/spool/locks` directories for leftover lock files. A lock file would have a name like `LCK.cua0`. If you find a lock file, remove it.

# Setting Up SAF for Character Terminals

The Solaris Operating Environment is automatically configured to work properly with Sun graphics display monitors. You do not need to do any additional SAF configuration to use them. The word *terminal* is used in this chapter to describe a *character terminal*—a serial port device that displays only letters, numbers, and other characters, such as those produced by a typewriter. The VT100 model, for example, is a popular type of character terminal that many other terminals can emulate.

Not all systems require character terminals. You may want to attach a character terminal to a server as an inexpensive control console or to a malfunctioning system's serial port to use for diagnostics.

If you do attach a character terminal to a system, you need to use the SAF to set it up. See Chapter 10, "Understanding the Service Access Facility," for background information about terminal control.

## Connecting the Terminal Cable

Use a null modem cable to connect a character terminal to serial ports on Sun systems. A null modem cable swaps lines 2 and 3 so that the proper transmit and receive signals are communicated between two DTE devices. Line 7 goes straight through, connecting pin 7 of the devices at each end of the null modem cable.

## Using Admintool: Serial Ports to Add a Character Terminal

You can use the Admintool: Serial Ports graphical user interface to add a character terminal. Table 54 shows the Admintool default settings for adding a character terminal.

*Table 54    Terminal—Hardwired Default Values*

| Item | Default Value |
|---|---|
| Port | a \| b \| other port identifier |
| Service | enabled |
| Baud rate | 9600 |
| Terminal type | tvi925 |
| Option: Initialize only | no |
| Option: Bidirectional | no |
| Option: Software carrier | yes |
| Login prompt | login: |
| Comment | Terminal—Hardwired |
| Service tag | tty*n* |
| Port monitor tag | zsmon |
| Create utmpx entry | yes |
| Connect on Carrier | no |
| Service | /usr/bin/login |
| Streams modules | ldterm,ttcompat |
| Timeout (secs) | never |

Use the following steps to configure SAF for a character terminal.

1. Start Admintool.
   See "Starting Admintool: Serial Ports" on page 258 for complete instructions on how to start Admintool.
2. In the Admintool: Serial Ports window, click on the port that will be used with a terminal.
3. From the Edit menu, choose Modify.

The Admintool: Modify Serial Port window is displayed showing the Basic settings. Click either More or Expert to display more settings.

4. Terminal—Hardwired is the default choice from the Template menu. If it is not displayed, choose it.

   Admintool: Modify Serial Port window displays default settings for the Terminal—Hardwired template shown in Table 54 on page 281.

5. Change values of template entries if desired.

   If you change the values, make sure that you change the comment field so that other users know that you have changed the default values.

6. Click on OK to configure the port.

## Initializing Ports with AdminTool Without Configuring

The Admintool: Modify Serial Port window enables you to initialize a port without configuring it. Table 55 shows the Admintool default values for initializing a port without configuring it.

*Table 55     Initialize Only—No Connection Default Values*

| Item | Default Value |
| --- | --- |
| Port | a \| b \| other port identifier |
| Service | enabled |
| Baud rate | 9600 |
| Terminal type | tvi925 |
| Option: Initialize only | yes |
| Option: Bidirectional | no |
| Option: Software carrier | no |
| Login prompt | ttyn login: |
| Comment | Initialize Only—No Connection |
| Service tag | ttyn |
| Port monitor tag | zsmon |
| Create utmpx entry | yes |
| Connect on carrier | no |
| Service | /usr/bin/login |
| Streams modules | ldterm,ttcompat |
| Timeout (secs) | never |

Use the following steps to initialize ports without configuring for a specific device.

1. From the Admintool: Serial Ports window, click on the port you want to initialize.
2. From the Edit menu, choose Modify.

   The Admintool: Modify Serial Port window is displayed.
3. Click Expert to display all of the settings.
4. Choose Initialize Only—No Connection from the Template menu.
5. Change values of template entries if desired.

   If you change the values, make sure that you change the comment field so that other users know that you have changed the default values.
6. Click OK to initialize the port.

### Removing Port Services with AdminTool

Use the following steps to delete services on configured ports with Admintool.

1. In the Admintool: Serial Ports window, click the port that you want to delete.
2. From the Edit menu, choose Delete.

   A confirmation window is displayed asking if you really want to delete the service for the specified port.
3. Click Cancel to stop the operation or Delete to delete the port.

## Using the SMC Serial Ports Tool to Add a Character Terminal

*New!*

You can use the SMC Serial Ports tool to configure SAF for character terminals within the current SMC management scope.

Use the following steps to configure SAF for modems with the SMC Serial Ports tool.

1. Start SMC.

   See "Starting the SMC Serial Ports Tool" on page 260 if you need instructions on how to start SMC.
2. Double-click on the Serial Ports icon.

   The Serial Ports window is displayed.
3. Click on the port to which the character terminal is connected and then from the Action menu, choose Configure > Terminal.

The Serial Port properties are displayed.

*NOTE. If you click on a port and choose Configure from the Action menu, only the basic options tab is displayed. You can display the Advanced options only by double-clicking on a port or by highlighting a port and clicking on the properties icon to the right of the View menu.*

4. Terminal—Hardwired is the default choice from the Template menu. If it is not displayed, choose it.

5. Change the values of template entries if desired.

   If you change the values, make sure that you change the comment field so that other users know that you have changed the default values.

6. Click on the OK button to configure the port.

## Using SAF Commands to Set Up Character Terminals

Solaris systems come with a `ttymon` port monitor named `zsmon` and with serial ports A and B already configured with default settings for terminals, as shown in the following example.

```
castle% /usr/sbin/sacadm -l
PMTAG          PMTYPE          FLGS RCNT STATUS       COMMAND
zsmon          ttymon          ttya          u     root      /dev/term/a I -
 /usr/bin/login - 9600 ldterm,ttcompat ttya login:  - tvi925 y  #
zsmon          ttymon          ttyb          u     root      /dev/term/b I -
 /usr/bin/login - 9600 ldterm,ttcompat ttyb login:  - tvi925 y  #
castle%
```

The I in the second field of the <PMSPECIFIC> column means that the service is initialized for the hardware configuration but connection to the service is not enabled.

You probably only need to add a login service to configure an existing port. Follow these steps to configure the SAF for a character terminal.

1. Become superuser.

2. Type **sacadm -l** and press Return.

   Check the output to make sure that a `ttymon` port monitor is configured. It is unlikely that you will need to add a new port monitor. If you do need to add one, type **sacadm -a -p *pmtag* -t *ttymon* -c /usr/lib/saf/ttymon -v `ttymon -V`** and press Return.

3. Type **pmadm -a -p** *pmtag* **-s** *svctag* **-i root -fu -v** **`ttymon -V`** **-m "`ttyadm -t** *terminfo-type* **-d** *dev-path* **-l** *ttylabel* **-s /usr/bin/login`"** and press Return.

   The port is configured for a login service.

4. Attach all of the cords and cables to the terminal and turn it on.

The following example creates a `ttymon` port monitor called `ttymon0` and enables a login for serial port `/dev/term/00`.

```
oak% su
Password:
# sacadm -l
PMTAG           PMTYPE         FLGS RCNT STATUS    COMMAND
zsmon           ttymon         -    0    ENABLED   /usr/lib/saf/ttymon #
# sacadm -a -p ttymon0 -t ttymon -c /usr/lib/saf/ttymon -v `ttyadm -V`
# sacadm -l
PMTAG           PMTYPE         FLGS RCNT STATUS    COMMAND
ttymonm0        ttymon         -    0    STARTING  /usr/lib/saf/ttymon #
zsmon           ttymon         -    0    ENABLED   /usr/lib/saf/ttymon #
# pmadm -a -p ttymon0 -s tty00 -i root -fu -v `ttyadm -V` -m "`ttyadm -t
  tvi925 -d /dev/term/00 -l 9600 -s
/usr/bin/login`"
# pmadm -l
PMTAG           PMTYPE         SVCTAG        FLGS ID      <PMSPECIFIC>
zsmon           ttymon         ttya          u    root    /dev/term/a I -
  /usr/bin/login - 9600 ldterm,ttcompat ttya login:  - tvi925 y  #
zsmon           ttymon         ttyb          u    root    /dev/term/b I -
  /usr/bin/login - 9600 ldterm,ttcompat ttyb login:  - tvi925 y  #
ttymon0         ttymon         tty00         u    root    /dev/term/00 - - -
  /usr/bin/login - 9600 login: - tvi925 - #
#
```

# Troubleshooting the Terminal Connection

When troubleshooting problems with terminal connections, first check the following list with the user.

- Was the correct login ID or password used?
- Is the terminal waiting for the xon flow control key?
- Is the serial cable loose or unplugged?
- Is the serial cable verified to work properly?
- Is the terminal configuration correct?
- Is the terminal turned off?

Continue troubleshooting by checking the configuration of the terminal.

- Was the proper *ttylabel* used?
- Does the *ttylabel* setting of the modem match the *ttylabel* of the SAF?

If the problem persists, check the system software.

- Was the port monitor configured to enable logins?
- Does it have the correct `ttylabel` associated with it?
- Is the port monitor enabled? (Use the `sacadm -l -p` *pmtag* command.)
- Is the service enabled? (Use the `pmadm -l -p` *pmtag* command.)

If the Service Access Controller is starting the `ttymon` port monitor, the service is enabled, and the configuration matches the port monitor configuration, continue to search for the problem by checking the serial connection. A serial connection consists of serial ports, cables, and terminals. Test each of these parts by using it with two other parts that are known to be reliable.

To check for cable problems, a breakout box is helpful. It plugs into the RS-232-C cable. A patch panel lets you connect any pin to any other pins. A breakout box often contains light-emitting diodes that show whether a signal is present on each pin.

If you cannot access a port and the `ps` command shows that a process is running on it, make sure that pin 8 in the cable is connected.

# 12

# SETTING UP PRINTING SERVICES

Sun recommends that you use the Solaris Print Manager, now available in the Solaris Operating Environment to set up printing on systems running the Solaris Operating Environment.

*New!*

This chapter describes how to set up network printing services with the Solaris Print Manager. The Solaris Print Manager issues the necessary SAF commands.

In the past, the term *network printer* was used to describe printers that were directly attached to a Sun print server. These printers were accessed over the network. In this book, the term network printer means a printer with an internal network card that has its own IP address and is directly connected to the network.

*New!*

You can connect printers to a network in the following ways, also illustrated in Figure 44.

- Connect a local printer to a user's system.
- Connect one or more printers to a print server.
- Connect a network printer directly to the network.

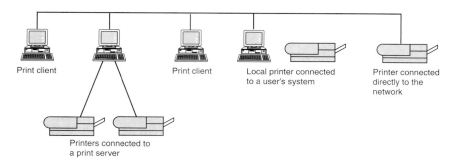

Figure 44    Three Ways to Connect Printers to a Network

**New!**    The network at your site may comprise many systems. A system that has the printer connected to it and makes the printer available to other systems is called a *print server*. Print servers also provide access to network printers. A system that has its printing needs met by a print server is called a *print client*. You need to decide which systems to designate as print servers with printers directly cabled to them, which systems to designate as print servers for network printers, and which systems to designate as print clients.

You perform the following basic tasks to set up printing services.

- Setting up local printers.
**New!**
- Setting up network printers.
- Setting up print servers.
- Setting up print clients.

# **New!** New Printing Features in the Solaris 8 Operating Environment

This section describes new printing features in the Solaris 8 Operating Environment.

## Solaris Print Manager

The Solaris Print Manager, previously available as part of the Solstice AdminSuite Package, is a Java-based graphical user interface that enables you to manage local and remote printers. You can use the Solaris Print Manager with NIS, NIS+, NIS+ with Federated Naming Service (xfn), and files nameservices. You must be superuser, have rights to administer printing, or be a member of a role that has rights to administer printing to use this tool. See Chapter 23, "Role-Based Access Control," for information about rights.

## Print Naming Enhancement to the Nameservice Switch File

The Solaris release supports the `printers` database in the `/etc/nsswitch.conf` nameservice switch file. The `printers` database provides centralized printer configuration information to print clients on the network. The Solaris Print Manager creates the `printers` database the first time you use it to configure a network printer. See "Enhanced Network Printer Support" on page 291 for more information.

## Enabling or Disabling Global Banner Page Printing

The Solaris 8 Operating Environment adds the `-banner` option with arguments of `always`, `never`, and `optional` to the `lpadmin` command. When banner page printing is set to `optional`, the banner is printed by default, but users can disable banner page printing with the `lp -o nobanner` command. See `lpadmin`(1M) for more information.

# Solaris Print Package Redesign

This section describes the redesign of the Solaris print packages starting with the Solaris 2.6 release and the additional features that were added with that release.

## Redesign of Print Packages

Starting with the Solaris 2.6 release, print packages are redesigned to provide greater flexibility and modularity of print software installation and to enable installation of a print client that takes up less disk space.

In the print package redesign, the default is to install all of the packages. Print servers require installation of all packages, including both client and server. For print clients, you can choose to install only the print client packages. PostScript filter software is provided in its own print package, which provides client configuration files and commands for the print service. Table 56 describes the redesigned set of print packages.

*Table 56    Solaris Redesigned Print Packages*

| Package | Base Directory | Description |
| --- | --- | --- |
| SUNWpcr | / (root) | Sun Print-Client. |
| SUNWpcu | /usr | Sun Print-Client. |
| SUNWpsr | / (root) | Sun Print-LP Server. |
| SUNWpsu | /usr | Sun Print-LP Server. |
| SUNWpsf | /usr | PostScript Filters. |
| SUNWscplp | /usr | Sun Print-Source Compatibility. |
| SUNWppm | /usr/sadm/admin/bin | Solaris Print Manager (new in the Solaris 8 release). |

*New!*

The following print packages have been removed from Solaris 2.6 and later releases.

- SUNWlpr—LP print service, (root).
- SUNWlpu—LP print service-Client, (usr).
- SUNWlps—LP print service-Server, (usr).

Print commands from SUNWscpu have been moved into the SUNWscplp (Sun Print-Source Compatibility) package.

## Print Protocol Adaptor

Starting with the Solaris 2.6 release, the print protocol adapter replaces the Service Access Facility (SAF), the network listener, and lpNet on the inbound side of the LP spooler with a more modular and modern design.

The print protocol adapter provides the following features.

- The complete BSD print protocol, plus extended Solaris functionality, is implemented.
- Multiple spooling systems can coexist on the same host and have access to the BSD print protocol.
- Third-party application developers can extend the print protocol adapter to support other printing protocols such as those of Apple and Novell.

The new print protocol adapter is compatible with print clients set up in previous Solaris releases if the BSD protocol was used to configure these clients. If the BSD protocol was not used, you must modify the previous Solaris print client configuration to use the BSD protocol with Admintool, the Solaris Print Manager, or the `lpsystem` command.

## Print Client Software

Starting with the Solaris 2.6 release, the Print Client software is bundled with the Solaris release as packages SUNWpcr and SUNWpcu. This software was previously released as an unbundled product.

The Print Client software uses an NIS map, NIS+ table, or a single file to provide centralized client administration in the Solaris release. The Print Client software includes the following features.

- Replaces the `/etc/lp` directory structure with a configuration database that can be stored in a user file (`$HOME/.printers`), a system file (`/etc/printers.conf`), an NIS map (`printers.conf.byname`), or an NIS+ FNS context.
- Uses a more streamlined implementation that provides reduced client overhead and quicker, more accurate responses to print status requests.
- Uses the `lpset(1M)` command to create the `printers.conf` file.
- Reduces the size of the package from previous Solaris releases.
- Provides interoperability with the BSD protocol, HP-UX, and other systems as described in RFC-1179.

## Enhanced Network Printer Support

Starting with the Solaris 2.6 release, print software provides better support for network printers than in previous Solaris releases.

Network printer support including the following features.

- A new interface script, `/usr/lib/lp/model/netstandard`, which is specifically designed to support network printers. This script collects the spooler and print database information necessary for performing network printing and passes that information to the print output module.
- A new print output module, `netpr`, is called from the `netstandard` interface script to print the print job. It opens a network connection to the printer, creates the correct protocol instructions, and sends the data to the printer. The `netpr` program currently supports two protocols: BSD print protocol and a TCP pass-through.

*NOTE. You should use this new support only as a last resort. Usually, the vendors of network printers provide their own printer drivers and*

*New!*

*interface scripts, which Sun recommends that you use in preference to the new functionality.*

New arguments to the `lpadmin -o` command are available for specifying destination name, protocol, and timeout values for the network printer.

**New!** The Solaris 8 Operating Environment supports the `printers` database in the `/etc/nsswitch.conf` nameservice switch file. The `printers` database provides centralized printer configuration information to print clients on the network. The Solaris Print Manager creates and manages the `printers` database.

With the `printers` database and corresponding sources of information in the nameservice switch file, print clients can automatically access centralized printer configuration information without having it added to their own systems. Table 57 shows the default `printers` entry for each of the nameservice environments.

*Table 57    Default printers Entries in the /etc/nsswitch.conf File*

| Nameservice | Default printers Entry |
|---|---|
| files | printers: user files |
| nis | printers: user files nis |
| nis+ | printers: user nisplus files xfn |

For example, if the nameservice is NIS, print client configuration information is looked up in the following order.

- user—The `$HOME/.printers` file for the user.
- files—The `/etc/printers.conf` file.
- nis—The `printers.conf.byname` table.

If the nameservice is NIS+, print client configuration information is looked up in the following order.

- user—The `$HOME/.printers` file for the user.
- nisplus—The `printers.org_dir` table.
- files—The `/etc/printers.conf` file.
- xfn—The FNS printer contexts.

See "Converting Printer Configuration in NIS+ (xfn) to NIS+ Format" on page 313 for more information about FNS printer contexts.

See "Adding a Network Printer" on page 313 for information about configuring network printers.

# Print Administration Tools in the Solaris Operating Environment

The Solaris printing software provides an environment for setting up and managing client access to printers on a network. It contains the following components.

- Solaris Print Manager—previously provided as the Solstice AdminSuite *New!* Printer Manager unbundled product—is a graphical user interface that enables you to manage printers in a nameservice environment and over the network.

- Admintool, a graphical user interface, enables you to manage printing on a local system.

- The LP print service command-line interface enables you to set up and manage printers that provide additional functionality that is not available with the other print management tools.

*NOTE. If you do not use the Solaris Print Manager to set up and manage printing, you must use some combination of the other components to completely manage printing in the Solaris Operating Environment.*

Table 58 summarizes the features of the Solaris printing components.

*Table 58   Solaris Printing Component Features*

| Component | Graphical User Interface | Configure Network Printers | Manage Print Clients and Servers | NIS, NIS+, or NIS+ (xfn) | |
|---|---|---|---|---|---|
| Solaris Print Manager | Yes | Yes | Yes | Yes | *New!* |
| Admintool | Yes | No | Yes | No | |
| LP commands | No | Yes | Yes | No | |

## Choosing a Method to Manage Printers

As you can see from the list of features in Table 58, the printing components provide overlapping functionality. Your site requirements and needs for centralized or decentralized printer administration determine the optimum combination of tools you use for print administration.

The Solaris Print Manager application provides a graphical solution for   *New!* setting up and managing printers on a network. The advantage of the Solaris

Print Manager is that it supports a nameservice—NIS, NIS+, or NIS+ (xfn)—which enables you to centralize print administration for a network. You can also use the lpadmin command to configure printers on individual systems.

You must run Admintool on the system to which the printer is connected. When you set up a printer, Admintool makes the appropriate changes in the /etc/printers.conf file and /etc/lp directories on the system as required. You can use Admintool to set up a system as a print server or print client only if it is running the Solaris operating system.

The Solaris Print Manager should meet most of your needs for setting up printing services. However, if you have special needs, such as writing scripts, you may want to use the LP print service commands directly.

# System Requirements for a Print Server

*New!*

You can attach a printer to a stand-alone system, or to any system on the network, or you can connect printers that have their own IP address directly to the network. You can make any networked system that has adequate system resources into a print server. A print server can have printers directly connected to it or can provide service for network printers.

Each print server should have the following system resources.

- Spooling directory space of 10 MB per user (or more).
- Memory of 128 MB (or more).
- Swap space of 512 MB (or more).

If the print server has a /var directory that resides in a small partition, and if a large amount of disk space is available elsewhere, you can use that space as spooling space by mounting it on the /var directory on the print server. Consult the *Solaris System Administrator's Guide,* Third Edition, for information about mounting file systems and editing the /etc/vfstab file.

# Printer Configuration Information

To configure a printer directly connected to a print server on the network, you need the following configuration information.

- A unique name for the printer (required).
- The serial (or parallel) device name (required), for example /dev/xxx.

- The printer type (required).
- The type of file content (required), for example, `PS` for PostScript, `simple` for ASCII, or both.
- The filter names for your printer (required).
- The description of the printer to convey to users (recommended, optional)
- The default printer for each system (recommended, optional).

Configuration information is stored in the LP configuration files in the `/etc/lp` directory.

## Printer Name

Choose a *printer name* for the printer you are adding to a system. A printer name must be unique among all printers known to the network and can contain a maximum of 14 alphanumeric characters and underscores.

You should also establish conventions when naming printers. Make your printer names meaningful and easy to remember. A printer name can identify the type of printer, its location, or the print server name. Establish a naming convention that works for your site. If you have different types of printers on the network, for example, including the printer type as part of the printer name can help users choose an appropriate printer. You could identify, for instance, PostScript printers with the letters `PS`. If all of the printers at your site are PostScript printers, however, you do not need to include `PS` as part of the printer name.

You use printer names when you perform the following tasks.

- Add the printer to the LP print service.
- Change the configuration of the printer.
- Monitor the print queue.
- Check the status of the printer.
- Accept or cancel print requests for the printer.
- Enable or disable the printer.
- Specify a default printer.
- Submit a print job to a particular printer.

## Printer Port

The printer *device name* identifies the port to which the printer is connected. The Solaris Print Manager, Admintool, and the `-v` option to the `lpadmin` command use the `stty` settings from the standard printer interface program to initialize the printer port.

When you install a printer or later change its setup, you can specify the device or the printer port to which the printer is connected with Solaris Print Manager, with Admintool, or with the `lpadmin -p` *printer-name* `-v` *device-name* command.

Most systems have two serial ports and a parallel port. Unless you add ports, you cannot connect more than two serial printers and a parallel printer to one system.

With Solaris Print Manager and Admintool, you can choose `/dev/term/a`, `/dev/term/b`, `/dev/bpp0`, or `/dev/printers/0` for the serial port, or choose Other and specify any port name that the print server recognizes. These options give you as much flexibility as the `lpadmin` command does.

The LP print service initializes the printer port with the settings from the standard printer interface program. If you have a parallel printer or a serial printer for which the default settings do not work, you need to adjust the printer port characteristics to use a custom setting.

*NOTE. If you use multiple ports on an IA microprocessor-based system, only the first port is enabled by default. To use more than one port, you must manually edit the device driver port configuration file for each additional asy (serial) port or lp (parallel) port. The path names for the IA port configuration files are shown below.*

```
/platform/i86pc/kernel/drv/asy.conf
/platform/i86pc/kernel/drv/lp.conf
```

*Refer to your IA documentation for information about configuring serial and parallel ports on IA systems.*

## Printer Type

A *printer type* is the generic name for a printer. By convention, it is often derived from the manufacturer's name. For example, the printer type for the Digital Equipment Corporation LN03 printer is `ln03`. However, one common printer type—`PS`, for PostScript laser printer—does not follow this convention. `PS` is used for many different models of PostScript printers.

For a local PostScript printer, use either `PS` or `PSR` (which reverses the pages) as the printer type. `PSR` works reliably only with PostScript files that conform to the standards in Appendix C of the *PostScript Language Reference Manual*. Refer to the bibliography at the back of this book for a complete reference.

The printer type must match an entry in the `terminfo` database. The LP print service uses the printer type to extract information about the capabilities of the printer from the `terminfo` database, as well as the control data, to initialize a particular printer before printing a file.

You specify the printer type with Solaris Print Manager, Admintool, or with the `-T` option of the `lpadmin` command, where *printer-type* matches the name of a file in the `terminfo` database, which contains compiled terminal information files. These files are located in the `/usr/share/lib/terminfo/*` directories. For example, the `terminfo` directory for the type name `PS` is `/usr/share/lib/terminfo/P/PS`.

*New!*

You can specify the following printer types from the Solaris Print Manager Printer Type menu.

*New!*

- PostScript (default).
- HP Printer.
- Reverse PostScript.
- Epson 2500.
- IBM Proprinter.
- Qume S print 5.
- Daisy.
- Diablo.

Not all available printer types are listed in the Solaris Print Manager Printer Type menu. If you need to specify a printer type that is not included in the Solaris Print Manager menu, use the `lpadmin -T` command.

If a printer can emulate more than one kind of printer, you can assign it several types. If you specify more than one printer type, the LP print service uses one of the types as appropriate for each print request.

If you don't specify a type with the `lpadmin` command, the default type is `unknown`, and the local printer does not get initialized before printing a file.

## File Content Type

The *file content type* tells the LP print service what types of files you can print directly on each printer. Print requests can ask for a type, and the LP print service uses this type to match jobs to printers. Most printers can print two types of files directly.

- The same type as the printer type (for example, `PS` for PostScript).
- The type `simple` (an ASCII file).

**New!**

Solaris Print Manager provides a list of file content types, listed in Table 59, that you can choose when installing or modifying a local printer. Solaris Print Manager translates the choices to the names that the LP print service uses.

*Table 59     Solaris Print Manager File Content Types*

| File Contents Menu Item | LP Print Service Name | Filtering Description |
|---|---|---|
| PostScript (the default) | `postscript` | PostScript files do not require filtering. |
| ASCII | `simple` | ASCII files do not require filtering. |
| Both PostScript and ASCII | `simple,postscript` | PostScript files and ASCII files do not require filtering. |
| None | `" "` | All files require filtering except those matching the type of the printer. |
| Any | `any` | No filtering required. If the printer cannot handle a file content type directly, the file is not printed. |

Not all available file content types are listed in the Solaris Print Manager File Content menu. If you need to specify file content types that are not included on the Solaris Print Manager menu, use the `lpadmin -I` command. The following paragraphs describe additional file content types.

Some printers can accept and print several types of files. You can specify the names of the content types as a list. Table 60 lists some common file content types for local printers.

*Table 60     Common File Content Types for Local Printers*

| Type | Description |
|---|---|
| `any` | Accept any file content type. |
| `cif` | Output of BSD `cifplot`. |
| `daisy` | Daisy wheel printer. |
| `dmd` | DMD. |
| `fortran` | ASA carriage control format. |
| `otroff` | Cat typesetter instructions generated by BSD or pre-System V `troff` (old `troff`). |

*Table 60    Common File Content Types for Local Printers (Continued)*

| Type | Description |
|------|-------------|
| `plot` | Plotting instructions from Tektronix displays and devices. |
| `PS` | PostScript language. |
| `raster` | Raster bitmap format for Varian raster devices. |
| `simple` | ASCII file. |
| `tex` | DVI format files. |
| `troff` | Device-independent output from `troff`. |

*NOTE. If you specify more than one printer type, you must specify*
`simple` *as one of the content types.*

Content type names may look like printer names, but you are free to choose content type names that are meaningful to you and the users of the printers. Use the following command to specify the file content type with the `lpadmin` command.

```
lpadmin -p printer-name -I file-content-type
```

The content types to use for a Solaris print client are `any`, `simple`, and `PS`. If you omit the content type, the default is `any`, which sends the file to the print server. Any required filtering is done on the print server, not on the print client. The type `PS` filters files on the client.

Table 61 lists the printer type and content type for frequently used PostScript printers.

*NOTE. The name* `simple` *means ASCII file, and* `any` *means any file content type. Be sure to use them consistently. The name* `terminfo` *is reserved as a reference to all types of printers.*

All printers in Table 61 are either `PS` or `PSR`. `PS` prints a banner page first and prints the document from front to back. `PSR` reverses the pagination, printing the pages in reverse order, with the banner page last. File content type is `PS` for all these models.

*Table 61    Frequently Used PostScript Printers*

| Manufacturer | Model |
|--------------|-------|
| Apple | Personal LW II<br>LaserWriterII<br>LaserWriter IINT<br>LaserWriter IINTX |

*Table 61*     *Frequently Used PostScript Printers (Continued)*

| Manufacturer | Model |
|---|---|
| Canon | BJ-10<br>BJ-130e<br>LBP-4<br>LBP-8 |
| Epson | All |
| GammaData | System300 |
| Hewlett Packard | II, IIP, IID<br>III, IIIP, IIID<br>Deskjet+ |
| Mitsubishi Electric | G650<br>G370<br>S340 |
| Pacific | Rim Data Sciences |
| QMS | PS 410<br>PS 810 |
| Raster Graphics | ColorStation |
| Seiko | 5504<br>5514 |
| Sharp | JX-730 |
| Shinko | CHC-635<br>CHC-645-2<br>CHC-645-4<br>CHC-345<br>CHC-445<br>CHC-445-4<br>CHC-745-2 |
| Talaris | 2090 |
| Talaris/Olympus | 3093<br>5093 |
| Talaris/Ricoh | 1590, 1590-T |
| Talaris/Xerox | 2492-B |
| Tektronix | Phaser DXN<br>Phaser SXS |

*Table 61     Frequently Used PostScript Printers (Continued)*

| Manufacturer | Model |
|---|---|
| Versatec | 8836<br>C25*xx* series<br>CE3000 series<br>7000 series<br>V-80 series<br>8200 series<br>8500 series<br>CADMate series<br>8600 series<br>8900 series |

Table 62 lists additional non-PostScript printers and shows the printer type to use for configuring each printer. The file content type is `simple` for all these printers.

*Table 62     Non-PostScript Printers*

| Printer | Printer Type |
|---|---|
| Daisy | `daisy` |
| Datagraphix | `datagraphix` |
| DEC LA100 | `la100` |
| DEC LN03 | `ln03` |
| DECwriter | `decwriter` |
| Diablo | `diablo`<br>`diablo-m8` |
| Epson 2500 variations | `epson2500`<br>`epson2500-80`<br>`epson2500-hi`<br>`epson2500-hi80` |
| Hewlett Packard HPCL printer | `hplaser` |
| IBM Proprinter | `ibmproprinter` |

# Print Filters

*Print filters* are programs that convert print requests from one format to another. The LP print service uses filters to perform the following tasks.

- Convert a file from one data format to another so that you print it properly on a specific type of printer.
- Handle the special modes of printing, such as two-sided printing, landscape printing, or draft- or letter-quality printing.
- Detect printer faults and notify the LP print service of them so that the print service can alert users and system administrators.

The Solaris Operating Environment provides a default set of PostScript filters. Table 63 lists and describes the default PostScript filters.

*Table 63*     *PostScript Filters*

| Filter | Action |
|---|---|
| download | Download fonts. |
| dpost | ditroff to PostScript. |
| postdaisy | daisy to PostScript. |
| postdmd | dmd to PostScript. |
| postio | Communicate with printer. |
| postior | Communicate with printer. |
| postmd | Matrix gray scales to PostScript. |
| postplot | plot to PostScript. |
| postprint | simple to PostScript. |
| postreverse | Reverse or select pages. |
| posttek | TEK4014 to PostScript. |

The Solaris Operating Environment does not provide the following filters.

- TEX
- oscat (NeWSprint™ opost)
- Enscript. The Enscript filters are freely available from prep.ai.mit.edu:/pub/gnu/enscript/.

## Printer Description (Optional)

You can define a *printer description* for a printer. The description can contain any helpful information that might benefit its users. For example, the description could say where the printer is located or whom to call when the printer has problems.

Users can display the printer's description with the following command.

```
% lpstat -D -p printername
```

## Default Printer (Optional)

You can specify a *default printer* for each system, even if it is the only printer connected to the system. When you specify a default printer, users do not need to type the default printer name when they use LP print service commands. However, they can override the default by explicitly naming another printer or setting the LPDEST environment variable. Before you can designate a default printer, it must be known to the LP print service on the system.

# Introducing Solaris Print Manager

New!

In the Solaris 8 release, the Solaris Print Manager is the preferred method for managing printers. This Java-based graphical user interface centralizes printing information when used in conjunction with a nameservice. Using a nameservice to store printer configuration information centralizes printer information and makes printer information available to all systems on the network.

You can use Print Manager in the following nameservice environments.

- files.
- NIS.
- NIS+.
- NIS+ with Federated Naming Service (xfn).

See "The Nameservice Switch" on page 144 and "Enhanced Network Printer Support" on page 291 for additional information about the /etc/nsswitch.conf file.

In the Solaris 8 release, you can use the Solaris Print Manager to manage printer configuration information in the NIS+ nameservice without the underlying xfn application layer. Eliminating the underlying xfn application layer provides better performance when accessing printer configuration information. See "Converting Printer Configuration in NIS+ (xfn) to NIS+ Format" on page 313 for more information.

You must be superuser, have rights to administer printers, or be a member of a role that grants you rights to manage printing functions to use the

Solaris Print Manager. See Chapter 23, "Role-Based Access Control," for information about rights.

Solaris Print Manager recognizes existing printer information on the printer servers, print clients, and in the nameservice databases. You do not need to convert print clients to use the new Solaris Print Manager as long as the print clients are running the Solaris 2.6 release or compatible versions.

Using Solaris Print Manager to perform printer-related tasks automatically updates the appropriate printer databases. Solaris Print Manager also includes a command-line console that displays the `lp` command line for the add, modify, and delete printer operations. Errors and warnings are also displayed when Printer Manager operations are performed.

You can run Solaris Print Manager on a remote system with the display sent to the local system. Use the following syntax to set the `DISPLAY` environment variable for the Bourne and Korn shells.

```
DISPLAY=hostname:display_number;export DISPLAY
```

*hostname* is the name of the remote system and *display_number* is the name of the display. For example, to display the Solaris Print Manager from `paperbark` on the system `castle`, type the following command on `castle`.

```
$ su
Password:
# DISPLAY=paperbark:0;export DISPLAY
$ /usr/sadm/admin/bin/printmgr&
```

## Solaris Print Manager Prerequisites

Before you use Solaris Print Manager to configure printers, verify that the following prerequisites are met.

- Use an X Window server, displaying Solaris Print Manager either remotely—by setting the `DISPLAY` environment variable to display the Print Manager on your screen—or locally.
- Log in as superuser to the print server to install an attached or network printer, or to the print client to add access to a printer.
- Have the required access privileges for the NIS, NIS+, or NIS+ (`xfn`) nameservice.
  - For NIS, you need the root password for the NIS master server.
  - For NIS+, you may need to identify the group that owns the `printers` table.

- For NIS+ (`xfn`), you may need to identify the group that owns the federated naming table.
- Make sure the `/etc/nsswitch.conf` file for each individual print server and client is configured to examine the nameservice you modified above.

*New!*

## Identifying the NIS+ Group That Owns the printers Table

Use the following steps to identify the NIS+ group that owns the `printers` table.

1. Log in as superuser to the NIS+ master server.
2. Type **niscat -o printers.org_dir.domainname** and press Return.

   The group that owns the `printers` table is displayed. In the following example, the `printers.org_dir` table is not found.

```
nismaster% su
Password:
# niscat -o printers.org_dir.wellard.com.
printers.org_dir.wellard.com.: Not found.
#
```

3. If you get a `Not Found` message, configure an NIS+ printer with the Solaris Print Manager.

   See "Adding a New Attached Printer with Print Manager" on page 308 for instructions. If the `printers.org_dir` table does not exist, Solaris Print Manager creates it when you add a printer and modifies it, as needed, when you change a printer configuration.

   The following example identifies the group that owns the `printers` table as `admin`. The group line is highlighted in bold.

```
nismaster# niscat -o printers.org_dir.wellard.com.
Object Name    : "printers"
Directory      : "org_dir.wellard.com."
Owner          : "nismaster.wellard.com."
Group          : "admin.wellard.com."
Access Rights  : r---rmcdrmcdr---
Time to Live   : 12:0:0
Creation Time  : Mon Oct 30 14:13:16 2000
Mod. Time      : Mon Oct 30 14:13:16 2000
Object Type    : TABLE
Table Type         : printers_tbl
Number of Columns  : 2
Character Separator :
Search Path        :
Columns            :
        [0]     Name       : key
                Attributes : (SEARCHABLE, TEXTUAL DATA, CASE SENSITIVE)
                Access Rights : ----------------
        [1]     Name       : datum
```

```
                    Attributes    : (TEXTUAL DATA)
                    Access Rights : ----------------
nismaster#
```

4. If the name of the system running Solaris Print Manager is not included as part of the Owner name in the output from the `niscat` command—`"nismaster.wellard.com."` in the previous example—add the system that runs Solaris Print Manager to the NIS+ `admin` group authorized to update the `printers.org_dir` table. Type **nisgrpadm -a admin.*domainname hostname*** and press Return.

5. Log in as superuser to the system that runs Solaris Print Manager. Depending on your NIS+ configuration, you may also need to run the `/usr/bin/keylogin` command. See `keylogin`(1) for more information.

See "Starting Solaris Print Manager" on page 307 for instructions on how to start Solaris Print Manager.

## Identifying the NIS+ (xfn) Group That Owns the printers Table

Use the following steps to identify the NIS+ (`xfn`) group that owns the `printers` table.

1. Log in as superuser to the NIS+ master server.
2. Type **niscat -o printers.org_dir.domainname** and press Return.
3. If the system name is not include as part of the Owner name in the output from the `niscat` command, add the system that runs Solaris Print Manager to the NIS+ `admin` group authorized to update the `fns.ctx_dir.`*wq* file, type **nisgrpadm -a admin.*domainname hostname*** and press Return.
4. Log in as superuser to the system that runs Solaris Print Manager. Depending on your NIS+ configuration, you may also need to run the `/usr/bin/keylogin` command. See `keylogin`(1) for more information.

## Starting Solaris Print Manager

Use the following steps to start Solaris Print Manager from the Workspace menu.

1. From the Workspace menu, choose Tools > Printer Administrator.
   The Action: Print Administrator window is displayed.

2. Type the name of the system you want to configure with Solaris Print Manager and click on the OK button.
   The Invoker—Password screen is displayed,

3. Type the root password for the system.

*NOTE. Alternatively, you can start Solaris Print Manager from a command line. Become superuser in a Terminal window and type* `/usr/sadm/admin/bin/printmgr&`. *If you use Solaris Print Manager frequently, you may want to add* `/usr/sadm/admin/bin` *to your root path.*

The Select Naming Service window is displayed, asking you to choose the nameservice, as shown in Figure 45.

*Figure 45    Print Manager Select Naming Service Window*

4. Choose the appropriate nameservice from the Naming Service menu and click on the OK button.
   The nameservice you choose should match the nameservice specified on the `printers` line in the `/etc/nsswitch.conf` file.
   The Print Manager window is displayed, as shown in Figure 46.

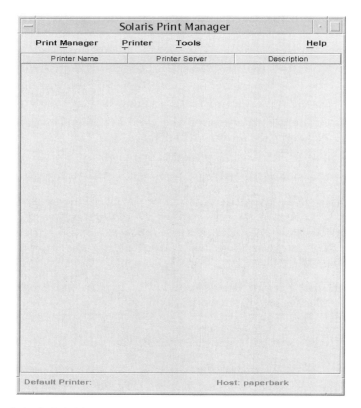

*Figure 46    Solaris Print Manager Window*

New!    ## Adding a New Attached Printer with Print Manager

The first task in setting up a print server is to set the printer up as a local Solaris printer. To add a new printer directly cabled to a print server, you need the following information.

- Printer name.
- Description.
- Printer port.
- Printer type.
- File contents.
- Fault notification policy.

- Whether this printer is the default.
- Whether to always print banners.
- User access list.

Once you have physically attached the printer to the computer, use the following steps to make the printer available to the local computer.

1.  Start the Solaris Print Manager (if necessary).

    See "Starting Solaris Print Manager" on page 307 for more information.

2.  From the Printer menu, choose New Attached Printer, as shown in Figure 47.

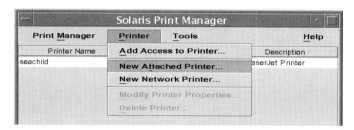

*Figure 47    Choose New Network Printer from the Printer Menu*

The New Attached Printer window is displayed, as shown in Figure 48.

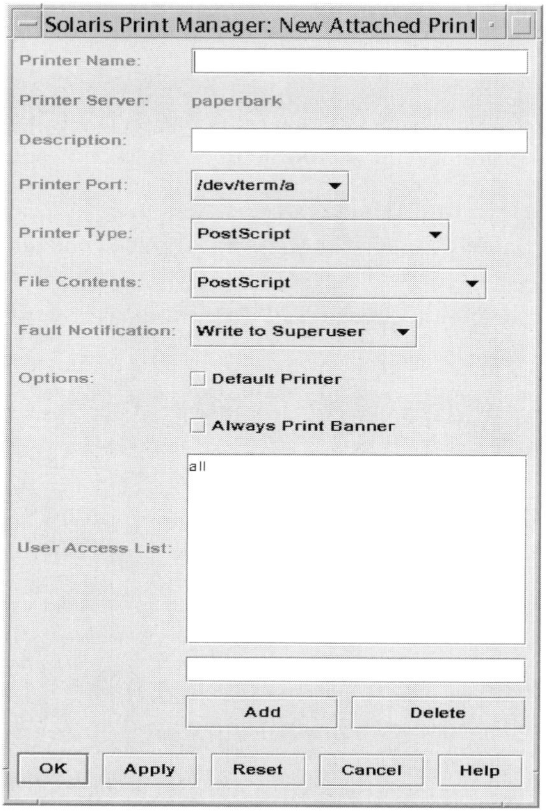

*Figure 48    New Attached Printer Window*

Click on the Help button if you need help with details about values that are required for the text fields.

3.  Fill in the form and click on the OK button.

    The printer is added to the Solaris Print Manager, and the appropriate databases and files are updated.

4.  If files do not print correctly or are not printed on the correct printer, see the section "Solving Printing Problems" on page 322 for help.

## New! Adding a New Network Printer with Print Manager

You can use Solaris Print Manager to configure a network printer—that is, a printer that is connected directly to the network as its own node. See "Adding a Network Printer" on page 313 for information about network printers and

"Adding a Network Printer with Solaris Print Manager" on page 315 for instructions on adding a network printer with Solaris Print Manager.

## Adding Access to a Printer with the Print Manager

*New!*

To add access to a printer, you need the following information.

- Printer name.
- Print server name.
- Description of the printer.
- Whether this printer is the default printer.

Use the following steps to add access to a printer.

1. Start the Print Manager (if necessary).

   See "Starting Solaris Print Manager" on page 307 for more information.

2. From the Printer menu, choose Add Access to Printer, as shown in Figure 49.

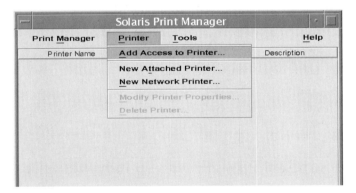

*Figure 49    Printer Menu*

The Solaris Print Manager Add Access to Printer window is displayed, as shown in Figure 50.

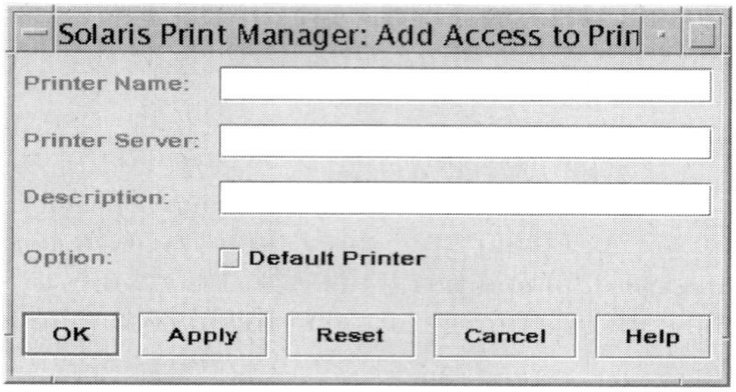

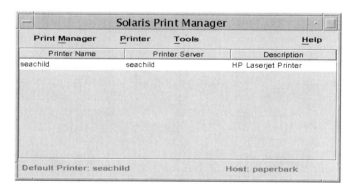

*Figure 50*   *Solaris Print Manager Add Access to Printer Window*

> 3.  Type the printer name, name of the printer server, and description in the text fields. If you want this printer to be the default printer, click on the Default Printer check box.
>
> 4.  Click on the OK button.
>
>     The printer is configured, the printer information is added to the list in the Solaris Print Manager window, and the relevant files are updated. The name of the default printer is displayed at the bottom of the window, as shown in Figure 51.

*Figure 51*   *Solaris Print Manager Window*

> 5.  If files do not print correctly or are not printed on the correct printer, see the section "Solving Printing Problems" on page 322 for help.

## Converting Printer Configuration in NIS+ (xfn) to NIS+ Format

New!

This section describes how to convert printer configuration information in NIS+ (xfn) format to NIS+ format. You can run the following conversion script only on a system running the Solaris 8 Operating Environment.

1. Log in as superuser to the NIS+ master.
2. Copy the following conversion script and name it something like /tmp/convert.

```sh
#!/bin/sh
#
# Copyright (C) 1999 by Sun Microsystems, Inc.
# All Rights Reserved
#
PRINTER=""
for LINE in `lpget -n xfn list | tr "\t " "Control A Control B?"` ; do
 LINE=`echo ${LINE} | tr "Control A ControlB" "\t " | sed -e 's/^
\t//g'`
    case "${LINE}" in
     *:)
       PRINTER=`echo ${LINE} | sed -e 's/://g'`
       ;;
     *=*)
       lpset -n nisplus -a "${LINE}" ${PRINTER}
       ;;
    esac
 done
```

3. Type **chmod 755 /tmp/convert** and press Return.

   The script is executable.
4. Type **/tmp/convert** and press Return.

# Adding a Network Printer

New!

A network printer is a hardware device that is connected directly to the network. A print server can access the network printer without actually being connected to it with a cable. The network printer has its own system name and IP address.

You should always set up a print server for each network printer so that print clients submit print jobs through the print server to the network printer.

*NOTE. Although you could configure every single system as a print server for a network printer so each system could submit print jobs directly, in practice, these printers tend to lock up or act strangely if you configure more than 16 systems as print servers.*

Figure 52 shows the path of a print request that is submitted from a print client through a print server to a network printer.

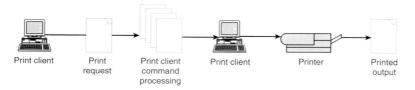

Print client    Print       Print client    Print client        Printer        Printed
                request     command                                              output
                            processing

*Figure 52    Printing to a Network Printer*

Network printers may use one or more special protocols that require a printing program supplied by the vendor. The procedures to set up the vendor-supplied printing program vary. If the printer does not come with vendor-supplied support, you can use the Solaris network printer support with most devices. Sun strongly advises that you use the print vendor software whenever possible.

If the vendor supplies an SVR4 printer interface script to replace the standard printer interface script, this interface script will call the vendor-supplied printing program to send the job to the printer. If the vendor does not provide an SVR4 printer interface script, you need to modify the standard interface script to call the vendor-supplied printing program.

## Adding a Network Printer with Vendor-Supplied Tools

Vendors who provide network printers usually provide an interface script. For example, for HP LaserJet printers, Hewlett Packard provides JetAdmin/JetDirect software and drivers for Solaris. JetAdmin/JetDirect includes the necessary filters and interface scripts to recognize pure text and PostScript jobs.

LPRng is an alternative print spooler that provides support for network printers. LPRng a descendant of the LPD/BSD family of spoolers that provides administrative control over printing operations. For example, LPRng provides IFHP, which is its own implementation of the HP JetAdmin/JetDirect software. LPRng is available free from www.lprng.org.

Use the following steps to add a network printer with vendor-supplied tools.

1.  Consult the vendor's installation documentation for information about the hardware switches and cabling requirement.
2.  Connect the printer to the network and turn on the power to the printer.

3.  Get an IP address and select a name for the printer node.

    This step is equivalent to adding any node to the network.

4.  Follow the printer vendor instructions to add the network printer to a Solaris system.

5.  Add client access to the new printer.

## Adding a Network Printer with Solaris Print Manager

You can use Solaris Print Manager to configure a network printer. To add a new network printer, you need the following information.

- Printer name.
- Description.
- Printer type.
- File contents.
- Fault notification policy.
- Destination—The internal name of the printer node that is used by the printer subsystem to access the printer. It is the name of the printer node or the name of the printer node with a printer vendor port designation. The print vendor documentation explicitly defines the printer vendor port designation.
- Protocol—The over-the-wire protocol used to communicate with the printer. The printer vendor documentation supplies the information about the protocol. The network printer support supplies both BSD Printer Protocol and raw TCP. Because of implementation variations, you may want to try both.
- Whether this printer is the default.
- Whether to always print banners.
- User access list.

Use the following steps to add a new network printer.

1.  Start the Print Manager (if necessary).

    See "Starting Solaris Print Manager" on page 307 for more information.

2.  From the Print menu, choose New Network Printer, as shown in Figure 53.

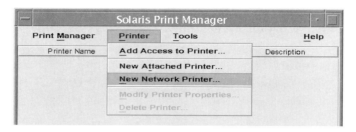

*Figure 53* Choose New Network Printer from the Print Menu

The New Network Printer window is displayed, as shown in Figure 54.

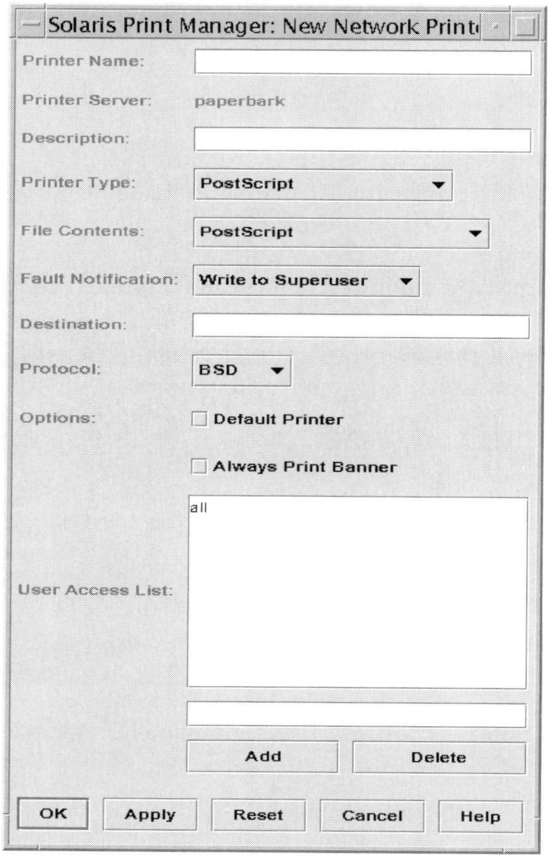

*Figure 54* New Network Printer Window

Click on the Help button if you need help with details about values that are required for the text fields.

3. Fill in the form and click on the OK button.

The printer is added to the Print Manager and the appropriate databases and files are updated.

4. If the file does not print correctly or is not printed on the correct printer, see the section "Solving Printing Problems" on page 322 for help.

## Adding a Network Printer with LP Commands

This section describes the steps needed to set up a network printer with the Solaris network printer support software. Use these steps only for printers that do not come with vendor-supplied software.

You need the following information to configure a network printer.

- Printer name—The name of the printer.
- Printer server name—The name of the print server that spools and schedules the jobs for a printer.
- Destination—The internal name of the printer node that is used by the printer subsystem to access the printer. It is the name of the printer node or the name of the printer node with a printer vendor port designation. The print vendor documentation explicitly defines the printer vendor port designation.
- Protocol—The over-the-wire protocol used to communicate with the printer. The printer vendor documentation supplies the information about the protocol. The network printer support supplies both BSD Printer Protocol and raw TCP. Because of implementation variations, you may want to try both.
- Timeout—A seed number specifying the number of seconds to wait between attempting connections to the printer. The timeout is the smallest amount of time to wait between attempted connections. It increases with an increase in failed connections. After repeated failures to connect to the printer, a message is returned to the user requesting possible human intervention. Attempts to reconnect continue until successful or the until the job owner cancels the job.

Use the following steps to add a network printer with the LP commands.

1. Consult the vendor's installation documentation for information about the hardware switches and cabling requirement.

2. Connect the printer to the network and turn on the power to the printer.

3. Get an IP address and select a name for the printer node.

    This step is equivalent to adding any node to the network.

4. Become superuser.

5. Type **lpadmin -p** *printer-name* **-v /dev/null** and press Return.

    This step defines the printer name and the port device the printer will use.

6. Type **lpadmin -p printer-name -m netstandard** and press Return.

    This step identifies the interface script the printer will use.

7. Type **lpadmin -p** *printer-name* **-o dest=***access-name***:***port* **-o protocol=***protocol* **-o timeout=***value* and press Return.

    This step sets the printer destination, protocol, and timeout values.

8. Type **lpadmin -p** *printer-name* **-I** *content-type* **-T** *printer-type* and press Return.

    This step specifies the file content type and the printer type.

9. Type **cd /etc/lp/fd** and press Return.

10. Type **for filter in *.fd;do**

    > **name=`basename $filter .fd`**
    > **lpfilter -f $name -F $filter**
    > **done**

    You have added the filters to the print server.

11. Type **accept** *printer-name* and press Return.

12. Type **enable** *printer-name* and press Return.

    You have enabled the printer to accept print requests.

13. Type **lpstat -p** *printer-name* and press Return.

    Verify that the printer is configured correctly.

14. Add client access to the new printer.

    The following example uses the following information. The information you provide will vary.

- Printer name: seachild
- Server: castle
- Network printer access name: seachild:9100
- Protocol: tcp
- Timeout: 5
- Interface: /usr/lib/lp/model/netstandard
- Printer type: PS

- Content types: `postscript`
- Device: `/dev/null`

```
castle% su
Password:
# lpadmin -p seachild -v /dev/null
# lpadmin -p seachild -m netstandard
# lpadmin -p seachild -o dest=seachild:9100 -o protocol=tcp -o timeout=5
# lpadmin -p seachild -I postscript -T PS
# cd /etc/lp/fd
# ls
catv.fd         postdaisy.fd    postior.fd      postplot.fd     posttek.fd
download.fd     postdmd.fd      postmd.fd       postprint.fd    pr.fd
dpost.fd        postio.fd       postpages.fd    postreverse.fd
# for filter in *.fd;do
> name=`basename $filter .fd`
> lpfilter -f $name -F filter
> done
# lpfilter -f all -l
(Filter "download")
Input types: postscript
Output types: postdown
Printer types: PS,PSR,PS-b,PS-r,PS-br
Printers: any
Filter type: fast
Command: /usr/lib/lp/postscript/download
Options: PRINTER * = -p*
...(Additional lines deleted from this example)
# lpadmin -p seachild accept
# lpadmin -p seachild enable
# lpadmin -d seachild
# lpstat -p seachild
printer seachild now printing seachild-3. enabled since Thu Jan 25 12:09:30
  WST 2001. available.
#
```

# Using Print Client Commands

A system becomes a print client when you install the Sun print client software and enable access to remote printers on the system. The Sun print client commands have the same names and produce the same output as the print commands of the previous Solaris releases.

The Solaris print client commands use a greater number of options to locate printer configuration information than in the previous Solaris Operating Environment, and the client communicates directly with the print server.

The `lp` print command locates a printer and printer configuration information in the following sequence.

- Users can specify the name of a printer as part of the `lp` print command.When the user specifies a printer, `lp` checks to see if the specified destination printer name or printer class is specified in one of the three valid styles—atomic, POSIX, or context-based. See "Print Request Submission" on page 321 for more information.

- If the user did not specify a printer name, the search for a suitable default printer follows the sequence below.

  - If the user did not specify a printer name or class in a valid style, the command checks the user's `PRINTER` or `LPDEST` environment variable for a default printer name. Note that `PRINTER` takes priority over `LPDEST` and is probably searched only if the `/etc/nsswitch.conf` file has a `printers: files` entry.

  - If neither environment variable for the default printer is defined, the command checks the `.printers` file in the user's home directory for the `_default printer` alias.

  - If the command does not find a `_default printer` alias in the `.printers` file, it then checks the Sun print client's `/etc/printers.conf` file for configuration information.

- If the printer is not found in the `/etc/printers.conf` file and the `printers:` entry in the `/etc/nsswitch.conf` file enables searches in the nameservices such as `nis`, `nisplus`, `xfn`, or `ldap`, then, the `lp` command checks them in the specified order.

The client does not have a local print queue. The Sun print client sends its requests to the queue on the specified print server. The client writes the print request to a temporary spooling area only if the print server is not available or if an error occurs. This streamlined path to the server decreases the print client's use of resources, reduces the chance for printing problems, and improves performance.

## Printer Configuration Resources

This section describes the resources that the print client commands use to locate printer names and printer configuration information.

The print client commands introduced in the Solaris release can use a nameservice, which is a shared network resource, for storing printer configuration information for all printers on the network. The nameservice—NIS, NIS+, or NIS+ (`xfn`)—simplifies the maintenance of printer configuration information. When you add a printer in the nameservice, all print clients on the network can access it.

The Sun print client software locates printers by checking the following resources.

- Atomic, POSIX, or context-based printer name or class (see "Print Request Submission" below for more information).
- User's PRINTER or LPDEST environment variable for the default printer.
- User's .printers file for a printer alias.
- Sun print client's /etc/printers.conf file.
- Name service—NIS, NIS+, or NIS+ (xfn).

## Print Request Submission

Users submit a print request from a print client by using either the lp or lpr command. The user can specify a destination printer name or class in any of the following three styles.

- Atomic style, which is the print command and option followed by the printer name or class and the file name.

  **lp -d *printer-name filename***

- POSIX style, which is the print command and option followed by *server:printer* and the file name.

  **lpr -P *server:printer filename***

- Context-based style, as defined in the *Federated Naming Service Guide* in the *Solaris Software Developer AnswerBook®*.

  **lpr -d *dept-name/service/printer filename***

## Summary of the Print Client Process

This section summarizes the print client process.

1. A user submits a print request from a print client with a print client command (lp or lpr).
2. The print client command checks a hierarchy of print configuration resources to determine where to send the print request.
3. The print client command sends the print request directly to the appropriate print server. A print server can be any server that accepts BSD printing protocol, including SVR4 (LP) print servers and BSD print servers.
4. The print server sends the print request to the appropriate printer.
5. The print request is printed.

# Solving Printing Problems

When you set up a printer, you may find that nothing prints the first time you try to print a file. Or you may get a little farther: Something prints, but it is not what you expect—the output is incorrect or illegible. Then, when you get past these problems, you may encounter other problems, such as those listed below.

- LP commands hang.
- Printers become idle.
- Users receive conflicting messages.

*NOTE. Although many of the suggestions in this chapter are relevant to parallel printers, they are specific to the more common serial printers.*

## No Output (Nothing Prints)

When nothing prints, check the following three basic areas.

- The printer hardware.
- The network.
- The LP print service.

### Check the Hardware

The hardware is the first thing to check. As obvious as it sounds, make sure that the printer is plugged in, turned on, and online. In addition, refer to the manufacturer's documentation for information about hardware settings. Some printers use hardware switches that change the characteristics of a printer port.

The printer hardware includes the printer, the cable that connects it to the computer, and the ports at each end of the cable. As a general approach, work your way from the printer to the system.

Use the following checklist to troubleshoot hardware problems.

1. Check that the printer is plugged in, turned on, and online.
2. Check that the cable is connected to the correct port on the printer and to the correct port on the workstation or server.
3. Check that the cable is the correct cable and that it is not defective.
4. Refer to the manufacturer's documentation.
5. Check that hardware switches for the ports are set properly.

6. Check that the printer is operational. Use the printer's self-test feature if the printer has one. (Check the printer documentation for information about printer self-testing.)

7. (Serial printers only) Check that the baud settings for the computer and the printer are correct. If the baud settings are not the same for both the computer and the printer, sometimes nothing prints, but more often you get incorrect output.

## Check the Network

Problems with remote jobs—those going from a print client to a print server—are common. Make sure that network access between the print clients and the print server is enabled.

If the network is running NIS+, check the following items.

1. Check NIS+ configurations and credentials.

2. Check to make sure the `printers.org_dir` table exists by typing **niscat -o printers.org_dir.*domainname*** and pressing Return. If you get a `Not found` error message, use Solaris Print Manager to add a network printer to the print server. Solaris Print Manager creates and maintains data in the `printers.org_dir` table.

3. If the `printers.org_dir` table exists, check the output of the **niscat -o printers.org_dir.*domainname*** command to make sure the table is configured correctly.

4. Check the `printers:` entry in the `/etc/nsswitch.conf` file to make sure that the NIS+ nameservice is being queried for printer information.

If the network is not running DNS, NIS, or NIS+, check to make sure that names and IP addresses of each client are correctly entered in the `/etc/inet/hosts` (for the IPv4 protocol) and `/etc/inet/ipnodes` (for the IPv6 protocol) files on the print server. Also check to be sure that the name and IP address of the print server are correctly entered in the `/etc/inet/hosts` or `/etc/inet/ipnodes` file of each print client system.

Use the following steps to check for problems with the network.

1. On a print client or server, type **ping *system-name*** and press Return.

This command helps you check that the network link between the print server and print clients is set up correctly.

```
pserver% ping pclient
pclient is alive
pserver%
pclient% ping pserver
pserver not available
pclient%
```

If the system is alive (answers the `ping`), the network connection is probably all right. Either a nameservice or the local `/etc/hosts` file has successfully translated the host (system) name you entered into an IP address.

If the system is not available (does not answer the `ping`), check the NIS or NIS+ setup at your site. You may need to take additional steps so that print servers and print clients can communicate with one another. For example, you may need to verify that a route exists between the server and client if they are on separate networks.

If your site is not running NIS or NIS+, make sure that you have entered the IP address for the print server in the `/etc/hosts` file for each print client, and that you have entered all of the names and IP addresses of the client systems in the `/etc/hosts` file of the print server.

2. For directly attached printers, check that the port monitor is configured correctly on the print server.

3. For directly attached printers, check that the network listen services are registered with the port monitor on the print server.

## Check the LP Print Service

For printing to work, the LP scheduler must be running on both the print server and print clients. In addition to the scheduler running, a printer must be enabled and accepting requests before it can produce output. If the LP print service is not accepting requests for a printer, the submitted jobs (print requests) are rejected. Usually, in that instance, the user receives a warning message when a job is submitted. If the LP print service is not enabled for a printer, jobs remain queued on the system until the printer is enabled. In general, use the following steps to analyze a printing problem.

1. Follow the path of the print request step by step.
2. Examine the status of the LP print service at each step.
3. Is the configuration correct?
4. Is the printer accepting requests?
5. Is the printer enabled to process requests?

6. If the request is hanging on transmission, examine the `lpsched` log (`/var/lp/logs/lpsched`).

7. If the request is hanging locally, have notification of the printer device errors (faults) mailed to you, and reenable the printer.

Ask the following additional questions.

- Did the printer ever work?
- Was something changed recently that might affect printing?

## How to Check and Start the Scheduler

The print scheduler must be running both on the print server and on each print client system. On the print server and on each print client, type **lpstat -r** and press Return. Check the output of the command to make sure that the LP print service is running.

The following example shows that the LP print service is running on the print server.

```
pserver% lpstat -r
scheduler is running
pserver%
```

The following example shows that the LP print service is running on a print client

```
pclient% lpstat -r
scheduler is running
pclient%
```

If the scheduler is not running, become superuser, type **/usr/lib/lp/lpsched**, and press Return.

## How to Enable Printers and Accept Print Requests

You must enable printers and tell them to accept print requests.

Use the following steps both on the print server and on each print client to make sure that the printer is enabled and is accepting print requests.

1. Type **lpstat -a** and press Return to make sure that the printer is accepting requests.

```
pclient% lpstat -a
_default accepting requests since Oct 31 16:45 2000
pclient%
```

If the printer is not accepting requests, become superuser on the print server and then type **accept** *printer-name* and press Return.

The printer you specify should now accept requests. Type **lpstat -a** and press Return again to make sure that the printer is accepting requests.

2.  Type **lpstat -p** *printer-name* and press Return to make sure that the printer is enabled to print requests.

In the following example, the printer pinecone is disabled.

```
pclient% lpstat -p pinecone
printer pinecone disabled since Oct 31 16:45 2000. available.
unknown reason
pclient%
```

If the printer is disabled, become superuser on the print server, then type **enable** *printer-name* and press Return.

Then, on the print server, type **accept** *printer-name* and press Return.

The printer you specify should be enabled and accepting requests. On either the print server or a print client, type **lpstat -p** *printer-name* and press Return again to make sure the printer is enabled and accepting requests.

```
pserver% su
Password:
# enable pinecone
printer "pinecone" now enabled and accepting requests.
#
```

## How to Check the Port Connection

Make sure that the cable is connected to the port that the LP print service is using. To find out which port is configured for the LP print service, type **lpstat -t** on the print server and press Return. In the following example, the printer is connected to /dev/term/a.

```
pserver% lpstat -t
scheduler is running
system default destination: pinecone
device for pinecone: /dev/term/a
pserver%
```

If the cable is connected to the right port, type **ls -l /devices** and press Return to check whether the device is owned by lp and that the permissions are set to 600. In the following example, the port (fourth entry from the bottom) is configured correctly.

```
pserver% ls -l /devices
total 12
crw-rw-rw-   1 root      sys       28,   0 Mar 24 10:22
   audio@1,f7201000:sound,audio
crw-rw-rw-   1 root      sys       28,128 Mar 24 10:22 audio@1,f7201000:sound,
Åaudioctl
crw-------   1 root      sys       68,  11 Mar 24 09:39 eeprom@1,f2000000:eeprom
brw-rw-rw-   1 root      sys       36,   0 Mar 24 09:39 fd@1,f7200000:a
crw-rw-rw-   1 root      sys       36,   0 Mar 24 09:39 fd@1,f7200000:a,raw
brw-rw-rw-   1 root      sys       36,   1 Mar 24 09:39 fd@1,f7200000:b
crw-rw-rw-   1 root      sys       36,   1 Mar 24 09:39 fd@1,f7200000:b,raw
brw-rw-rw-   1 root      sys       36,   2 Mar 24 09:39 fd@1,f7200000:c
crw-rw-rw-   1 root      sys       36,   2 Mar 24 09:39 fd@1,f7200000:c,raw
drwxr-xr-x   2 root      sys         4608 Mar 24 10:22 pseudo
drwxr-xr-x   3 root      sys          512 Mar 24 11:41 sbus@1,f8000000
crw-------   1 lp        sys       29,   0 Mar 24 09:39 zs@1,f1000000:a
crw-rw-rw-   1 root      sys       29,131072 Mar 24 09:39 zs@1,f1000000:a,cu
crw-rw-rw-   1 root      sys       29,   1 Mar 24 09:39 zs@1,f1000000:b
crw-rw-rw-   1 root      sys       29,131073 Mar 24 09:39 zs@1,f1000000:b,cu
pserver%
```

If you are not certain which device is the serial port, you can type **ls -l /dev/term** and press Return to display the link to the /devices file.

```
pserver% ls -l /dev/term
total 4
lrwxrwxrwx   1 root      root          38 Oct 23 17:52 a ->
   ../../devices/sbus@1f,0/zs@f,1100000:a
lrwxrwxrwx   1 root      root          38 Oct 23 17:52 b ->
   ../../devices/sbus@1f,0/zs@f,1100000:b
pserver%
```

Use the following steps on the print server if you need to change the ownership or permissions for the device.

1. Become superuser.
2. Type **chown lp** *device-name* and press Return.

   The lp process now owns the port device file.
3. Type **chmod 600** *device-name* and press Return.

   Only lp or root can access the printer port device file.

## How to Check Printer Configurations

Check to make sure the printer type and file content type are configured properly on the print server and on each print client. Type **lpstat -p** *device-name* **-l** and press Return. In the following example, a remote printer is configured properly and is available to process print requests.

```
pserver% lpstat -p seachild -l
printer seachild unknown state. enabled since Oct 31 16:52 2000. available.
        Remote Name: seachild
        Remote Server: seachild
pserver%
```

If the printer type or file content type is incorrect, use **lpadmin -p**
**device-name -T *printer-type* -I *file-content-type*** and press
Return to change it. On the print client, try setting the print type to unknown
and the content type to any.

## How to Check for Printer Faults on the Print Server

Print jobs may be waiting in the queue because of a printer fault on the
print server. Use the following steps to make sure that the printer is not
waiting because of a printer fault.

1.  On the print server, become superuser.

2.  Type **lpadmin -p *printer-name* -F continue** and press Return.

    You have instructed the LP print service to continue if it is waiting
    because of a fault.

3.  Type **enable *printer-name*** and press Return.

    This command forces an immediate retry.

4.  (Optional) Type **lpadmin -p *printer-name* -A 'write root'**
    and press Return.

    You have instructed the LP print service to set a default policy of
    sending the printer fault message to the terminal on which root is
    logged in if the printer fails. This policy may help you to get quick
    notification of faults as you try to fix the problem.

It is easy to set up a printer port as a login terminal by mistake. To check
that the printer port is not incorrectly set up as a login terminal, type **ps -ef**
and press Return. Look for the printer port entry. In the example, port
/dev/term/a is incorrectly set as a login terminal. You can tell by the
"passwd\n## information at the end of the line.

```
pserver% ps -ef
  root    169    167  0   Apr 04 ?        0:08 /usr/lib/saf/listen tcp
    root    939      1  0 19:30:47 ?        0:02 /usr/lib/lpsched
    root    859    858  0 19:18:54 term/a   0:01 /bin/sh -c /etc/lp/interfaces/
pinecone pinecone-294 pine!winsor "passwd\n##
pserver%
```

If the port is set up as a login port, use the following steps to disable the
login.

1. Become superuser.
2. Type **cancel** *request-id* and press Return.

   The request ID is shown in the output of the ps -ef command. In the following example, request-id pinecone-294 is canceled.

```
pserver% su
# cancel pinecone-294
request "pinecone-294" canceled
#
```

3. Type **lpadmin -p** *printer-name* **-h** and press Return.

   The printer port is set to be a non-login device.
4. Type **ps -ef** and press Return. Verify that the printer port is no longer a login device.

If you do not find the source of the printing problem in the basic LP print service functions, use one of the following procedures for the specific client or server case that applies.

## How to Check Printing from a Print Client to a Print Server

Before you follow the steps in this section, you should already have checked the basic functions of the LP print service on both the print server and the print client. Make sure that the printer works locally before trying to diagnose problems with a print client.

On the print client, type **ping** *print-server-name* and press Return. This command checks to make sure that the systems are connected and available on the network.

```
pclient% ping pserver-1
pserver-1 is alive
pclient% ping pserver-2
pserver-2 not available
pclient%
```

If you receive the message *system* not available, you have a network connection problem.

Use the following steps to check the print server type for a print client.

1. On the print client, become superuser.
2. Type **lpsystem -l** and press Return. Check the output to make sure that the print server is identified as type bsd (for Solaris).

In the following example, the print server is properly identified as type `bsd`.

```
pclient% su
Password
# lpsystem -l
System:                    +
Type:                      bsd
Connection timeout:        never
Retry failed connections:  after 10 minutes
Comment:                   Allow all connections

#
```

If the print server is not identified correctly, type **lpsystem -t bsd** *print-server-name* and press Return, as shown in the following example.

```
pserver% lpsystem -t bsd pserver
pserver%
```

Use the following steps to check the print queue on the print client.

1. Type **cd /var/spool/lp/requests/***system-name* and press Return.

   This directory contains a record of print requests still in the queue.

2. Type **ls -l** and press Return.

   A list of the print jobs is displayed.

3. For the print job you want to check, type **lpstat -o** *request-id* and press Return.

   In the following example, the job is queued successfully.

```
pclient% lpstat -o seachild-10
seachild-10            paperbark!winsor   137359   Oct 31 17:03
pclient%
```

If the job is not queued successfully, the client-server connection may be faulty. Use the following steps to make sure that the client-server connection is not faulty:

1. On the print client, type **tail /var/lp/logs/lpsched** and press Return.

   The output of this command shows whether `lpsched` can connect to the print server. In the following example, the log does not indicate any problems.

```
pclient% tail /var/lp/logs/lpsched
10/28 12:25:13: Print services started.
10/28 17:29:29: Print services stopped.
```

```
10/29 09:44:36: build info: 04/07/00:07:20:52
10/29 09:44:36: Print services started.
10/29 16:46:42: Print services stopped.
10/30 10:36:58: build info: 04/07/00:07:20:52
10/30 10:36:58: Print services started.
10/30 17:09:28: Print services stopped.
10/31 09:21:25: build info: 04/07/00:07:20:52
10/31 09:21:25: Print services started.
pclient%
```

2. If the connection is not being made, on the print server, type **lpstat -t** and press Return.

The output of this command shows you whether the print server is operating properly. In the following example, printers `pinecone` and `red` are up and running on the print server.

```
pserver% lpstat -t
scheduler is running
system default destination: pinecone
device for pinecone: /dev/term/a
pinecone accepting requests since Thu May 23 20:56:26 PDT 1991
printer red is idle. enabled since Sun May 19 17:12:24 PDT 1991. available.
printer pinecone now printing pinecone-314. enabled since Fri May 24 16:10:39
  PDT 1991. available.
pinecone-129              root              488   May 23 20:43 filtered
pserver%
```

3. On the print server, type **tail /var/lp/logs/lpsched** and press Return. Examine the `lpsched` log to see if the print server is connecting to the client. If there is no entry or if the server cannot complete the connection to the print client, `lpsched` is not transmitting correctly.

The following example shows the log for two jobs. The first job, from the system `elm`, completed successfully. The second job could not complete because the print server could not connect to the system `opus`.

```
pserver% tail /var/lp/logs/lpsched
05/17/93 09:39 c   834 elm Starting.
05/17/93 09:39 c   834 elm Normal process termination.
05/17/93 09:41 p   162 <none> Started child for elm, pid = 902
05/17/93 09:41 c   902 elm Starting.
05/17/93 09:41 c   902 elm Connected to remote child.
05/17/93 09:41 c   341 opus Could not connect to remote child.
05/17/93 09:51 c   341 opus Could not connect to remote child.
05/17/93 10:01 c   341 opus Could not connect to remote child.
05/17/93 10:11 c   341 opus Could not connect to remote child.
05/17/93 10:21 c   341 opus Could not connect to remote child.
pserver%
```

4. On the print server, type **lpsystem -l** and press Return. Check the output to make sure that the print client is correctly identified as type bsd. In the following example, the print client clobber is configured correctly.

```
pserver% lpsystem -l
System:                       clobber
Type:                         bsd
Connection timeout:           never
Retry failed connections:     after 10 minutes
Comment:                      none
pserver%
```

If the print client configuration is incorrect, become superuser and type **lpsystem -t bsd** *client-system-name* and press Return, as shown in the following example.

```
pserver% su
Password
# lpsystem -t bsd oak
#
```

5. On the print server, as superuser, type **sacadm -l** and press Return. Make sure that the port monitor and network listen service are set up properly.

   The following example shows a print server that is configured correctly.

```
# sacadm -l
PMTAG           PMTYPE          FLGS RCNT STATUS       COMMAND
tcp             listen      -   9999 ENABLED    /usr/lib/saf/listen tcp #
#
```

6. Type **pmadm -l** and press Return.

   The following example shows a print server with attached printers that is configured for lp and lpd.

```
pserver# pmadm -l
PMTAG     PMTYPE    SVCTAG    FLGS ID        <PMSPECIFIC>
tcp       listen    lp    - root    - - p - /var/spool/lp/fifos/listenS5 #
tcp       listen    lpd   - root     \x000202038194143a0000000000000000 - p -
 /var/spool/lp/fifos/listenBSD #
tcp       listen    0     - root     \x00020ACE8194143a0000000000000000 - c -
 /usr/lib/saf/nlps_server #
pserver#
```

If the service and port monitors are not configured correctly, use Solaris Print Manager to reconfigure the printer port.

## Incorrect Output

If the printer and the print service software are not configured correctly, the printer may print but it may provide output that is not what you expect.

### Check the Printer Type

If you used the wrong printer type when you set up the printer with the LP print service, inappropriate printer control characters may be sent to the printer. The results are unpredictable: Nothing may print, output may be illegible, or output may be printed in the wrong character set or font.

To check the printer type, type **lpstat -p** *printer-name* **-l** and press Return.

A list of the printer characteristics is displayed.

```
pserver% lpstat -p pinecone -l
printer pinecone is idle. enabled since Wed Jan  2 18:20:22 PST 1991. available.
        Content types: PS
        Printer types: PS
        Description:
        Users allowed:
                (all)
        Forms allowed:
                (none)
        Banner not required
        Character sets:
                (none)
        Default pitch:
        Default page size:
pserver%
```

If the printer type is not correct, become superuser and type **lpadmin -p** *printer-name* **-T** *printer-type* and press Return.

### Check the STTY Settings (Serial Printers Only)

Many formatting problems can result when the default STTY (standard terminal) settings do not match the settings required by the printer. The following sections describe what happens when some of the settings are incorrect. Read the printer documentation to determine the correct STTY settings for the printer port.

To display the current STTY settings for the printer port, as superuser, type **stty -a <** *device-name* and press Return. The current STTY settings for the printer port are displayed.

```
pserver# stty -a < /dev/term/a
speed 9600 baud;
rows = 0; columns = 0; ypixels = 0; xpixels = 0;
eucw 1:0:0:0, scrw 1:0:0:0
intr = ^c; quit = ^|; erase = ^?; kill = ^u;
eof = ^d; eol = <undef>; eol2 = <undef>; swtch = <undef>;
start = ^q; stop = ^s; susp = ^z; dsusp = ^y;
rprnt = ^r; flush = ^o; werase = ^w; lnext = ^v;
```

```
parenb -parodd cs7 -cstopb -hupcl cread -clocal -loblk -parext
-ignbrk brkint -ignpar -parmrk -inpck istrip -inlcr -igncr icrnl -iuclc
ixon -ixany -ixoff imaxbel
isig icanon -xcase echo echoe echok -echonl -noflsh
-tostop echoctl -echoprt echoke -defecho -flusho -pendin iexten
opost -olcuc onlcr -ocrnl -onocr -onlret -ofill -ofdel tab3
pserver#
```

To change the STTY settings, type **lpadmin -p *printer-name*
-o "stty=*options*"** and press Return.

You can change more than one option setting by including the options in
single quotation marks and separating them by spaces. For example, suppose
the printer requires you to enable odd parity and set a 7-bit character size.
You would type a command such as the following.

```
# lpadmin -p clobber -o "stty='parenb parodd cs7'"
```

The STTY option parenb enables parity checking/generation, parodd sets
odd parity generation, and cs7 sets the character size to 7 bits.

To send a document to the printer, type **lp -d *printer-name filename***
and press Return. Look at the document to verify that it is printing correctly.

Table 64 shows the default STTY options used by the LP print service's
standard printer interface program.

*Table 64*     *Default STTY Settings Used by the Standard Interface
              Program*

| Option | Meaning |
|--------|---------|
| 9600 | Set baud rate to 9600. |
| cs8 | Set 8-bit bytes. |
| -cstopb | Send 1 stop bit per byte. |
| -parity | Do not generate parity. |
| ixon | Enable XON/XOFF (also known as START/STOP or DC1/DC3). |
| opost | Do "output post-processing." |
| -olcuc | Do not map lower case to upper case. |
| onlcr | Change line feed to carriage return/line feed. |
| -ocrnl | Do not change carriage returns into line feeds. |
| -onocr | Output carriage returns even at column 0. |
| nl0 | No delay after line feeds. |

*Table 64    Default STTY Settings Used by the Standard Interface Program (Continued)*

| Option | Meaning |
|--------|---------|
| cr0 | No delay after carriage returns. |
| tab0 | No delay after Tabs. |
| bs0 | No delay after backspaces. |
| vt0 | No delay after vertical Tabs. |
| ff0 | No delay after form feeds. |

Use Table 65 to choose STTY options to correct various problems affecting print output.

*Table 65    STTY Options to Correct Print Output Problems*

| STTY Values | Result | Possible Problem from Incorrect Setting |
|-------------|--------|------------------------------------------|
| 300, 600, 1200, 1800, 2400, 4800, 9600, 19200, 38400 | Set baud rate to the specified value (enter only one baud rate). | Random characters and special characters may be printed and spacing may be inconsistent. |
| oddp<br>evenp<br>-parity | Set odd parity.<br>Set even parity.<br>Set no parity. | Characters are randomly missing or appear incorrectly. |
| -tabs | Set no Tabs. | Text is jammed against right margin. |
| tabs | Set Tabs every eight spaces. | Text has no left margin, is run together, or is jammed together. |
| -onlcr | Set no Return at the beginning of lines. | Text has incorrect double spacing. |
| onlcr | Set Return at beginning of lines. | Zigzags print down the page. |

## Check the Baud Settings

When the baud setting of the computer does not match the baud setting of the printer, you usually get some output, but it does not look like what you submitted for printing. Random characters show up, with an unusual mixture of special characters and undesirable spacing. The default for the LP print service is 9600 baud.

*NOTE. If a printer is connected to a parallel port, the baud setting is irrelevant.*

## Check the Parity Setting

Some printers use a parity bit to ensure that data received for printing has not been garbled during transmission. The parity bit settings for the computer and for the printer must match. If they do not match, some characters do not print at all or are replaced by other characters. The output will look only approximately correct, with the word spacing all right and many letters in their correct place. The LP print service does not set the parity bit by default.

## Check the Tab Settings

If Tabs are set but the printer expects no Tabs, the printed output may contain the complete contents of the file, but the text may be jammed against the right margin. Also, if the Tab settings for the printer are incorrect, the text may not have a left margin, may run together, may be concentrated in a portion of the page, or may be incorrectly double-spaced. The default is for Tab settings every eight spaces.

## Check the Return Setting

If the output is double-spaced but should be single-spaced, either the Tab settings for the printer are incorrect or the printer is adding a line feed after each Return. The LP print service adds a Return before each line feed, so the combination causes two line feeds.

If the print zigzags down the page, the STTY option `onlcr`, which sends a Return before every line feed, is not set. The `stty=onlcr` option is set by default, but you may have cleared it while trying to solve other printing problems.

# Hung LP Print Service Commands

If you type any of the `lp` commands (`lpsystem`, `lpadmin`, `lpstat`, `lpshut`) and nothing happens (you get no error message, status information, or prompt), chances are that something is wrong with the LP scheduler. You usually can resolve such a problem by stopping and restarting the LP scheduler.

Use the following steps to free hung `lp` commands.

1. Become superuser.
2. Type **lpshut** and press Return.

   If this command hangs, press Control-C and proceed to the next step. If this command succeeds, skip to step 5.

3. Type **ps -e | grep lpsched** and press Return.

Note the process ID numbers (PID) from the first column. You use the PID number in the next step.

```
# ps -e | grep lpsched
134 term/a   0:01 lpsched
#
```

4. Type **kill -9 *pid*** and press Return.

All the **lp** processes are terminated.

```
# kill -9 134
#
```

5. Type **rm /usr/spool/lp/SCHEDLOCK** and press Return.

You have removed the SCHEDLOCK file so that you can restart the LP print service.

6. Type **/usr/lib/lp/lpsched** and press Return.

The LP print service restarts.

# Idle (Hung) Printers

You may find a printer that is idle even though print requests have been queued to it. A printer may seem idle when it shouldn't be for one of the following reasons.

- The current print request is being filtered.
- The printer has a fault.
- Networking problems may be interrupting the printing process.

## Check the Print Filters

Slow print filters run in the background to avoid tying up the printer. A print request that requires filtering does not print until it has been filtered. To check the print filters, type **lpstat -o *printer-name*** and press Return. See if the first waiting request is being filtered. If the output looks like the following example, the file is being filtered. The printer is not hung; it just is taking a while to process the request.

```
pserver% lpstat -o pinecone
pinecone-10         fred        1261    Mar 12 17:34 being filtered
pinecone-11         iggy        1261    Mar 12 17:36 on pine
pinecone-12         jack        1261    Mar 12 17:39 on pine
pserver%
```

## Check Printer Faults

When the LP print service detects a fault, printing resumes automatically, but not immediately. The LP print service waits about five minutes before trying again and continues trying until a request is printed successfully. You can force a retry immediately by enabling the printer.

Use the following steps to resume printing after a printer fault.

1. Look for a message about a printer fault and try to correct the fault if you find one.

   Depending on how printer fault alerts have been specified, messages may be sent to root by e-mail or may be written to a terminal on which you (root) are logged in.

2. Type **enable *printer-name*** and press Return.

   If a request was blocked by a printer fault, this command forces a retry. If this command doesn't work, continue with other procedures in this section.

## Check Network Problems

When printing files over a network, you may encounter the following types of problems.

- Requests sent to print servers may back up in the client system (local) queue.
- Requests sent to print servers may back up in the print server (remote) queue.

Use the following steps to check that the printer is ready to print.

1. Type **lpstat -p *printer-name*** and press Return.

   The information that is displayed tells you whether the printer is idle or active, enabled or disabled, or available or not accepting print requests. If everything looks all right, continue with other procedures in this section.

2. If the printer is not available (is not accepting requests), become superuser on the print server and type **accept *printer-name*** and press Return.

   The printer begins to accept requests to its print queue.

3. If the printer is disabled, as superuser on the print server, type **enable *printer-name*** and press Return.

   This command reenables the printer so that it can act on the requests in its queue.

## Check for Jobs Backed Up in the Local Client Queue

Jobs earmarked for a print server may back up in the client system queue for the following reasons.

- The print server is down.
- The printer is disabled on the print server.
- The network between the print client and print server is down.
- Underlying Solaris network software was not set up properly.

While you are tracking down the source of the problem, use the `disable` command on the print server to stop new requests from being added to the queue.

## Check for Jobs Backed Up in the Remote Server Queue

If jobs back up in the print server queue, the printer probably has been disabled. When a printer is accepting requests but not processing them, the requests are queued to print. After you enable the printer, the print requests in the queue should print—unless there is an additional problem.

Use the following steps to send jobs to a remote printer when they back up in the local queue.

1. On the print client, type **reject *printer-name*** and press Return.
   Additional queuing of print requests from the print client to the print server ceases.
2. Type **ping *print-server-name*** and press Return to check that the print server and the network between the print client and the print server is up.
3. Type **tail /var/lp/logs/lpsched** and press Return.
   The resulting information may help you pinpoint what is preventing the transmission of print requests from the print client to the print server.
4. After you fix the problem, on the print client, type **accept *printer-name*** and press Return.
   New jobs can begin to queue.
5. (If necessary) On the print client type **enable *printer-name*** and press Return.
   The printer is enabled.

Use the following steps to free from a print client the jobs that back up in the print server queue.

1. On the print server, type **reject *printer-name*** and press Return.
   Additional print requests are not queued.

2. Type **tail /var/lp/logs/lpsched** and press Return.

   The information that is displayed may help you pinpoint what is preventing the print requests that have been transmitted from the print client to the print server from being printed.

3. After you fix the problem, on the print server type **accept** *printer-name* and press Return.

   The printer accepts new jobs in the print queue.

4. (If necessary) On the print server, type **enable** *printer-name* and press Return.

   The printer is enabled.

## Conflicting Status Messages

A user may enter a print request and be notified that the client system has accepted it, then receive mail from the print server that the job has been rejected. These conflicting messages may occur for the following reasons.

- The print client may be accepting requests, but the print server is rejecting requests.
- The definition of the printer on the print client might not match the definition of that printer on the print server. More specifically, the definitions of the print job components, such as filters, character sets, print wheels, and forms, are not the same on the client and server systems.

Make sure that identical definitions of these job components are registered on both the print clients and print servers so that local users can access printers on the print servers.

Use the following steps to resolve conflicting status messages.

1. Type **lpstat -p** *printer-name* and press Return. Check that the printer connected to the print server is enabled and accepting requests.

   Users see conflicting status messages when the print client accepts requests but the print server rejects them.

2. On the print server and on each print client, type **lpstat -p -l** *printer-name* and press Return. Check that the definition of the printer on the print client matches the definition of the printer on the print server.

   Look at the definitions of the print job components, such as print filters, character sets, print wheels, and forms, to be sure they are the same on both the client and server systems, so that local users can access printers on print server systems.

# Part Five

# Application Software

The five chapters in this part describe how to install and delete application software and how to install system software patches.

Chapter 13 provides an overview of the installation process, introduces the package commands and the Software Manager for installation, recommends policy for installing software on an application server, and describes how to access files from a CD-ROM drive.

Chapter 14 describes how to use the package commands to administer application software and how to set up the users' environment.

Chapter 15 describes how to use the Admintool: Software manager to administer application software.

Chapter 16 describes how to use the Solaris Product Registry tool to administer system software.                                            *New!*

Chapter 17 describes how to use the `patchadd` and `patchrm` commands that are now bundled with the Solaris Operating Environment to administer system software patches.

# 13

# INSTALLING AND MANAGING APPLICATION SOFTWARE

When you support a network that provides application software to users, your responsibilities include the following tasks.

- Setting up the software installation environment.
- Installing the software on a server or on the users' local system.
- Setting up the users' environment to access software.
- Removing software that is obsolete or no longer used.

This chapter introduces the package commands and Admintool—two alternative ways to install and manage application software. It also describes how to set up an application server and access files from a remote and a local CD-ROM drive. Chapter 14 describes how to use the package commands. Chapter 15 describes how to use Admintool. Although you can install application software on a user's local system, the information in this chapter describes how to set up the software on an application server and share the files so that they are available over the network to make software administration and upgrades easier.

# Overview of Installing and Managing Application Software

With the Solaris Operating Environment, installation is managed by packages of information. A software package contains the components of a software product that are delivered on the CD-ROM installation medium. The components typically contain groups of files such as compiled programs, files, and installation scripts.

Software packages are installed from the CD-ROM onto a system, and are removed from a system, in one of the following ways.

- With the package commands from a command line. See Chapter 14, "Package Commands," for more information.
- With Admintool (which calls the package commands). See Chapter 15, "Admintool: Software Manager," for more information.
- With Solaris Product Registry, which launches an installer to install and remove products. See Chapter 16, "Solaris Product Registry," for more information.
- With an installation script provided by the application vendor (which calls the package commands). Some vendors may also provide a deinstallation script.

*NOTE. Before the Solaris 2.5 release, Software Manager, accessed with the* swmtool *command, provided the graphical tool for adding and removing software. Starting with the Solaris 2.5 release, Admintool, accessed with the* admintool *command, provides the same capability. If you use the* swmtool *command on a system running Solaris 2.5 or later, it starts the Software portion of Admintool.*

You can use the package commands, Admintool, and Solaris Product Registry interchangeably. For example, you can install software with Admintool and remove the software with the pkgrm(1M) command or Solaris Product Registry. Alternatively, you can install software with the pkgadd(1M) command and remove that software with Admintool or Solaris Product Registry.

Starting with the Solaris 2.6 release, new patchadd and patchrm commands are provided to support adding and removing patches from a Solaris system. See Chapter 17, "Installing and Managing System Software Patches," for more information about these commands.

*New!*

## Using Package Commands

You manage software from a command line with the commands shown in Table 66.

*Table 66 Package Commands*

| Command | Task |
|---|---|
| vi(1)<br>admin(4) | Set installation defaults. |
| pkgask(1M) | Create a script to define installation parameters. |
| pkgadd(1M) | Install software package or store files for installation at a later time. |
| pkgchk(1M) | Check accuracy of installation. |
| pkginfo(1M) | List installed packages. |
| pkgrm(1M) | Remove packages. |

Chapter 14, "Package Commands," describes these tasks in detail.

## Using Admintool

Admintool is a graphical user interface tool that you can use to perform the same tasks that you would perform from a command line with the package commands. For easier administration, you can group packages into clusters that are slated for installation with Admintool. Admintool calls the package commands to perform the requested functions. Figure 55 shows the Admintool: Software window. Refer to Chapter 15, "Admintool: Software Manager," for instructions on how to use this tool.

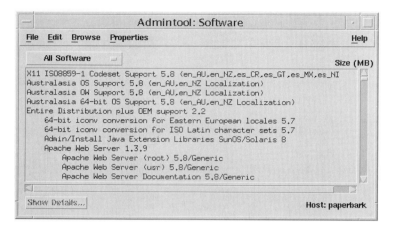

*Figure 55    The Admintool: Software Window*

You can view more detailed information about each package by clicking on a package to highlight it and then clicking on the Show Details button. Figure 56 shows the details for the SUNWwsrv package, which is part of the Solaris Product Registry tools.

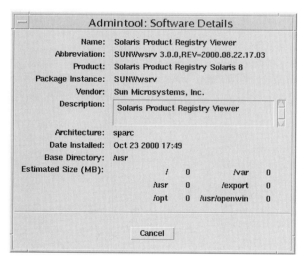

*Figure 56    Package Details for the SUNWwsrv Package*

## Using Installation Scripts

Although Sun recommends a policy on how to create packages for installation, some software products from application vendors provide their own installation scripts. The installation scripts may call the package commands to perform setup and installation of the software. Always read the installation instructions from the vendor to make sure that you follow the vendor's recommended installation procedure. For information about how to create packages for installation, refer to the *Application Packaging Developer's Guide* available at http://docs.sun.com.

# User Access to Applications

Making applications available to users is a major task for system administrators. Most users depend on reliable access to application software to get their jobs done. The demands of creating and maintaining user access to application software can easily consume a quarter or more of system administration time.

You may need to perform any or all of the following tasks to administer user access to applications.

- Acquire software.
- Locate space for the software.
- Install the software on multiple local systems or on an NFS server.
- Set up user environments, such as paths, links, and environment variables that are specific to each application.
- Revise user environments each time the software version changes or new software is added.

Anything that you can do to leverage these tasks will increase productivity.

The first step to manage software access is to use the automounter to match users with the proper binary version of applications. After setting up the automounter, you need to perform an additional step to provide a complete solution to this problem.

The following paragraphs describe four alternative approaches to providing a complete solution. Each solution has its own particular caveat.

The first approach is to use scripts that are run once on each system to set up the user environment for an application. Subsequently, when the user starts the application, the environment is already properly prepared. A disadvantage to this approach is that it introduces additional command names that users must learn to prepare for running an application. An additional drawback is that some programs use the same environment variable names as other programs with different values. When users run a script for a specific application but do not start the application until later, other packages that use the same environment variable may be affected. (See "Wrappers and Dot Files" on page 353 for an example.)

The second approach is to have user `.login` or `.profile` files "source" a global configuration file that sets up the user's environment.

The third approach is to use *wrappers* to manage access to software. Wrappers are tailored application startup scripts. These scripts set up the user's environment at runtime and start the application. Wrappers perform the setup that you otherwise would need to hardcode in individual users' dot files.

Using wrappers together with standard application server layouts and simplified user mount and path setups can produce an environment in which you need to do very little, if any, administrative maintenance of the end user environment. Users can have as few as one software access mount and one software access path component.

Most application access at Sun is based on this last approach, which was developed by Sun Information Resources. Sun recommends that you consider dedicating servers to provide access to application software over the network, in the manner proposed in the following sections.

*NOTE. A comprehensive description of how to configure and manage application servers is beyond the scope of this book. However, the approaches and examples cited here provide you with a foundation based on sound principles and real-world experience.*

**New!**

The fourth approach is to create *site initialization files* that contain initialization information or wrappers for applications. See "Wrappers and Site Initialization Files" on page 353 for more information.

## Automating Your Application Environment

The information in the following sections provides suggestions for ways that you can automate your application environment. The key technologies and techniques are introduced in Table 67 and described in the following sections.

*Table 67    Key Elements for an Application Server*

| Element | Used to |
|---|---|
| NFS/automounter | Share application file systems across the network; guarantee consistency and integrity with read-only access. |
| Veritas Volume Manager or File System or Online: DiskSuite™ | Permit file systems larger than individual disks; enable a single mount to access a huge distribution. |

**New!**

*Table 67    Key Elements for an Application Server (Continued)*

| Element | Used to |
|---------|---------|
| Wrappers | Remove setup requirements from the end-user environment; provide all users with consistent behavior. |
| Site initialization files | Centrally manage wrappers and application setup scripts; provide all users with consistent behavior. |
| Symbolic links or hard links (note that symbolic links can cross file system boundaries) | Enable one executable to have many startup names; permit generic path references to version-named locations; control default application versions. |
| Common command directory | Make all commands accessible with a single path component. |
| `rdist` command | Facilitate replication of file systems across application servers. |
| NIS/NIS+ nameservice | Facilitate sharing files in a network environment. |

When you set up an application server, you dedicate a single volume to contain the applications and wrappers. You create two (or more) directories in the volume. The *application directory* contains the applications and wrappers, as well as a symbolic link directory that you can use to determine the default version of the application. The *common command directory* contains symbolic links in the form of command names that link to the wrappers for each application. You can use a product such as Veritas Volume Manager or Sun Online: DiskSuite to create a large file system that spans more than one slice or disk.

Veritas Volume Manager provides the following capabilities, although you still write generic Solaris UFS file systems on top of these volumes.

- Enables you to mirror your OS boot disk in case it fails.
- Enables you to slice up or combine physical disks to create "virtual" disks called *volumes*. You can treat these volumes as though they are physical disks and can write file systems on them.
- Enables you to mirror data on a volume so that failure of one physical disk that is part of the volume does not interrupt service.
- Enables you to dynamically grow volumes on the fly without any downtime.

Veritas File System provides the following capabilities, which complement those of Volume Manager.

- Enables you to create a VXFS file system, in addition to UFS, which can be written on a Veritas Volume.

- Enables you to grow and shrink VXFS file systems on the fly, with no downtime.

- Provides two- to fourfold performance improvement over UFS.

- Provides a much faster `fsck` after system crash. On a VXFS file system, `fsck` takes only a few seconds, regardless of the size of the file system. On a large UFS file system, `fsck` could take hours.

- Provides plug-ins to the VXFS file system that increase performance by bypassing all kernel buffering for applications like NFS file service and databases for which kernel buffering makes no sense.

- Enables you to take a snapshot of a production file system, mount it at another location, and back it up while the production file system remains active

Online: DiskSuite provides similar capabilities.

When you have installed the application packages, you write a wrapper that sets up the environment for the application. If you want to copy the setup to another server, you can do so with the `rdist` command. Refer to "Designing an Application Server" on page 356 for a detailed description of these tasks.

## Benefits of a Standardized Application Server Setup

The information in the following sections describe the administrative benefits that you gain from a standardized application server setup.

**Use NFS**     Installing the same application for multiple users on local disks uses extra disk space, requires more time, and becomes a support burden. You must perform upgrades at multiple locations. When problems arise, you may have to deal with multiple versions of the same application.

When you provide an NFS-shared installation, you reduce local disk installations. You save time by reducing the number of systems that you must support. When multiple users share access to a single read-only copy of an application, you perform fewer installations and upgrades and simplify troubleshooting by ensuring that users are executing the same code.

**Consolidate Your Installations**     Even NFS-shared applications can be difficult to maintain if they are scattered among too many locations. Sometimes applications have been installed on a user's system or on a server. As demand for the application develops, users share it from the original location. Users frequently pass the word to other users about where they can mount the application. In such a situation, users may draw on inconsistent or unreliable sources and experience confusion regarding where they should get applications.

To solve this problem, designate dedicated application servers. Sharing all standard applications from the same server offers users a reliable source and lets you keep track of where maintenance is needed.

**Standardize Server Layouts** Your environment, like that at Sun, may require many application servers to service different networks, buildings, and regions. If so, commit to using the same file system layout on all application servers. Although the contents of different application servers may vary from one server to another, the locations of individual applications should be consistent. A unified file system naming scheme simplifies user paths and reduces the updates required when users move and must change from one application server to another. This approach also simplifies the process of copying (distributing) applications from a master installation server to production servers, because the destination file system is the same.

Sometimes in comparing two locations where a product has been installed, you cannot tell whether the contents of like-named directories are intended to be the same or different; you have no outward clue. Sun recommends that you install applications in directories with names that identify both the product and the version. That practice lets you and others know what the directories contain. In addition, you can maintain multiple versions of an application at the same directory level.

In some environments, you must perform maintenance at numerous locations for each change. Using wrappers and a common command directory reduces the number of locations where attention is needed, limits them to servers, and leverages the results for all users.

**Synchronize Version Cutovers** In the traditional UNIX environment, you may find it difficult to convert to a new application version quickly because of the number of changes to the user environment that may be required. Using symbolic links to control all the versioning at this level, and using wrappers that immediately provide any necessary user setups can help to speed up and synchronize cutovers. It can be difficult to know who is using particular applications or whether some applications are being used at all.

Wrappers can increase usage visibility if you code them to report to a central location by e-mail each time the user starts a product.

## Benefits of a Standardized User Environment

The information in these sections describes the administrative benefits you gain from a standardized user environment setup.

**Simplified User Mount Points**     When users access applications from a variety of locations or even from multiple file systems on a dedicated server, they need a variety of mount points. You, as system administrator, probably have to maintain the information that supports these mounts. Regardless of whether you perform this maintenance on individual user systems or with automounter maps, the fewer times you need to update the user environment, the more time you save.

**Simplified User Path Requirements**     When you configure dedicated application servers so that all applications are accessible from a single file system, users need only one mount point, which may not need to be updated. Even when the contents of the file system that users are mounting change, the mount point remains the same.

Maintaining path updates for users can be an unnecessary burden. If users have the "right" path, you do not need to change it. The *right path* is one whose standard component(s) provide ongoing access to all applications.

**Reduced Runtime Conflicts**     The settings that some applications need at runtime may be in conflict with those needed by others. Wrappers tailor one process environment without affecting others.

**Simplified User Relocations**     User moves can impose a tremendous burden, because many user setups in a nonstandard environment are customized. Using wrappers and simplified user mount points and paths can drastically reduce the updates required to reinstate application service after a move. In some cases, you need change only the server name for the user's mount. Alternatively, you can let the automounter decide the server name based on the network topology. Refer to Part 3 for information about the automounter.

## Using Wrapper Technology

Wrappers are custom startup scripts for applications, and have been used for quite some time. Many application vendors, such as Frame Technology, use wrappers to tailor their application startup.

Vendors cannot, however, anticipate the full range of startup decisions and settings that are needed in every customer environment. You can add value by developing wrappers that are truly customized to your own end-user environment. It may be worth writing your own wrapper—even to serve as a front end to a vendor-designed application wrapper. Wrappers can leverage your system administration expertise and hard-won knowledge of the application requirements in a consistent way, to the benefit of all your users.

## Wrappers and Dot Files

Ordinarily, user dot files (for example, `.login` and `.cshrc` for the C shell or `.profile` for the Bourne and Korn shells) try to provide for what users may do after they log in. The goal is to define a comprehensive environment that supports all requests to access applications. It is not only difficult, but in some cases impossible, to provide for all cases: Some applications need a different value for an environment variable than do other applications that use the same variable name.

For example, to run a given Sybase application, users may need to set the `DSQUERY` variable to identify the back-end database server for the application. If this variable is set from dot files at login time, it extends throughout subsequent shell environments. However, other Sybase applications may require different `DSQUERY` values. If, instead, you write a wrapper for each Sybase application, each wrapper can set `DSQUERY` to the value needed for the application that is associated with it.

When you use wrappers, the environment for each application is set up as needed. Wrappers construct the needed environment at runtime, before executing the application. In addition, the settings are visible to the resulting application process only; they do not interact with the rest of the user's environment. This encapsulation of runtime environment is a significant advantage of wrappers.

Likewise, users' paths frequently must be updated as applications come and go, in an effort to provide for what the user may decide to run.

Consider this analogy: In a given year, you plan to go running, hiking, skating, scuba diving, and snow skiing. (Forget for a moment that, as a system administrator, you're too busy.) Doesn't it seem more practical to don the special equipment for each activity just before you need it (and take it off when you're done), rather than trying to put it all on at the beginning of the year "just so you'll be ready"? Clearly, the latter approach can generate conflicts. And in choosing where to go skiing, for instance, you probably would prefer to choose your destination based on where the snow is at the time you are ready to go.

## Wrappers and Site Initialization Files *New!*

You can incorporate wrappers in site initialization files. Site initialization files locate initialization files centrally and distribute them globally. With site initialization files, you can continue to introduce new functionality to the user's work environment and also enable the user to customize individual user initialization files.

You create a site initialization file and add a reference to it in each user's initialization file. When you reference a site initialization file in a user initialization file, all updates to the site initialization file are automatically reflected when the user logs in to the system or when a user starts a new shell.

You can do any customization in a site initialization file that you can do in a user initialization file. Site initialization files typically reside on a server or a set of servers and appear as the first statement in a user initialization file. Each site initialization file must be the same type of shell script as the user initialization file that references it. In other words, you must write two versions of the site initialization file and keep them in sync. One version would handle users of the C shell or tcsh, the other version would handle users of the Bourne/Korn/Bash shells. It can, however, be a challenge to keep these two versions in sync.

To reference a site initialization file for a C shell user initialization file, put a line similar to the following example at the beginning of each user's .cshrc initialization file.

```
source /net/machine-name/export/site-files/site-init-file
```

To reference a site initialization file in a Bourne or Korn shell user initialization file, put a line similar to the following example at the beginning of each user's .profile initialization file.

```
. /net/machine-name/export/site-files/site-init-file
```

**Example of a Site Initialization File**    The following example shows a C shell site initialization file named site.login in which a user can choose a particular version of an application.

```
# @(#)site.login
main:
echo "Application Environment Selection"
echo ""
echo "1. Application, Version 1"
echo "2. Application, Version 2"
echo ""
echo -n "Type 1 or 2 and press Return to set your
application environment: "
set choice = $<
if ( $choice !~ [1-2] ) then
goto main
endif
switch ($choice)
case "1":
setenv APPHOME /opt/app-v.1
breaksw
case "2":
setenv APPHOME /opt/app-v.2
endsw
```

You would reference the `site.login` site initialization file located on a server named `server2` in the user's `.cshrc` file (C shell users only) with the following line. The automounter must be running on the user's system.

```
source /net/server2/site-init-files/site.login
```

## Additional Wrapper Advantages

With wrappers, you can provide sensible default values for variables while still allowing users the option to override those settings. You can automate user installation steps that some applications require when first run and know that you are producing consistent results. You can also generate usage information about the application.

## Wrapper Overhead and Costs

Some administrators question whether the merits of a wrapper approach justify the overhead imposed each time an application starts up. After all, an additional shell script runs ahead of the normal application startup. Several years of experience with complex wrappers at Sun have shown that the delay in startup time is trivial and the benefits overwhelming.

The biggest cost to consider is the flip side of the greatest benefit—wrappers are powerful, so they require care. Wrappers present consistent behavior to large numbers of users. If wrappers are well produced and maintained, they deliver gratifyingly reliable service and prevent many problems. On the other hand, if wrappers are broken, service to large numbers of users may be impacted.

## Introduction of Wrappers into an Existing Environment

One of the great advantages of wrappers is that you can introduce them immediately into almost any application environment. Once you develop a wrapper for a given application, if the command names that link to it are installed in a location already in the users' paths (for example, `/usr/local/bin`), you can make the application immediately available without needing to do anything to set up the user environment.

To provide a limited implementation, you can decide how many wrappers you want to provide, and for which applications. You can write wrappers as you add new packages, and you can write wrappers for older applications as well. You can create links to the wrappers in a directory already in the users' paths. Alternatively, you can create a new directory that contains the links to the wrappers.

The following tasks are required in setting up a limited implementation of an application server with wrappers.

- Installing packages by using vendor instructions.
- Creating wrappers for applications, to eliminate or minimize any requirement for hard-coded setup by individual users.
- Creating all application command names as symbolic links in a directory that is already on the users' paths (or in a new directory to be added to their paths).
- Creating symbolic links to point to the application wrapper.

## Designing an Application Server

To provide a complete implementation of these techniques throughout an environment, you perform the following tasks on the server.

- Identifying servers to specialize in providing application access.
- Implementing the fewest possible slices (partitions) to contain the software packages.
- Performing software installations on these servers in a consistent file system layout.

*New!*
- Sharing the application server file system read-only to users if possible. Some applications must write into their library areas (although it is bad practice) and require their application area to be readable and writable by at least a group.
- Naming package directories in a way that reflects both the application name and the version.
- Installing packages initially per vendor instructions and then (if necessary) adjusting them to simplify and encapsulate their structure.
- Creating wrappers for applications, to eliminate or minimize any requirement for hard-coded setup on the part of individual users.

*New!*
- If you use site initialization files, creating or modifying the appropriate site initialization file.
- Creating all application command names as symbolic links in a common directory, and creating symbolic links to point to the application wrapper.
- As applications are added to a server, using the `rdist` command to update other servers that mirror this central application server's applications.
- Separating servers for network services (NIS/NIS+, DNS, NTP, mail, and so on) from application servers in all but the smallest environments.

You perform the following tasks in the user environment.

- Setting up users with the appropriate mount point and mount to access the application server.
- Setting up users with a path that includes the common command directory.
- If you use site initialization files, adding the reference to the appropriate  *New!*
server site initialization file to users' initialization files.

The following sections describe in greater detail the basic tasks involved in a general implementation. However, coverage of many topics necessarily is superficial and the overall model is simplified.

## Server Configuration

Consider the following points when designating servers to act as application servers.

- Choose server configurations that you believe to be robust. Consolidating applications into one location simplifies life only to the extent that the system provides ongoing, reliable service. Typically, when application service is down, users are down.
- Choose servers that can retain their identities for reasonable lengths of time. Host name changes require mount maintenance, and host ID changes can make licensed passwords obsolete.

Alternatively, you can use DNS CNAMEs (aliases) for each service (for  *New!*
example, `dns.`*`domainname`*, `nisplus.`*`domainname`*, `apps.`*`domainname`*). If you want to migrate the service to another host, you can move it while keeping the original host up. For a brief time, two hosts are running the same application. Change the DNS CNAME and wait for all clients to roll over to the new host. Then, retire the old host server.

## User Capacity

It is impossible to offer specific guidelines concerning the number of servers you will require. Your goal is to provide reasonable NFS response time to all clients served. The user ratio you can support depends on many factors, such as the server characteristics, network characteristics, the types of applications being served, and the number of clients.

Try to locate application servers on the same network segments as the bulk of their clients. As a rule, you obtain the best response if you minimize NFS traffic through routers and other store-and-forward network devices.

Automounter maps for application directories are especially useful when applications are moved from one server to another.

**New!**

For example, with the automounter, you could change application servers with the following steps.

1.  Create a new application server and load the new software.
2.  Update the NIS/NIS+ automounter map with the information for the new application server.
3.  Wait for all automounter clients to unmount the old application server, then start mounting these file systems from the new application server.

    Wait a week or so for those users who run applications such as FrameMaker for days at a time, thus holding down the mount point.
4.  Retire the old application server.

### Compatible Services

It is probably simplest to dedicate a server exclusively as an application server. If, however, it is impossible or impractical to do so in your environment, you may need to implement a multipurpose server. Note that a multipurpose server is a bad practice because it provides a single point of failure.

Certain services present little conflict with NFS service because of their lightweight or typical scheduling. Examples include DNS or NIS/NIS+ servers. Additional, nonapplication NFS roles, such as sharing client root or home directory file systems, may have some impact on application response time.

> *NOTE. For its role as an NFS server, a platform need not be typical of the user base platforms. However, if an application server is also to act as a license server, it must be capable of running the license support binaries provided by the application vendors.*

Other functions are incompatible with optimum NFS performance because they make heavy CPU and I/O demands. Examples of incompatible functions include back-end database engines, development activity such as compiling and debugging, and routing.

### Disk Allocation

You need to allocate adequate space for applications on the server, allowing ample space to accommodate future additions. Also remember that you may need space for multiple versions of some applications as you transition users to newer versions.

As noted earlier, you want to serve applications from a single file system to minimize user mounts. If your overall application space requirements exceed the size of your largest disk, you may want to use the Veritas Volume

Manager or Online: DiskSuite product. These products let you concatenate (group together) multiple physical disk slices into one logical metaslice. They also offer other performance and high-availability enhancements, such as striping, mirroring and "hot spare" capability.

Contrary to system defaults, put /, /usr, and /opt into a single partition large enough to hold dozens or hundreds of patches as well as providing enough room for an OS upgrade.

## File System Configuration

The following sections suggest a basic file system configuration for application servers. When you create one or more application servers, you generally provide a single file system with a consistent directory hierarchy. In that way, you create an environment that is consistent throughout your organization.

**Base Directories**    When you have a server with a disk slice (partition) that you consider adequate for long-term use as an application server, you can begin to implement the file system itself. As a foundation, Sun recommends that you create a minimum of two standard directories, which, in this model, we name /usr/apps/exe and /usr/apps/pkgs.

You install symbolic links or wrappers that represent all the available commands used to execute applications in /usr/apps/exe, the common command directory. You install all of the applications that the symbolic links and wrappers point to in the /usr/apps/pkgs directory.

**Parallel Hierarchies**    You may want to create one or more parallel file systems. For example, you might want to make a distinction between packages implemented by central administration and packages introduced by regional administration. You also might want to distinguish between production and beta versions of software.

If you want to create such parallel hierarchies, you could designate them as follows.

```
/usr/apps/local/pkgs
/usr/apps/local/exe
```

The /usr/apps/local/pkgs directory contains the applications, and the corresponding /usr/apps/local/exe directory contains the symbolic links to the wrappers for those applications. Under this type of arrangement, you need to add a second path (/usr/apps/local/exe) to the users' environment. If you arrange the directory as a parallel hierarchy under a single file system instead of a separate file system, you can use a single mount point. If you create a separate file system, users need to have a second mount point.

Clearly there are more variations not presented here. It is important for you to determine your needs. Try to plan for the long term, and try to keep your setup as simple and as consistent as possible. At Sun it has, indeed, been possible to provide most application services through a single mount.

**Transitory Names**    If you use wrappers, avoid the temptation to create a file system with directories that are named after architectures or other transitory distinctions; for example, /usr/apps/sun4u. Packages are always present, but other distinctions come and go. Confine file system distinctions to individual application directories (which come and go themselves) where the changes impact only the wrapper.

**Permissions**    Unless you have good reasons not to do so, permissions should be mode 755 for directories you create and for those within applications, so that they are writable by owner, with read and execute for group and world. Sometimes vendors ship nonwritable directories that interfere with your ability to transfer the contents to another system. In general, make other files writable by owner and readable by all, and leave execute permissions intact. You can use the following commands to change a directory hierarchy to the recommended permissions.

*New!*

The arguments to the find -perm option must be octal only. -perm takes two kinds of arguments: The first lists an absolute octal permission (for example -perm 0777), so it locates any file or directory that has those exact permissions. The second lists an octal permission preceded by a minus sign that finds any file or directory that has the mentioned permission bits turned on, even if other permission bits are turned on too (for example, -perm -0020 matches any file or directory that has the group write bit turned on).

*New!*

Use the following command to change permissions only on directories that do NOT have the setuid, setgid, or sticky bits set.

```
/usr/bin/find directory-name -type d ! \( -perm -4000 -o -perm -2000 -o -perm
  -1000 \) -exec /usr/bin/chmod 755 {} \;
```

*New!*

Use the following command to find all files that are *not* writable by their owners and make them writable.

```
/usr/bin/find directory-name -type f ! -perm -0200 -exec /usr/bin/chmod u+w {} \;
```

*New!*

Use the following command to find all files that are *not* readable by user, group *and* other, and make them readable by all three.

```
/usr/bin/find directory-name -type f ! \( -perm -0400 -perm -0040 -perm -0004 \)
  -exec /usr/bin/chmod ugo+r {} \;
```

**Ownership**     If you set up or maintain an extensive network of application servers and update them using trusted host relationships, consider what account should own the software distribution. In general, you do not need to have root be the owner. You may find some security advantages to creating a special, nonprivileged ownership account for managing application servers.

## File System Sharing

Before users can access files on the application server, you must share (export) the file system to make it available to other systems on the network. Sun strongly recommends that you share the application's file system read-only.

Use the following steps on the application server to share the file system.

1.  Become superuser.
2.  Edit the `/etc/dfs/dfstab` file and add the following line.

```
share -F nfs -o ro pathname
```

3.  Type **share _pathname_** (or **shareall**) and press Return.

In the following example, the path name `/usr/apps` is shared.

```
oak% su
Password
# vi /etc/dfs/dfstab
[Add the following line]
share -F nfs -o ro /usr/apps
[Quit the file and save the changes]
# share /usr/apps
#
```

Edit the `/etc/init.d/nfs.server` file and increase the `/usr/lib/nfsd -a 16` value—which represents the number of potential threads within a single `nfsd` program—to anything up to 512 to improve NFS performance. For an application server, 16 is inadequate.

*New!*

In the following example, the value for starting `/usr/lib/nfsd` in the `/etc/init.d.nfs.server` file is changed to `256`.

```
        # If /etc/rmmount.conf exists and contains share commands
        # then start up mountd and nfsd

        if [ $startnfsd -eq 0 -a -f /etc/rmmount.conf ] && \
            /usr/bin/grep '^[    ]*share' \
            /etc/rmmount.conf > /dev/null 2>&1; then
                startnfsd=1
        fi

        if [ $startnfsd -ne 0 ]; then
                /usr/lib/nfs/mountd
                /usr/lib/nfs/nfsd -a 256
        elif [ ! -n "$_INIT_RUN_LEVEL" ]; then
                echo "NFS service was not started because" \
```

```
                              "/etc/dfs/dfstab has no entries."
        fi
```

If you must start the NFS service manually, use the following steps. Otherwise, the services start up at boot time.

1. Type **/usr/lib/nfs/nfsd 64** and press Return.

   You have started the NFS daemons.

2. Type **/usr/lib/nfs/mountd** and press Return.

   You have started the mount daemon.

3. Type **share -F nfs -o ro *pathname*** and press Return.

   *pathname* is the name of the mount point file system. For example, if you have mounted the partition as /usr/apps, type **share -F nfs -o ro /usr/apps** and press Return.

## Installing and Configuring Packages

If you want to install the application in the /usr/apps directory instead of /opt, you need to set up either the package commands or Admintool to install the software in a different directory and then install the software.

Sun suggests that you use a name for the application directory that reflects the actual product name (in lower case for simplicity), with some sort of version suffix. For example, following the proposed naming convention, you might install version 2.0 of FooTool in the /usr/apps/pkgs/footool,v2.0 directory.

Follow the vendor's directions to install the software. If the vendor's or developer's install procedure does not use the package commands, you may need to rename the directory after completing the vendor installation process. See Chapter 14, "Package Commands," for instructions on how to use the package commands. See Chapter 15, "Admintool: Software Manager," for instructions on how to use Admintool.

Normally you should minimize any changes that you make to the original installed software. The flexibility of the wrapper helps you adapt to unusual requirements. You do, however, typically want to add some things to the package—at least, the wrapper itself. Create a subdirectory at the top level of the package to contain the wrapper and other possible additions. Such additions might include site-specific README files, announcements, and scripts that complete server-specific setup for the package. In the following example, the subdirectory is called dist.

```
$ cd /usr/apps/pkgs/footool,v2.0
$ /usr/bin/mkdir dist
$
```

Determine whether you think this directory requires additional subdivision. If so, be sure to use a consistent naming convention. The location of the wrapper determines the form of the command name links that must connect to it. For the purpose of this example, refer to the wrapper as being in the top level of this subdirectory and name it simply `wrapper`, as shown in the following example.

```
/usr/apps/pkgs/footool,v2.0/dist/wrapper
```

In many application packages, you must configure some of the files before the package can be run. If you are maintaining multiple application servers, consider the following issues.

- Once you modify the original files, you may not have generic copies left. If you copy the package to another server, you may want the original files to match the vendor's setup documentation.

- If you synchronize the package between servers after setup, be careful not to overwrite the server-specific setups with those from another server.

Consider how you want to handle such files. One way is to identify the files that are candidates for modification and to make copies of them where they reside, using a suffix such as `.orig`. This convention preserves generic copies. You still must avoid shipping the modified versions of these files to other servers so that you do not overwrite local configurations that are already established.

## Changes to the Default Package Version

When you install applications in directories that identify their versions, multiple versions can coexist at the same directory level. To identify the default version of a given application, create a generic directory name as a symbolic link pointing to the version-named directory that you want to serve as the default.

In the following example, the `/usr/apps/pkgs` directory contains two versions of FooTool and a generic `footool` name link.

```
$ cd /usr/apps/pkgs
$ ls -ld footool*
lrwxrwxrwx   1 nobody    nobody       12 Jun 19  1992 /usr/apps/pkgs/footool ->
  footool,v1.0
```

```
drwxr-xr-x   9 nobody    nobody     512 Jun 18  1992 /usr/apps/pkgs/footool,v1.0
drwxr-xr-x   9 nobody    nobody     512 May  3 21:23 /usr/apps/pkgs/footool,v2.0
$
```

The default version is `footool,v1.0`. If you want to change the default version to 2.0, remove the existing link and create a new link to version 2.0, as shown in the following example.

```
$ /usr/bin/rm footool
$ /usr/bin/ln -s footool,v2.0 footool
$ ls -ld footool*
lrwxrwxrwx   1 nobody    nobody      12 Jul 19 07:32 /usr/apps/pkgs/footool ->
  footool,v2.0
drwxr-xr-x   9 nobody    nobody     512 Jun 18  1992 /usr/apps/pkgs/footool,v1.0
drwxr-xr-x   9 nobody    nobody     512 May  3 21:23 /usr/apps/pkgs/footool,v2.0
$
```

The version `footool,v2.0` is the default for all users because the symbolic links in `/usr/apps/exe` point to a wrapper by using a path that refers to the directory named `footool`. This path now leads to the wrapper in `footool,v2.0`.

## Developing Wrappers

The following sections describe some basic information about how to develop wrappers. Refer to Part 6 of this book for an introduction to shell programming.

### Interpreter Choice

You typically write wrapper scripts in an interpreted language so that they can execute on the various platform configurations in the environment. If you are going to write wrappers, you must decide which interpreter to use. The Solaris Operating Environment provides three shells that make suitable interpreters for wrappers, as noted in Table 68.

*Table 68    Available Shells*

| Shell | Description |
|---|---|
| `/bin/sh` | Bourne shell. |
| `/bin/ksh` | Korn shell. |
| `/bin/csh` | C shell. |

*New!*

*NOTE. The Solaris 8 Operating Environment also includes three freeware shells: The Bourne-Again shell (`bash`), the TC shell (`tcsh`), and the Z shell (`zsh`).*

Sun recommends that you use the Bourne shell to write wrappers. Although the C shell is popular for interactive use, the Bourne shell is more advanced as a programming language. The C shell is also less portable because there are more feature variations between UNIX platforms. The Bourne shell supports functions—which result in code that is reusable in other wrappers—and the ability to pipe into and out of control constructs. The examples in this chapter use Bourne shell syntax.

*NOTE. In an environment that is so heterogeneous that even the Bourne shell is not universally available, you would have to seek yet another interpreter, possibly Perl.*

As with all shell scripts, the first line in the script specifies the shell. The following example shows the first line in a Bourne shell wrapper script.

```
#!/bin/sh
```

## Wrapper Directory and Naming

Create a subdirectory in the application directory, for example, `/usr/apps/pkgs/`*application-name*`/dist`. Within that directory, create a wrapper that has the same name as the other wrappers. For example, name each wrapper `wrapper` (for example, `/usr/apps/pkgs/`*application-name*`/dist/wrapper`). When you use the same name for each application wrapper, it simplifies administration because you do not need to remember a host of different wrapper names. You can easily create links to any wrapper.

## Command Name Evaluation

One of the first things a wrapper must do is evaluate the name that was used to invoke it. The wrapper has its own name. The wrapper name is different from any of the application command names, but the wrapper must know which command name it is being asked to represent.

For example, for package `footool,v2.0`, the `foo` command is a link to the script called `wrapper` that is located in the `/usr/apps/pkgs/footool,v2.0/dist` directory. When a user types **foo**, the wrapper learns the name used to invoke it from the construct `$0`. In this case, `$0` is `/usr/apps/exe/foo`. The `/bin/basename` command is used to strip the leading path, and `foo` is assigned to the variable `cmd`, as shown below.

```
cmd=`/bin/basename $0`
```

## Environment Variables

Many applications require that you assign environment variables before you can execute the application. Environment variables usually are values that cannot be reliably predicted by the compiled code, such as the directory where the application is installed. Such variables must be set and exported to be available to subsequently executing processes, just as they would be from a user's dot files. The Bourne shell syntax is shown below.

```
export FOOHOME
FOOHOME=/usr/apps/pkgs/footool,v2.0
```

*NOTE. You can export the environment variable either before or after you assign it a value. Once you export an environment variable, it remains exported for the remainder of the script, even if you modify it. So, you need to export an environment variable only once within a script.*

## Platform Evaluation

Not all applications support all combinations of hardware platforms and operating systems that may be in your environment. Therefore, you need to evaluate the user's platform to see if service can be provided.

For example, if `footool,v2.0` supports only the `sun4u` platform, the code shown here declines service (politely) to all other platforms.

```
case `uname -m` in
    sun4u)
            ;;
    *)
            echo >&2 "Sorry, $cmd not available for `uname -m`
  architecture."
            exit 1
            ;;
esac
```

## Command Path Construction

Next, you define the variable command in terms of code that yields the complete execution path to the application binary.

*NOTE. The wrapper may not, in fact, execute the binary itself but instead may invoke a link that the vendor has routed through its own wrapper, as is the case with the FrameMaker product.*

In the `footool,v2.0` wrapper, you might write a command path definition, as shown in the following example.

```
command=$FOOHOME/bin.`uname -m`/$cmd
```

The command path definition could be more complex, or it could be as simple as that shown in the following example.

```
command=$FOOHOME/bin/$cmd
```

## Exec/Argument Passing

The wrapper has now made its assignments and calculations and has determined that the service is available for this user. It is time to hand off execution to the application and get out of the way, via the `exec` statement. The wrapper process has navigated to the correct binary and passed on the necessary environment. It then vanishes and imposes no further burden.

The last action of the wrapper is to make sure that any arguments the user included on the original command line get through exactly as expressed, which is the purpose of the ${1+"$@"} construct at the end of the `exec` statement shown in the following example.

```
exec $command ${1+"$@"}
```

## A Basic Wrapper

At this point, the basic wrapper looks like the example below.

```
#!/bin/sh
     cmd=`/bin/basename $0`
     export FOOHOME
     FOOHOME=/usr/apps/pkgs/footool,v2.0
     case `uname -m` in
          sun4u)
                    ;;
          *)
                    echo >&2 "Sorry, $cmd not available for `uname -m`
                    architecture."
                    exit 1
                    ;;
     esac
     command=$FOOHOME/bin/$cmd
     exec $command ${1+"$@"}
```

The wrapper example is not quite complete; it does not consider how `uname -m` gets defined. The code necessary to assess architecture varies depending on the mix of platforms in the environment. However, in a given environment, you would need to use this same code for many wrappers. You can create the code as a Bourne shell function that can be replicated in as many wrappers as necessary.

In fact, for ease of maintenance, you might choose to make this code one function among others in a library external to the wrappers themselves. The wrappers requiring this function then merely source it from the library and execute it at the appropriate point in the wrapper. In this way, you often can carry out maintenance required by the wrappers by updating the library that supports all the wrappers. See Chapter 19 for some examples of wrapper functions.

If you provide a function library, be sure to use a consistent naming convention so that the wrappers can access and source the wrapper functions. You may want to apply the version-naming convention to this directory as well. For example, you might create a directory named `/usr/apps/library,v1.0`.

When a function library exists, you use the functions in scripts by defining the library location and sourcing the function script at the beginning of the wrapper. Next, you would execute the function at the appropriate point in the wrapper to return the values required. Remember, our wrapper example here is intentionally basic. The bold lines in the following example show the additions made to the basic script. See "arch.sh.fctn Function" on page 503 for an example of the function `arch.sh.fctn`.

```
#!/bin/sh
library=/usr/apps/pkgs/library,v1.0
. $library/sh/arch.sh.fctn
cmd=`/bin/basename $0`
export FOOHOME
FOOHOME=/usr/apps/pkgs/footool,v2.0
case `uname -m` in
    sun4u)
        ;;
    *)
        echo >&2 "Sorry, $cmd not available for `uname -m` architecture."
        exit 1
        ;;
esac
command=$FOOHOME/bin/$cmd
exec $command ${1+"$@"}
```

## Using a Common Command Directory

You should create symbolic links for all application command names in the `/usr/apps/exe` directory. When you do so, users can access all of the software in the distribution with a single, unchanging path component.

If you choose to have a common command directory for a parallel hierarchy, as mentioned previously, two path components are sufficient to access the entire distribution.

The command names are symbolic links that point to the location of the wrapper for their application. Many applications, such as MatLab and FrameMaker, come with separate subprograms, and you need to create symbolic links to the wrapper for each subprogram For example, if the package FooTool 2.0 has the commands `foo` and `bar`, create these names as symbolic links in `/usr/apps/exe`, as follows.

```
$ cd /usr/apps/exe
$ /usr/bin/ln -s /usr/apps/pkgs/footool/dist/wrapper foo
$ /usr/bin/ln -s /usr/apps/pkgs/footool/dist/wrapper bar
$ ls -l foo bar
lrwxrwxrwx   1 nobody    nobody       35 Apr  6  1992 foo ->
  /usr/apps/pkgs/footool/dist/wrapper

lrwxrwxrwx   1 nobody    nobody       35 Apr  6  1992 bar ->
  /usr/apps/pkgs/footool/dist/wrapper
$
```

Notice that the link destinations refer to the generic directory name link, `footool`, instead of the `footool,v2.0` directory. Use the generic directory name link for each package in this way to determine the version of the package to which the commands are connected. The users start the default version of the software, and you can change the default version simply by changing the link that determines it. Alternatively, the wrapper could accept options that would enable a user to specify the version of the program to use. If the user specifies no options, the latest version is run.

You could link the command names via the specific version-named directory instead, but you would find that changing from one version to another, when that time inevitably arrives, requires more work and more exposure. This extra work might not be obvious when packages have only one or two commands, but some applications have many. FrameMaker, for instance, has more than 80 commands and all of them should be handled by one wrapper.

It is a good idea to create a help function for each wrapper to display usage *New!* information about the possible options that the wrapper command accepts. The user could then type the wrapper name with a -h (help) option to display usage information for the wrapper.

## Setting User Configurations

The following sections describe what you need to do to set up the user environment to access files on the application server.

### Mount Points

In a general implementation, each user system needs to have a mount point directory; for example, `/usr/apps`.

## Mounts

You can mount files from an application server when you use NFS. You can mount files either by editing the `/etc/vfstab` or with the automounter.

If you use the `/etc/vfstab` file, edit it on each user's system and add a line that looks like the following.

```
#device        device       mount      FS     fsck    mount     mount
#to mount      to fsck      point      type   pass    at boot   options
#
server-name:/usr/apps -     /usr/apps  nfs    -       yes       ro
```

For example, to mount from an application server named oak, become superuser and add the following line to the user's `/etc/vfstab` file.

```
oak:/usr/apps  -  /usr/apps  nfs  -  yes  ro
```

Refer to Part 3 of this book for information about setting up the automounter to perform these mounts automatically when they are needed.

## Path

Each user typically needs either one or two path components to access applications, depending on whether you implement a parallel hierarchy. The name of the second component depends on the naming scheme applied to the parallel hierarchy. Suppose the path components are as follows.

```
/usr/apps/exe
/usr/apps/local/exe
```

The order in which you put the directories in the path is up to you. If you have applications that share the same name in both directories, you may want priority applied to either the global or the local distribution. The placement in the path relative to the standard OS directories is significant only if you expect to encounter name conflicts with commands in those locations.

A path for Solaris users could conceivably be as simple as the following.

```
/usr/dt/bin /usr/bin /usr/sbin /usr/apps/exe /usr/apps/local/exe
```

## Migration Considerations

In migrating existing users to a new software scheme, you must (carefully) simplify their existing setups. Of course, they need the mount point and mount and the path component(s). Beyond these, you must remove most of the other hard-coded settings, to allow the dynamic connections to operate. There are always exceptions, though, and some hard-coded setups remain appropriate.

## Understanding Distribution Issues

If you must maintain multiple application servers and need to copy application packages (or entire file systems) from one to another, you probably want to become familiar with the rdist(1) command. It is a standard command specially designed for synchronizing file systems or portions of file systems between remote hosts. One of rdist's great advantages is that it compares the status of files between the source and destination systems and copies only those files that need updating. This procedure is more efficient in many cases than using tar, for example, which copies all files unconditionally.

Unfortunately, the manual page for rdist does not provide clear guidelines for how to begin simply and scale to more sophisticated formats. The following paragraphs provide some suggestions for how to begin.

*NOTE. Be sure to begin with controlled experimentation in a test environment and study of the* rdist *manual page so that you are not unpleasantly surprised by unexpected results.*

To be able to use rdist to copy from one system to another depends on some level of trusted host relationship. (That is, the UID using rdist must be able to log in to the remote system without a password.) You may want this account to be owned by a UID other than root.

Once this privilege exists, you can use rdist to copy a hierarchy from the local system to the same destination on the remote system with a command as simple as the following.

```
$ rdist -c /usr/apps remote-system
```

Perhaps the most common form of rdist is to refer to a file that lists the target host systems and the path names to be synchronized. When the file has been created, use the following syntax.

```
$ rdist -f distfile
```

You may encounter limitations because rdist distfiles cannot use actual shell variables for flexibility. You can work around this limitation, however, by creating a script in which the shell expands variables before feeding the resulting syntax to rdist. The format of such a script, shown here, is the beginning of the power needed to use `rdist` to perform flexible, selective updates.

```
#!/bin/sh
files="
pathname1
pathname2
. . .
"
hosts="
host1
host2
. . .
"
rdist -f - <<-EOrdist
("$files") -> ("$hosts")
EOrdist
```

*NOTE. Beware of using `rcp` `-r` to copy hierarchies. In the process, symbolic links get converted to actual copies of their destination files. This conversion not only can affect the amount of space occupied, but can produce unexpected behavior. You may later make changes to link destination files, such as wrappers, not realizing that command names have become outdated copies of the script itself. Also, `rcp` does not replicate UID, GID, or permissions.*

## Licensing

Many Sun unbundled products and application software packages require software licenses that control the number of users who can access the product at the same time. If the application software has a floating license system, you can also designate the application server as a license server. Preferably, a single license server can manage licenses for multiple application servers, provided the license server is accessible to all the application servers across an existing network.

A full description of all the available types of licenses and license servers is beyond the scope of this book. Following are three possible configurations for setting up license servers.

- Single independent license server: All licenses are handled by a single server.
- Multiple independent license servers: You can have as many independent license servers as you have systems on the network. Each license server is configured independently, and you must obtain individual license passwords for each independent server system. Multiple independent license servers are bad practice. They are very difficult to administer, require a lot of paperwork to track the license

*New!*

keys and the host IDs they are bound to, provide a fragile infrastructure, and make it difficult to migrate license service as a contiguous unit.

- Multiple redundant license servers: You can define a set of servers that operate together to emulate a single independent license server configuration. A redundant license server configuration improves the stability of a license system and ensures that licensed products are not shut down as long as the majority of your license servers are running. You must obtain a license password for each set of redundant license servers. When you define a set of redundant license servers, you must administer them as a set. If you add a license password to one of the servers in the set, you must add it to all other license servers in the set.

# 14

# *PACKAGE*
# *COMMANDS*

This chapter describes how to use the Solaris package commands to install, remove, and administer software.

## Reviewing Package Commands

You manage software from a command line with the commands shown in Table 69. You must have superuser privileges to use the `pkgadd` and `pkgrm` commands.

*Table 69    Package Commands*

| Command | Task |
|---|---|
| vi(1)<br>admin(4) | Set installation defaults. |
| /bin/pkgadd(1M) | Install software package or store files for installation at a later time. |
| /usr/sbin/pkgask(1M) | Create a script to define installation parameters. |
| /usr/sbin/pkgchk(1M) | Check accuracy of installation. |
| /bin/pkginfo(1) | List installed packages. |

*Table 69     Package Commands (Continued)*

| Command | Task |
|---------|------|
| /bin/pkgparam(1) | Display software package parameter values. |
| /usr/sbin/pkgrm(1M) | Remove packages. |
| /bin/pkgtrans(1) | Translate an installable package from one format to another. |

*New!* (beside pkgparam row)
*New!* (beside pkgtrans row)

## *New!* Package Formats

Packages can be provided in the following configurations.

- In a CD-ROM file system.
- On raw media such as a tape.
- In a raw package file, which is written into a file system.

Most packages come as a directory tree, where the top-level directory is the name of the package. One or more packages can be bundled inside a package file that is created with the pkgtrans command. See "Translating Package Formats" on page 392 for more information about the pkgtrans command.

*NOTE. You may experience problems with adding and removing some packages that were developed before the Solaris 2.5 release. If adding or removing a package fails during user interaction or if you are prompted for user interaction and your responses are ignored, set the following environment variable to:*

NONABI_SCRIPTS=TRUE

# Setting Up Package Administration Files

The pkgadd and pkgrm files, by default, use information from the /var/sadm/install/admin/default file, as shown below.

```
oak% more /var/sadm/install/admin/default
#ident      "@(#)default1.4   92/12/23 SMI"/* SVr4.0  1.5.2.1*/
mail=
instance=unique
partial=ask
runlevel=ask
idepend=ask
rdepend=ask
space=ask
setuid=ask
```

```
conflict=ask
action=ask
basedir=default
oak%
```

The parameters in this file are a set of *parameter=value* pairs, each on a separate line. If you do not want to use the default values, you can create an `admin` file and set different values. Table 70 lists and describes the parameters and shows the available values.

*Table 70    Package Administration Options*

| Parameter | Description | Possible Value |
|---|---|---|
| mail | Who will receive mail about installation or removal? | *username* |
| instance | Package already installed. | ask<br>overwrite<br>unique*<br>quit |
| partial | Partial package installed. | ask*<br>nocheck<br>quit |
| runlevel | Is run level correct? | ask*<br>nocheck<br>quit |
| idepend | Are package dependencies met? | ask*<br>nocheck<br>quit |
| rdepend | Is there a dependency on other packages? | ask*<br>nocheck<br>quit |
| space | Is disk space adequate? | ask*<br>nocheck<br>quit |
| setuid | Ask permission to set UID? | ask*<br>nocheck<br>quit<br>nochange |
| conflict | Will overwriting a file cause conflict with other packages? | ask*<br>nocheck<br>quit<br>nochange |

*Table 70      Package Administration Options (Continued)*

| Parameter | Description | Possible Value |
|---|---|---|
| `action` | Check for security impact? | `ask*`<br>`nocheck`<br>`quit` |
| `basedir` | Set base install directory. (`$PKGINST` creates a default directory with the same name as the package.) | `default*`<br>`$PKGINST`<br>`/path`<br>`/path/$PKGINST` |

\* Indicates the default value.

New!    Table 71 describes the possible values for the parameters in the `admin` file described in Table 70.

*Table 71      Description of Possible Parameter Values*

| Possible Value | Description |
|---|---|
| `ask` | Notify the installer when the situation occurs and ask for instructions. |
| `default` | Install packages in the base directory specified by the `BASEDIR` parameter in the `pkginfo` file. |
| `nocheck` | Do not check for the specified parameter. |
| `nochange` | Override installation of the specified parameter. |
| `overwrite` | Overwrite an existing package if only one instance exists. If there is more than one instance but only one has the same architecture, overwrite that instance. Otherwise, prompt the installer with existing instances asking which to overwrite. |
| `quit` | Abort installation if the parameter condition is detected. |
| `unique` | Do not overwrite an existing instance of a package. Instead, create a new instance of the package. Assign the new instance the next available instance identifier. |
| `username` | User login name. |
| `$PKGINST` | Create a default directory with the same name as the package. |
| `/path` | Use the specified path as the base directory. |

*Table 71    Description of Possible Parameter Values (Continued)*

| Possible Value | Description |
|---|---|
| /path/$PKGINST | Use the specified path as the base directory and create a default directory with the same name as the package at the end of the specified path. |

*CAUTION. Do not edit the* /var/sadm/install/admin/default *file. If you want to change the defaults, create your own* admin *file.*

If you create a custom admin file and specify it from the command line with the -a admin option, the pkgadd and pkgrm commands automatically look for the file first in the current working directory and then in the /var/sadm/install/admin directory. If you put the admin file in another directory, you must specify the path name for the file as part of the command-line argument. The following example specifies an admin file in the /var/tmp directory.

```
# pkgadd -a /var/tmp/admin -d /cdrom/cdrom0
```

To create an admin file, use any editor. Define each *parameter=value* pair, one per line. You do not need to assign values to all 11 parameters. If you do not assign a value and *pkgadd* needs one, it uses the default value ask.

The following example shows an administration file that prevents pkgadd *New!* from prompting the user for any confirmation before installing the package. Without prompting, you can start the installation and it completes without requiring any further user input. This file does no checking of any of the parameters, overwrites an existing instance of the package, and installs the package in the default base directory.

```
mail=
instance=overwrite
partial=nocheck
runlevel-nocheck
idepend=nocheck
rdepend=nocheck
space=nocheck
setuid=nocheck
conflict=nocheck
action=nocheck
basedir=default
```

The following example of an administration file runs without user interaction but quits the installation if it encounters an error for any of the parameters.

```
mail=
instance=quit
partial=quit
runlevel-quit
idepend=quit
rdepend=quit
space=quit
setuid=quit
conflict=quit
action=quit
basedir=default
```

*CAUTION. Because the* ask *value asks for user input, when you specify it in an* admin *file, you cannot use that* admin *file for a noninteractive installation.*

The following example shows an admin file created to install files in the /usr/apps/pkgs directory and to use the name of the package as the name of the directory—as specified by the $PKGINST variable as part of the value for the basedir parameter. Because no other parameters are specified, pkgadd uses the default values for other parameters.

```
oak% more /var/sadm/install/admin/admin
basedir=/usr/apps/pkgs/$PKGINST
oak%
```

## Setting Up the Installation Base Directory

Before you begin software installation, decide where you want to install the software. If you want to install in a directory other than /opt, create an admin file in the /var/sadm/install/admin directory and set the basedir parameter to the directory where you want to install the software. If basedir is the only parameter you want to change, you can create an admin file that contains only that parameter. All other parameters use the default values. Refer to Table 70 on 377 for a description of the other parameters you can customize.

The following steps show how to create an admin file that installs files in the /usr/apps/pkgs directory and uses the name of the package as the directory name.

1. Become superuser.
2. Type **cd /var/sadm/install/admin** and press Return.
3. Use any editor to create a file.

   Assign the file any name you like, other than the name default. A suggested file name is admin.

4.  Add the line **basedir=/usr/apps/pkgs/$PKGINST** to the file.

5.  Save the changes and quit.

## Installing a Package with an Alternative Administration File

Unless you specify a different administration file, the pkgadd command uses the /var/sadm/install/admin/default file, which specifies the base directory as /opt. To use an alternative admin file, use the following syntax.

```
pkgadd -d device -a admin-file pkgid
```

The following example installs the package SUNWssser from the CD-ROM file system mounted at the /cdrom/cdrom0 mount point with an administration file named admin in the /var/sadm/install/admin directory.

```
# pkgadd -d /cdrom/cdrom0 -a admin SUNWssser
```

# Adding Packages

Use the pkgadd command to install software packages. The default pkgadd command is interactive and can inform you of potential problems in the installation as they occur.

*NOTE. You must have superuser privileges to use the* pkgadd *command.*

The pkgadd command has the following syntax.

```
pkgadd -d device-name [ -a admin-file ] pkgid
```

*New!*

The -d device-name option of the `pkgadd` command enables you to specify three different types of locations. Table 72 describe these locations and provides an example of the -d *device-name* option for each location.

*Table 72      Examples of -d Option Locations*

| Location | Example of Command Syntax |
|----------|---------------------------|
| Packages stored in a CD-ROM file system. | `pkginfo -d /cdrom/cdrom0` |
| Packages stored on raw media such as a tape. | `pkginfo -d /dev/rmt/0` |
| Packages stored in a raw package file that is written into a file system. | `pkginfo -d /tmp/raw-pkg-file` |

For example, to interactively install a software package named SUNWpkgA from a directory named /cdrom/cdrom0, type **/usr/sbin/pkgadd -d /cdrom/cdrom0 SUNWssser** and press Return. To install the a software package stored on a tape with an alternative administrative file named admin located in the /var/sadm/install/admin directory, type **/usr/sbin/pkgadd -d /dev/rmt/0 -a admin SUNWssser** and press Return. See "Setting Up Package Administration Files" on page 376 for information about package administrative files.

You can install multiple packages from the command line by typing a list of *pkgids* separated by spaces. The following example shows an edited example of installation of SearchIt 2.0 software from the /cdrom/cdrom0 directory.

```
# pkgadd -d /cdrom/cdrom0 SUNWssser SUNWsssra SUNWsssrb SUNWsssrc SUNWsssrd
  SUNWssstr

Processing package instance <SUNWssser> from </cdrom/cdrom0>

SearchIt Text Messages and Handbook
(sparc) 2.0

(C) 1992, 1993 Sun Microsystems, Inc. Printed in the United States of America.
  2550 Garcia Avenue, Mountain View, California, 94043-1100
U.S.A.

(Additional copyright information not shown)

Using </opt> as the package base directory.
## Processing package information.
## Processing system information.
## Verifying package dependencies.
WARNING:
The <SUNWsssra> package "SearchIt Runtime 1 of 3" is a prerequisite package
  and should be installed.

Do you want to continue with the installation of this package [y,n,?] y
## Verifying disk space requirements.
## Checking for conflicts with packages already installed.

The following files are already installed on the system and are being
used by another package:
```

```
/opt <attribute change only>

Do you want to install these conflicting files [y,n,?,q] y
## Checking for setuid/setgid programs.

Installing SearchIt Text Messages and Handbook as <SUNWssser>

## Installing part 1 of 1.
/opt/SUNWssoft/SearchIt/share/locale/C/LC_HELP/Home.info
/opt/SUNWssoft/SearchIt/share/locale/C/LC_HELP/Index.info
/opt/SUNWssoft/SearchIt/share/locale/C/LC_HELP/Search.info
/opt/SUNWssoft/SearchIt/share/locale/C/LC_HELP/SearchIt.handbook
/opt/SUNWssoft/SearchIt/share/locale/C/LC_HELP/SearchIt.info
/opt/SUNWssoft/SearchIt/share/locale/C/LC_HELP/Viewer.info
/opt/SUNWssoft/SearchIt/share/locale/C/LC_MESSAGES/SUNW_SEARCHIT_LABELS.po
/opt/SUNWssoft/SearchIt/share/locale/C/LC_MESSAGES/SUNW_SEARCHIT_MESSAGES.po
/opt/SUNWssoft/SearchIt/share/locale/C/LC_MESSAGES/SUNW_SEARCHIT_XVBROWSER.po
[ verifying class <none> ]

Installation of <SUNWssser> was successful.

Processing package instance <SUNWsssra> from </cdrom/cdrom0>

SearchIt Runtime 1 of 3
(sparc) 2.0

(Copyright information not shown)

Using </opt> as the package base directory.
## Processing package information.
## Processing system information.
   3 package pathnames are already properly installed.
## Verifying package dependencies.
WARNING:
The <SUNWsssrb> package "SearchIt Runtime 2 of 3" is a prerequisite package
   and should be installed.
WARNING:
The <SUNWsssrc> package "SearchIt Runtime 3 of 3" is a prerequisite package
   and should be installed.

Do you want to continue with the installation of this package [y,n,?] y
## Verifying disk space requirements.
## Checking for conflicts with packages already installed.
## Checking for setuid/setgid programs.

Installing SearchIt Runtime 1 of 3 as <SUNWsssra>
## Installing part 1 of 1.
/opt/SUNWssoft/SearchIt/README
/opt/SUNWssoft/SearchIt/bin/auto_index
/opt/SUNWssoft/SearchIt/bin/browseui
/opt/SUNWssoft/SearchIt/bin/catopen
/opt/SUNWssoft/SearchIt/bin/collectionui
(Additional files not shown)
[ verifying class <none> ]

Installation of <SUNWsssra> was successful.

Processing package instance <SUNWsssrb> from </cdrom/cdrom0>

SearchIt Runtime 2 of 3
(sparc) 2.0

(Copyright information not shown)

Using </opt> as the package base directory.
## Processing package information.
## Processing system information.
   4 package pathnames are already properly installed.
## Verifying package dependencies.
## Verifying disk space requirements.
## Checking for conflicts with packages already installed.
## Checking for setuid/setgid programs.

Installing SearchIt Runtime 2 of 3 as <SUNWsssrb>
```

```
## Installing part 1 of 1.
/opt/SUNWssoft/SearchIt/lib/fultext/fultext.ftc
/opt/SUNWssoft/SearchIt/lib/fultext/fultext.stp
/opt/SUNWssoft/SearchIt/lib/libft.so.1
[ verifying class <none> ]

(Additional package installations not shown)
```

The pkgadd command, by default, looks for packages in the
/var/spool/pkg directory. In this context, any packages that you have
copied into that directory are "spooled" and waiting for installation. If the
/var/spool/pkg directory contains no packages, installation fails, as shown
in the following example.

```
castle# pkgadd
pkgadd: ERROR: no packages were found in </var/spool/pkg>
castle#
```

To install packages from a CD-ROM, a tape, or a raw package file in a file
system, you must use the -d option to specify a full (absolute) path name to
the directory on the device that contains the packages that you want to
install.

If pkgadd encounters a problem, information about the problem is
displayed along with the prompt Do you want to continue with this
installation of the package?. Type **yes**, **no**, or **quit** and press
Return. Typing **yes** continues with the installation. If you have specified
more than one package, typing **no** stops the installation of the package that
failed, but does not stop the installation of the other packages. Typing **quit**
stops installation of all packages.

In the following example, although the command-line argument specifies a
valid directory on the CD-ROM, that directory contains no packages and the
pkgadd command returns an error message.

```
castle# pkgadd -d /cdrom/cdrom0
pkgadd: ERROR: no packages were found in </cdrom/sol_8_1000_doc>
castle#
```

```
castle# pkgadd -d /cdrom/sol_8_1000_doc/Solaris_8_Doc/sparc/Product

The following packages are available:
  1  SUNWab2r     AnswerBook2 Documentation Server
                  (sparc) 3.0,REV=2000.0804
  2  SUNWab2s     AnswerBook2 Documentation Server
                  (sparc) 3.0,REV=2000.0804
  3  SUNWab2u     AnswerBook2 Documentation Server
                  (sparc) 3.0,REV=2000.0804

Select package(s) you wish to process (or 'all' to process
all packages). (default: all) [?,??,q]:
```

In the following example, the command-line argument specifies a path to a valid directory on the CD-ROM that contains multiple packages.

```
castle# pkgadd -d /cdrom/sol_8_1000_doc/Solaris_8_Doc/sparc/Product

The following packages are available:
  1  SUNWab2r     AnswerBook2 Documentation Server
                  (sparc) 3.0,REV=2000.0804
  2  SUNWab2s     AnswerBook2 Documentation Server
                  (sparc) 3.0,REV=2000.0804
  3  SUNWab2u     AnswerBook2 Documentation Server
                  (sparc) 3.0,REV=2000.0804

Select package(s) you wish to process (or 'all' to process
all packages). (default: all) [?,??,q]:
```

Alternatively, you can use the cd command to change to the directory that contains the packages, and then type **pkgadd -d .** and press Return to proceed with installation, as shown in the following example.

```
castle# cd /cdrom/sol_8_1000_doc/Solaris_8_Doc/sparc/Product
castle# pkgadd -d .

The following packages are available:
  1  SUNWab2r     AnswerBook2 Documentation Server
                  (sparc) 3.0,REV=2000.0804
  2  SUNWab2s     AnswerBook2 Documentation Server
                  (sparc) 3.0,REV=2000.0804
  3  SUNWab2u     AnswerBook2 Documentation Server
                  (sparc) 3.0,REV=2000.0804

Select package(s) you wish to process (or 'all' to process
all packages). (default: all) [?,??,q]:
```

# Checking the Installation of a Package

You can use the pkgchk command to check the completeness, specific path name, file contents, and file attributes of an installed package.

The pkgchk command has the following syntax.

```
pkgchk pkgid
```

For example, to check the package SUNWman, the online manual pages, type **pkgchk SUNWman** and press Return. If the prompt comes up without any messages, the package has installed properly.

```
oak% pkgchk SUNWman
oak%
```

If you do get messages, however, the package has not installed properly, as shown in the following example.

```
oak% pkgchk SUNWssoft
WARNING: no pathnames were associated with <SUNWssoft>
oak%
```

*New!*

> *NOTE.* pkgchk *also reports errors if the package was installed correctly but any files or directories that are part of the package subsequently had their contents or attributes modified.*

You can specify more than one package identifier by typing a list separated by spaces. If you do not specify a *pkgid*, the complete list of packages on a system is checked.

You can check the installation completeness of a specific path name—where the path name refers either to an absolute path name to a file or to a directory—with the pkgchk -p option, which has the following syntax.

```
pkgchk -p pathname
```

If you want to check more than one path, provide the paths as a comma-separated list.

You can check the installation completeness of just the file attributes with the pkgchk -a option. You can check the installation completeness of just the file contents with the pkgchk -c option. The syntax for these options is shown below.

```
/usr/sbin/pkgchk [ -a | -c ] pkgid
```

*New!*

You can use the -d option to pkgchk to display information about packages stored in a file system, in a raw package datastream on a device, or the same raw package datastream saved in a file in a file system. To check the completeness of a spooled package, use the pkgchk -d option. This option looks in the specified directory or on the specified device and performs a check of the package. In the following example, the pkgchk command looks in the spool directory spool-dir and checks the completeness of the package named pkgA.

```
# /usr/sbin/pkgchk -d spool-dir pkgA
```

> *NOTE. Spooled package checks are limited because not all information can be audited until a package is installed.*

# Displaying Package Parameters

You can use the `pkgparam` command to display the parameter values for a package.

If you specify no parameters on the command line, values for all parameters associated with a package are displayed. The following example displays the parameters for the `SUNWdthj` package.

```
castle% pkgparam SUNWdthj
base docs runtime
/usr
Australia/West
/sbin:/usr/sbin:/usr/bin:/usr/sadm/install/bin
/usr/sadm/sysadm
sparc
SUNWdthj
HotJava Browser for Solaris
1.0.1,REV=1998.02.13
HotJava
1.0.1
usr
1000
system
HotJava Browser for Solaris
Sun Microsystems, Inc.
Please contact your local service provider

dt/appconfig/hotjava
pavoni980213183227
SUNWdthj
/var/sadm/pkg/SUNWdthj/save
Mar 03 1999 17:51
castle%
```

If you use the `-v` option, the output of the `pkgparam` command shows the name of the parameter and its value. The following example shows the output for the `SUNWdthj` package.

```
castle% pkgparam -v SUNWdthj
CLASSES='base docs runtime'
BASEDIR='/usr'
TZ='Australia/West'
PATH='/sbin:/usr/sbin:/usr/bin:/usr/sadm/install/bin'
OAMBASE='/usr/sadm/sysadm'
ARCH='sparc'
PKG='SUNWdthj'
NAME='HotJava Browser for Solaris'
VERSION='1.0.1,REV=1998.02.13'
PRODNAME='HotJava'
PRODVERS='1.0.1'
SUNW_PKGTYPE='usr'
MAXINST='1000'
CATEGORY='system'
DESC='HotJava Browser for Solaris'
VENDOR='Sun Microsystems, Inc.'
HOTLINE='Please contact your local service provider'
EMAIL=''
HOTJAVA='dt/appconfig/hotjava'
PSTAMP='pavoni980213183227'
PKGINST='SUNWdthj'
PKGSAV='/var/sadm/pkg/SUNWdthj/save'
```

```
INSTDATE='Feb 15 1999 09:33'
castle%
```

The following example displays the value for the VENDOR parameter.

```
castle% pkgparam SUNWab2r VENDOR
Sun Microsystems, Inc.
castle%
```

# Listing Packages

If you need to check which packages are installed on a system, use the pkginfo command. By default, it displays information about currently installed packages. You can also use the pkginfo command to display packages that are on mounted distribution media.

Use the pkginfo command with no arguments to list all installed packages. The following example shows the first few packages from a system.

```
48]castle{winsor}% pkginfo
system      SUNWadmap      System & Network Administration Applications
system      SUNWadmfw      System & Network Administration Framework
system      SUNWadmr       System & Network Administration Root
system      SUNWarc        Archive Libraries
system      SUNWaudio      Audio Applications
system      SUNWbcp        Binary Compatibility
system      SUNWbtool      CCS tools bundled with SunOS
system      SUNWcar        Core Architecture, (Root)
(Additional packages not shown in this example)
```

You can display information about a single package with the following syntax.

```
pkginfo pkgid
```

In the following example, information is displayed for the SUNWppm package.

```
oak% pkginfo SUNWppm
application SUNWppm      Solaris Print Manager
oak%
```

To display information about packages on a CD-ROM, mount the CD-ROM. Then use the following syntax to display a complete list of packages on the CD-ROM.

```
pkginfo -d /cdrom/cdrom-name
```

You can display information about single packages on a CD-ROM with the following syntax.

```
pkginfo -d /cdrom/cdrom-name pkgid
```

# Removing Packages

In previous releases of SunOS, you could remove unbundled software packages with the `rm(1)` command, which simply removed the files associated with a file system. Chances are that you would not know the names of all the files associated with a package. The Solaris packaging system, on the other hand, keeps track of all the files, directories, and their permissions for any application package. Therefore, you should always use the provided package commands, especially when removing a package. The `pkgrm` command makes administration easier by removing a complete unbundled package with a single command.

Use the following syntax to remove a package in interactive mode.

```
/usr/sbin/pkgrm pkgid
```

In the following example, the package `SUNWdiag` is removed.

```
oak% su
Password:
# pkgrm SUNWdiag

The following package is currently installed:
   SUNWdiag          Online Diagnostics Tool
(sparc) 2.1

Do you want to remove this package [y,n,?,q] y

## Removing installed package instance <SUNWdiag>
## Verifying package dependencies.
## Processing package information.
## Removing pathnames in <none> class
/opt/SUNWdiag/lib/libtest.a
/opt/SUNWdiag/lib
/opt/SUNWdiag/include/sdrtns.h
/opt/SUNWdiag/include
/opt/SUNWdiag/bin/what_rev
/opt/SUNWdiag/bin/vmem
```

```
/opt/SUNWdiag/bin/tapetest
/opt/SUNWdiag/bin/sunlink
/opt/SUNWdiag/bin/sundials
/opt/SUNWdiag/bin/sundiagup
/opt/SUNWdiag/bin/sundiag.info
/opt/SUNWdiag/bin/sundiag
/opt/SUNWdiag/bin/sunbuttons
/opt/SUNWdiag/bin/sptest
/opt/SUNWdiag/bin/revision_ref_file
/opt/SUNWdiag/bin/rawtest
/opt/SUNWdiag/bin/prp
/opt/SUNWdiag/bin/probe
/opt/SUNWdiag/bin/pmem
/opt/SUNWdiag/bin/nettest
/opt/SUNWdiag/bin/music.au
/opt/SUNWdiag/bin/mptest
/opt/SUNWdiag/bin/lpvitest
/opt/SUNWdiag/bin/isdntest
/opt/SUNWdiag/bin/gttest.data
/opt/SUNWdiag/bin/gttest
/opt/SUNWdiag/bin/fstest
/opt/SUNWdiag/bin/fputest
/opt/SUNWdiag/bin/fbtest
/opt/SUNWdiag/bin/dispatcher
/opt/SUNWdiag/bin/diagscrnprnt
/opt/SUNWdiag/bin/cg6test
/opt/SUNWdiag/bin/cg12.data.gsxr
/opt/SUNWdiag/bin/cg12.data
/opt/SUNWdiag/bin/cg12
/opt/SUNWdiag/bin/cdtest
/opt/SUNWdiag/bin/cbrtest
/opt/SUNWdiag/bin/bpptest
/opt/SUNWdiag/bin/autest.data
/opt/SUNWdiag/bin/autest
/opt/SUNWdiag/bin/audbri
/opt/SUNWdiag/bin/57fonts.400
/opt/SUNWdiag/bin/57fonts.300
/opt/SUNWdiag/bin
/opt/SUNWdiag
## Updating system information.

Removal of <SUNWdiag> was successful.
#
```

To remove a package in noninteractive mode, use the `pkgrm -n` option, as shown below.

```
/usr/sbin/pkgrm -n pkgid
```

To remove a package that was spooled to a directory, use the `pkgrm -s` option, as shown below.

```
/usr/sbin/pkgrm -s spooldir [ pkgid ]
```

In this example, *spooldir* is the name of the spool directory to which the unbundled package was spooled and *pkgid* is the name of the package specified for removal. When you do not supply a package identifier, `pkgrm` interactively prompts you to remove or preserve each package listed in the spool directory.

# Using the Package System Log File

The package commands maintain a list of installed packages in the /var/sadm/install/contents file. You can use the pkgchk -v *pkgid* command to list the files contained in a package. The following example (truncated to save space) lists the files contained in the SUNWebnfs package.

```
castle# pkgchk -v SUNWebnfs
/opt/SUNWebnfs
/opt/SUNWebnfs/JFileChooser-patch
/opt/SUNWebnfs/JFileChooser-patch/com
/opt/SUNWebnfs/JFileChooser-patch/com/sun
/opt/SUNWebnfs/JFileChooser-patch/com/sun/java
/opt/SUNWebnfs/JFileChooser-patch/com/sun/java/swing
/opt/SUNWebnfs/JFileChooser-patch/com/sun/java/swing/plaf
/opt/SUNWebnfs/JFileChooser-patch/com/sun/java/swing/plaf/windows
/opt/SUNWebnfs/JFileChooser-patch/com/sun/java/swing/plaf/windows/WindowsFileC
  hooserUI$DirectoryComboBoxModel.class
...(Additional lines deleted from this example)
castle#
```

The following example shows the first ten lines of the /var/sadm/install/contents file.

```
castle# head /var/sadm/install/contents
/bin=./usr/bin s none SUNWcsr
/dev d none 0755 root sys SUNWcsr SUNWcsd
/dev/arp=../devices/pseudo/arp@0:arp s none SUNWcsd
/dev/conslog=../devices/pseudo/log@0:conslog s none SUNWcsd
/dev/console=../devices/pseudo/cn@0:console s none SUNWcsd
/dev/dsk d none 0755 root sys SUNWcsd
/dev/eri=../devices/pseudo/clone@0:eri s none SUNWcsd
/dev/fd d none 0555 root root SUNWcsd
/dev/hme=../devices/pseudo/clone@0:hme s none SUNWcsd
/dev/icmp=../devices/pseudo/icmp@0:icmp s none SUNWcsd
castle#
```

If you need to determine which package contains a particular file, you can use the pkgchk -l -p *filename* command to search the package system file. The following example searches for information about the pkgadd command. The output shows that the command is located in /usr/sbin and is part of the SUNWcsu package.

```
castle% pkgchk -l -p /usr/sbin/pkgadd
Pathname: /usr/sbin/pkgadd
Type: regular file
Expected mode: 0555
Expected owner: root
Expected group: sys
Expected file size (bytes): 105196
Expected sum(1) of contents: 52501
Expected last modification: Jan 06 07:59:42 2000
Referenced by the following packages:
        SUNWcsu
Current status: installed

castle%
```

# New! Translating Package Formats

You can use the `pkgtrans` command to translate an installable package from one format to another. `pkgtrans` performs the following translations.

- A file system format to a datastream.
- A datastream to a file system format.
- One file system format to another file system format.

The `pkgtrans` command uses the following syntax.

```
/usr/bin/pkgtrans [-inos= device1 device2 [pkginst]
```

Table 73 describes the `pktrans` options.

*Table 73     Options to the pkgtrans Command*

| Option | Description |
|--------|-------------|
| `-i` | Copy only the `pkginfo`(4) and `pkgmap`(4) files. |
| `-n` | Create a new instance of the package on the destination device if any instance of this package already exists, up to the number specified by the `MAXINST` variable in the `pkginfo`(4) file. |
| `-o` | Overwrite the same instance on the destination device if it already exists. |
| `-s` | Write the package to *device2* as a datastream instead of as a file system. The default behavior is to write a file system format on devices that support both formats. |

The *device1* operand specifies the source device. The package or packages on this device are translated and placed on *device2*. *device2* specifies the destination device. Translated packages are placed on this device. *pkginst* specifies which package instance or instances on *device1* should be translated. You can use the token `all` to indicate all packages. You can use *pkginst.\** to indicate all instances of a package. If no packages are defined, a prompt shows all packages on the device and asks which to translate.

The following example creates a file named `raw-pkg-file` from the packages contained in `/var/spool/pkg`.

```
castle# pkgtrans -s /var/spool/pkg /tmp/raw-pkg-file

The following packages are available:
  1  SUNWab2r     AnswerBook2 Documentation Server
                  (sparc) 3.0,REV=2000.0804
  2  SUNWab2s     AnswerBook2 Documentation Server
                  (sparc) 3.0,REV=2000.0804
  3  SUNWab2u     AnswerBook2 Documentation Server
                  (sparc) 3.0,REV=2000.0804

Select package(s) you wish to process (or 'all' to process
all packages). (default: all) [?,??,q]: all
Transferring <SUNWab2r> package instance
Transferring <SUNWab2s> package instance
Transferring <SUNWab2u> package instance
castle#
```

You are prompted to ask which packages you want to transfer. You can use the `all` token to specify all packages.

You can also use the `pkgtrans` command to write the packages to a raw tape device. The following example writes the packages to the `/dev/rmt/0` tape drive.

```
castle# pkgrans -s /var/spool/pkg /dev/rmt0
```

You can then use the `pkgadd` command with the `-d` option to install the datastream packages, as shown in the following example.

```
castle# pkgadd -d /tmp/raw-pkg-file

The following packages are available:
  1  SUNWab2r     AnswerBook2 Documentation Server
                  (sparc) 3.0,REV=2000.0804
  2  SUNWab2s     AnswerBook2 Documentation Server
                  (sparc) 3.0,REV=2000.0804
  3  SUNWab2u     AnswerBook2 Documentation Server
                  (sparc) 3.0,REV=2000.0804

Select package(s) you wish to process (or 'all' to process
all packages). (default: all) [?,??,q]:
```

# 15

# *ADMINTOOL: SOFTWARE MANAGER*

Admintool is a graphical user interface to the package commands. You can use Admintool: Software Manager to install and remove unbundled software packages on a Solaris system.

Starting with the Solaris 2.5 release, the Admintool: Software functionality replaces Software Manager (swmtool). The swmtool command is a link to the admintool command and displays the Admintool: Software portion of Admintool.

Software that is designed to be managed with Admintool groups the packages into a set of clusters to make software management easier. Admintool calls the package commands. You can use the package commands and Admintool interchangeably. For example, you can install software with Admintool and remove the software with the pkgrm command. Alternatively, you can install software with the pkgadd command and remove that software with Admintool. Admintool displays all packages installed on a system, regardless of how they were installed.

Admintool: Software provides the following functionality.

- Displays a list of the software packages installed on a local system, showing the full title, package names, icons, and the size of each package.
- Installs and removes software on a local Solaris system.
- Enables you to specify the directory from which to install the software.

It is easy to use Admintool to add and remove software from a local system. Admintool provides a graphical user interface to the `pkgadd` and `pkgrm` commands. It also includes online help that provides general information on using the tool. Admintool enables you to view a descriptive list of software that is already installed on a system or to list the software on the installation media. It also enables you to view detailed information about each package, including the package name.

Admintool does not enable you to add packages to a spool directory or to eliminate user interaction with an administration file. You must use `pkgadd` command for those tasks.

*NOTE. Before the Solaris 2.5 release, Software Manager (accessed with the* `swmtool` *command) was the graphical tool for adding and removing software. With Solaris 2.5 and later releases, Admintool (accessed with the* `admintool` *command) provides that capability. The* `swmtool` *command in the Solaris 2.5 and 2.6 releases is linked to the* `admintool` *command.*

# Starting Admintool

The Admintool executable, `admintool`, is located in the `/bin` directory. The obsolete Software Manager executable, `swmtool` (located in the `/usr/sbin` directory) is linked to the `/bin/admintool` command. If you type **swmtool&**, the Admintool window opens. Use the following steps to start Admintool.

New!

*NOTE. To install or remove software, you must run Admintool as superuser, be a member of the UNIX* `sysadmin` *group (GID 14), have rights to install or remove software, or be a member of a role that has rights to install or remove software. See Chapter 23, "Role-Based Access Control," for information about rights.*

New!

1. From the CDE Application Manager window, double-click on the System_Admin folder, then double-click on the Admintool icon.

   You can also start Admintool from the Workspace Menu > Tools > Admintool. Or, from a Terminal window, type **admintool &** and press Return. The Admintool: Users window is displayed, as shown in Figure 57.

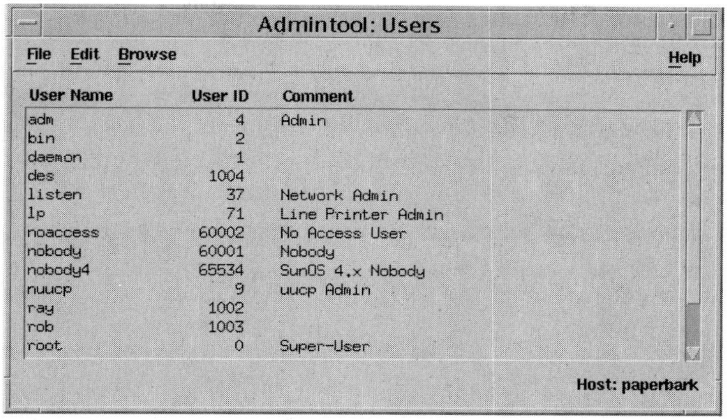

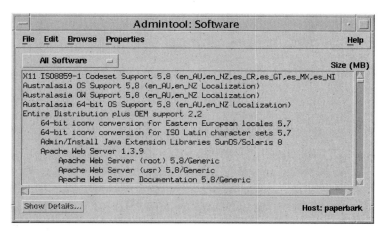

*Figure 57   Admintool: Users Window*

    2.   From the Browse menu, choose Software.

        The Admintool: Software window is displayed, as shown in Figure 58.

*Figure 58   Admintool: Software Window*

# Installing Software

The following sections describe how to access files from a local CD-ROM, how to set up custom installation, and how to choose an alternative location for installation.

## Accessing Files from a Local CD-ROM Drive

Use the following steps to access software from a local CD-ROM.

1.  Insert the CD in the CD-ROM drive.

    After a few moments, a File Manager window displays the contents of the CD-ROM.

2.  Start Admintool if necessary and, from the Browse menu, choose Software.

    The Admintool: Software window is displayed, as shown in Figure 58 on page 397.

3.  From the Admintool: Software Edit menu, choose Add.

    The Set Source Media window is displayed, as shown in Figure 59.

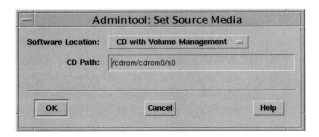

*Figure 59    Admintool: Set Source Media Window*

4.  (If necessary) From the Software Location list, choose Hard Disk or CD without Volume Management.

    CD with Volume Management is the default.

5.  (If necessary) In the CD Path field, type the path to the subdirectory that contains the packages on the media.

    If volume management can read the CD-ROM and the packages are at the CD path level, the Admintool: Add Software window is displayed, as shown in Figure 60.

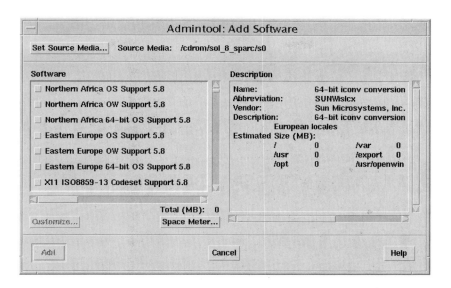

*Figure 60    Admintool: Add Software Window*

## Customizing Installation

Before you begin installing software, you can customize some of the installation parameters to minimize or maximize the amount of operator intervention required during installation.

Use the following steps to customize installation.

1. In the Software pane, click on the check box of the package you want to customize.

   The package name is highlighted and the Customize button is activated.

2. Click on the Customize button.

   The Admintool: Customize Installation window is displayed, as shown in Figure 61.

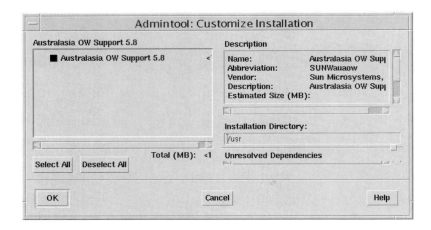

*Figure 61    Admintool: Customize Installation Window*

A description of the package is displayed in the Description pane.

3.  By default, all packages are selected. Click individual packages to deselect them or use the Deselect All button to deselect all of the packages.

4.  The default location for installing packages is the /opt directory. If you want to specify an alternative location for installation, type it into the Installation Directory text field.

5.  When all of the settings are correct, click on the OK button.

    The customization settings you specified are set and the Customize Installation window closes.

## Beginning Installation

Before you follow the steps in this section, check to make sure that you have performed the following tasks.

*   Set the source media properties to the CD-ROM mount point directory or any other directory that contains packages.

*   Specify a base directory for installation (if you do not want to use the default installation directory).

After you set up all properties and specify the base directory (if desired), you are ready to install software. Use the following steps to install software.

1.  In the Admintool: Add Software window, click on the Add button.

    A Terminal window opens, revealing additional instructions.
    Figure 62 shows instructions for the SUNWsadma package.

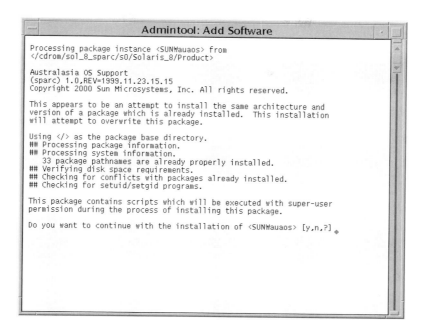

Figure 62    *Admintool: Add Software Terminal Window*

2.  Answer the questions generated by the package you are installing.

    When the installation is complete, the packages are installed and listed in the Admintool: Software window. When you press Return in the Admintool: Add Software terminal window, the window closes.

# Removing Software

You can use the Admintool: Software window to display installed packages and to remove software from a system.

Use the following steps to remove software from a system.

1.  If Admintool is not running, start it.
2.  From the Browse menu, choose Software.
3.  In the Admintool: Software window, click on the package you want to remove.

    The package is highlighted.

4.  From the Edit menu, choose Delete.

An Admintool: Warning window is displayed, asking you to confirm the delete, as shown in Figure 63.

*Figure 63    Admintool: Warning Window*

5.  Click on the Cancel button to cancel, or click on the Delete button to delete the package.

    The Admintool: Delete Software Terminal window is displayed, as shown in Figure 64.

*Figure 64    Admintool: Delete Software Window*

6.  To delete, type **Y** and press Return. Continue to answer any additional questions that the package displays.

7.  When you press Return after the delete is complete, the Admintool: Delete Software window closes.

# 16

# *SOLARIS PRODUCT REGISTRY*

Solaris Product Registry is a graphical user interface tool to enable you to manage installed software. Once Solaris is installed, Product Registry lists all the software that was installed with Solaris Web Start 3.0 or with Solaris package management commands.

*New!*

You can perform the following tasks with the Solaris Product Registry tool.

- View a list of installed and registered software and some software attributes.
- Find and launch an installer.
- Install additional software products.
- Uninstall software.

## Introducing the Product Registry Tool

To start the Product Registry tool, at a command line, type `/usr/bin/prodreg&` and press Return. The Solaris Product Registry window is displayed, as shown in Figure 65.

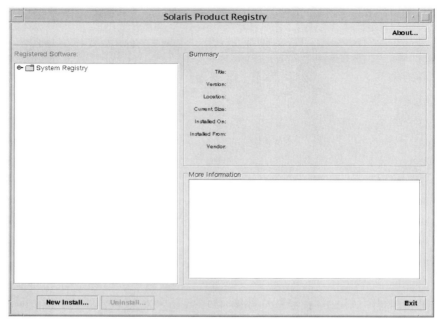

*Figure 65    The Solaris Product Registry Window*

The Solaris Product Registry window has three information areas.

* A list of installed, registered, and removed software.
* A summary of attributes of the current selection.
* Additional attributes and attributes internal to the registered software.

To view the items in the Product Registry, click on the control, called a *turner*, to the left of the System Registry folder. Notice that the turner control now points down instead of to the right and the contents of the folder are displayed, as shown in Figure 66.

*Figure 66     Software Installed in the Registered Software View*

You can expand or collapse any item in the registry except items with a text file icon.

The Solaris 8 System Software folder always contains the configuration software group that you chose when installing Solaris and an additional folder for additional system software. In the example shown in Figure 67, the Solaris 8 System Software folder contains the Entire Distribution plus OEM support folder and the System Software Localizations folder.

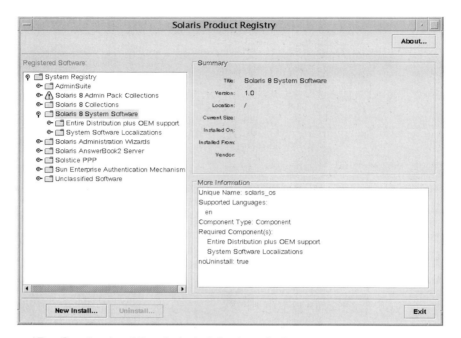

*Figure 67    Contents of the Solaris 8 System Software Folder*

Software groups include Core, End User System Support, Developer System Support, Entire Distribution, or Entire Distribution plus OEM support.

The additional system software folder contains Solaris products that are not part of the software group you chose. Additionally, Unclassified Software contains any package installed with the pkgadd command that is not a Solaris product or part of the software group.

Product registry attributes are displayed in the Summary area to the right of the scrolling list. For product items installed with Solaris Web Start, the Product Registry displays values for Title, Version, Location, and Installed On. Items in an expanded list below a product or software group inherit the version information of the product. Click on an item to view its attribute values.

Sometimes an item is displayed in the Product Registry window when the corresponding software has been removed with the pkgrm command. In this case, the Installed From information displays the message Missing files in one or more components. When you remove software with AdminSuite, the Summary information remains available. In the example shown in Figure 68, the Solaris Admin Pack Collection was removed with AdminSuite. As you can see, a warning icon is displayed to the left of the product name, but the package Summary information is still displayed.

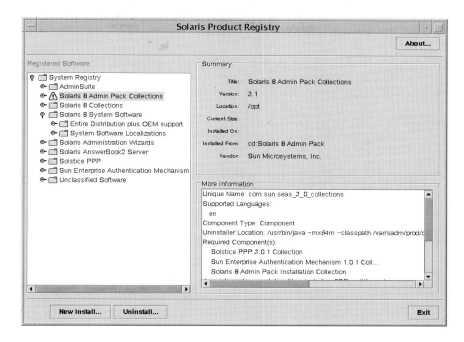

*Figure 68     Warning Icon Displayed Next to Removed Software*

# Installing Software with the Product Registry Tool

Use the following steps to install software with the Product Registry tool.

1.  If necessary, type `prodreg&` and press Return.
    The Product Registry tool is started.
2.  Locate the net image of the software you want to install or insert the software CD into the CD-ROM drive attached to the system.
3.  Click on the New Install button at the bottom of the window.
    The Select Installer window is displayed, as shown in Figure 69.

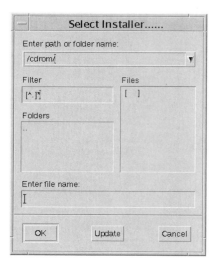

*Figure 69*   *Select Installer Window*

The default installer location is the /cdrom directory.

4. Type the path to the packages contained in any file system—such as a mounted CD-ROM, the /var/spool/pkg directory, or anywhere else a package may have been copied to—and click on the Update button.

    Alternatively, click on a path in the Folders pane and then click on the Update button.

5. Choose the installer from the list in the Files box and click on the OK button.

6. If you were not superuser when you started the Product Registry tool, a Terminal window is displayed asking you to type your root password.

7. Type your root password and press Return.

    Solaris Product Registry opens the installer you chose. Note that the Solaris Web Start installer is named Installer or installer.

# Uninstalling Products with the Product Registry Tool

Use the following steps to remove a product with the Product Registry tool.

1. If necessary, type prodreg& and press Return.

    The Product Registry tool is started.

2. Locate and click on the software package you want to remove, then click on the Uninstall button at the bottom of the window.

   If you were not superuser when you started the Product Registry tool, a Terminal window is displayed asking you to type your root password.

3. Type your root password and press Return.

   The Web Start Uninstaller is launched, as shown in Figure 70.

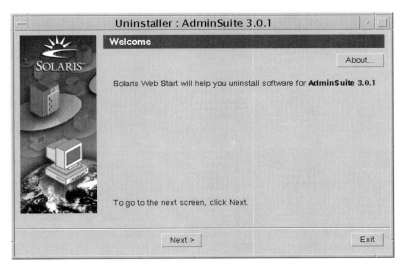

*Figure 70    Web Start Uninstaller Window*

4. If you want to see more information about the package, click on the About button.

5. Click on the Next button to go to the next screen.

   You are asked to choose whether you want to do a complete or a partial uninstall, as shown in Figure 71.

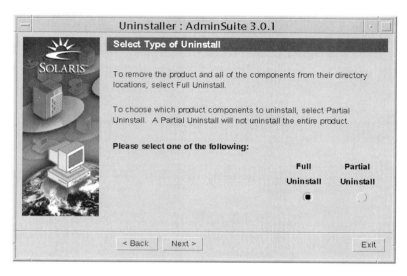

*Figure 71    Web Start Uninstaller Window*

6.   If you click on Partial Uninstall and the software package has more
     than one component, a list of the components is displayed, as shown
     in Figure 72. (Note that the example in Figure 72 is of Solaris
     Administration Wizards deinstallation because AdminSuite—shown
     in the other examples—has only one component to uninstall.)

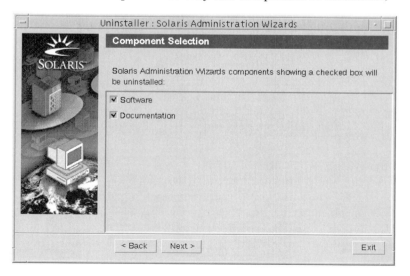

*Figure 72    Web Start Partial Uninstall Window*

If you want to exclude any of the packages from the deinstallation, click on the check box next to the package and then click on the Next button.

You are asked to begin the uninstallation, as shown in Figure 73.

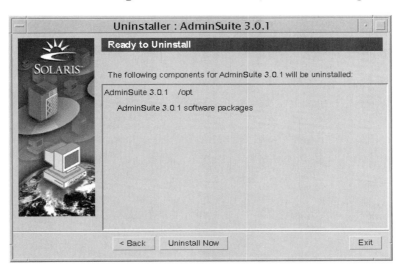

*Figure 73*   *Web Start Uninstaller Window*

7. Click on the Back button to go back, on the Exit button to cancel the uninstallation, or on the Uninstall Now button to begin the uninstallation.

   The software is removed from the system.

# 17

# INSTALLING AND MANAGING SYSTEM SOFTWARE PATCHES

Patch administration involves installing or removing Solaris patches from a running Solaris system. It may also involve removing or backing out unwanted or faulty patches.

A *patch* is a collection of files and directories that replaces or updates existing files and directories to facilitate proper execution of the software. The existing software is derived from a specific package format, which conforms to the Application Binary Interface. See Chapter 14, "Package Commands," for more information about packages.

The Solaris Operating Environment includes the following two commands for administering patches.

- `patchadd`—Use to install directory-format patches to a Solaris system.
- `patchrm`—Use to remove patches installed on a Solaris system. This command restores the file system to its state before a patch was applied.

These commands replace the `installpatch` and `backoutpatch` commands that previously shipped with each individual patch.

Detailed information about how to install and back out a patch is provided in the `Install.info` file that accompanies each patch. Each patch also contains a `README` file that contains specific information about the patch.

*NOTE. Some patches require you to take special actions. These instructions may be in the* README *file or in the* Install.info *file.*

Before installing patches, you need to know what patches have previously been installed on the system. Table 74 shows commands that provide useful information about existing patches.

*Table 74     Useful Commands for Patch Administration*

| Command | Description |
|---|---|
| showrev -p | Show all patches applied to a system. |
| patchadd -p | Show all patches applied to a system. |
| pkgparam *pkgid* PATCHLIST | |
| | Show all patches applied to the package identified by *pkgid*. |
| pkgparam *pkgid* PATCH_INFO_*patch-number* | |
| | Show the installation date and time of the host from which the package was applied. *pkgid* is the name of the package; for example, SUNWadmap. |
| patchadd -R *client_root_path* -p | |
| | Show all patches applied to a client from the server's console. |

*New!*

The showrev -p command is part of the old way of installing and managing packages, along with the self-contained patch installation scripts that came with every patch. The patchadd -p is part of the new patch maintenance scheme introduced in the Solaris 2.6 release with the patchadd and patchrm commands. Both commands show the same information for each patch—Patch, Obsoletes, Requires, Incompatibles, and Packages—but sort the patches differently.

The following example shows the beginning of the output of the showrev -p command for the system castle. You do not need superuser privileges to run the showrev command.

```
castle% showrev -p
Patch: 109134-05 Obsoletes:  Requires: 110113-01, 109318-06 Incompatibles:
 Packages: SUNWwbapi, SUNWwbcor, SUNWwbcou, SUNWmgapp
Patch: 109965-01 Obsoletes:  Requires:  Incompatibles:  Packages: SUNWpamsx,
 SUNWpamsc
Patch: 109889-01 Obsoletes: 109353-04 Requires:  Incompatibles:  Packages:
 SUNWkvmx, SUNWkvm, SUNWctu, SUNWhea, SUNWmdb, SUNWpstl, SUNWpstlx
Patch: 110131-01 Obsoletes:  Requires:  Incompatibles:  Packages: SUNWkvmx,
 SUNWkvm, SUNWhea, SUNWmdb, SUNWpstl, SUNWpstlx
Patch: 110132-02 Obsoletes:  Requires:  Incompatibles:  Packages: SUNWkvmx,
 SUNWkvm, SUNWhea
Patch: 110229-01 Obsoletes:  Requires:  Incompatibles:  Packages: SUNWkvmx,
 SUNWkvm, SUNWhea, SUNWmdb, SUNWpstl, SUNWpstlx
```

```
Patch: 110096-04 Obsoletes: 110118-02, 110201-01, 110121-01, 110134-02, 110141-02
 Requires:  Incompatibles:  Packages: SUNWkvmx, SUNWcsu, SUNWcsr, SUNWcslx,
 SUNWcsl, SUNWcarx, SUNWcar, SUNWcpr, SUNWcprx, SUNWcsxu, SUNWdrr, SUNWdrrx,
 SUNWidn, SUNWidnx, SUNWarc, SUNWarcx, SUNWcstl, SUNWcstlx, SUNWhea, SUNWtnfc,
 SUNWtnfcx
Patch: 110135-01 Obsoletes:  Requires:  Incompatibles:  Packages: SUNWkvmx,
 SUNWcsr, SUNWcarx
...(Additional lines deleted from this example)
```

The following example shows the output of the `patchadd -p` command for the system castle. You must be superuser to run the `patchadd` command.

```
castle% patchadd -p
You must be root to execute this script.

Patchadd is terminating.
castle% su
Password:
# patchadd -p

Patch: 108528-03 Obsoletes: 109153-01, 109656-01, 109291-06, 109663-01, 109309-02,
 109345-02 Requires:  Incompatibles:  Packages: FJSVhea, SUNWcar, SUNWcarx, SUNWcpr,
 SUNWcprx, SUNWcsr, SUNWcsu, SUNWcsxu, SUNWdrr, SUNWdrrx, SUNWhea, SUNWidn,
 SUNWidnx, SUNWmdb, SUNWmdbx, SUNWpmr, SUNWpmu, SUNWpmux, SUNWsrh, SUNWtnfc,
 SUNWtnfcx
Patch: 108979-10 Obsoletes: 109296-05, 109348-05, 109350-06 Requires: 108528-03
 Incompatibles:  Packages: FJSVhea, SUNWcar, SUNWcarx, SUNWcsl, SUNWcslx, SUNWcsr,
 SUNWcstl, SUNWcstlx, SUNWcsu, SUNWcsxu, SUNWhea
Patch: 109888-02 Obsoletes: 109352-05 Requires: 108979-08 Incompatibles:  Packages:
 FJSVhea, SUNWcar, SUNWcarx, SUNWcsr, SUNWhea
Patch: 108664-04 Obsoletes:  Requires:  Incompatibles:  Packages: SMEvplr, SMEvplu
Patch: 109221-04 Obsoletes: 108960-01 Requires:  Incompatibles:  Packages: SUNWadmap,
 SUNWadmc
...(Additional lines deleted from this example)
```

The following example shows the output for the `SUNWcsr` package with the `pkgparam` *pkgid* `PATCHLIST` command. You do not need superuser privileges to run the `pkgparam` command.

```
castle% pkgparam SUNWcsr PATCHLIST
108723-01 108725-02 108875-07 108901-03 109041-02 109147-06 109181-02 109202-01
 109236-01 109279-06 109324-01 109454-01 109458-01 109472-03 109576-01 109657-01
 109740-02 109742-02 109764-02 109877-01 109883-01 109898-01 109920-03 110075-01
 108528-03 108727-04 108964-03 108966-05 108974-06 108977-01 108979-10 108983-04
 108984-03 108989-02 108991-05 108993-01 108995-01 108997-03 108999-01 109003-01
 109005-01 109009-01 109785-01 109874-02 109876-01 109879-01 109882-02 109885-02
 109888-02 109894-01 109896-02 109900-01 109904-01 109906-01 109954-01 108968-02
 108972-04 110122-02 110180-01 110182-01 110186-01 110196-01 110225-01 110096-04
 110113-02 110135-01 110136-02 110137-01 110138-01 110139-03 110140-01 110228-01
 110233-01 110234-01 110246-01 110144-04 110146-02
castle%
```

The following example shows the output for patch 108723-01 for the `SUNWcsr` package with `pkgparam` *pkgid* `PATCH_INFO_`*patchno*.

```
castle% pkgparam SUNWcsr PATCH_INFO_108723-01
Installed: Mon Sep 18 15:39:13 PDT 2000 From: fern Obsoletes:  Requires:
  Incompatibles:
castle%
```

# Patch Distribution

All Sun customers can access security patches and other recommended patches from the World Wide Web. Sun customers who have purchased a service contract can access an extended set of patches and a complete database of patch information. This information is available on the World Wide Web and is regularly distributed on a CD-ROM. Table 75 summarizes customer access to patch information.

*Table 75     Customer Access to Patch Information*

| Status | Patch Access |
|---|---|
| Sun Service customer | The SunSolve database provides access to all patch information. Public patches are available from the Web or by anonymous `ftp`. |
| Not a Sun Service customer | Customers can access a limited set of security patches and other recommended patches from the Web or by anonymous `ftp`. |

## Requirements to Access Sun Patches

You can access Sun patches from the World Wide Web or by anonymous `ftp`. If you have purchased a Sun service contract, you also can get patches from the regularly distributed patch CD-ROM.

To access patches from the Web, you need a system that is connected to the Internet and capable of running Web browsing software such as Netscape.

## Accessing Patches from the Web

To access patches from the Web, use the following URL.

**New!**

```
http://sunsolve.sun.com/
```

The SunSolve home page is shown in Figure 74.

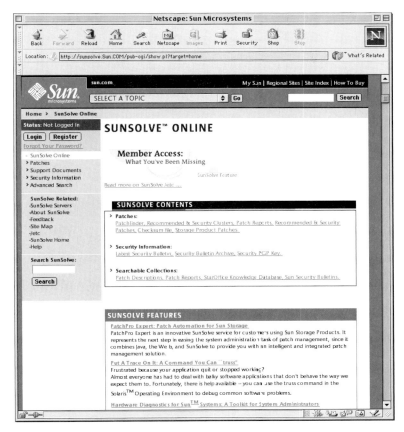

*Figure 74    The SunSolve Online Web Page*

Click on the Patches link. The SunSolve Online Patches window is displayed, as shown in Figure 75.

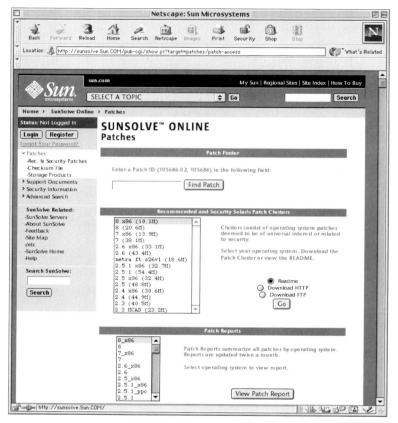

*Figure 75    The SunSolve Online Patch Web Page*

If you are a contract customer, you can log in by clicking on the Login button to access all patch information. If you are not a contract customer, your login status is always "Not Logged In" and you can access only the limited number of patches that have been marked for public access.

# Patch Numbering

Patches are identified by unique alphanumeric strings with the patch base code first, a dash, and a number that represents the patch revision number.

**New!**        Each version of Solaris can have patches for virtually every package. Each of these patches is assigned a number that is unique for each version of Solaris. Thus, the patch for the core Solaris user package, `SUNWcsu`, has a different number assigned to it for each version of Solaris. This numbering scheme prevents you from applying a Solaris 2.6 patch for the SUNWcsu package to a system running Solaris 7 or 8.

The sendmail package, for example, has a released patch for each version of Solaris. For Solaris 2.5.1 the patch number is 103594-19; for Solaris 2.6, 105395-06; for Solaris 7, 107684-01. At the time of this writing, Sun has not released a sendmail patch for Solaris 8.

Some patches, when applied, affect multiple packages simultaneously. An example of this kind of patch is the kernel update patch released for each version of Solaris.

As time goes on, Sun releases multiple revisions of a patch. The revision number is reflected in the number following the dash. Thus, the patch identification number for the sendmail patch for Solaris 2.6 (105395-06) indicates that this patch has been released six times since Solaris 2.6 was shipped.

# Installing a Patch

When you install a patch, the patchadd command copies files from the patch directory to a local system disk. The patchadd command does the following tasks.

- Determines the Solaris version number of the managing host and the target host.
- Updates the pkginfo file of the patch package with information about patches that are rendered obsolete by the patch being installed, other patches required by this patch, and patches that are incompatible with this patch.
- In the backout area, saves a copy of all of the files that the patch replaces or modifies.

*New!*

During patch installation, the patchadd command keeps a log of the patch installation in /var/sadm/patch/*patch-number*/log for the Solaris 2.4 and earlier operating environments. The Solaris 2.5 and later releases also store log files in this location, but only in the event of installation errors.

The patchadd command does not install a patch under the following conditions.

- The package is not fully installed on the host.
- The patch architecture differs from the system architecture.
- The patch version does not match the installed package version.

- A patch is already installed with the same base code and a higher version number.
- The patch is incompatible with another, already installed patch. (This information is stored in the pkginfo file for each patch.)
- The patch being installed requires another patch that is not installed.

**New!**

The patchadd command has the following syntax.

```
/usr/sbin/patchadd [-d][-u][-B backout-dir][-C net-install-image |
 -R client-root-path | -S service] patch
/usr/sbin/patchadd [-d][-u][-B backout-dir][-C net-install-image |
 -R client-root-path | -S service] -M patch-dir | patch-id... | patch-dir
 patch-list
/usr/sbin/patchadd [-C net-install-image | -R client-root-path | -S service] -p
```

Table 76 lists the options to the patchadd command.

*Table 76    Options to the patchadd Command*

| Option | Description |
|---|---|
| -B *backout-dir* | |
| | Save backout data to a directory other than the package database. This data is used by the patchrm command. Specify *backout-dir* as an absolute path name. |
| | Backout data is a list of files and directories that are removed or modified by a patch. Backout data can consume vast quantities of disk space in the root partition, which is a good reason to use the first drive in the system as the root file system (/) without a separate /var, /usr, or other partition on the boot device. For example, the 40th 32-MB kernel update patch to Solaris 8 would eat up 41 * 32 Mbytes = 1.32 Gbytes of disk space. |
| -C *net-install-image* | |
| | Patch the files located on the miniroot on a Net Install Image created by setup_install_server. Specify *net-install-image* as the absolute path name to a Solaris 2.6 or compatible version Net Install Image created by setup_install_server. |
| -d | Do not back up the files to be patched. If you use this option, you cannot remove the patch with the patchrm command. |

*Table 76    Options to the patchadd Command (Continued)*

| Option | Description |
|---|---|
| `-M patch-dir patch-id... | patch-dir patch-list` | |
| | Specify the patches to be installed. Specify patches to the `-M` option in one of the following ways. |
| | By directory location and patch number. To use the directory location and patch number, specify `patch-dir` as the absolute path name of the directory that contains spooled patches. Specify `patch-id` as the patch number of a given patch. Specifying multiple `patch-id`s is recommended. |
| | By directory location and the name of a file containing a patch list. To use the directory location and a file containing a patch list, specify `patch-dir` as the absolute path name of the directory containing the file with a list of patches to be installed. Specify `patch-list` as the name of the file containing the patches to be installed. |
| `-p` | Display a list of the patches currently applied. |
| `-u` | Install unconditionally, turn off file validation. Apply the patch even if some of the files to be patched have been modified since their original installation. |
| `-R client-root-path` | |
| | Locate all patch files generated by `patchadd` under the directory `client-root-path`. `client-root-path` is the directory that contains the bootable root of a client from the server's perspective. Specify `client-root-path` as the absolute path name to the beginning of the directory tree under which all patch files generated by `patchadd` are to be located. You cannot specify `-R` with the `-S` option. |
| `-S service` | Specify an alternate service (for example, `Solaris_2.3`). This service is part of the server and client model and can be used only from the server's console. Servers can contain shared `/usr` file systems that are created by Host Manager. You can then make these service areas available to the clients they serve. You cannot specify `-S` with the `-R` option. |

Table 77 lists the operands to the `patchadd` command.

*Table 77*     *Operands to the patchadd Command*

| Operand | |
|---------|--|
| *patch-id* | The patch number of a given patch, for example, `104945-02`. |
| *patch-list* | The name of a file that contains a list of patches to install. *patch-list* files contain one *patch-id* on each line. |
| *patch* | The absolute path name to *patch-id*, for example, `/var/sadm/spool/patch/104945-02`. |
| *patch-dir* | The absolute path name to the directory that contains all the spooled patches, for example, `/var/sadm/spool/patch`. |

The following example installs a patch to a stand-alone system.

```
# patchadd /var/spool/patch/104945-02
```

The following example installs a patch to a client system, `client1`, from the server's console.

```
# patchadd -R /export/root/client1 /var/spool/patch/104945-02
```

The following example installs a patch to a service from the server's console.

```
# patchadd -S Solaris_2.3 /var/spool/patch/104945-02
```

The following example installs multiple patches in a single `patchadd` invocation.

```
# patchadd -M /var/spool/patch 104945-02 104946-02 102345-02
```

The following example installs multiple patches, specifying a file that contains the list of patches to install.

```
# patchadd -M /var/spool/patch patchlist
```

The following example installs multiple patches to a client and saves the backout data to a directory other than the default.

```
# patchadd -M /var/spool/patch -R /export/root/client1 -B
  /export/backoutrepository 104945-02 104946-02 102345-02
```

The following example installs a patch to a Solaris 2.6 or later Net Install Image.

```
# patchadd -C /export/Solaris_2.6/Tools/Boot /var/spool/patch/104945-02
```

The following example installs a patch to a Solaris 2.6 or later Net Install Image but instructs the `patchadd` command not to save copies of files that are updated or replaced.

```
# patchadd -d /export/Solaris_2.6/Tools/Boot /var/spool/patch/104945-02
```

*CAUTION. Never use the* -d *option because it makes it difficult to remove or back out patches that become obsolete.*

## Removing Patches

When you remove, or back out, a patch, the `patchrm` command restores all files modified by that patch, unless any of the following conditions are true.

- The patch was installed with `patchadd -d`, which instructs `patchadd` not to save copies of files that are updated or replaced.
- The patch has been obsoleted by a later patch.
- The patch is required by another patch.

The `patchrm` command calls `pkgadd` to restore packages that were saved from the initial patch installation.

The `pkgrm` command has the following syntax.                    *New!*

```
/usr/sbin/patchrm [-f][-B backout-dir][-C net-install-image |
  -R client-root-path | -S service] patch-id
```

Table 78 lists the options to the pkgrm command.

*Table 78     Options to the pkgrm Command*

| Option | Description |
|---|---|
| -f | Force the patch removal regardless of whether the patch was superseded by another patch. |
| -B *backout-dir* | Remove a patch whose backout data has been saved to a directory other than the package database. You need this option only if the original backout directory, supplied to the patchadd command at installation time, has been moved. Specify *backout-dir* as an absolute path name. |
| -C *net-install-image* | |
| | Remove the patched files located on the miniroot on a Net Install Image created by setup_install_server. Specify *net-install-image* as the absolute path name to a Solaris 2.6 or compatible version Net Install Image created by setup_install_server. |
| -R *client-root-path* | |
| | Locate all patch files generated by patchrm under the directory *client-root-path.client-root-path* is the directory that contains the bootable root of a client from the server's perspective. Specify *client-root-path* as the absolute path name to the beginning of the directory tree under which all patch files generated from patchrm are located. You cannot specify -R with the -S option. |
| -S *service* | Specify an alternate service (for example, Solaris_2.3). This service is part of the server and client model and can be used only from the server's console. Servers can contain shared /usr file systems that are created by Host Manager. You can then make these service areas available to the clients they serve. You cannot specify -S with the -R option. |

During the patch removal, patchrm keeps a log of the patch installation in /tmp/backoutlog.*pid*. This log is removed if the patch backs out successfully.

The following example removes a patch from a stand-alone system.

```
# patchrm 104945-02
```

The following example removes a patch from a client's system from the server's console.

```
# patchrm -R /export/root/client1 104945-02
```

The following example removes a patch from a server's service area.

```
# patchrm -S Solaris_2.3 104945-02
```

The following example removes a patch from a Net Install Image.

```
# patchrm -C /export/Solaris_2.6/Tools/Boot 104945-02
```

# Part Six

# Introducing
# Shell
# Programming

This part introduces shell programming in two chapters: Chapter 18 introduces the basic concepts of shell programming and the three basic shells available with the Solaris Operating Environment. It describes how shells work, describes the programming elements, and provides reference tables comparing shell syntax. Chapter 19 contains examples of shell scripts.

Understanding shell programs can help you interpret system scripts, such as the run control (rc) scripts, and write your own scripts to automate system administration tasks. Refer to these two chapters if you want to familiarize yourself with the basics of shell programming and to decide which shell language you want to use to perform a specific task. This book does not provide in-depth instructions for writing scripts in the Bourne, Korn, and C shell programming languages. Refer to one of the many books that have been written on the subject for complete instructions on how to use any of the shell programming languages. Refer to the Bibliography at the end of this book for a partial list of references.

# 18

# *WRITING SHELL SCRIPTS*

The Solaris Operating Environment includes three shells: Bourne, Korn, and C. Each shell has its own high-level programming language that you can use to execute sequences of commands, select among alternative operations, perform logical tests, and repeat program actions. The Bourne and Korn shells use almost identical syntax, although the Korn shell is a superset of the Bourne shell and provides more functionality, including history and array capability. The Bourne shell is used for most scripts that are distributed with the Solaris Operating Environment. The C shell uses a syntax that is similar to C programming language syntax, and it has built-in capabilities not provided with the Bourne shell, such as history and array capability.

> *NOTE. The Solaris 8 Operating Environment also includes three freeware shells: The Bourne-Again shell (*bash*), the TC shell (*tcsh*), and the Z shell (*zsh*). For information about these shells, refer to the manual pages.*

New!

This chapter introduces the basic concepts of shell programming and the three shells, describes how shells work, and compares the syntax of the three basic shells; reference tables are provided throughout this chapter and are repeated in Chapter 19, "Reference Tables and Example Scripts."

# Basic Concepts

A *shell* is a specialized Solaris command that provides an interface between the user and the operating system kernel. The *kernel* is the central core of the operating system and controls all basic aspects of a computer's operation. The kernel coordinates all of the executing commands and manages the system's resources. The shell is a special command interpreter that invokes and interacts with the kernel to provide a way for users to execute commands and other programs.

Each user is assigned a default shell that starts each time the user logs in to a system or opens a new Command Tool, Shell Tool, or CDE Terminal window. The shell interprets the commands that it reads. You can type those commands directly into the shell at the prompt, or the shell can read the commands from a file. A file that contains shell commands is called a *shell script*.

Shell scripts are interpreted, not compiled: The commands are read and executed one by one, in sequence. A compiled program, on the other hand, is initially read and converted to a form that can be directly executed by the CPU and thereafter executed all at once. Because shell scripts are interpreted, even the fastest shell script always runs more slowly than an equivalent program written in a compiled language such as C.

## Introducing the Bourne, Korn, and C Shells

The Bourne, Korn, and C shells each have their own environment and syntax. Table 79 compares the initialization files that define the shell environment at startup.

*Table 79     Shell Initialization Files*

| Feature | Bourne | Korn | C |
| --- | --- | --- | --- |
| Read at login | `.profile` | `.profile` | `.login` |
| Read at invocation of shell | N/A | Any file specified in `.profile` with ENV=*file*. By convention, *file* is usually `.kshrc`. | `.cshrc` |

The initialization files contain environment variables and other settings that configure the user's environment when a shell starts. Refer to the section "Environment Variables" on page 446 for more information. The `.profile` (Bourne and Korn shells) and `.login` (C shell) files execute when a user logs in to a system. The Korn shell and .cshrc (C shell) environment files execute each time a new shell starts. Use these environment files to define aliases and functions for interactive use and to set variables that you want to apply to the current shell.

## Bourne Shell

The Bourne shell, written by Steve Bourne when he was at AT&T Bell Laboratories, is the original UNIX shell. This shell is preferred for shell programming because of its programming capabilities and its universal availability. It lacks features for interactive use, such as built-in arithmetic and recall of previous commands (history). The Bourne shell is the default login shell for the root account, and it serves as the default user login shell if you do not specify another shell in the user's passwd file. The Bourne shell is used for all system-supplied administration scripts.

The Bourne shell command is /bin/sh. The default prompt for the Bourne shell is a dollar sign ($). The root prompt is a pound sign (#).

## Korn Shell

The Korn shell, written by David Korn of AT&T Bell Laboratories, was designed to be compatible with the Bourne shell and to offer interactive features comparable to the C shell. The Korn shell includes convenient programming features such as built-in integer arithmetic, arrays, and string-manipulation facilities. The Korn shell runs faster than the C shell and runs virtually all scripts that are written for the Bourne shell.

The Korn shell command is /bin/ksh. The default prompt for the Korn shell is a dollar sign ($). The root prompt is a pound sign (#).

## C Shell

The C shell, written by Bill Joy when he was at the University of California at Berkeley, was designed to incorporate features such as aliases and command history for interactive use. The syntax for its programming features is similar to that for the C programming language.

The C shell command is /bin/csh. The default prompt for the C shell is the system name followed by a percent sign (%). The root prompt is the system name followed by a pound sign (#).

*NOTE. For many reasons, you should use the C shell only as a login shell. For more information, see Chapter 47, "C Shell Programming...NOT," in UNIX Power Tools, Second Edition.*

*New!*

## Understanding How Shells Process Commands

Each shell creates *subshells* and *child processes*—subordinate shells and processes that are under the control of the originating, or *parent,* shell—to interpret and execute commands. For example, the following list shows a simplified version of the order in which the Korn shell processes commands. The shell parses (divides up) the command into units—such as words, keywords, I/O redirectors, and semicolons—separated by the fixed set of metacharacters: Space Tab Newline ; ( ) < > | &.

1. Checks the first part of each unit for shell keywords, such as `function` or `if` statements, with no quotes or backslashes. When it finds a keyword, the shell processes the compound command.
2. Searches the list of aliases.
3. Expands any tilde (~) expressions.
4. Substitutes variables.
5. Substitutes commands.
6. Substitutes arithmetic expressions.
7. Splits the items that result from parameter, command, and arithmetic substitution and splits them into words again.
8. Expands wildcards.
9. Looks up built-in commands, functions, and executable files.
10. Sets up I/O redirection.
11. Runs the command.

The Bourne shell interprets commands similarly but does not check for aliases, tildes, or arithmetic. The C shell interprets commands in a different order.

## Naming Shell Scripts

When you assign a name to a shell script, follow the general rule for naming Solaris files. Make a script name as descriptive as possible so that you can easily remember its designated function. Be careful to avoid names that the Solaris Operating Environment itself uses for its own programs unless you intend to replace those commands with your own scripts.

Each shell has a list of built-in commands. You should also avoid using built-in shell commands as script names. If you name a file with one of the shell built-in commands—such as `alias`, `break`, `case`, `cd`, `continue`, `echo`, `else`, `exit`, or `history` for the C shell—the shell interprets the script name as one of its own built-in commands and runs the built-in command instead of executing the script. For example, with the Bourne or Korn shell, you will run into trouble if you name a script `test`—which you might easily do if you are testing something—because `test` is a built-in Bourne and Korn shell command. Refer to "Reference Tables" starting on page 485 and to the `sh(1)`, `ksh(1)`, and `csh(1)` manual pages for a complete list of built-in commands.

## Identifying the Shell

The first line of each shell script determines the shell that runs—or interprets—the script. Always identify the interpreting shell on the first line of the script, using the information from Table 80.

*Table 80    First Line of Script*

| Shell | Syntax |
|-------|--------|
| Bourne | `#!/bin/sh` |
| Korn | `#!/bin/ksh` |
| C | `#!/bin/csh -f` |

The `-f` (fast) option to `/bin/csh` runs the script without sourcing the `.cshrc` file.

If you do not specify the shell in the first line of the script and it is an executable script, the current shell interprets the contents of the script.

After the first line of a script, any line beginning with a pound sign (#) is treated as a comment line and is not executed as part of the script.

## Making Scripts Executable

Before you can run a shell script, it is customary to change its permissions so that it has at least read and execute permissions (`chmod 555`). When you write and debug the script, give yourself write permission to the file (`chmod 755`) so that you can edit it and, subsequently, execute it. When assigning permissions to a completed shell script, consider the scope of access that you want to permit to this script. Use restrictive permissions if the script is proprietary or individual, and use more relaxed permissions if many users who are not in the same group will use the script.

## Storing Shell Scripts

After you create a shell script, you can execute it only from the directory in which it resides or by using the full path name, unless you set your PATH variable to include the directory that contains the script.

If you write many scripts, you may want to create a `~/bin` directory in your home directory and update your search path to include this directory. In this way, your scripts are available to you regardless of where you are working in the directory hierarchy. If you provide scripts for more general use, be sure to debug them before you put them in a directory where they are more accessible.

## Writing Shell Scripts: The Process

The following checklist describes the process to follow when writing any shell script.

1. Decide what you want the script to do. Establish a list of the commands you need to use to accomplish the desired task.
2. Use an editor to put the commands into a file. Give the file a name that indicates what the script does.
3. Identify the shell in the first line of the script.
4. Include comments at the beginning of the script to describe its purpose and to annotate each individual part of the script. These comments can aid in debugging the script and in interpreting a script that may be used only occasionally. Comments are also invaluable in helping others to interpret scripts that you have written.
5. Save the file and quit the editor.
6. Change the permissions so that the file has, at a minimum, read and execute permissions.
7. Check your path or the `PATH` variable to make sure that the directory that contains the script is in the search path.
8. Type the name of the script as a command. The script executes one line at a time.
9. If errors occur, debug the script.
10. When the script is complete, decide where you want to store the command (for example, in your home directory, your local `~/bin` directory, or in a more globally available directory).

# Variables

A *variable* is a name that refers to a temporary storage area in memory. A variable holds a value. Changing a variable's value is called *assigning* a value to the variable. Shell programming uses two types of variables: shell variables and environment variables. By convention, you write shell variables in lower case and environment variables in upper case.

*Shell variables* are maintained by the shell and are known only to the shell. Shell variables are always local and are not passed on from parent to child processes.

To display the value for any shell variable, type **echo $*variable*.**

## Displaying Bourne and Korn Shell Variables

Although the Korn shell recognizes the echo command, print *$variable* is the preferred syntax. Optionally, you can enclose the name of the variable in curly braces ({}). You may want to use curly braces if you are concatenating strings and want to separate the name of the variable from the information that follows it. In the following example, a variable named flower is set to rose. If you want to add an "s" at the end of the variable name when it is displayed on-screen, you must enclose the variable in curly braces and add the s.

```
$ flower=rose
$ echo $flower
rose
$ echo $flowers

$ echo ${flower}s
roses
$
```

You can use the set command with no arguments to display a list of current shell and environment variables. The Bourne and Korn shells display variables in the format shown in the following example.

```
$ set
AB_CARDCATALOG=/usr/dt/share/answerbooks/C/ab_cardcatalog
DISPLAY=:0.0
DTAPPSEARCHPATH=/export/home/winsor/.dt/appmanager:/etc/dt/appconfig/appmanager/%L:
 /etc/dt/appconfig/appmanager/C:/usr/dt/appconfig/appmanager/%L:/usr/dt/appconfig/a
 ppmanager/C
DTDATABASESEARCHPATH=/export/home/winsor/.dt/types,/etc/dt/appconfig/types/%L,/etc/
 dt/appconfig/types/C,/usr/dt/appconfig/types/%L,/usr/dt/appconfig/types/C
DTHELPSEARCHPATH=/export/home/winsor/.dt/help/winsor-paperbark-0/%H:/export/home/wi
 nsor/.dt/help/winsor-paperbark-0/%H.sdl:/export/home/winsor/.dt/help/winsor-paperb
 ark-0/%H.hv:/export/home/winsor/.dt/help/%H:/export/home/winsor/.dt/help/%H.sdl:/e
 xport/home/winsor/.dt/help/%H.hv:/usr/dt/appconfig/help/%L/%H:/usr/dt/appconfig/he
 lp/%L/%H.sdl:/usr/dt/appconfig/help/%L/%H.hv:/usr/dt/appconfig/help/C/%H:/usr/dt/a
 ppconfig/help/C/%H.sdl:/usr/dt/appconfig/help/C/%H.hv
DTSCREENSAVERLIST=StartDtscreenSwarm StartDtscreenQix      StartDtscreenFlame
 StartDtscreenHop StartDtscreenImage StartDtscreenLife     StartDtscreenRotor
 StartDtscreenPyro StartDtscreenWorm StartDtscreenBlank
DTSOURCEPROFILE=true
DTUSERSESSION=winsor-paperbark-0
DTXSERVERLOCATION=local
EDITOR=/usr/dt/bin/dtpad
HELPPATH=/usr/openwin/lib/locale:/usr/openwin/lib/help
HOME=/export/home/winsor
```

*New!*

```
IFS=

LANG=C
LOGNAME=winsor
MAIL=/var/mail/winsor
MAILCHECK=600
MANPATH=/usr/dt/man:/usr/man:/usr/openwin/share/man
OPENWINHOME=/usr/openwin
OPTIND=1
PATH=/usr/openwin/bin:/usr/dt/bin:/export/home/opt/SUNWadm/bin:/bin:/usr/bin:/usr/s
  bin:/usr/ucb:/etc:/usr/proc/bin:/usr/ccs/bin:/opt/hpnp/bin:/opt/NSCPcom:/usr/local
  /games:.
PS1=$
PS2=>
PWD=/export/home/winsor
SESSION_SVR=paperbark
SHELL=/bin/csh
TERM=dtterm
TERMINAL_EMULATOR=dtterm
TZ=Australia/West
USER=winsor
WINDOWID=71303231
XFILESEARCHPATH=/usr/openwin/lib/locale/%L/%T/%N%S:/usr/openwin/lib/%T/%N%S
XMBINDDIR=/usr/dt/lib/bindings
XMICONBMSEARCHPATH=/export/home/winsor/.dt/icons/%B%M.bm:/export/home/winsor/.dt/ic
  ons/%B%M.pm:/export/home/winsor/.dt/icons/%B:/usr/dt/appconfig/icons/%L/%B%M.bm:/u
  sr/dt/appconfig/icons/%L/%B%M.pm:/usr/dt/appconfig/icons/%L/%B:/usr/dt/appconfig/i
  cons/C/%B%M.bm:/usr/dt/appconfig/icons/C/%B%M.pm:/usr/dt/appconfig/icons/C/%B
XMICONSEARCHPATH=/export/home/winsor/.dt/icons/%B%M.pm:/export/home/winsor/.dt/icon
  s/%B%M.bm:/export/home/winsor/.dt/icons/%B:/usr/dt/appconfig/icons/%L/%B%M.pm:/usr
  /dt/appconfig/icons/%L/%B%M.bm:/usr/dt/appconfig/icons/%L/%B:/usr/dt/appconfig/ico
  ns/C/%B%M.pm:/usr/dt/appconfig/icons/C/%B%M.bm:/usr/dt/appconfig/icons/C/%B
dtstart_sessionlogfile=/dev/null
$
```

## Displaying C Shell Environment Variables

For the C shell, use the `set` command with no arguments to display a list of
current shell and environment variables in the following format.

*New!*

```
paperbark% set
argv     ()
cwd      /export/home/winsor
filec
history 32
home     /export/home/winsor
manpath (/usr/openwin/share/man /usr/openwin/man /usr/share/man /usr/dt/share/man
  /usr/dt/man /usr/man /opt/SUNWrtvc/man /opt/hpnp/man /opt/SUNWadm/man)
path    (/usr/openwin/bin /usr/dt/bin /export/home/opt/SUNWadm/bin /bin /usr/bin
  /usr/sbin /usr/ucb /etc /usr/proc/bin /usr/ccs/bin /opt/hpnp/bin /opt/NSCPcom
  /usr/local/games .)
prompt  paperbark%
shell   /bin/csh
status  0
term    dtterm
user    winsor
paperbark%
```

## Setting Bourne and Korn Shell Variables

To create a Bourne or Korn shell variable, you simply assign the value of the
variable to the name. If the value contains spaces or characters that the shell

interprets in a special way, you must enclose the value in quotes. Refer to the section "Quoting" on page 456 for more information. Use the following syntax to assign the value of the variable to a name.

```
variable=value
```

In the following Bourne or Korn shell example, the variable `today` is set to Tuesday.

```
$ today=Tuesday
$ echo $today
Tuesday
$
```

You can also set the value of a variable to return the output of a command. To do so, enclose the name of the command in backquotes (` `` `). The following Bourne shell example sets the variable `today` to display the output of the `date` command.

```
$ today = `date`
S echo $today
Wed Feb 14 12:41:27 WST 2001
S
```

The Korn shell also supports the notation `$(command)`, as shown in the following exmaple

```
$ today = $(date)
S echo $today
Wed Feb 14 12:41:27 WST 2001
S
```

You can set local variables from the command line, as shown in the previous examples, or within a script.

## Unsetting Bourne and Korn Shell Variables

You can use the `unset` command to remove any shell variable, as shown in the following Bourne shell example.

```
$ unset today
$ echo $today

$
```

## Setting C Shell Variables

Use the following syntax to set a C shell variable. If the value contains spaces or characters that the shell interprets in a special way, you must enclose the value in quotes. Refer to the section "Quoting" on page 456 for more information.

```
set variable=value
```

You can also set the value of a variable to return the output of a command. To do so, enclose the name of the command in backquotes ( `  ` ). See "Command Substitution" on page 457 for more information. The following C shell example sets the variable today to display the output of the date command.

```
oak% set today = `date`
oak% echo $today
Wed Feb 14 12:41:27 WST 2001
oak%
```

## Unsetting C Shell Variables

Use the unset command to remove any C shell variable. See "Unsetting Bourne and Korn Shell Variables" on page 437 for an example.

# File Name Stripping

Sometimes you want to modify a path name in a script to strip off unneeded parts. With the Bourne shell, you can use the basename(1) command to return only the file name, and the dirname(1) command to return only the directory prefix. The Korn and C shells provide a built-in way for you to modify path names.

## Korn Shell Path Stripping

The Korn shell provides pattern-matching operators, shown in Table 81, that you can use to strip off components of path names.

*Table 81    Korn Shell Pattern-Matching Operators*

| Operator | Description |
|---|---|
| `${variable# pattern}` | Delete the shortest part at the beginning of the variable that matches the pattern and return the rest. |
| `${variable## pattern}` | Delete the longest part at the beginning of the variable that matches the pattern and return the rest. |
| `${variable% pattern}` | Delete the shortest part at the end of the variable that matches the pattern and return the rest. |
| `${variable%% pattern)` | Delete the longest part at the end of the variable that matches the pattern and return the rest. |

The following example shows how all of the operators work, using the pattern `/*/` to match anything between two slashes, and `.*` to match a dot followed by anything.

```
$ pathname=/home/winsor/Design.book.new
$ echo ${pathname#/*/}
winsor/Design.book.new
$ echo ${pathname##/*/}
Design.book.new
$ echo ${pathname%.*}
/home/winsor/Design.book
$ echo ${pathname%%.*}
/home/winsor/Design
$
```

## C Shell Path Stripping

The C shell provides a set of modifiers that you can use to strip off unneeded components. These modifiers are quite useful in stripping path names, but can also be used to modify variable strings. Table 82 lists the C shell variable modifiers.

*Table 82*     *C Shell File-Name Modifiers*

| Modifier | Description |
|----------|-------------|
| :e | Extension—Remove prefix ending with a dot. |
| :h | Head—Remove trailing path-name components. |
| :r | Root—Remove suffixes beginning with a dot. |
| :t | Tail—Remove all leading path-name components. |
| :q | Quote—Force variable to be quoted. (Used to quote $argv.) |
| :x | Like q, but break into words at each space, Tab, or newline. |

    The following example shows the results of the first four variable modifiers.

```
oak% set pathname = /home/winsor/Design.book
oak% echo $pathname:e
book
oak% echo $pathname:h
/home/winsor
oak% echo $pathname:r
/home/winsor/Design
oak% echo $pathname:t
Design.book
oak%
```

# Built-in Shell Variables

All three shells have a set of single-character variables that are set initially by the shell, as shown in Table 83. You can use these variables to access words in variables and return other information about the variable. These variables are used differently in the C shell than they are in the Bourne and Korn shells.

## Bourne and Korn Shells Built-in Variables

Table 83 describes the built-in variables initialized by the Bourne and Korn shells.

*Table 83*   *Built-in Variables Initialized by the Bourne and Korn Shells*

| Variable | Explanation |
| --- | --- |
| $* | List the value of all command-line parameters. This variable is useful only in scripts because the login shell has no arguments associated with it. |
| $# | Return the number of command-line arguments (in decimal). Useful only in scripts. |
| $? | Return the exit status (in decimal) of the last command executed. Most commands return a zero exit status if they complete successfully; otherwise a non-zero exit status is returned. This variable is set after each command is executed. |
| $$ | Return the process ID (PID) number of the current shell (in decimal). |
| $! | Return the process number (in decimal) of the last process run in the background. |

You can use the $* variable to list the values of command-line arguments within a script, and the $# variable to hold the number of arguments. In the following example, the shell expands the $* variable to list all of the command-line arguments to the script.

```
#!/bin/sh

echo $#
for var in $*
do
        echo $var
done
```

If you named the script **tryit** and executed it with three arguments, it echoes the number of arguments from $# and then displays the list of arguments from $*, one on each line. The input string can contain quotes. Refer to the sh(1) manual page for information about how quoted strings are interpreted.

```
$ tryit one two three
3
one
two
three
$
```

For the Bourne shell, the `$?` variable displays exit status for the last command executed. Refer to the section "Exit Status" on page 475 for an example.

The `$$` variable returns the PID number of the current shell process, as shown in the following example.

```
$ echo $$
392
$
```

Because process numbers are unique, you can use this string to generate unique temporary file names. For example, when a script assigns a file name of `tmp.$$`, that file rarely is confused with another file.

*NOTE. If you are concerned about generating unique file names, you can use the format feature of the* `date`(1) *command to generate a temporary file name that includes both a process ID and a time and date stamp.*

## C Shell Built-in Variables

Table 84 describes the built-in variables initialized by the C shell.

*Table 84     Variables Initialized by the C Shell*

| Variable | Explanation |
|---|---|
| `$*` | List the value of all command-line parameters. This variable is useful only in scripts because the login shell has no arguments associated with it. Some people prefer to use `$argv` instead of `$*`. |
| `$#` | Check to see if a variable of that name has been set. |

For the C shell, the $#*variable* command holds the number of words in a variable array, as shown in the following example.

```
oak% set var = (a b c)
oak% echo $#var
3
oak%
```

You can use the variable $?*variable* to test whether a variable is set. $?*variable* returns a 1 if a named variable exists, or 0 if the named variable does not exist.

```
oak% set var="a b c"
oak% echo $?var
1
oak% unset var
oak% echo $?var
0
oak%
```

*NOTE. The numbers returned by* $?*variable are the opposite from status numbers, where 0 is success and 1 is failure.*

The $$ variable returns the PID number of the current shell process, as shown in the following examples. Because process numbers are unique, you can use this string to generate unique temporary file names. For example, when a script assigns a file name of tmp.$$, that file rarely is confused with another file.

*NOTE. If you are concerned about generating unique file names, you can use the format feature of the* date(1) *command to generate a temporary file name that includes both a process ID and a time and date stamp.*

```
oak% echo $$
364
oak% sh
```

# Built-in Commands

Each shell also includes built-in commands for efficiency. Table 85 lists the built-in commands. The Bourne shell relies more on using external commands to do the work, and thus has the fewest built-in commands. The additional built-in commands for the Korn shell are shown by (K) following the command name. The job control variant of the Bourne shell, jsh, has the same job control features as the Korn shell.

*CAUTION. Do not use any of the built-in commands as names for shell scripts. If you use one of the built-in commands as a shell script name, the shell will execute the built-in command instead of running the script.*

Table 85    *Shell Built-In Commands*

| Purpose | Bourne or Korn Shell | C Shell |
|---|---|---|
| Null command. | : | : |
| Create a command name alias. | alias (K) | alias |
| Run current command in background. | bg (K) | bg |
| Exit enclosing for or while loop. | break | break |
| Break out of a switch. | N/A | breaksw |
| Change directory. | cd | cd |
| Continue next iteration of for or while loop. | continue | continue |
| Default case in switch. | N/A | default |
| Print directory stack. | N/A | dirs |
| Write arguments on standard output. | echo, print (K) | echo |
| Evaluate and execute arguments. | eval | eval |
| Execute the arguments. | exec | exec |
| Return or set shell variables. | set | @ |
| Exit shell program. | exit | exit |
| Create an environment variable. | export | setenv |
| Bring a command into foreground. | fg (K) | fg |
| Execute foreach loop. | for | foreach |
| Perform file-name expansion. | N/A | glob |
| Go to label within shell program. | N/A | goto |
| Display history list. | fc -l (K) | history |
| if-then-else decision. | if | if |
| List active jobs. | jobs (K) | jobs |
| Send a signal. | kill | kill |
| Set limits for a job's resource use. | ulimit | limit |

*New!*

*Table 85     Shell Built-In Commands (Continued)*

| Purpose | Bourne or Korn Shell | C Shell |
|---|---|---|
| Terminate login shell and invoke `login`. | N/A | `login` |
| Terminate a login shell. | N/A | `logout` |
| Change to a new user group. | `newgrp (K)` | N/A |
| Change priority of a command. | N/A | `nice` |
| Ignore hang up. | N/A | `nohup` |
| Notify user when job status changes. | N/A | `notify` |
| Control shell processing on receipt of a signal. | `trap` | `onintr` |
| Pop the directory stack. | N/A | `popd` |
| Push a directory onto the stack. | N/A | `pushd` |
| Read a line from standard input. | `read` | `$<` |
| Change a variable to read-only. | `readonly` | N/A |
| Repeat a command *n* times. | N/A | `repeat` |
| Set shell environment variables. | `=` | `setenv` |
| Set a local C shell variable. | N/A | `set` |
| Shift positional parameters $* or $argv. | `shift` | `shift` |
| Read and execute a file. | `. (dot)` | `source` |
| Stop a background process. | N/A | `stop` |
| Stop the shell. | `suspend` (**K**) | `suspend` |
| Case statement. | `case ... esac` | `switch ... endsw` |
| Evaluate conditional expressions. Note that test is normally an external program except for the Korn shell. | `test` `[ ]` `[[ ]]` (**K**) `\` | N/A |
| Display execution times. | `times` | `time` |
| Set default security for creation of files and directories. | `umask` | `umask` |
| Discard aliases. | `unalias` (**K**) | `unalias` |

*Table 85*     *Shell Built-In Commands (Continued)*

| Purpose | Bourne or Korn Shell | C Shell |
|---|---|---|
| Remove limitations on resources. | `ulimit` | `unlimit` |
| Unset a variable. | `unset` | `unset` |
| Unset an environment variable. | `unset` | `unsetenv` |
| `until` loop. | `until` | N/A |
| Wait for background process to complete. | `wait` | N/A |
| `while` loop. | `while` | `while` |

# Environment Variables

Environment variables are often used to define initialization options such as the default login shell, user login name, search path, and terminal settings. Some environment variables are set for you each time you log in. You can also create your own variables and assign values to them. By convention, environment variable names are in capital letters.

Environment variables are passed on from parent to child processes. For example, an environment variable set in a shell is available to any program started in that shell, to any additional program started by the initial program, and so on. In other words, environment variables are inherited from parent to child, from child to grandchild, and so on. They are not inherited backward from parent to grandparent or child to parent.

Use the `env` command to display a list of current environment variables. Consult the *Solaris System Administrator's Guide,* Third Edition, for more information about environment variables.

## Bourne and Korn Shell Environment Variables

For the Bourne and Korn shells, use the following syntax to assign environment variables and export them. You must export the variable before it can be put into the environment of child processes.

```
VARIABLE=value;export VARIABLE
```

For the Korn shell, you can also use the following syntax.

```
export VARIABLE=value
```

For the Bourne and Korn shells, use the `unset` command with the following syntax to remove an environment variable.

```
unset VARIABLE
```

## C Shell Environment Variables

For the C shell, use the `setenv` command with the following syntax to assign environment variables.

```
setenv VARIABLE value
```

Use the `unsetenv` command with the following syntax to remove the environment variable.

```
unsetenv VARIABLE
```

# Input and Output

When you write shell scripts, you want to be able to obtain input from sources outside your scripts; for example, from another file or from keyboard input. You also want to be able to generate output both for use within the script and for display on-screen.

The following sections describe how to control input and output of a shell script, using standard input, output, error, and redirection; how to accept user input (input from the keyboard) to a script; how to create "here" documents; and how to generate output to the screen.

## Standard In, Standard Out, and Standard Error

When writing shell scripts, you can control input/output redirection. *Input redirection* forces a command to read any necessary input from a file instead of from the keyboard. *Output redirection* sends the output from a command into a file or pipe instead of to the screen.

Each process created by a shell script begins with three file descriptors associated with it, as shown in Figure 76.

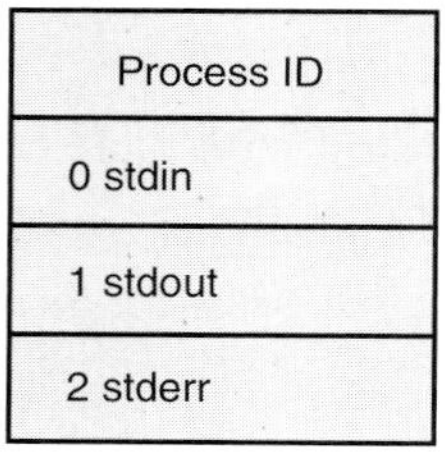

| |
|---|
| Process ID |
| 0 stdin |
| 1 stdout |
| 2 stderr |

*Figure 76    File Descriptors*

These file descriptors—*standard input*, *standard output*, and *standard error*—determine where input to the process comes from and where the output and error messages are sent.

Standard input (STDIN) is always file descriptor 0. Standard input is the place where the shell looks for its input data. Usually data for standard input comes from the keyboard. You can specify standard input to come from another source with input/output redirection.

Standard output (STDOUT) is always file descriptor 1. Standard output (default) is the place where the results of the execution of the program are sent. Usually, the results of program execution are displayed on the terminal screen. You can redirect standard output to a file or suppress it completely by redirecting it to /dev/null.

Standard error (STDERR) is always file descriptor 2. Standard error is the place where error messages are sent as they are generated during command processing. Usually, error messages are displayed on the terminal screen. You can redirect standard error to a file or suppress it completely by redirecting it to /dev/null.

You can use the file descriptor numbers 0 (standard input), 1 (standard output), and 2 (standard error) together with the redirection metacharacters to control input and output in the Bourne and Korn shells. Table 86 shows the common ways you can redirect file descriptors.

*Table 86     Bourne and Korn Shell Redirection*

| Command | Description |
|---|---|
| <*file*, or<br>0<*file* | Take STDIN from file. |
| > *file*, or<br>1> *file* | Redirect STDOUT to file. |

*Table 86    Bourne and Korn Shell Redirection (Continued)*

| Command | Description |
|---------|-------------|
| `2> file` | Redirect STDERR to file. |
| `>> file` | Append STDOUT to end of file. |
| `2>&1` | Redirect STDERR to the location where STDOUT is currently directed. |
| `cmd1 \| cmd2` | Pipe standard output of `cmd1` as standard input to `cmd2`. |
| `<> file` | Use `file` as both STDIN and STDOUT. |
| `<&-` | Close STDIN. |
| `>&-` | Close STDOUT. |
| `2>&-` | Close STDERR. |

*New!*

When redirecting STDIN and STDOUT in the Bourne and Korn shells, you can omit the file descriptors 0 and 1 from the redirection symbols. You must always use the file descriptor 2 with the redirection symbol to denote STDERR.

The 0 and 1 file descriptors are implied and not used explicitly for the C shell, as shown in Table 87. The C shell representation for standard error (2) is an ampersand (&). STDERR can only be redirected when redirecting STDOUT.

*Table 87    C Shell Redirection*

| Command | Description |
|---------|-------------|
| `> file` | Redirect STDOUT to file. |
| `< file` | Take input from file. |
| `>> file` | Append STDOUT to end of file. |
| `>& file` | Redirect STDOUT and STDERR to file. |
| `>>& file` | Append STDOUT and STDERR to file. |
| `2>&-` | Close STDERR. |

## Command-Line Input

You can ask users to provide input to a script as part of the command-line argument when the script is run. All three shells use the positional parameter $n$ to specify as many as nine command-line arguments (for example, $1, $2, $3, up to $9). $0 is a legitimate variable; it returns the name of the command.

You can use each of these command-line arguments to pass file names or other information into a shell script from a command line.

## Bourne Shell Command-Line Input

The following Bourne shell script, named `tryit`, returns the number of command-line arguments and echoes each argument.

```
#!/bin/sh

echo $#
for var in $*
do
        echo $var
done
```

The following example shows the output for seven command-line arguments.

```
$ tryit one two three four five six seven
7
one
two
three
four
five
six
seven
$
```

Instead of using `$#`, the following example uses `echo $0` (which displays the name of the script) and `echo $1`, `echo $2`, and `echo $3` to display up to three command-line arguments.

```
#!/bin/sh

echo $0
echo $1
echo $2
echo $3
```

The following example provides four command-line arguments, but the `tryit` script processes only three of those arguments. The `echo$0` line echoes the name of the script.

```
$ tryit one two three four
tryit
one
two
three
$
```

*NOTE. The $n notation does not return an error if no parameters are provided as part of the command. Users do not need to supply*

*command-line arguments, so you cannot be sure that $n will contain*
*a value unless you check the number of positional parameters with $#*
*for the Bourne and Korn shells.*

## Korn Shell Command-Line Input

The scripts shown in "Bourne Shell Command-Line Input," above, also work
with the Korn shell. In addition, with the Korn shell, you can use `${10}`,
`${11}` ... notation to recognize more than the nine command-line arguments
permitted by the `$1` ... `$9` syntax.

## C Shell Command-Line Input

For the C shell, instead of the `echo $#` statement shown in the first example
in "Bourne Shell Command-Line Input" on page 450, use `$#argv` to hold the
number of command-line arguments.

The C shell provides additional syntax for positional parameters, as shown
in Table 88.

*Table 88      C Shell $argv Notation*

| Notation | Description |
| --- | --- |
| `$#argv`<br>`$*` | Count the number of command-line arguments. |
| `$argv` | Return the value of all arguments. |
| `$argv[1-3]` | Return the value of arguments 1 through 3. |
| `$0` | Return the command used to run the shell script. |
| `$argv[n]` | Return the *n*th argument. |
| `$argv[$#argv}` | Return the last argument. |

The shell performs range checking on the `$argv[n]` syntax, but it does not
on the `$n` syntax. If the shell does not find the word, you get the message
`Subscript out of range`.

*NOTE. `$argv[0]` is not defined and does not return the name of the*
*script.*

The following example script shows different ways you can use the `argv`
syntax.

```
#!/bin/csh -f
echo Number of args = $#argv
echo All args = $*
echo All args = $argv
echo Args 1-3 = $argv[1-3]
echo Name of script file = $0
echo Script file\? = $argv[0]
```

```
echo Second arg = $argv[2]
echo Last arg = $argv[$#argv]
echo Fifth arg = $5
echo Fifth arg = $argv[5]
```

The following example shows the output of the example script. Note that the incorrect $argv[0] argument on the 7th line of the script is ignored and produces no output. The $5 on the 9th line also produces no output because there is no fifth command-line argument.

```
castle% example one two three four
Number of args = 4
All args = one two three four
All args = one two three four
Args 1-3 = one two three
Name of script file = tryit
Script file? =
Second arg = two
Last arg = four
Fifth arg =
Subscript out of range
castle%
```

## Shifting Command-Line Arguments

You can use the shift command, which is built into all three shells, to manipulate the positional parameters in a script. The shift command moves each argument from $1 through $n to the left, changing the previous argument list. The shift command is particularly useful in processing positional parameters in while loops; you can use these commands together to process each positional parameter in turn.

In the following Bourne shell example, each argument is displayed in turn. The shift command shifts the list to the left, removing the leftmost value in the list, as shown in the following script.

```
#!/bin/sh
while [ $# -ne 0 ]
do
    echo argument: $1
    shift
done
The following example shows the output of this script:
$ tryit one two three
argument: one
argument: two
argument: three
$
```

Because the shift command shifts the positional parameters, you need to use $1 in the script only if you want to display (or process) the command-line

arguments. The following example shows how to shift positional parameters
from a Bourne shell command line.

```
$ set a b c d e f g h i
$ while [ $# -gt 0 ]; do
> echo $*
> shift
> done
a b c d e f g h i
b c d e f g h i
c d e f g h i
d e f g h i
e f g h i
f g h i
g h i
h i
i
$
```

Refer to the section "Using while Loops" on page 472 for more information
about `while` loops.

## Interactive Input

You can ask the user to type a single line of input anywhere in a script.

**Bourne and Korn Shell Interactive Input**     For the Bourne and Korn shells,
use the `read` command followed by a variable name for interactive input.

*NOTE. You do not need to assign the variable before you use it as an
argument to the* read *command. The following example shows the
Bourne and Korn shell syntax for interactive input.*

*To suppress the newline at the end of the prompt, use* \c *at the end of
the string when* /usr/bin *is in the path before* /usr/ucb*. Then,
users will type the input on the same line as the string that is
displayed. The SunOS 4.x* echo  -n *command works only if you have*
/usr/ucb *in the path before* /usr/bin*. Otherwise, the script uses the
Solaris version of the* echo *command. Refer to the* echo(1) *manual
page for more information.*

*Alternatively, you can set the* PATH *environment variable in the script
so that you are assured of getting the version of* echo *that you want.
The script* PATH *setting overrides the user's* PATH *settings to make
sure the script works as you intended.*

New!

```
#!/bin/sh

echo "Enter search pattern and press Return: \c"
read filename
```

When the prompt is displayed, the script waits for input from the keyboard. When the user types input and presses Return, the input is assigned to the variable and the script continues to execute.

*NOTE. Be sure to always include a descriptive screen prompt as part of the script before you request input so that users know that the script is waiting for screen input before it continues.*

**C Shell Interactive Input**     For the C shell, the special variable $< waits for a value from STDIN. You can use $< anywhere you would use a variable.

For the C shell, use $< as a value to a variable, as shown below.

```
#!/bin/csh -f
echo "Enter search pattern and press Return: \c"
set pattern = $<
```

When the prompt is displayed, the script waits for input from the keyboard. When the user types input and presses Return, the input is assigned to the variable and the script continues to execute.

## Here Documents

Sometimes a shell script requires data. Instead of having the data in a file somewhere in the system, you can include the data as part of the shell script. Including the data in the script makes it simpler to distribute and maintain the script. Such a collection of data is called a *here document*—the data (document) is right here in the shell script. Another advantage of a here document is that shell parameters can be substituted in the document as the shell is reading the data.

The general format of a here document is shown below. The format is the same for all three shells.

```
    lines of shell commands
    ...
command << delimiter
lines of data belonging
to the here document
delimiter
    ...
    more lines of shell commands
```

The here document operator << signals the beginning of the here document. The operator must be followed by a special string that delimits the input, for example <<DONE. Follow the here document operator with the list of input you want to use. The input can consist of any text and can include variables because the shell does variable substitution on a here document.

*NOTE. The shell can perform variable interpolation and substitution, but only if the keyword in the here document has the proper quotes around it. Certain quoting prevents the shell from performing variable substitution. See "Quoting" on page 456 for more information about quoting.*

At the end of the here document, you must include the delimiter at the left margin on a single line. The shell sends everything between the two delimiters to be processed as standard input.

In the following example, the mail message specified in the here document is sent to members of the staff whose names are contained in a file named stafflist, and invites them to a party. The delimiter used is the string EOF.

```
#!/bin/sh

time="7:00 p.m."
mail -s "staff party" `cat stafflist` << EOF
Please come to our staff party being held
in the cafeteria at $time tomorrow night
EOF
```

## Output Generation

The following sections describe how to use the echo command, quoting, and command substitution.

*NOTE. Although the* echo *command works in Korn shell scripts, the* print *command is preferred. The syntax for the* print *command is the same as for the* echo *command.*

### The echo and print Commands

Use the echo command to generate messages to display on a terminal screen. You have already seen some examples of using the echo command to display the value for a variable. You can also use the echo command to display text messages, as shown in the following portion of an interactive Bourne shell script.

```
#!/bin/sh
echo "Enter a pathname and press Return:"
read pathname
```

If you want to echo more than one message on the same line, use the \c string at the end of the line to leave the cursor at the end of the output line and to suppress the newline. The following example modifies the previous

Bourne shell script so that the user types the input following the colon, instead of on the line beneath the prompt message.

```
#!/bin/sh
echo "Enter a pathname and press Return: \c"
read pathname
```

If you need to display control characters or metacharacters, you can *escape* them (that is, get the shell to interpret the character literally) by putting a backslash (\) in front of the character. Refer to the echo(1) manual page for information about special backslash characters (for example, \c, \n).

The Bourne and Korn shell echo command has fewer restrictions on quoting metacharacters than does the C shell echo command. The following Bourne shell script displays an error message only for the parentheses in the last line, which are not escaped with backslashes. Note that the dollar sign ($) followed by a space does not need to be escaped.

```
$ more echodemo
#!/bin/sh

echo Type a pathname and press Return:
echo You owe me \$35 \(Please pay\).
echo This is a $ sign (not a variable)
$ echodemo
Type a pathname and press Return:
You owe me $35 (Please pay).
This is a $ sign (Not a variable).
anything: syntax error at line 6: `(' unexpected
$
```

## Quoting

All three shells use the same syntax for quoting, as shown in Table 89. Quoting a string incorrectly can produce many unexpected results.

*Table 89    Quoting Characters*

| Character | Term | Description |
|---|---|---|
| \ | Backslash | Nullify the special meaning of any shell metacharacter, including another backslash. |
| ` ` | Backquotes | Substitute the output of the command enclosed in backquotes as if it were typed in place of the command. Refer to the shell manual pages for more information. |

*Table 89    Quoting Characters (Continued)*

| Character | Term | Description |
|-----------|------|-------------|
| ' ' | Single quotes | Nullify the special meaning of all characters except bang ( ! ), the backslash ( \ ), and the single quote itself ( ' ). Single quotes are more restrictive than double quotes and do not permit variable or backquote expansion. |
| " " | Double quotes | Nullifies the special meaning of all special characters except bang ( ! ), backquote ( ` ` ), and dollar sign ( $ ). Permits variable and backquote expansion. |

*NOTE. The bang ( ! ) is not used as a metacharacter in the Bourne and Korn shells. If it is not quoted properly, it is likely to cause problems mostly in the C shell.*

The following examples demonstrate the result of different forms of quotation.

```
$ name=Fred
$ echo "My name is $name"
My name is Fred
$ echo 'My name is $name'
My name is $name
$ echo "Today is `date`"
Today is Tue Oct 31 12:12:35 PDT 2000
$ echo 'Today is `date`'
Today is `date`
$ echo 'Use metacharacters * ? < > | & and $ often'
Use metacharacters * ? < > | & and $ often
$ echo "It's hard to turn off"!
It's hard to turn off!
```

## Command Substitution

You can substitute the output of the command in place of the command itself. This process is called *command substitution*. Use backquotes ( ` ` ) to surround the desired command. You can use command substitution to return the output of the command or to use it as the value for a variable.

*NOTE. In the Korn shell, you can use the $ (command) syntax instead of backquotes.*

In the first example following, the output of the date command is used as part of a larger output string, and the output of the who command is filtered through `wc`, which counts the number of lines in the output of `who` to determine how many users are logged in. The second example pipes the output of the `who` command to the `cut` command to display only the list of user names and uses the `uname -n` command to display the name of the system.

```
$ echo Today is `date` and there are `who | wc -l` users logged in
Today is Wed Feb 14 13:12:41 WST 2001 and there are 5 users logged in

$ echo `who | cut -f1 -d" "` logged in to `uname -n`
winsor newton fred george anna logged in to seachild
$
```

# Testing for Conditions

When writing scripts, you frequently want to test for conditions. The simplest test is to determine whether a condition is true or false. If the expression is true, execute any subsequent commands (shown indented in Table 90); if not, continue with the script. Table 90 shows the syntax for conditional tests.

*Table 90    Conditional Test Syntax*

| Bourne and Korn Shells | C Shell |
|---|---|
| if *command* | if (*cond*) then |
| then |    *commands* |
|   *commands* | else if (*cond*) then |
| elif *command* |    *commands* |
|   *commands* | else |
| else |    *commands* |
|   *commands* | endif |
| fi | |

## if-then-else-elif

For the Bourne and Korn shells, use the `if-then-else-elif-fi` syntax to test for conditions. You can follow the `if` statement with the `test` command and its argument(s) to test for conditions. As an alternative to typing the `test` command, you can enclose the test condition in square brackets `[ ]`.

You must put a space after the first bracket and before the last one for the characters to be interpreted correctly—as shown in the following example.

```
if [ -r filename ]
then
```

The results of test `-r filename` and `[ -r filename ]` are identical. Refer to the section "Test and C Shell Built-in Test" on page 495 for `test` command options.

The Bourne shell fragment shown next uses the simplest form of the `if` statement to test whether a user has entered at least one command-line argument following the name of the script.

```
#!/bin/sh
#
# Test for at least one command-line argument
#
if test $# -lt 1
then
     echo Usage: $0 name requires one command-line argument
     exit 1
fi
```

If you want the script to perform additional actions if the first conditional test fails, use the `else` clause, as shown in the following Bourne shell fragment.

```
#!/bin/sh

if test $# -lt 1
then
     echo Usage: $0 name requires one command-line argument
     exit 1
else
     echo "Thank you for entering arguments"
     echo "You entered $# arguments"
fi
```

You can use the `elif` conditional (a combination of `else` and `if`) to test for additional conditions within the `if` statement. The `elif` clause is performed only if the previous `if` or `else` fails. Each `elif` clause lists another command to be tested. The following Bourne shell example has one `elif` and one `else` clause.

```
#!/bin/sh
#
# Time of day greetings
#
hour=`date +%H`

if [ $hour -H 12 ]
then
     echo "Good Morning!"
elif [ $hour -H 17 ]
```

```
then
    echo "Good Afternoon!"
else
    echo "Good Night!"
fi
```

# if-else-else if-endif

The C shell has built-in constructs that you can use to test conditions. Refer to "Test and C Shell Built-in Test" on page 495 for C shell test command options.

The C shell fragment shown next tests whether a user has entered one or more command-line arguments following the name of the script.

```
#!/bin/csh -f

if ($#argv == 0) then
    echo Usage: $0 name requires one command-line argument
    exit 1
endif
```

> *NOTE. The* then *statement for the C shell, if present, must be positioned at the end of the* if *line.*

If you want the script to perform additional actions if the first conditional test fails, use the else clause, as shown in the following C shell fragment.

```
#!/bin/csh -f

if ($#argv == 0) then
    echo Usage: $0 requires command-line arguments
    exit 1
else
    echo "Thank you for entering arguments"
    echo "You entered $# arguments"
endif
```

You can use the else if conditional to test for additional conditions within the if statement. The else if clause is performed only if the previous if or else if fails (is false). Each else if statement lists another conditional to be tested. The following C shell example has one else if and one else statement.

```
#!/bin/csh -f
#
# Time of day greetings
#
set d=`date +%H`
set hour = $d[4]

if ($hour < 12) then
    echo "Good Morning\!"
else if ($hour < 17) then
```

```
    echo "Good Afternoon\!"
else
    echo "Good Night\!"
endif
```

# Nested if Constructs

if statements can contain additional if statements; such containment is called nesting. When you write a script that contains nested if statements, be sure to indent the statements to make it easier to follow the logic of the statements and to check that you have included all the required elements.

## Bourne and Korn Shell Nesting Constructs

The syntax for nesting if statements in the Bourne and Korn shells is shown below.

```
if command
then
    if command
    then
        command
        ...
    else
        command
        ...
    fi
elif command
then
    command
    ...
else
    command
    ...
fi
```

## C Shell Nesting Constructs

The syntax for nesting if statements in the C shell is shown below.

```
if (expression) then
    if (expression) then
        if (expression) then
            command
            ...
        else
            command
            ...
        endif
    else if (expression) then
        command
        ...
    else
        command
        ...
    endif
endif
```

## Multibranching

You may want to take several different types of action depending on the value of a variable or a parameter. Although you can use conditional testing to test each value and take action, you can more easily perform such tests with the Bourne and Korn shell `case` statement or the C shell `switch` statement.

### Bourne and Korn Shell Multibranching

The syntax for the Bourne and Korn Shell `case` statement is shown below.

```
case value in
  pattern1)
    command
    command ;;
  pattern2)
    command ;;
    *)
    default action ;;
esac
```

The value of the variable is successively compared against patterns until a match is found. The commands immediately following the matching pattern are executed until `;;` is found. The last test `*)` is a default action. If no other values match, the shell executes the default action. In many scripts, the default action displays an error message and exits from the shell.

`case` statements can be especially helpful for processing parameters to a function.

The following Bourne script example displays information based on the current value of the $TERM environment variable.

```
#!/bin/sh
#
# Set the terminal type
#
case $TERM in
    tvi???)
        echo $TERM
        echo Probably the system console ;;
    vt[12][02]0)
        echo A VT terminal ;;
    Wyse40 | Wyse75)
        echo A Wyse terminal ;;
    sun)
        echo Aha!! a workstation ;;
    *)
        echo surprise! it's a $TERM ;;
esac
```

### C Shell Multibranching

The syntax for the C shell `switch` statement is shown below.

```
switch (value)
case pattern:
    commands
    breaksw
default:
commands
    breaksw
endsw
```

The value of the variable is successively compared against patterns until a match is found. The commands immediately following the matching pattern are executed until a `breaksw` is found. The last `default:` (C shell) is a default action. If no other values match, the shell executes the default action. In many scripts, the default action displays an error message and exits from the shell.

The following interactive C shell script example sets the terminal type.

```
#!/bin/csh -f
#
# Set the terminal type
#
echo "Do you want to see the present setting? \c"
set input = $<
switch ("$input")
    case [Yy]*:
        echo "term =" $TERM
        breaksw
endsw
echo "Terminal type? \c"
set term = $<
switch ($term)
    case sun:
        setenv TERM $term
        breaksw
    default:
        echo "I don't know that one."
        breaksw
endsw
```

## The Bourne Shell test Command

*New!*

The Bourne shell uses the external `test(1)` command to evaluate a condition and indicate the result of the evaluation by its exit status. You can use the test command with a *condition* argument or enclose *condition* in square brackets, as shown below.

```
test condition
[ condition ]
```

You must separate the square brackets with a space, and *condition* is optional.

You can use the primitives listed in Table 91 to construct *condition*.

*Table 91    test Command Primitives*

| | |
|---|---|
| -b *filename* | true if *filename* exists and is a block special file. |
| -c *filename* | true if *filename* exists and is a character special file. |
| -d *filename* | true if *filename* exists and is a directory. |
| -f *filename* | true if *filename* exists and is a regular file. Alternatively, if /usr/bin/sh users specify /usr/ucb before /usr/bin in their PATH environment variable, then test returns true if *filename* exists and is not a directory. This behavior is also the default for /usr/bin/csh users. The not-a-directory alternative to the -f option is a transition aid for BSD applications and may not be supported in future releases. |
| -g *filename* | true if *filename* exists and its set-group-ID bit is set. |
| -h *filename* | true if *filename* exists and is a symbolic link. With all other primitives (except -L *filename*), follow the symbolic links by default. |
| -k *filename* | true if *filename* exists and its sticky bit is set. |
| -L *filename* | true if *filename* exists and is a symbolic link. With all other primitives (except -h *filename*), follow the symbolic links by default. The -L option is a migration aid for users of other shells that have similar options. It may not be supported in future releases. |
| -n *s1* | true if the length of the string *s1* is non-zero. |
| -p *filename* | true if *filename* exists and is a named pipe (fifo). |
| -r *filename* | true if *filename* exists and is readable. |
| -s *filename* | true if *filename* exists and has a size greater than 0. |
| -t [*fildes*] | true if the open file whose file descriptor number is *fildes* (1 by default) is associated with a terminal device. |
| -u *filename* | true if *filename* exists and its set-user-ID bit is set. |
| -w *filename* | true if *filename* exists and is writable. |
| -x *filename* | true if *filename* exists and is executable. |
| -z *s1* | true if the length of string *s1* is zero. |

*Table 91     test Command Primitives (Continued)*

| | |
|---|---|
| `n1 -eq n2` | `true` if the integers *n1* and *n2* are algebraically equal. |
| `n1 -ge n2` | `true` if the *integer n1* is algebraically greater than or equal to the integer *n2*. |
| `n1 -gt n2` | `true` if the integer *n1* is algebraically greater than the integer *n2*. |
| `n1 -le n2` | `true` if the integer *n1* is algebraically less than or equal to the integer *n2*. |
| `n1 -lt n2` | `true` if the integer *n1* is algebraically less than the integer *n2*. |
| `n1 -ne n2` | `true` if the integers *n1* and *n2* are not algebraically equal. |
| `s1` | `true` if *s1* is not the null string. |
| `s1 != s2` | `true` if strings *s1* and *s2* are not identical. |
| `s1 = s2` | `true` if strings *s1* and *s2* are identical. |

You can combine these primaries with the operators listed in Table 92.

*Table 92     test Command Operators*

| | |
|---|---|
| `!` | Unary negation operator. |
| `-a` | Binary and operator. |
| `-o` | Binary or operator (`-a` has higher precedence than `-o`). |
| `(condition)` | Parentheses for grouping. Notice also that parentheses are meaningful to the shell and, therefore, must be quoted. |

If you test a file you own (the `-r` `-w` or `-x` tests) but the permission tested does not have the owner bit set, a non-zero (`false`) exit status is returned even though the file may have the group or other bit set for that permission. The correct exit status is set if you are superuser.

*NOTE. If more than one argument follows the `-r` through `-n` operators, only the first argument is examined; the others are ignored, unless `-a` or `-o` is the second argument.*

*The `=` and `!=` operators have a higher precedence than the `-r` through `-n` operators, and `=` and `!=` always expect arguments; therefore, you cannot use `=` and `!=` with the `-r` through `-n` operators.*

The following example performs a mkdir if a directory does not exist.

```
test ! -d tempdir && mkdir tempdir
```

The following example waits for a file to become nonreadable.

```
while test -r thefile
do
  sleep 30
done
echo '"thefile" is no longer readable'
```

The following example uses the [ *command* ] syntax to perform *command* if the argument is one of three strings (two variations).

```
if [ "$1" = "pear" ] || [ "$1" = "grape" ] || [ "$1" = "apple" ]
then
  command
fi
case "$1" in
  pear|grape|apple) command ; ;
esac
```

## The Korn Shell ((...)) Command

**New!**

The Korn shell accepts the external test(1) command. It also provides its own internal test command with the following syntax.

```
[[ expression ]]
```

You must use a space after the opening brackets and before the closing brackets. You must also use a space to separate the expression arguments and operators within the double square brackets. The [[...]] command is similar in function to the test command except that it provides additional operators. You can use [[...]] to test for strings, patterns, file attributes, integer attributes, and file descriptors.

Table 93 lists the [[...]] string operators.

*Table 93*      *((...)) Command String Operators*

| | |
|---|---|
| -n *string* | true if length of *string* is not zero. |
| -o *option* | true if *option* is set. |
| -z *string* | true if length of *string* is zero. |

*Table 93* *((...)) Command String Operators (Continued)*

| *string1 = string2* | |
|---|---|
| | true if *string1* is equal to *string2*. |
| *string1 != string2* | |
| | true if *string1* is not equal to *string2*. |
| *string1 = pattern* | |
| | true if *string1* is equal to *pattern*. |
| *string1 != pattern* | |
| | true if *string1* is not equal to *pattern*. |
| *string1 < string2* | |
| | true if *string1* is less than *string2*. |
| *string1 > string2* | |
| | true if *string1* is greater than *string2*. |
| *string1 = string2* | |
| | true if *string1* is equal to *string2*. |

The following example checks to see if the variable x is set to the value abc.

```
$ x=abc
$ [[ $x = abc ]] && print "x is set to abc."
x is set to abc.
$
```

Table 94 lists some of the `[[...]]` file operators.

*Table 94* *((...)) Command File Operators*

| -a *file* | true if *file* exists. |
|---|---|
| -d *file* | true if *file* exists and is a directory. |
| -f *file* | true if *file* exists and is a regular file. |
| -G *file* | true if *file* exists and its group ID matches the effective group ID of the current process. |
| -L *file* | true if *file* exists and is a symbolic link. |
| -O *file* | true if *file* exists and its user ID matches the effective user ID of the current process. |
| -r *file* | true if *file* exists and is readable. |

*Table 94     ((...)) Command File Operators (Continued)*

| | |
|---|---|
| `-s file` | true if `file` exists and its size is greater than zero. |
| `-S file` | true if `file` exists and is a socket. |
| `-u file` | true if `file` exists and its user-ID bit is set. |
| `-w file` | true if `file` exists and is writable. |
| `-x file` | true if `file` exists and is executable. If `file` is a directory, then `true` indicates that the directory is searchable. |
| `file1 -ef file2` | |
| | true if `file1` exists and is another name for `file2`. |
| `file1 -nt file2` | |
| | true if `file1` exists and is newer than `file2`. |
| `file1 -ot file2` | |
| | true if `file1` exists and is older than `file2`. |

The following example uses the `-a` operator to check that a file exists.

```
$ touch tmp
$ [[ -a tmp ]] && print "File tmp exists."
File tmp exists.
$
```

Table 95 lists the `[[ ... ]]` integer operators.

*Table 95     ((...)) Command Integer Operators*

| | |
|---|---|
| `exp1 -eq exp2` | |
| | true if `exp1` is equal to `exp2`. |
| `exp1 -ne exp2` | |
| | true if `exp1` is not equal to `exp2`. |
| `exp1 -le exp2` | |
| | true if `exp1` is less than or equal to `exp2`. |
| `exp1 -lt exp2` | |
| | true if `exp1` is less than `exp2`. |
| `exp1 -ge exp2` | |
| | true if `exp1` is greater than or equal to `exp2`. |

*Table 95    ((...)) Command Integer Operators (Continued)*

| *exp1* -gt *exp2* | |
|---|---|
| | true if *exp1* is greater than *exp2*. |

The following example can be used to check the number of command-line arguments. This expression evaluates to true if the positional parameters are less than or equal to three.

```
[[ $# -le 3 ]] && print "3 or fewer args are given."
```

Table 96 lists the [[ ... ]] other operators.

*Table 96    ((...)) Command Other Operators*

| [[ *exp1* && *exp2* ]] | |
|---|---|
| | true if both *exp1* and *exp2* are true. |
| [[ *exp1* \|\| *exp2* ]] | |
| | true if either *exp1* or *exp2* are true. |
| [[ (*expression*) ]] | |
| | true if *expression* evaluates to true. Use the parentheses to override the precedence rules. |
| [[ !*expression* ]] | |
| | true if *expression* evaluates to false. |

The following example checks whether two variables were set to specific examples.

```
$ x=abc y=def
$ [[ $x = abc && $y = def ]] && print "x-abc and y=def."
x=abc and y=def.
$
```

# Controlling the Flow

You can use loops to control the flow of execution in a script. A *loop* is an iterative mechanism that repeats a sequence of instructions until a predetermined condition is met. You can use different forms of loops. The for/foreach loop executes a list of commands one time for each value of a loop variable. The while loop repeatedly executes a group of commands within the body of the loop until the test condition in the expression is no longer true. The Bourne and Korn shells provide an `until` loop that continues to execute until a command executes successfully. Table 97 shows the syntax for `for/foreach`, `while`, and `until` loops.

*Table 97     Looping Syntax*

| Feature | Bourne/Korn Shell | C Shell |
|---|---|---|
| `for/foreach`<br>`loops` | `for` *variable* `in` *list*<br>`do`<br>    *commands*<br>`done` | `foreach` *variable* `(`*list*`)`<br>    *commands*<br>`end` |
| `while loops` | `while` *command*<br>`do`<br>    *commands*<br>`done` | `while` `(`*cond*`)`<br>    *commands*<br>`end` |
| `until loops` | `until` *command*<br>`do`<br>    *commands*<br>`done` | N/A |

## Using Bourne and Korn Shell for Loops

Use the `for` loop to process items from a fixed list or from a command-line argument. The Bourne and Korn shell `for` loop executes the commands between the `do` and the `done` statement as many times as there are words or strings listed after the `in` statement.

The `for` loop has the following basic syntax.

```
for variable in word1 word2 word3 . . . wordn
do
    command $variable
    command
done
```

The following Bourne shell script contains two examples of `for` loops. The first example copies files into a backup directory. The second removes all files that contain a `.o` suffix.

```
#!/bin/sh
#
# Backup files
#
dir=/home/winsor/backup
for file in ch1 ch2 ch3 ch4
do
    cp $file $dir/${file}.back
```

```
        echo $file has been backed up in directory $dir
done

for file in *.o
do
    echo removing $file
    rm $file
done
```

## Using C Shell foreach Loops

In the C shell, use the `foreach` loop to process items from a fixed list or to execute commands interactively from a command line. The `foreach` construct executes a list of commands one time for each value specified in the (*list*).

The following C shell script contains two examples of `foreach` loops. The first example copies `$file` into a backup directory. The second example removes all files that contain a `.o` suffix.

```
#!/bin/csh -f
#
# Backup files
#
set dir=/home/winsor/backup
foreach file (ch1 ch2 ch3 ch4)
    cp $file $dir/${file}.back
    echo $file has been backed up in directory $dir
end

foreach file (*.o)
    echo removing $file
    rm $file
end
```

You can type the `foreach` loop statement at the command-line prompt. The secondary prompt (`?`) is displayed. At the prompt, type the commands you want to execute in the loop. After you complete the list of commands, type **end** and press Return. The commands are executed in sequence and the C shell prompt is redisplayed. The following example displays and compiles the name of each C source file in the directory and renames the binary output file. The `:r` modifier removes the `.c` extension. If there are 10 source files in the current working directory, the loop executes 10 times. When there are no more C source files, the loop ends.

```
oak% foreach file (*.c)
? echo $file
? cc -o $file:r $file
? end
oak%
```

The following example converts raster files to GIF format, strips off the
.rs suffix, and adds a .gif suffix:

```
oak% foreach file (*.rs)
? cat $file | rasttoppm | ppmtogif > ${file:r}.gif
? end
oak%
```

## Using while Loops

Use while loops to repeatedly execute a group of commands within the body of a
loop until the test condition in the expression is no longer true. In other words,
the while loop says, "While the expression is true, execute these commands."

### Bourne and Korn Shell while Loops

For the Bourne and Korn shells, the while loop executes the commands
between the do and the done statements as long as the initial command exits
with a status of zero.

The while loop has the following basic syntax.

```
while command
do
     command
     command
done
```

In the following Bourne shell script, the first example sets the variable num
equal to 0 and adds 1 to it as long as the number is less than or equal to 4.

```
#!/bin/sh

num=0
while [ $num -le 4 ]
do
        num=`expr $num + 1`
        echo number: $num
done
```

Refer to "Mathematical Operations" on page 476 for information on how to
use the expr command.

The next example displays the command-line arguments in sequence when
any arguments are given. Refer to "Shifting Command-Line Arguments" on
page 452 for information about the shift command.

```
#!/bin/sh

while [ $# -ne 0 ]
do
```

```
        echo argument: $1
        shift
done
```

## C Shell while Loops

For the C shell, the `while` loop executes the commands between the `while` and the `end` statement as long as the expression evaluates to true.

The `while` loop has the following basic syntax.

```
while (expression)
    command
    command
end
```

In the following C shell script, the first example uses the `@` built-in command to set the variable `num` equal to `0` and adds `1` to it as long as the number is less than or equal to `4`. See "C Shell Mathematical Operations" on page 478 for more information about the `@` command.

```
#!/bin/csh -f

@ num = 0
while ($num <= 4)
    @ num++
    echo "number: $num"
end
```

The output of this script is shown below.

```
oak% tryit
number: 0
number: 1
number: 2
number: 3
number: 4
```

The next example displays the command-line arguments in sequence when any arguments are given.

```
#!/bin/csh -f
#
while ($#argv != 0)
        echo "argument: $1"
        shift
end
```

## Using Bourne and Korn Shell until Loops

Use Bourne or Korn shell `until` loops to test an expression until the command returns a successful status. The syntax for the `until` loop is similar to the `while` loop.

```
until command
do
      command
      command
done
```

> NOTE. *The* `until` *condition is checked at the top of the loop, not at the bottom.*

The following example prints the numbers 1 through 5.

```
#!/bin/sh

num=0
until [ $num -gt 4 ]
do
        num=`expr $num + 1`
        echo number: $num
done
```

The results of this script are the same as the example shown for the `while` loop. Refer to the section "Mathematical Operations" on page 476 for a description of the `expr` command used in the preceding example.

## Breaking Loops

All three shells have built-in `break` and `continue` commands that you can use to break out of a `for/foreach`, `while`, or `until` loop. The `break` command forces premature termination of the loop and transfers control to the line after the `done` (for the Bourne and Korn shells) or `end` (for the C shell) statement. In the following C shell example, the script continues running the `while` loop until the user answers `Yes` (or `yes`, `y`, `Y`, or any word beginning with `y` or `Y`). When the user does answer `yes`, the break terminates the `while` loop and, in this case, exits because there are no additional commands to execute.

```
#!/bin/csh -f
#
while (1)
        echo "Finished yet? \c"
        set answer = $<
        if ($answer =~ [Yy]*) break
end
```

You can use the `continue` command in a similar way to control for/foreach and `while` loops. The `continue` command operates on the innermost loop with which it is associated. The `continue` statement transfers execution immediately back to the `while` test, skipping all subsequent commands in the innermost loop. If `continue` is used with a `foreach` loop, the `continue` statement quits the current iteration of the loop and processes the next item in the list.

# Exit Status

When a command or shell function terminates, it returns an exit status to the invoking shell. The *exit status* is a numeric value that indicates whether the program ran successfully and whether certain events occurred in the command.

Every command that runs has an exit status, which is set by the programmer when writing the command. Usually, an exit status of 0 means that the program executed successfully. Any non-zero value (usually 1 or −1) means that the program failed. Programmers may not always follow this convention. Check the manual page for a given command to determine its exit status. For example, the `grep` command returns one of three exit status values: 0 means that the search pattern was found, 1 means that the pattern could not be found, and 2 means that the `grep` command could not open or find the file(s) to be searched.

## Bourne Shell Exit Status

For the Bourne shell, the `$?` variable holds exit status for the last command executed. Usually, 0 indicates success and 1 indicates failure.

```
$ pwd
/home/seachild/winsor
$ echo $?
0
$ cd /home3
/home3: bad directory
$ echo $?
1
$
```

## C Shell Exit Status

The C shell variable named `status` is automatically set by the shell to the exit status of the last command executed. You can use the `echo` command to display the exit status at the prompt.

```
oak% grep root /etc/passwd
root:x:0:1:0000-Admin(0000):/:/sbin/sh
oak% echo $status
0
oak% grep anthonly /etc/passwd
oak% echo $status
1
oak% grep root /etc/password
grep: can't open /etc/password
oak% echo $status
2
oak%
```

When writing shell scripts, you can add an `exit 0` to the end of the script to indicate successful completion. Exiting with any other value will let any program or script that calls your script know that something went wrong.

# Mathematical Operations

You can do mathematical operations only on integers (whole numbers) for all three shells. If you want to do more complicated arithmetic, use the `awk` or the `bc` command.

To perform mathematical operations in the Bourne shell, use the `expr` command. The `expr` command has the following syntax.

```
expr arguments
```

You must separate the mathematical operators (shown in Table 98) and the operand with white space.

*Table 98     Mathematical Operators*

| Operator | Description |
| --- | --- |
| + | Addition. |
| – | Subtraction. |
| * | Multiplication. |
| / | Division. |
| % | Remainder (modulus). |

The multiplication, division, and remainder operators have higher precedence than do the addition or subtraction operators. Use parentheses for grouping.

## Bourne Shell Mathematical Operations

The following Bourne shell example uses the `expr` command.

```
$ i=4
$ expr $i + 1
5
$ expr $i - 1
3
$ expr $i \* 2
8
$ expr $i / 2
2
$ expr $i % 2
0
$ j=2
$ expr $i + $j
6
$
```

## Korn Shell Mathematical Operations

The Korn shell has `let` and built-in `$((...))` expressions for doing arithmetic.

You can use the `let` command to do integer arithmetic. The syntax for the `let` command is `let "arithmetic-expression"`. `arithmetic-expression` can contain constants, operators, and Korn shell variables. Use double quotes with arithmetic expressions that contain white space or operators that have special meanings to the Korn shell.

*New!*

The following example sets variable x to the sum of 2 + 2.

```
$ let "x=2 + 2"
$ print $x
4
$
```

You can then increment the value of x, as shown below.

```
$ let "x=x + 1"
$ print $x
5
$
```

Note that you can reference regular variables by name only in arithmetic expressions. You do not need to precede them with $ for substitution to be performed. You can precede variables with $ in arithmetic expressions, but parameter execution is slower than if you reference the variables directly.

The $((*arithmetic-expression*)) is replaced by the value of the arithmetic expression within the double parentheses. *arithmetic-expression* is treated as if it were in double quotes except that a double quote inside the expression is not treated specially. The shell expands all tokens in the expression for parameter expansion, command substitution, and quote removal. Next, the shell treats the expression as an arithmetic expression and substitutes the value of the expression.

The following simple examples use the $(( . . . )) expression for arithmetic expansion.

```
$ echo $((2+2))
4
$ echo $((8192*16384%23))
9
$
```

## C Shell Mathematical Operations

The C shell @ command is similar to the Bourne and Korn shell `expr` command. The @ command evaluates an expression mathematically and then assigns the resulting value to a shell variable, as shown in Table 99.

The expressions can be mathematical or logical. Mathematical expressions typically use the operators shown in Table 99. Logical expressions typically use one of the following operators and yield a 1 (true) or 0 (false) value.

```
> < >= <= == !=
```

The following example shows C shell numeric values.

```
oak% @ total = 5 + 3
oak% echo $total
8
oak% @ total++
oak% echo $total
9
oak% @ total += 4
oak% echo $total
13
oak% @ newtotal = ($total > 5)
oak% echo $newtotal
1
oak%
```

*Table 99    C Shell Mathematical Operators*

| Syntax | Description |
|---|---|
| @ *variable* = (*expression*) | Set value of variable equal to the expression. |
| @ *variable* += (*expression*) | Perform addition. |
| @ *variable* -= (*expression*) | Perform subtraction. |
| @ *variable* *= (*expression*) | Perform multiplication. |
| @ *variable* /= (*expression*) | Perform division. |
| @ variable ++ | Add 1. |
| @ variable -- | Subtract 1. |

# User-Defined Functions

You can write your own functions in the Bourne and Korn shells and use them as part of other scripts.

*NOTE. Not all Bourne shells support functions. However, the Solaris Bourne shell does support functions.*

*User-defined functions* are useful if you have a series of commands that you want to use repeatedly. The functions written for an application server are an example of user-defined functions. Some examples of functions are provided in "Example Scripts" on page 498. When you define a function, you use the name of the function at the place where you want to execute the series of commands contained in the function.

Typically, you define functions at the beginning of a script, but you can define them in separate files and share them between scripts. Once the function has been defined, you can use it any number of times.

Use the following syntax to define functions.

```
function_name() {
    (body of the function)
}
```

*Shell functions* use positional parameters and special variables such as * and # in the same way that shell scripts do. Typically, you define several shell functions within a single shell script. Each function receives arguments as positional parameters. These positional parameters "overlay" command-line parameters.

To call the function, use the *function_name* as if it were a normal command at the place in the script where you want to use the function. The following Bourne shell script defines and uses a simple function.

```
#!/bin/sh
#
printlist() {
        echo The current list of arguments is:
        echo $*
}
while [ $# -gt 0 ]
do
        printlist $*
        shift 2
done
```

The following example shows the result of running this script.

```
oak% doit one two three four
The current list of arguments is:
one two three four
The current list of arguments is:
three four
oak%
```

# Debugging Shell Scripts

The following sections provide some suggestions for debugging shell scripts.

## Using Debugging Flags

A common problem when writing shell scripts is that the shell does not interpret the command in exactly the way that you expect. When the shell interprets a command line, it substitutes variables with values, replaces file-name wildcards with the appropriate file names, and performs command substitution. If the interpretation transforms a command line into something unexpected, the command most likely will not execute the way you intend it to.

All three shells provide -x (echo) and -v (verbose) options that you can use to help pinpoint where problems are occurring in a script. The -v option displays each line of the script as it is read from the file. The -x option shows each line after it has been processed by the shell and is ready for execution. The combination of these two options provides you with much useful information for debugging your scripts.

You can use the options from the command line, as shown below.

```
oak% csh -xv script-name
$ sh -xv script-name
$ ksh -xv script-name
```

Alternatively, you can set the flag options in the first line of the script, as follows.

```
#!/bin/sh -xv
#!/bin/csh -f -xv
#!/bin/ksh -xv
```

The following example shows the time-of-day greeting script with the -x option in the command line, followed by the screen output.

```
#!/bin/sh -x
#
# Time of day greetings
#
hour=`date +%H`

if [ $hour -le 12 ]
then
        echo "Good Morning!"
elif [ $hour -le 17 ]
then
        echo "Good Afternoon!"
else
        echo "Good Night!"
fi

$ greetings
+ date +%H
hour=11
+ [ 11 -le 12 ]
+ echo Good Morning!
Good Morning!
$
```

The following example shows the output for the same script with the -v option set.

```
$ greetings
#!/bin/sh -v
#
# Time of day greetings
#
hour=`date +%H`

if [ $hour -le 12 ]
then
        echo "Good Morning!"
elif [ $hour -le 17 ]
then
        echo "Good Afternoon!"
else
        echo "Good Night!"
fi
Good Morning!
$
```

The following example shows the screen output of the same script with -xv set.

```
$ greetings
#!/bin/sh -xv
#
# Time of day greetings
#
hour=`date +%H`
+ date +%H
hour=11

if [ $hour -le 12 ]
then
        echo "Good Morning!"
elif [ $hour -le 17 ]
then
        echo "Good Afternoon!"
else
        echo "Good Night!"
fi
+ [ 11 -le 12 ]
+ echo Good Morning!
Good Morning!
$
```

## Understanding Shell Parsing Order

Each shell analyzes commands, whether from the command line or in a script, and then parses them (divides them up) into recognizable parts. Shells can perform many kinds of substitutions and expansions. These operations are carried out in a very specific order for each shell. The parsing order for a shell can definitely impact shell programs that you write. Understanding the parsing order can help you determine where a script may be broken. Figure 77 shows a simplified version of Korn shell parsing order. When a command or string is quoted, the parsing order is affected. It can be difficult to understand exactly how the evaluation process works. Nevertheless, sometimes understanding the order in which a shell performs its operation can provide some insight into a problem. The Bourne shell parses in a similar order to the Korn shell, omitting history and alias substitution.

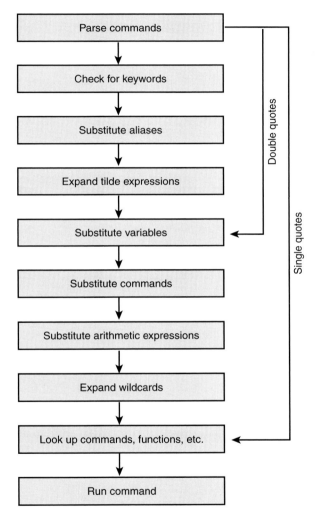

*Figure 77    Korn Shell Parsing Order*

Figure 78 shows a simplified version of C shell parsing order.

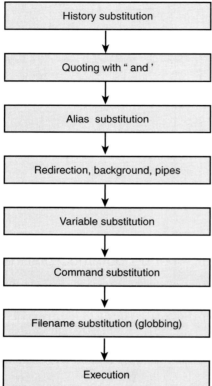

Figure 78   *C Shell Parsing Order*

The following Bourne shell script fails because variables are substituted *after* redirection.

```
$ moreit='| more'
$ cat    /etc/passwd $moreit
ppp:x:12881:1:PPP:/tmp:/usr/etc/ppp-listen
root:x.:0:1:Operator:/:/bin/csh
nobody:x:65534:65534::/:
(Lines omitted from example)
+::0:0:::
cat: |: No such file or directory
cat: more: No such file or directory
```

For shell programming reference tables and for examples of more complex shell scripts see Chapter 19, "Reference Tables and Example Scripts."

# 19

# *REFERENCE TABLES AND EXAMPLE SCRIPTS*

## Reference Tables

This chapter contains tables of syntax elements for all three shells and examples of shell scripts.

### Environment Files

| Description | Bourne | Korn | C |
|---|---|---|---|
| Read at login. | `.profile` | `.profile` | `.login` |
| Read at invocation of shell. | | Any file specified in `.profile` with `ENV=`*file*. By convention, *file* is usually `.kshrc` | `.cshrc` |

## First Line of Script

| Shell | Syntax |
|-------|--------|
| Bourne | `#!/bin/sh` |
| Korn | `#!/bin/ksh` |
| C | `#!/bin/csh -f` |

## Korn Shell Path Operators

| Operator | Description |
|----------|-------------|
| `${variable# pattern}` | Delete the shortest part at the beginning of the variable that matches the pattern and return the rest. |
| `${variable## pattern}` | Delete the longest part at the beginning of the variable that matches the pattern and return the rest. |
| `${variable% pattern}` | Delete the shortest part at the end of the variable that matches the pattern and return the rest. |
| `${variable%% pattern}` | Delete the longest part at the end of the variable that matches the pattern and return the rest. |

## C Shell Path Modifiers

| Modifier | Meaning | Description |
|----------|---------|-------------|
| `:e` | Extension | Remove prefix ending with a dot. |
| `:h` | Head | Remove trailing path-name component. |
| `:r` | Root | Remove suffixes beginning with a dot ( . ). |
| `:t` | Tail | Remove all leading path-name components. |
| `:q` | Quote | Force variable to be quoted. Used to quote `$argv`. |
| `:x` | Quote | Like q, but break into words at each space, Tab, or newline. |

## Bourne and Korn Shell Built-in Variables Initialized by Shell

| Variable | Explanation |
|----------|-------------|
| $* | List the value of all command-line parameters. This variable is useful only in scripts because the login shell has no arguments associated with it. |
| $# | Return the number of command-line arguments (in decimal). Useful only in scripts. |
| $? | Return the exit status (in decimal) of the last command executed. Most commands return a zero exit status if they complete successfully; otherwise a non-zero exit status is returned. This variable is set after each command is executed. |
| $$ | Return the process ID (PID) number of the current shell (in decimal). |
| $! | Return the process number (in decimal) of the last process run in the background. |

## C Shell Built-in Variables Initialized by Shell

| Variable | Explanation |
|----------|-------------|
| $* | List the value of all command-line parameters. This variable is useful only in scripts because the login shell has no arguments associated with it. Some people prefer to use $argv instead of $*. |
| $# | Check whether a variable of that name has been set. |

## Shell Built-in Commands

The (K) in the Bourne or Korn Shell column indicates commands that are available only with the Korn shell.

| Purpose | Bourne or Korn Shell | C Shell |
|---------|----------------------|---------|
| Null command. | : | : |
| Create a command name alias. | alias (K) | alias |
| Run current command in background. | bg (K) | bg |

| Purpose | Bourne or Korn Shell | C Shell |
|---|---|---|
| Exit enclosing `for` or `while` loop. | `break` | `break` |
| Break out of a switch. | N/A | `breaksw` |
| Change directory. | `cd` | `cd` |
| Continue next iteration of `for` or `while` loop. | `continue` | `continue` |
| Default `case` in switch. | N/A | `default` |
| Print directory stack. | N/A | `dirs` |
| Write arguments on STDOUT. | `echo`, `print` (**K**) | `echo` |
| Evaluate and execute arguments. | `eval` | `eval` |
| Execute the arguments. | `exec` | `exec` |
| Return or set shell variables. | `set` | `@` |
| Exit shell program. | `exit` | `exit` |
| Create an environment variable. | `export` | `setenv` |
| Bring a command into foreground. | `fg` (**K**) | `fg` |
| Execute `foreach` loop. | `for` | `foreach` |
| Perform file name expansion. | N/A | `glob` |
| Go to label within shell program. | N/A | `goto` |
| Display history list. | `fc -l`(**K**) | `history` |
| `if-then-else` decision. | `if` | `if` |
| List active jobs. | `jobs` (**K**) | `jobs` |
| Send a signal. | `kill` | `kill` |
| Set limits for a job's resource use. | `ulimit` | `limit` |
| Terminate login shell and invoke login. | N/A | `login` |
| Terminate a login shell. | `exit` | `logout` |
| Change to a new user group. | `newgrp` | N/A |
| Change priority of a command. | N/A | `nice` |
| Ignore hang up. | N/A | `nohup` |
| Notify user when job status changes. | N/A | `notify` |
| Control shell processing on receipt of a signal. | `trap` | `onintr` |

| Purpose | Bourne or Korn Shell | C Shell |
|---|---|---|
| Pop the directory stack. | N/A | `popd` |
| Push a directory onto the stack. | N/A | `pushd` |
| Read a line from standard input. | `read` | `$<` |
| Change a variable to read-only. | `readonly` | N/A |
| Repeat a command *n* times. | N/A | `repeat` |
| Set shell environment variables. | `=` | `setenv` |
| Set a local C shell variable. | | `set` |
| Shift positional parameters `$*` or `$argv`. | `shift` | `shift` |
| Read and execute a file. | `. (dot)` | `source` |
| Stop a background process. | N/A | `stop` |
| Stop the shell. | `suspend` (**K**) | `suspend` |
| `case` statement. | `case` | `switch` |
| Evaluate conditional expressions. | `test`<br>`[ ]`<br>`[[ ]]` (**K**) | N/A |
| Display execution times. | `times` | `time` |
| Set default security for creation of files and directories. | `umask` | `umask` |
| Discard aliases. | `unalias` (**K**) | `unalias` |
| Remove limitations on resources. | `ulimit` | `unlimit` |
| Unset a variable. | `unset` | `unset` |
| Unset an environment variable. | `unset` | `unsetenv` |
| `until` loop. | `until` | N/A |
| Wait for background process to complete. | `wait` | N/A |
| `while` loop foreground. | `while` | `while` |

## Bourne and Korn Shell Redirection

| Command | Description |
|---------|-------------|
| `<file`, or `0< file` | Take standard input from `file`. |
| `> file`, or `1> file` | Redirect STDOUT to `file`. |
| `2> file` | Redirect STDERR to `file`. |
| `>> file` | Append STDOUT to `file`. |
| `2>&1` | Redirect STDERR to the place where STDOUT is directed. |
| `cmd1 | cmd2` | Pipe standard output of `cmd1` as standard input to `cmd2`. |
| `<> file` | Use `file` as both STDIN and STDOUT. |
| `<&-` | Close STDIN. |
| `>&-` | Close STDOUT. |
| `2>&-` | Close STDERR. |

## C Shell Redirection Metacharacters

| Command | Description |
|---------|-------------|
| `> file` | Redirect STDOUT to file. |
| `< file` | Take input from file. |
| `>> file` | Append STDOUT to end of file. |
| `>& file` | Redirect STDOUT and STDERR to file. |
| `>>& file` | Append STDOUT and STDERR to file. |
| `2>&-` | Close STDERR. |

## C Shell $argv Notation

| Notation | Description |
|----------|-------------|
| `$#argv` | Count the number of command-line arguments. |
| `$*` | Display all arguments. |
| `$argv` | Display all arguments. |
| `$argv[1-3]` | Display arguments 1 through 3. |

| Notation | Description |
|---|---|
| `$0` | Display the command used to run the shell script. |
| `$argv[n]` | Display the nth argument. |
| `$argv[$#argv}` | Display the last argument. |

## Quoting

| Character | Term | Description |
|---|---|---|
| `\` | Backslash | Nullify the special meaning of the following shell metacharacter, including another backslash. |
| `` ` ` `` | Backquotes | Substitute the output of the command enclosed in backquotes as if it were typed in place of the command. Refer to the shell manual pages for more information. |
| `' '` | Single quote | Nullify the special meaning of all characters except bang (`!`), the backslash (`\`), and the single quote itself (`'`). Single quotes are more restrictive than double quotes and do not permit variable or backquote expansion. |
| `" "` | Double quotes | Nullify the special meaning of all special characters except bang (`!`), backquote (`` ` ` ``), and dollar sign (`$`). Permits variable and backquote expansion. |

## Metacharacter Shell Syntax

| Feature | Bourne and Korn | C |
|---|---|---|
| Single-character wildcard. | ? | ? |
| Any number of characters. | * | * |
| Any one of the characters in the set of characters. | `[abc]` | `[abc]` |
| Any one character in the range of characters. | `[a-c]` | `[a-c]` |

| Feature | Bourne and Korn | C |
|---|---|---|
| Any one character not in the range of characters specified. | `[!a-c]` | N/A |

## Variable Shell Syntax

| Feature | Bourne | Korn | C |
|---|---|---|---|
| Assigning regular variables. | `x=1` | `x=1` | `set x = 1` |
| Accessing regular variables. | `echo $x` | `echo $x` | `echo $x` |
| Assigning arrays. | N/A | `y[0]=1; y[1]=2` | `set y=(1 2)` |
| Accessing array elements. | N/A | `echo $y`<br>`echo ${y[1]}` | `echo $y[1]`<br>`$y[2]` |
| Accessing entire array. | N/A | `echo ${y[*]}` | `echo $y` |
| Exporting variables (make global). | `export var` | `export var` | `setenv command` |
| Command-line arguments. | N/A | N/A | `$argv,`<br>`$#argv,`<br>`$argv[1]` |
| Positional parameters. | `$*, $#, $1` | `$*, $#, $1` | `$*, $1` |
| Setting positional parameters. | `set a b c` | `set a b c` | N/A |

## I/O Redirection and Piping

| Feature | Bourne | Korn | C |
|---|---|---|---|
| STDOUT to file. | `> filename` or<br>`1> filename` | `> filename` or<br>`1> filename` | `> filename` |
| STDIN from file. | `< filename` or<br>`0< filename` | `< filename` or<br>`0< filename` | `< filename` |
| STDERR to file. | `2> filename` | `2> filename` | N/A |

| Feature | Bourne | Korn | C |
|---|---|---|---|
| Output and errors to file. | 2>&1 | 2>&1 | >& *filename* |
| Output to next command. | \| *cmd* | \| *cmd* | \| *cmd* |
| Output and errors to next command. | 2>&1 \| | 2>&1 \| | \|& |

## Printing to the Screen

| Feature | Bourne | Korn | C |
|---|---|---|---|
| Display text and variables. | echo | print **or** echo | echo |

## Reading from the Keyboard

| Feature | Bourne | Korn | C |
|---|---|---|---|
| Read keyboard input. | read *name1* *name2* . . . | read *name1* *name2* . . . | set var = $< |

## Math and Calculations

| Feature | Bourne | Korn | C |
|---|---|---|---|
| Perform a calculation. | var=`expr a + b` | let var= a + b | @ var = (a + b) |
| Test a relational condition. | var=`expr a < b` | let var=a < b | @ var = (a < b) |

## Command Substitution

| Feature | Bourne | Korn | C |
|---|---|---|---|
| Command substitution. | `command` | $(command) **or** `command` | `command` |

## Tilde Expansion

| Feature | Korn | C |
|---|---|---|
| Tilde represents user's home directory. | `~loginid` | `~ ~loginid` |
| Tilde represents current and previous directories. | `~+ ~- -` | N/A |

## Alias Syntax

| Feature | Korn | C |
|---|---|---|
| Create new alias. | `alias name=value` | `alias name value` |
| Display current list of values. | `alias` | `alias` |
| Remove alias from list. | `unalias name` | `unalias name` |

## History Syntax

| Feature | Korn | C |
|---|---|---|
| Turn on history. | `automatic` | `set history = num` |
| Display history list. | `history` or `fc -l` | `history` |
| Display partial listing. | `history n m`<br>`history -n` | `history n` |
| Reexecute a command. | `r string`<br>`r number`<br>`r` | `!string`<br>`!number`<br>`!!` |

## Function Syntax

| Feature | Bourne and Korn | C |
|---|---|---|
| Create a function. | `func() {commands}`<br>`function func {commands}` | `func() {commands}` |
| Use a function. | Use `func` as a command | Use `func` as a command |

## Programming Statement Syntax

| Feature | Bourne and Korn | C |
|---------|-----------------|---|
| `if` conditional. | `if command` | `if (cond) then` |
| | `then`<br>  `commands`<br>`elif command`<br>`commands`<br>`else`<br>  `commands`<br>`fi` |   `commands`<br>`else if (cond) then`<br>  `commands`<br>`else`<br>  `commands`<br>`endif` |
| `switch` and `case` pattern. | `case variable in`<br>  `pattern)`<br>    `commands;;`<br>`*)`<br>    `commands;;`<br>`esac` | `switch (variable)`<br>  `case pattern:`<br>    `commands`<br>  `default:`<br>    `commands`<br>`endsw` |
| `while` loops. | `while command`<br>`do`<br>  `commands`<br>`done` | `while (cond)`<br>  `commands`<br>`end` |
| `for/foreach` loops. | `for variable in list`<br>`do`<br>  `commands`<br>`done` | `foreach variable (list)`<br>  `commands`<br>`end` |

## Test and C Shell Built-in Test

| What Is Tested | Test Command | C Shell Built-In |
|----------------|--------------|------------------|
| `file` is block device. | `-b file` | N/A |
| `file` is character device. | `-c file` | N/A |
| `file` is directory. | `-d file` | `-d file` |
| `file` or directory exists. | `-e file` (Korn shell only) | `-e file` |
| `file` is a file. | `-f file` | `-f file` |

| What Is Tested | Test Command | C Shell Built-In |
|---|---|---|
| *file* has *set-group-id* bit set. | `-g` *file* | N/A |
| *file* has sticky bit set. | `-k` *file* | N/A |
| *file* is owned by executing user. | N/A | `-o` *file* |
| *file* is a named pipe. | `-p` *file* | N/A |
| Current user can read *file*. | `-r` *file* | `-r` *file* |
| *file* exists and has size >0. | `-s` *file* | N/A |
| *n* is a terminal file descriptor. | `-t` *n* | N/A |
| *file* has set-user-id bit set. | `-u` *file* | N/A |
| Current user can write to *file*. | `-w` *file* | `-w` *file* |
| Current user can execute *file*. | `-x` *file* | N/A |
| *file* has zero size. | N/A | `-z` *file* |
| *string* is NULL. | `-z` *string* | *string* `== ""` |
| *string* is NOT NULL. | *string* `!= ""` | `-n` *string*, *string* |
| *strings* are equal. | *string* `=` *string* | *string* `==` *string* |
| *strings* are not equal. | *string* `!=` *string* | *string* `!=` *string* |

| What Is Tested | Test Command | C Shell Built-In |
|---|---|---|
| *string* matches file name wildcard pattern. | N/A | *string =~ pattern* |
| *string* does not match file name wildcard pattern. | N/A | *string !~ pattern* |
| *num1* is equal to *num2*. | *num1* -eq *num2* | *num1* == *num2* |
| *num1* is not equal to *num2*. | *num1* -ne *num2* | *num1* != *num2* |
| *num1* is less than *num2*. | *num1* -lt *num2* | *num1* < *num2* |
| *num1* is less than or equal to *num2*. | *num1* -le *num2* | *num1* <= *num2* |
| *num1* is greater than *num2*. | *num1* -gt *num2* | *num1* > *num2* |
| *num1* is greater than or equal to *num2*. | *num1* -ge *num2* | *num1* >= *num2* |
| Logical AND. | -a | && |
| Logical OR. | -o | \|\| |
| Logical NEGATION. | ! | !! |

## Bourne Shell Mathematical Operators

| Operator | Description |
|---|---|
| + | Addition. |
| − | Subtraction. |
| * | Multiplication. |
| / | Division. |
| % | Remainder (modulus). |

## C Shell Mathematical Operators

| Syntax | Description |
|---|---|
| @ *variable* = (*expression*) | Set value of *variable* equal to the *expression*. |
| @ *variable* += (*expression*) | Addition. |
| @ *variable* -= (*expression*) | Subtraction. |
| @ *variable* *= (*expression*) | Multiplication. |
| @ *variable* /= (*expression*) | Division. |
| @ *variable* ++ | Add 1. |
| @ *variable* -- | Subtract 1. |

# Example Scripts

These sections contain some examples of Bourne shell scripts.

## Anonymous ftp Script

A script named `fez` performs an anonymous `ftp get` or `list`. Refer to the Description comments in the script for information about how the FTP site is determined.

```
#!/bin/sh
#
#       @(#)fez,v1.0                        (me@anywhere.EBay.Sun.COM) 08/29/92
#
PATHNAME=anywhere.EBay:/home/me/bin/fez
MYNAME=`basename $0`
#
# Author:
#       Wayne Thompson
#
# Synopsis:
usage=`/bin/sed -e "s/^ *//" << endusage
        usage: $MYNAME [-h] [-abfglmprR] [[login@]hostname:[sourcepath]]
endusage`
#
# Description:
#       This script will perform an anonymous ftp get or list.
#
#       If the hostname is not specified on the command line, then
#       it is derived from the basename(1) of the current directory.
#       This provides for a hierarchy of hostnames within which to
#       get files or directory listings.
#
#       If no flags and arguments are given or a single argument of
#       the form "hostname:" is given, the default action will be
#       to retrieve a recursive directory listing from the remote
#       host into the file "./ls-lR.".
#
```

```
#       Directory listings are named in the following manner:
#           <the command used to produce the listing w/spaces collapsed>
#           followed by the path it was produced from with slashes(/)
#           transliterated to dots(.). e.g.
#               ls-1.           (ls -l /)
#               ls-1R.a.b       (ls -1R /a/b)
#
#       When mirroring is enabled (default), the directory listing
#       "ls-1R.a.b" would be placed in the directory "./a/b" which
#       would be created if necessary.
#       Likewise, "fez export.lcs.mit.edu:/contrib/3dlife.c" would
#       get "/contrib/3dlife.c" from "export.lcs.mit.edu" and place
#       it into "./contrib/3dlife.c".
#       An alternative behavior is provided by the "-f" flag, which
#       serves to flatten the destination hierarchy.
#       "fez -f export.lcs.mit.edu:/contrib/3dlife.c" would get
#       "/contrib/3dlife.c" into "./3dlife.c"
#
#       The default user is "anonymous".
#       The default password is one of:
#           internal to Sun = $USER@hostname
#           external to Sun = $USER@Sun.Com
#       You may override these in $HOME/.netrc (see netrc(5))
#       or from the command line.
#
# Options:
#       -a          ascii mode
#       -b          binary mode                         (default)
#       -f          flatten hierarchy
#       -g          get                                 (default w/arg)
#       -h          print command description.
#       -l          list                                (default w/o arg)
#       -m          mirror hierarchy                    (default)
#       -p passwd   password
#       -(r|R)      recursive                           (default w/o arg)
#
# Environment:
#
# Files:
#       $HOME/.netrc                file for ftp remote login data
#
# Diagnostics:
#       Exit Status:
#           0       normal termination
#           1       abnormal termination
#
#       Errors (stderr):
#           usage
#
#       Warnings (stderr):
#
#       Info (stdout):
#
# Dependencies:
#       Fez only knows how to talk to UNIX(R) hosts.
#
# Caveats:
#       A recursive directory get will not fetch subdirectories unless
#       they already exist.
#
# Bugs:
#

# >> BEGIN parse options >>>>>>>>>>>>>>>>>>>>>>>>>>>>>>>>>>>>>>>>>>>> #
while [ $# -gt 0 ]
do
    case $1 in
        -??*)                                           # bundled options
            opts=$1
            while [ $opts ]
            do
                opts=`/bin/expr $opts : '.\(.*\)'`
                case $opts in
                    a*)                                 # ascii mode
                        mode=asci
```

```
                               ;;
            b*)                           # binary mode
                mode=binary
                ;;
            f*)                           # flatten remote hierarchy
                flat=true
                ;;
            g*)                           # get
                ;;
            l*)                           # list
                list=true
                ;;
            p)
                passflg=true
                shift
                if [ $# -eq 0 ]
                then
                    echo >&2 "$MYNAME: error: no passwd"
                    echo >&2 "usage"
                    exit 1
                fi
                passwd=$1
                ;;
            p*)
                echo >&2 "$MYNAME: error: p: must be last element of
                 bundled options"
                exit 1
                ;;
            [rR]*)                        # recursive
                recurse=true
                ;;
            ?*)
                echo >&2 "$MYNAME: error: -`/bin/expr $opts :
'\(.\)'`:
                 unknown option."
                echo >&2 "$usage"
                exit 1
                ;;
        esac
    done
    shift
    ;;

    -a)                                   # ascii mode
    mode=ascii
    shift
    ;;

    -b)                                   # binary mode
    mode=binary
    shift
    ;;

    -f)                                   # flatten remote hierarchy
    flat=true
    shift
    ;;

    -g)                                   # get
    shift
    ;;

    -h)                                   # help
    /bin/awk '
        /^$/ {
            exit;
        }
```

```
                      /^[# :]/ && NR > 1 {
                          print substr ($0, 3);
                      }
                  ' $0 |
              /bin/sed "
                  /^$/{
                      N
                      /^\n$/D
                  }
                  s/\$MYNAME/$MYNAME/
              "
              exit 0
              ;;

    -l)                                           # list
          list=true
          shift
          ;;

    -m)                                           # mirror remote hierarchy
          mirror=true
          shift
          ;;

    -p)
          passflg=true
          shift
          if [ $# -eq 0 ]
          then
              echo >&2 "$MYNAME: error: no passwd"
              echo >&2 "usage"
              exit 1
          fi
          passwd=$1
          shift
          ;;

    -[rR])                                        # recursive
          recurse=true
          shift
          ;;

    --)                                           # end of options
          shift
          break
          ;;

    -*)
          echo >&2 "$MYNAME: error: $1: unknown option."
          echo >&2 "$usage"
          exit 1
          ;;

    *)                                            # end of options
          break
          ;;
    esac
done

# << END parse options <<<<<<<<<<<<<<<<<<<<<<<<<<<<<<<<<<<<<<<<<<<< #

# >> BEGIN parse arguments >>>>>>>>>>>>>>>>>>>>>>>>>>>>>>>>>>>>>>>> #

case $# in
    0)
        list=true
        recurse=true
        ;;

    1)
        case $1 in
            *:)
                list=true
                recurse=true
                ;;
        esac
```

```
        ;;
    *)
        echo >&2 "$MYNAME: error: unexpected argument(s)."
        echo >&2 "$usage"
        exit 1
        ;;
esac

# << END parse arguments <<<<<<<<<<<<<<<<<<<<<<<<<<<<<<<<<<<<<<<<<< #

# >> BEGIN initialization >>>>>>>>>>>>>>>>>>>>>>>>>>>>>>>>>>>>>>>>> #

[ umask -ge 700 ] && umask `/bin/expr \`umask\` - 0700`

# return unrooted dirname
dirname () {
    expr \
    './'${1-.}'/' : '\(\.\)/[^/]*/$' \
    \| ${1-.}'/' : '/*\(.*[^/]\)//*[^/][^/]*//*$' \
    \| .
}
[ ${1-.} = / ] && set .
host=`/bin/expr \
    "$1" : '[^@]*@\(.*\):' \
    \| "$1" : '\(.*\):' \
    \| \`/bin/basename \\\`pwd\\\`\``
path=`/bin/expr "$1" : '[^:]*:\(.*\)' \| $1. : '[^:]*:\(.*\)' \| ${1-.}`
dir=`dirname $path`
file=`/bin/basename $path`
login=`/bin/expr "$1" : '\([^@]*\)@' \| anonymous`
if /bin/ypmatch $host hosts.byname 2>&- 1>&- ||
   /bin/ypmatch $host hosts.byaddr 2>&- 1>&-
then
    port=21
    passwd=${passwd-USER@`hostname`}
else
    port=4666
    passwd=${passwd-USER@Sun.COM}
    machine=$host
    host=sun-barr.EBay
fi

if [ $list ]
then
    cmd="ls -l${recurse+R}"
    file=ls-l${recurse+R}`expr \
        $path : '\(\.\)$' \
        \| $dir$file : '\(\..*\)' \
        \| /$dir/$file | tr / .`

    dir=$path
else
    cmd=${recurse+m}get
    [ $recurse ] && dir=$path && file=\*
fi

case $1 in
    *@*:*)
        ;;
    *)
        [ $passflg ] ||
        eval `
            /bin/awk '
                /machine *'"${machine-$host}"'/ {
                    for (i = 1; i <= NF; i++) {
                        if ($i == "login") print "login="$++i";";
                        if ($i == "password") print "passwd="$++i";";
                    }
                    exit;
                }
            ' $HOME/.netrc 2>&-`
        ;;
esac
```

```
# << END initialization <<<<<<<<<<<<<<<<<<<<<<<<<<<<<<<<<<<<<<<<< #

# >> BEGIN verify prerequisites >>>>>>>>>>>>>>>>>>>>>>>>>>>>>>>> #

if [ ! "$flat" ]
then
    /bin/mkdir -p $dir 2>&-
    cd $dir
fi

# << END verify prerequisites <<<<<<<<<<<<<<<<<<<<<<<<<<<<<<<<< #

# >> BEGIN main >>>>>>>>>>>>>>>>>>>>>>>>>>>>>>>>>>>>>>>>>>>>>>> #

/usr/ucb/ftp -i -n -v $host $port << EOFTP
    user $login${machine+@$machine} $passwd
    ${mode-binary}
    cd $dir
    $cmd $file
    quit
EOFTP
echo ""

# << END main <<<<<<<<<<<<<<<<<<<<<<<<<<<<<<<<<<<<<<<<<<<<<<<< #
```

# arch.sh.fctn Function

The `arch.sh.fctn` script emulates SunOS 4.x system architecture.

```
#
#  %M%:    Version:  %I%    Date:    %G%
#

[ $_Arch_loaded ] || {

# Function:
#     @(#)Arch                     (Wayne.Thompson@Sun.COM) 05/14/92
#
# Description:
#     This function emulates 4.x arch(1).
#
# Variables:
#
# Usage:
#     Arch
#     Arch -k
#     Arch archname
#
# Return:
#     0 success
#     1 non-success
#
# Dependencies:
#     This function works under SunOs 3.x - 5.x.
#
# Bugs:
#

Arch () {
    case $1 in
        '')
            /bin/arch $* 2>&- || /bin/expr `/bin/uname -m` : '\(sun[0-9]*\)'
            ;;

        -k)
            /bin/arch $* 2>&- || /bin/uname -m
            ;;
```

```
        *)
            if [ -x /bin/arch ]
            then
                /bin/arch $*
            else
                [ $* = `/bin/expr \`/bin/uname -m\` : '\(sun[0-9]*\)'` ]
            fi
            ;;
    esac
}

_Arch_loaded=1
}
```

# array.sh.fctn Function

The following function extends the functionality of the Bourne shell to include associative arrays.

```
## >> BEGIN package: arrays >>>>>>>>>>>>>>>>>>>>>>>>>>>>>>>>>>>>>>>> ##

# Package:
#     @(#)arrays,v1.0                    (Wayne.Thompson@Sun.COM) 05/02/93
#
# Description:
#     This package contains functions that emulate associative arrays.
#     Keys are limited to letters, digits, underscores, hyphens and periods.
#
# Variables:
#     __array_size_<array>
#     __array_keys_<array>
#     __array__<array>_<key>
#     __array_filename
#     __array_name
#     __array_key
#     __array_keys
#     __array_cell
#
# Usage:
#     setarray array key [value ...]
#     getarray array key
#     unsetarray array [key ...]
#     keys array
#     sizearray array
#     defined array [key]
#     dumparray pathname [array ...]
#
# Dependencies:
#     Array names and keys are combined to form strings which are
#     evaluated as parameters.
#
# Bugs:
#

### >> BEGIN function: setarray >>>>>>>>>>>>>>>>>>>>>>>>>>>>>>>>>>>> ###

# Function:
#     @(#)setarray,v1.0                  (Wayne.Thompson@Sun.COM) 05/16/93
#
# Description:
#     This function assigns values to array elements. If more than one
#     value is provided and the key is an integer, values will be
#     assigned to successive elements beginning with the initial key.
#
# Variables:
#     __array_size_<array>
#     __array_keys_<array>
#     __array__<array>_<key>
```

```
#       __array_name
#       __array_key
#       __array_cell
#
# Usage:
#     setarray array key [value ...]
#     setarray pathname
#
# Return:
#
# Dependencies:
#
# Bugs:
#
setarray () {
    case $# in
        0)
            echo >&2 setarray: error: "$@"
            echo >&2 usage: setarray array key '[value ...]'
            exit 1
            ;;

        1)
            if [ -f $1 ]
            then
                while read __array_name __array_key __array_value
                do
                    setarray $__array_name $__array_key $__array_value
                done < $1
                return
            else
                echo >&2 setarray: error: $1: no such file
                exit 1
            fi
            ;;

        2|3)
            ;;

        *)
            case $2 in
                [0-9]*)
                    ;;

                *)
                    echo >&2 setarray: error: "$@"
                    echo >&2 setarray: error: 2nd argument must be an integer
                    exit 1
                    ;;
            esac
            ;;
    esac
    __array_name=$1
    __array_key=$2
    case $2 in
        *[-.]*)
            __array_cell=`echo $2 | /bin/tr '[-.]' __`
            shift 2
            set $__array_name $__array_cell "$@"
            ;;
    esac
    eval "
        if [ \${__array_size_$1+1} ]
        then
            [ \${__array__$1_$2+1} ] || {
                __array_size_$1=\`/bin/expr \$__array_size_$1 + 1\`
                __array_keys_$1=\"\$__array_keys_$1 \$__array_key \"
            }
        else
            __array_size_$1=1
            __array_keys_$1=\$__array_key
        fi
        __array__$1_$2=\$3
    "
    case $# in
```

```
        2)
            shift 2
            ;;

        *)
            shift 3
            ;;
    esac
    while [ $# -gt 0 ]
    do
        __array_key=`/bin/expr $__array_key + 1`
        eval "
            [ \${__array__${__array_name}_$__array_key+1} ] || {
                __array_size_$__array_name=\`/bin/expr
\$__array_size_$__array_name + 1\`
                __array_keys_$__array_name=\"\$__array_keys_$__array_name
\$__array_key\"
            }
            __array__${__array_name}_$__array_key=\$1
        "
        shift
    done
}

### << END function: setarray <<<<<<<<<<<<<<<<<<<<<<<<<<<<<<<<<<<<< ###

### >> BEGIN function: getarray >>>>>>>>>>>>>>>>>>>>>>>>>>>>>>>>>>>>>>> ###

# Function:
#     @(#)getarray,v1.0                   (Wayne.Thompson@Sun.COM) 05/02/93
#
# Description:
#     This function prints array values.
#
# Variables:
#     __array__<array>_<key>
#     __array_name
#
# Usage:
#     getarray array [key ...]
#
# Return:
#
# Dependencies:
#
# Bugs:
#

getarray () {
    case $# in
        0)
            echo >&2 getarray: error: "$@"
            echo >&2 usage: getarray array '[key ...]'
            exit 1
            ;;

        1)  # entire array
            set $1 `keys $1`
            ;;
    esac
    __array_name=$1
    shift
    while [ $# -gt 0 ]
    do
        case $1 in
        *[-.]*)
            eval echo \$__array__${__array_name}_`echo $1 |
            /bin/tr '[-.]' __`
            ;;

        *)
            eval echo \$__array__${__array_name}_$1
            ;;
        esac
        shift
```

```
    done
}

### << END function: getarray <<<<<<<<<<<<<<<<<<<<<<<<<<<<<<<<< ###

### >> BEGIN function: unsetarray >>>>>>>>>>>>>>>>>>>>>>>>>>>>> ###

# Function:
#     @(#)unsetarray,v1.0                    (Wayne.Thompson@Sun.COM) 05/02/93
#
# Description:
#     This function unsets (undefines) one or more array elements
#     or an entire array.
#
# Variables:
#     __array_size_<array>
#     __array_keys_<array>
#     __array_<array>_<key>
#     __array_name
#     __array_key
#     __array_keys
#
# Usage:
#     unsetarray array [key ...]
#
# Return:
#
# Dependencies:
#
# Bugs:
#
unsetarray () {
    case $# in
        0)
            echo >&2 unsetarray: error: "$@"
            echo >&2 usage: unsetarray array '[key ...]'
            exit 1
            ;;

        1)  # entire array
            set $1 `keys $1`
            ;;
    esac

    __array_name=$1
    shift

    while [ $# -gt 0 ]
    do
        eval "
            __array_keys=
            [ \${__array__${__array_name}_$1+1} ] &&
            for __array_key in \$__array_keys_$__array_name
            do
                case \$__array_key in
                    \$1)
                        case \$1 in
                            *[-.]*)
                                unset __array__${__array_name}_\`echo \$1 |
                                /bin/tr '[-.]' __\`
                                ;;

                            *)
                                unset __array__${__array_name}_$1
                                ;;
                        esac
                        __array_size_$__array_name=\`/bin/expr
                        \$__array_size_$__array_name - 1\`
                        ;;

                    *)
                        case \$__array_keys in
                            '')
                                __array_keys=\$__array_key
                                ;;
```

```
                              *)
                                  __array_keys=\"\$__array_keys \$__array_key\"
                                  ;;
                        esac
                        ;;
                esac
            done
            __array_keys_$__array_name=\$__array_keys
        "
        shift
    done
    eval "
        case \$__array_size_$__array_name in
            0)
                unset __array_size_$__array_name __array_keys_$__array_name
                ;;
        esac
    "
}

### << END function: unsetarray <<<<<<<<<<<<<<<<<<<<<<<<<<<<<<<<< ###

### >> BEGIN function: keys >>>>>>>>>>>>>>>>>>>>>>>>>>>>>>>>>>>>> ###

# Function:
#     @(#)keys,v1.0                        (Wayne.Thompson@Sun.COM) 05/02/93
#
# Description:
#     This function prints the keys of an array.
#
# Variables:
#     __array_keys_<array>
#
# Usage:
#     keys array
#
# Return:
#
# Dependencies:
#
# Bugs:
#

keys () {
    case $# in
        1)
            eval echo \$__array_keys_$1
            ;;

        *)
            echo >&2 keys: error: "$@"
            echo >&2 usage: keys array
            exit 1
            ;;
    esac
}

### << END function: keys <<<<<<<<<<<<<<<<<<<<<<<<<<<<<<<<<<<<<<< ###

### >> BEGIN function: sizearray >>>>>>>>>>>>>>>>>>>>>>>>>>>>>>>> ###

# Function:
#     @(#)sizearray,v1.0                   (Wayne.Thompson@Sun.COM) 05/02/93
#
# Description:
#     This function prints the number of defined array elements.
#
# Variables:
#     __array_size_<array>
#
# Usage:
#     sizearray array
#
# Return:
#
```

```
# Dependencies:
#
# Bugs:
#
sizearray () {
    case $# in
        1)
                eval echo \${__array_size_$1:-0}
                ;;

        *)
                echo >&2 sizearray: error: "$@"
                echo >&2 usage: sizearray array
                exit 1
                ;;
    esac
}

### << END function: sizearray <<<<<<<<<<<<<<<<<<<<<<<<<<<<<<<<<<< ###

### >> BEGIN function: defined >>>>>>>>>>>>>>>>>>>>>>>>>>>>>>>>>> ###

# Function:
#     @(#)defined,v1.0                    (Wayne.Thompson@Sun.COM) 05/02/93
#
# Description:
#     This function returns whether an array element or array is defined.
#
# Variables:
#     __array_size_<array>
#     __array__<array>_<key>
#
# Usage:
#     defined array [key]
#
# Return:
#     0           defined
#     1           undefined
#
# Dependencies:
#
# Bugs:
#
defined () {
    case $# in
        1)
                eval set \${__array_size_$1+0} 1
                ;;

        2)
                case $2 in
                    *[-.]*) set $1 `echo $2 | /bin/tr '[-.]' __`;;
                esac
                eval set \${__array__$1_$2+0} 1
                ;;

        *)
                echo >&2 defined: error: "$@"
                echo >&2 usage: defined array '[key]'
                exit 1
                ;;
    esac
    return $1
}

### << END function: defined <<<<<<<<<<<<<<<<<<<<<<<<<<<<<<<<<<< ###

### >> BEGIN function: dumparray >>>>>>>>>>>>>>>>>>>>>>>>>>>>>>>>>> ###

# Function:
#     @(#)dumparray,v1.0                  (Wayne.Thompson@Sun.COM) 05/02/93
#
# Description:
#     This function dumps arrays in file in a format readable by
```

```
#       shell dot (.) command.
#
# Variables:
#       __array_filename
#
# Usage:
#       dumparray pathname [array ...]
#
# Return:
#       0               success
#       1               failure
#
# Dependencies:
#
# Bugs:
#       Since this depends on the output of set, and set does not preserve
#       quoting, the resultant file may be unusable. Use of
#       storearray/setarray is safer, albeit slower.
#

dumparray () {
    case $# in
        0)
            echo >&2 dumparray: error: "$@"
            echo >&2 usage: dumparray pathname '[array ...]'
            exit 1
            ;;
    esac

    __array_filename=$1
    shift

    set |
    /bin/awk '
        /\(\)$/ { exit }                    # functions follow parameters

        /^__array_(filename|name|key|keys|cell)=/ { next }      # temp storage

        /^__array_(size|keys)*_(`echo ${*:-.\*} | /bin/tr " " \|`)(_|=)/ {
            if (NF > 1) {
                n = index($0, "=");
                print substr($0 , 1, n)"'\''"substr($0, n+1)"'\''";
            }
            else {
                print;
            }
        }
    ' > $__array_filename
}

### << END function: dumparray <<<<<<<<<<<<<<<<<<<<<<<<<<<<<<<<< ###

## << END package: arrays <<<<<<<<<<<<<<<<<<<<<<<<<<<<<<<<<<<<<<<< ##
```

The function scripts `arch.sh.fctn` (displayed earlier in this chapter), `hostname.sh.fctn`, `osr.sh.fctn`, and `whoami.sh.fctn` are used to help in the transition from SunOS 4.*x* to Solaris 2.*x*.

## hostname.sh.fctn Function

The `hostname.sh.fctn` script emulates the SunOS 4.x `hostname` command.

```
#
# %M%:    Version:  %I%    Date:    %G%
#
```

```
[ $_Hostname_loaded ] || {

# Function:
#     @(#)hostname                      (Wayne.Thompson@Sun.COM) 02/15/92
#
# Description:
#     This function emulates 4.x hostname(1) given no arguments.
#
# Variables:
#
# Usage:
#     Hostname
#
# Return:
#
# Dependencies:
#     This funcion works under SunOs 3.x - 5.x.
#
# Bugs:
#

Hostname () {
    /bin/hostname 2>&- || /bin/uname -n
}

_Hostname_loaded=1
}
```

## osr.sh.fctn Function

The `osr.sh.fctn` script outputs the numeric portion of the current
operating system release—for example, 5.2 for Solaris 5.2 system software.

```
#
#   %M%:    Version:  %I%    Date:      %G%
#

[ $_Osr_loaded ] || {

# Function:
#     @(#)Osr                           (Wayne.Thompson@Sun.COM) 02/08/92
#
# Description:
#     This function outputs the numeric portion of the current OS release.
#
# Variables:
#
# Usage:
#     os=`Osr`
#
# Return:
#     0 success
#     1 non-success
#
# Dependencies:
#     This funcion works under SunOs 3.x - 5.x.
#
# Bugs:
#

Osr () {
    /bin/expr `
        {
            /bin/uname -r ||
            /bin/cat /usr/sys/conf*/RELEASE
        } 2>&- ||
        /etc/dmesg |
```

```
        /bin/awk '
            BEGIN { status = 1 }
            /^SunOS Release/ { print $3; status = 0; exit }
            END { exit status }
        ' ||
        /bin/expr "\`
            /usr/ucb/strings -50 /vmunix |
            /bin/egrep '^SunOS Release'
        \`" : 'SunOS Release \([^ ]*\)'
    ` : '\([.0-9]*\)'
}

_Osr_loaded=1
}
```

# whoami.sh.fctn Function

The whoami.sh.fctn emulates the SunOS 4.x whoami command.

```
#
#  @(#)  whoami.sh.fctn        1.2     Last mod: 6/4/93
#

[ $_Whoami_loaded ] || {

# Function:
#     @(#)whoami                      (Wayne.Thompson@Sun.COM) 03/20/92
#
# Description:
#     This function emulates 4.x whoami(1).
#
# Variables:
#
# Usage:
#     whoami
#
# Return:
#
# Dependencies:
#     This funcion works under SunOs 3.x - 5.x.
#
# Bugs:
#

Whoami () {
    /usr/ucb/whoami 2>&- ||
    /bin/expr "\`/bin/id\`" : '[^(]*(\([^)]*\)'
}

_Whoami_loaded=1
}
```

# Part Seven

# System Security

This part introduces system security in four chapters. Chapter 20 introduces the basic concepts of system security, including file, system, and network security. Chapter 21 describes how to use ASET. Chapter 22 describes authentication methods. It provides an overview of DES encryption and Diffie-Hellman authentication. It also explains how to use pluggable authentication modules (PAM). Chapter 23 describes the new Role-Based Access Control (RBAC) functionality available in the Solaris 8 Version 3 release.

*New!*

Refer to these chapters if you want to familiarize yourself with the basics of system security, if you want to use authentication services and ASET security, and if you want to assign system administrators rights to perform certain sets of system administration tasks.

# 20

# *UNDERSTANDING SYSTEM SECURITY*

Managing system security is an important part of system administration. This chapter provides information about managing system security at the file, system, and network level.

At the file level, the Solaris Operating Environment provides some standard security features that you can use to protect files, directories, and devices. At the system and network levels, the security issues are similar. In the workplace, a number of systems connected to a server can be viewed as a large, multifaceted system. When you are responsible for the security of this larger system or network, it is important for you to defend the network from outsiders trying to gain access. In addition, it is important to ensure the integrity of the data on the systems within the network.

## New Security Features in the Solaris 8 Release

This section describes security features introduced in the Solaris 8.

### New Default Ownership and Permissions on System Files and Directories

The Solaris 8 release provides stricter default ownership and permissions than in previous releases. The following list describes the changes to default ownership and permissions.

*NOTE. These changes apply to only some files and directories in the Solaris 8 release. For example, the changes do not apply to OpenWindows or CDE files and directories.*

- Default file and directory ownership is changed from `bin` to `root`.
- Files and directories have default permissions of `755` instead of `775`.
- Files and directories have default permissions of `644` instead of `664`.
- The default system `umask` is `022`.

When creating a package to be added to a system running the Solaris 8 release, keep the following in mind.

- All files and directories must have root as the default owner.
- Directories and executables must have default permissions of `555` or `755`.
- Ordinary files must have default permissions of `644` or `444`.
- Files with setuid or setgid ownership cannot be writable by the owner unless the owner is root.

## Role-Based Access Control

Role-based access control (RBAC) provides a flexible way to package superuser privileges for assignment to user accounts or to role accounts so that you can grant partial superuser privileges to a user who needs to solve a specific problem.

RBAC was introduced in the Solaris 8 release. With the Solaris 8 Version 3 release, the Solaris Operating Environment provides a set of graphical user interface tools in the Solaris Management Console (SMC) to administer RBAC. See Chapter 23, "Role-Based Access Control," for more information about RBAC and a description of how to use the SMC tools with RBAC.

## Sun Enterprise Authentication Mechanism (SEAM) or Kerberos V5 Client Support

The Solaris 8 release provides the Kerberos V5 client-side infrastructure, an addition to the Pluggable Authentication Module (PAM), and commands that you can use to secure RPC-based applications such as the NFS service. Kerberos provides selectable strong user or server level authentication, integrity, or privacy support. You can use the Kerberos client in conjunction with Sun Enterprise Authentication Mechanism (SEAM), a part of Sun Easy Access Server (SEAS) 3.0, or other Kerberos V5 software (for example, the M.I.T. distribution) to create a complete, single-network, sign-on solution.

Note that the Solaris 8 release provides only the client-side part of the SEAM product. To use this product you must install the Key Distribution Center (KDC) with either the SEAS 3.0 release, Solaris 8 Admin Pack, the M.I.T. distribution, or Windows2000.

SEAM is available as a free download from `www.sun.com/bigadmin/content/adminPack` as part of the Solaris 8 Admin Pack.

Describing how to administer SEAM is beyond the scope of this book. For more information, refer to the Sun SEAM documentation or to the *Solaris System Administration Guide, Volume II*. Sun documentation is available online at `http://docs.sun.com`.

# New Security Features in the Solaris 2.6 Release

Starting with the Solaris 2.6 release. the following new features are provided to enhance security.

- The Pluggable Authentication Module (PAM) framework.

- A `noexec_user_stack` variable, set in the `/etc/system` file, which enables you to specify whether stack mappings are executable.

## Pluggable Authentication Module (PAM)

PAM enables you to plug in new authentication technologies without changing the `login`, `ftp`, or `telnet` commands. You can also use PAM to integrate UNIX login with other security mechanisms, such as data encryption standard (DES) or Kerberos. You can also use this framework to plug in mechanisms for account, session, and password management. See Chapter 22, "Using Authentication Services," for more information.

## Executable Stacks and Security

A number of security bugs are related to default executable stacks when permissions are set to read, write, and execute. Although the SPARC and Intel application binary interface (ABI) mandates that stacks have execute permissions, most programs can function correctly without using executable stacks.

Starting with the Solaris 2.6 release, a `noexec_user_stack` variable enables you to specify whether stack mappings are executable. By default, the value for the variable is 0, which provides ABI-compliant behavior. If the variable is set to non-zero, the system marks the stack of every process in the system as readable and writable but not executable.

## Disabling Programs from Using Executable Stacks

Use the following steps to disable programs from using executable stacks.

1. Become superuser.
2. Edit the `/etc/system` file and add the following two lines.

   **`set noexec_user_stack=1`**
3. Save the changes and reboot the system.

*New!*

When the `noexec_user_stack` variable is set to a non-zero value, programs that execute code on their stack are sent a `SIGSEGV` signal, which usually terminates the program with a core dump. When the `noexec_user_stack_log` variable is set to a non-zero value, core dump programs also generate a warning message, which includes the name of the program, the PID, and the UID of the user who ran the program, as shown in the following example.

```
a.out[347] attempt to execute code on stack by uid 555
```

The message is logged by the `syslogd`(1M) daemon when the `syslog` kern facility is set to `notice` level. This logging is set by default in the `syslog.conf`(4) file, which means that the message is sent to both the console and to the `/var/adm/messages` file.

When you have set the `noexec_user_stack` variable, you can monitor these messages to observe potential security problems. You can also monitor the messages to identify valid programs that depend on executable stacks and have been prevented from correct operation.

You can explicitly mark program stacks as executable with the `mprotect`(2) function. See the `mprotect`(2) manual page for more information.

> *NOTE. Because of hardware limitations, executable stack problems can be caught and reported only on sun4m, sun4d, and sun4u platforms.*

## Disabling Executable Stack Message Logging

If you do not want to log executable stack messages, you can set the `noexec_user_stack_log` variable to zero in the `/etc/system` file. Note that even if you disable executable stack message logging, the `SIGSEGV` signal may continue to dump core for the executing program.

Use the following steps to disable executable stack message logging.

1. Become superuser.
2. Add the line **set noexec_user_stack_log=0** to the /etc/system file.
3. Reboot the system.

# Overview of System Security

The first line of security defense is to control access to systems. You can control and monitor system access in the following ways.

- Maintain physical site security.
- Maintain login control.
- Restrict access to data in files.
- Maintain network control.
- Monitor system use.
- Set the path variable correctly.
- Monitor setuid and setgid programs.
- Track superuser (root) login.
- Install a firewall.
- Report security problems.
- Use the Automated Security Enhancement Tool (ASET).
- Use role-based access control (RBAC) to grant users rights to perform specific system administration tasks without full superuser access.

*New!*

## Maintaining Physical Site Security

To control access to systems, your company must maintain the physical security of the computer environment. For instance, if a user logs in to a system and leaves it unattended, anyone who can use that system can gain access to the operating system and the network. Be aware of your users' surroundings and educate users to physically protect the computers from unauthorized access.

## Maintaining Login and Access Control

Use password and login control to restrict unauthorized logins to a system or to the network. All accounts on a system should have a password. A single account without a password makes your entire network accessible to anyone who knows or can guess a user name.

The Solaris Operating Environment restricts control of certain system devices to the user login account. Only a process running as superuser or console user can access a system mouse, keyboard, frame buffer, or audio device unless `/etc/logindevperm` is edited. See the `logindevperm`(4) manual page for more information.

## Restricting Access to Data in Files

Use UNIX directory and file permissions to control access to the data on your users' systems. You may want to enable some people to read certain files and grant other people permission to change or delete certain files. You may have data that you do not want anyone else to see. See "File Security" on page 523 for information on how to set file permissions.

## Maintaining Network Control

Computers are often part of a configuration of systems called a network. A *network* enables connected systems to exchange information and access data and other resources that are available from systems connected to the network. Networking has created a powerful and sophisticated way of computing. However, networking introduces the opportunity for breaches in computer security.

For example, within a network of computers, individual systems are open to enable sharing of information. Because many people have access to the network, the opportunity for unwanted access is increased, especially through user error, such as a poor choice of passwords.

## Monitoring System Use

Be aware of all aspects of the systems that are your responsibility, including the following.

- What is the normal load?
- Who has access to the system?
- When do individuals access the system?

Use the available tools to audit system use and monitor the activities of individual users. Monitoring is useful when you suspect a breach in security.

## Setting the Correct Path

Path variables are important. They can prevent users from accidentally running a program introduced by someone else that harms data on a system. A program that creates a security hazard is referred to as a *Trojan horse*. For example, a substitute switch user (su) program could be placed in a public directory where you, as system administrator, might run it. Such a script would look like the regular su command that you use to gain superuser access. Because it removes itself after execution, it is difficult to tell that you have actually run a Trojan horse.

The path variable is automatically set at login time through the .login, .profile, and .cshrc startup files. Set up the user search path so that the current directory (.) comes last to prevent you or your users from running this type of Trojan horse. Never include a publicly writable directory in root's search path. The path variable for superuser should not include the current directory at all. The ASET command examines the startup files to ensure that the path variable is set up correctly and that it does not contain a dot (.) entry. See Chapter 21, "Using the Automated Security Enhancement Tool (ASET)," for more information.

## Monitoring setuid and setgid Programs

Many executable programs must be run as root or superuser to work properly. These executables run with the UID set to 0 (setuid=0). Anyone running these programs runs them with the root ID, which creates a potential security problem if the programs are not written with security in mind.

You should not allow the use of setuid programs except for executables shipped with setuid to root. At the least, you should restrict and keep these programs to a minimum.

Setgid programs enable a running program to change its group ID from that of the user running to the group ID of the running program, which creates a potential security problem if the programs are not written with security in mind. Setgid programs are just as dangerous as setuid programs.

*New!*

## Installing a Firewall

Another way to protect your network is to use a firewall or secure gateway system. A *firewall* is a dedicated system that separates two networks, each of which approaches the other as untrusted. Consider a firewall setup as mandatory between your internal network and any external networks, such as the Internet, with which you want internal network users to communicate.

A firewall can also be useful between some internal networks. For example, the firewall or secure gateway computer does not send a packet between two networks unless the gateway computer is the origin or the destination address of the packet. Set up a firewall to forward packets for particular protocols only. For example, you may allow packets for transferring mail, but not for `telnet` or `rlogin`. The ASET command, when run at high security, disables the forwarding of Internet Protocol (IP) packets. See Chapter 21, "Using the Automated Security Enhancement Tool (ASET)," for more information.

## Reporting Security Problems

If you experience a suspected security breach, you can contact the Computer Emergency Response Team/Coordination Center (CERT/CC), which is a project funded by the Defense Advanced Research Projects Agency (DARPA) located at the Software Engineering Institute at Carnegie Mellon University. It can assist you with any security problems you are having. It can also direct you to other CERTs that may be more appropriate for your particular needs. You can contact them in the following ways.

- CERT/CC 24-hour hotline: 412-268-7090.
- E-mail: `cert@cert.org`.
- URL: `http://www.cert.org/`.

*New!*

## Using the Automated Security Enhancement Tool (ASET)

The automated security enhancement tool (ASET) enables you to monitor and control system security by automatically performing tasks that you would otherwise do manually.

ASET consists of seven tasks, each performing specific checks and adjustments to file systems.

- System files permissions verification.
- System files checks.
- User/group checks.
- System configuration files check.
- Environment check.
- EEPROM check.
- Firewall setup.

The ASET tasks tighten file permissions, check the contents of critical system files for security weaknesses, and monitor crucial areas. ASET can safeguard a network by applying the basic requirements of a firewall system to a system that serves as a gateway system. See Chapter 21, "Using the Automated Security Enhancement Tool (ASET)," for more information.

## Using Role-Based Access Control (RBAC)

Role-based access control (RBAC)—introduced in the Solaris 8 release and enhanced with a set of graphical user interface tools in the Solaris 8 Version 3 release—enables the *primary administrator* (one with root privileges) to divide superuser capabilities into several packages and assign them separately to individuals sharing administrative responsibilities. When you separate superuser privileges with RBAC, users can have a variable degree of access and you can control delegation of privileged operations to other users. See Chapter 23, "Role-Based Access Control," for more information.

# File Security

All of the users logged into the Solaris operating system can read and use files belonging to one another as long as they have permission to do so. UNIX file security is based on a combination of user classes and file and directory permissions, as described briefly in the following sections.

> *NOTE. In most cases, you can keep sensitive files in an inaccessible directory (700 mode) and make such files unreadable by others (600 mode). However, anyone who guesses your password or has access to the root password can read and write to any file on the local system. In addition, the sensitive file is preserved on backup tapes every time you back up the system. Sensitive files can be retrieved by anyone having access to the backup media.*

> *All Solaris users in the United States have an additional layer of security available—the optional file encryption kit. The encryption kit includes the* crypt *command, which scrambles the data to disguise the text.*

In addition to basic UNIX file security, you can implement Access Control Lists (ACLs, pronounced "ackkls") to provide greater control over file permissions. For more information about ACLs, see "Access Control Lists (ACLs)" on page 537.

## User Classes

Each UNIX file has three classes of users.

- Users.
- Members of a group.
- All others who are not the file or group owner.

New!

*NOTE. The Solaris 8 release introduces role accounts, which are similar to user accounts See "What Is a Role?" on page 614 for more information about role accounts.*

Only the owner of the file or root can assign or modify file permissions.

## File Permissions

File permissions, listed in Table 100, apply to regular files and to special files, such as devices, sockets, and named pipes (FIFOs). When a file is a symbolic link, the permissions that apply are those of the file to which the link points.

*Table 100    File Permissions*

| Symbol | Permission | Description |
| --- | --- | --- |
| r | Read | Can open and read the contents of a file. |
| w | Write | Can write to the file (modify its contents), add to it, or delete it. |
| x | Execute | Can execute the file (if it is a program or shell script) or run it with one of the exec(1) system calls. |
| – | Denied | Cannot read, write, or execute the file. |

## Directory Permissions

Directory permissions, listed in Table 101, apply to directories.

*Table 101    Directory Permissions*

| Symbol | Permission | Description |
| --- | --- | --- |
| r | Read | List the files in the directory. |
| w | Write | Add or remove files or links in the directory. |
| x | Execute | Open or execute files in the directory and change into the directory. |
| – | Denied | Cannot list, write, or open the files in the directory. |

You can protect the files in a directory and its subdirectories by denying access to that directory. Note, however, that superuser has access to all files and directories on the system, regardless of permission settings. Other permission values and their meanings are discussed in the section "Special File Permissions (Setuid, Setgid, and Sticky Bit)" on page 532.

## Octal Values for Permissions

Instead of using the letter symbol, you can use a numeric argument for file and directory permissions. Table 102 shows the octal values for setting file permissions. You can use these numbers in sets of three to set permissions for owner, group, and other. For example, the value 644 sets permissions to rw-r--r--: read/write permissions for owner and read-only permissions for group and other.

*Table 102   Octal Values for File and Directory Permissions*

| Value | Permissions | Description |
|-------|-------------|-------------|
| 0 | --- | No permissions. |
| 1 | --x | Execute-only. |
| 2 | -w- | Write-only. |
| 3 | -wx | Write, execute. |
| 4 | r-- | Read-only. |
| 5 | r-x | Read, execute. |
| 6 | rw- | Read, write. |
| 7 | rwx | Read, write, execute. |

## Default umask

When a user creates a file or directory, it is created with a default set of permissions. These default permissions are determined by the value of umask that is set in the /etc/profile system file or in the user's .cshrc, .login, or .profile file. If no umask is explicitly set by the user, the system sets the default permissions with the default umask.

> *NOTE. In the Solaris 8 release, the default* umask *is changed from* 002 *to* 022.

New!

A text file is set to 644, granting read and write permission to user and read permission to group and other. Directory or executable file permissions are set to 755.

```
777 full permissions
-022 umask
755 allowed permissions
```

The value assigned by umask is subtracted from full permissions for all newly created files and directories. It denies permissions in the same way that the chmod command grants them. For example, while the command chmod 022 grants write permission to group and others, umask 022 denies write permission for group and others.

Table 103 shows some typical umask settings and describes the effect on an executable file.

*Table 103   umask Settings for Different Security Levels*

| Security Level | umask | Disallows |
|---|---|---|
| 744 (Permissive) | 022 | Write for group and others. |
| 740 (Moderate) | 027 | Write for group; read, write, execute for others. |
| 741 (Moderate) | 026 | Write for group; read, write for others. |
| 700 (Severe) | 077 | Read, write, execute for group and others. |

## File Types

A file can be one of the six types listed in Table 104.

*Table 104   File Types*

| Symbol | Description |
|---|---|
| – | Text or program. |
| d | Directory. |
| b | Block special file. |
| c | Character special file. |
| p | Named pipe (FIFO). |
| l | Symbolic link. |

The file type is displayed in the first column of the output of the `ls -l`    *New!*
command. The following example shows one of each of the six file types
described in Table 104.

```
-rw-------   1 root     other      220200 Jan 25 12:40 core
drwxr-xr-x   2 root     root          512 Jan 17 16:16 TT_DB
br--r--r--   1 nobody   nobody     91,  1 Feb 16 10:11 seas_3_0_update_1
crw-------   1 root     sys        111,  0 Jan 17 16:11 pci@1f,0:devctl
prw-------   1 root     root            0 Feb 16 10:16 utmppipe
lrwxrwxrwx   1 root     root            9 Jan 17 15:52 bin -> ./usr/bin
```

## File Administration Commands

Table 105 lists the file administration commands that you can use on files or
directories.

*Table 105   File Administration Commands*

| Command | Description |
|---|---|
| ls(1) | List the files in a directory and display information about them. |
| chown(1) | Change the ownership of a file. |
| chgrp(1) | Change the group ownership of a file. |
| chmod(1) | Change permissions on a file. |

### Displaying File Information

Use the `ls` command to display information about files in a directory. The `-l`
(long) option to the `ls` command displays the following information.

- Type of file and its permissions.
- Number of hard links.
- Owner of the file.
- Group of the file.
- Size of the file, in bytes.
- Date the file was created or the last date it was changed.
- Name of the file.

The `-a` option to the `ls` command displays all files, including hidden files
that begin with a dot ( . ). To display information about files, type the
following command.

```
castle% ls -la
```

The following example shows a partial listing of the files in the root directory ( / ).

```
paperbark% cd /
paperbark% ls -la
total 961
drwxr-xr-x  24 root      root          512 Nov 11 11:33 .
drwxr-xr-x  24 root      root          512 Nov 11 11:33 ..
-rw-------   1 root      other          73 Oct 24 07:31 .TTauthority
-rw-------   1 root      other         103 Oct 24 07:31 .Xauthority
drwxr-xr-x  12 root      other         512 Oct 24 08:56 .dt
-rwxr-xr-x   1 root      other        5111 Oct 23 18:34 .dtprofile
drwxr-xr-x   2 root      root          512 Oct 23 17:57 TT_DB
lrwxrwxrwx   1 root      root            9 Oct 23 16:59 bin -> ./usr/bin
drwxr-xr-x   3 root      nobody        512 Nov  6 10:47 cdrom
-rw-------   1 root      root       400180 Nov 11 11:33 core
drwxr-xr-x  15 root      sys          3584 Nov 11 11:33 dev
drwxr-xr-x   4 root      sys           512 Oct 23 17:52 devices
drwxr-xr-x  40 root      sys          3584 Nov 11 11:33 etc
drwxr-xr-x   3 root      sys           512 Oct 23 16:52 export
dr-xr-xr-x   1 root      root            1 Nov 11 11:33 home
drwxr-xr-x   9 root      sys           512 Oct 23 16:59 kernel
(Additional lines not shown in this example)
```

## Changing File Ownership

Use the chown command to change file ownership. Only the owner of the file or superuser can change the ownership of a file.

*New!*

The operating system has a configuration option, {_POSIX_CHOWN_RESTRICTED}, to restrict ownership changes. When this option is in effect, even the owner of the file cannot change the owner ID of the file. Only superuser can arbitrarily change owner IDs regardless of whether this option is in effect. To set the {_POSIX_CHOWN_RESTRICTED} configuration option, include the following line in the /etc/system file.

```
set rstchown = 1
```

To disable the {_POSIX_CHOWN_RESTRICTED} option, include the following line in /etc/system.

```
set rstchown = 0
```

{_POSIX_CHOWN_RESTRICTED} is enabled by default. See system(4) and fpathconf(2).

Use the following steps to change the ownership of a file.

1. Type **ls -l** *filename* and press Return.
   The owner of the file is displayed in the third column.
2. Become superuser if necessary.
3. Type **chown** *username* *filename* and press Return.
4. Type **ls -l** *filename* and press Return to verify that the owner of the file has changed.

You can change ownership on groups of files or on all of the files in a directory by using metacharacters such as * and ? in place of file names or in combination with them.

You can change ownership recursively with the chown -R option. When you use the -R option, the chown command descends through the directory and any subdirectories, setting the ownership ID. If a symbolic link is encountered, the ownership is changed only on the target file itself.

The following example changes the ownership of the file local.cshrc from root to winsor.

```
paperbark% ls -l local.cshrc
-rw-r--r--   1 root       sys           124 Oct 23 17:00 local.cshrc
paperbark% su
Password:
# chown winsor local.cshrc
# ls -l local.cshrc
-rw-r--r--   1 winsor     sys           124 Oct 23 17:00 local.cshrc
# exit
paperbark%
```

*NOTE. You can also change file ownership by specifying the UID number as the first argument to the* chown *command.*

## Changing Group Ownership of a File

Only the owner of the file or superuser can change the group ownership of a file.

The operating system has a configuration option, {_POSIX_CHOWN_RESTRICTED}, to restrict ownership changes. When this option is in effect, even the owner of the file cannot change the owner ID of the file. Only superuser can arbitrarily change owner IDs regardless of whether this option is in effect. To set the {_POSIX_CHOWN_RESTRICTED} configuration option, include the following line in the /etc/system file.

*New!*

set rstchown = 1

To disable the {_POSIX_CHOWN_RESTRICTED} option, include the following line in /etc/system.

set rstchown = 0

{_POSIX_CHOWN_RESTRICTED} is enabled by default. See system(4) and fpathconf(2).

Use the following steps to change the ownership of a file.

1. Type **ls -l *filename*** and press Return.

   The owner of the file is displayed in the third column.

2. Become superuser if necessary.

3. Type **chgrp** *groupname* *filename* and press Return.

4. Type **ls -l** *filename* and press Return to verify that the group owner of the file is changed.

*NOTE. You can also change group ownership by specifying the group number as the first argument to the* chgrp *command.*

You can change group ownership on a set of files or on all of the files in a directory with metacharacters such as * and ? in place of file names or in combination with them.

You can change group ownership recursively with the chgrp -R option. When you use the -R option, the chgrp command descends through the directory and any subdirectories, setting the group ownership ID. If a symbolic link is encountered, the group ownership is changed only on the target file itself.

The following example changes the group ownership of the file local.cshrc from sys to staff.

```
paperbark% ls -l local.cshrc
-rw-r--r--   1 winsor      sys          124 Oct 23 17:00 local.cshrc
paperbark% su
Password:
# chgrp staff local.cshrc
# ls -l local.cshrc
-rw-r--r--   1 winsor     staff         124 Oct 23 17:00 local.cshrc
# exit
paperbark%
```

## Changing File Permissions

Use the chmod command to change the permissions on a file or directory. Only the owner of a file or superuser can change file and directory permissions.

You can set permissions with the chmod command in one of two ways.

- Absolute mode—Use numbers to represent file permissions. When you change permissions with the absolute mode, you represent permissions by specifying an octal mode triplet, such as 700 or 666.

- Symbolic mode—Use combinations of letters and symbols to add or remove permissions.

Refer to Table 102 on page 525 for the octal values used to set file permissions in absolute mode.

Table 106 lists the symbols for setting file permissions in symbolic mode. You can use symbols to specify whose permissions are to be set or changed, the operation to be performed, or the permissions being assigned or changed.

*Table 106   Symbolic Values for File and Directory Permissions*

| Symbol | Function* | Description |
|--------|-----------|-------------|
| u | Who | User (owner). |
| g | Who | Group. |
| o | Who | Others. |
| a | Who | All. |
| = | Operation | Assign. |
| + | Operation | Add. |
| – | Operation | Remove. |
| r | Permission | Read. |
| w | Permission | Write. |
| x | Permission | Execute. |
| l | Permission | Mandatory locking, setgid bit is on, group execution bit is off. |
| s | Permission | Setuid or setgid bit is on. |
| S | Permission | Setuid bit is on, user execution bit is off. |
| t | Permission | Sticky bit is on, execution bit for others is on. |
| T | Permission | Sticky bit is on, execution bit for others is off. |

\* The who, operator, and permissions designations in the function column specify the symbols that change the permissions on the file or directory.

Use the following steps to change permissions in absolute mode.

1.  If you are not the owner of the file or directory, become superuser.
2.  Type **chmod *nnn filename*** and press Return.
3.  Type **ls -l *filename*** and press Return to verify that the permissions of the file have changed.

Use the following steps to change permissions in symbolic mode.

1. If you are not the owner of the file or directory, become superuser.
2. Type **chmod *who operator permission filename*** and press Return.
3. Type **ls -l *filename*** and press Return to verify that the permissions of the file have changed.

The following example changes permissions in absolute mode for the file local.cshrc to 666.

```
paperbark% chmod 666 local.cshrc
castle% ls -l local.cshrc
-rw-rw-rw-   1 winsor    staff          124 Oct 23 17:00 local.cshrc
paperbark%
```

The following example removes read permission from others for the file filea.

```
castle% chmod o-r filea
```

The following example adds read and execute permissions for user, group, and others for the file fileb.

```
castle% chmod a+rx fileb
```

The following example adds read, write, and execute permissions for group for the file filec.

```
castle% chmod g=rwx filec
```

## Special File Permissions (Setuid, Setgid, and Sticky Bit)

Three special types of permissions are available for executable files and public directories.

- Setuid permission.
- Setgid permission.
- Sticky bit.

When setuid or setgid permissions are set for an executable file, any user who runs that file assumes the permissions of the owner or group of the executable file. See "Setuid Permission" (below) for information about setuid permissions. See "Setgid Permission" on page 534 for information about setgid permissions. When the sticky bit is set on a directory, it prevents users from removing files owned by other users. See "Sticky Bit" on page 535 for information about sticky bits.

> *CAUTION. Be extremely careful when setting special permissions because they constitute a security risk. For example, a user can gain superuser permission by executing a program that sets the UID to root.*

Monitor your system for any unauthorized use of the setuid and setgid permissions to gain superuser privileges. See "Searching for Files with Special Permissions" on page 535 for information on how to search for file systems and print a list of all of the programs using these permissions. A suspicious listing would be one that grants ownership of such a program to a user rather than to bin or sys. Only superuser can set these permissions.

## Setuid Permission

When setuid (set user identification) permission is set on an executable file, a process that runs this file is granted access based on the owner of the file (usually root), instead of the user who created the process. This permission enables a user to access files and directories that are normally available only to the owner.

The setuid permission is shown as an s in the file permissions. For example, the setuid permission on the admintool command enables a user to use Admintool, assuming the permissions of the root ID are the following.

```
paperbark% ls -l /bin/admintool
-r-s--x--x   1 root      sys        341204 Jan 15  2000 /bin/admintool
paperbark%
```

> *NOTE. Using setuid permissions with the reserved UIDs (0–99) from a program may not set the effective UID correctly. Instead, use a shell script to avoid using the reserved UIDs with setuid permissions.*

You set UID permissions with the chmod command to assign the octal value 4 as the first number in a series of four octal values. Use the following steps to set UID permissions.

1. If you are not the owner of the file or directory, become superuser.
2. Type **chmod 4nnn filename** and press Return.
3. Type **ls -l filename** and press Return to verify that the permissions of the file have changed.

The following example sets setuid permission on the `myprog` file.

```
# chmod 4555 myprog
-r-sr-xr-x  1 winsor     staff      12796 Jul 15 21:23 myprog
#
```

To minimize setuid problems, restrict the number of local setuid programs. If you write a setuid program, use the following guidelines to minimize security problems.

- Do not write setuid shell scripts for any shell.
- Do not use library routines that start slave shells.
- Do not use `execlp`(3) and `execvp()` routines that duplicate the path-searching functionality of a shell.
- Use full path names to identify files.
- Only set UID to root when you need to.
- Use the set effective user ID function, `seteuid`(2), to control setuid use.
- Keep permissions on setuid programs restrictive.
- Avoid secret back-door escapes in your code.

## Setgid Permission

The setgid (set group identification) permission is similar to setuid, except that the effective group ID for the process is changed to the group owner of the file and a user is granted access based on permissions granted to that group. The `/usr/bin/mail` program has setgid permissions, as shown below.

```
paperbark% ls -l /usr/bin/mail
-r-x--s--x  1 root       mail       61288 Jan  6  2000 /usr/bin/mail
paperbark%
```

When setgid permission is applied to a directory, files subsequently created in the directory belong to the group the directory belongs to, not to the group the creating process belongs to. Any user who has write permission in the directory can create a file there; however, the file does not belong to the group of the user, but instead belongs to the group of the directory.

You can set setgid permissions with the `chmod` command to assign the octal value 2 as the first number in a series of four octal values. Use the following steps to set setgid permissions:

1. If you are not the owner of the file or directory, become superuser.
2. Type **chmod 2*nnn* *filename*** and press Return.
3. Type **ls -l *filename*** and press Return to verify that the permissions of the file have changed.

The following example sets setgid permission on the `myprog2` file.

```
# chmod 2551 myprog2
# ls -l myprog2
-r-xr-s--x   1 winsor      staff   26876 Jul 15 21:23 myprog2
#
```

## Sticky Bit

The sticky bit on a directory is a permission bit that protects files within that directory. If the directory has the sticky bit set, only the owner of the file, the owner of the directory, or root can delete the file. The sticky bit prevents a user from deleting other users' files from public directories, such as /tmp.

```
drwxrwxrwt   7 root      sys           718 Feb 16 10:16 tmp
```

When you set up a public directory on a TMPFS temporary file system, make sure that you set the sticky bit manually.

You can set sticky bit permissions with the `chmod` command to assign the octal value 1 as the first number in a series of four octal values. Use the following steps to set the sticky bit on a directory.

1. If you are not the owner of the file or directory, become superuser.
2. Type **chmod 1*nnn* filename** and press Return.
3. Type **ls -l *filename*** and press Return to verify that the permissions of the file have changed.

The following example sets the sticky bit permission on the `pubdir` directory.

```
castle% chmod 1777 pubdir
castle% ls -l pubdir
drwxrwxrwt   2 winsor      staff      512 Jul 15 21:23 pubdir
castle%
```

## Searching for Files with Special Permissions

You should monitor your systems for any unauthorized use of the setuid and setgid permissions to gain superuser privileges. A suspicious listing would be one that grants ownership of a setuid or setgid program to a user other than bin or sys.

You can use the permissions (-perm) option to the `find` command to search for files with setuid, setgid, or sticky bit permissions. Use the following steps to search for files with setuid permissions.

1. Become superuser.
2. Type **find *directory* -user root -perm -4000 -print** and press Return.

The following example lists the system files that have setuid permissions.

```
# paperbark% su
Password:
# find / -user root -perm -4000 -print
/usr/lib/lp/bin/netpr
/usr/lib/fs/ufs/quota
/usr/lib/fs/ufs/ufsdump
/usr/lib/fs/ufs/ufsrestore
/usr/lib/pt_chmod
/usr/lib/utmp_update
/usr/lib/fbconfig/SUNWifb_config
/usr/lib/sendmail
/usr/lib/acct/accton
/usr/openwin/bin/xlock
/usr/openwin/bin/ff.core
/usr/openwin/bin/sys-suspend
/usr/openwin/bin/kcms_configure
/usr/openwin/bin/kcms_calibrate
/usr/openwin/bin/sparcv9/kcms_configure
/usr/openwin/lib/mkcookie
/usr/bin/sparcv7/ps
/usr/bin/sparcv7/uptime
/usr/bin/sparcv7/w
/usr/bin/at
/usr/bin/atq
/usr/bin/atrm
/usr/bin/crontab
/usr/bin/eject
/usr/bin/fdformat
/usr/bin/login
/usr/bin/newgrp
/usr/bin/newtask
/usr/bin/passwd
/usr/bin/pfexec
/usr/bin/rcp
/usr/bin/rdist
/usr/bin/rlogin
/usr/bin/rsh
/usr/bin/su
/usr/bin/yppasswd
/usr/bin/admintool
/usr/bin/sparcv9/ps
/usr/bin/sparcv9/uptime
/usr/bin/sparcv9/w
/usr/bin/chkey
/usr/bin/nispasswd
/usr/bin/cancel
/usr/bin/lp
/usr/bin/lpset
/usr/bin/lpstat
/usr/bin/rmformat
/usr/bin/volcheck
/usr/bin/volrmmount
/usr/bin/ct
/usr/bin/pppconn
/usr/bin/pppdisc
/usr/bin/ppptool
/usr/sbin/sparcv7/whodo
/usr/sbin/allocate
/usr/sbin/mkdevalloc
/usr/sbin/mkdevmaps
/usr/sbin/ping
/usr/sbin/sacadm
/usr/sbin/traceroute
/usr/sbin/deallocate
/usr/sbin/list_devices
/usr/sbin/afbconfig
```

```
/usr/sbin/sparcv9/whodo
/usr/sbin/ffbconfig
/usr/sbin/igsconfig
/usr/sbin/m64config
/usr/sbin/lpmove
/usr/sbin/pmconfig
/usr/sbin/aspppls
/usr/sbin/static/rcp
/usr/dt/bin/dtaction
/usr/dt/bin/dtappgather
/usr/dt/bin/sdtcm_convert
/usr/dt/bin/dtprintinfo
/usr/dt/bin/dtsession
/usr/ucb/sparcv7/ps
/usr/ucb/sparcv9/ps
/etc/sysevent/sysevent_door
/proc/317/object/a.out
/proc/388/object/a.out
#
```

## Access Control Lists (ACLs)

*Access Control Lists* (ACLs, pronounced "ackkls") can provide greater control over file permissions when traditional UNIX file permissions are not enough. UNIX file protection provides read, write, and execute permissions for three user classes: owner, group, and other. An ACL provides better file security by enabling you to define file permissions for the owner, owner's group, others, specific users, and groups. It also enables you to define default permissions for each of these categories.

For example, you might have two groups that need permission to access a file: one to read it and one to write to it. Alternatively, you might have a file that you wanted everyone in a group to be able to read, so you would give group read permissions on that file. Suppose that you want only two people in the group to be able to write to that file. With standard UNIX permissions, you cannot give write permission to only two members of a group. You can, however, set up an ACL for that file to grant only two people in the group write permissions on that file.

ACLs are extensions to standard UNIX file permissions. The ACL information is stored and associated with each file individually.

## ACL Commands

You define an ACL for a file or directory with the ACL commands and options listed in Table 107. Each ACL entry consists of the following fields, which are separated by colons.

*Table 107   ACL Commands and Options*

| Command/ Option | Description |
|---|---|
| `getfacl` | Display ACL entries. |
| `-a` | Display the file name, owner, group, and ACL of the file. |
| `-d` | Display the file name, owner, and group of the file. The information is displayed even if the file does not have an ACL. |
| `setfacl` | Set, add, modify, and delete ACL entries. |
| `-s acl-entries` | Set the ACL for the file, removing all old entries and replacing them with the newly specified ACL. |
| `-m acl-entries` | Add one or more new ACL entries to the file or modify one or more existing ACL entries for the file. If an entry already exists, the specified permissions replace the current permissions. If no entry exists, a new entry is created. |
| `-d acl-entries` | Delete one or more entries from the file. You cannot delete entries for the file owner, the owning group, and other. Note that deleting an entry does not necessarily have the same result as removing all permissions from the entry. |
| `-f acl-file` | Specify a file containing the ACL entries to be used as arguments to the `setfacl` command. |
| `-r` | Recalculate permissions for the ACL mask. Permissions specified in the mask are ignored and replaced by the maximum permissions needed to give access to any additional user, owning group, and additional group entries in the ACL. |

```
entry-type:[UID] | [GID]:perms
```

Table 108 explains each of the elements of the syntax for ACL commands.

*Table 108   ACL Argument Syntax*

| Argument | Description |
|---|---|
| *entry-type* | Type of ACL entry on which to set file permissions. For example, *entry-type* can be user (the owner of a file) or mask (the ACL mask). |
| *UID* | User name or identification number. |
| *GID* | Group name or identification number. |
| *perm* | Permissions set for the *entry-type*. You can set permissions symbolically with the characters r, w, x, and – or with octal values from 0 to 7. |

*NOTE. ACLs are supported in UFS file systems only. If you restore or copy files with ACL entries in the* /tmp *directory, which is usually mounted as a TMPFS file system, the ACL entries are lost. If you need to temporarily store UFS files containing ACLs, use the* /var/tmp *directory instead.*

## ACL Permissions for Files

You can set the following permissions for UFS files.

- u[ser]::*perm*—Set the permissions for the owner of the file.

- g[roup]::*perm*—Set the permissions for the group that owns the file.

- o[ther]::*perm*—Set the permissions for users other than the owner or members of the group that owns the file.

- m[ask]::*perm*—Set the ACL mask. The mask entry indicates the maximum permissions allowed for users other than the owner and for groups. Using the mask is a quick way to change permissions on all of the users and groups. For example, the mask:r-- or mask:4 entry means that users and groups cannot have more than read permissions, even though they may have write/execute permissions.

- u[ser]:*UID* | *username*:*perm*—Set the permissions for a specific user.

- g[roup]:*GID* | *groupname*:*perm*—Set the permissions for a specific group.

## ACL Permissions for Directories

You can set default ACL entries on a directory that apply to files subsequently created within the directories. Files created in a directory that has default ACL entries have the same ACL entries as the directory.

When you set default ACL entries for specific users and groups on a directory for the first time, you must also set default ACL entries for the owner, owner's group, others, and the mask.

- d[efault]:u[ser]::*perm*—Set the default permissions for the owner of the directory.

- d[efault]:g[roup]::*perm*—Set the default permissions for the group that owns the directory.

- d[efault]:o[ther]::*perm*—Set the default permissions for users other than the owner or members of the group that owns the directory.

- d[efault]:m[ask]::*perm*—Set the default ACL mask.

- d[efault]:u[ser]:UID:*perm*—Set the default permissions for a specific user.

- d[efault]:g[roup]:GID:*perm*—Set the default permissions for a specific group.

## Determining Whether a File Has an ACL

You can determine whether a file has an ACL in one of two ways.

- With the ls -l command.
- With the getfacl command.

When you use the ls -l command, any file that has an ACL displays a plus (+) sign to the right of the mode field.

> *NOTE. If you define an ACL for a file and do not specify any additional users or groups, the plus sign is not displayed to the right of the mode field even though the file has a basic ACL. The plus sign is displayed only if additional users or groups are included in the ACL.*

In the following example, the file foo has an ACL and at least one entry in the list.

```
castle% ls -l foo
-rwxrw----+  1 winsor    staff         0 Oct  3 14:22 foo
castle
```

When you use the `getfacl` *filename* command with no options, the ACL information for the file is displayed in the following format.

```
# file: filename
# owner: uid
# group: gid
user::perm
user:uid:perm
group::perm
group:gid:perm
mask:perm
other:perm
default:user::perm
default:v:uid:perm
default:group::perm
default:group:gid:perm
```

The ACL for the file `foo` in the following example gives the owner of the file `rwx` permissions and user `ray` read-only permissions.

```
castle% getfacl foo

# file: foo
# owner: winsor
# group: staff
user::rwx
user:ray:r--              #effective:r--
group::rw-               #effective:rw-
mask:rw-
other:---
castle%
```

*NOTE. You can use the `getfacl` command to display permissions on any UFS file or directory in the same format. The file does not need to have an ACL.*

For comparison, the following example shows the output of the `ls -l` and `getfacl` commands for the file `bar`, which does not have an ACL.

```
castle% ls -l bar
-rwxrw----   1 winsor   staff           0 Oct  3 14:22 bar
castle% getfacl bar

# file: bar
# owner: winsor
# group: staff
user::rwx
group::rw-               #effective:rw-
mask:rw-
other:---
castle%
```

## Setting ACL File Permissions

Use the `setfacl` command to set ACL permissions on a file. You can set the permissions for a file or a group of files from a command line or by listing the permissions in a file and using the file as an argument to the `setfacl` command. You can specify the permissions with the following syntax.

```
u[ser]::perm
u[ser]:uid:perm
g[roup]::perm
g[roup]:gid:perm
m[ask]:perm
o[ther]:perm
d[efault]:u[ser]::perm
d[efault]:u[ser]:uid:perm
d[efault]:g[roup]::perm
d[efault]:g[roup]:gid:perm
d[efault]:m[ask]:perm
d[efault]:o[ther]:perm
```

*NOTE. You can use either octal or symbolic values to set permissions.*

On a command line, use a comma to separate each permission statement. In an ACL file, put each statement on a separate line. The statements do not need to be in any particular order.

## Setting Permissions for a File from a Command Line

To set ACL permissions from a command line, you must specify at least the basic set of user, group, other, and mask permissions. Type the following command to set ACL permissions: **setfacl -s u::*perm*,g::*perm*,o:*perm*,m:*perm*,[u:*UID*:*perm*],[g:*GID*:*perm*]**

You can set users with either their user name or their UID number. Note that before you can use the *username* argument, the user account must already exist in the `Passwd` database or in the local `/etc/passwd` file. You can assign permissions to any UID by number, regardless of whether a user account exists.

In the same way, you can set group names with either the group name or the GID number.

The following example assigns all of the permissions to the user, restricts group permissions to read-only, and denies permissions to other. The default mask sets read-write permissions, and user `ray` is assigned read-write permissions to the file `foo`.

First, take a look at the current permissions for the file.

```
castle% ls -l foo
-rw-rw-rw-   1 winsor    staff        0 Oct  3 14:22 foo
```

Then, set permissions for user, group, owner, and the mask and add one user to the ACL.

```
castle% setfacl -s u::rwx,g::r--,o:---,mask:rw-,u:ray:rw- foo
```

Using octal values, as shown in the following example, yields the same result.

```
castle% setfacl -s u::7,g::4,o:0,mask:6,u:ray:6 foo
```

Next, verify that the permissions have been set and that the file has an ACL.

```
castle% ls -l foo
-rwxrw----+  1 winsor    staff         0 Oct  3 14:22 foo
```

As you can see, the permissions for the file are changed and the plus sign after the permission field shows that the file has an ACL. Last, use the getfacl command to verify that everything has been set correctly.

```
castle% getfacl foo

# file: foo
# owner: winsor
# group: staff
user::rwx
user:ray:rw-          #effective:rw-
group::rw-            #effective:r--
mask:rw-
other:---
castle%
```

The getfacl command always displays ACL permissions symbolically, regardless of how you specify the values from the command line.

## Using an ACL Configuration File to Set Permissions

You can create an ACL configuration file that contains a list of the permissions you want to set and then use that file name as an argument to the setfacl -f command.

*NOTE. You can use a configuration file only with the -f option to the* setfacl *command.*

Use the following steps to set up the ACL configuration file.

1. Use any editor to create a file.
2. Edit the file to include the permissions you want to set, putting each statement on a separate line. As a minimum set, be sure to include permissions for user, group, other, and mask.
3. Save the file with any file name you choose.
4. Type **setfacl -f *acl-file filename1* [*filename2*] [*filename3*]...** and press Return.

   The ACLs from *acl-file* are applied to subsquent files listed on the command line.
5. Type **getfacl *filename1* [*filename2*] [*filename3*]...** and press Return to verify that the permissions are set correctly.

*NOTE. If you make typographical errors in the configuration file, the command could return a prompt without displaying any error messages. If you make syntax errors, the* setfacl *command could display an error message. Be sure to use the* getfacl *command to check that the permissions are set properly.*

In the following example, the owner has rwx permissions, group has rw-, other has ---, and the mask is rw-. Three users with different permissions are also granted access to the file. *acl-file* (named anything) contains the following access list.

```
u::rwx
g::rw-
o:---
m:rw-
u:ray:rwx
u:des:rw-
u:rob:r--
```

Once you have set up the ACL for the file named anything, you can use the setfacl -f option to assign those same permissions to one more file. In the following example, the file named anything is used as the argument to the -f option to change ACLs for the files foo and bar so that they match the file anything.

```
castle% setfacl -f anything foo bar
castle% getfacl foo bar

# file: foo
# owner: winsor
# group: staff
user::rwx
user:ray:rwx          #effective:rwx
user:des:rw-          #effective:rw-
user:rob:r--          #effective:r--
group::rw-            #effective:rw-
mask:rw-
other:---

# file: bar
```

```
# owner: winsor
# group: staff
user::rwx
user:ray:rwx                    #effective:rwx
user:des:rw-                    #effective:rw-
user:rob:r--                    #effective:r--
group::rw-                      #effective:rw-
mask:rw-
other:---
castle%
```

## Adding and Modifying ACL Permissions

You can add and modify ACL permissions for a file that already has an ACL or for any existing UFS file or directory with the setfacl -m command. Arguments to the setfacl -m command use the same syntax and structure as arguments to the setfacl -s command.

Because each file already has a default owner, group, other, and mask setting, you can use the setfacl -m command on any UFS file without first using the setfacl -s command to specify an owner, group, other, or mask setting. If the file already has the permissions you want to use, you can simply use the setfacl -m command to modify (and create) the ACL for any file or directory.

When you use the -m option, if an entry already exists for a specified UID or GID, the permissions you specify replace the current permissions. If an entry does not exist, it is created.

Use the following syntax to add and modify permissions for a file or files.

```
setfacl -m acl-file filename1 [filename2] [filename3]
```

In the following example, permissions for user ray are modified from rwx to rw- for the file foo.

```
castle% setfacl -m u:ray:rw- foo
castle% getfacl foo

# file: foo
# owner: winsor
# group: staff
user::rw-
user:ray:rw-                    #effective:rw-
group::rw-                      #effective:rw-
mask:rw-
other:rw-
castle%
```

## Deleting an ACL Entry

Use the setfacl -d command to delete an ACL entry. To delete the entry, you can specify the entry type and the UID or GID. You do not need to include the permissions as part of the argument to the -d option.

Use the following syntax to delete an ACL entry.

```
setfacl -d entry-type:UID | GID filename1 [filename2] [filename3]
```

In the following example, user `ray` is deleted from the ACL of the file `foo`.

```
castle% setfacl -d u:ray foo
castle% getfacl foo

# file: foo
# owner: winsor
# group: staff
user::rw-
group::rw-              #effective:rw-
mask:rw-
other:rw-
castle%
```

## Copying ACL File Permissions

You can copy ACL file permissions from one file to another without specifying them on the command line: pipe the output of `getfacl` *filename* to another file with the following syntax.

```
getfacl filename1 | setfacl -f - filename2
```

In the following example, the ACL for file `foo` is used as the template for the ACL for file `bar`.

First, use the `getfacl` command to verify that the files have different ACL permissions.

```
castle% getfacl foo bar

# file: foo
# owner: winsor
# group: staff
user::rw-
user:ray:rwx            #effective:rw-
group::rw-              #effective:rw-
mask:rw-
other:rw-

# file: bar
# owner: winsor
# group: staff
user::rw-
group::rw-              #effective:rw-
mask:rw-
other:rw-
```

Then, list the ACL with the `getfacl` command and pipe the output to the `setfacl -f` command. The dash (-) tells the `setfacl` command to take its standard input from the standard output of the preceding `getfacl` command. Essentially, you list the ACLs for one file and use them to set the ACLs on another file.

```
castle% getfacl foo | setfacl -f - bar
```

Finally, use the `getfacl` command to verify that both files now have the same ACL permissions.

```
castle% getfacl foo bar

# file: foo
# owner: winsor
# group: staff
user::rw-
user:ray:rwx              #effective:rw-
group::rw-                #effective:rw-
mask:rw-
other:rw-

# file: bar
# owner: winsor
# group: staff
user::rw-
user:ray:rwx              #effective:rw-
group::rw-                #effective:rw-
mask:rw-
other:rw-
castle%
```

# Network Security

Networks create an interesting access and security paradox. Users on a network almost always push for freer access to information and files. System administrators almost always push for more restrictive access to information and files so that they can more effectively monitor use and secure access to sensitive information.

Network security is usually based on limiting or blocking operations from remote systems.

Network security comprises three aspects: firewall, authentication, and authorization.

## Firewall Systems

The purpose of creating a firewall network security system is to ensure that all of the communication between a local network and an external network conforms to your local network security policy. A network security policy can be permissive or restrictive. A permissive policy might allow access to all services unless specifically denied. A restrictive policy might deny access to all services unless specifically allowed.

You can set up a firewall system to help protect the resources in your network from outside access. A firewall system acts as a barrier between your internal network and outside networks, as illustrated in Figure 79.

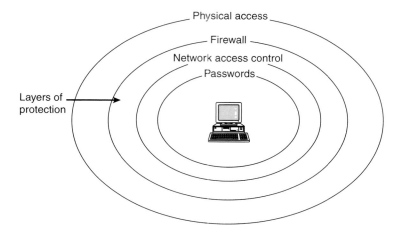

*Figure 79   Firewall Security Protects in Layers*

The firewall has two functions.

• It acts as a gateway that passes data between the networks.
• It acts as a barrier that blocks the free passage of data to and from the network.

*CAUTION. A firewall prevents unauthorized users from accessing hosts on your network. Maintain strict and rigidly enforced security on the firewall. However, an intruder who can break into your firewall system may be able to gain access to all of the other hosts on the internal network.*

A firewall system should not have any trusted hosts. A *trusted host* is one from which a user can log in without being required to type in a password. The firewall system should not share any of its file systems or mount any file systems from other servers.

You can use ASET to make a system into a firewall and to enforce high security on a firewall system. Refer to Chapter 21, "Using the Automated Security Enhancement Tool (ASET)," for more information on ASET.

Good reference books on firewalls are *Firewalls & Internet Security: Repelling the Wily Hacker* by Steven Cheswick and William Bellovin and

*Building Internet Firewalls* by D. Brent Chapman and Elizabeth D. Zwicky. Also refer to *Solaris Security* by Peter H. Gregory. (See the bibliography at the end of the book.)

## Authentication and Authorization

*Authentication* is the method used to verify the identity of a user so that you can allow or deny access because you know the person is who he says he is. You can set up authentication at both the system and the network level. Once a user gains access to a remote system, *authorization* is a list of actions that are allowed or denied for users who have been authenticated. Then, their authorizations can be determined based on their verified identities.

The types of authentication and authorization that can help protect your systems on the network against unauthorized use are listed in Table 109.

*Table 109    Types of Authentication and Authorization*

| Type | Description |
| --- | --- |
| NIS+ | The NIS+ name service can provide both authentication and authorization at the network level. |
| Remote login programs | The remote login programs (`rlogin`) enable users to log in to a remote system over the network and use its resources. If you are a trusted host, authentication is automatic; otherwise, you are asked to authenticate yourself. |
| Secure RPC | Secure RPC improves the security of NFS network environments by authenticating users who make Remote Procedure Calls to remote systems. You can use either the UNIX, DES, or Kerberos authentication system for Secure RPC. |
| DES encryption | The Data Encryption Standard (DES) encryption functions use a 56-bit key to encrypt a secret key. Although DES is an encryption algorithm, it can be used as part of data authentication. |
| Diffie-Hellman authentication | This authentication method is based on the capability of the sending system to use the common key to encrypt the current time, which the receiving system can decrypt and check against its current time. |
| Kerberos Version 4 | Used to authenticate a user logging in to the system. |

## Monitoring Login Security Information

The following sections describe the following ways to monitor login information.

- Display a user's login status.
- Temporarily disable user logins.
- Save failed login attempts.

## Displaying a User's Login Status

Use the `logins` command to display the status of logged in users. Using the `logins` command with no arguments displays a list of all user and system login accounts. Use the options listed in Table 110 to control the output displayed by the `logins` command.

*Table 110   Options to the logins Command*

| Option | Description |
|--------|-------------|
| `-a` | Add two password expiration fields to the display. The fields show how many days a password can remain unused before it automatically becomes inactive; they also show the date that the password expires. |
| `-d` | List logins with duplicate UIDs. |
| `-m` | Display multiple group membership information. |
| `-o` | Format the output into one line of colon-separated fields. |
| `-p` | Display logins with no passwords. |
| `-s` | Display all system logins. |
| `-t` | Sort output by login name instead of by UID. |
| `-u` | Display all user logins. |
| `-x` | Print an extended set of information about each specified user. The extended information displays the home directory, login shell, and password aging information, each on a separate line.  The password information includes password status (`PS` for password, `NO` for no password, or `LK` for locked). If the login is password protected, status is followed by the date the password was last changed, the number of days required between changes, and the number of days allowed before a change is required. |

*Table 110   Options to the logins Command (Continued)*

| Option | Description |
|--------|-------------|
|        | The password aging information shows the time interval during which the user will receive a password expiration warning message at logon before the password expires. |
| -g group | List all users belonging to the group, sorted by login. You can specify multiple groups as a comma-separated list. |
| -l login | List the requested login. You can specify multiple logins as a comma-separated list. Depending on the nameservice lookup types set in /etc/nsswitch.conf, the information can come from the /etc/passwd and /etc/shadow files and other nameservices. |

The logins command has the following syntax.

```
/usr/bin/logins [-admopstux] [-g group1,group2...] [-l login1,login2...]
```

You can group options. When you group options, any login that matches any criteria is displayed. When you combine the -l and -g options, a user is listed only once, even if the user belongs to more than one of the specified groups.

*NOTE. You must be superuser to run the* logins *command.*

The following example shows the output of the logins command, which is used with no arguments.

```
paperbark% su
Password:
# logins
root          0       other       1       Super-User
daemon        1       other       1
bin           2       bin         2
sys           3       sys         3
adm           4       adm         4       Admin
uucp          5       uucp        5       uucp Admin
nuucp         9       nuucp       9       uucp Admin
ppp           10      uucp        5       Solstice PPP 3.0 pppls
listen        37      adm         4       Network Admin
lp            71      lp          8       Line Printer Admin
printadm      100     sysadmin    14      Grant solaris.admin.printer* rights
sysadmin      101     sysadmin    14      System Administrator rights
winsor        1001    staff       10
ray           1002    staff       10
des           1003    staff       10
rob           1004    staff       10
nobody        60001   nobody      60001   Nobody
noaccess      60002   noaccess    60002   No Access User
nobody4       65534   nogroup     65534   SunOS 4.x Nobody
#
```

*New!*

**New!**

*NOTE. The* `printadm` *and* `sysadm` *logins shown in the above example are actually role login accounts that grant specific system administration rights to users assigned to those roles. See Chapter 23, "Role-Based Access Control," for more information about role accounts and rights.*

The following example displays an extended set of login status information for user `winsor`.

```
# logins -x -l winsor
winsor          1001    staff           10
                        /export/home/winsor
                        /bin/csh
                        PS 000000 -1 -1 -1
#
```

The following example shows a list of user accounts with no password.

```
# logins -p
ray             1002    staff           10
des             1003    staff           10
rob             1004    staff           10
#
```

The following example shows extended login status for all user accounts on a stand-alone system.

```
# logins -xu
printadm        100     sysadmin        14      Grant solaris.admin.printer* rights
                        /home/printadm
                        /bin/pfsh
                        PS 000000 -1 -1 -1
sysadmin        101     sysadmin        14      System Administrator rights
                        /home/sysadmin
                        /bin/pfsh
                        PS 000000 -1 -1 -1
winsor          1001    staff           10
                        /export/home/winsor
                        /bin/csh
                        PS 000000 -1 -1 -1
ray             1002    staff           10
                        /export/home/ray
                        /bin/csh
                        NP 000000 -1 -1 -1
des             1003    staff           10
                        /export/home/des
                        /bin/csh
                        NP 000000 -1 -1 -1
rob             1004    staff           10
                        /export/home/rob
                        /bin/csh
                        NP 000000 -1 -1 -1
nobody          60001   nobody          60001   Nobody
                        /
                        /sbin/sh
                        LK 082587 -1 -1 -1
noaccess        60002   noaccess        60002   No Access User
                        /
                        /sbin/sh
                        LK 082587 -1 -1 -1
nobody4         65534   nogroup         65534   SunOS 4.x Nobody
                        /
```

```
                            /sbin/sh
                            LK 082587 -1 -1 -1
   #
```

*NOTE. The* `logins` *command lists role accounts—such as* `printadm`          New!
*and* `sysadm` *in the previous example—as user accounts. See*
*Chapter 23, "Role-Based Access Control," for more information about*
*role accounts and rights.*

## Temporarily Disabling User Logins

You can temporarily disable logins in one of two ways to prevent new login
sessions.

- Bring the system to run level 0 (single-user mode).
- Create an `/etc/nologin` file.

When a system will not be available for an extended time, you can create
an `/etc/nologin` file to prevent users from logging in to the system. When a
user logs in to a system that has an `/etc/nologin` file, the message in the
`/etc/nologin` file is displayed and the user login is terminated. Superuser
logins are not affected by the `/etc/nologin` file.

Use the following steps to create an `/etc/nologin` file.

1. Become superuser.
2. Use any editor to create a file named `/etc/nologin`.
3. Type the message to display to users when they log in to the system.
   If possible, include specific information about when logins will be
   permitted or how users can find out when they can access the system
   again.
4. Save the changes and close the file.

The following example shows the text of a `nologin` file.

```
# cat /etc/nologin
No Logins Are Currently Permitted

The system will be unavailable until 12 noon on Friday, October 24.
#
```

## Saving Failed Login Attempts

You can use the `syslog` subsystem if it is important for you to track whether      New!
users are trying to log in to your user accounts. Check to make sure the
`/etc/syslog.conf` file is set up properly so that you can use it to track user
logins. Once the `syslog` subsystem is set up, you can create a
`/var/adm/loginlog` file with read and write permissions for root only. After

you create the `loginlog` file, all failed login activity is written to this file automatically after five failed attempts. The five-try limit avoids recording failed attempts that are the result of typographical errors.

The `loginlog` file contains one entry for each failed attempt. Each entry contains the user's login name, TTY device, and time of the attempt.

*NOTE. The `loginlog` file may grow quickly. To use the information in this file and prevent it from getting too large, check and clear its contents regularly. If this file shows a lot of activity, it may suggest that someone is trying to break into the computer system. If you regularly track information from the `loginlog` file, consider creating a `cron` entry to track and clear out the `loginlog` file.*

Use the following steps to create a `loginlog` file.

1. Become superuser.
2. Type **touch /var/adm/loginlog** and press Return.
3. Type **chmod 700 /var/adm/loginlog** and press Return.
4. Type **chgrp sys /var/adm/loginlog** and press Return.
5. Make sure the log works by trying to log in to the system six times with the wrong password.
6. Type **more /var/adm/loginlog** and review the output to make sure the login attempts are being logged successfully.

## Sharing Files

A network server can control which files are available for sharing via NFS. It can also control which clients have access to the files and what type of access is permitted to those clients. In general, the file server can grant read/write or read-only access either to all clients or to specific clients. Access control is specified when resources are made available with the `share` command.

A server can use the `/etc/dfs/dfstab` file to list the file systems it makes available to clients on the network. See the *Solaris System Administrator's Guide,* Third Edition for more information about sharing files (see bibliography at the end of this book).

## Restricting Superuser (root) Access

In general, superuser on a local system is not allowed root access to file systems shared across the network. Unless the server specifically grants superuser privileges, a user who is logged in as superuser on a client cannot gain root access to file systems that are remotely mounted on the client. The NFS system implements this restriction by changing the user ID (usually

60001) of the requester to the user ID of the user named `nobody`. The access rights of user `nobody` are the same as those given to the public or to a user without credentials for a particular file. For example, if the public has only execute permission for a file, then user `nobody` can execute only that file.

An NFS server can grant superuser privileges on a shared file system on a per-host basis, using the `root=hostname` option to the `share` command.

## Controlling and Monitoring Superuser Access

The next sections describe the following ways to restrict and monitor superuser access.

- Restrict superuser login to the console.
- Monitor who is using the `su` command.
- Grant only specific rights to specific users or roles.

*New!*

**Restricting Superuser Logins to the Console**     The superuser account has complete control over the entire operating system. It has access to and can execute essential system programs. For this reason, there are almost no security restraints for any program that is run by superuser.

You can protect the superuser account on a system by restricting access to a specific device through the `/etc/default/login` file. For example, if superuser access is restricted to the console, root can log in to a system only from the console. If individuals remotely log in to the system to perform administrative functions, they must first log in with their user logins and then use the `su` command to become superuser.

> *NOTE. Restricting superuser login to the console is the default setup when a system is installed.*

Use the following steps to restrict superuser (root) login to the console.

1. Become superuser.
2. Edit the `/etc/default/login` file and remove the # comment from the beginning of the `#CONSOLE=/dev/console` line.
3. Save the changes to the file.
4. Use `rlogin` to try to log in remotely to the system as superuser and verify that the operation fails.

**Monitoring Who Is Using the su Command**     You can monitor `su` attempts with the `/etc/default/su` file, which is part of the `syslog` subsystem. By using this file, you can enable the `/var/adm/sulog` file to monitor each time the `su` command is used to change to another user.

> *NOTE. Enabling the `/var/adm/sulog` file to monitor `su` use is the default setup when a system is installed.*

The `sulog` file lists all uses of the `su` command, not only those used to switch user to superuser. The entries show the date and time the command was used, whether or not it was successful (+ or -), the port from which the command was issued, and the name of the user and the switched identity.

Use the following steps to monitor who is using the `su` command.

1.  Become superuser.
2.  Edit the `/etc/default/su` file and remove the remove the # comment from the beginning of the `#SULOG=/var/adm/sulog` line.
3.  Save the changes to the file.
4.  Use the `su` command several times and, as superuser, display the contents of the `/var/adm/sulog` file.

The following example shows the tail of the `/var/adm/sulog` file.

```
castle% su
Password:
# tail -20 /var/adm/sulog
SU 10/07 10:35 + pts/3 winsor-root
SU 10/07 15:05 + console root-daemon
SU 10/07 15:54 + console root-daemon
SU 10/07 16:28 + pts/3 winsor-root
SU 10/08 08:23 + console root-daemon
SU 10/08 09:43 + pts/3 winsor-root
SU 10/08 12:39 + pts/3 winsor-des
SU 10/08 12:39 - pts/3 winsor-ray
SU 10/08 12:40 - pts/3 winsor-ray
SU 10/08 12:40 - pts/3 winsor-ray
SU 10/08 12:40 + pts/3 winsor-root
SU 10/08 12:44 + console root-daemon
SU 10/08 12:56 + pts/3 winsor-root
#
```

*New!*     **Grant Only Specific Rights to Specific Users or Roles.**     Starting with the Solaris 8 release and enhanced in the Solaris 8 Update 3 release, you can grant specific rights to users or to roles to perform specific system administration tasks. See Chapter 23, "Role-Based Access Control," for more information about rights and roles.

## Using Privileged Ports

Secure RPC is a method of providing additional security that authenticates both the host and the user making a request. Refer to Chapter 22, "Using Authentication Services," for more information about Secure RPC. If you do not want to run Secure RPC, a possible substitute is the Solaris *privileged port* mechanism. A privileged port is built by the superuser with a port number of less than 1024. After a system has authenticated the client's credentials, it builds a connection to the server via the privileged port. The server then verifies the client credential by examining the connection's port number.

Non-Solaris clients might not, however, be able to communicate through the privileged port. If they cannot, you might see error messages such as `Weak Authentication NFS request from unprivileged port.`

## Automated Security Enhancement Tool (ASET)

The ASET security package provides automated administration tools that enable you to control and monitor system security. You specify a security level—low, medium, or high— at which ASET runs. At each higher level, ASET's file control functions increase to reduce file access and tighten your system security. See Chapter 21, "Using the Automated Security Enhancement Tool (ASET)," for more information.

# 21

# *USING THE AUTOMATED SECURITY ENHANCEMENT TOOL (ASET)*

The automated security enhancement tool (ASET) enables you to monitor and control system security by automatically performing tasks that you would otherwise do manually.

ASET consists of seven tasks, each performing specific checks and adjustments to file systems.

- System files permissions verification.
- System files checks.
- User/group checks.
- System configuration files check.
- Environment check.
- `eeprom` check.
- Firewall setup.

The ASET tasks tighten file permissions, check the contents of critical system files for security weaknesses, and monitor crucial areas. ASET can contribute to safeguarding a network by applying the basic requirements of a firewall system to a system that serves as a gateway system.

Each task generates a report noting detected security weaknesses and changes the task has made to the system files. When run at the highest security level, ASET tries to modify all system security weaknesses. If it cannot correct a potential security problem, ASET reports the existence of the problem.

# ASET Master Files

ASET uses master files for configuration. Master files, reports, and other files are available in the /usr/aset directory. You can change these files to suit the particular requirements of your site.

The contents of the /usr/aset directory are listed in Table 111.

*Table 111   Contents of the /usr/aset Directory*

| Files and Directories | Description |
| --- | --- |
| archives | Directory ASET uses to store archive files. The aset.restore script uses the original files from this directory to restore a system to its pre-ASET state. |
| aset | The ASET shell script. |
| aset.restore | Script used to restore a system to its original condition before ASET was run. It also deschedules ASET if it is scheduled. |
| asetenv | Script that controls and sets ASET environment variables. |
| masters | Directory containing a list of master files that control the three levels of ASET security. |
| reports | Directory ASET uses to store reports. |
| tasks | Directory containing shell scripts and C executables that perform ASET tasks. |
| tmp | Temporary directory. |
| util | Directory containing ASET shell scripts and ELF executable utilities. |

To administer ASET, if you want to change any of the ASET defaults, first you edit the asetenv file. Next, you initiate an ASET session at one of the three levels of security. You can set the security level interactively with the /user/aset/aset command. Alternatively, use the proper option to the aset command to put an entry into root's crontab file to periodically run ASET. Finally, you review the contents of the reports in the /usr/aset/reports directory to monitor and fix any security problems reported by ASET.

*CAUTION. ASET tasks are disk intensive and can interfere with regular system and application activities. To minimize the impact on system performance, schedule ASET to run when system activity level is lowest—for example, once every 24 or 48 hours at midnight or on weekends.*

## ASET Security Levels

You can set ASET to operate at one of three security levels: low, medium, or high. At each higher level, ASET increases its file-control functions to reduce file access and heighten system security. These functions range from monitoring system security without limiting file access to users to increasingly tightening access permissions until a system is as secure as file permissions protection can make it.

The following list provides more information about the three ASET security levels.

- *Low security*—Ensures that attributes of system files are set to standard release values. ASET performs several checks and reports potential security weaknesses. At this level, ASET takes no action and does not affect system services.
- *Medium security*—Provides adequate security control for most environments. ASET modifies some of the system file settings and parameters, restricting system access to reduce the risks from security attacks. ASET reports security weaknesses and any modification it makes to restrict access. At this level, ASET does not affect system services.
- *High security*—Provides a highly secure system. ASET adjusts many system files and parameter settings to minimize access permissions. Most system applications and commands continue to function normally, but at this level, security considerations take precedence over other system behavior.

*NOTE. ASET does not change the permissions of a file to make it less secure unless you downgrade the security level or intentionally revert the system to the settings that existed before you ran ASET.*

## How ASET Tasks Work

This section describes what ASET does. You should understand each ASET task to interpret and use the reports effectively.

- The objective of the task.
- Operations the task performs.
- System components that are affected by the task.

ASET report files contain messages that describe as specifically as possible any problems discovered by each ASET task. These messages can help you diagnose and correct these problems. Successful use of ASET assumes that you understand system administration and system components.

Reports are generated by the `taskstat` command, which identifies the tasks that have been completed and the ones that are still running. Each completed task produces a report file. For a complete description of the `taskstat` command, refer to the `taskstat`(1M) manual page.

You set up tasks and choose the files to be checked for each security level by setting environment variables in the `User Configurable Parameters` part of the `/usr/aset/asetenv` script, shown below.

```
#############################################
#                                           #
#       User Configurable Parameters        #
#                                           #
#############################################

CKLISTPATH_LOW=${ASETDIR}/tasks:${ASETDIR}/util:${ASETDIR}/masters:/etc
CKLISTPATH_MED=${CKLISTPATH_LOW}:/usr/bin:/usr/ucb
CKLISTPATH_HIGH=${CKLISTPATH_MED}:/usr/lib:/sbin:/usr/sbin:/usr/ucblib
YPCHECK=false
UID_ALIASES=${ASETDIR}/masters/uid_aliases
PERIODIC_SCHEDULE="0 0 * * *"
TASKS="firewall env sysconf usrgrp tune cklist eeprom"
```

For more information about ASET environment variables, see "ASET Environment File (asetenv)" on page 572.

## System Files Permissions Verification

The `tune` task sets the permissions on system files to the security level you designate. It is run when the system is installed. If you decide later to alter the previously established levels, you must run this task again. At low security, the permissions are set to values that are appropriate for an open information-sharing environment. At medium security, the permissions are tightened to produce adequate security for most environments. At high security, they are tightened to severely restrict access.

Any modifications that this task makes to system files permissions or parameter settings are reported in the `tune.rpt` file.

## System Files Checks

The `cklist` task examines system files and compares each one with a description of that file listed in a master file. The master file is created the first time ASET runs the task. The master file contains the system file settings enforced by `cklist` for the specified security level.

ASET defines a default list of directories whose files are to be checked for each security level. You can use the default list or you can modify it, specifying different directories for each level.

For each file, the following criteria are checked.

- Owner and group.
- Permission bits.
- Size and checksum.
- Number of links.
- Last modification time.

Any discrepancies are reported in the `cklist.rpt` file. This file contains the results of comparing system file size, permission, and checksum values to the master file.

## User/Group Checks

The `usrgrp` task checks the consistency and integrity of user accounts and groups as defined in the `passwd` and `group` files. It checks the local and NIS or NIS+ password files. NIS+ password file problems are reported but not corrected.

This task checks for the following violations.

- Duplicate names or IDs.
- Entries in incorrect format.
- Accounts without a password.
- Invalid login directories.
- Presence of a `nobody` account.
- Null group password.
- A plus sign (+) in the `/etc/passwd` file on an NIS or NIS+ server.

Discrepancies are reported in the `usrgrp.rpt` file.

## System Configuration Files Check

The `sysconf` task checks various system tables, most of which are in the `/etc` directory.

- `/etc/default/login`
- `/etc/hosts.equiv`
- `/etc/inetd.conf`
- `/etc/aliases`
- `/var/adm/utmp`
- `/var/adm/utmpx`
- `/.rhosts`
- `/etc/vfstab`
- `/etc/dfs/dfstab`
- `/etc/ftpusers`

ASET performs various checks and modifications on these files and reports all problems in the `sysconf.rpt` file.

## Environment Check

The `env` task checks how the `PATH` and `UMASK` environment variables are set for `root` and other users in the `/.profile`, `/.login`, and `/.cshrc` files.

The results of checking the environment for security are reported in the `env.rpt` file.

## eeprom Check

The `eeprom` task checks the value of the `eeprom` security parameter to ensure that it is set to the appropriate security level. You can use one of the following values to set the `eeprom` security parameter.

- `none`
- `command`
- `full`

ASET does not change the `eeprom` setting but reports its recommendations in the `eeprom.rpt` file.

## Firewall Setup

The firewall task ensures that the system can be safely used as a network relay. It protects an internal network from external public networks by setting up a dedicated system as a firewall. The firewall system separates two networks, each of which approaches the other as untrusted. The firewall setup task disables the forwarding of Internet Protocol (IP) packets and hides routing information from the external network.

The firewall task runs at all security levels but takes action only at the highest level. If you want to run ASET at high security but find that your system does not require firewall protection, you can eliminate the firewall task; simply remove it from the list of tasks specified by the TASKS environment variable in the asetenv file.

Any changes made by this task are reported in the firewall.rpt file.

# ASET Execution Log

ASET generates an *execution log* whether it runs interactively or in the background. By default, ASET generates the log file on standard output. The execution log confirms that ASET ran at the designated time. It also contains any execution error messages. The -n option of the aset command directs the log to be delivered by electronic mail to a designated user. For a complete list of ASET options, refer to the aset(1M) manual page.

The following example shows an execution log running at low-level security.

```
castle% su
Password:
# /usr/aset/aset -l low
======= ASET Execution Log =======

ASET running at security level low

Machine = castle; Current time = 1015_09:29

aset: Using /usr/aset as working directory

Executing task list ...
        firewall
        env
        sysconf
        usrgrp
        tune
        cklist
        eeprom

All tasks executed. Some background tasks may still be running.

Run /usr/aset/util/taskstat to check their status:
    /usr/aset/util/taskstat     [aset_dir]

where aset_dir is ASET's operating directory,currently=/usr/aset.
```

```
When the tasks complete, the reports can be found in:
    /usr/aset/reports/latest/*.rpt
You can view them by:
    more /usr/aset/reports/latest/*.rpt
#
```

The log first shows the system and the time that ASET was run. Then it lists each task as it is started.

ASET invokes a background process for each of the tasks. The task is listed in the execution log when it starts. The log does not indicate when the task has been completed. To check the status of the background tasks, type **/usr/aset/util/taskstat** and press Return.

The following example shows that four tasks—firewall, env, sysconf, and usrgrp—have been completed and that three tasks—tune, cklist, and eeprom—are not finished.

```
# /usr/aset/util/taskstat

Checking ASET tasks status ...
Task firewall is done.
Task env is done.
Task sysconf is done.
Task usrgrp is done.

The following tasks are done:
        firewall
        env
        sysconf
        usrgrp

The following tasks are not done:
        tune
        cklist
        eeprom
#
```

# ASET Reports

All report files generated from ASET tasks are stored in subdirectories under the /usr/aset/reports directory. This section describes the structure of the /usr/aset/reports directory and provides guidelines on managing the report files.

ASET puts the report files in subdirectories that are named to reflect the time and date when the reports are generated. This structure enables you to keep an orderly set of records documenting the system status as it varies between ASET executions. You can monitor and compare the reports to determine the soundness of your system security.

The `/usr/aset/reports` directory contains a subdirectory named `latest` that is a symbolic link to the most recent set of reports generated by ASET.

The following example shows contents of the `/usr/aset/reports` directory with two subdirectories and the `latest` directory.

```
# ls -l /usr/aset/reports
total 6
drwxrwxrwx   2 root     other         512 Oct 15 09:30 1015_09:29
drwxrwxrwx   2 root     other         512 Oct 15 09:41 1015_09:41
lrwxrwxrwx   1 root     other          28 Oct 15 09:41 latest ->
 /usr/aset/reports/1015_09:41
#
```

The subdirectory name indicates the date and time the reports were generated, in the following format.

```
monthdate_hour:minute
```

where *month*, *date*, *hour*, and *minute* are all two-digit numbers. For example, `1015_09:41` represents October 15 at 9:41 a.m.

Each of the report subdirectories contains a collection of reports generated from one execution of ASET. To look at the latest reports that ASET has generated, you can always review the reports in the `/usr/aset/reports/latest` directory. The following example shows the contents of the `/usr/aset/reports/latest` directory.

```
# ls -l /usr/aset/reports/latest
total 14
-rw-rw-rw-   1 root     other         383 Oct 15 09:41 env.rpt
-rw-rw-rw-   1 root     other         622 Oct 15 09:41 execution.log
-rw-rw-rw-   1 root     other         306 Oct 15 09:41 firewall.rpt
-rw-rw-rw-   1 root     other         631 Oct 15 09:41 sysconf.rpt
-rw-rw-rw-   1 root     other          84 Oct 15 09:41 taskstatus
-rw-rw-rw-   1 root     other         114 Oct 15 09:41 tune.rpt
-rw-rw-rw-   1 root     other         256 Oct 15 09:41 usrgrp.rpt
castle#
```

*NOTE. Because ASET was not run at the highest security level, this listing does not contain the* `cklist.rpt` *and* `eeprom.rpt` *reports.*

Each report is named after the task that generates it. The complete list of reports is shown in Table 112 along with the task that generates the report.

*Table 112  ASET Reports and Tasks*

| Report | Task |
|---|---|
| cklist.rpt | System files checklist (cklist). |
| eeprom.rpt | EEPROM check (eeprom). |
| env.rpt | Environment check (env). |
| execution.log | Messages displayed by the taskstat command. |
| firewall.rpt | Firewall setup (firewall). |
| sysconf.rpt | System configuration files check (sysconf). |
| taskstatus | Messages displayed by the taskstat command on the status of the tasks. |
| tune.rpt | System file permissions tuning (tune). |
| usrgrp.rpt | User/group checks (usrgrp). |

## Format of Report Files

Within each report file, messages are bracketed by a beginning and ending banner line. Sometimes a task terminates prematurely—for example, when a component of ASET is accidentally removed or damaged. In most cases, the report file contains a message near the end that indicates the reason for the premature exit.

The following example of the usrgrp.rpt file reports that user rob has no password in the /etc/shadow file.

```
castle# more /usr/aset/reports/latest/usrgrp.rpt

*** Begin User And Group Checking ***

Checking /etc/passwd ...

Checking /etc/shadow ...

Warning!  Shadow file, line 17, no password:
      rob::::::::

... end user check.

Checking /etc/group ...

... end group check.

*** End User And Group Checking ***
#
```

## Examining and Comparing Report Files

After you run ASET the first time or when you reconfigure it, you should examine the report files closely.

Reconfiguration includes modifying the `asetenv` file or the master files in the `masters` subdirectory, or changing the security level at which ASET operates. The reports record any errors introduced when you reconfigured. By watching the reports closely, you can diagnose and solve problems as they arise.

You should routinely monitor the report files to check for security breaches. You can use the `diff` command to compare reports.

# ASET Master Files

The ASET master files—`tune.high`, `tune.low`, `tune.med`, and `uid_aliases`—are located in the `/usr/aset/masters` directory. ASET uses the master files to define security levels. The checklist files `cklist.high`, `cklist.med`, and `cklist.low` are also located in the `/usr/aset/masters` directory. The checklist files are generated when you execute ASET and are used by ASET to check file permissions.

## File Tuning

The `tune.low`, `tune.med`, and `tune.high` master files define the available ASET security levels. They specify the attributes of system files at each level and are used for comparison and reference.

The `tune.high` file, shown below, specifies the most restrictive level of security.

```
#
# Copyright 1990,1991,1999 by Sun Microsystems, Inc.
# All rights reserved.
#
#ident  "@(#)tune.high 1.10    99/04/14 SMI"
#
# Tune list for level high
#
# The original list was largely obsoleted by the
# "Safe Default File Permissions" project.
#
# Format:
#       pathname mode owner group type

/.cshrc 0600 root ? file
/.login  0600 root ? file
/.profile 0600 root ? file
/.logout 0600 root ? file
#
```

*NOTE. With the change in default file permissions introduced in the Solaris 8 release, the long list in previous* tune.high *files is now obsolete.*

The entries have the following syntax.

```
pathname mode owner group type
```

The following rules apply to the entries in the tune files.

- You can use regular shell wildcard characters such as an asterisk (*) and a question mark (?) in the path name for multiple references.
- *mode* represents the least allowable value. If the current setting is already more restrictive than the specified value, ASET does not loosen the permission settings. For example, if the specified value is 0777, the permission remains unchanged, because 0777 is always less restrictive than the current setting.

  When you decrease the security level from what it was for the previous execution or when you want to restore the system files to the state they were in before ASET was first executed, ASET recognizes what you are doing and decreases the protection level.
- You must use names for *owner* and *group* instead of numeric IDs.
- You can use a question mark (?) in place of *owner*, *group*, and *type* to prevent ASET from changing the existing values of these parameters.
- *type* can be symlink (symbolic link), directory, or file (everything else).
- Higher security level tune files reset file permissions to be at least as restrictive as they are at lower levels. Also, at higher levels, additional files are added to the list.
- A file can match more than one tune file entry. For example, /etc/passwd matches /etc/pass* and /etc*.
- Where two entries have different permissions, the more restrictive file permission applies. In the following example, the permission of /etc/passwd is set to 00755, which is the more restrictive of 00755 and 00770.

```
/etc/pass* 00755 ? ? file
/etc/* 00770 ? ? file
```

- If two entries have different *owner* or *group* designations, the last entry takes precedence.

You modify settings in the tune file by adding or deleting file entries.

*NOTE. Setting a permission to a less restrictive value than the current setting has no effect; the ASET tasks do not relax permissions unless you downgrade your system security to a lower level.*

## The uid_aliases File

The uid_aliases file contains a list of multiple user accounts sharing the same ID. Normally, ASET warns about such multiple user accounts because this practice lessens accountability. You can allow for exceptions to this rule by listing the exceptions in the uid_aliases file. ASET does not report entries in the passwd file with duplicate user IDs if these entries are specified in the uid_aliases file.

The default /usr/aset/masters/uid_aliases file is shown below.

```
#
# Copyright 1990, 1991 Sun Microsystems, Inc.  All Rights Reserved.
#
#
# sccsid = @(#) uid_aliases 1.1 1/2/91 14:39:52
#
# format:
#      uid=alias1=alias2=alias3= ...
# allows users "alias1", "aliase2", "alias3" to share the same uid.
0=+=root=checkfsys=makefsys=mountfsys=powerdown=setup=smtp=sysadm=umountfsys
1=sync=daemon
```

The default entry is to make UID 0 equivalent to user accounts root, checkfsys, makefsys, mountfsys, powerdown, setup, smpt, sysadm, and umountfsys. UID1 is equivalent to the user accounts sync and daemon.

Each entry has the following format.

```
uid=alias1=alias2=alias3-...
```

where *uid* is the shared UID number and *aliasn* is the name of the user account that shares the UID.

## The Checklist Files

The master files cklist.high, cklist.med, and cklist.low are generated when you first execute ASET or when you run ASET after you change the security level.

The following environment variables determine the files that are checked by this task.

- CKLISTPATH_LOW
- CKLISTPATH_MED
- CKLISTPATH_HIGH

Refer to the following section for more information about ASET environment variables.

## ASET Environment File (asetenv)

The environment file `asetenv` contains a list of environment variables that affect ASET tasks. You can change these variables to modify ASET operation.

The default `/usr/aset/asetenv` file is shown below.

```
#!/bin/sh
#
# Copyright 1990, 1991 Sun Microsystems, Inc.  All Rights Reserved.
#
#ident   "@(#)asetenv.sh 1.2     92/07/14 SMI"

# This is the "dot" script for ASET and should be invoked before
# running any ASET tasks.

###########################################
#                                         #
#       User Configurable Parameters      #
#                                         #
###########################################

CKLISTPATH_LOW=${ASETDIR}/tasks:${ASETDIR}/util:${ASETDIR}/masters:/etc
CKLISTPATH_MED=${CKLISTPATH_LOW}:/usr/bin:/usr/ucb
CKLISTPATH_HIGH=${CKLISTPATH_MED}:/usr/lib:/sbin:/usr/sbin:/usr/ucblib
YPCHECK=false
UID_ALIASES=${ASETDIR}/masters/uid_aliases
PERIODIC_SCHEDULE="0 0 * * *"
TASKS="firewall env sysconf usrgrp tune cklist eeprom"

###########################################
#                                         #
# ASET Internal Environment Variables     #
#                                         #
# Don't change from here on down ...      #
# there shouldn't be any reason to.       #
#                                         #
###########################################

export YPCHECK UID_ALIASES PERIODIC_SCHEDULE

# full paths of system utilites
AWK=/bin/awk
LS=/bin/ls
RM=/bin/rm
MV=/bin/mv
MKDIR=/bin/mkdir
LN=/bin/ln
SUM=/bin/sum
CUT=/bin/cut
GREP=/bin/grep
EGREP=/bin/egrep
DIFF=/bin/diff
MAIL=/bin/mail
CHGRP=/bin/chgrp
```

```
CHMOD=/bin/chmod
CHOWN=/usr/bin/chown
SORT=/bin/sort
UNIQ=/bin/uniq
YPCAT=/bin/ypcat
PS=/bin/ps
CP=/bin/cp
REALPATH=${ASETDIR}/util/realpath
ADDCKSUM=${ASETDIR}/util/addcksum
MINMODE=${ASETDIR}/util/minmode
FILE_ATTR=${ASETDIR}/util/file_attr
STR_TO_MODE=${ASETDIR}/util/str_to_mode
IS_WRITABLE=${ASETDIR}/util/is_writable
IS_READABLE=${ASETDIR}/util/is_readable
HOMEDIR=${ASETDIR}/util/homedir
SED=/bin/sed
ED=/bin/ed
CAT=/bin/cat
EXPR=/bin/expr
CRONTAB=/bin/crontab
TOUCH=/bin/touch

sysutils="AWK LS RM MV MKDIR LN SUM CUT GREP EGREP DIFF MAIL CHGRP CHMOD CHOWN \
PS \
CP SORT UNIQ YPCAT REALPATH ADDCKSUM MINMODE FILE_ATTR STR_TO_MODE \
ED SED CAT IS_WRITABLE IS_READABLE HOMEDIR EXPR CRONTAB TOUCH"

progs="$AWK $LS $RM $MV $MKDIR $LN $SUM $CUT $GREP $EGREP \
$DIFF $MAIL $CHGRP $CHMOD $CHOWN $PS $CRONTAB $TOUCH \
$CP $SORT $UNIQ $YPCAT $REALPATH $ADDCKSUM $MINMODE $FILE_ATTR \
$STR_TO_MODE $ED $SED $CAT $IS_WRITABLE $IS_READABLE $HOMEDIR $EXPR"

noprog=false
for i in $progs
do
        if [ ! -x $i ]
        then
                if [ "$noprog" = "false" ]
                then
                        noprog=true
                        echo
                        echo "ASET startup unsuccessful:"
                else
                        echo "Could not find executable $i."
                fi
        fi
done
if [ "$noprog" = "true" ]
then
        echo "Unable to proceed."
        exit
fi

export $sysutils

TIMESTAMP=`date '+%m%d_%H:%M'`
QUIT="ASET: irrecoverable error -- exiting ..."

case $ASETSECLEVEL in
low)    CKLISTPATH=`echo "${CKLISTPATH_LOW}"`;;
med)    CKLISTPATH=`echo "${CKLISTPATH_MED}"`;;
high)   CKLISTPATH=`echo "${CKLISTPATH_HIGH}"`;;
*)      echo $QUIT;
        exit 3;;
esac

# Set up report directory
$RM -rf ${ASETDIR}/reports/${TIMESTAMP}
$MKDIR ${ASETDIR}/reports/${TIMESTAMP}
REPORT=${ASETDIR}/reports/${TIMESTAMP}
$RM -rf ${ASETDIR}/reports/latest
$LN -s $REPORT ${ASETDIR}/reports/latest

# temorary files directory
TMP=${ASETDIR}/tmp
```

```
export TASKS TIMESTAMP QUIT REPORT CKLISTPATH
export TMP
```

Table 113 lists the ASET environment variables and the values that they specify.

*Table 113   ASET Environment Variables*

| Environment Variable | Default Value | Description |
|---|---|---|
| ASETDIR | Optional (set from shell). If not defined in the user environment, ASETDIR uses /usr/aset. | ASET working directory. |
| ASETSECLEVEL | Optional (set from shell). If not defined in the user environment, ASETSECLEVEL uses /usr/aset. | Security level (low, med, high). |
| CKLISTPATH_HIGH | ${CKLISTPATH_MED}: /usr/lib:/sbin: /usr/sbin: /usr/ucblib | Directory list for high security. |
| CKLISTPATH_LOW | ${ASETDIR}/tasks:$ {ASETDIR}/util: ${ASETDIR}/masters :/etc | Directory list for low security. |
| CKLISTPATH_MED | ${CKLISTPATH_LOW}: /usr/bin:/usr/ucb | Directory list for medium security. |
| PERIODIC_SCHEDULE | "0 0 * * *" | Periodic schedule for running crontab entries. |
| TASKS | "firewall env sysconf usrgrp tune cklist eeprom" | Tasks to run. |
| UID_ALIAS | ${ASETDIR}/masters /uid_aliases | Aliases file. |
| YPCHECK | false | Extends check to NIS and NIS+. |

## ASET Shell Environment Variables

ASET provides two optional environment variables that you can set through a shell.

- ASETDIR specifies an ASET working directory.
- ASETSECLEVEL specifies a security level at which ASET tasks are executed: low, medium, or high.

You set these environment variables in the same way you set any other shell environment variable.

From the C shell, type

```
castle% setenv ASETDIR pathname
```

From the Bourne or Korn shell, type

```
$ ASETDIR=pathname
$ export ASETDIR
$
```

## PERIODIC_SCHEDULE Variable

ASET uses the cron scheduling system to set its periodic schedule. Thus, the value of the PERIODIC_SCHEDULE variable that you set in the asetenv file uses the crontab file format (see crontab(1)). You specify the variable values as a string of five fields enclosed in double quotation marks, each field separated by a space.

```
"minutes hours day-of-month month day-of-week"
```

Table 114 explains the values used for the PERIODIC_SCHEDULE variable.

*Table 114   PERIODIC_SCHEDULE Variable Values*

| Variable | Value |
|---|---|
| minutes | Specify start time in number of minutes after the hour, with values from 0 through 59. |
| hours | Specify the start time hour, with values from 0 through 23. |
| day-of-month | Specify the day of the month when ASET should be run, with values from 1 through 31. |

*Table 114   PERIODIC_SCHEDULE Variable Values (Continued)*

| Variable | Value |
|----------|-------|
| *month* | Specify the month of the year when ASET should be run, with values from 1 through 12. |
| *day-of-week* | Specify the day of the week when ASET should be run, with values from 0 through 6. In this scheme, Sunday is day 0. |

The following rules apply.

• For any field, you can specify a list of values, each delimited by a comma.

• You can specify a value as a number or as a *range* (a pair of numbers joined by a dash). A range states that the ASET tasks should be executed for every time included in the range.

• You can specify an asterisk (*) as the value of any field. An asterisk specifies all possible values of the field, inclusive.

The default entry for PERIODIC_SCHEDULE executes ASET daily at midnight.

## TASKS Variable

The TASKS variable in the asetenv file lists the tasks that ASET performs. The default is to list all seven tasks.

• firewall
• env
• sysconf
• usrgrp
• tune
• cklist
• eeprom

If you want to skip any of the tasks, simply remove the task from the list. To add a task, edit the asetenv file and include the task name in the quoted string following the TASK environment variable, using a space as the separator.

## UID_ALIASES Variable

The UID_ALIASES variable in the asetenv file specifies which aliases file to use. If the file is present, ASET consults it for a list of permitted multiple aliases. The format is shown below.

```
UID_ALIASES=pathname
```

where *pathname* is the full path name of the aliases file.

The default is the uid_aliases file in the /usr/aset/masters directory.

## YPCHECK Variable

The YPCHECK variable in the asetenv file extends the task of checking system tables to include NIS or NIS+ tables. The variable accepts a Boolean value, which can be set to either true or false. The default is false, confining checking to local system tables. To extend checking, edit the asetenv file and change the value for the variable to true.

## CKLISTPATH_level Variable

The three checklist path variables list the directories to be checked by the checklist task.

The values for the checklist path environment variables are similar to those of shell path variables. They are a list of directory names separated by colons (:). You use an equal sign (=) to assign the value to the variable name.

# Running ASET

This section describes how to run ASET either interactively or periodically.

## Running ASET Interactively

You can run ASET interactively from the command line any time you want to monitor system security; use the `/usr/aset/aset` command. Table 115 lists the options to the `aset` command.

*Table 115   Options to the aset Command*

| Option | Description |
|---|---|
| `-p` | Schedule `aset` to be executed periodically. This command adds an entry for `aset` to the `/var/spool/cron/crontabs/root` file. The option uses the value from the `PERIODIC_SCHEDULE` environment variable in the `/usr/aset/asetenv` file to define the time for execution. |
| `-d` *aset-dir* | Specify a working directory other than the default `/usr/aset` for ASET. ASET is installed by default in `/usr/aset`, which is the root directory of all ASET commands and data files. If you use another directory as the ASET working directory, either define it with the `-d` option from the command line or set the `ASETDIR` environment variable before running `aset`. The command-line option, if specified, overwrites the environment variable. |
| `-l` *sec-level* | Specify a security level (`low`, `med`, or `high`). The default level is low. You can also specify the level by setting the `ASETSECLEVEL` environment variable before running `aset`. The command-line option, if specified, overwrites the environment variable. |
| `-n` *user@host* | Notify *user* at system *host*. Send the output of `aset` to the user by e-mail. If you do not specify this option, the output is sent to the standard output. Note that this information is not the ASET report, but, instead, is an execution log that includes any error messages. |
| `-u` *userlist-file* | Specify a file containing a list of users for ASET to perform environment checks on. By default, ASET only checks for root. *userlist-file* is an ASCII text file. Each entry in the file is a line that contains only one user name (login name). |

New!

Use the following steps to run ASET interactively.

1. Become superuser.
2. Type **/usr/aset/aset -l low | med | high [-d *pathname*]** and press Return. You use the -d *pathname* option to specify the ASET working directory if it is located somewhere else than the default /usr/aset directory.
3. Review the ASET execution log that is displayed on the screen.
4. Type **/usr/aset/util/taskstat** and press Return to verify that all tasks running in background are completed.
5. When tasks are completed, review the contents of the reports in the /usr/aset/reports/latest directory.

The following example runs ASET at low security with the default working directory. Notice that if you run the aset command with no arguments, the default is to run at low security level.

```
# /usr/aset/aset
======= ASET Execution Log =======

ASET running at security level low

Machine = castle; Current time = 1015_13:45

aset: Using /usr/aset as working directory

Downgrading security level:
Previous level = high; Current level = low

Executing task list ...
        firewall
        env
        sysconf
        usrgrp
        tune
        cklist
        eeprom

All tasks executed. Some background tasks may still be running.

Run /usr/aset/util/taskstat to check their status:
    /usr/aset/util/taskstat     [aset_dir]

where aset_dir is ASET's operating directory,currently=/usr/aset.

When the tasks complete, the reports can be found in:
    /usr/aset/reports/latest/*.rpt
You can view them by:
    more /usr/aset/reports/latest/*.rpt
# /usr/aset/util/taskstat

Checking ASET tasks status ...
Task firewall is done.

The following tasks are done:
        firewall

The following tasks are not done:
        env
        sysconf
        usrgrp
        tune
        cklist
```

```
          eeprom
# cd /usr/aset/reports/latest
# ls
env.rpt          firewall.rpt    taskstatus      usrgrp.rpt
execution.log  sysconf.rpt     tune.rpt
# more env.rpt

*** Begin Enviroment Check ***

Warning! umask set to umask 022 in /etc/profile - not recommended.
chmod: WARNING: can't access /tmp/tmppath.24379
Ambiguous output redirect
Can't open /tmp/tmppath.24379
Can't open /tmp/tmppath.24379
Can't open /tmp/tmppath.24379
Can't open /tmp/tmppath.24379
Can't open /tmp/tmppath.24379
cat: cannot open /tmp/tmppath.24379

*** End Enviroment Check ***
# more firewall.rpt

*** Begin Firewall Task ***

Beginning firewall.restore...

Restored ip_forwarding to previous value - 0.

Restored /usr/sbin/in.routed.

firewall.restore completed.
# more sysconf.rpt

Beginning sysconf.restore...

Restoring /etc/inetd.conf. Saved existing file in /etc/inetd.conf.asetbak.

Restoring /etc/aliases. Saved existing file in /etc/aliases.asetbak.

sysconf.restore completed.

*** Begin System Scripts Check ***

*** End System Scripts Check ***
# more tune.rpt

*** Begin Tune Task ***

Beginning tune.restore...
(This may take a while.)
# more usrgrp.rpt

Beginning usrgrp.restore...

Restoring /etc/passwd. Saved existing file in /etc/passwd.asetbak.

Restoring /etc/group. Saved existing file in /etc/group.asetbak.

Restoring /etc/shadow. Saved existing file in /etc/shadow.asetback.

usrgrp.restore completed.

*** Begin User And Group Checking ***

Checking /etc/passwd ...

Checking /etc/shadow ...

Warning!  Shadow file, line 17, no password:
       rob::::::::

... end user check.

Checking /etc/group ...

... end group check.
```

```
*** End User And Group Checking ***
```

## Running ASET Periodically

To run ASET periodically, first you edit the PERIODIC_SCHEDULE variable in
the /usr/aset/asetenv file, then you run the aset -p command, which
adds an ASET entry to the crontab file.

*NOTE. Schedule ASET to run when system demand is light. The
default setting for the* PERIODIC_SCHEDULE *environment variable is
to run ASET every 24 hours at midnight.*

Use the following steps to run ASET periodically.

1. Become superuser.
2. Review the settings in the /usr/aset/asetenv file for the
   PERIODIC_SCHEDULE environment variable, and modify them as
   appropriate.
3. Type **/usr/aset/aset -p** and press Return.

   The -p (periodic) option edits the crontab file, using the values from
   the asetenv file.
4. Type **crontab -l root** and press Return to verify that the
   crontab entry for ASET has been added.

The following example uses the default values for PERIODIC_SCHEDULE
from the asetenv file to schedule when ASET will run.

```
# crontab -l root
#ident    "@(#)root        1.19     98/07/06 SMI"    /* SVr4.0 1.1.3.1        */
#
# The root crontab should be used to perform accounting data collection.
#
# The rtc command is run to adjust the real time clock if and when
# daylight savings time changes.
#
10 3 * * 0,4 /etc/cron.d/logchecker
10 3 * * 0   /usr/lib/newsyslog
15 3 * * 0 /usr/lib/fs/nfs/nfsfind
1 2 * * * [ -x /usr/sbin/rtc ] && /usr/sbin/rtc -c > /dev/null 2>&1
30 3 * * * [ -x /usr/lib/gss/gsscred_clean ] && /usr/lib/gss/gsscred_clean
#
```

```
castle% su
Password:
# /usr/aset/aset -p
======= ASET Execution Log =======

ASET running at security level low

Machine = castle; Current time = 1015_14:22

aset: Using /usr/aset as working directory
```

```
ASET execution scheduled through cron.

# crontab -l root
#ident  "@(#)root       1.19    98/07/06 SMI"  /* SVr4.0 1.1.3.1       */
#
# The root crontab should be used to perform accounting data collection.
#
# The rtc command is run to adjust the real time clock if and when
# daylight savings time changes.
#
10 3 * * 0,4 /etc/cron.d/logchecker
10 3 * * 0   /usr/lib/newsyslog
15 3 * * 0 /usr/lib/fs/nfs/nfsfind
1 2 * * * [ -x /usr/sbin/rtc ] && /usr/sbin/rtc -c > /dev/null 2>&1
30 3 * * * [ -x /usr/lib/gss/gsscred_clean ] && /usr/lib/gss/gsscred_clean
0 0 * * * /usr/aset/aset  -d /usr/aset
#
```

## Stopping Running ASET Periodically

If you want to stop running ASET from crontab, edit the crontab file to remove the ASET entry.

Use the following steps to stop running ASET periodically.

1.  Become superuser.
2.  Type **crontab -e root** and press Return.

    A text editor window opens, displaying the contents of the crontab file.
3.  Delete the ASET entry.
4.  Save the changes and close the file.
5.  Type **crontab -l root** and press Return to verify that the ASET entry is deleted.

## Collecting Reports on a Server

You can collect reports from a number of client systems into a directory on the server to make comparing ASET reports easier.

Use the following steps to collect reports on a server.

1.  Become superuser.
2.  Type **cd /usr/aset** and press Return.
3.  Type **mkdir *rptdir*** and press Return to create a report directory.
4.  Type **cd *rptdir*** and press Return.
5.  Type **mkdir *client-rpt*** and press Return for each client system for which you want to collect reports.

6. Edit the `/etc/dfs/dfstab` file and add the `client-rpt` directories with read/write options.

```
share -F nfs -o rw=client-hostname /usr/aset/rptdir/client-rpt
```

7. Type **shareall** and press Return.
8. On each client, become superuser.
9. Type **mount server:/usr/aset/*rptdir*/*client-rpt*** **/usr/aset/reports** and press Return. The file system is mounted
10. On each client, also add a line to the `/etc/vfstab` file on the mount point `/usr/aset/reports`. The next time the system is booted, the reports are automatically mounted.

*NOTE. You may want to use the automounter to decrease the amount of manual mounting. Refer to Part 3, Automounter and WebNFS Services, for more information.*

The following example collects ASET reports from the client `seachild` on the server `castle`.

```
castle% su
Password:
castle# cd /usr/aset
castle# mkdir all_reports
castle# cd all_reports
castle# mkdir seachild_rpt
castle# vi /etc/dfs/dfstab
share -F dfs -o rw=seachild /usr/aset/all_reports/seachild_rpt
ZZ (Writes changes and quites vi)
castle# shareall
castle#
```

On the client, `seachild`.

```
seachild% su
Password:
seachild# mount castle:/usr/aset/all_reports/seachild_rpt /usr/aset/reports
seachild# vi /etc/vfstab
castle:/usr/aset/all_reports/seachild_rpt /usr/aset/reports nfs - yes hard
ZZ (Writes changes and quites vi)
seachild#
```

# Restoring System Files Modified by ASET

When ASET is executed for the first time, it saves and archives the original system files in the `/usr/aset/archive` directory. You can use the `/usr/aset/aset.restore` command to reinstate these files. If ASET is currently scheduled for periodic execution, it also removes the line from the `crontab` entry.

Any changes made to system files are lost when you run `aset.restore`.

Use the `aset.restore` command at the following times.

- When you want to remove ASET changes and restore the original system. If you want to deactivate ASET permanently, you can remove it from `cron` scheduling if the `aset` command has been added to root's `crontab`.
- After a brief period of experimenting with ASET, to restore the original system state.
- When some major functionality is not working properly and you suspect that ASET may be causing the problem.

Use the following steps to restore system files modified by ASET.

1. Become superuser.
2. Type **/usr/aset/aset.restore** and press Return.

   Informational messages are displayed while the script is restoring system files to their original state.
3. If there is an ASET `crontab` entry, you are prompted to verify you want to remove it. Type **y** and press Return to remove the entry.

The following example restores system files to their pre-ASET state.

```
# /usr/aset/aset.restore
aset.restore: beginning restoration ...

Executing /usr/aset/tasks/firewall.restore

Beginning firewall.restore...

firewall.restore failed:
/usr/sbin/in.routed.asetoriginal not found.

Executing /usr/aset/tasks/sysconf.restore

Beginning sysconf.restore...

Restoring /etc/inetd.conf. Saved existing file in /etc/inetd.conf.asetbak.

Restoring /etc/aliases. Saved existing file in /etc/aliases.asetbak.

sysconf.restore completed.

Executing /usr/aset/tasks/tune.restore

Beginning tune.restore...
(This may take a while.)

tune.restore completed.

Executing /usr/aset/tasks/usrgrp.restore

Beginning usrgrp.restore...
```

```
Restoring /etc/passwd. Saved existing file in /etc/passwd.asetbak.

Restoring /etc/group. Saved existing file in /etc/group.asetbak.

Restoring /etc/shadow. Saved existing file in /etc/shadow.asetback.

usrgrp.restore completed.

Descheduling ASET from crontab file...
The following is the ASET schedule entry to be deleted:
1 2 * * * [ -x /usr/sbin/rtc ] && /usr/sbin/rtc -c  /dev/null 2&10 0 * * *
 /usr/aset/aset  -d /usr/aset
Proceed to deschedule: (y/n) y

Resetting security level from low to null.

aset.restore: restoration completed.
#
```

Note that the firewall restore was not successful in this example.

The aset.restore script does not remove files from the /usr/aset/reports and the /usr/aset/archive directories. If you want to reclaim that file system space, you may want to delete the contents of these directories.

# ASET Error Messages

This section documents the error messages generated by ASET.

| ASET failed: no mail program found. | |
|---|---|
| | ASET is directed to send the execution log to a user, but no mail program can be found. To fix the problem, install a mail program. |
| USAGE: aset [n user[@host]] in /bin mail or /usr/ucb/mail Cannot decide current and previous security levels. | |
| | ASET cannot determine what the security levels are for the current and previous invocations. To fix the problem, ensure that the current security level is set either with the command-line option or with the ASETSECLEVEL environment variable from a shell. Also, ensure that the last line of the ASETDIR/archives/asetseclevel.arch file correctly reflects the previous security level. If these values are not set or are incorrect, specify them correctly. |

| |
|---|
| `ASET working directory undefined.`<br>`To specify, set ASETDIR environment variable or use`<br>`command line option -d`<br>`ASET startup unsuccessful.` |

| | |
|---|---|
| | The ASET working directory is not defined or is defined incorrectly. To fix the problem, use the `ASETDIR` environment variable or the `-d` command line option to correctly specify the ASET working directory and restart ASET. |

| |
|---|
| `ASET working directory $ASETDIR missing.`<br>`ASET startup unsuccessful.` |

| | |
|---|---|
| | The ASET working directory is not defined or it is defined incorrectly. This may be because the `ASETDIR` variable refers to a nonexistent directory. Ensure that the correct directory—the directory containing the ASET directory hierarchy—is referred to correctly. |

| |
|---|
| `Cannot expand $ASETDIR to full pathname.` |

| | |
|---|---|
| | ASET cannot expand the directory name given by the `ASETDIR` variable or the `-d` command line option to a full path name. To fix the problem, ensure that the directory name is correct and that it refers to an existing directory to which the user has access. |

| |
|---|
| `aset: invalid/undefined security level.`<br>`To specify, set ASESTSECLEVEL environment variable or use`<br>`command line option -l, with argument= low/med/high.` |

| | |
|---|---|
| | The security level is not defined or it is defined incorrectly. Only the values `low`, `med`, or `high` are acceptable. To fix the problem, use the `ASETSECLEVEL` variable or the `-l` command-line option to specify one of the three values. |

| |
|---|
| `ASET environment file asetenv not found in $ASETDIR.`<br>`ASET startup unsuccessful.` |

| | |
|---|---|
| | ASET cannot locate an `asetenv` file in its working directory. To fix the problem, ensure that there is an `asetenv` file in the ASET working directory. |

| |
|---|
| `filename doesn't exist or is not readable.` |

| | |
|---|---|
| | The file referred to by `filename` doesn't exist or is not readable. This problem can occur with the `-u` option with which you can specify a file that contains a list of users whom you want to check. To fix the problem, ensure the argument to the `-u` option exists and is readable. |

| ASET task list TASKLIST undefined. |
| --- |
| The ASET task list, which should be defined in the asetenv file, is not defined. Your asetenv file may be bad, or the entry may be missing. To fix the problem, examine your asetenv file. Ensure the task list is defined in the User Configurable section. Also check other parts of the file to ensure that the file is intact. Refer to the asetenv(4) manual page for the content of a good asetenv file. |
| ASET task list TASKLIST missing.<br>ASET startup unsuccessful. |
| The ASET task list, which should be defined in the asetenv file, is not defined. Your asetenv file may be bad, or the entry may be missing. To fix the problem, check the User Configurable section of the asetenv file to ensure that the variable is defined and is in the proper format. |
| Warning! Duplicate ASET execution scheduled.<br>Check crontab file. |
| ASET is scheduled more than once. In other words, scheduling is requested while a schedule is already in effect. This conflict may not necessarily be an error if you want more than one schedule. If you want more than one schedule, use crontab(1) scheduling. To fix the problem, check your crontab file to make sure that the correct schedule is in effect and that no duplicate crontab entries for ASET exist. |

# 22

# USING
# AUTHENTICATION
# SERVICES

Secure RPC is a method of providing additional security that authenticates the host and the user making a request. Secure RPC uses Diffie-Hellman keypairs. This authentication mechanism uses DES (data encryption standard) public key encryption. Applications that use Secure RPC include NFS and the NIS+ name service.

> *NOTE. Starting with the Solaris 8 release, Kerberos V5 support is no longer provided as part of Secure RPC. However, a client-side implementation of Kerberos V5, which uses RPCSEC_GSS, is included with the Solaris 8 release.*

*New!*

The NFS software enables several hosts to share files over the network. The clients have access to the file systems that the server exports to the clients. Users logged in to the client system can access the file systems by mounting them from the server. To the user on the client system, the files seem to be local. One of the most common uses of the NFS environment is to enable systems, which act as NFS clients, to be installed for each user. However, each user's files are actually kept on a central NFS server. The file systems that contain these files are mounted to the clients as needed.

The NFS environment can use Secure RPC to authenticate users who make requests over the network. This combination is known as *Secure NFS*. The authentication mechanism, AUTH_DH, uses DES encryption with Diffie-Hellman authentication to ensure authorized access. The AUTH_DH mechanism has also been called AUTH_DES. As a whole, this method is called public key encryption, because it authenticates with the Diffie-Hellman keypairs, then encrypts everything after that with the DES algorithm.

*New!*

**New!**

Two kinds of encryption are in use today.

- Symmetric encryption.
- Asymmetric or public key encryption.

In symmetric encryption, a single secret key is shared by two parties (hence, the name symmetric). Any data encrypted with the secret key can be decrypted by anyone who has the secret key. Thus, it is important that only the parties involved possess the key. The algorithms that implement this type of encryption are very fast and efficient. However, the main problem with symmetric encryption is that the key must remain secret, which makes it difficult to transmit the key safely to the parties that need it. The key can be intercepted, thus defeating the encryption process.

In asymmetric encryption, each party generates a "keypair," that consists of a public key and a private or secret key. The public key is made available to the universe, and the private key is available only to the party that created it. In fact, the private key is encrypted with a password so that it cannot be used directly if it is stolen. The a person's public key is used by *other parties* to encrypt information that can be decrypted only with the private key. For example, user A and user B generate keypairs for themselves and make their public keys available to each other. User A encrypts a message with user B's public key. This message can be decrypted only with user B's private key. In fact, even user A cannot decrypt this message because he didn't encrypt it with his own public key.

This process provides a safe method of encryption because each person exposes only his public key. The public keys can be used only to encrypt messages that are destined for themselves. Asymmetric encryption has another side benefit: only the owner of the private key can decrypt messages encrypted with his associated public key. Thus, by responding to an encrypted message, he can prove—or authenticate—his identity to the person that encrypted the message in the first place. The only problem with this form of encryption is that it is several orders of magnitude slower than symmetric encryption. Because of the slow speed, asymmetric encryption is useless for transmitting large amounts of data over a network.

So what do you do to transmit large amounts of information? You use both kinds of encryption.

## Example: Diffie-Hellman

For example, user A wants to exchange a lot of data with user B on another system but wants to encrypt all of it as it passes over the network. Ultimately, both users want to use symmetric encryption for speed but don't want to pass the secret key over the network link. User A and user B have each other's public keys. User A can create a secret symmetric key and encrypt it with user B's public key. He then transmits the encrypted secret key to user B. User B uses his password-protected private key (which he has to unprotect with its password each time he uses it) to decrypt the incoming secret key. Now users A and B both have the secret symmetric key and can start a symmetric encryption session. Notice that they used asymmetric encryption to get the symmetric key safely over the network.

## Example: Secure RPC

To use asymmetric and symmetric encryption with NIS+ and Secure RPC credentials, every individual and system is first given an asymmetric keypair. In NIS+, the keypair is called an NIS+/Secure RPC "credential" (the DES one, not the LOCAL one). The public key and the password-encrypted private key for the credential are put in the NIS+ `cred` table. In this way, the public key is available to everyone and the private key is protected with a password.

Normally, whenever users log in to a system, they provide their password to do so. The `keylogin` program is also run as part of the login process. The user's Secure RPC password is the password that protects his private key in the `cred` table. If the user's login password is the same as his secure RPC password, then his private key is automatically unlocked whenever he logs in and the unlocked and unprotected private key is stored in the `keyserv` program. Thus, the user does not need to type in his private key password whenever he wants to start a public key asymmetric encryption session.

When an individual wants to start a Secure RPC session with a server, the Secure RPC subsystem automatically looks up the server's public key in the `cred` table and then generates the common key, which is really just a symmetric encryption key combined with other information, such as time. The symmetric common key is encrypted with the server's public key and passed to the server. The server can decrypt the common key with its own private asymmetric key. The user and server now share a symmetric encryption with each other.

This chapter describes the following elements of Secure RPC.

- Data Encryption Standard (DES) encryption.
- Diffie-Hellman keypair authentication.
- Pluggable Authentication Module (PAM).

# DES Encryption

The data encryption standard (DES) functions use a 56-bit key to encrypt user data. If two credential users (or principals) know the same DES key, they can communicate in private, using the key to encrypt and decrypt data. DES is a relatively fast encryption mechanism. A DES chip makes the encryption even faster; if the chip is not present, though, a software implementation is substituted.

The risk of using just DES is that, with enough time, an intruder can collect enough cipher-text messages encrypted with the same key to be able to discover the key and decipher the messages. For this reason, security systems such as Secure RPC change the keys frequently.

# Diffie-Hellman Authentication

The Diffie-Hellman method of authenticating a user is nontrivial for an intruder to crack. The client and the server each have their own private key (sometimes called a *secret key*) which they use together with the public key to devise a *common key*. They use the common key to communicate with each other, with an agreed-upon encryption/decryption function such as DES. This method was identified as *DES authentication* in previous Solaris releases.

*Authentication* is based on the capability of the sending system to use the common key to encrypt the current time, which the receiving system can decrypt and check against its current time. Because Diffie-Hellman depends on the current times matching, the keyserver program first synchronizes the time between the client and server.

The public and private keys are stored in an NIS or NIS+ database. NIS stores the keys in the publickey map, and NIS+ stores the keys in the cred table. These files contain the public key and the private key for all potential users.

The system administrator is responsible for setting up NIS or NIS+ tables and generating a public key and a private key for each user. The private key is stored, encrypted, with the user's password. This makes the private key known only to the user.

## How Diffie-Hellman Authentication Works

This section describes the series of transactions in a client-server session where DH authentication (AUTH_DH) is used.

### Generating the Public and Secret Keys

Some time before a transaction, the administrator runs either the newkey or nisaddcred commands that generate a public key and a secret key. Each user has a unique public key and secret key. The public key is stored in a public database; the secret key is stored in encrypted form in the same database. To change the key pair, use the `chkey` command.

## Running the keylogin Command

Normally, the login password is identical to the secure RPC password. In this case, a `keylogin` is not required. If the passwords are different, the users have to log in and then do an explicit `keylogin`.

The `keylogin` program prompts the user for a secure RPC password and uses the password to decrypt the secret key. The `keylogin` program then passes the decrypted secret key to a program called the keyserver. The *keyserver* is an RPC service with a local instance on every computer. The keyserver saves the decrypted secret key and waits for the user to initiate a Secure RPC transaction with a server.

If the passwords are the same, the login process passes the secret key to the keyserver automatically whenever the user logs in. If the passwords are required to be different and the user must always run `keylogin`, then the `keylogin` program can be included in the user's environment configuration file such as `~/.login`, `~/.cshrc`, or `~/.profile`, so that it runs automatically whenever the user logs in.

## Generating the Conversation Key

The following sequence occurs when the user initiates a transaction with a server.

1. The keyserver randomly generates a conversation key.
2. The keyserver uses the conversation key to encrypt the client's timestamp (among other things).
3. The keyserver looks up the server's public key in the public-key database (see the `publickey`(4) manual page).
4. The keyserver uses the client's secret key and the server's public key to create a common key.
5. The keyserver encrypts the conversation key with the common key.

## First Contact with the Server

The transmission, including the encrypted timestamp and the encrypted conversation key, is then sent to the server. The transmission includes a credential and a verifier. The credential has three components.

- The client's Net name.
- The conversation key, encrypted with the common key.
- A "window," encrypted with the conversation key.

The *window* is the difference the client says should be allowed between the server's clock and the client's timestamp. If the difference between the server's clock and the timestamp is greater than the window, the server rejects the client's request. Under normal circumstances, the request is not rejected because the client first synchronizes with the server before starting the RPC session.

The client's verifier contains the following elements.

- The encrypted timestamp.
- An encrypted verifier of the specified window, decremented by 1.

The *window verifier* is needed in case an outsider wants to impersonate a user and writes a program that, instead of filling in the encrypted fields of the credential and verifier, just stuffs in random bits. The server decrypts the conversation key into some random key and uses it to try to decrypt the window and timestamp. The result is random numbers. After a few thousand trials, however, there is a good chance that the random window/timestamp pair will pass the authentication system. The window verifier makes guessing the right credential much more difficult.

## Decrypting the Conversation Key

The following sequence occurs when the server receives the transmission from the client.

1. The keyserver local to the server looks up the client's public key in the public-key database.
2. The keyserver uses the client's public key and the server's secret key to deduce the common key—the same common key computed by the client. Only the server and the client can calculate the common key because doing so requires knowing one secret key or the other.
3. The kernel uses the common key to decrypt the conversation key.
4. The kernel calls the keyserver to decrypt the client's timestamp with the decrypted conversation key.

## Storing Information on the Server

After the server decrypts the client's timestamp, it stores four items of information in a credential table.

- The client's computer name.
- The conversation key.
- The window.
- The client's timestamp.

The server stores the first three items for future use. It stores the timestamp to protect against replays. The server accepts only timestamps that are chronologically greater than the last one seen, so any replayed transactions are guaranteed to be rejected.

*NOTE. Implicit in these procedures is the name of the caller, who must be authenticated in some manner. The keyserver cannot use DES authentication to do this because it would create a deadlock. To solve this problem, the keyserver stores the secret keys by UID and grants requests only to local root processes.*

### Verifier Returned to the Client

The server returns a verifier to the client, which includes the following elements.

- The index ID, which the server records in its credential cache.
- The client's timestamp minus 1, encrypted by the conversation key.

1 is subtracted from the timestamp to ensure that the timestamp is invalid and cannot be reused as a client verifier.

### Client Authenticates the Server

The client receives the verifier and authenticates the server. The client knows that only the server could have sent the verifier because only the server knows what timestamp the client sent.

### Additional Transactions

With every transaction after the first, the client returns the index ID to the server in its second transaction and sends another encrypted timestamp. The server sends back the client's timestamp minus 1, encrypted by the conversation key.

## Administering Diffie-Hellman Authentication

This section describes the commands used to administer Secure RPC and provides instructions for the following tasks associated with network security.

- Restarting the keyserver.
- Setting up NIS+ credentials for Diffie-Hellman authentication.
- Setting up NIS credentials for Diffie-Hellman authentication.
- Sharing and mounting files with Diffie-Hellman authentication.

## Secure RPC Commands

Table 116 lists manual pages that provide useful reference information about Secure RPC.

*Table 116   Secure RPC Manual Page References*

| Command | Description |
|---|---|
| secure_rpc(3N) | Description of Secure RPC library routines for secure remote procedure calls. |
| rpc(3N) | Description of RPC library routines for secure remote procedure calls. |
| attributes(5) | Characteristics of commands and device drivers. |

Table 117 lists commands used to administer Diffie-Hellman authentication.

*Table 117   Secure RPC Commands*

| Command | Description |
|---|---|
| chkey | Change user's Secure RPC key pair. |
| getpublickey | Retrieve public key. |
| getsecretkey | Retrieve secret key. |
| keylogin | Decrypt and pass secret key into keyserv for storage. |
| keylogout | Delete secret key stored inside keyserv. |
| keyserv | Daemon for storing private encryption keys. |
| login | Sign on to a system. |
| newkey | Create a new Diffie-Hellman keypair in the public-key database. |
| nisaddcred | Create NIS+ credentials. |
| nisclient | Initialize NIS+ credentials for NIS+ principals. |
| publickey | Retrieve public or secret key. |

## Restarting the Keyserver

The keyserv daemon must be running before Diffie-Hellman authentication can work properly. Normally, the keyserver is started at boot time by the rc2 script that runs the /etc/rc2.d/S71rpc script.

If the keyserv daemon dies or is not running on a system, use the following steps to restart it.

1. Become superuser.
2. Type **ps -ef | grep keyserv** and press Return. Check the output to verify that the keyserv daemon is not running.
3. Type **/usr/sbin/keyserv** and press Return.

In the following example, the ps -ef command is used to verify that the keyserv daemon is not running, the keyserv daemon is restarted, and the ps -ef command is used again to verify that it is now running.

```
castle% su
Password:
castle# ps -ef | grep keyserv
    root   727   722  0 12:58:25 pts/3     0:00 grep keyserv
castle# /usr/sbin/keyserv
castle# ps -ef | grep keyserv
    root   729     1  0 12:58:46 ?         0:00 /usr/sbin/keyserv
    root   733   722  0 12:58:57 pts/3     0:00 grep keyserv
castle#
```

*NOTE. If you start the* keyserv *daemon when it is already running, the message* /usr/sbin/keyserv: unable to create service *is displayed.*

## Setting Up NIS+ Credentials for Diffie-Hellman Public Key Authentication

To set up Diffie-Hellman authentication for the NIS+ nameservice, you must set up a new key for both root and user accounts. This section describes how to set up a new key for these two accounts.

Use the following steps to set up a new key for root on an NIS+ client.

1. Become superuser on the client.
2. Edit the publickey entry in the /etc/nsswitch.conf file to read **publickey: nisplus**.
3. Type **nisinit -cH *hostname*** and press Return to initialize the NIS+ client.
4. Type **nisaddcred local** and press Return.
5. Type **nisaddcred des** and press Return.
   The client is added to the cred table.
6. When prompted, type the network password.
7. When prompted, retype the network password.
8. Type **keylogin** and press Return.
   If you are prompted for a password, the procedure succeeded.

The following example sets up the system seachild as an NIS+ client. It uses the host castle as the argument to the nisinit command. You can ignore the warnings. The `keylogin` command is accepted, verifying that `seachild` is correctly set up as a secure NIS+ client.

```
seachild# nisinit -cH castle
NIS Server/Client setup utility.
This machine is in the Castle.Abc.COM. directory.
Setting up NIS+ client ...
All done.

seachild# nisaddcred local
seachild# nisaddcred des
DES principal name: unix.seachild@Castle.Abc.COM (seachild.Castle.Abc,COM.)

Network password: xxx Press Return
Warning, password differs from login password.
Retype password: xxx Press Return

seachild# keylogin
Password:
seachild#
```

To set up a new key for an NIS+ user.

1.  On the root master server, type **nisaddcred -p unix.*UID*@*domainname* -P *username.domainname* des** and press Return. Note that the *username. domainname* must end with a dot ( . ).
2.  Log in remotely (with `rlogin`) to the root master server as the client, type **keylogin**, and press Return. If you are prompted for a password, the procedure succeeded.

The following example gives DES security authorization to user `ray` and connects to the system named `rootmaster` as login `ray` to check the connection.

```
# nisaddcred -p unix.1002@Castle.Abcv.COM -P ray.Castle.Abc.COM. des
DES principal name : unix.1002@ Castle.Abc.COM
Adding new key for unix.1002@Castle.Abc.Com (ray.Castle.Abc.COM.)

Password:
Retype password:

# rlogin rootmaster -l ray
# keylogin
Password:
#
```

## Setting Up NIS Credentials for Diffie-Hellman Authentication

This section describes how to set up NIS credentials for Diffie-Hellman authentication. You must set up a new key for both root and user accounts.

Use the following steps to create a new key for superuser on a client.

1. Become superuser on the client.
2. Edit the `publickey` entry in the `/etc/nsswitch.conf` file to read **publickey: nis**.
3. Type **newkey -h *hostname*** and press Return.
   This command creates a new key pair.
4. When prompted, type the password.
5. When prompted, retype the password.

The following example sets up `seachild` as a secure NIS client.

```
# newkey -h seachild
Adding new key for unix.seachild@Castle.Abc.COM
New Password:
Retype Password:
Please wait for the database to get updated...
Your new key has been successfully stored away
#
```

Only the system administrator who is logged into the NIS server can generate a new key for a user.

Use the following steps to create a new key for a user.

1. Log in to the NIS server as superuser.
2. Type **newkey -u *username*** and press Return.
   The system prompts for a password. You can type a generic password.
3. When prompted, type the password.
4. When prompted, retype the password.
5. Instruct the user to log in and type the **chkey -p** command.

The following example creates a new key for user `ray`.

```
# newkey -u ray
Adding a new key for unix.1002@Castle.Abc.COM
New Password:
Retype password:
Please wait for the database to get updated...
Your new key has been successfully stored away.
#

seachild% chkey -p
Updating nis publickey database.
Reencrypting key for unix.1002@Castle.Abc.COM
Please enter the Secure-RPC password for ray:
Please enter the login password for ray:
Sending key change request to castle...
seachild%
```

### Sharing and Mounting Files with Diffie-Hellman Authentication

Before you can share files from a server and mount file systems on clients with Diffie-Hellman authentication, the Diffie-Hellman public key authentication must be enabled on the network.

Use the following steps to share a file system with Diffie-Hellman authentication.

1. On the server, become superuser.
2. Type **share -F nfs -o sec_dh** */filesystem* and press Return.

To mount a file system with Diffie-Hellman authentication, specify the -o sec=dh option to the mount command.

1. On the client, become superuser.
2. Check to make sure the mount point is available. If not, type **mkdir** *directory-name* and press Return to create the mount point.
3. Type **mount -F nfs -o sec=dh** *server:resource mountpoint* and press Return.

# The Pluggable Authentication Module (PAM) Framework

PAM enables you to "plug in" new authentication technologies without changing system entry services such as login, ftp, and telnet. You can also use PAM to integrate UNIX login with other security mechanisms such as DES or Kerberos. You can also plug in mechanisms for account, session, and password management by using this framework. The PAM framework enables you to choose any combination of system entry services (for example, ftp, login, telnet, or rsh) for user authentication.

## PAM Module Types

PAM uses runtime pluggable modules to provide authentication for system entry services. These modules are broken down into the following four different types based on their function.

- The *authentication modules* provide authentication for users and enables credentials to be set, refreshed, or destroyed. They provide a valuable administration tool for user identification.

- The *account modules* check for password aging, account expiration, and access hour restrictions. After the user is identified through the authentication modules, the account modules determine if the user should be given access.
- The *session modules* manage the opening and closing of an authentication session. They can log activity or provide for cleanup after the session is over.
- The *password modules* enable changes to the actual password.

## Stacking Feature

A *stacking* feature is provided to let you authenticate users through multiple services. Depending on the configuration, users can be prompted for passwords for each authentication method. The order in which the authentication services are used is determined by the PAM configuration file, `/etc/pam.conf`.

## Password-Mapping Feature

The stacking method can require that a user remember several passwords. With the *password-mapping* feature, the primary password is used to decrypt the other passwords so that the user does not need to remember or enter multiple passwords. The other option is to synchronize the passwords across each authentication mechanism. Note that synchronizing passwords can increase the security risk, because the security of each mechanism is limited by the least secure password method used in the stack.

## How PAM Works

The PAM software consists of a library, several modules, and a configuration file. New versions of several system entry commands or daemons that take advantage of the PAM interfaces are also included.

Figure 80 shows the relationship between the applications, the PAM library, the `pam.conf` file, and the PAM modules.

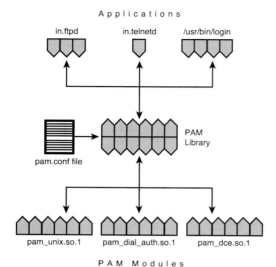

Applications

*Figure 80    How PAM Works*

The `in.ftp` and `in.telnetd` daemons and the `/usr/bin/login` binary use the PAM library to access the appropriate module. When a client tries to contact one of these daemons or use the `login` program, the daemons load the PAM dynamic library on the fly (if it isn't already loaded). Then, the daemon or `login` program reads the `pam.conf` file to determine which authentications and authorizations to take for this particular device. Responses from the modules are passed back through the library to the application.

## PAM Library and Modules

The PAM library files found in the `/usr/lib/security` directory provide the framework to load the appropriate modules and manage the stacking process. They provide a generic structure to which all of the modules can plug in.

Each PAM module implements a specific mechanism. When setting up PAM authentication, you need to specify both the module and the module type, which defines what the module will do. More than one module type (auth, account, session, or password) can be associated with each module. The following list describes each of the PAM modules:

- The `pam_unix` module, `/usr/lib/security/pam_unix.so.1`, provides support for authentication, account management, session management, and password management. You can use any of the four module type definitions with this module. This module uses UNIX passwords for authentication. The Solaris environment uses the

`/etc/nsswitch.conf` file to control the choice of appropriate name services to get password records. For complete information, refer to the pam_unix(5) manual page.

- The `dial_auth` module, `/usr/lib/security/pam_dial_auth.so.1`, can be used only for authentication. This module, used mainly by the `login` command, uses data stored in the `/etc/dialups` and `/etc/d_passwd` files for authentication. For complete information, refer to the pam_dial_auth(5) manual page.

- The `rhosts_auth` module, `/usr/lib/security/pam_rhosts_auth.so.1`, can be used only for authentication. This module, used mainly by the `rlogin` and `rsh` commands, uses data stored in the `~/.rhosts` and `/etc/host.equiv` files through `ruserok`. For compete information, refer to the pam_rhosts_auth(5) manual page.

## PAM Configuration File

The PAM configuration file, `/etc/pam.conf`, determines the authentication services to be used and in the order in which they must be used. You can edit this file to choose authentication mechanisms for each system-entry application.

Each entry in the PAM configuration file has the following syntax.

```
service-name module-type control-flag module-path [module-options]
```

These elements are described in Table 118.

*Table 118    PAM Configuration File Syntax*

| Element | Description |
|---|---|
| `service-name` | Name of the service. Use values such as `ftp`, `login`, `telnet`. |
| `module-type` | Module type for the service. Use one of the following values: `auth`, `account`, `session`, or `password`. |
| `control-flag` | Determine the continuation or failure semantics for the module. Use the values `required`, `requisite`, `optional`, or `sufficient`. For more information, see "Control Flags" on page 605. |
| `module-path` | Path to the library object that implements the service functionality. |

*Table 118    PAM Configuration File Syntax (Continued)*

| Element | Description |
|---------|-------------|
| [*module-options*] | Specify options that are passed to the service module, such as debug and nowarn. You do not need to specify module options. Refer to the manual page of the specific module for a complete list of module options. |

You can add comments to the pam.conf file by starting the line with a pound sign (#). Use white space to delimit fields.

Each line must specify the first four elements. *module-options* are optional.

> *NOTE. An entry in the PAM configuration file is ignored if the line has fewer than four fields, if an invalid value is given for* module-type *or* control-flag, *or if the named module is not found.*

## Valid Service Names

Table 119 lists some of the valid service names, the module types that can be used with that service, and the daemon or command associated with the service name.

Several module types are not appropriate for each service. For example, the password module type is only specified to go with the passwd command. There is no auth module type associated with this command because it is not concerned with authentication.

*Table 119    Valid Service Names for /etc/pam.conf*

| Service Name | Daemon or Command | Module Type |
|--------------|-------------------|-------------|
| dtlogin | /usr/dt/bin/dtlogin | auth, account, session |
| ftp | /usr/sbin/in.ftpd | auth, account, session |
| init | /usr/sbin/init | session |
| login | /usr/bin/login | auth, account, session |
| passwd | /usr/bin/passwd | password |
| rexd | /usr/sbin/rpc.rexd | auth |

*Table 119   Valid Service Names for /etc/pam.conf (Continued)*

| Service Name | Daemon or Command | Module Type |
|---|---|---|
| rlogin | /usr/sbin/in.rlogind | auth, account, session |
| rsh | /usr/sbin/in.rshd | auth, account, session |
| sac | /usr/lib/saf/sac | session |
| su | /bin/su | auth, account, session |
| telnet | /usr/sbin/in.telnetd | auth, account, session |
| ttymon | /usr/lib/saf/ttymon | session |
| uucp | /usr/sbin/in.uucpd | auth, account, session |

## Control Flags

You must specify one of four control flags, listed below, for each entry in the pam.conf file to determine continuation or failure behavior from a module during authentication. The *control flags* specify how to handle a successful or failed attempt for each module. Even though the flags apply to all module types, the following explanation assumes that these flags are being used for authentication modules.

- required
- requisite
- optional
- sufficient

### The required Flag

When the required flag is used, the module must return success for the overall result to be successful.

- If all of the modules are labeled as required, then authentication through all modules must succeed for the user to be authenticated.
- If some of the modules fail, then an error value from the first failed module is reported.
- If a failure occurs for a module flagged as required, all modules in the stack are still tried, but failure is returned.

- If none of the modules are flagged as `required`, then at least one of the entries for that service must succeed for the user to be authenticated.

### The requisite Flag

When the `requisite` flag is used, the module must return `success` for additional authentication to occur.

- If a module flagged as `requisite` fails, an error is immediately returned to the application and no additional authentication is performed.
- If the stack does not include preceding modules labeled as `required` that failed, then the error from this module is returned.
- If an earlier module labeled as `required` fails, the error message from the `required` module is returned.

### The optional Flag

When the `optional` flag is used and a module fails, the overall result can be successful if another module in the stack returns `success`. Use the `optional` flag only when one success in the stack is enough for a user to be authenticated. Only use this flag if it is not important for the particular mechanism to succeed.

> *NOTE. If your users need to have permission associated with a specific mechanism to get their work done, you should not label that mechanism as* `optional`.

### The sufficient Flag

When the `sufficient` flag is used and the module returns `success`, the remaining modules in the stack are skipped, even if they are labeled as `required`. The `sufficient` flag indicates that one successful authentication is enough for the user to be granted access.

An example of the generic `/etc/pam.conf` file is shown below.

**New!**

```
#
#ident  "@(#)pam.conf   1.15    00/02/14 SMI"
#
# Copyright (c) 1996-1999 by Sun Microsystems, Inc.
# All rights reserved.
#
# PAM configuration
#
# Authentication management
#
login   auth required    /usr/lib/security/$ISA/pam_unix.so.1
login   auth required    /usr/lib/security/$ISA/pam_dial_auth.so.1
#
rlogin  auth sufficient  /usr/lib/security/$ISA/pam_rhosts_auth.so.1
rlogin  auth required    /usr/lib/security/$ISA/pam_unix.so.1
#
dtlogin auth required    /usr/lib/security/$ISA/pam_unix.so.1
```

```
#
rsh     auth required    /usr/lib/security/$ISA/pam_rhosts_auth.so.1
other   auth required    /usr/lib/security/$ISA/pam_unix.so.1
#
# Account management
#
login   account requisite    /usr/lib/security/$ISA/pam_roles.so.1
login   account required     /usr/lib/security/$ISA/pam_projects.so.1
login   account required     /usr/lib/security/$ISA/pam_unix.so.1
#
dtlogin account requisite    /usr/lib/security/$ISA/pam_roles.so.1
dtlogin account required     /usr/lib/security/$ISA/pam_projects.so.1
dtlogin account required     /usr/lib/security/$ISA/pam_unix.so.1
#
other   account requisite    /usr/lib/security/$ISA/pam_roles.so.1
other   account required     /usr/lib/security/$ISA/pam_projects.so.1
other   account required     /usr/lib/security/$ISA/pam_unix.so.1
#
# Session management
#
other   session required     /usr/lib/security/$ISA/pam_unix.so.1
#
# Password management
#
other   password required    /usr/lib/security/$ISA/pam_unix.so.1
dtsession auth required /usr/lib/security/$ISA/pam_unix.so.1
#
# Support for Kerberos V5 authentication (uncomment to use Kerberos)
#
#rlogin auth optional    /usr/lib/security/$ISA/pam_krb5.so.1 try_first_pass
#login  auth optional    /usr/lib/security/$ISA/pam_krb5.so.1 try_first_pass
#dtlogin        auth optional    /usr/lib/security/$ISA/pam_krb5.so.1 try_first pass
#other  auth optional    /usr/lib/security/$ISA/pam_krb5.so.1 try_first_pass
#dtlogin        account optional /usr/lib/security/$ISA/pam_krb5.so.1
#other  account optional /usr/lib/security/$ISA/pam_krb5.so.1
#other  session optional /usr/lib/security/$ISA/pam_krb5.so.1
#other  password optional /usr/lib/security/$ISA/pam_krb5.so.1 try_first_pass
#SEAM rlogin auth optional /usr/lib/security/$ISA/pam_krb5.so.1 try_first_pass
#SEAM login auth optional /usr/lib/security/$ISA/pam_krb5.so.1 try_first_pass
#SEAM dtlogin auth optional /usr/lib/security/$ISA/pam_krb5.so.1 try_first_pass
#SEAM dtsession auth required /usr/lib/security/$ISA/pam_unix.so.1
#SEAM krlogin auth required /usr/lib/security/$ISA/pam_krb5.so.1 acceptor
#SEAM ktelnet auth required /usr/lib/security/$ISA/pam_krb5.so.1 acceptor
#SEAM krsh auth required /usr/lib/security/$ISA/pam_krb5.so.1 acceptor
#SEAM other auth optional /usr/lib/security/$ISA/pam_krb5.so.1 try_first_pass
#SEAM dtlogin account optional /usr/lib/security/$ISA/pam_krb5.so.1
#SEAM other account optional /usr/lib/security/$ISA/pam_krb5.so.1
#SEAM other session optional /usr/lib/security/$ISA/pam_krb5.so.1
#SEAM other password optional /usr/lib/security/$ISA/pam_krb5.so.1 try_first_pass
```

The generic pam.conf file specifies the following.

- For login, authentication must succeed for both the pam_unix and the pam_dial_auth modules.

- For rlogin, authentication through the pam_unix module must succeed if authentication through pam_rhosts_auth fails.

- The sufficient control flag indicates that for rlogin, the successful authentication provided by the pam_rhosts_auth module is sufficient and the next entry is ignored.

- Most of the other commands require successful authentication through the pam_unix module.

- Authentication for rsh must succeed through the pam_rhosts_auth module.

The `other` service name enables a default to be set for any other commands requiring authentication that are not included in the file. The `other` option makes it easier to administer the file because many commands that are using the same module can be covered with only one entry. Also, the `other` service name when used as a catch-all can ensure that each access is covered by one module. By convention, the `other` entry is included at the bottom of the section for each module type.

The rest of the entries in the file control the `account`, `session`, and `password` management.

**New!**

Normally the entry for *module-path* is "root relative." If the file name you enter for *module-path* does not begin with a slash (`/`), it is assumed to be relative to `/usr/lib/security/$ISA/`. If the path name contains the `$ISA` token, that token is replaced by an implementation-defined directory name that defines the path relative to the calling program's instruction set architecture. You must use a full path name for modules located in other directories.

You can find the values for *module-options* in the manual page for the specific module; for example, `pam_unix(5)` provides the following options.

- `debug`
- `nowarn`
- `use_first_pass`
- `try_first_pass`

If `login` specifies authentication through both `pam_local` and `pam_unix`, then the user is prompted to enter a password for each module. For situations in which the passwords are the same, the `use_first_pass` module option prompts for only one password and uses that password to authenticate the user for both modules. If the passwords are different, the authentication fails. In general, use this option with an `optional` control flag to make sure that the user can still log in, as shown in the following example.

```
# Authentication management
#
login auth required /usr/lib/security/pam_unix.so.1
login auth optional /usr/lib/security/pam_local.so.1 use_first_pass
```

If you use the `try_first_pass` module option instead, the local module prompts for a second password if the passwords do not match or if an error is made. If both methods of authentication are needed for a user to get access to all the tools needed, using this option could cause some confusion for the user because the user could get access with only one type of authentication.

## Planning for PAM

When deciding how best to use PAM in your environment, start by focusing on the following issues.

- Determine what your needs are, especially which modules you should use.
- Identify the services that need special attention. Use `other` if appropriate.
- Decide on the order in which the modules should be run.
- Choose the control flag for that module.
- Choose any options needed for the module.

Consider the following suggestions before changing the configuration file.

- Use the `other` entry for each module type so that you do not have to include every application.
- Make sure to consider the security implications of the `sufficient` and `optional` control flags.
- Review the manual pages associated with the modules to understand how each module functions, what options are available, and how the stacked modules interact.

  *CAUTION. If the PAM configuration file is misconfigured or becomes corrupted, it is possible that even the superuser would not be able to log in. If the configuration file does become corrupted, you can boot in single-user mode and fix the problem because* `sulogin` *does not use PAM.*

  After you change the `/etc/pam.conf` file, review it carefully while still logged in as superuser. Test all of the commands that might have been affected by your changes. For example, if you added a new module to the `telnet` service, use the `telnet` command and verify that the changes you made behave as expected.

## Configuring PAM

This section describes how to prevent unauthorized access from remote systems, initiate PAM error reporting, and add a PAM module.

### Preventing Unauthorized Access from Remote Systems with PAM

To prevent unauthorized access from remote systems with PAM, remove the `rlogin auth rhosts_auth.so.1` entry from the `/etc/pam.conf` configuration file. Without this entry, the `~/.rhosts` files are not read during an `rlogin` session. Unauthenticated access to the local system from remote systems is prevented. All `rlogin` access requires a password, regardless of the presence or contents of any `~/.rhosts` or `/etc/hosts.equiv` files.

> *NOTE. To prevent other unauthenticated access to the `~/.rhosts` files, remember to also disable the `rsh` service. The best way to disable a service is to comment out or remove the service entry from the `/etc/inetd.conf` file. Changing the PAM configuration file does not prevent the service from being started.*

### Initiating PAM Error Reporting

You can display five different levels of PAM error reporting by adding entries to the `/etc/syslog.conf` file.

> *NOTE. The `/etc/syslog.conf` file is actually an m4 macro. The `syslogd` program runs the file through m4 with some predefined macros for preprocessing and uses the output as the actual `syslog.conf` file. You must use Tabs to separate the fields. If you do not use Tabs to separate the fields, m4 considers the entire file corrupt.*

- `auth.alert` displays messages about conditions that should be fixed immediately.
- `auth.crit` displays critical messages.
- `auth.err` displays error messages.
- `auth.info` displays informational messages.
- `auth.debug` displays debugging messages.

As with any other configuration entry in the `syslog.conf` file, the entry consists of two Tab-separated fields.

```
selector    action
```

The *selector* field is one of the five levels of PAM error reporting. The *action* field indicates where to forward the message. Values for this field can have one of the following four forms.

- A file name, beginning with a leading slash, which indicates that messages specified by the selector are to be written to the specified file. The file is opened in append mode.
- A comma-separated list of user names, which indicates that messages specified by the selector are to be written to the named users if they are logged in.
- An asterisk, which indicates that messages specified by the selector are to be written to all logged-in users.

- The name of a remote host, prefixed with an at sign (@), such as @*server*, which indicates that messages specified by the selector are to be forwarded to the syslogd on the named host.

Blank lines are ignored. Lines with a pound sign (#) as the first non-white character are treated as comments. Refer to the syslog.conf(4) manual page for more information.

Use the following steps to initiate PAM error reporting.

1. Edit the /etc/syslog.conf file and add a line for the *selector* and *action* you want to use for error reporting.

   Remember to use a tab as the separator character.

2. Restart the syslog daemon or send a SIGHUP signal to it to activate the PAM error reporting.

The following example displays all alert messages on the console. Critical messages are mailed to root. Informational and debug messages are added to the /var/log/pamlog file.

```
auth.alert   /dev/console
auth.crit   'root'
auth.info;auth.debug   /var/log/pamlog
```

Each line in the log contains a timestamp, the name of the system that generated the message, and the message itself. syslogd is capable of logging huge amounts of information into the pamlog file. Be sure to monitor the size of the log and prune it periodically to delete old information.

## Adding a PAM Module

You can add new PAM modules. The /usr/lib/security model contains a pam_sample.so.1 ELF executable file that you can use as a model for creating new modules.

*CAUTION. Before you reboot the system, it is very important to test any changes to the /etc/pam.conf configuration file to detect any misconfiguration errors. Run rlogin, su, and telnet to test and verify expected access results before you reboot the system. However, if the service is a daemon spawned only once when the system is booted, you may need to stop and restart individual services or reboot the system before you can verify that module.*

Use the following steps to add a PAM module.

1. Become superuser.
2. Determine which control flags and other options you want to use.

3. Create the new module.

4. Copy the new module to `/usr/lib/security`.

5. Set permissions so that the module file is owned by root and permissions are set to `555`.

6. Edit the `/etc/pam.conf` file and add the module to the appropriate services.

# 23

# ROLE-BASED ACCESS CONTROL

The Solaris 8 Operating Environment provides role-based access control *New!* (RBAC). RBAC is new security feature that provides a flexible way to package certain superuser privileges for assignment to user accounts. You no longer need to give users all superuser privileges to enable them to perform a set of tasks that require superuser privileges.

With traditional security models, superuser has full superuser privileges and other users do not have enough power to fix their own problems. With role-based access control (RBAC), you now have an alternative to the traditional all-or-nothing security model.

With RBAC, those with Primary Administrator (one with root privileges) and User Security rights can divide superuser capabilities into several packages and assign them separately to individuals sharing administrative responsibilities. When you separate superuser privileges with RBAC, users can have a variable degree of access and you can control delegation of privileged operations to other users.

RBAC includes the following features.

- Authorization—A right used to grant access to a restricted function.

- Rights profile (or just profile)—A bundling mechanism for grouping authorizations and commands with special attributes; for example, user and group IDs.

- Role—A special type of user account that can be used to perform a set of administrative tasks.

Starting with the Solaris 8 Update 3 release, you use the Users > Rights tool in the Solaris Management Console (SMC) to manage RBAC databases. This chapter describes the Solaris 8 Update 3 version of RBAC.

This chapter introduces the elements of RBAC, describes how to use the SMC tools to administer RBAC, and then describes the databases and files used to administer RBAC. It also lists RBAC commands.

# What Is a Role?

A role is an account with all the attributes of a user account, including a name, user ID (UID), password, and home directory. A role also has a specific set of administrative rights. Instead of a login shell, a role has a *role shell* (for example, Administrator's Bourne instead of Bourne shell). The `root` account is a role with all rights, whereas other roles have more limited rights.

When a user is associated with a role, that user first logs in as usual, with the individual's user name and password. The user can log in to the SMC Users tools with the role ID and role password. Alternatively, from a command line, the user can type **su  *rolename*** and type the role password to assume the rights of the specific role.

# Administrative Rights

For convenience in assigning rights, the SMC Users tools group individual rights into three overall categories: Primary Administrator, System Administrator, and Operator.

- The *Primary Administrator* has all the rights of the root user and is responsible for assigning rights to users, assigning users to roles, creating new roles, and changing the rights associated with administrative roles. The Primary Administrator can designate other users as a Primary Administrator. The Primary Administrator can also grant Rights Delegation, which gives other administrators the limited ability to grant to others only rights they already have or rights to roles to which they are already assigned.

- The *System Administrator* has an extensive set of rights but has no security-related rights. For example, the System Administrator can add new user accounts but cannot change a user's password. The System Administrator cannot grant rights to another user.

- The *Operator* performs tasks such as media backup and printer administration.

# Primary Administrator Capabilities

With RBAC, the Primary Administrator can provide all other administrators with tools and commands to perform specific jobs and can restrict the other administrator's access to additional tools and commands.

A right is a named collection that includes three components.

- Commands.
- Authorizations to use specific applications or to perform specific functions within an application.
- Other previously created rights.

The Primary Administrator can grant or deny rights to other administrators.

The Primary Administrator uses the Solaris Management Console (SMC) to grant rights in the following two ways.

- Assign the rights directly to users, who can then perform their administrative tasks. Assigning rights directly to users is recommended in small companies where system administrators perform a wide range of administrative tasks.
- Assign the rights to roles and associate users with those roles. To perform administrative tasks, users assume the role login and gain the rights assigned to that role. Assigning rights to roles is recommended for large organizations with many administrators, each with specific administrative tasks to perform.

By default all users who can log in are granted the right of simply viewing data. See "Policy Configuration File (policy.conf)" on page 650 for information on how to deny all regular users the right to view SMC information. See "Rights Profiles (prof_attr)" on page 643 for information on how to deny regular users from viewing a specific SMC tool.

When the Solaris Management Console (SMC) and User Management tools are installed, a comprehensive default set of rights is included. Only the special accounts included in the Solaris Operating Environment exist and no administrator has the rights needed to begin creating users, assigning roles, and administering RBAC.

To begin adding groups and users, assigning rights, and creating roles, the first administrator to log in to SMC must log in as root on the local system and then give himself or herself the right of Primary Administrator.

## Granting Primary Administrator Rights

Use the following steps to grant Primary Administrator rights.

1.  From the Tools menu in the CDE Front Panel, choose Solaris Management Console.

    The Solaris Management Console window is displayed, as shown in Figure 81.

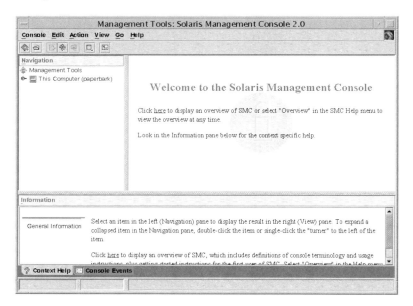

*Figure 81    Solaris Management Console Window*

Alternatively, you can open SMC from the Applications menu in the CDE Front Panel by choosing Applications and then double-clicking on the Solaris Management Console icon in the Application Manager window.

2.  If you want to switch to a different system, from the Console menu, choose Open Toolbox.

    The Open Toolbox window is displayed, as shown in Figure 82.

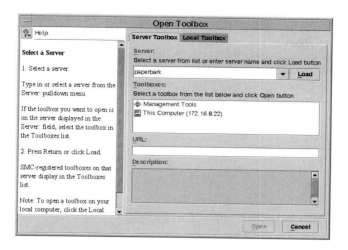

*Figure 82    Open Toolbox Window*

3. Type the name of the server or click on the name of the server in the list and then click on the Load button.

The toolbox for the system you chose is displayed.

4. In the SMC window, click on the control to the left of the This Computer icon, then click on the control next to the System Configuration item in the navigation pane.

The Users tool is displayed. Figure 83 shows all of the SMC tools in the navigation pane.

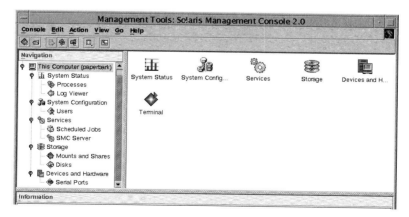

*Figure 83    SMC Tools*

5. Double-click on the Users icon.

The Users Login window is displayed, as shown in Figure 84.

*Figure 84    Users Login Window*

6. Log in as user root, type the root password, and click on the OK button.

After a few moments, the Users tools are displayed in the right pane, as shown in Figure 85.

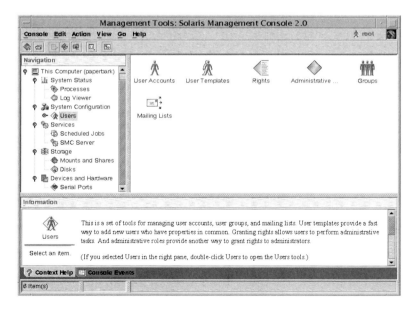

*Figure 85    Users Tools*

7.  If you do not have a user account on this server, double-click on User Accounts and from the Action menu, choose Add User > With Wizard. If you already have a user account on this server, double-click on the icon for your user account.

    The User Properties for your account are displayed, as shown in Figure 86.

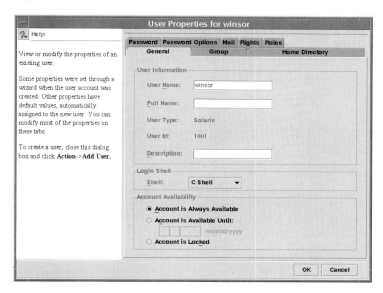

*Figure 86    User Properties Window*

8.  Click on the Rights tab.

    The Rights tab is displayed, as shown in Figure 87.

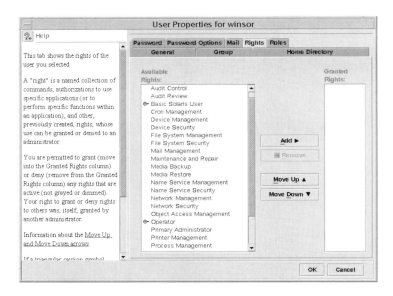

*Figure 87    Rights Tab in the User Properties Window*

9.  Click on Primary Administrator and then click on the Add button.

    Information about the Primary Administrator is displayed in the help
    pane. The Primary Administrator right is added to the Granted
    Rights list, as shown in Figure 88.

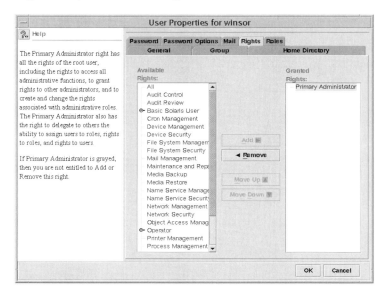

*Figure 88    Granting Primary Administrator Rights*

10. Click on the OK button.

    The Primary Administrator rights are granted for the user account. This user account now has all the rights of the root user when logged in with their user name.

11. You can verify the rights for the user in a Terminal window by typing **profiles** *username* and pressing Return.

    The following example shows that user winsor has Primary Administrator rights (just granted), Basic Solaris User (the default), and All profiles (the default). The All profile makes all commands available but without any attributes.

```
paperbark% profiles winsor
Primary Administrator
Basic Solaris User
All
paperbark%
```

# Granting Rights to a User

Granting rights to users is similar to granting Primary Administrator rights except that you log in as a user who has Primary Administrator rights instead of as root. See "Granting Primary Administrator Rights" on page 616 for illustrations of the screens.

Use the following steps to grant rights to a user.

1. From the CDE Applications menu, open the Application Manager.
   The Application Manager window is opened.

2. Double-click on the Solaris Management Console icon.
   The Solaris Management Console window is displayed.

3. Click on the control to the left of the System Configuration item in the navigation pane.
   The Users tool is displayed.

4. Double-click on the Users icon.
   The Users Login window is displayed.

5. Log in as a user who has Primary Administrator rights, type your password, and click on the OK button.
   After a few moments, the Users tools are displayed in the right pane.

6. If the user does not already have a user account on this server, double-click on User Accounts and from the Action menu, choose Add User > With Wizard. If the user already has a user account on this server, double-click on the icon for the user account.

   The User Properties for the user account is displayed.

7. Click on the Rights tab.

   The Rights tab is displayed.

8. Click on the right you want to grant to this user and click on the Add button. You can add more than one set of user rights.

9. When the list is complete, click on the OK button.

   The rights are granted for the user account. This user account now has all the rights that you assigned when logged in with the user name.

10. You can verify the rights for the user in a Terminal window by typing **profiles** *username* and pressing Return.

## Creating a Role

Use the following steps to create a role and assign users to it.

1. From the Solaris Management Console window, click on the control to the left of the System Configuration item in the navigation pane.

   The Users tool is displayed.

2. Double-click on the Users icon.

   The Users Login window is displayed.

3. Log in as a user who has `solaris.role.write` authorization rights, type your password, and click on the OK button.

   By default, Primary Administrator and User Security have `solaris.role.write` rights.

   After a few moments, the Users tools are displayed in the right pane.

4. Double-click on the Administrative Roles tool.

   The Administrative Roles window is displayed, as shown in Figure 89. If the Primary Administrator has not created any roles, the right pane of the Administrative Roles window contains no entries.

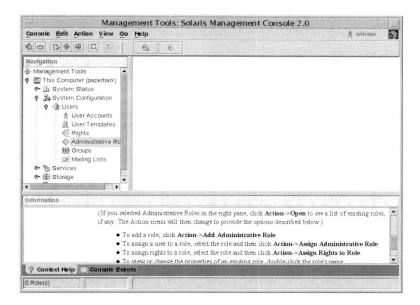

*Figure 89    Administrative Roles Window*

5.  From the Action menu, choose Add Administrative Role.

    The Add Administrative Role window is displayed, as shown in Figure 90.

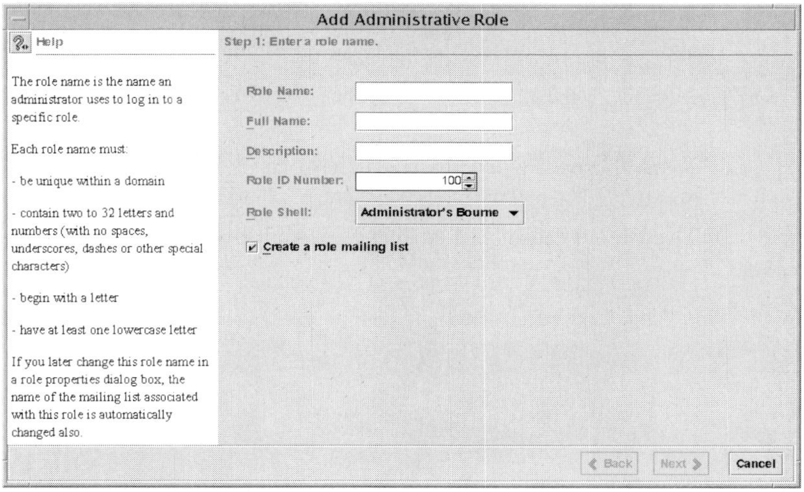

*Figure 90    Add Administrative Role Window*

6.   Type a unique role name (2 to 32 alphanumeric characters, no spaces, dashes, or other special characters, the unique full name of the role (no limitations on length or characters), a longer description of the role (no colons or returns), and choose a role shell. The default is to create a role mailing list. If you do not want to create a mailing list, click to turn off the check box.

Review the information in the Help pane on the left if you need more details for each of the entries.

7.   When the information is complete, click on the Next button.

The password screen is displayed, as shown in Figure 91.

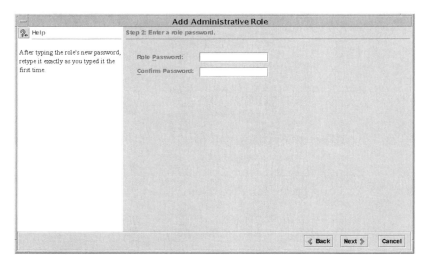

*Figure 91    Password Screen*

8.   Type the password for the role once in each of the text fields and click on the Next button.

The Select Role Rights screen is displayed, as shown in Figure 92.

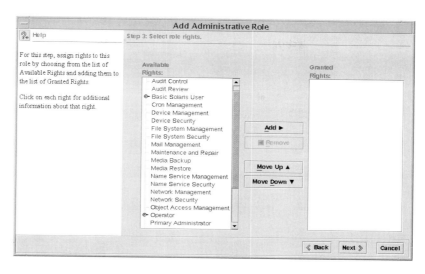

*Figure 92    Select Role Rights Screen*

9.  Click on the right you want to add to the role and then click on the
    Add button. Repeat the process as many times as needed until all of
    the rights you want to grant are listed in the Granted Rights pane.

    The rights are listed in the Granted Rights pane. In Figure 93,
    Printer Management rights are granted to the `printadm` role.

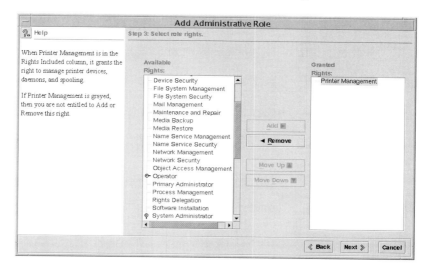

*Figure 93    Rights Granted to printadm Role*

10. When you have granted the appropriate rights, click on the Next
button.

The Select a Home Directory screen is displayed, as shown in
Figure 94. The default is to create the home directory for the role on
the current server in the `/export/home` directory.

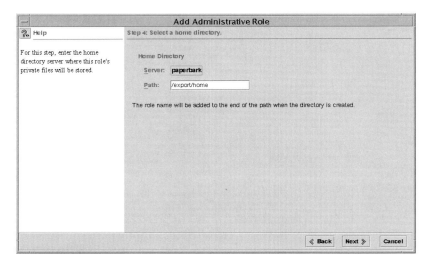

*Figure 94    Select a Home Directory Screen*

11. Change the server or path, if necessary, and click on the Next
button.

The Assign Users to This Role screen is displayed, as shown in
Figure 95.

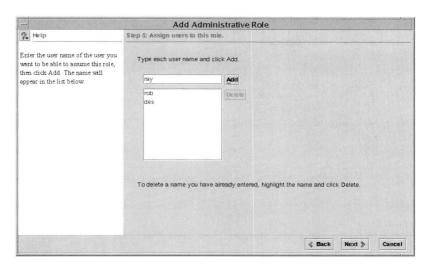

*Figure 95    Assign Users to This Role Screen*

12. For each user you want to assign to this administrative role, type the user name in the top text field and click on the Add button.

    Each user name is added to the list. If you want to delete a user, highlight the user name in the list and click on the Delete button.

13. When all users are assigned, click on the Next button.

    A summary screen displays the settings for the role, as shown in Figure 96. The list of users assigned to the role is not displayed on this screen.

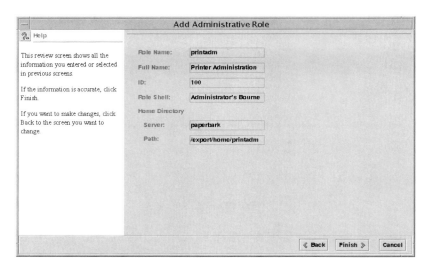

*Figure 96    Summary Screen*

14. If you want to change any of the information, click on the Back button to go back to the appropriate screen and enter the correct information. If the information is correct, click on the Finish button.

    The role is created, the users are assigned, and the role is listed in the Administrative Role screen, as shown in Figure 97.

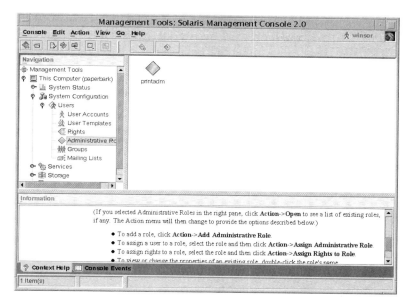

Figure 97    Administrative Role Window with printadm Role

15. You can verify the rights granted to the role by typing
    **profiles** *rolename* and pressing Return.

    The following example shows the rights granted to the printadm
    role. The rights include the default Basic Solaris User and All rights
    as well as the Printer Management rights.

```
paperbark% profiles printadm
Printer Management
Basic Solaris User
All
paperbark%
```

# Regular User Rights

By default, any user can list and read information in the SMC tools. This
default authorization is provided through the PROFS_GRANTED=Basic
Solaris User in the /etc/security/policy.conf file. See "Policy
Configuration File (policy.conf)" on page 650 for more information about the
policy.conf file.

The Primary Administrator can prevent regular users from using a specified SMC tool by removing the Read authorization from the Basic Solaris User right.

Use the following steps to remove the Read authorization from the Basic Solaris User right.

1.  From the SMC Users window, click on the Rights icon.

    The Rights window is displayed, as shown in Figure 98.

*Figure 98    Rights Window*

2.  Double-click on the Basic Solaris User right.

    The Basic Solaris User Properties window is displayed, as shown in Figure 99.

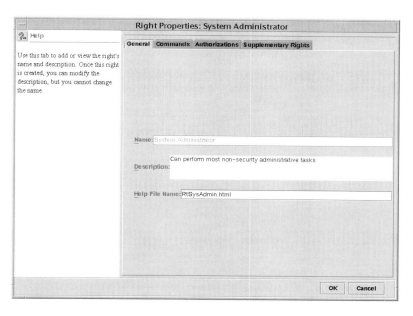

*Figure 99   Basic Solaris User Rights Properties Window*

3.   Click on the Authorizations tab.

The Authorizations tab is displayed, as shown in Figure 100.

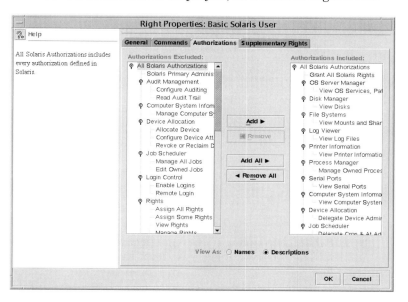

*Figure 100  Basic Solaris User Rights Authorizations Tab*

You can view the authorizations by authorization name or by description by clicking on the appropriate View As radio button. The default is to view authorizations by description.

4. Click on the authorization you want to exclude in the Authorizations Included list and click on the Remove button.

The authorization is moved to the Authorizations Excluded list. In Figure 101, the View Users and Roles authorization has been excluded.

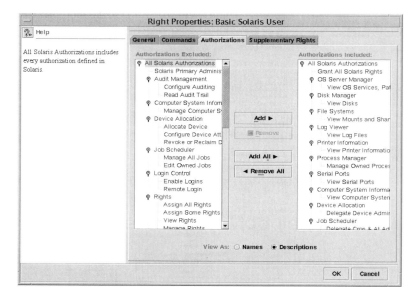

*Figure 101  Changing Default Authorizations for All Users*

5. When you have modified the appropriate authorizations, click on the OK button.

The authorizations are changed and the Properties window is closed.

# Rights Hierarchies

With the Rights tool, you can add a right to a right, which means the same command could be included more than once in a right. The order of rights is important. Just as with searches for the PATH variable, searches for commands in a right use the first occurrence of the command it finds. For example, you might specify the /usr/bin/date command in one right with an effective UID of root but specify it in another right to run as the normal user. Always list the most specific and powerful rights first, followed by subordinate rights. Any wildcard entries should be last in the list.

You can change the order of rights within rights from the Rights tool.

Use the following steps to change the order of rights within rights.

1. From the SMC Users window, click on the Rights icon.

   The Rights window is displayed.

2. Double-click on the name of the right containing the command you want to change.

   The Rights Properties window for that right is displayed. Figure 102 shows the Rights Properties for System Administrator window.

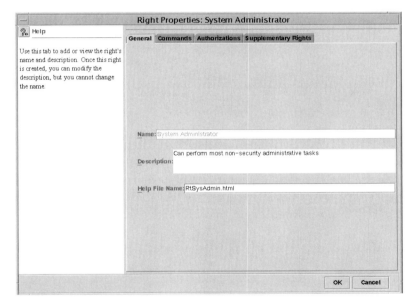

*Figure 102  System Administrator Rights Properties Window*

3. Click on the Supplementary Rights tab.

   The Supplementary Rights information is displayed, as shown in Figure 105.

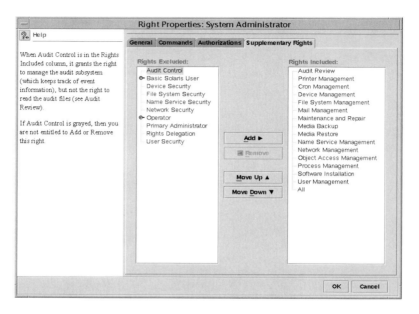

*Figure 103  Supplementary Rights Tab*

4. Click on a right and use the Move Up and Move Down buttons to change the order of the supplementary rights.

5. When the supplementary rights are in the correct sequence, click on the OK button.

   The supplementary rights hierarchy is set.

# Real and Effective UIDs and GIDs

If the user has been associated with a role and its attendant rights, all commands affected by these rights have two types of user IDs (UIDs) and group IDs (GIDs)—effective and real.

Effective UIDs and GIDs are used for access control to protected resources. Real UIDs and GIDs are used to establish ownership and responsibility (for logging purposes). For example, when users create files, the files are created with the real UID and GID; however, the ability to open a file is based on the effective UID and GID.

In most cases, effective IDs are sufficient to grant access to restricted system resources. In other cases, the real IDs are required.

Commands are executed under the real or effective UID and GID established for the command, whether launched by SMC or executed in an administrator's shell.

Try effective IDs first; if the command does not perform as expected, real IDs are probably necessary. You can change the real and effective UID and GID from the SMC Rights tool.

Use the following steps to change the real and effective UID and GID for a command.

1. From the SMC Users window, click on the Rights icon.

   The Rights window is displayed.

2. Double-click on the name of the right containing the command you want to change.

   The Rights Properties window for that right is displayed. Figure 104 shows the Rights Properties for Process Management window.

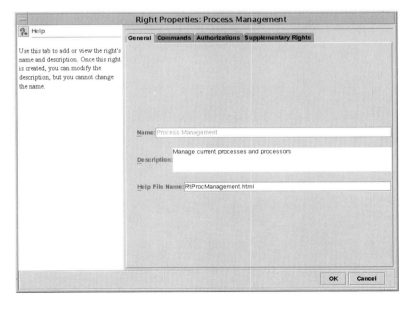

*Figure 104  Process Management Rights Properties Window*

3. Click on the Commands tab.

   The Commands information is displayed. as shown in Figure 105.

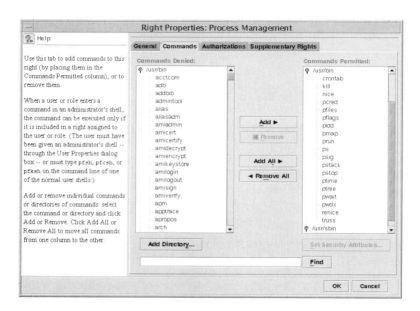

*Figure 105  Commands Tab*

4.  Click on the command you want to change and then click on the Set
    Security Attributes button.

    The Set Security Attributes window is displayed, as shown in
    Figure 106.

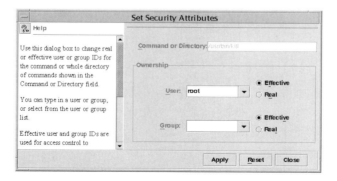

*Figure 106  Set Security Attributes Window*

5.  Click on the settings you want for the command and then click on the
    Apply button.

    The security attributes are set for the command.

# The RBAC Databases

The following sections describe the underlying RBAC databases and the `policy.conf` file that provide users access to privileged operations.

- `/etc/user_attr` (extended user attributes database)—Associates users and roles with authorizations and rights profiles.

- `/etc/security/auth_attr` (authorization attributes database)—Defines authorizations and their attributes and identifies the associated help file.

- `/etc/security/prof_attr` (rights profile attributes database)—Defines profiles, lists the profile's assigned authorizations, and identifies the associated help file.

- `/etc/security/exec_attr` (profile execution attributes database)—Defines the privileged operations assigned to a profile.

- `/etc/security/policy.conf`—Provides the security policy configuration for user-level attributes.

You can directly assign authorizations and profiles to users in the `user_attr` database. You can also assign the user to a role to give the user access to any privileged operations associated with that role.

Profiles are defined in the `prof_attr` database and can include authorizations defined in `auth_attr` and commands with attributes defined for that profile in `exec_attr`.

The `pfexec`(1) command is used to execute commands with the attributes specified by the user profiles in the `exec_attr`(4) database. Commands that are assigned to profiles are run in special shells called *profile shells*.

- `pfsh` corresponds to the Bourne shell (`sh`).
- `pfcsh` corresponds to the C shell (`csh`).
- `pfksh` corresponds to the Korn (`ksh`) shell.

See the `pfexec`(1) manual page for more information.

## Extended User Attributes Database (user_attr)

The `/etc/user_attr` database supplements the `passwd` and `shadow` databases. It contains extended user attributes such as authorizations and rights profiles. It also enables you to assign roles to a user.

Once associated with a role account, a user can access commands with special attributes, typically the root user ID, that are not available to users whose accounts are not associated with any extra role accounts.

## Syntax of the user_attr Database

The default `/etc/user_attr` database is shown below.

```
# Copyright (c) 1999 by Sun Microsystems, Inc. All rights reserved.
#
# /etc/user_attr
#
# user attributes. see user_attr(4)
#
#pragma ident      "@(#)user_attr      1.2      99/07/14 SMI"
#
root:::::type=normal;auths=solaris.*,solaris.grant;profiles=All
```

Each entry consists of a single line with five fields separated by colons (`:`). You can continue lines by using the backslash character (`\`). Each entry has the following form.

```
user:qualifier:res1:res2:attr
```

The fields are described in Table 120.

*Table 120    Fields in the user_attr Database*

| | |
|---|---|
| *user* | The name of the user as specified in the `passwd`(4) database. |
| *qualifier* | Reserved for future use. |
| *res1* | Reserved for future use. |
| *res2* | Reserved for future use. |
| *attr* | An optional list of semicolon-separated (`;`) key-value pairs that describe the security attributes to apply to the object when it is executed. You can specify zero or more keys. The four valid keys are `auths`, `profiles`, `roles`, and `type`. |
| | `auths` | Specify a comma-separated list of authorization names chosen from the names defined in the `auth_attr`(4) database. You can specify authorization names by using the asterisk (`*`) character as a wildcard. For example, `solaris.printer.*` grants all Sun printer authorizations. |

*Table 120    Fields in the user_attr Database (Continued)*

| | profiles | Specify an ordered, comma-separated list of profile names chosen from prof_attr(4). A profile determines which commands a user can execute and which command attributes can be specified. At a minimum, each user in user_attr should have the All profile, which makes all commands available but without any attributes. |
|---|---|---|
| | | The order of profiles is important; it works similarly to UNIX search paths. The first profile in the list that contains the command to be executed defines which (if any) attributes are applied to the command. Profiles are enforced by the profile shells (see pfexec(1)). If no profiles are assigned, the profile shells do not permit the user to execute any commands. |
| | roles | Specify an optional, comma-separated list of role names from the set of user accounts in this database whose type field indicates the account is a role. If the role's key value is not specified, the user cannot assume any role. You cannot assign roles to other roles. |
| | type | Specify either normal to specify that this account is for a normal user—in which case the user can assume a role only after logging in—or role to specify that this account is for a role. |

*NOTE. Because the list of legal keys is likely to expand, any code that parses this database must be written to ignore unknown key-value pairs without error. When you create new keywords, prefix the names with a unique string, such as the company's stock symbol, to avoid potential naming conflict. All of the Solaris keys except those in the* user_attr *database are prefixed with the string* solaris.

## Examples of user_attr Database Entries

The entry in the default `user_attr` database is shown below.

```
root::::type=normal;auths=solaris.*,solaris.grant;profiles=All
```

This entry assigns to root the `All` profile, which enables root to use all commands in the system. It also assigns two authorizations. The `solaris.*` wildcard authorization grants root all of the `solaris` authorizations. The `solaris.grant` authorization grants root the right to grant to others any `solaris` authorizations that root has. This combination of authorizations enables root to grant to others any or all `solaris` authorizations.

The following example shows the entries in the `auth_attr` database that were created by the examples shown earlier in this chapter.

```
paperbark% more /etc/user_attr
# Copyright (c) 1999 by Sun Microsystems, Inc. All rights reserved.
#
# /etc/user_attr
#
# user attributes. see user_attr(4)
#
#pragma ident   "@(#)user_attr   1.2      99/07/14 SMI"
#
root::::type=normal;auths=solaris.*,solaris.grant;profiles=All
winsor::::profiles=Primary Administrator;type=normal
printadm::::profiles=Printer Management;type=role
rob::::roles=printadm;type=normal
des::::roles=printadm;type=normal
paperbark%
```

# Authorizations Database (auth_attr)

An authorization is a user right that grants access to a restricted function. It is a unique string that identifies what is being authorized and who created the authorization.

Certain privileged programs check authorizations to determine whether users can execute restricted functionality. For example, the `solaris.jobs.admin` authorization is required for one user to edit the `crontab` file of another user.

All authorizations are stored in the `/etc/security/auth_attr` database. When you assign authorizations directly to users or roles, the authorizations are entered in the `user_attr` database. You can also assign authorizations to rights profiles, which in turn are then assigned to users.

## Syntax of the auth_attr Database

The default `/etc/security/auth_attr` database is shown below.

```
#
# Copyright (c) 2000 by Sun Microsystems, Inc. All rights reserved.
#
# /etc/security/auth_attr
#
# authorization attributes. see auth_attr(4)
#
#pragma      ident     "@(#)auth_attr 1.8     00/07/10 SMI"
#
solaris.admin.usermgr.:::Users, Groups & Mailing Lists::help=UserMgrHeader.html
solaris.admin.usermgr.write:::Add, Modify & Delete::help=UserMgrWrite.html
solaris.admin.usermgr.read:::View Users and Roles::help=AuthUsermgrRead.html
solaris.admin.usermgr.pswd:::Change User Passwords::help=UserMgrPswd.html
solaris.admin.logsvc.:::Log Viewer::help=LogSvcHeader.html
solaris.admin.logsvc.write:::Change Log Settings::help=LogSvcWrite.html
solaris.admin.logsvc.purge:::Backup & Delete Log Files::help=LogSvcPurge.html
solaris.admin.logsvc.read:::View Log Files::help=AuthLogsvcRead.html
solaris.admin.fsmgr.:::File Systems::help=FsMgrHeader.html
solaris.admin.fsmgr.write:::Mount/Share File Systems::help=FsMgrWrite.html
solaris.admin.fsmgr.read:::View Mounts and Shares::help=AuthFsmgrRead.html
solaris.admin.serialmgr.:::Serial Ports::help=SerialPortMgrHeader.html
solaris.admin.serialmgr.modify:::Modify Serial Port
  information::help=SerialMgrModify.html
solaris.admin.serialmgr.delete:::Delete Serial Ports::help=SerialMgrDelete.html
solaris.admin.serialmgr.read:::View Serial Ports::help=AuthSerialmgrRead.html
solaris.admin.diskmgr.:::Disk Manager::
solaris.admin.diskmgr.write:::Manage Disks::help=AuthDiskmgrWrite.html
solaris.admin.diskmgr.read:::View Disks::help=AuthDiskmgrRead.html
solaris.admin.procmgr.:::Process Manager::
solaris.admin.procmgr.admin:::Manage All Processes::help=AuthProcmgrAdmin.html
solaris.admin.procmgr.user:::Manage Owned Processes::help=AuthProcmgrUser.html
solaris.compsys.:::Computer System Information::
solaris.compsys.read:::View Computer System Information::help=AuthCompSysRead.html
solaris.compsys.write:::Manage Computer System
  Information::help=AuthCompSysWrite.html
solaris.admin.printer.:::Printer Information::
solaris.admin.printer.read:::View Printer Information::help=AuthPrinterRead.html
solaris.admin.printer.modify:::Update Printer
  Information::help=AuthPrinterModify.html
solaris.admin.printer.delete:::Delete Printer
  Information::help=AuthPrinterDelete.html
solaris.admin.dcmgr.:::OS Server Manager::
solaris.admin.dcmgr.admin:::Manage OS Services and
  Patches::help=AuthDcmgrAdmin.html
solaris.admin.dcmgr.clients:::Manage Diskless Clients::help=AuthDcmgrClients.html
solaris.admin.dcmgr.read:::View OS Services, Patches and Diskless
  Clients::help=AuthDcmgrRead.html
solaris.profmgr.:::Rights::help=ProfmgrHeader.html
solaris.role.delegate:::Assign Some Roles::help=AuthRoleDelegate.html
solaris.profmgr.write:::Manage Rights::help=AuthProfmgrWrite.html
solaris.system.shutdown:::Shutdown the System::help=SysShutdown.html
solaris.device.grant:::Delegate Device Administration::help=DevGrant.html
solaris.:::All Solaris Authorizations::help=AllSolAuthsHeader.html
solaris.jobs.grant:::Delegate Cron & At Administration::help=JobsGrant.html
solaris.device.revoke:::Revoke or Reclaim Device::help=DevRevoke.html
solaris.role.assign:::Assign All Roles::help=AuthRoleAssign.html
solaris.jobs.user:::Edit Owned Jobs::help=AuthJobsUser.html
solaris.profmgr.read:::View Rights::help=AuthProfmgrRead.html
solaris.audit.:::Audit Management::help=AuditHeader.html
solaris.profmgr.delegate:::Assign Some Rights::help=AuthProfmgrDelegate.html
solaris.device.config:::Configure Device Attributes::help=DevConfig.html
solaris.role.write:::Manage Roles::help=AuthRoleWrite.html
solaris.role.:::Roles::help=RoleHeader.html
solaris.system.:::Machine Administration::help=SysHeader.html
solaris.device.allocate:::Allocate Device::help=DevAllocate.html
solaris.device.:::Device Allocation::help=DevAllocHeader.html
solaris.login.enable:::Enable Logins::help=LoginEnable.html
solaris.system.date:::Set Date & Time::help=SysDate.html
solaris.login.remote:::Remote Login::help=LoginRemote.html
```

```
solaris.audit.read::::Read Audit Trail::help=AuditRead.html
solaris.jobs.admin::::Manage All Jobs::help=AuthJobsAdmin.html
solaris.audit.config::::Configure Auditing::help=AuditConfig.html
solaris.profmgr.execattr.write::::Manage
  Commands::help=AuthProfmgrExecattrWrite.html
solaris.jobs.::::Job Scheduler::help=JobHeader.html
solaris.grant::::Grant All Solaris Rights::help=PriAdmin.html
solaris.login.::::Login Control::help=LoginHeader.html
solaris.profmgr.assign::::Assign All Rights::help=AuthProfmgrAssign.html
solaris.*::::Solaris Primary Administrator::help=PriAdmin.html
solaris.admin.hostmgr.::::Computers/Networks::help=HostMgrHeader.html
solaris.admin.hostmgr.write::::Write Computer & Network
  Information::help=HostMgrWrite.html
```

Each entry consists of a single line with six fields separated by colons (:). You can continue lines by using the backslash character (\). Each entry has the following form.

```
authname:res1:res2:short_desc:long_desc:attr
```

The fields are described in Table 121.

*Table 121    Fields in the auth_attr Database*

| `authname` | The name of the authorization as a unique string in the format `prefix.[suffix]`. Authorizations for the Solaris Operating Environment use `solaris.` as the prefix. All other authorizations should use a prefix that begins with the reverse-order Internet domain name of the organization that creates the authorization (for example, `com.wellard`). The suffix indicates what is being authorized, which is typically the functional area and operation. |
|---|---|
| | When `authname` has no suffix (that is, the name consists of a prefix and functional area and ends with a period), the `authname` serves as a heading for use by applications in their GUIs instead of as an authorization. `solaris.printmgr.` is an example of a heading. |
| | When `authname` ends with the word `grant`, the `authname` serves as a grant authorization and lets the user delegate related authorizations to other users—that is, authorizations with the same prefix and functional area. `solaris.printmgr.grant` is an example of a grant authorization. It gives the user the right to delegate such authorizations as `solaris.printmgr.admin` and `solaris.printmgr.nobanner` to other users. |

*Table 121    Fields in the auth_attr Database (Continued)*

| | |
|---|---|
| `res1` | Reserved for future use. |
| `res2` | Reserved for future use. |
| `short_desc` | A short name for the authorization that is suitable for display in user interfaces such as in a scrolling list in a GUI. |
| `long_desc` | A long description that identifies the purpose of the authorization, the applications in which it is used, and the type of user interested in using it. The long description can be displayed in the help text of an application. |
| `attr` | An optional list of semicolon-separated (`;`) key-value pairs that describe the attributes of an authorization. You can specify zero or more keys. You can use the `help=` keyword to identify an HTML help file. A Web browser can read the help file with the following URL. `file:/usr/lib/help/auths/locale/C/index.html` |

## Rights Profiles (prof_attr)

With rights profiles, you can group authorizations and commands with special attributes and assign them to users or roles. The special attributes include real and effective UIDs and GIDs. The most common attribute is to set the real or effective UID to root. Definitions of rights profiles are stored in the `prof_attr` database.

`/etc/security/prof_attr` is a local source for rights profile names, descriptions, and other attributes of rights profiles. You can use `prof_attr` with other profile sources, including the `prof_attr` NIS map and NIS+ table.

### Syntax of the prof_attr Database

The default `/etc/security/prof_attr` database is shown below.

```
#
# Copyright (c) 2000 by Sun Microsystems, Inc. All rights reserved.
#
# /etc/security/prof_attr
#
# profiles attributes. see prof_attr(4)
#
#pragma     ident      "@(#)prof_attr 1.12     00/07/10 SMI"
#
Primary Administrator:::Can perform all administrative
  tasks:auths=solaris.*,solaris.grant;help=RtPriAdmin.html
```

```
System Administrator:::Can perform most non-security administrative
  tasks:profiles=Audit Review,Printer Management,Cron Management,Device
  Management,File System Management,Mail Management,Maintenance and Repair,Media
  Backup,Media Restore,Name Service Management,Network Management,Object Access
  Management,Process Management,Software Installation,User
  Management,All;help=RtSysAdmin.html
Operator:::Can perform simple administrative tasks:profiles=Printer
  Management,Media Backup,All;help=RtOperator.html
Audit Control:::Configure BSM
  auditing:auths=solaris.audit.config,solaris.jobs.admin,solaris.admin.logsvc.purge,
  solaris.admin.logsvc.read;help=RtAuditCtrl.html
Basic Solaris User:::Automatically assigned
  rights:auths=solaris.profmgr.read,solaris.jobs.users,solaris.admin.usermgr.read,
  solaris.admin.logsvc.read,solaris.admin.fsmgr.read,solaris.admin.serialmgr.read,
  solaris.admin.diskmgr.read,solaris.admin.procmgr.user,solaris.compsys.read,solaris
  .admin.printer.read,solaris.admin.prodreg.read,solaris.admin.dcmgr.read;profiles=
  All;help=RtDefault.html
Device Management:::Control Access to Removable
  Media:auths=solaris.device.*,solaris.admin.serialmgr.*;help=RtDeviceMngmnt.html
Device Security:::Manage devices and Volume
  Manager:auths=solaris.device.*,solaris.admin.serialmgr.*;help=RtDeviceSecurity.
  html
File System Management:::Manage, mount, share file
  systems:help=RtFileSysMngmnt.html;auths=solaris.admin.fsmgr.*,solaris.admin.
  diskmgr.*
File System Security:::Manage file system security
  attributes:help=RtFileSysSecurity.html;auths=solaris.admin.fsmgr.*,solaris.admin.
  diskmgr.*
Maintenance and Repair:::Maintain and repair a
  system:help=RtMaintAndRepair.html;auths=solaris.admin.logsvc.write,solaris.admin.
  logsvc.read,solaris.compsys.write,solaris.compsys.read
Process Management:::Manage current processes and
  processors:help=RtProcManagement.html;auths=solaris.admin.procmgr.*
User Management:::Manage users, groups, home
  directory:auths=profmgr.read,solaris.admin.usermgr.write,solaris.admin.usermgr.
  read;help=RtUserMngmnt.html
User Security:::Manage passwords,
  clearances:auths=solaris.role.*,solaris.profmgr.*,solaris.admin.usermgr.*;help=
  RtUserSecurity.html
Printer Management:::Manage printers, daemons,
  spooling:help=RtPrntAdmin.html;auths=solaris.admin.printer.read,solaris.admin.
  printer.modify,solaris.admin.printer.delete
Software Installation:::Add application software to the
  system:help=RtSoftwareInstall.html;auths=solaris.admin.prodreg.read,solaris.admin.
  prodreg.modify,solaris.admin.prodreg.delete,solaris.admin.dcmgr.admin,solaris.
  admin.dcmgr.read
Network Management:::Manage the host and network
  configuration:help=RtNetMngmnt.html;auths=solaris.admin.dcmgr.clients,solaris.
  admin.dcmgr.read
Media Restore:::Restore files and file systems from
  backups:help=RtMediaRestore.html
Name Service Security:::Security related name service
  scripts/commands:help=RtNameServiceSecure.html
Media Backup:::Backup files and file systems:help=RtMediaBkup.html
Mail Management:::Manage sendmail & queues:help=RtMailMngmnt.html
Audit Review:::Review BSM auditing
  logs:auths=solaris.audit.read;help=RtAuditReview.html
Network Security:::Manage network and host security:help=RtNetSecure.html
Cron Management:::Manage at and cron
  jobs:auths=solaris.jobs.*;help=RtCronMngmnt.html
Name Service Management:::Non-security name service
  scripts/commands:help=RtNameServiceAdmin.html
Object Access Management:::Change ownership and permission on
  files:help=RtObAccessMngmnt.html
Rights Delegation:::Delegate ability to assign rights to users and
  roles:auths=solaris.role.delegate,solaris.profmgr.delegate,solaris.grant;help=
  RtRightsDelegate.html
All:::Execute any command as the user or role:help=RtAll.html
```

Each entry consists of a single line with five fields separated by colons ( : ). You can continue lines by using the backslash character ( \ ). Each entry has the following form.

```
profname:res1:res2:desc:attr
```

The fields are described in Table 122.

*Table 122    Fields in the prof_attr Database*

| *profname* | The name of the profile. Profile names are case sensitive. |
|---|---|
| *res1* | Reserved for future use. |
| *res2* | Reserved for future use. |
| *desc* | A long description that explains the purpose of the profile, including what type of user would be interested in using it. The long description should be suitable for display in the help text of an application. |
| *attr* | An optional list of semicolon-separated ( ; ) key-value pairs that describe the security attributes to apply to the object when it is executed. You can specify zero or more keys. The two valid keys are `help` and `auths`. |
| | `help` | Assign the name of a file ending in `.htm` or `.html`. |
| | `auths` | Specify a comma-separated list of authorization names chosen from those names defined in the `auth_attr`(4) database. You can specify authorization names with the asterisk (*) character as a wildcard. For example, `solaris.printer.*` means all Sun authorizations for printing. |

## Execution Attributes (exec_attr)

An execution attribute associated with a profile is a command with any special security attributes that can be run by those users or roles to whom the profile is assigned. Special security attributes refer to such attributes as UID, EUID, GID, and EGID that can be added to a process when the command is run.

## Syntax of the exec_attr Database

Definitions of executions attributes are stored in the /etc/security/exec_attr database. The default exec_attr database is shown below.

```
#
# Copyright (c) 2000 by Sun Microsystems, Inc. All rights reserved.
#
# /etc/security/exec_attr
#
# execution attributes for profiles. see exec_attr(4)
#
#pragma     ident     "@(#)exec_attr 1.2     00/05/22 SMI"
#
Primary Administrator:suser:cmd:::*:uid=0;gid=0
Name Service Security:suser:cmd:::/usr/sadm/bin/smattrpop:uid=0;gid=sys
Software Installation:suser:cmd:::/usr/bin/pkgparam:uid=0
Network Management:suser:cmd:::/usr/sbin/in.named:uid=0
File System Management:suser:cmd:::/usr/sbin/mount:uid=0
Software Installation:suser:cmd:::/usr/bin/pkgtrans:uid=0
Name Service Security:suser:cmd:::/usr/bin/nisaddcred:euid=0
Software Installation:suser:cmd:::/usr/sbin/install:euid=0
Process Management:suser:cmd:::/usr/bin/crontab:euid=0
Audit Review:suser:cmd:::/usr/sbin/praudit:euid=0
Media Backup:suser:cmd:::/usr/bin/mt:euid=0
Object Access Management:suser:cmd:::/usr/bin/chmod:euid=0
Network Management:suser:cmd:::/usr/sbin/snoop:uid=0
Process Management:suser:cmd:::/usr/bin/pmap:euid=0
File System Management:suser:cmd:::/usr/sbin/dfshares:euid=0
Network Management:suser:cmd:::/etc/init.d/nscd:uid=0;gid=sys
Printer Management:suser:cmd:::/usr/sbin/accept:euid=lp
Process Management:suser:cmd:::/usr/bin/truss:euid=0
Process Management:suser:cmd:::/usr/bin/psig:euid=0
Maintenance and Repair:suser:cmd:::/etc/init.d/syslog:uid=0;gid=sys
Maintenance and Repair:suser:cmd:::/usr/sbin/syslogd:euid=0
Device Security:suser:cmd:::/etc/init.d/mkdtab:uid=0;gid=sys
Maintenance and Repair:suser:cmd:::/usr/sbin/init:euid=0
Media Backup:suser:cmd:::/usr/sbin/tar:euid=0
Device Management:suser:cmd:::/usr/sbin/allocate:uid=0
Media Restore:suser:cmd:::/usr/sbin/tar:euid=0
Process Management:suser:cmd:::/etc/init.d/perf:uid=0;gid=sys
Software Installation:suser:cmd:::/usr/bin/pkgmk:uid=0
Network Management:suser:cmd:::/etc/init.d/inetsvc:uid=0;gid=sys
Audit Control:suser:cmd:::/usr/sbin/audit:euid=0
Mail Management:suser:cmd:::/usr/bin/mconnect:euid=0
Maintenance and Repair:suser:cmd:::/usr/sbin/halt:euid=0
User Management:suser:cmd:::/usr/sbin/grpck:euid=0
File System Management:suser:cmd:::/usr/sbin/format:uid=0
Process Management:suser:cmd:::/usr/bin/pstop:euid=0
Name Service Management:suser:cmd:::/usr/lib/nis/nisping:euid=0
Maintenance and Repair:suser:cmd:::/usr/sbin/prtconf:euid=0
Process Management:suser:cmd:::/usr/bin/prun:euid=0
Name Service Security:suser:cmd:::/usr/bin/nischgrp:euid=0
Process Management:suser:cmd:::/usr/bin/nice:euid=0
Name Service Management:suser:cmd:::/usr/lib/nis/nisshowcache:euid=0
Network Management:suser:cmd:::/usr/bin/ruptime:euid=0
Name Service Security:suser:cmd:::/usr/bin/nispasswd:euid=0
Media Backup:suser:cmd:::/usr/lib/fs/ufs/ufsdump:euid=0;gid=sys
File System Management:suser:cmd:::/usr/sbin/devinfo:euid=0
Device Security:suser:cmd:::/usr/sbin/eeprom:uid=0
Name Service Security:suser:cmd:::/usr/bin/nisrmdir:euid=0
Audit Control:suser:cmd:::/etc/security/bsmunconv:uid=0
Process Management:suser:cmd:::/usr/bin/renice:euid=0
Audit Control:suser:cmd:::/usr/sbin/auditd:uid=0
Mail Management:suser:cmd:::/usr/lib/sendmail:uid=0
File System Management:suser:cmd:::/usr/sbin/mkfs:euid=0
Network Management:suser:cmd:::/usr/sbin/spray:euid=0
File System Management:suser:cmd:::/etc/init.d/standardmounts:uid=0;gid=sys
User Management:suser:cmd:::/usr/sbin/pwck:euid=0
User Security:suser:cmd:::/usr/bin/passwd:euid=0
Network Management:suser:cmd:::/usr/sbin/ifconfig:uid=0
File System Management:suser:cmd:::/usr/sbin/shareall:uid=0;gid=root
```

```
Name Service Management:suser:cmd:::/usr/sbin/nscd:euid=0
Name Service Security:suser:cmd:::/usr/bin/nismkdir:euid=0
Process Management:suser:cmd:::/etc/init.d/power:euid=0
Maintenance and Repair:suser:cmd:::/usr/sbin/poweroff:uid=0
Process Management:suser:cmd:::/etc/init.d/cvc:uid=0;gid=root
File System Management:suser:cmd:::/usr/sbin/clri:euid=0
Device Security:suser:cmd:::/etc/init.d/volmgt:uid=0;gid=sys
Software Installation:suser:cmd:::/usr/sbin/pkgrm:uid=0;gid=bin
Name Service Management:suser:cmd:::/usr/bin/nisln:euid=0
Printer Management:suser:cmd:::/usr/ucb/lpq:euid=0
File System Management:suser:cmd:::/usr/bin/rmdir:euid=0
Process Management:suser:cmd:::/usr/bin/pfiles:euid=0
File System Management:suser:cmd:::/usr/lib/autofs/automountd:euid=0
Printer Management:suser:cmd:::/etc/init.d/lp:euid=0
File System Management:suser:cmd:::/usr/sbin/unshareall:uid=0;gid=root
Software Installation:suser:cmd:::/usr/bin/pkginfo:uid=0
File System Management:suser:cmd:::/etc/init.d/buildmnttab:uid=0;gid=sys
File System Management:suser:cmd:::/usr/lib/fs/autofs/automount:euid=0
Name Service Security:suser:cmd:::/usr/bin/nischown:euid=0
File System Management:suser:cmd:::/usr/sbin/share:uid=0;gid=root
Software Installation:suser:cmd:::/usr/sbin/pkgadd:uid=0;gid=bin
File System Management:suser:cmd:::/usr/bin/mkdir:euid=0
Network Management:suser:cmd:::/usr/bin/rup:euid=0
Network Management:suser:cmd:::/etc/init.d/uucp:uid=0;gid=sys
Maintenance and Repair:suser:cmd:::/usr/bin/ldd:euid=0
File System Management:suser:cmd:::/usr/lib/fs/ufs/tunefs:uid=0
Object Access Management:suser:cmd:::/usr/bin/getfacl:euid=0
Device Security:suser:cmd:::/etc/init.d/keymap:uid=0;gid=sys
Name Service Security:suser:cmd:::/usr/bin/nisgrpadm:euid=0
Device Security:suser:cmd:::/usr/sbin/list_devices:euid=0
Network Management:suser:cmd:::/etc/init.d/inetinit:uid=0;gid=sys
Network Management:suser:cmd:::/etc/init.d/rpc:uid=0;gid=sys
Name Service Security:suser:cmd:::/usr/lib/nis/nisserver:uid=0
Device Security:suser:cmd:::/etc/init.d/dtlogin:uid=0;gid=sys
File System Management:suser:cmd:::/usr/sbin/fstyp:euid=0
File System Management:suser:cmd:::/usr/sbin/ff:euid=0
Name Service Security:suser:cmd:::/usr/bin/nischmod:euid=0
File System Management:suser:cmd:::/usr/sbin/fuser:euid=0
Mail Management:suser:cmd:::/usr/bin/mailq:euid=0
File System Management:suser:cmd:::/usr/sbin/fsck:euid=0
Printer Management:suser:cmd:::/usr/bin/lpstat:euid=0
File System Management:suser:cmd:::/usr/bin/eject:euid=0
File System Management:suser:cmd:::/usr/sbin/umountall:uid=0
Mail Management:suser:cmd:::/usr/bin/newaliases:euid=0
Printer Management:suser:cmd:::/usr/lib/lp/lpsched:uid=0
Device Security:suser:cmd:::/etc/init.d/drvconfig:uid=0;gid=sys
Process Management:suser:cmd:::/usr/bin/pstack:euid=0
Network Management:suser:cmd:::/usr/bin/netstat:uid=0
User Security:suser:cmd:::/usr/sbin/pwck:euid=0
Name Service Security:suser:cmd:::/usr/sbin/nisinit:euid=0
Printer Management:suser:cmd:::/usr/sbin/lpfilter:euid=lp
Maintenance and Repair:suser:cmd:::/usr/sbin/eeprom:euid=0
Process Management:suser:cmd:::/usr/sbin/fuser:euid=0
Audit Control:suser:cmd:::/etc/init.d/audit:euid=0;egid=3
File System Management:suser:cmd:::/usr/sbin/mountall:uid=0
File System Management:suser:cmd:::/usr/sbin/unshare:uid=0;gid=root
Maintenance and Repair:suser:cmd:::/usr/bin/adb:euid=0
Printer Management:suser:cmd:::/usr/bin/lpset:egid=14
Printer Management:suser:cmd:::/usr/sbin/lpadmin:egid=14
Name Service Security:suser:cmd:::/usr/bin/chkey:euid=0
Cron Management:suser:cmd:::/etc/init.d/cron:uid=0;gid=sys
File System Management:suser:cmd:::/etc/init.d/ufs_quota:uid=0;gid=sys
Name Service Security:suser:cmd:::/usr/bin/nisrm:euid=0
Software Installation:suser:cmd:::/usr/sbin/pkgmv:uid=0;gid=bin
Maintenance and Repair:suser:cmd:::/usr/sbin/reboot:uid=0
File System Management:suser:cmd:::/usr/sbin/fsdb:euid=0
Process Management:suser:cmd:::/usr/bin/pwdx:euid=0
Name Service Management:suser:cmd:::/usr/lib/nis/nisctl:euid=0
Name Service Security:suser:cmd:::/usr/lib/nis/nisaddent:euid=0
Maintenance and Repair:suser:cmd:::/usr/bin/date:euid=0
Name Service Management:suser:cmd:::/usr/bin/nischttl:euid=0
Software Installation:suser:cmd:::/usr/ccs/bin/make:euid=0
Process Management:suser:cmd:::/usr/bin/pldd:euid=0
Device Security:suser:cmd:::/etc/init.d/pcmcia:uid=0;gid=sys
File System Management:suser:cmd:::/usr/lib/fs/ufs/newfs:euid=0
User Management:suser:cmd:::/etc/init.d/utmpd:uid=0;gid=sys
```

```
All:suser:cmd:::*:
Software Installation:suser:cmd:::/usr/sbin/pkgchk:uid=0
Process Management:suser:cmd:::/usr/bin/pcred:euid=0
Process Management:suser:cmd:::/usr/bin/pflags:euid=0
Software Installation:suser:cmd:::/usr/bin/admintool:uid=0;gid=bin
File System Management:suser:cmd:::/usr/lib/fs/ufs/fsirand:euid=0
Printer Management:suser:cmd:::/usr/sbin/lpsystem:uid=0
Media Restore:suser:cmd:::/usr/bin/cpio:euid=0
Printer Management:suser:cmd:::/usr/sbin/lpmove:euid=1p
User Security:suser:cmd:::/usr/sbin/pwconv:euid=0
Printer Management:suser:cmd:::/usr/sbin/lpshut:euid=1p
Device Security:suser:cmd:::/etc/init.d/devlinks:uid=0;gid=sys
Device Security:suser:cmd:::/usr/sbin/strace:euid=0
Mail Management:suser:cmd:::/etc/init.d/sendmail:uid=0;gid=sys
Name Service Security:suser:cmd:::/usr/lib/nis/nisupdkeys:euid=0
Process Management:suser:cmd:::/usr/bin/ps:euid=0
Maintenance and Repair:suser:cmd:::/etc/init.d/sysetup:uid=0;gid=sys
Process Management:suser:cmd:::/usr/bin/kill:euid=0
Object Access Management:suser:cmd:::/usr/bin/chgrp:euid=0
Network Management:suser:cmd:::/etc/init.d/asppp:uid=0;gid=sys
Name Service Security:suser:cmd:::/usr/lib/nis/nisclient:uid=0
Process Management:suser:cmd:::/etc/init.d/cron:uid=0;gid=sys
Printer Management:suser:cmd:::/usr/bin/cancel:euid=0
Name Service Security:suser:cmd:::/usr/bin/nistbladm:euid=0
Software Installation:suser:cmd:::/usr/sbin/pkgask:uid=0
Software Installation:suser:cmd:::/usr/bin/pkgproto:uid=0
Printer Management:suser:cmd:::/usr/bin/disable:euid=1p
Process Management:suser:cmd:::/usr/bin/pwait:euid=0
Name Service Security:suser:cmd:::/usr/lib/nis/nispopulate:euid=0
Media Restore:suser:cmd:::/usr/bin/mt:euid=0
Printer Management:suser:cmd:::/usr/sbin/reject:euid=1p
Printer Management:suser:cmd:::/usr/sbin/lpforms:euid=1p
Network Management:suser:cmd:::/etc/init.d/sysid.net:uid=0;gid=sys
Audit Control:suser:cmd:::/usr/sbin/auditconfig:euid=0
Audit Review:suser:cmd:::/usr/sbin/auditreduce:euid=0
Printer Management:suser:cmd:::/usr/ucb/lprm:euid=0
Software Installation:suser:cmd:::/usr/bin/ln:euid=0
Name Service Security:suser:cmd:::/usr/lib/nis/nissetup:euid=0
File System Management:suser:cmd:::/usr/sbin/swap:euid=0
Name Service Security:suser:cmd:::/usr/sbin/nislog:euid=0
File System Management:suser:cmd:::/usr/sbin/umount:uid=0
Object Access Management:suser:cmd:::/usr/bin/setfacl:euid=0
Cron Management:suser:cmd:::/usr/bin/crontab:euid=0
File System Management:suser:cmd:::/etc/init.d/autofs:uid=0;gid=sys
Media Restore:suser:cmd:::/usr/lib/fs/ufs/ufsrestore:euid=0
Process Management:suser:cmd:::/usr/bin/ptime:euid=0
Audit Control:suser:cmd:::/etc/security/bsmconv:uid=0
Process Management:suser:cmd:::/usr/bin/ptree:euid=0
Network Security:suser:cmd:::/etc/init.d/rootusr:uid=0;gid=sys
Network Management:suser:cmd:::/etc/init.d/sysid.sys:uid=0;gid=sys
Device Management:suser:cmd:::/usr/sbin/deallocate:uid=0
Maintenance and Repair:suser:cmd:::/usr/bin/vmstat:euid=0
Maintenance and Repair:suser:cmd:::/usr/sbin/crash:euid=0
Name Service Management:suser:cmd:::/usr/lib/nis/nisstat:euid=0
Device Security:suser:cmd:::/etc/init.d/initpcmcia:uid=0;gid=sys
File System Management:suser:cmd:::/usr/lib/fs/nfs/showmount:euid=0
Audit Review:suser:cmd:::/usr/sbin/auditstat:euid=0
Object Access Management:suser:cmd:::/usr/bin/chown:euid=0
Network Management:suser:cmd:::/usr/sbin/route:uid=0
Printer Management:suser:cmd:::/usr/bin/enable:euid=1p
File System Management:suser:cmd:::/usr/sbin/mkfile:euid=0
File System Management:suser:cmd:::/usr/sbin/dfmounts:euid=0
Name Service Security:suser:cmd:::/usr/sbin/rpc.nisd:uid=0;gid=0
Name Service Security:suser:cmd:::/usr/sbin/newkey:euid=0
Printer Management:suser:cmd:::/usr/sbin/lpusers:euid=1p
Network Management:suser:cmd:::/usr/bin/setuname:euid=0
```

Each entry consists of a single line with seven fields separated by colons (:). You can continue lines by using the backslash character (\). Each entry has the following form.

```
name:policy:type:res1:res2:id:attr
```

The fields are described in Table 123.

*Table 123    Fields in the exec_attr Database*

| name | The name of the profile. Profile names are case sensitive. |
|---|---|
| policy | The security policy associated with this entry. Currently, suser—the superuser policy model—is the only valid policy entry. |
| type | The type of entry whose attributes are specified. Currently, cmd—command—is the only valid type. |
| res1 | Reserved for future use. |
| res2 | Reserved for future use. |
| id | A string identifying the entity. You can use the asterisk wildcard character. Commands should have the full path or a path with a wildcard character. To specify arguments, write a script with the arguments and point id to the script. |
| attr | An optional list of semicolon-separated (;) key-value pairs that describe the security attributes to apply to the entity when it is executed. You can specify zero or more keys. The list of valid keywords depends on the policy being enforced. euid, uid, egid, and gid are the four valid keys. |
|  | euid and uid contain a single user name or a numeric user ID. Commands designated with euid run with the effective UID indicated, which is similar to setting the setuid bit on an executable file. Commands designated with uid run with both the real and effective UIDs. |
|  | egid and gid contain a single group name or numeric group ID. Commands designated with egid run with the effective GID indicated, which is similar to setting the setgid bit on an executable file. Commands designated with gid run with both the real and effective GIDs. |

## Policy Configuration File (policy.conf)

The `/etc/security/policy.conf` file provides the security policy configuration for user-level attributes.

### Syntax of the policy.conf File

The default `/etc/security/policy.conf` file is shown below.

```
#
# Copyright (c) 1999-2000 by Sun Microsystems, Inc. All rights reserved.
#
# /etc/security/policy.conf
#
# security policy configuration for user attributes. see policy.conf(4)
#
#ident      "@(#)policy.conf    1.3     00/03/30 SMI"
#
#AUTHS_GRANTED=
PROFS_GRANTED=Basic Solaris User
```

Each entry consists of a *key=value* pair on a single line. The key must start the line. Comment lines starting with a pound sign (#) are ignored.

The keys listed in Table 124 are defined.

*Table 124   Defined Keys for the policy.conf File*

| Key | Description |
|---|---|
| AUTHS_GRANTED | Specify the default set of authorizations granted to all users. This entry is interpreted by `chkauthattr`(3SECDB). The value is one or more comma-separated authorizations defined in the `auth_attr`(4) database. |
| PROFS_GRANTED | Grant rights profiles by default. This key is available starting with the Solaris 8 Update 3 release. The default `Basic Solaris User` value is assigned. |

You can deny all regular users the ability to view the information in the Solaris Management Console by setting `PROFS_GRANTED=` with no value.

### Example of the policy.conf File

The following example grants authorization to set the system date and denies all regular users the capability of viewing information in the Solaris Management Console.

```
AUTHS_GRANTED=com.sun.date
PROFS_GRANTED=
```

# Commands That Use Role-Based Access Control Authorizations

Table 125 lists the commands that use RBAC authorizations.

*Table 125   Commands That Use RBAC Authorizations*

| Command | Authorizations |
|---|---|
| allocate(1M) | solaris.device.allocate, solaris.device.revoke |
| at(1) | solaris.jobs.user |
| atq(1) | solaris.jobs.admin |
| crontab(1) | solaris.jobs.user, solaris.jobs.admin |
| deallocate(1M) | solaris.device.allocate, solaris.device.revoke |
| list_devices(1M) | solaris.device.revoke |
| rdate(1M) | solaris.system.date |
| smcron(1M) | solaris.jobs.admin, solaris.jobs.user |
| smdiskless(1M) | solaris.admin.dcmgr.clients, solaris.admin.dcmgr.read |
| smexec(1M) | solaris.profmgr.read, solaris.profmgr.write |
| smgroup(1M) | solaris.admin.usermgr.read, solaris.admin.usermgr.write |
| smmaillist(1M) | solaris.admin.usermgr.read, solaris.admin.usermgr.write |
| smmultiuser(1M), smuser(1M) | solaris.admin.usermgr.pswd, solaris.admin.usermgr.read, solaris.admin.usermgr.write, solaris.profmgr.assign, solaris.profmgr.delegate, solaris.role.assign, solaris.role.delegate |
| smosservice(1M) | solaris.admin.dcmgr.admin, solaris.admin.dcmgr.read |
| smprofile(1M) | solaris.profmgr.read, solaris.profmgr.write |

*Table 125   Commands That Use RBAC Authorizations (Continued)*

| Command | Authorizations |
|---|---|
| smrole(1M) | solaris.admin.usermgr.pswd,<br>solaris.admin.usermgr.read,<br>solaris.admin.usermgr.write,<br>solaris.profmgr.assign,<br>solaris.profmgr.delegate,<br>solaris.role.assign,<br>solaris.role.delegate |

# Commands for Managing Role-Based Access Control

The commands listed in Table 126 have options for managing role-based access control from a command line. See the appropriate manual page for more information.

*NOTE. The recommended way to manage RBAC is with the tools in the Solaris Management Console. Direct editing of the databases is not recommended.*

*Table 126   Commands for Managing Role-Based Access Control*

| Command | Description |
|---|---|
| auths(1) | Display authorizations for a user. |
| makedbm(1M) | Make a dbm file. |
| ncsd(1M) | Nameservice cache daemon. This daemon is useful for caching the user_attr, prof_attr, and exec_attr databases. |
| pam_roles(5) | Role account management module for PAM. Checks for the authorization to assume a role. |
| pfexec(1)<br>pfsh(1)<br>pfcsh(1)<br>pfksh(1) | Profile shells, used to execute commands with attributes specified in the exec_attr database. |
| policy.conf(4) | Configuration file for security policy. Lists granted authorizations. |

*Table 126*   *Commands for Managing Role-Based Access Control (Continued)*

| Command | Description |
|---------|-------------|
| profiles(1) | Display profiles for a specified user. |
| roles(1) | Display roles granted to a user. |
| roleadd(1M) | Add a role account on the system. |
| roledel(1M) | Delete a role's account from the system. |
| rolemod(1M) | Modify a role's account information on the system. |
| useradd(1M) | Add a user account on the system. The -P option assigns a policy, the -R option assigns a role, the -A option assigns an authorization. |
| userdel(1M) | Delete a user's login from the system. |
| usermod(1M) | Modify a user's account information on the system. The -P option modifies a policy, the -R option modifies a role, the -A option modifies an authorization. |

# A

# *VOLUME MANAGEMENT*

Volume management automates the mounting of CD-ROMs and diskettes; users no longer need to have superuser permissions to mount a CD-ROM or a diskette.

Volume management provides users with a standard interface for dealing  with diskettes and CD-ROMs. Starting with the Solaris 8 release, volume management also manages DVD-ROMs, Iomega Universal Serial Bus (USB) Zip, and Iomega Jaz Drives.

Volume management provides three major benefits.

- Automatically mounting diskettes, CDs, DVD-ROMs, Zip, and Jaz disks simplifies their use.
- Users can access the media without having to become superuser.
- Users on the network can gain automatic access to the media mounted on remote systems.

With volume management, you mount devices automatically with the following steps.

1. Insert media.
2. For diskettes, the `volcheck` command.
3. Work with files on media.
4. Eject media.

## New! What's New with Volume Management

Volume management functionality continues to evolve with the Solaris 8 and update releases. With the Solaris 8 6/00 release, volume management features are improved to fully support removable media that can be connected to relevant hardware platforms. This improvement means that DVD-ROMs, Iomega USB Zip and Jaz drives, CD-ROMs, and diskettes are mounted and available for reading when inserted. For example, if a system has a DVD-ROM drive, volume management automatically mounts discs in the drive and displays information in the CDE File Manager. As another example, if a system has a USB port, you can connect third-party devices such as an Iomega Zip drive to the USB port. The Solaris 8 volume management software enables you to automatically access such third-party devices.

Both the Common Desktop Environment (CDE) volume management and Solaris command-line features are updated to provide full support.

With the volume management improvements you can perform the following tasks.

- Use the new `rmformat` command to format, label, and set read or write software protection on removable media. The `rmformat` command replaces the `fdformat` command for formatting removable media. See "Using the rmformat Command to Format Diskettes" on page 671 and the `rmformat`(1) manual page for more information.
- Use the `mkfs_pcfs`(1M) and `fsck_pcfs`(1M) commands to create and verify a PCFS file system on removable media.
- Create an `fdisk` partition and a PCFS file system on removable media on a SPARC-based system to facilitate data transfers to IA-based systems. See "Creating An Alternate fdisk Partition" on page 680 for more information.
- Use the CDE Removable Media Manager to format, protect, and view data on removable media devices such as diskettes, CD-ROM, DVD-ROM, Iomega Zip, and Iomega Jaz devices.

*NOTE. Zip drives work with the Solaris 7 release, with the Solaris 8 and Solaris 8 6/00 release with a workaround. Bug 4365456 reports that Zip drives don't work with the Solaris 8 10/00 release. At the time of writing, no workaround exists to enable Zip drivers to work with the Solaris 8 10/00 or Solaris 8 01/01 release. These problems are fixed in the Solaris 8 04/01 release. See "Accessing Jaz or Zip Drives" on page 678 for more information.*

Use the following guidelines for removable media.

- Use UDFS and PCFS to transfer data between DVD media.

- Use the `tar` or `cpio` commands to transfer files between rewritable media such as a PCMCIA memory card or diskette with a UFS file system. Note that a UFS file system created on a SPARC system is not identical to a UFS file system on PCMCIA or to a diskette created on an IA system.

- Set write protection to protect important files on Jaz or Zip drives or diskettes. Apply a password to Iomega media.

# Volume Management Files

Volume management consists of the following elements.

- The `/usr/sbin/vold` volume management daemon.

- The `/etc/vold.conf` configuration file that is used by the `vold` daemon to determine which devices to manage.

- The `/etc/rmmount.conf` file that is used to configure removable media mounts and actions in `/usr/lib/rmmount`.

- The volume daemon logs messages in the `/var/adm/vold.log` file.

## The /etc/vold.conf File

The default `/etc/vold.conf` file is shown below.

```
# @(#)vold.conf 1.25     99/11/11 SMI
#
# Volume Daemon Configuration file
#

# Database to use (must be first)
db db_mem.so

# Labels supported
label cdrom label_cdrom.so cdrom
label dos label_dos.so floppy rmdisk pcmem
label sun label_sun.so floppy rmdisk pcmem

# Devices to use
use cdrom drive /dev/rdsk/c*s2 dev_cdrom.so cdrom%d
use floppy drive /dev/rdiskette[0-9] dev_floppy.so floppy%d
use pcmem drive /dev/rdsk/c*s2 dev_pcmem.so pcmem%d forceload=true
use rmdisk drive /dev/rdsk/c*s2 dev_rmdisk.so rmdisk%d

# Actions
eject dev/diskette[0-9]/* user=root /usr/sbin/rmmount
eject dev/dsk/* user=root /usr/sbin/rmmount
insert dev/diskette[0-9]/* user=root /usr/sbin/rmmount
insert dev/dsk/* user=root /usr/sbin/rmmount
notify rdsk/* group=tty user=root /usr/lib/vold/volmissing -p
remount dev/diskette[0-9]/* user=root /usr/sbin/rmmount
remount dev/dsk/* user=root /usr/sbin/rmmount

# List of file system types unsafe to eject
```

*New!*

```
unsafe ufs hsfs pcfs udfs
```

The syntax for the `/etc/vold.conf` file is shown below.

```
# Database to use
db database

# Labels supported
label label_type shared_object device

# Devices to use
use device type special shared_object symname [ options ]

# Actions
insert regex [ options ] program program args
eject regex [ options ] program program args
notify regex [ options ] program program args

# List of file system types unsafe to eject
unsafe fs_type fs_type
```

You can safely modify only the `Devices to use` and `Actions` fields. You should not make changes to any of the other fields.

If you modify the `vold.conf` file, you must send `vold` a HUP signal to tell it to reread `vold.conf`, as shown below.

```
# ps = -ef _ grep vold
    root    252    1  0 10:38:29 ?        0:02 /usr/sbin/vold
  winsor    500  422  0 11:08:38 pts/4    0:00 grep vold
# kill -HUP 252
#
```

If a system has additional diskette drives, volume management automatically creates two subdirectories in `/vol/dev` for each additional drive—one to provide access to any file systems that might be written on the media inserted into these drives, and the other to provide access to the raw device itself. For a second diskette drive, volume management creates directories named `diskette1` and `rdiskette1`. For a third diskette drive, it creates directories named `diskette2` and `rdiskette2`. And so on for additional drives.

> NOTE. If you want additional CD-ROM drives on a system, you must edit the `/etc/vold.conf` file and add the new devices to the `Devices to use` list.

The syntax for a `Devices to use` entry is shown below.

```
use device type special shared-object symname options
```

Table 127 describes each of the fields for the `Devices to use` syntax.

*Table 127   Device Control Syntax Descriptions*

| Field | Supported Default Values | Description | |
|---|---|---|---|
| *device* | cdrom, floppy, pcmem, rmdisk | The removable media device. | New! |
| *type* | drive | The type of device—multiple or single media support. | |
| *special* | /dev/dsk/c0t6, /dev/diskette, /dev/rdsk/c*s2, /dev/rmdisk/jaz, /dev/rmdisk/zip | Path name of the device to be used in the /dev directory. | New! |
| *shared-object* | /usr/lib/vold/ shared-object-name | Location of the code that manages the device. | |
| *symname* | cdrom0, cdrom1, floppy0, rmdisk, jaz0, zip0 | The symbolic name that refers to this device. The *symname* is placed in the device directory. | New! |
| *options* | user=nobody group=nobody mode=0666 | The user, group, and mode permissions for the inserted media. | |

The *special* and *symname* parameters are related. If *special* contains any shell wildcard characters—for example, if it has one or more asterisks or question marks in it—then the *symname* field must have a %d at its end. In this case, the devices that match the regular expression are sorted, then numbered. The first device has a 0 for the %d, the second device has a 1, and so on. If the *special* specification does not have any shell wildcard characters, then you must explicitly specify a number at the end of the *symname* parameter.

New!

The syntax for an `Action` entry is shown below.

```
insert | eject | notify regex [options] program program_args
```

Table 128 describes each of the fields for the Actions syntax.

*Table 128   Actions Syntax Descriptions*

| Field | Description |
|---|---|
| insert \| eject \| notify | The media event prompting the event. |
| regex | This sh(1) regular expression is matched against each entry in the /vol file system that is being affected by this event. |
| options | (Optional) Specify what user or group name is to be used to run this event. |
| program | The full path name of an executable program to be run when regex is matched. |
| program_args | Arguments to the program. |

## The /etc/rmmount.conf File

The default /etc/rmmount.conf file is shown below.

```
# @(#)rmmount.conf 1.10      00/02/14 SMI
#
# Removable Media Mounter configuration file.
#

# File system identification
ident udfs ident_udfs.so cdrom floppy rmdisk
ident hsfs ident_hsfs.so cdrom
ident ufs ident_ufs.so cdrom floppy rmdisk pcmem
ident pcfs ident_pcfs.so floppy rmdisk pcmem

# Actions
action cdrom action_filemgr.so
action floppy action_filemgr.so
action rmdisk action_filemgr.so

# Mount
mount * hsfs udfs ufs -o nosuid
```

## Volume Management Files

This section lists the files and shared libraries used by volume management. The following example shows the files in the /usr/lib/vold directory.

```
paperbark% ls -1 /usr/lib/vold
db_mem.so.1
db_nis.so.1
dev_cdrom.so.1
dev_cdtest.so.1
dev_floppy.so.1
dev_pcmem.so.1
```

```
dev_rmdisk.so.1
dev_test.so.1
eject_popup
label_cdrom.so.1
label_dos.so.1
label_sun.so.1
label_test.so.1
volcancel
volmissing
volmissing_popup
volstat
paperbark%
```

The following example lists the files in the /usr/lib/rmmount directory.

```
paperbark% ls -1 /usr/lib/rmmount
action_dvdvideo.so.1
action_filemgr.so.1
action_workman.so.1
paperbark%
```

*New!*

## Volume Management Log Messages

If you encounter problems with volume management, check the
/var/adm/vold.log file for information. The following example shows the
contents of the vold.log file.

```
paperbark% more /var/adm/vold.log
Thu Nov 16 08:18:25 2000 warning: either couldn't find a driver for cdrom
  "/dev/rdsk/c*s2", or it's already managed
Thu Nov 16 08:18:25 2000 warning: either couldn't find a driver for floppy
  "/dev/rdiskette[0-9]", or it's already managed
Thu Nov 16 08:18:26 2000 warning: either couldn't find a driver for rmdisk
  "/dev/rdsk/c*s2", or it's already managed
Thu Nov 16 10:41:44 2000 warning: either couldn't find a driver for cdrom
  "/dev/rdsk/c*s2", or it's already managed
Thu Nov 16 10:41:44 2000 warning: either couldn't find a driver for floppy
  "/dev/rdiskette[0-9]", or it's already managed
Thu Nov 16 10:41:44 2000 warning: either couldn't find a driver for rmdisk
  "/dev/rdsk/c*s2", or it's already managed
Sat Nov 18 13:32:44 2000 warning: either couldn't find a driver for cdrom
  "/dev/rdsk/c*s2", or it's already managed
Sat Nov 18 13:32:44 2000 warning: either couldn't find a driver for floppy
  "/dev/rdiskette[0-9]", or it's already managed
Sat Nov 18 13:32:45 2000 warning: either couldn't find a driver for rmdisk
  "/dev/rdsk/c*s2", or it's already managed
Mon Nov 20 08:59:02 2000 warning: either couldn't find a driver for cdrom
  "/dev/rdsk/c*s2", or it's already managed
Mon Nov 20 08:59:02 2000 warning: either couldn't find a driver for floppy
  "/dev/rdiskette[0-9]", or it's already managed
Mon Nov 20 08:59:03 2000 warning: either couldn't find a driver for rmdisk
  "/dev/rdsk/c*s2", or it's already managed
paperbark%
```

*New!*

If you want to display debugging messages from the volume daemon, you
can start the daemon by typing **/usr/sbin/vold -v -L 10**. With these
options, the volume daemon logs quite a bit of information in
/var/adm/vold.log.

Another way to gather debugging information is to run the `rmmount` command with the debug option. To do so, edit `/etc/vold.conf` and change the lines that have `/usr/sbin/rmmount` to include the `-D` option, as shown in the following example.

```
insert /vol*/dev/diskette[0-9]/* user=root /usr/sbin/rmmount -D
```

# Volume Management Mount Points

Volume management automatically mounts CD-ROM file systems on the `/cdrom` mount point when you insert the media into the drive.

*New!*

When you insert a diskette in the diskette drive, a Zip disk in a Zip drive, or a Jaz disk in a Jaz drive, you must ask the system to check the drive. You can check for a disk in any one of the following ways.

- From the command line, type **volcheck** and press Return.
- From the CDE front panel, click on the Folders menu and then click on Open Floppy.
- From the CDE File Manager File menu, choose Open Floppy.

*New!*

When you use any one of these methods, `vold` mounts the file system/device at a particular direct path and then creates a symbolic link that points to it. The pattern used to create the symbolic link is defined in the `/etc/vold.conf` file.

Table 129 describes the mount points and how volume management uses them.

*Table 129   Volume Management Mount Points*

| Media | Mount Point | State of Media |
|---|---|---|
| Diskette | `/floppy/floppy0` | Symbolic link to mounted diskette in local diskette drive. |
| | `/floppy/`*floppy-name* | Mounted named diskette. |
| | `/floppy/unnamed_floppy` | Mounted unnamed diskette. |
| CD-ROM | `/cdrom/cdrom0` | Symbolic link to mounted CD-ROM in local CD-ROM drive. |
| | `/cdrom/`*CD-ROM-name* | Mounted named CD-ROM. |
| | `/cdrom/`*CD-ROM-name*`/` *partition* | Mounted named CD-ROM with partitioned file system. |
| | `/cdrom/unnamed_cdrom` | Mounted unnamed CD-ROM. |

*Table 129  Volume Management Mount Points (Continued)*

| Media | Mount Point | State of Media | |
|-------|-------------|----------------|---|
| DVD-ROM | `/cdrom/cdrom1`<br>`/cdrom/`*DVD-ROM-name* | Mount a DVD-ROM drive. If the system has no CD-ROM drive, the mount point may be `/cdrom/cdrom0`. | *New!* |
| Zip | `/rmdisk/jaz` | Mount a Zip drive. | *New!* |
| Jaz | `/rmdisk/zip` | Mount a Jaz drive. | *New!* |

If the media does not contain a file system, volume management provides block and character devices in the `/vol` file system, as shown in Table 130.

*Table 130  CD-ROM and Diskette Device Locations When No File System Is Present*

| Media | Device Location | State of Media |
|-------|-----------------|----------------|
| Diskette | `/vol/dev/diskette0/`<br>`unnamed_floppy` | Formatted unnamed diskette-block device access. |
| | `/vol/dev/rdiskette0/`<br>`unnamed_floppy` | Formatted unnamed diskette—raw device access. |
| | `/vol/dev/diskette0/`<br>`unlabeled` | Unlabeled diskette—block diskette-raw device access. |
| CD-ROM | `/vol/dev/dsk/c0t6/`<br>`unnamed_cdrom` | CD-ROM—block device access. |
| | `/vol/dev/rdsk/c0t6/`<br>`unnamed_cdrom` | CD-ROM—raw device access. |

# Removable Media Manager

*New!*

You can use CDE Removable Media Manager to format, protect, and view data on removable media devices such as diskettes, CD-ROM, DVD-ROM, Iomega Zip, and Iomega Jaz devices.

> *NOTE. Removable Media Manager was introduced in the Solaris 8 6/00 release and updated in the Solaris 8 10/00 release.*

When you start Removable Media Manager, it displays all media currently loaded into the drives. If none of the drives contain any media, nothing is displayed in the Removable Media Manager window. The different forms of devices are represented by icons and are unlimited. For example, if a system has three drives loaded with diskettes, three diskette icons are displayed and the icon view is updated each time you insert or eject a device. Each class of media is represented by a different icon.

## Starting Removable Media Manager

You can open the Removable Media Manager in any of the following ways.

- From the File Manager File menu, choose Removable Media Manager.
- From the Front Panel Files subpanel, click on the Removable Media Manager icon.
- From the Workspace menu Folders menu, choose Removable Media Manager.

Figure 107 shows the Removable Media Manager window with one CD-ROM device and one diskette.

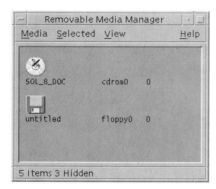

*Figure 107  Removable Media Manager Window*

A device is displayed with a nickname (cdrom0), an optional volume name (SOL_8_DOC), and an optional partition or slice number (0). You can view additional information about a device and set properties. You can select one or more devices and perform operations on them such as formatting and slicing devices, creating Solaris slices, and write-protecting a device either with or without a password.

## Supported Media Classes

Removable Media Manager supports the following devices.

- Diskette.
- CD-ROM.
- DVD-ROM.
- Iomega Zip drive.
- Iomega Jaz drive.
- Rmdisk (generic call that includes Syquest devices).

# Local and Remote CD-ROMs

The following sections describe how to access files from local and remote CD-ROM drives.

## Mounting a Local CD-ROM

Use the following procedure to mount a CD-ROM from a local drive.

1. Insert the CD-ROM in the CD-ROM drive.

   `vold` automatically mounts the file system on the CD-ROM at
   `/cdrom/`*cdlabel*, where *cdlabel* is the label written on the CD.
   Then `vold` creates the symbolic link `/cdrom/cdrom0`, which points
   to `/cdrom/`*cdlabel*. If you have more than one CD drive on a
   system, each drive gets its own symbolic link: `/cdrom/cdrom0`,
   `/cdrom/cdrom1`, and so on.

   *New!*

   If File Manager is running, a window displays the contents of the
   CD-ROM, as shown in Figure 108.

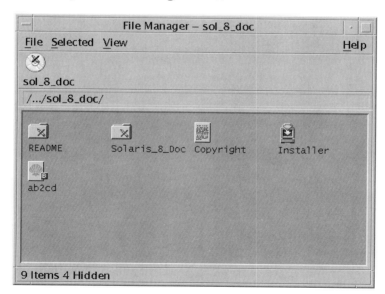

*Figure 108  The File Manager CD-ROM Window*

2. To access files on the CD-ROM from File Manager, click on the
   appropriate folders to navigate through the directory structure.

   In the example shown in Figure 108, double-click on the Installer icon
   to start the Installer.

3.  To access files on the CD-ROM from a command line, type
    **cd /cdrom/cdrom0** and press Return.

4.  Type **ls -L** and press Return.

    The list of files in the /cdrom/cdrom0 directory is displayed. Use the
    -L option because some of the files on the CD may be symbolic links.

*NOTE. You can use the File Manager CD-ROM window and the
command line interchangeably. For example, you can eject a CD-ROM
either from a command line by typing* **eject cdrom** *or by clicking
SELECT on the Eject button in the File Manager CD-ROM window.*

## Sharing Files from a Remote CD-ROM Drive

Before you can share CD-ROM files from a command line, the mountd
daemon must be running. On the system with the CD-ROM drive attached,
type **ps -ef | grep mountd** and press Return.

If the mountd daemon is running, other systems can access shared files. If
the mountd daemon is not running, you need to start NFS services.

Use the following steps to start NFS services.

1.  Become superuser.

2.  Type **/etc/init.d/nfs.server start** and press Return.

    NFS services are started.

```
oak% ps -ef | grep mountd
    root  4571  4473  5 12:53:51 pts/3     0:00 grep mountd
oak% su
Password:
# /etc/init.d/nfs.server start
```

Use the following steps to share CD files from a remote CD-ROM drive.

1.  Insert the CD-ROM into the drive.

    The CD-ROM file system is mounted.

2.  Become superuser on the system with the CD-ROM drive attached.

3.  Type **share -F nfs -o ro /cdrom/cdrom0** and press Return.

```
oak% su
Password:
# share -F nfs -o ro /cdrom/cdrom0
# ps -ef | grep mountd
    root  4655  4473  6 12:56:05 pts/3     0:00 grep mountd
    root  4649     1 47 12:55:25 ?        0:00 /usr/lib/nfs/mountd
#
```

*NOTE. Volume management does not recognize entries in the* /etc/dfs/dfstab *file. With Solaris 2.3 and later releases of volume management, you can set up remote CD-ROM mounts to be automatically shared by editing the* /etc/rmmount.conf *file. Refer to the* rmmount.conf *manual page for more information.*

## How to Access a Shared CD-ROM File System

You can use the /mnt directory as the mount point for the CD-ROM file system or create another directory.

*CAUTION. Do not use the* /cdrom *mount point to mount local file systems. Volume management may interfere with accessing files that have been manually mounted on the volume management* /cdrom *mount point.*

Once the CD-ROM is in the remote drive and the files are shared, follow these steps to access the shared files on another system via NFS.

1. Become superuser on the local system.
2. Type **mount *remote-system-name*:/cdrom/cdrom0 */mount-point*** and press Return.

   The file system from the remote system directory /cdrom/cdrom0 is mounted on the /mount-point directory. The cdrom0 subdirectory is symbolically linked to the actual name of the CD-ROM, which is assigned by the application vendor.

In the following example, the files from the remote system castle are mounted on the /mnt mount point.

```
oak% su
Password:
# mount castle:/cdrom/cdrom0 /mnt
# cd /mnt
# ls
SUNWssser   SUNWsssra   SUNWsssrb   SUNWsssrc   SUNWsssrd   SUNWssstr
#
```

## How to Unmount Shared CD-ROM File Systems

When you are through using the remote CD-ROM file system, use the following steps to unmount it.

1. On the local system, become superuser.
2. Type **cd** and press Return.
3. Type **umount */mount-point*** and press Return.

   The file system from the remote system directory /cdrom/cdrom0 is unmounted.

# Diskettes and Volume Management

When you insert a diskette into the diskette drive, volume management does not mount the diskette automatically; this prevents excessive reads, which can quickly wear out the diskette drive. You must use the `volcheck` command or choose a menu option that checks for the presence of a diskette in the diskette drive.

## Formatting Diskettes

You can format diskettes in three ways.

- With Removable Media Manager.
- With the `fdformat` command.
- With the `rmformat` command.

### *New!* Using Removable Media Manager to Format Diskettes

You can use the Removable Media Manager graphical user interface to create the following formats and file systems on a diskette.

- PCFS (DOS).
- UFS (UNIX).
- UDFS.
- NEC DOS.

You can format an unformatted diskette or reformat a formatted diskette.

*CAUTION. Reformatting a diskette destroys any existing data on the diskette.*

Use the following steps to format a diskette with Removable Media Manager.

1. Insert the diskette you want to format in the diskette drive.
2. Choose Open Floppy from the CDE Front Panel Files menu or, in a Terminal window, type `volcheck` and press Return.

   The command checks the diskette drive and mounts a formatted diskette, if found. If volume management finds an unformatted diskette in the drive, the diskette is not mounted. Instead, it is made visible as a raw device to the Removable Media Manager, as indicated by the `(...unformatted)` message and a dash (-) instead of the normal number used to indicate which instance of the diskette is mounted.

3. From the CDE Front Panel Files menu, choose Removable Media Manager.

   The Removable Media Manager window opens and displays any mounted media on the system. In the example shown in Figure 109, an unformatted diskette is the only available media.

*Figure 109 Removable Media Manager Window*

4. Click on the diskette icon.

   The diskette is highlighted to show that you selected it.

5. From the Selected menu, choose Format.

   The Media Format window is displayed, as shown in Figure 110.

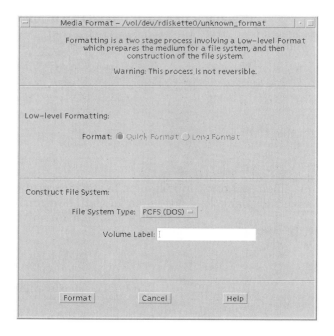

*Figure 110  Removable Media Manager Media Format Window*

6. Choose the file system type from the File System Type menu.

7. (Optional) Type a label in the Volume Label field if you want to assign a name to the device.

8. Click on the Format button.

   The diskette icon is removed from the Removable Media Manager window, and the Format button in the Format window is dimmed. No other status information is displayed while the diskette is formatting. When the diskette is formatted, a notice is displayed, as shown in Figure 111.

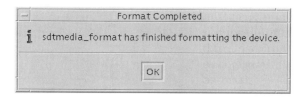

*Figure 111  Notice of Successful Formatting*

The icon in the Removable Media Manager window is updated to show the new format and volume name (if assigned), as shown in Figure 112.

*Figure 112  Removable Media Manager Window*

## Using the fdformat Command to Format Diskettes

You can use the fdformat command to format a UFS or MS-DOS file system on a diskette.

Use the following steps to format a diskette with the fdformat command.

1.  Insert a diskette into the diskette drive.
2.  Type **volcheck** and press Return.
    The system has access to the unformatted diskette.
3.  To format an MS-DOS file system, type **fdformat  -d** and press Return. If you want to create a UFS file system on the diskette at a later time, type **fdformat** and press Return.
4.  When prompted, type **y** and press Return to begin formatting the diskette.

Use the following commands to create a UFS file system on a formatted diskette.

1.  Become superuser.
2.  Type **newfs /vol/dev/rdiskette0/unnammed_floppy** and press Return.

## Using the rmformat Command to Format Diskettes              *New!*

Starting with the Solaris 8 06/00 release, you can use the rmformat command to format removable media, including the following types of diskettes.

- Double-density—720 Kbytes (3.5 inch).
- High-density—1.44 Mbytes (3.5 inch).

The `rmformat` command can format and protect rewritable removable media without requiring superuser privileges. It has the following formatting options.

- `quick`—Format removable media without certification or with limited certification of certain tracks on the media.
- `long`—Format removable media completely. For some devices, this might include the certification of the whole media by the drive itself.
- `force`—Format completely without confirmation. For media with password protection, clear the password before formatting. This feature is useful when you have forgotten or do not know the password. On media without password protection, this option forces a long format.

*NOTE. At the time of writing, the* `rmformat` *command has numerous reported bugs. This author was unable to get any of the following examples to work.*

Use the following steps to format a diskette from a command line.

1. Insert a diskette into the diskette drive.
2. Type **rmformat -F [quick | long | force]** *device-name* and press Return.
3. When prompted, type **y** and press Return to begin formatting the diskette.

Use the following commands to create a UFS file system on a formatted diskette.

1. Become superuser.
2. Type **newfs /vol/dev/rdiskette0/unnamed_floppy** and press Return.

## Diskette Command-Line Access

Use the following steps to access files on a formatted diskette.

1. Insert a formatted diskette in the diskette drive.
2. Type **volcheck** and press Return.

   If there is a formatted diskette in the drive, volume management mounts it on the `/floppy` mount point. If no diskette is in the drive, no error message is displayed. The `volcheck` command redisplays the prompt. Once the diskette is mounted on the `/floppy` mount point, you can access files on it either from the command line or from the File Manager Floppy window, which is described in "Diskette CDE File Manager Access" on page 676.

3.  Type **cd /floppy** and press Return.

4.  Type **ls** and press Return.

The name of the diskette is displayed as the name of a directory.

5.  Type **cd *diskette-name*** and press Return.

6.  Type **ls** and press Return.

The names of the files on the diskette are displayed. You can copy files to and from the diskette with the cp command.

In the following example, the diskette is not mounted, so the only directory in /floppy is ms-dos_5, which is the name of the last mounted diskette. After volcheck mounts the diskette, the directory with the name of the diskette is displayed. The diskette in this example contains only a lost+found directory.

```
oak% cd /floppy
oak% ls
ms-dos_5
oak% volcheck
oak% ls
ms-dos_5          unnamed_floppy
oak% cd unnamed_floppy
oak% ls
lost+found
oak% cp /home/winsor/Appx/appxA.doc .
oak% ls
appxA.doc lost+found
oak%
```

You cannot unmount a file system when that file system is in use by any process. If you get the message Device busy, a process may have its current working directory on the diskette, or some process has opened a file on the diskette. Use the fuser command to find out what processes are using the diskette. See the fuser(1M) manual page for information.

If you have more than one media device connected to the system, you may need to specify the device name to the eject command. If you are not sure which device name to use, you can display device names for all removable media devices with the eject -n command, as shown in the following example.

```
paperbark% eject -n
       fd -> floppy0
       fd0 -> floppy0
       fd1 -> floppy1
       diskette -> floppy0
       diskette0 -> floppy0
       diskette1 -> floppy1
       rdiskette -> floppy0
       rdiskette0 -> floppy0
       rdiskette1 -> floppy1
       cd -> cdrom0
       cd0 -> cdrom0
```

```
        cd1 -> cdrom1
        sr -> cdrom0
        sr0 -> cdrom0
        /dev/sr0 -> cdrom0
        /dev/rsr0 -> cdrom0
        cdrom0 -> /vol/dev/rdsk/c0t6d0/sol_8_doc
paperbark%
```

Use the following steps to eject the diskette.

1. Type **cd** and press Return.

   You have changed out of the /floppy directory.

2. Type **eject [*device-name*]** and press Return.

   After a few seconds, the diskette is ejected from the drive.

   On systems with diskette drives with an eject button, a message is displayed telling you that it's OK to manually eject the diskette from the drive.

## Diskette CDE Front Panel Access

If you are running CDE, you can use the Folders menu on the front panel to display the contents of a diskette. Follow these steps to open a diskette from the front panel.

1. Insert a formatted or unformatted diskette into the diskette drive.

2. From the front panel, open the Folders menu, shown in Figure 113, and click on Open Floppy.

*Figure 113  The Front Panel Folders Menu*

3.  After the light on the CDE front panel stops flashing (about five to ten seconds), the floppy is mounted to /floppy and a File Manager window opens. Figure 114 shows an example of the File Manager Floppy window for a formatted floppy.

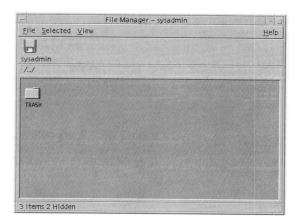

*Figure 114  The CDE File Manager Floppy Window*

## Diskette CDE File Manager Access

If you are running CDE File Manager, you can use it to format a diskette, display the contents, and copy files to and from the diskette. Follow these steps to open a diskette from the CDE File Manager.

1.  Insert a formatted or unformatted diskette into the diskette drive.

2.  From the File Manager File menu, shown in Figure 115, choose Open Floppy.

    After the light on the CDE front panel stops flashing (about five to ten seconds), the floppy is mounted to /floppy and a File Manager window opens.

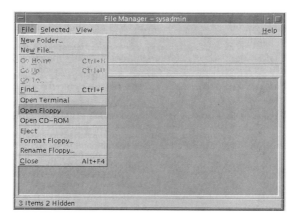

*Figure 115   The CDE File Manager Menu*

3.  From the File Manager File menu note that you can also format, rename, and eject the diskette by clicking on the respective options.

## Using the tar and cpio Commands with Diskettes

If a diskette contains a tar or cpio data stream (or archive) instead of a file system, volume management does not mount it. You cannot access raw data on the diskette from the old /dev/rdiskette device name because volume management provides access to the file system (if present) written on the diskette, not to raw diskette device itself.

You can access tar and cpio data streams that are written on a diskette by using the symbolic link to the character device for the media that is in floppy drive 0, as shown in the following example.

```
/vol/dev/aliases/floppy0
```

Use the following steps to copy a file into a `tar` archive that is written as a raw data stream on a diskette.

1. Insert a formatted diskette into the diskette drive.
2. Type **volcheck** and press Return.
3. Type **tar cvf /vol/dev/aliases/floppy0** *filename* and press Return.

   The file is copied to the diskette.
4. Type **eject [*device-name*]** and press Return.

   After a few seconds, the diskette is ejected.

   On systems with diskette drives with an eject button, a message is displayed telling you that it's OK to manually eject the diskette from the drive.

New!

Use the following steps to extract all files contained in a raw `tar` archive data stream from a diskette into the current directory.

1. Insert the diskette containing your `tar` archive into the diskette drive.
2. Change to the directory where you want to put the files.
3. Type **volcheck** and press Return.

   The diskette is now available for raw access because it has no file system written on it.
4. Type **tar xvf /vol/dev/aliases/floppy0** and press Return.

   The files are extracted from the tar archive data stream on the diskette.
5. Type **eject [*device-name*]** and press Return.

   After a few seconds, the diskette is ejected.

   On systems with diskette drives with an eject button, a message is displayed telling you that it's OK to manually eject the diskette from the drive.

New!

Alternatively, with Solaris 2.2 (and later) systems, you can access `tar` or `cpio` files with the following device name syntax.

```
/vol/dev/rfd0/media-name
```

The most common *media-name* is `unlabeled`.

Starting with the Solaris 2.3 release, the device name syntax is changed. You access `tar` or `cpio` files with the following device name syntax.

```
/vol/dev/rdiskette0/media-name
```

The most frequent `media-name` for media without a file system is `unlabeled`.

For example, to create a `tar` archive data stream on a diskette, type **tar cvf /vol/dev/rdiskette0/unlabeled *filename*** and press Return. To extract all the files contained in the `tar` archive data stream on a diskette and put these files in the current directory, type **tar xvf /vol/dev/rdiskette0/unlabeled** and press Return.

# New! Accessing Jaz or Zip Drives

You can connect Iomega USB Jaz or Zip drives to systems that have a USB port. If you connected a Jaz or Zip drive to a system with the Solaris 7 or Solaris 8 release and have upgraded the system to the Solaris 8 6/00 release, users can continue to access Jaz and Zip drives the same way as in previous releases.

If you are freshly installing the Solaris 8 6/00 release, you must use the following procedure to access a Jaz or Zip drive in the same way as previous releases.

1.  Become superuser.
2.  Edit the **/etc/vold.conf** file and comment out the `rmdisk drive` line, as shown below.

```
# use rmdisk drive /dev/rdsk/c*s2 dev_rmdisk.so rmdisk%d
```

3.  Type **init 6** and press Return.

    The system reboots.

*NOTE. If the system has the Solaris 8 10/00 or Solaris 8 01/01 release installed, Jaz or Zip drives do not work. At the time of writing, no workaround exists. These problems are fixed in the Solaris 8 04/01 release.*

See "Using the rmformat Command to Format Diskettes" on page 671 for instructions on how to use the `rmformat` command to format Jaz or Zip disks. You can also use Removable Media Manager to format Jaz or Zip disks. The procedure is similar to formatting diskettes. See "Using Removable Media Manager to Format Diskettes" on page 668 for more information.

To access information on a Jaz or Zip drive insert a disk into the drive. The file systems on the drive are mounted and a File Manager window opens showing the contents, as shown in Figure 116.

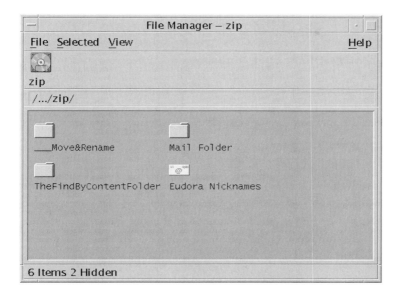

*Figure 116 File Manager Window with Mounted Zip Disk File Systems*

You can also access the file systems on a Zip or Jaz drive from the command line with the following steps.

1. Type **ls /rmdisk** and press Return.

   The contents of the /rmdisk drive are displayed.

2. Type **cd /rmdisk/zip** or **cd /rmdisk/jaz** and press Return.

   The file systems on the Zip or Jaz drive are displayed. The following example shows the contents of a Zip disk

```
mopoke% ls /rmdisk
zip    zip0
mopoke% cd /rmdisk/zip
mopoke% ls
___Move&Rename          Mail Folder
Eudora Nicknames        TheFindByContentFolder
mopoke%
```

You can also use the Removable Media Manager to format, protect, and view data on removable media devices. See "Removable Media Manager" on page 663 for more information.

## Creating An Alternate fdisk Partition

You can create an fdisk partition and a PCFS file system on removable media such as diskettes, Zip, or Jaz disks on a SPARC-based system to facilitate data transfers to IA-based systems.

Use the following steps to format removable media for a PCFS file system and create an alternate fdisk partition.

*NOTE. If you want to create a PCFS file system without an* fdisk *partition, skip step 4.*

1. Type **rmformat -F quick** *device-name* and press Return.
2. When prompted, type **y** and press Return.

   The disk is formatted.
3. Become superuser.
4. Type **fdisk** *device-name* and press Return.
5. Type **mkfs -F pcfs** *device-name* and press Return.
6. When prompted, type **y** and press Return.

   A new FAT file system is created in the specified partition.

The following example creates an alternate fdisk partition on /dev/rdsk/c0t4d0s2:c.

```
paperbark% rmformat -F quick /dev/rdsk/c0t4d0s2:c
Formatting will erase all the data on disk.
Do you want to continue? (y/n) y
paperbark% su
Password:
# fdisk /dev/rdsk/c0t4d0s2:c
# mkfs -F pcfs /dev/rdsk/c0t4d0s2:c
Construct a new FAT file system on /dev/rdsk/c0t4d0s2:c (y/n)? y
#
```

# *New!* Accessing DVD-ROM Drives

The Solaris 8 Operating Environment includes support for the Universal Disk Format (UDFS) file system, which is the industry-standard format for storing information on the optical media technology called DVD (Digital Versatile Disc or Digital Video Disc).

UDFS is provided as dynamically loadable 32-bit and 64-bit modules, with system administration commands that you can use to create, mount, and check the file system on both SPARC and IA platforms. The Solaris UDFS works with supported ATAPI and SCSI DVD drives, CD-ROM devices, and disk and diskette drives. In addition, the Solaris UDFS is fully compliant with the UDF 1.50 specification.

## Hardware and Software Requirements

The UDF file system requires the following components.

- The Solaris 7 11/99 or Solaris 8 Operating Environment.
- Supported SPARC or Intel platforms.
- Supported CD-ROM or DVD-ROM device.

## UDF Compatibility Issues

This first Solaris UDF file system implementation provides support for industry-standard read-write UDF version 1.50 and fully internationalized file system commands.

## Connecting a DVD-ROM Device

Use the following steps to connect a DVD-ROM device.

1. Become superuser.
2. Type **touch /reconfigure** and press Return.

   The /reconfigure file is created.
3. Type **telinit 0** and press Return to shut down the system and turn off power.
4. Connect the DVD-ROM device.
5. Turn on power to the system.

## Accessing Files on a DVD-ROM Device

Use the following steps to access files on a DVD-ROM device.

*NOTE. If a system has both a CD-ROM and a DVD-ROM device, the CD-ROM might be named* /cdrom/cdrom0 *and the DVD-ROM might be named* /cdrom/cdrom1. *If the system has only a DVD-ROM device, try using* /cdrom/cdrom0.

1. Type **ls /cdrom** and press Return.

   The contents of the /cdrom directory are displayed.
2. Type **ls /cdrom/cdrom1** (or **ls /cdrom/cdrom0** if the system has no CD-ROM device) and press Return.

The following example displays the contents of a DVD-ROM device.

```
$ ls /cdrom/cdrom1
Copyright  install.sh  product.gz
$
```

   Automatic display with the CDE File Manager was not implemented in the initial Solaris 8 release. You can use all other CDE File Manager functions, such as drag and drop for copying and imagetool features. Starting with the Solaris 8 6/00 release and continuing with the Solaris 8 10/00 release, CDE is updated to handle DVD-ROM devices.

## Troubleshooting

*New!*

From time to time, you may encounter problems with mounting diskettes (or, less frequently, a CD-ROM, DVD-ROM, or Iomega Zip or Jaz drive). If you encounter a problem, first check to find out if volume management knows about the device. The best way to check is to look in the mount point directory to see if something is there. If the files are not mounted, you may have forgotten to run the `volcheck` command, you may have a hardware problem, or the media may be corrupted. If references to `/vol` hang, the `/usr/sbin/vold` daemon has probably died, and you should restart it.

   If you find a name in the mount point directory and nothing is mounted, it is likely that the data on the media is not a recognized file system. It may contain a raw data stream such as a `tar` or `cpio` archive, or it may contain a Macintosh file system. For diskettes, you can access these media through the block or character devices found in `/vol/dev/rdiskette0` or `/vol/dev/diskette0` and use your own tools to interpret the data on them.

## Using Workman with Volume Management

Many people use the `workman` program to play music from their CD-ROM drive. Workman is not a Sun product, but it is in wide use. To use `workman` with volume management, add the line shown in bold to the `/etc/rmmount.conf` file. Be sure the line comes before the `action_filemgr` line.

```
# @(#)rmmount.conf 1.2     92/09/23 SMI
#
# Removable Media Mounter configuration file.
#

# File system identification
ident hsfs ident_hsfs.so cdrom
ident ufs ident_ufs.so cdrom floppy
ident pcfs ident_pcfs.so floppy

# Actions
action cdrom action_workman.so pathname
```

```
action cdrom action_filemgr.so
action floppy action_filemgr.so
```

The *pathname* is the name of the path where users access the `workman` program—for example, `/usr/apps/pkgs/exe/workman`.

When you have made this change, audio CD-ROMs are automatically detected and the `workman` program is started when the CD-ROM is inserted into the CD-ROM drive.

*NOTE. When you set up* `workman` *in the way described in this chapter, users should not try to start* `workman` *application manually because volume management may become confused. In addition, with Solaris 2.2 (and later) volume management, if you are using* `workman`, *you must eject the CD-ROM from the* `workman` *application. If you eject the CD-ROM from another window,* `workman` *hangs. This problem has been fixed in Solaris 2.3 and later releases.*

# Disabling Volume Management

You may want to disable volume management completely for some users. To do so, use the following steps.

1. Become superuser.
2. Rename the `/etc/rc2.d/S92volmgt` script as `/etc/rc2.d/XS92volmgt`.

   With the `X` prefix, the file is never started and you can always remove the `X` at a later time to restore volume management functionality.
3. Type **/etc/init.d/volmgt stop** and press Return.

You could also disable only part of volume management and leave other parts functional. You may, for example, want to automatically mount CD-ROMs but use the Solaris 2.0 method for accessing files on a diskette. You can do so by commenting out the lines for diskettes in the `/etc/vold.conf` file, as shown below.

```
# @(#)vold.conf 1.21     96/05/10 SMI
#
# Volume Daemon Configuration file
#

# Database to use (must be first)
db db_mem.so

# Labels supported
label dos label_dos.so floppy rmscsi pcmem
label cdrom label_cdrom.so cdrom
label sun label_sun.so floppy rmscsi pcmem

# Devices to use
```

```
use cdrom drive /dev/rdsk/c*s2 dev_cdrom.so cdrom%d
# use floppy drive /dev/rdiskette[0-9] dev_floppy.so floppy%d
use pcmem drive /dev/rdsk/c*s2 dev_pcmem.so pcmem%d forceload=true
# use rmscsi drive /dev/rdsk/c*s2 dev_rmscsi.so rmscsi%d

# Actions
insert dev/diskette[0-9]/* user=root /usr/sbin/rmmount
insert dev/dsk/* user=root /usr/sbin/rmmount
eject dev/diskette[0-9]/* user=root /usr/sbin/rmmount
eject dev/dsk/* user=root /usr/sbin/rmmount
notify rdsk/* group=tty user=root /usr/lib/vold/volmissing -p

# List of file system types unsafe to eject
unsafe ufs hsfs pcfs
```

# B

## CELESTE'S TUTORIAL ON SOLARIS 2.X MODEMS AND TERMINALS

This document—Revision 1.13 5/20/2000—is a tutorial written by Celeste Stokely that will teach you everything you need to know about connecting asynchronous modems and terminals to a Sun SPARC or IA workstation under Sun's Solaris 2.0–2.8 (Solaris 8). It does not cover the specifics of setting up PPP nor Sun's 4.x releases. An abridged version of this information has been published in some 1995 issues of *Unix Review*. Refer to the Copyright page of this book for copyright restrictions on the information in this appendix.

## Introduction

You must execute the commands as root, and you probably will have to reboot the machine. So, plan the system's downtime accordingly.

You may distribute this information to anyone who wants it, as long as you never attempt to copyright it in any way. If you find errors in it or have suggestions for changes in future revisions, please let Celeste know via e-mail (celeste@stokely.com). Go for it—you can do it!

Setting up modems and terminals under UNIX is often painful. If you had modem and terminal connection down to a science in SunOS 4.x, you're probably having trouble understanding it in Solaris 2.x. Solaris 2.x uses the SYSV-ish approach instead of the SunOS 4.x BSD approach. BSD uses getty and friends to spawn login, whereas SYSV uses port monitors and new friends.

If this is your first attempt at hooking up a modem or terminal to a UNIX machine, I'll give you a sound strategy to use and walk you through it. It's not really hard once you learn a few basics.

The Sun manuals and AnswerBook have had a few incorrect back quotes in vital places. Following their instructions probably won't give you error messages, but they may not work, either. However, AnswerBook does explain all the details of port monitors, if you want to understand them in detail.

Sun's `admintool` Serial Port Manager works for many simple modem and terminal setups. But when it doesn't work, you need to know how to run the various setup commands by hand.

> *WARNING. I have very strong feelings about modems and serial ports, their uses, their manufacturers, and their support. My clients ask me to make their modems work and keep working, so I tend to use only modems that are robust, highly configurable, fast, and well supported. They're not cheap, but neither is a System Administrator's time. I use cheap modems for doorstops and bookends.*

## Which Modem Should You Use?

Hundreds of Hayes-compatible, asynchronous modems are on the market today. Most of them can be made to work on a Sun system for dial-out. Many can work for dial-in. Several work gracefully for bidirectional (dial-in and dial-out) use. Fewer still bring a smile to a sysadmin's heart.

If you're trying to connect a non-Hayes-compatible modem to your Sun system, this article won't work for you.

This article covers the basic setup for many common serial port usages, such as the following.

- Dial-in-only access for human login accounts.
- Dial-out-only access for humans and programs using `tip`.
- Dial-in and dial-out setups for UUCP (e-mail, Usenet NetNews, file transfer).
- Bidirectional modem use—dialing in and out on the same port.
- Basic dumb terminal connection, ("dumb terminal" == vt100, Wyse-50, and other plain, character-based terminals).

This article specifically does not cover the following issues.

- Setting up PPP or SLIP. See the PPP and SLIP FAQs and how-tos at
  `http://www.stokely.com/unix.serial.port.resources/ppp.slip.html`—
  Using your modem to send faxes. See "FAX and Unix" at the following URL.
  `http://www.stokely.com/unix.serial.port.resources/fax.pager.html`
- Communicating with a pager. See "Pagers with Unix Connections" at the following URL.
  `http://www.stokely.com/unix.serial.port.resources/fax.pager.html`
- X Terminal setup.

In general, you get what you pay for. A $49 modem will cost you a fortune in the time it takes to get it running. A $499 modem can often be configured and running in under 20 minutes and gives you little grief in day-to-day use.

## Types of Modem Usage

Match your modem to your intended use for it. Don't buy a cheap 2400 bps modem to transfer all your company's mail and net news. If your Internet service provider offers UUCP connection only over Telebit WorldBlazers, you should strongly consider buying a Telebit WorldBlazer and dedicate it to that use. If they're not a Telebit site and plan on staying that way, there are faster, more widely compatible modems available for a *lot* less money.

My current favorite is the USRobotics Courier V.Everything. Next month, who knows what will be the darling? I have so many "former favorite" modems in my office that it's starting to look like a modem museum.

If you have to support a lot of dial-in users with a wide collection of random modems, then you need something that can happily work with all the possible user modems. That means you need one that runs at least 28800 bps. The 56K modem manufacturers have finally agreed on a single standard, so these modems will become great for your users, in time. Plan on spending $250–$600 for a solid, production-quality modem.

## Modem Programming

In deciding which modem to buy, a key consideration is how you program the modem. Some modems use DIP switches, some are programmed by connecting to the modem and setting software registers, some use both methods. You get more programming flexibility with software registers, and this is important when you'll be connecting to a lot of different modem types.

If a modem has only DIP switches available, it probably will be hard to make it do everything you need for lots of different connections. It's probably also an old, slow modem. I call these "cheap PC modems" and avoid them like Internet spam get-rich-quick schemes.

## Modem Speed

One of the most important features to look for is the modem's ability to run at split speeds. You really want to run the computer-to-modem connection at a fixed speed (the "DTE rate" or "serial rate") all the time, and let the modem negotiate the modem-to-modem speed ("DCE rate" or "line speed") independently.

Beware, because many inexpensive modems can't run at split speeds. If your modem doesn't do this, you and your users will have to press the Break key until the speeds sync up. This drives users (and you) crazy!

You should try to run the computer-to-modem (DTE) connection at 9600 bps, 19200 bps, or 38400 bps. A Sun system *cannot* run the CPU serial port at 14400 bps. But, that's OK because all the 14400 modems I've ever seen can run at 19200 bps DTE speed. You can also run at slower speeds, but why bother? Buy a faster modem than you think you need; you'll get more use out of it in the long run.

A few kernel hacks are available to run the Sun CPU serial ports at higher speed. Use them at your own risk. I do *not* recommend them—they're too unstable for most purposes. The Sun CPU serial ports and their drivers are bad enough without hacking on them yourself.

> *NOTE. Sun Ultra 2 and newer machines are reported to be able to run the CPU serial ports faster than 38400 bps with Solaris 2.6 and greater. Your line speed may vary.*

If you crave more speed than 38400 bps, you need to look into SBus serial port expander cards with DMA, or even network-connected terminal servers, and modems which are even *more* expensive. If you need a lot of high-speed serial connections, network terminal servers are probably the way you should go.

## Flow Control and Parity

When you run at higher speeds (9600 bps and above), you *must* worry about flow control. Ideally, you want hardware flow control where the Sun system and modem play the right games with the RTS/CTS lines to say "shut up" and "give me more."

Historically, the Sun CPU ports have not been able to use incoming hardware flow control, only outgoing. Sun has released some patches to enable incoming flow control. For Solaris 2.4, use Patch # 102845, available from `http://sunsolve.sun.com` to Sun Support contract customers. Sometimes, the patch just doesn't work. Sometimes it does. It's worth a try for 2.4. If it doesn't work and you must have hardware flow control, look into the higher-end SBus-based serial port expander cards. I don't know if this problem is fixed in later versions of Solaris.

If the patch doesn't work for you, you can consider using software (XON/XOFF) flow control. But, *never* use software flow control with UUCP/PPP or the protocol will go nuts from the unexpected XON and XOFF characters. If you can't use hardware flow control with UUCP/PPP, it's better to use no flow control at all and let UUCP/PPP do its own packet throttling.

If hardware flow control is a must-have (and it's becoming that way for most of us), then buy a DMA-type SBus serial port card with hardware flow control from a reputable vendor. I do not recommend the Sun SPC card for this use. I have some suggestions for vendors in "Vendor List" on page 717 and on our Unix Serial Port Resources WWW page at the following URL.
`http://www.stokely.com/unix.serial.port.resources/`

I run my own communications server without port-level flow control on my 13 UUCP connections at 38400 bps and all the mail and NetNews gets delivered just fine.

Try to always run your ports and modems at 8 bits, no parity. Parity on serial port transmissions is an outdated concept when you're using modern, error-correcting modem protocols. By default, most Sun CPU ports run at 7 bits, even parity (7E1). I'll explain how to run them at 8 bits, no parity (8N1). If you've got a legitimate use for odd, mark, or space parity, I want to hear from you!

## Celeste's Strategy for Configuring Modems and Terminals

This strategy gives you flexibility and maintainability in your serial port configurations. It works for nearly all configurations.

> *IMPORTANT RULE. Add and configure only one modem or terminal at a time. Get it working, then move on to the next one. Any other approach will result in madness. I've been there, done that. Trust me.*

There are actually very few steps.

- To configure the port for a terminal, set up the port monitor, then configure the terminal.
- To configure the port for a modem, get `tip` working, program the modem, make sure your logical port devices have the proper permissions, then enable a bidirectional port monitor.

- Then, if you only want to use the modem port for incoming connections, disable `tip` for everyone but root.
- Or, if you only want to use the modem port for outgoing connections, remove the port monitor and turn off auto-answer on the modem.

Purists may argue that this modem-port configuration has extra, unneeded steps or leaves the port monitor in bidirectional mode for incoming-only connections. I find that if a sysadmin sets up a port for only dial-in or dial-out, someday he or she will want the port to be bidirectional. Setting things up for this in the beginning means you'll have easier success in the future. And, it doesn't hurt anything.

## Ok, So What Do I Do?

To use a port for dial-out only:

- Configure `/etc/remote` for `tip`. (See "Tip and /etc/remote" on page 691.)
- Set up the word length and parity for the port. (See "Setting Serial Port Modes" on page 703.)
- Program the modem. (See "Basic Modem Programming" on page 694.)
- Remove any port monitor which may be on the serial port. (See "Enabling Solaris for a Dial-out-only Modem" on page 699.)

To use a port for dial-in only:

- Configure `/etc/remote` for `tip`. (See "Tip and /etc/remote" on page 691.)
- Set up the word length and parity for the port. (See "Setting Serial Port Modes" on page 703.)
- Program the modem. (See "Basic Modem Programming" on page 694.)
- Configure the port monitor to spawn a login correctly. (See "Enabling Solaris for a Bidirectional Modem" on page 697.)
- Make `/bin/tip` owner-executable only. Don't delete it, you'll need it someday. And remember to leave it setuid-uucp!

To use a port for bidirectional operations—both dial-in and dial-out use:

- Configure `/etc/remote` for `tip` (See "Tip and /etc/remote" on page 691.)
- Set up the word length and parity for the port. (See "Setting Serial Port Modes" on page 703.)
- Program the modem. (See "Basic Modem Programming" on page 694.)

- Configure the port monitor to spawn a login correctly (See "Enabling Solaris for a Bidirectional Modem" on page 697.)

To configure a dumb terminal on a port instead of a modem:

- Ignore `tip`. (That should be easy!)
- Set up the word length and parity for the port. (See "Setting Serial Port Modes" on page 703.)
- Configure the port monitor to spawn a login correctly. (See "Setting Up a Terminal on Solaris 2.x" on page 700.)
- Configure the terminal itself, setting up the baud rate, word length parity, and flow control.

If you want to use UUCP or PPP, you must configure it as well. This article tells you about setting up parity and flow control in UUCP, but doesn't cover all the other UUCP file changes. For UUCP, get the O'Reilly and Associates book, *Using and Managing UUCP*, by Ed Ravin, Tim O'Reilly, Dale Dougherty, and Grace Todino, if you can find it. It's out of print. For PPP FAQs and how-tos, see the following URL.

```
http://www.stokely.com/unix.serial.port.resources/ppp.slip.html
```

Simple, huh? Find the parts of this article that do the pieces you want, modify the scripts as needed, and go for it!

# Tip and /etc/remote

You may hate `tip` and love `kermit` or `pcomm`. I understand. But, do this next procedure via `tip` to keep it simple, OK?

Decide which serial port you want to use. (One with no cable already plugged in is often a good bet.) The port will be labeled A, B, A/B or could even be C or higher.

If you use one labeled A/B and have no Y-type splitter cable plugged into it, you'll have access only to port A. With the splitter, you'll get ports A and B on separate sockets of the splitter cable. The pinout of the splitter cable can be found at the following URL.

```
http://www.stokely.com/unix.serial.port.resources/A-B-Ycablepinout.html
```

The Sun serial port device driver splits each physical port into two logical devices, `/dev/term/a` or `/dev/term/b` for incoming transmission, and `/dev/cua/a` or `/dev/cua/b` for outgoing transmission.

The speed referred to in this section is the DTE or computer-to-modem speed. It is *not* the modem-to-modem speed. A 14400 bps modem may have a 19200 bps DTE speed.

Make sure you have your serial port permissions right. UUCP should own the outgoing side, and root should own the incoming side.

1. Execute these commands as root, substituting your port name (a, b, c, or d) where needed.

```
prompt# chown uucp /dev/cua/a; chgrp tty /dev/cua/a
prompt# chown root /dev/term/a; chgrp tty /dev/term/a
```

2. Edit the tip configuration file, /etc/remote, and find the entry beginning with hardwire:. This entry is the one you use to program the modem and is not usually used for dialing out directly, unless you enjoy AT commands. (If this is the second modem you're adding, clone the entire hardwire entry and label the new entry hardwire2.) Change it from an entry like the following

```
hardwire:\
    :dv=/dev/????/?:br#????:el=^C^S^Q^U^D:ie=%$:oe=^D:
```

to one set to your port (like /dev/cua/a) and baud rate (like 9600).

```
hardwire:\
    :dv=/dev/cua/a:br#9600:el=^C^S^Q^U^D:ie=%$:oe=^D:
```

3. Run tip.

*NOTE. Never run tip from a cmdtool. Use a shelltool, xterm, or some other window without scrollbars. The scrollbars can confuse tip's Return processing.*

*There are exceptions to this caveat, but if you never run tip in a scrollbar-type window, you won't have to remember all the ways it does and does not work.*

a. Now, use your edited hardwire entry from /etc/remote, type **tip hardwire** (or **tip hardwire2**), and press Return.
   You should see connected.

b. Type **ATE1V1** and press Return.
   (This will work for all Hayes-compatible modems, even cheapies.) You should see OK. Congratulations! You're talking with the modem!

c. Now, issue the appropriate AT commands to program the modem. (See "Basic Modem Programming" on page 694.)

    d.  Don't forget to write the new settings out to the modem's NonVolatile RAM.

If you don't see OK, you are not communicating with the modem. See if the modem is plugged in, verify the baud rate of the modem and the hardwire entry in /etc/remote, and verify the modem cable.

  4.  Exit tip by pressing Return ~.

(This means to type three separate keys, one at a time, of Return, tilde, period.)

This step also exits rlogin, so if you're running tip through an rlogin, make that Return ~~. (Return, tilde, tilde, period) or you'll exit only rlogin.

The cuaa entry (in the /etc/remote example below) allows you to type **tip cuaa** and talk directly to a modem on port A at 19200 bps, using 7 bits, even parity.

The cuab entry (in the example below) allows you to type **tip cuab** and talk directly to a modem on port A at 9600 bps, using 8 bits, no parity.

**tip *some_phone_number*** looks for the tip0 entry and uses that definition to dial ***some_phone_number***. (In the /etc/remote example below, it uses tip0, which points to UNIX-19200, which sets up a dial-up 19200 bps, 7 bits, even parity, Hayes-compatible modem. UNIX-19200 points to diala, which references /dev/cua/a. Convoluted, eh?)

**tip *mysystem*** (below) looks up the ***mysystem*** entry and dials the number 14155551234 via a 19200 bps, 7 bits, no parity connection on /dev/cua/a.

## /etc/remote Example

The following sample /etc/remote file is set up for:

- Port a, 19200 bps, Hayes-compatible modem, 7 bits, even parity. (It's 7E1 because there is no p8 entry.)

- Port b, 9600 bps, Hayes-compatible modem, 8 bits, no parity. (It's 8N1 because there is a p8 entry.)

See the remote(4) manual page for all the possible options.

```
cuaa:dv=/dev/cua/a:br#19200:
cuab:dv=/dev/cua/b:p8:br#9600
mysystem:pn=14155551234:tc=UNIX-19200:
hardwire:\
        :dv=/dev/cua/b:p8:br#9600:el=^C^S^Q^U^D:ie=%$:oe=^D:
tip0|tip19200:tc=UNIX-19200:
tip9600:tc=UNIX-9600:
UNIX-9600:\
        :el=^D^U^C^S^Q^O@:du:at=hayes:ie=#$%:oe=^D:br#9600:tc=dialb:
UNIX-19200:\
        :el=^D^U^C^S^Q^O@:du:at=hayes:ie=#$%:oe=^D:br#19200:tc=diala:
diala:\
```

```
        :dv=/dev/cua/a:
dialb:\
        :p8:dv=/dev/cua/b:
```

The attributes are listed in Table 131.

*Table 131   /etc/remote Attributes*

| Attribute | Description |
|---|---|
| dv | Device to use for the TTY. |
| du | Make a call flag (dial-up). |
| pn | Phone numbers (@ =>'s search phones file; possibly taken from PHONES environment variable). |
| at | ACU type. |
| ie | Input EOF marks (default is NULL). |
| oe | Output EOF string (default is NULL). |
| cu | Call unit (default is dv). |
| br | Baud rate (default is 300). |
| tc | Continue a capability. |

# Basic Modem Programming

Dust off your modem manual and have it handy. Use tip to connect to the modem and program the modem registers. Be sure to write out the modem's registers to NonVolatile RAM when you're done. Program the modem with the following settings.

- Hardware DTR, Normal DTR, or Reset When DTR Toggles.

  When the Sun system drops DTR, the modem should hang up the phone line and reset the modem to NonVolatile RAM settings.

- Hardware Carrier Detect or Normal Carrier Detect.

  The modem should raise Carrier Detect (known as CD or DCD) only when there is an active carrier signal on the phone connection. You'll set up the port monitor so that when CD goes active, the Sun system spawns a login.

  When carrier drops, either when the other end of the connection terminated or if the phone connection is broken, the Sun system will be notified and act appropriately. The CD signal is also used for coordinating dial-in and dial-out use on a single serial port.

- Respond with numeric result codes if this procedure is for `tip`'s use. (Usually this is `ATV0`.)

  If you're setting the modem for UUCP/PPP dial-out, then program the modem to use English result codes (like `CONNECT`). (Usually, this is `ATV1`.)

  If you're using the modem for both `tip` and UUCP, set it up with numeric result codes, and have UUCP's chat script set it to English result codes for the duration of the UUCP connection. See the Ed Ravin out-of-print book, *Using and Managing UUCP*, for the nitty-gritties.

- Send *basic* result codes *only*.

  `tip` only wants to see result codes 0 through 4. If it sees other result codes, it calls them an error. (Sometimes this is `ATX0` or `ATQ0`.)

- Do not echo commands. (Usually this is `ATE0`.)

- Modem is locked at a single-speed setting between the Sun system and the modem.

  The speed may vary as needed between local and remote modem, but should remain constant between the Sun system and the modem. (If your modem can't do this, use it for a paperweight and buy one that allows split speeds If your boss won't let you do this, OK, but you should whine loudly.)

- If this modem is used for dial-in, turn on Auto-Answer. (Sometimes, this is `ATS0=1`.) If the modem is not used for dial-in, turn off Auto-Answer. (Sometimes, this is `ATS0=0`.)

- Set the modem to your parity and word-length requirements. Use 8 bits, no parity if you can.

- Set the modem to your flow control scheme. Use hardware flow control (CTS/RTS) if you can, software flow control (XON/XOFF) if you must, or no flow control if you just have to.

## Useful Modem Register Settings

The USR Courier V.34 and Telebit WorldBlazer modem settings are our own work. The USR V.Everything settings are courtesy of Doug Hughes at Auburn University. These settings have worked well in bidirectional, interactive dial-in, UUCP, and PPP applications. Other modem settings can be found at the following URL.

`http://www.stokely.com/unix.serial.port.resources/modem.mfg.reg.isdn.html`

It will probably take a few tries to get all the right settings into your modem. No, you don't need to set *all* the S registers this way. These have been tweaked for the client's application. Your mileage will definitely vary, but the entries below on these modems, from the B0 (or B1) C1 through the S00=001 are very good ones to use, IMHO.

### USRobotics Courier V.32bis V.34 Fax Settings

```
B0  C1  E1  F1  M1  Q2  V0  X0
BAUD=38400   PARITY=N  WORDLEN=8
DIAL=TONE    ON HOOK    TIMER
&A0  &B1  &C1  &D2  &G0  &H1  &I0  &K1  &L0  &m4  &N0
&P0  &R1  &S0  &T5  &X0  &Y1  %N6
S00=001  S01=000  S02=255  S03=013  S04=010  S05=008  S06=002  S07=060
S08=002  S09=006  S10=007  S11=070  S12=255  S13=000  S14=000  S15=000
S16=000  S17=000  S18=000  S19=000  S20=000  S21=010  S22=017  S23=019
S24=150  S25=005  S26=001  S27=000  S28=008  S29=020  S30=000  S31=000
S32=009  S33=000  S34=000  S35=000  S36=000  S37=000  S38=000  S39=000
S40=000  S41=000  S42=126  S43=200  S44=015  S45=000  S46=000  S47=000
S48=000  S49=000  S50=000  S51=000  S52=000  S53=000  S54=064  S55=000
S56=000  S57=000
```

Dip Switches: (UP = dip switch up, DN = dip switch down).

Table 132 lists the dip switch settings for the USRobotics Courier V.32.

*Table 132   USRobotics Courier V.32 Dip Switch Settings*

| Switch | Position | Description |
|---|---|---|
| 1 | UP | DTR normal. |
| 2 | DN | Numeric messages (a starting point for tip usage). |
| 3 | DN | Display result codes. |
| 4 | UP | Modem does not echo commands. |
| 5 | UP | Modem answers on first ring, or DN for no auto-answer. |
| 6 | UP | CD indicates the modem is online and carrier signal is present. |
| 7 | DN | Suppress result codes in answer mode. |
| 8 | DN | Normal AT command set recognition. |
| 9 | DN | On Escape code (+++), modem stays online. |
| 10 | UP | Power-on loads registers from NFRAM. |

## USRobotics Courier V.Everything Settings

```
B0   C1  E1  F1  M1  Q0  V1  X7
BAUD=115200 PARITY=N  WORDLEN=8
DIAL=HUNT    ON HOOK    TIMER

&A3  &B1  &C1  &D2  &G0  &H1  &I0  &K3  &L0  &m4  &N0
&P0  &R2  &S0  &T5  &X0  &Y1  %N6  #CID=0
```

```
S00=003   S01=000   S02=043   S03=013   S04=010   S05=008   S06=002   S07=060
S08=002   S09=006   S10=007   S11=070   S12=050   S13=000   S14=001   S15=000
S16=000   S17=000   S18=000   S19=000   S20=000   S21=010   S22=017   S23=019
S24=150   S25=005   S26=001   S27=000   S28=008   S29=020   S30=000   S31=000
S32=005   S33=000   S34=000   S35=000   S36=000   S37=000   S38=000   S39=000
S40=000   S41=000   S42=126   S43=200   S44=015   S45=000   S46=000   S47=000
S48=000   S49=000   S50=000   S51=001   S52=000   S53=000   S54=064   S55=000
S56=000   S57=000   S58=000   S59=000   S60=000   S61=000   S62=000   S63=000
S64=000   S65=000   S66=000   S67=000   S68=000   S69=000   S70=000

3. Telebit WorldBlazer Settings

 B1  E1  L1  M0  Q2  T   V0  X0  Y0
&C1 &D3 &G0 &J0 &L0 &Q0 &R3 &S4 &T4 &X0
S000=1    S001=0    S002=43   S003=13   S004=10   S005=8    S006=2    S007=90
S008=2    S009=6    S010=14   S011=70   S012:255  S018=0    S025=5    S026=1
S038=0    S041:1    S045=0    S046=0    S047=4    S048=0    S050=0    S051:253
S056=17   S057=19   S058:2    S059:15   S060=0    S061:0    S062=15   S063=0
S064:1    S068=255  S069=0    S090=0    S092:1    S093=8    S094=1    S100=0
S104=0    S105=1    S111:30   S112=1    S151=4    S155=0    S180=2    S181=1
S183=25   S190=1    S191:6    S253=10   S254=1    S255=255
```

# Enabling Solaris for a Bidirectional Modem

The following list contains important notes.

- All single quotes in these directions are *back quotes*, not *forward quotes*, except where specifically noted.

- Be sure to execute these commands as root, from a *Bourne* shell (`sh`), not `ksh`, `tcsh`, or `csh`. (If you use a Bourne shell script, that's good.)

- If, after following these instructions, you get modem failures, or if the `add_modem` script gives an error message about `ttyadm: -V: invalid parameter`, then make sure that root's default shell is `/sbin/sh` and not `csh`.

- You want to have a maximum of one port monitor running on a given port. If you accidentally have two or more running on the port, your machine will probably panic.

- There is much disagreement over whether these EEPROM settings are required. They are not used, once a port monitor is running. Just use them and it won't hurt anything.

1. Log in as root, type **eeprom ttya-ignore-cd=true**, and press Return.

   The command means use HW carrier detect.

2. Type **eeprom ttya-rts-dtr-off=true** and press Return.

3. To reboot the system, type **init 6** and press Return.

   Is it critical to reboot now? No, but you'll need to reboot at some time.

4.  Make sure the modem is properly connected to your port and already programmed. Make sure the cable is OK. Your cable needs at least lines 1, 2, 3, 4, 5, 6, 7, 8, and 20, all straight through, with none crossed. A 25-pin cable, wired straight through is fine. A null modem cable will *not* work.

5.  Is the Solaris 2.x port monitor, `ttymon`, configured and running? Log in as root, type **`sacadm -l -t ttymon`**, and press Return.

    If you get a message like `Invalid request, ttymon does not exist`, the `ttymon` port monitor is not configured. Go to the next step.

    If you get a result like the following, go to step 7.

```
PMTAG    PMTYPE    FLGS RCNT STATUS     COMMAND
zsmon    ttymon     -    0   ENABLED    /usr/lib/saf/ttymon
```

6.  Configure an instance of `ttymon` called `zsmon`. Type
    **`sacadm -a -p zsmon -t ttymon -c /usr/lib/saf/ttymon -v`**
    **`` `ttyadm -V` ``** and press Return.

    Note: The string `zsmon` is known as a PMTAG.

7.  Is there a service running on the `zsmon` port monitor? Type
    **`pmadm -l`** and press Return.

    If you get a result like the following

```
PMTAG    PMTYPE    SVCTAG    FLGS ID     <PMSPECIFIC>
zsmon    ttymon    ttya      u    root   /dev/term/a I - ........
```

    then you need to remove the existing service. Issue the command and insert the PMTAG and SVCTAG found in the previous command by typing **`pmadm -r -p zsmon -s ttya`** and pressing Return.

    pmadm is the PMTAG, zsmon is the SVCTAG.

    If you don't see your port (like `/dev/term/a`) listed, then you're OK.

8.  Make a script that removes any existing port monitor and creates a new bidirectional port service.

    Putting this information in a script is a Very Good Idea because if you make a mistake, you can easily fix the problem and rerun the script. Don't try to do this without a script—there are too many typing errors waiting to be made in these commands.

Type the following script as a file (for instance, `/sbin/add_modem`), make it executable, then run it.

```
#!/sbin/sh
# add_modem shell script. Must be run as root from bourne shell
```

```
# Change these parameters as needed for your particular needs.
#
# PARAMETER                 MEANING
# ---------                 -------
# PORT                      Port you want to set up. "a" or "b"
# TTYSPEED                  Speed setting, from /etc/ttydefs
# LOGINMSG                  The login message which will be displayed.
# -p zsmon                  PMTAG, name of this port monitor
# -s ttya                   SVCTAG, modem is on ttya. You may want ttyb
# -d /dev/term/$PORT        Actual port device.
# -l contty5H               Ttylabel, defined in /etc/ttydefs file. (speed
#                           setting. contty5H=19200 baud)
# -b                        Flag for bidirectional port use
# -S n                      Turn software carrier off (modem supplies
#                           hardware carrier detect signal)
# "dial in/out on serial port" This is a comment you'll see on pmadm -l
####################################################################
LOGINMSG="Always be nice to your sysadm. login: "
# set PORT = either a or b
PORT="a"
#----------------------------------------
# Choose your speed setting. See /etc/ttydefs for more, or build your
# own from the examples in the rest of this article.
#       contty5H = 19200bps, 7 bits even parity, as supplied by Sun
#       conttyH =   9600bps, 7 bits even parity, as supplied by Sun
TTYSPEED="contty5H"
#----------------------------------------
# Change ownership of outgoing side of port to user uucp, group tty.
# Change ownership of incoming side of port to user root, group tty.
chown uucp /dev/cua/$PORT; chgrp tty /dev/cua/$PORT
chown root /dev/term/$PORT; chgrp tty /dev/term/$PORT
#----------------------------------------
# Remove any existing port monitor on this port.
# You can ignore any error messages from this next command.
# If you see the message "Invalid request, ttya does not exist under zsmon",
# You may be trying to remove a port monitor which does not exist.
/usr/sbin/pmadm -r -p zsmon -s tty$PORT
#----------------------------------------
# Create the new port monitor.
/usr/sbin/pmadm -a -p zsmon -s tty$PORT -i root \
-v `/usr/sbin/ttyadm -V` -fu -m "`/usr/sbin/ttyadm \
-p "$LOGINMSG" -d /dev/term/$PORT -s /usr/bin/login -l $TTYSPEED -b \
-S n -m ldterm,ttcompat`" -y "dial in/out on serial port"
########### end of add_modem script ###############################
```

Make the script executable by typing **chmod 700 /sbin/add_modem** and pressing Return. Then, run it by typing **/sbin/add_modem** and pressing Return.

For more information, see "Tip and /etc/remote" on page 691.

# Enabling Solaris for a Dial-out-only Modem

*IMPORTANT RULE. If no port monitor is running on the port, then the Sun system will not try to spawn a login. So, you have to remove any port monitor on the port. There is much disagreement over whether these EEPROM settings are required. They are not used once a port monitor is running. Just use them and it won't hurt anything.*

1.  Log in as root, type **eeprom ttya-ignore-cd=true**, and press Return.

This command means use HW carrier detect.

2. Type **eeprom ttya-rts-dtr-off=true** and press Return.

3. To reboot the system, type **init 6** and press Return.

   Is it critical to reboot now? No, but you'll need to reboot at some time.

4. Make sure the modem is properly connected and already programmed. Make sure the cable is OK. Your cable needs at least lines 1, 2, 3, 4, 5, 6, 7, 8, and 20, all straight through, with none crossed. A 25-pin cable, wired straight through is fine. A null modem cable does *not* work.

5. Is there a service running on the zsmon port monitor? Type **pmadm -l** and press Return.

   If you get a result like the following

```
PMTAG     PMTYPE    SVCTAG    FLGS ID     <PMSPECIFIC>
zsmon     ttymon    ttya      u    root   /dev/term/a I - /.....
```

   then you need to remove the existing service. Insert the PMTAG and SVCTAG tokens with the output of the command above. Type **pmadm -r -p zsmon -s ttya** and press Return.

   pmadm is the PMTAG, zsmon is SVCTAG.

   If you haven't already programmed the modem, go to "Tip and /etc/remote" on page 691.

   If you see nothing listed for the port you're dealing with, then the Sun system will not spawn a login on that port.

# Setting Up a Terminal on Solaris 2.x

The following list contains important notes.

- All single quotes in these directions are *back quotes*, not *forward quotes*, except where specifically noted.

- Be sure to execute these commands as root, from a *Bourne* shell (sh), not ksh, tcsh, or csh. (If you use a Bourne shell script, that's good.)

- If, after following these instructions, you get modem failures or if the add_terminal script gives an error message about ttyadm: -V: invalid parameter, then make sure that root's default shell is /sbin/sh and not csh.

- You want to have a maximum of one port monitor running on a given port. If you accidentally have two or more running on the port, your machine will probably panic.

Is the Solaris 2.x port monitor, `ttymon`, configured and running?

1. Log in as root, type **sacadm -l -t ttymon**, and press Return.

   If you get a message like `Invalid request, ttymon does not exist`, then the `ttymon` port monitor is not configured. Go to the next step.

   If you get a result like the following, skip to step 3.

   ```
   PMTAG    PMTYPE   FLGS RCNT STATUS    COMMAND
   zsmon    ttymon    -    0   ENABLED   /usr/lib/saf/ttymon
   ```

2. Configure an instance of `ttymon` called `zsmon`. Type **sacadm -a -p zsmon -t ttymon -c /usr/lib/saf/ttymon -v `ttyadm -V`** and press Return.

   Note: The string `zsmon` is known as a PMTAG.

3. Is there a service running on the `zsmon` port monitor? Type **pmadm -l** and press Return.

   If you got a result like the following

   ```
   PMTAG    PMTYPE   SVCTAG   FLGS ID      <PMSPECIFIC>
   zsmon    ttymon   ttya     u    root    /dev/term/a I - .........
   ```

   then you need to remove the existing service. Type **pmadm -r -p zsmon -s ttya** and press Return. `pmadm` is PMTAG, `zsmon` is SVCTAG.

   If you don't see your port (like `/dev/term/a`) listed, then you're OK.

4. Set up the terminal

   a. Set the terminal for the speed you want (The `add_terminal` script below assumes you are using 9600 baud.)

   b. The only lines you really need in the terminal-to-computer cable are 2, 3, and 7. Be sure to cross lines 2 and 3 in your cable. A null modem cable will work well for this.

   c. Set the terminal for XON/XOFF flow control

   d. Set the terminal for 7 bits, Even Parity (1 stop bit, if you have that setting). If you want a different parity or word length, see "Setting Serial Port Modes" on page 703.

5. Enable Solaris for the terminal.

   a. Edit and save the following script as `add_terminal`.

b.  To make the script executable, type **chmod 700 add_terminal**
and press Return.

c.  Edit `add_terminal` to meet your particular needs.

d.  Execute `add_terminal` as root.

e.  If the terminal doesn't give you a login when you press Return,
try rebooting the machine once.

```
Create the following shell script.
#!/sbin/sh
# add_terminal shell script. Must be run as root.
# This script invokes pmadm with the following parameters.
# Change these parameters as needed for your particular needs.
#
# PARAMETER                      MEANING
# ---------                      -------
# PORT                           Port you want to set up. "a" or "b"
# TTYSPEED                       Speed setting, from /etc/ttydefs
# LOGINMSG                       The login message which will be displayed.
# -s tty$PORT                    Terminal is on tty$PORT
# -d /dev/term/$PORT             Actual port device. you may want
# -l $TTYSPEED                   Speed/stty setting from /etc/ttydefs. Choose a
#                                $TTYSPEED entry that meets your needs
# -T vt100                       Your default terminal type for this port. This
#                                is a terminfo terminal type
# -i 'terminal disabled'         Message sent to the tty port if the port is
#                                ever disabled
# -S y                           Turn on software carrier
##############################################################################
LOGINMSG="Always be nice to your sysadm. login: "
PORT="a"
#-------------------------------------
# choose your speed setting. See /etc/ttydefs for more settings,
# or build your own from the examples in the rest of this article.
#       conttyH =   9600bps, 7 bits even parity, as supplied by Sun
TTYSPEED="conttyH"
#-------------------------------------
# Change ownership of outgoing side of port to user uucp, group tty.
# Change ownership of incoming side of port to user root, group tty.
# (Yes, I know you're not using the outgoing side of the port, but if you
# do this now, it will be ready when you someday put a modem on the port.)
chown uucp /dev/cua/$PORT; chgrp tty /dev/cua/$PORT
chown root /dev/term/$PORT; chgrp tty /dev/term/$PORT
#-------------------------------------
# Remove any existing port monitor on the port
# You can ignore any error messages from this next command.
# You may be trying to remove a port monitor which does not exist.
/usr/sbin/pmadm -r -p zsmon -s tty$PORT
#-------------------------------------
# Create the new port monitor.
#       QUOTE-ALERT: The single quotes delimiting the port-disabled message
#                    [terminal disabled] are FORWARD QUOTES
/usr/sbin/pmadm -a -p zsmon -s tty$PORT -i root -fu \
-v `/usr/sbin/ttyadm -V` -m "`/usr/sbin/ttyadm -l $TTYSPEED \
-p "$LOGINMSG" -d /dev/term/$PORT -T vt100 -i 'terminal disabled' \
 -s /usr/bin/login -S y`"
############ end of add_terminal script ###################################
```

f.  To make the script executable, type **chmod 700
/sbin/add_terminal** and press Return.

g.  To run the script, type **/sbin/add_terminal** and press Return.

# Setting Serial Port Modes

Sun doesn't supply all the serial ports modes you're likely to want as stock entries in /etc/ttydefs. (Sun seems to think that the whole world wants to run as 7 bits, even parity.) I'll show you how to set up the entries in /etc/ttydefs to match your own needs.

Serial port modes (the terminal I/O options found in stty(1)) are set in the file /etc/ttydefs. The name of the serial port mode (like contty5H) is used as the argument to the -l option in the ttyadm portion of the pmadm -a command. (This is the speed setting you use when you add a new port monitor.) See the stty manual page for all the available terminal I/O options.

The format of the entries in ttydefs is shown below and described in Table 133.

```
ttylabel:initial-flags:final-flags:autobaud:nextlabel
```

*Table 133   Entries in the /etc/ttydefs File*

| | |
|---|---|
| *ttylabel* | The string ttymon tries to match against the TTY port's *ttylabel* field in the port monitor administrative file. It often describes the speed at which the terminal is supposed to run, for example, 1200. |
| *initial-flags* | Contains the initial termio(7) settings to which the terminal is to be set. For example, the system administrator can specify the default erase and kill characters. *initial-flags* must be specified in the syntax recognized by the stty command. |
| *final-flags* | *final-flags* must be specified in the same format as *initial-flags*. ttymon sets these final settings after a connection request has been made and immediately before invoking a port's service. |
| *autobaud* | If the *autobaud* field contains the character A, autobaud is enabled. Otherwise, autobaud is disabled. ttymon determines what line speed to use to set the TTY port by analyzing the Returns entered. If autobaud has been disabled, the hunt sequence is used for baud rate determination. (This works intermittently for me, so use at your own risk.) |

*Table 133   Entries in the /etc/ttydefs File (Continued)*

| | |
|---|---|
| `nextlabel` | If the user indicates that the current terminal setting is not appropriate by sending a Break, `ttymon` searches for a `ttydefs` entry whose `ttylabel` field matches the `nextlabel` field. If a match is found, `ttymon` uses that field as its `ttylabel` field. A series of speeds is often linked together in this way into a closed set called a hunt sequence. For example, 4800 may be linked to 1200, which in turn is linked to 2400, which is finally linked to 4800. If you have been clever enough to buy a modem that can handle split baud rates, then you and your users will never have to press Break again to match up the baud rate between modems. |
| | These `stty` modes are processed from left to right within each set of *initial-flags* or *final-flags*. So, the order of the modes in each entry is significant. |

*IMPORTANT RULE. When setting the mode to 8 bits, do* not *enter it as* ... -parity ... sane, *but as* ... sane... -parity *because* sane *resets the port to 7 bits.*

## /etc/ttydefs Examples

These examples should make you comfortable with the basics. I've been advocating the use of 8 bits, no parity; the 38400 bps, 8 bits, no parity example (below) shows you how to set that up. (Each entry should be on one line. Some are split here just so this document will print correctly.)

1.  19200 bps, 7 bits, even parity example.
    `contty5H`, as supplied by Sun, is 19200 bps, 7 bits even parity
    **contty5H:19200 opost onlcr:19200 hupcl sane::contty6H**
    This is equivalent to

```
contty5H:19200 evenp opost onlcr:19200 sane evenp hupcl::contty6H
```

    or

```
contty5H:19200 parenb -parodd opost onlcr:19200 sane parenb -parodd hupcl::contty6H
```

2.  19200 bps, 7 bits, no parity example.

    To change `contty5H` to 7 bits, no parity (`-parenb`):

```
contty5H:19200 -parenb opost onlcr:19200 sane -parenb hupcl::contty6H
```

3.  19200 7 bits, odd parity example.

    To change `contty5H` to 7 bits, odd parity (`parenb parodd`, or `oddp`):

```
contty5H:19200 parenb parodd opost onlcr:19200 sane parenb parodd
 hupcl::contty6H
```

    or

```
contty5H:19200 oddp opost onlcr:19200 sane oddp hupcl::contty6H
```

4.  38400 bps, 8 bits, no parity example.

    To make a 38400 bps, 8 bits no parity, hardware flow control entry with no chance of selecting another DTE rate—my own personal favorite:

```
contty6H:38400 -parity opost onlcr:38400 sane -parity crtscts
 hupcl::contty6H
```

5.  Unmodified `/etc/ttydefs` from Solaris 8.

    Note the higher speeds Solaris 8 can use if you have an Ultra 10 or better. (Perhaps the Ultra 5 can do these speeds, I'm not sure.)

```
# VERSION=1
460800:460800 hupcl:460800 hupcl::307200
307200:307200 hupcl:307200 hupcl::230400
230400:230400 hupcl:230400 hupcl::153600
153600:153600 hupcl:153600 hupcl::115200
115200:115200 hupcl:115200 hupcl::76800
76800:76800 hupcl:76800 hupcl::57600
57600:57600 hupcl:57600 hupcl::38400
38400:38400 hupcl:38400 hupcl::19200
19200:19200 hupcl:19200 hupcl::9600
9600:9600 hupcl:9600 hupcl::4800
4800:4800 hupcl:4800 hupcl::2400
2400:2400 hupcl:2400 hupcl::1200
1200:1200 hupcl:1200 hupcl::300
300:300 hupcl:300 hupcl::460800
460800E:460800 hupcl evenp:460800 evenp::307200
307200E:307200 hupcl evenp:307200 evenp::230400
230400E:230400 hupcl evenp:230400 evenp::153600
153600E:153600 hupcl evenp:153600 evenp::115200
115200E:115200 hupcl evenp:115200 evenp::76800
76800E:76800 hupcl evenp:76800 evenp::57600
57600E:57600 hupcl evenp:57600 evenp::38400
38400E:38400 hupcl evenp:38400 evenp::19200
19200E:19200 hupcl evenp:19200 evenp::9600
9600E:9600 hupcl evenp:9600 evenp::4800
```

```
4800E:4800 hupcl evenp:4800 evenp::2400
2400E:2400 hupcl evenp:2400 evenp::1200
1200E:1200 hupcl evenp:1200 evenp::300
300E:300 hupcl evenp:300 evenp::19200
auto:hupcl:sane hupcl:A:9600
console:9600 hupcl opost onlcr:9600::console
console1:1200 hupcl opost onlcr:1200::console2
console2:300 hupcl opost onlcr:300::console3
console3:2400 hupcl opost onlcr:2400::console4
console4:4800 hupcl opost onlcr:4800::console5
console5:19200 hupcl opost onlcr:19200::console
contty:9600 hupcl opost onlcr:9600 sane::contty1
contty1:1200 hupcl opost onlcr:1200 sane::contty2
contty2:300 hupcl opost onlcr:300 sane::contty3
contty3:2400 hupcl opost onlcr:2400 sane::contty4
contty4:4800 hupcl opost onlcr:4800 sane::contty5
contty5:19200 hupcl opost onlcr:19200 sane::contty
4800H:4800:4800 sane hupcl::9600H
9600H:9600:9600 sane hupcl::19200H
19200H:19200:19200 sane hupcl::38400H
38400H:38400:38400 sane hupcl::2400H
2400H:2400:2400 sane hupcl::1200H
1200H:1200:1200 sane hupcl::300H
300H:300:300 sane hupcl::4800H
conttyH:9600 opost onlcr:9600 hupcl sane::contty1H
contty1H:1200 opost onlcr:1200 hupcl sane::contty2H
contty2H:300 opost onlcr:300 hupcl sane::contty3H
contty3H:2400 opost onlcr:2400 hupcl sane::contty4H
contty4H:4800 opost onlcr:4800 hupcl sane::contty5H
contty5H:19200 opost onlcr:19200 hupcl sane::conttyH
```

# Configuring Serial Ports for UUCP

The following sections describe how to configure serial ports for UUCP.

## Parity in UUCP

People often get confused about running UUCP in 7 bits vs. 8 bits vs. even vs. odd parity. Here's what's really going on and how to deal with it. Both the caller and receiver must agree on parity (even, odd, none) during the login sequence. Seven- or 8-bit word length often doesn't matter if you "do the right thing" with parity.

Once the `uucico`'s are running, UUCP's own protocol handles all these issues for you, but you need to be concerned with it during login.

You can set up four parity-related options during the login chat.

- `P_ZERO`—8 bits, no parity.
- `P_EVEN`—7 bits, even parity.
- `P_ODD`—7 bits, odd parity.
- `P_ONE`—7 bits, "1" or Mark parity.

It is usually safest to set up parity on a per-system-to-call basis in the `/etc/uucp/Systems` file, but it can also be set for all uses of the port in `/etc/uucp/Dialers` file.

### UUCP Parity-per-system Example

To set up a port within UUCP to run with 8 bits, no parity, on a per-system-connect basis:

In the file `/etc/uucp/Systems`, include `P_ZERO` in the chat script, as in

```
outhost Any ACU 9600 5551212 "" P_ZERO ogin: mylogin ssword: mypass
```

This means that when you first start trying to contact the machine `outhost`, uucp expects nothing (`""`) and sets `P_ZERO` (8 bits, no parity or 8N1).

### UUCP Parity-for-all-systems Example

To set up a port within UUCP to run with no parity, for all uses of this port:

(This example assumes you are using the `tbfast` entry in your `/etc/uucp/Devices` file.)

In `/etc/uucp/Dialers`,

```
tbfast  =W-,    "" P_ZERO "" \dA\pA\pA\pTE1V1X1......
```

## Flow Control with UUCP

With UUCP, either use hardware flow control or no flow control. Please remember that there is no incoming hardware flow control on Sun CPU serial ports, only outgoing hardware flow control. (There is no such limitation on non-CPU ports, which claim to have hardware flow control.)

Sun has released a patch for some releases of Solaris 2.x to enable hardware flow control on some systems' CPU serial ports. It may work on your system, but it may not.

The lack of incoming hardware flow control is not a problem with UUCP, usually because the UUCP protocol is robust enough to request retransmission of packets when the data isn't correct.

Using a good modem that has built-in UUCP protocol support (also known as *spoofing*) may also help your throughput. (This is a good use for a Telebit WorldBlazer.) If all else fails, slow down the connection between the Sun system and the modem to a speed you can support in your environment.

The string `STTY=crtscts` tells UUCP to use hardware flow control. It's usually better to set this up on a per-port basis rather than on a per-system basis, but UUCP will let you configure it however you want.

### UUCP HW Flow for All Systems

To set up a port with UUCP to use hardware flow control for all uses of this port (preferred way):

(This example assumes you are using the `tbfast` entry in your `/etc/uucp/Devices file`.)

```
tbfast  =W-,  "" \dA\pTE1.... \EATDT\T\r\c CONNECT STTY=crtscts
```

In `/etc/uucp/Dialers`, add `STTY=crtscts` after the `CONNECT`.

### UUCP HW Flow for Some Systems

To set up a port with UUCP to use hardware flow control, on a per-system-connect basis: (Do this if you feel you must, but there are very few good reasons for it).

In the file `/etc/uucp/Systems`, include `STTY=crtscts` in the chat script, as in

```
outhost Any ACU 9600 5551212 ogin: mylog ssword: mypass "" STTY=crtscts
```

# File format: /etc/saf/{pmtag}/_pmtab and /etc/saf/_sactab

Sometimes, it's easier to just edit the `_pmtab` file directly and restart the port monitor, rather than fussing with `pmadm`.

*WARNING. This is not for the faint of heart or those not feeling confident about their ability to recover from trashing their Solaris system.*

If you're comfortable with hacking the file yourself, you'll need to know the format of the `_pmtab` file. Many thanks to Andrew Miller (`amiller@snm.com`) for providing this dissection! I haven't exhaustively tested this, but I trust Mr. Miller's work. Refer to the `pmadm`(1M) manual page for more discussion of these fields.

```
/etc/saf/*/_pmtab:
  {svc_tag}:{flags}:{id}:reserved:reserved:reserved:
  {device_path}:{tty_flags}:{return_count}:{service_path}:{timeout_seconds}:
  {tty_def}:{streamio_modules}:{login_prompt}:{disabled_msg}:{term_type}:
  {softcar_yn}:# {comment}

/etc/saf/_smtab:
  {pm_tag}:{pm_type}:{flags}:{restart_count}:{monitor_path args} # comment
```

This is one of my own `/etc/saf/zsmon/_pmtab` lines. (This is really one line, but you'll get the idea.)

```
ttya:u:root:reserved:reserved:reserved:/dev/term/a:b::/usr/bin/login
  ::contty5H:ldterm,ttcompat:Please login and be nice. :::n:#dial in/out  on
  serial port a
```

And here are my own `/etc/saf/_sactab`. lines.

```
tcp:listen::999:/usr/lib/saf/listen tcp #
zsmon:ttymon::0:/usr/lib/saf/ttymon     #
```

# Customizing the Login Message (Solaris 2.0–2.3)

Solaris versions 2.0–2.3 and Solaris 2.4 differ in how they set up the pre-login message. These instructions are for Solaris 2.0–2.3. For Solaris 2.4, see "Customizing the Login Message (Solaris 2.4–higher)" on page 710.

You can change the message displayed when login executes by using the `-p` option of `ttyadm`. This option can be used to display a fixed string (`Login please`), to display the contents of a file (`` `cat /etc/myloginmsg` ``) or to run a text-producing program (`` `uname -n` login``).

In fact, Sun's default `/etc/inittab` produces the console login prompt with a combination of a fixed string and a program's output.

```
co:234:respawn:/usr/lib/saf/ttymon -g -h -p "`uname -n` console login: "
 -T sun -d /dev/console -l console -m ldterm,ttcompat
```

*WARNING. I haven't tested this completely. There is probably a maximum amount of text that can be displayed. Use caution. And, let me know if you find other good tricks to use with the login message.*

1.  Setting the login prompt to a fixed string (as seen in the `add_modem` script in "Enabling Solaris for a Bidirectional Modem" on page 697 and the `add_terminal` script in "Setting Up a Terminal on Solaris 2.x" on page 700.

```
#!/sbin/sh
LOGINMSG="Welcome to ACME Widget Corp. Please login. "
/usr/sbin/pmadm -r -p zsmon -s ttya
/usr/sbin/pmadm -a -p zsmon -s ttya -i root -v \
`/usr/sbin/ttyadm -V` -fu -m "`/usr/sbin/ttyadm \
-p "$LOGINMSG" -d /dev/term/a \
-s /usr/bin/login -l conttyH -b -S n -m ldterm,ttcompat`" -y "comment"
```

2. Setting the login prompt to the contents of a file (`/etc/myloginmsg`).

```
#!/sbin/sh
LOGINMSG="`cat /etc/myloginmsg`"
/usr/sbin/pmadm -r -p zsmon -s ttya
/usr/sbin/pmadm -a -p zsmon -s ttya -i root -v \
`/usr/sbin/ttyadm -V` -fu -m "`/usr/sbin/ttyadm \
-p "$LOGINMSG" -d /dev/term/a \
-s /usr/bin/login -l conttyH -b -S n -m ldterm,ttcompat`" -y "comment"
```

3. Setting the login prompt to the output of a program and a fixed string.

```
#!/sbin/sh
LOGINMSG="Please login to the `uname -n` machine: "
/usr/sbin/pmadm -r -p zsmon -s ttya
/usr/sbin/pmadm -a -p zsmon -s ttya -i root -v \
`/usr/sbin/ttyadm -V` -fu -m "`/usr/sbin/ttyadm \
-p "$LOGINMSG" -d /dev/term/a \
-s /usr/bin/login -l conttyH -b -S n -m ldterm,ttcompat`" -y "comment"
```

# Customizing the Login Message (Solaris 2.4–higher)

Solaris versions 2.0–2.3 and Solaris 2.4–higher differ in how they set up the pre-login message. These instructions are for Solaris 2.4–higher. For Solaris 2.0–2.3, see "Customizing the Login Message (Solaris 2.0–2.3)" on page 709.

The contents of the file `/etc/issue` are displayed before the login prompt of all incoming serial port dial-in and `telnet` connection by the program `login`. `/etc/issue` is a plain, ASCII file and can be edited with any text editor.

Example: If `/etc/issue` contains the following information

```
This is the contents
of the /etc/issue
file on sunhost.
```

then a user initiating a `telnet` session to sunhost (**telnet sunhost**) would see the following output.

```
Trying 192.9.200.2 ...
Connected to sunhost.
Escape character is '^]'.

UNIX(r) System V Release 4.0 (sunhost)

This is the contents
of the /etc/issue
file on sunhost.

login:
```

# Solaris IA Issues

The following sections discuss Solaris IA issues.

## Solaris IA 2.0–2.5 and COM2

By default, versions of Solaris IA prior to 2.6 enable only COM1. If you are adding an internal modem to an existing system with two COM ports, be sure to set the modem to a valid COM setting and nonconflicting interrupt, or disable COM2 in the system and configure the modem to standard COM2 settings (io=2f8 irq=3). See Sun's *X86 Device Configuration Guide* for further details.

1. Boot Solaris 2.x IA and log in as root.
2. Edit the asy.conf file.

   (for Solaris 2.4 IA) # vi /kernel/drv/asy.conf
   (for Solaris 2.5 IA) # vi /platform/i86pc/kernel/drv/asy.conf

3. Uncomment second entry for COM2.

   (The following is for Solaris 2.4 IA.)

```
#
# Copyright (c) 1992 Sun Microsystems, Inc.  All Rights Reserved.
#

#ident "@(#)asy.conf    1.6    94/05/17 SMI"

name="asy" class="sysbus" interrupts=12,4 reg=0x3f8,0,0 ioaddr=0x3f8;
#
# Note: To enable COM2 uncomment the following entry, and it may require
#       reconfiguration of SMC device if you are using SMC Enet with
#       default configuration (which also uses IRQ 3).  (See smc.conf file.)
#
#name="asy" class="sysbus" interrupts=12,3 reg=0x2f8,0,0 ioaddr=0x2f8;
```

4. Remove the comment sign (#) before the second name="asy" . . . line.
5. Save and exit the file.

6.  To enable reconfiguration reboot, type **touch  /reconfigure** and press Return.
7.  To reboot the system, type **sync;reboot** and press Return.

## Solaris IA 2.6 and COM2

A serial or modem device is not automatically recognized by Solaris. Normally, Solaris 2.6 will find the COM1 and COM2 ports for a system and enable them by default. If you have a COM3 or COM4, some or all of the ports may not be recognized by Solaris. This can even happen with some serial devices at the standard COM1 and COM2 settings with all other serial devices in the system disabled.

The ultimate cause of this recognition failure may be fixed in a future Driver Update, so only try this if the latest Driver Update from http://access1.sun.com or the SunSoft CompuServe forum has been applied and you are still experiencing the problem.

Do not share IRQs from an ISA device, like a serial port, with any other device. If you are adding a COM3 or COM4 device, as is typical for a plug-in modem card, use an IRQ (5 is often available) that is not being used by another card in your system.

If it is not possible to set the IRQ to a nonstandard COM port IRQ, you may have to disable one of the built-in COM ports for your system. At boot time, Solaris probes COM1 for a mouse and COM2—if enabled in /platform/i86pc/kerne/drv/asy.conf—for a modem. This probe can cause problems with a lot of modems. It certainly causes problems with any UPS installed on COM2. If using an internal modem on COM2, disable the onboard COM port in the BIOS to avoid IRQ conflicts.

For Solaris IA 2.5.1 and earlier, these problems were handled by edits to the asy.conf file. While Solaris 2.6 does not come with such a file, it does honor it just as the previous versions did. Note that our example below has COM2 disabled by default. You should only enable devices that actually exist on your system.                    •

If you use this technique, save your existing asy.conf as asy.conf.orig in the /platform/i86pc/kernel/drv directory.

1.  Boot Solaris 2.6 IA and log in as root.
2.  Locate the asy.conf file.
    /platform/i86pc/kernel/drv/asy.conf
3.  Replace it with the following asy.conf file.

```
#
# Copyright (c) 1992 Sun Microsystems, Inc.  All Rights Reserved.
#
#ident "@(#)asy.conf   1.7     96/12/18 SMI"

name="asy" class="sysbus" interrupts=12,4 reg=0x3f8,0,0 ioaddr=0x3f8;
ignore-hardware-nodes=1;
#
# Note: To enable COM2 uncomment the following entry; you may need to
#       reconfigure the SMC device if you are using SMC Enet with
#       default configuration (which also uses IRQ 3). (See smc.conf file.)
#
#name="asy" class="sysbus" interrupts=12,3 reg=0x2f8,0,0 ioaddr=0x2f8;

# COM3:
#   To enable COM3, the following entry must be uncommented and
#   possibly edited.
#   You must ensure that the "interrupts," "reg," and "ioaddr" values
#   correspond to your hardware.  See the section on configuring additional
#   serial ports in your IA device configuration manual or AnswerBook for
#   further details.
#
# This entry uses its own unique interrupt (IRQ5)
#name="asy" class="sysbus" interrupts=12,5 reg=0x3e8,0,0 ioaddr=0x3e8;

# COM4:
#   In order to enable COM3, the following entry must be uncommented and
#   possibly edited.
#
#   You must ensure that the "interrupts," "reg," and "ioaddr" values
#   correspond to your hardware.  See the section on configuring additional
#   serial ports in your IA device configuration manual or AnswerBook for
#   further details.
#
# This entry uses its own unique interrupt (IRQ9)
#name="asy" class="sysbus" interrupts=12,9 reg=0x2e8,0,0 ioaddr=0x2e8;
```

4. Use `vi` to edit the `asy.conf` file and uncomment the second entry for COM2, shown below.

```
name="asy" class="sysbus" interrupts=12,3 reg=0x2f8,0,0 ioaddr=0x2f8;
```

5. Save and exit the file.

6. To enable reconfiguration on reboot, type **touch /reconfigure** and press Return.

7. To halt and reboot the system, type **sync;reboot** and press Return.

Further information is available from Sun's `http://access1.sun.com` site, in `http://access1.sun.com/cgi-bin/rinfo2html?226002.faq`, "How to Add a Serial Port at a Non-standard IRQ," and `http://access1.sun.com/cgi-bin/rinfo2html?223402.faq`, "Adding New Plug-N-Play Devices to Solaris 2.6."

## Solaris 7 IA (2.7) and COM2

*NOTE. This section, added in February 1999, would not have been possible without the help of many of our readers. Contributors include*

*Cagri Yucel (*`cyucel@is.ku.edu.tr`*) and Jim McCusker* (`puppy@biosys.net`*). Thanks, folks!*

Choose either the automatic or more manual methods below, depending on how much you like fussing with files versus point-and-click.

## Automatic Method, Using Device Configuration Assistant

1. Boot your machine, and press the ESC (escape) key to enter the Device Configuration Assistant during the boot.
2. Choose Add Device or View/Edit Devices and add a Serial Port with the IO = 2F8 and IRQ = 3.
3. Continue with the reboot, Solaris automatically performs a reconfigure boot. The new port should magically appear.

## More Manual Method, Using Device Configuration Assistant

1. Make sure the com port the internal modem corresponds to is *disabled* in the BIOS.
2. Boot the system, log in as root, and add these lines to `/platform/i86pc/kernel/drv/asy.conf`.

```
name="asy" class="sysbus" interrupts=12,4 reg=0x3f8,0,0 ioaddr=0x3f8;
ignore-hardware-nodes=1;
name="asy" class="sysbus" interrupts=12,3 reg=0x2f8,0,0 ioaddr=0x2f8;
```

3. In a window, type **reboot** and press Return.
4. While the system is booting, press ESC to enter the Device Configuration Assistant.
5. Press F2 to scan the system bus. Press F4 to select Device Tasks.
6. Select View/Edit Devices, then press F2 again to see a list of system devices and cards. Look for something that slightly resembles an internal modem, like this for a modem on `cua/b - com 2`.

```
PnP ISA ETT0001 port 2F8-2FF IRQ3
```

7. Confirm that the I/O address matches a COM port (either `2f8` for COM1 or `3f8` for COM2) and that the interrupt request is OK (3 for COM2 or 4 for COM1).
8. Press F2 to continue, press F3 for back, press F2 to continue again.

9. On the next screen, select the default boot device (marked with an asterisk *), then press F2 to boot the kernel.

10. When the machine is booted, log in as root, go to Application Manager, then to Admintool.

11. In Admintool select Browse, then select Serial Ports. Then, at last you can set up your internal modem as you so desire.

## PC Serial Ports and Internal Modems

*NOTE. This section was contributed in October 1998 by Jay Ts of Metran Technology. Jay Ts is a Linux and UNIX consultant with many years of experience in system administration and programming. He can be reached at* jayts@bigfoot.com, http://jayts.cx, *1-888-282-0549.*

The design of the PC architecture includes up to four "standard" serial ports with interrupts (IRQs) 3 and 4 and different I/O Ports, as shown in Table 134.

*Table 134   PC Serial Ports*

| COM# | IRQ | I/O Port | Comment |
|------|-----|----------|---------|
| COM1 | 4 | 0x3f8 | Look at those numbers carefully. They're not exactly intuitive. ;-) |
| COM2 | 3 | 0x2f8 | |
| COM3 | 4 | 0x3e8 | |
| COM4 | 3 | 0x2e8 | |

Usually, modern PC motherboards have two serial ports included on the motherboard, with a default configuration of COM1 and COM2. This configuration, along with many other hardware parameters, and the date and time are stored in a small area of battery-backed RAM (separate from main memory), sometimes referred to as CMOS, because early implementations (at least) were done with CMOS static RAM. Another term used for the hardware parameters is BIOS settings, because they are set using the system's built-in (ROM) firmware, the BIOS setup program. (BIOS stands for Basic Input/Output System; it was originally used by MS-DOS to perform low-level hardware access, and controls the initial boot procedures when the system is powered on or reset.)

There are a large number of PC motherboard manufacturers, and more than one company that develops BIOS ROMs (notably, AMI, Award and Phoenix), all with a plethora of revisions, so the details of how the setup program works varies considerably from one motherboard model to another.

However, there are some common functions. When you boot the computer, there usually is a message reporting how to enter the BIOS setup program. Once you have done that, you will need to use the setup program's menu selections to find the screen where you have options regarding how to configure the serial ports. Sometimes, you may only be able to enable or disable them, and in other cases, you may be able to configure each to be COM1, COM2, COM3, COM4, or disabled.

Now, about those internal modems. Typically, they are implemented to look like one of the standard serial ports, probably COM2 by default (because COM1 is almost always used for the mouse).

There are some exceptions to this implementation, notably the USR WinModem, which is a cost-reduced design that moves much of the modem's functions out of hardware and into software that is provided with the product; WinModem runs only under Windows. My advice is that if your system has a WinModem, that you remove it from the system, return it for a refund if possible, and if not, chuck it into the trash, and get yourself a real modem. So far, I do not know of one single case of a WinModem working with any version of UNIX. Likewise, if you have a modem that is not implemented to act like a serial port, your best option is probably to replace it with one that has a more standard implementation.

If your internal modem is configured as COM2, you'd better make sure that neither of the "normal" serial ports on the motherboard is also configured as COM2. That would be an obvious hardware conflict, which shouldn't be expected to work. Often (always?) this conflict will be detected by the BIOS during system boot-up, and you will be asked to enter the setup program to correct it. In any case, either reconfigure the conflicting motherboard serial port or just disable it.

Another conflict may happen if one of the motherboard's serial ports shares an IRQ with the modem. Note in the above listing that COM1 shares IRQ4 with COM3, and COM2 shares IRQ3 with COM4. This is a notorious source of difficulty. Theoretically, it is possible to have devices sharing an interrupt, as long as they use different I/O ports, but in practice, the implementations of specific motherboards and operating systems may prevent them from actually working together. The result of an incompatibility can be as minor as a flaky serial port or as major as a system crash or lockup.

You might think that it would be safe to configure the "extra" serial port on the motherboard as COM3 or COM4 and not plug anything (terminal, external modem, whatever) into it. Or only use it when the internal modem is not in use. But this configuration can still be a problem.

If you want to be safe, make sure that COM1 is enabled for the mouse, COM2 is reserved for the modem, and that no serial port in the system is configured as COM3 or COM4. Check your modem card to see if there are jumpers to allow you to configure the COM port that it uses. And of course, make sure that no other hardware in the system is using the same IRQ as the modem.

If none of this works, I can make the following suggestions.

1. Try different BIOS settings, even if they are not what I recommend. (And be prepared to reboot your system without using the mouse, if necessary.)
2. Try a different modem.
3. Contact the motherboard vendor to see if they have an update for the BIOS ROM chip(s).
4. Try a different motherboard.
5. Find a patch that updates the operating system's serial port driver.
6. Give up. :)

## Serial Device Naming in Solaris IA

The kind folks at Progressive Systems (`http://www.progressive-systems.com`) have alerted us that the serial device naming scheme is different in SPARC Solaris and IA Solaris, at least for Solaris 2.6–2.7. For Solaris 8 (2.8) the IA names match the SPARC names. So, make changes to the `add_modem` and `add_terminal` scripts in this appendix as necessary, as shown in Table 135.

*Table 135   Solaris Serial Device Naming*

| SPARC Name (all releases) | IA Name (Solaris 2.6–2.7) | IA Name (Solaris 8) |
| --- | --- | --- |
| `/dev/term/n` | `/dev/ttynn` | `/dev/term/n` |
| `/dev/ttyn` | `/dev/ttydn` | `/dev/ttyn` |
| `/dev/cua/n` | `/dev/cuan` | `/dev/cua/n` |

# Vendor List

This list of vendors is vastly incomplete. These are just some of the companies whose products and/or services my readers, clients, and I have been usually satisfied with.

A longer list of vendors and other UNIX Serial Port information can be found on our WWW page at the following URL.

`http://www.stokely.com/unix.serial.port.resources`

If you have had a happy experience with other vendors of serial-port-based products for Sun systems, send me the info and I'll include them in this list.

Companies, their products, and their support staffs change regularly, so your "satisfaction mileage" may vary. (I don't receive any money or special favors from any of these folks, nor would I consider it. I'm just a picky consumer, like you.)

## Serial Cards

- `http://www.stokely.com/unix.serial.port.resources/serial.card.code.html`
- MAGMA, 6725 Mesa Ridge Rd., #100, San Diego, CA 92121
  Voice: 800-285-8990 or 619-457-0750, Fax: 619-457-0798,
  `http://www.magma.com`

## Modems

- US Robotics/3Com, `http://www.3com.com`.
- Telebit Corporation/ITK, bought by Digi International
  `http://www.digi.com`

## PPP

- `http://www.stokely.com/unix.serial.port.resources/ppp.slip.html`

### Public Domain Versions

- dp-3.x available from `http://www.acn.purdue.edu/dp/dp.html`
- ppp-2.* available from `ftp://cs.anu.edu.au/pub/software/ppp` and
  `http://www.phase-one.com.au/solaris-x86/pppd/`

### Commercial Version

- Progressive Systems, 2000 W. Henderson Rd., Suite 400, Columbus, OH 43220, Voice: 1-800-558-7827, Fax: 614-326-4601,
  `ftp.Progressive-Systems.Com`, `http://www.Progressive-Systems.Com`

*NOTE. Progressive Systems was bought by Cobalt, which was bought by Sun Microsystems, Inc. Sun is no longer marketing Progressive's PPP product. You can, however, obtain a Progressive license from Sun. The Progressive URL still works but may not be available in the future.*

## Kermit/C-Kermit

Available from `http://www.columbia.edu/kermit/`

Zmodem (rzsz) Version 3.xx. Available from
`http://agora.rdrop.com/users/caf/rzsz3.html`

## Terminal Servers

- `http://www.stokely.com/unix.serial.port.resources/serial.card.code.html`
- Xylogics/Bay Networks Annex and micro Annex (WWW at `http://www.xylogics.com`).
- Xyplex (WWW at `http://www.xyplex.com`).
- Livingston/Lucent Portmasters (WWW at `http://www.livingston.com`).

## Publishers

- O'Reilly and Associates (*Using and Managing UUCP* is a great book, though now out of print.) `http://www.ora.com`
- This document on ftp servers: (Thanks to the ftp-server managers!)
  - `ftp://ftp.stokely.com/pub/` (always has the latest version)
  - `ftp://ftp.adee.net/pub/doc/tutorials`
  - `ftp://ugle.unit.no/info/unix`
  - `ftp://beatles.cselt.it/pub/info/`
  - `ftp://ftp.csv.warwick.ac.uk/pub/solaris2`
  - `ftp://ftp.cs.utwente.nl/pub/doc/SysAdmin`

Celeste Stokely is an outspoken and pro-user Web Architecture and Project Management consultant who has been trying to make the world safer for UNIX system administrators since 1983.

She lives in southwestern New Mexico, USA, near the Gila Wilderness Area, and runs Stokely Consulting with her husband, Peter, two bouncy cats named L.B. and Sparcy, and an ever-increasing number of cheerful tropical fish. Celeste can be reached via e-mail at `celeste@stokely.com`.

# GLOSSARY

### access rights

The four types of operations—read, modify, create, and destroy—that control access to NIS+ objects for each of the authorization rights categories.

### Admintool

A graphical user interface tool that you can use to manage local systems.

### AutoClient system

A system that caches all of its needed system software from a server.

### alias

An alternative name or names assigned to a program or to an electronic mail address.

### application server

A server set up and administered exclusively to provide application services to users over the network.

### asymmetric encryption

*New!*

See public key encryption.

*New!* *authentication*

> The process of identifying the principal who made a request to a server by checking the principal's credentials. For NIS+, these credentials are based on encrypted verification information stored in the NIS+ `cred` table.

*authorization rights*

> The four categories—nobody, owner, group, and world—that control access to NIS+ tables.

*Auto_home database*

> The database that you use to add home directories to the automounter. In SunOS 4.x releases, this database was a file or NIS+ table named `auto.home`.

*automounter*

> Solaris software that automatically mounts a directory when a user changes into it. The automounter automatically unmounts the directory when it is no longer in use.

*automount maps*

> The local files or nameservice tables that the automounter consults to determine which directories to mount, which system to mount them from, and where to mount them on the user's local system.

*back file system*

> The file system on the server from which a cache file system is mounted on a client.

*bang*

> An exclamation point (!) that acts as a single-character UNIX command or as a separator between the routes of a route-based electronic mail address such as the ones used in UUCP.

*base directory*

> The directory into which the package commands and Admintool: Packages GUI install software packages. The default base directory is `/opt`.

*baud rate*

> The transmission speed of a serial communications channel, expressed in bits per second.

*Bourne shell*

One of the Solaris command interpreters. The Bourne shell is the default user shell, and it is the shell language in which most system administration shell scripts are written. See also C shell, Korn shell.

*breakout box*

A diagnostic device that plugs into an RS-232-C cable; it is used to test whether a signal is present on each cable pin.

*cache*

A small, fast memory area that holds the most frequently referenced portions of a larger and/or slower memory. A cache is used to increase program or system performance. Examples include a disk cache where frequently referenced disk blocks are stored in RAM and a browser cache where frequently referenced Web pages and graphics objects are stored locally on a user's computer.

*CDE*

Common Desktop Environment. A windowing system based on the Motif graphical user interface.

*CD-ROM*

An acronym for compact disc, read-only memory. CD-ROM is a read-only storage medium for digital data.

*character terminal*

A serial port device that displays only letters, numbers, and other characters, such as those produced by a typewriter.

*child process*

A process that is created by another process. The process that creates the environment for the child is called the parent.

*client*

A system or program that receives system resources from a remote system—called a server—over the network.

*compiler*

A program that translates human-readable source code into a machine-readable form in preparation for creating directly executable programs. For example, a C compiler translates a human-readable C program into a machine-readable executable program.

### concatenation

The combining of two or more files to create one larger file. Also, with Online: DiskSuite, the combining of separate component disks into a sequential system of disk blocks.

### C shell

One of the Solaris command interpreters. See also Bourne shell, Korn shell.

### daemon

A special type of program that, once activated, carries out a specific task without any need for user intervention. Daemons typically are used to handle jobs that have been queued, such as printing, mail, and communication. Daemons are usually started when the system is booted. Because they typically are not started by a user, daemons communicate by means other than terminal I/O, such as log files, signals, and configuration files.

### direct map

An automount map that specifies absolute paths as the mount point.

### *New!* directory objects

The framework of the NIS+ namespace that contains the `org_dir` and `groups_dir` administrative directories that contain the NIS+ tables.

### diskette

A portable, nonvolatile storage medium used to store and access data magnetically. The Solaris Operating Environment supports 3.5-inch, double-sided, high-density (DS, HD) diskettes in raw and MS-DOS (PCFS) formats.

### domain

A directory structure for electronic mail addressing, network address naming, and NIS+ hierarchy naming. Within the United States, top-level Internet domains include `com` for commercial organizations, `edu` for educational organizations, `gov` for governments, `mil` for the military, `net` for networking organizations, and `org` for nonprofit organizations. `us` is used as the top-level domain for a U.S. geographical hierarchy; two-letter state codes are the second level in the geographic hierarchy, with cities, counties, or parishes following. Outside of the United States, top-level Internet domains designate the country. Subdomains designate the organization and the individual system. See also generic top-level domain (gTLD).

### domain addressing

Using a domain address to specify the destination of an electronic mail message or NIS+ table.

### DVD-ROM

New!

Digital Versatile Disc-read-only memory or Digital Video Disc-read-only memory. The Solaris 8 Operating Environment includes support for the Universal Disk Format (UDFS) file system, which is the industry-standard format for storing information on the optical media technology called DVD.

### electronic mail

A set of programs that transmit mail messages from one system to another, usually over communications lines. Electronic mail is frequently referred to as e-mail.

### e-mail

See electronic mail.

### environment variable

A system- or user-defined variable that provides information about the operating environment to a program or shell.

### exit status

A numeric value assigned in a program or a shell script to indicate whether it ran successfully. An exit status of 0 usually means that the program executed successfully. Any non-zero value usually means that the program failed, but it can also indicate various conditions of success.

### export

See share.

### file descriptor

A set of information, kept by the UNIX kernel, that is related to a file opened by a process. A file descriptor is represented by an integer. The file descriptor for STDIN is 0, for STDOUT is 1, and for STDERR is 2.

### file handle

New!

A kernel-generated address that identifies a file for NFS clients.

### file system

A hierarchical arrangement of directories and files.

### floppy diskette

See diskette.

*fork*

> A function used by a parent process to create a separate, but initially identical copy of itself. The copy is known as a child process, which can either perform activity on behalf of the parent or load another process on top of itself to carry out actions completely independenly of the parent process. See also child process and parent process.

*fully qualified domain name*

> A domain name that contains all of the elements needed to specify where an electronic mail message should be delivered or where an NIS+ table is located. NIS+ and DNS fully qualified domain names always have a dot at the end. See also domain.

*gateway*

> A connection between differing communications networks. Also a system that handles electronic mail traffic between differing communications networks.

*generic top-level domain (gTLD)*

> The seven new domains that are being added to the existing set to accommodate increased demand for domains because of the popularity of the Internet. The seven new domains are `.arts`, `.firm`, `.info`, `.nom`, `.rec`, `.store`, and `.web`.

*GID*

> The group identification number used by the system to control access to information owned by other users.

*group*

> A defined collection of users on a system who can access common data.

*Group database*

> The database that you use to create new group accounts or to modify existing group accounts. You access the Group database from the SMC Users tool.

*here document*

> A format used within a shell script to provide a collection of data within the shell script.

*home directory*

> The part of the file system that is allocated to an individual user for private files.

## Hosts database

A directory service that holds names and addresses for lookup of other hosts on a network.

## indirect map

An automount map that contains relative path names as mount points.

## init states

One of the seven states, or run levels, a system can be running. A system can run in only one init state at a time.

## inode

An entry in a predesignated area of a disk that describes where a file is located on that disk, the size of the file, when it was last used, and other identifying information.

## interpreter

A program that reads and executes programming commands in sequence—one by one as they are encountered. Shell scripts are an example of interpreted programs.

## IP address

A unique Internet address number that identifies each system or device in a network.

## kernel

The master program set of SunOS software that manages all of the physical resources of the computer, including file system management, virtual memory, reading and writing of files to disks and tapes, scheduling of processes, and communications over a network.

## Korn shell

One of the Solaris command interpreters. The Korn shell is upwards-compatible with the Bourne shell and provides an expanded set of features. See also Bourne shell, C shell.

## license server

A server process that provides users access to software licenses to enable users to access software programs. Licenses are frequently used to enforce a license agreement, whereby a maximum number of users are permitted to run a commercial software program concurrently.

### listenBSD

An LP print service daemon that is run on a Solaris print server to listen for print requests from SunOS 4.x print clients on the network.

### listenS5

An LP print service daemon that is run on a print server to listen for print requests from Solaris print clients on the network.

### login name

The name assigned to an individual user to control that user's access to a system.

### *New!* m4 macro processor

A standard UNIX tool, unrelated to sendmail, used as a front end to different compilers to expand easy-to-remember macro expresssions into "canned" complex constructs. Starting with version 8.9.3, sendmail uses the m4 macro processor to generate the sendmail.cf file from a macro configuration file.

### mail address

The name of the recipient and the location to which an electronic mail message is delivered.

### mail alias

See alias.

### mailbox

A file on a mail hub where mail messages are stored for a user.

### mail client

A system that does not provide mail spooling for its users. Mail is spooled on a mail server.

### mailer

A protocol that specifies the policy and mechanics used by sendmail when it delivers mail.

### mail host

See mail hub.

### mail hub

The main mail system on a network that receives and distributes mail outside of the network or the domain. A mail hub can also be a mail server.

*mail server*

> Any system that stores mailboxes in the /var/mail directory. A mail server can also serve as a mail hub.

*mail services*

> Services provided by a set of programs and daemons that transmit electronic mail messages between systems and distribute them to individual mailboxes.

*masquerading*

*New!*

> The process by which sendmail rewrites the sender's e-mail addresses in outging messages so that they seem to come from the domain itself instead of from any specific host within that domain.

*master map*

> The automount map consulted by the automounter when a system starts up. The automount map contains the default mount points /net and /home and the names of the direct and indirect maps that the automounter consults.

*metadevice*

> A logical device that is created with the Sun Online: DiskSuite product to concatenate or stripe one or more disks into a single logical device unit.

*MNTFS file system*

*New!*

> The mount table file system, introduced in the Solaris 8 release, that provides read-only information to /etc/mnttab directly from the kernel about mounted file systems for the local system.

*modem*

> A peripheral device that modulates a digital signal so that it can be transmitted across analog telephone lines and then demodulates the analog signal to a digital signal at the receiving end. The name is a contraction for modulate/demodulate. A modem is one way to connect a UNIX workstation or PC to a remote server or network.

*mount*

> To extend a file system directory hierarchy by attaching a file system from somewhere else in the hierarchy. See also mount point.

*mount point*

> A directory in the file system hierarchy where another file system is attached to the hierarchy.

**New!** *mount table*

>    The system file (`/etc/mnttab`) that keeps track of currently mounted file
>    systems. Starting with the Solaris 8 release, the `/etc/mnttab` file is no
>    longer a text-based file. Instead, it is an MNTFS file system. See also MNTFS
>    file system.

**New!** *multicomponent lookup*

>    A feature of the WebNFS service that enables the `LOOKUP` command to
>    evaluate an entire path name with a single transaction. See also WebNFS
>    service.

*namespace*

>    A hierarchical arrangement of domains and subdomains, similar to the
>    hierarchical UNIX file system, used by NIS+ and the automounter.

**New!** *network printer*

>    A printer with an internal network card that has its own IP address and is
>    directly connected to the network.

*NFS*

>    The default Solaris distributed file system that provides file sharing among
>    systems. NFS servers can also provide kernels and swap files to diskless
>    clients.

*NIS*

>    The SunOS 4.x network information service.

*NIS+*

>    The Solaris network information service.

**New!** *NIS+ principal*

>    A user or system whose credentials have been stored in an NIS+ namespace.

*null modem cable*

>    A cable that swaps RS-232 Transmit and Receive signals so that the proper
>    transmit and receive signals are communicated between two data termination
>    equipment (DTE) devices. The RS-232 Ground signal is wired straight
>    through.

*OpenWindows*

>    A windowing system based on the OPEN LOOK® graphical user interface.

*package commands*

> The set of Solaris commands—pkgadd, pkgask, pkgchk, pkginfo, and pkgrm—that install, query, and remove software packages.

*parent process*

> A process that can create a new process, called a child.

*parse*

> To resolve a string of characters or a series of words into component parts to determine their collective meaning. Virtually every program that accepts command input must do some sort of parsing before the commands can be acted upon. For example, the sendmail program divides an e-mail address into its component parts to decide where to send the message.

*partially qualified domain name*

> An NIS+ domain name that specifies the local directory only and does not contain the complete domain name. For example, hosts.org_dir is a partially qualified domain name that specifies the hosts table in the org_dir directory of the default NIS+ domain. See also domain.

*partition*

> A discrete portion of a disk, configured with the format program. A partition is the same as a slice.

*Passwd database*

> The database that you use to add, modify, or delete user accounts.

*path*

> A list of directories that is searched to find a file. PATH is a shell environment variable used to find user commands.

*path name*

> A list of directory names, separated with slashes ( / ), that specifies the location of a particular file or directory.

*PCFS*

> Personal computer file system. A file system type for diskettes in MS-DOS-compatible format.

*port*

> A physical connection between a peripheral device such as a terminal, printer, or modem and the device controller. Also, a logical access point on a system used to accept connections over a network.

*port monitor*

A program that continuously watches for requests to log in or requests to access printers or files. The `ttymon` and `listen` port monitors are part of the Service Access Facility (SAF).

*positional parameter*

A shell script notation—$1, $2, $*n*—used to access command-line arguments.

*principals*

Individuals or systems within the NIS+ namespace that have been "registered" with the NIS+ service.

*process*

A program in operation. See also fork, child process, parent process.

*New!* *public file handle*

A file handle with a predefined value so the server does not need to generate a file handle for the client. See also file handle.

*New!* *public key encryption*

A data protection method whereby each party generates a "keypair" that consists of a public key and a private or secret key. The public key is made available to the universe and the private key is available only to the party that created it.

*RFC*

Request for Comments, specifically Internet protocols and standards. RFCs are submitted to SRI-NIC, where they are assigned numbers and are distributed by electronic mail to the Internet community. The most important RFCs (through 1985) are available in a three-volume publication, *The DDN Protocol Handbook*, which is available from SRI International in Menlo Park, California. RFCs are also available online at `http://ds.internic.net/`.

*root*

The highest level of a hierarchical system. As a login ID, the user name of the system administrator or superuser who has responsibility for an entire system. Root has permissions for all users' files and processes on the system.

*New!* *root domain*

The top-level domain in an NIS+ hierarchy.

*run level*

See init state.

*SAC*

> See Service Access Controller.

*SAF*

> See Service Access Facility.

*script*

> See shell script.

*sendmail*

> The mail transport agent used by Solaris system software. See also transport agent.

*server*

> A system that provides network service, such as disk storage and file transfer or access to a database. Alternatively, a program that provides such a service. See client.

*service*

> A process that is started in response to a connection request.

*Service Access Controller (SAC)*

> The process that manages access to system services provided by the Service Access Facility.

*Service Access Facility (SAF)*

> The part of the system software that is used to register and monitor port activity for modems, terminals, and printers. SAF replaces `/etc/getty` as a way to control logins.

*share*

> To make a file system available (mountable) to other systems on the network. See mount, NFS.

*shell*

> The command interpreter for a user, specified in the `Passwd` database. The Solaris Operating Environment supports the Bourne (default), C, and Korn shells.

*shell script*

> A file containing a set of executable commands that are taken as input to the shell.

**shell variable**

> Local variables maintained by a shell. They are not passed on from parent to child processes.

*New!* **site initialization files**

> Initialization files that are managed centrally and distributed globally by being referenced in users' `.cshrc` or `.profile` files.

**slice**

> An alternate name for a partition. See partition.

*New!* **Solaris Management Console (SMC)**

> A set of graphical user interface tools—available in the Solaris 8 Update 3 release—that enable you to perform key system administration tasks. Most of the SMC tools can be used to manage both local and remote systems.

**spooling directory**

> A directory where files are stored until they are processed.

**spooling space**

> The amount of space allocated on a print server for storing requests in a queue.

**stand-alone system**

> A system that has a local disk and that can boot without relying on a server.

**standard error**

> The location where error messages are sent. The file descriptor for stderr is 2. The default device for stderr is the terminal screen. See also file descriptor.

**standard input**

> The location where input is received from. The file descriptor for stdin is 0. The default device for stdin is the keyboard. See also file descriptor.

**standard output**

> The part of a process that determines where the results of commands are displayed. The file descriptor for stdout is 1. The default device for stdout is the terminal screen.

**stderr**

> See standard error.

### stdin

See standard input.

### stdout

See standard output.

### striping

Interlacing two or more disk partitions that make a single logical slice of up to 1 terabyte. With the Sun Online: DiskSuite product, the addressing of blocks is interlaced on the resulting metadevice to improve performance.

### superuser

A user with special privileges granted if the correct password is supplied when the user is logging in as root or using the su command. For example, only the superuser can edit major administrative files in the /etc directory. The superuser has the user name root.

### symbolic link

A special file that contains a pointer to the name of another file or directory.

### symmetric encryption

*New!*

A data protection method whereby a single secret key is shared by two parties. See also public key encryption.

### system

Another name for a computer, PC, or workstation. A system can have either local or remote disks and may have additional peripheral devices, such as CD-ROM players, DVD-ROM drives, tape drives, diskette drives, modems, and printers.

### terminfo database

The database that describes the characteristics of terminal devices and printers.

### third-party software

Application software that is not included as part of the basic system software.

### transport agent

The program that is responsible for receiving and delivering e-mail messages. The Solaris transport agent is sendmail.

*New!* *UDFS file system*

> Universal Disk Format file system, which is the industry-standard format for storing information on the optical media technology called DVD.

*UFS (UNIX file system)*

> The default disk-based file system for the Solaris operating system.

*UID number*

> The user identification number assigned to each login name. UID numbers are used by the system to identify, by number, the owners of files and directories. The UID of root is 0.

*uncommitted interface*

> An interface in the `sendmail.cf` file that is a de facto industry standard. Uncommitted interfaces have never had a formal architectural review, and they may be subject to change.

*unmount*

> To remove a file system from a mount point so that the files are no longer accessible. See also mount, NFS.

*unresolved mail*

> Mail with an address for which `sendmail` cannot find a recipient in the specified domain.

*user account*

> An account set up for an individual user in the `/etc/passwd` file or the `Passwd` database that specifies the user's login name, full name, password, UID, GID, login directory, and login shell.

*User Account Manager*

> A graphical user interface tool accessed from Admintool to add users to a local system. You can also use the SMC Users tool to add users to an NIS+ environment or to a local system.

*user agent*

> A program that acts as the interface between the user and the `sendmail` program. The user agents for the Solaris Operating Environment are `/usr/bin/mail, /usr/bin/mailx, /usr/dt/bin/dtmail,` and `$OPENWINHOME/bin/ mailtool`.

*value*

> Data, either numeric or alphanumeric.

*variable*

A name that refers to a temporary storage area in memory. A variable holds a value.

*virtual file system table*

The file (`/etc/vfstab`) that specifies which file systems are mounted by default. Local UFS file systems and NFS file systems that are mounted automatically when a system boots are specified in this file.

*virtual memory*

A memory management technique used by the operating system for programs that require more space in memory than can be allotted to them. The kernel moves only pages of the program currently needed into memory, while unneeded pages remain on the disk. Virtual memory extends physical memory over disk. See also kernel.

*volume management*

System software available with Solaris 2.2 and later releases that mounts CD-ROM and diskettes automatically without requiring superuser permission. Starting with the Solaris 8 release, volume management supports DVD-ROM devices and USB Iomega Jaz and Zip drives.

*WebNFS Service*                                                                                    *New!*

An extension to NFS version 3 and version 2 that enables servers to make files in a directory available with a public file handle. See also file handle, public file handle.

*wrapper*

A shell script installed on an application server that is used to set up the environment for that application; the wrapper then executes the application.

*write-through cache*

A type of cache that immediately updates its data source as data is changed or added to the cache.

# BIBLIOGRAPHY

## General References

Coffin, Stephen. *UNIX System V Release 4: The Complete Reference.* Osborne McGraw-Hill, 1990.

Garfinkel, Simson, and Gene Spifford. *Practical UNIX Security.* O'Reilly & Associates, 1991.

Gregory, Peter H., *Sun Certified System Administrator for Solaris 8 Study Guide.* Sun Microsystems Press, June 2001.

Loukides, Mike. *System Performance Tuning.* O'Reilly & Associates, 1990.

Nemeth, Evi, Garth Snyder, and Scott Seebass. *UNIX System Administration Handbook,* Third Edition. Prentice Hall Software Series, 2000.

Rosen, Kenneth H., Richard R. Rosinski, and James M. Farber. *UNIX System V Release 4: An Introduction.* Osborne McGraw-Hill, 1990.

Stern, Hal. *Managing NFS and NIS.* O'Reilly & Associates, 1991.

Winsor, Janice. *Solaris System Administrator's Guide, Third Edition.* Sun Microsystems Press/Prentice Hall Publishing, 2000.

All Sun Online Documentation is available at `http://docs.sun.com`.

## Electronic Mail References

*DDN Protocol Handbook, The.* 1985. Three-volume set of RFCs, available from SRI International, 333 Ravenswood Avenue, Menlo Park, CA 94025.

Frey, Donnalyn, and Rick Adams. *!%@:: A Directory of Electronic Mail Addressing and Network,* Fourth Edition. O'Reilly & Associates, 1994. Out of print.

All e-mail RFCs are available at `http://www.ietf.org/rfc.html` and `http://www.cis.ohio-state.edu/hypertext/information/rfc.html`

`http://www.sendmail.org/vendor/sun/` contains links to several documents that address various Sun-specific `sendmail` issues.

`http://www.sendmail.org/m4/cf-readme.txt` contains information about the m4 macro and the `/etc/mail/*` tables you can configure.

Costales, Bryan, and Eric Allman, *sendmail, Second Edition.* O'Reilly, 1997.

# SAF References

`http://www.stokely.com/unix.serial.port.resources/modem.html` contains useful information about configuring and troubleshooting modems.

Ravin, Ed, Tim O'Reilly, Dale Dougherty, and Grace Todino, *Using and Managing UUCP.* O'Reilly and Associates, 1996. Out of print.

# NIS+ Reference

Ramsey, Rick. *All About Administering NIS+, Second Edition.* Sun Press/Prentice Hall, 1994.

Sun Microsystems, *Solaris Naming Setup and Configuration Guide.*

Sun Microsystems, *NIS+ Transition Guide.*

# Printing Reference

*PostScript Language Reference Manual.* Adobe Systems Incorporated, October 1990.

`http://www.lprng.com/LISA98.ppt` is a link to a PowerPoint document that contains information about using LPRng to manage network printers and print spoolers.

# Patch Reference

You can access patches from `http://sunsolve.sun.com`.

# Shell References

Anderson, Gail, and Paul Anderson. *The UNIX C Shell Field Guide.* Prentice Hall, 1986.

Arick, Martin R. *UNIX C Shell Desk Reference.* QED Technical Publishing Group, 1992.

Arthur, Lowell Jay. *UNIX Shell Programming,* Second Edition. John Wiley & Sons, Inc., 1990.

Bolsky, Morris I., and David G. Korn. *The New Korn Shell Command and Programming Language., Second Edition* Prentice Hall, 1995.

Olczak, Anatole. *The Korn Shell User and Programming Manual.* Addison-Wesley Publishing Company, 1992.

Peek, Jerry D., Tim O'Reilly, and Mike Loukides, *UNIX Power Tools*, Second Edition. O'Reilly & Associates, 1997.

Rosenblatt, Bill. *Learning the Korn Shell.* O'Reilly & Associates, 1993.

# Programming Languages

Aho, Alfred V., Brian W. Kernighan, and Peter J. Weinberger. *The AWK Programming Language.* Addison-Wesley Publishing Company, 1988.

Dougherty, Dale. *sed and awk.* O'Reilly & Associates, 1991.

# System Security

Chapman, D. Brent, and Elizabeth D. Zwicky, *Building Internet Firewalls.* O'Reilly& Associates, 1995.

Cheswick, Steven, and William Bellovin, *Firewalls and Internet Security: Repelling the Wily Hacker.* Addison-Wesley Publishing Company, 1996.

Gregory, Peter H., *Solaris Security*, Sun Microsystems Press and Prentice Hall, 2000.

# INDEX